# ARIZONA
T · R · A · V · E · L · E · R · S
# HANDBOOK
Second Edition

*Eleanore Brown*

# ARIZONA

TRAVELER'S

# HANDBOOK

## BILL WEIR

moon
PUBLICATIONS

# ARIZONA TRAVELER'S HANDBOOK

Please send all comments,
corrections, additions,
amendments and critiques to:

**BILL WEIR**
**MOON PUBLICATIONS**
**722 Wall Street**
**Chico, CA 95928, USA**

*Published by*
Moon Publications
722 Wall Street
Chico, California 95928, USA
tel. (916) 345-5473/5413

*Printed by*
Colorcraft Ltd., Hong Kong

© Copyright 1987 Bill Weir

Library of Congress Cataloging in Publication Data

Weir, Bill, 1951 —
    [Arizona handbook]
    Arizona traveler's handbook / Bill Weir.

    Bibliography: p. 425
    Includes index.
    ISBN 0-918373-16-6
    1. Arizona—Description and travel—1981-  — —Guide-books.
I. Title.
F809.3.W44  1987            87-19994
917.91'0453—dc19            CIP

PRINTING HISTORY
SEPTEMBER 1986
AUGUST 1987

Printed in Hong Kong

# ACKNOWLEDGEMENTS

Many thanks go to the hundreds of people who assisted in making the *Arizona Traveler's Handbook* as complete and accurate as it is. I am expecially indebted to the National Park Service people, whose high standards make Arizona's national parks and monuments such wonderful places to visit. Staff at the U.S. Forest Service, Bureau of Land Management, and U.S. Fish and Wildlife Service gave me considerable help in visiting lands under their care. State government officials helped too, and extra thanks go to Carol Downey of the research library in the Capitol and to staff of the Fort Verde and Jerome State Historic Parks for generous use of their historic photos. Chambers of commerce, from the tiniest communities to the big cities, supplied valuable maps, ideas, and advice. The *Arizona Traveler's Handbook* manuscript showed some dramatic improvements from the first drafts to the last, thanks to the enthusiasm and editorial skills of Deke Castleman at Moon Publications, who also proofread the final version, Dr. Thomas Kreider at Berea College, Kentucky, and my mohter, Doris Weir. Most of the Arizona animals and birds that grace these pages were drewn by fellow Flagstaff hiker Kay Stephenson. Diana Lasich also put her brush to work when additional drawings were needed at the last moment. Barton Wright kindly gave permission to use his excellent Hopi Reservation map. The other top-notch maps came from the steady hands of Dave Hurst and Louise Foote at Moon Publications. Louise Shannon typeset the text on a mad-hatter schedule so Dave Hurst could do the production. Much of the credit for getting this book to you goes to Sales Manager Donna Galassi. And lastly, appreciation is due my publisher, Bill Dalton, who inspired *Arizona Traveler's Handbook* and helped bring it to a successful completion.

# ILLUSTRATIONS AND PHOTOS

**front cover:** View of Howlands Butte in the Grand Canyon; taken by the author from East Tonto Trail. **black and white photos:** Arizona Office of Tourism—pages 39, 78, 94, 139, 222, 244, 321; Arizona State Archives—pages 9 (right), 13, 14, 19, 34 (bottom), 87, 89, 108 (bottom), 109, 207 (right), 233, 318, 351 (left & right), 404, 405 (top), 407, 411, 414, 417, 422 (right), 423 (top); Flagstaff Chamber of Commerce—pages 24, 29, 93, 119, 125 (top), 126, 131, 132, 137, 138, 164, 165, 169, 173 (U.S. Forest Service); Fort Verde State Historic Park—pages 11, 163, 176 (National Archives), 177 (Mearns Collection, Library of Congress), 178 (left: Mearns Collection, Library of Congress), 181, 243 (right: Carter Collection, National Archives), 315, 335 (Carter Collection, National Archives); Grand Canyon National Park—pages 3 (neg. #2784), 33 (neg. #5117), 35 (neg. #826), 41 (neg. #3121), 45 (neg. #5130), 52 (neg. #2361), 58 (neg. #5563), 59 (neg. #7080); Jerome State Historic Park—pages 185, 186 (left & right), 187 (top & bottom), 188, 189, 190; Metropolitan Tucson Convention and Visitors Bureau, Inc.—pages 365, 366, 373, 380 (top & bottom), 381 (bottom), 391, 408; Mohave County Historical Society (Kingman)—pages 68 (top), 201, 205 (left & right), 206, 207 (left), 208, 216, 219 (top), 229; *Phoenix Gazette* (reprinted with permission)—page 253; Pimeria Alta Historical Society (Nogales)—pages 110, 396 (Rochlin Archives), 397 (Ellen Underwood Collection), 399 (Rochlin Archives), 401 (left & right); Tony Rose—pages 63, 64; Bill Weir—pages 6 (right), 7 (top), 9 (left), 10 (right), 17, 21, 22, 23, 44, 48, 49, 56, 57, 65, 66, 67, 68 (bottom), 69, 73, 77, 79, 86, 90, 92, 96, 98, 99, 100 (left & right), 101, 103, 105, 106, 125 (bottom), 127, 129, 133, 135, 141, 142, 143, 144, 148, 149, 161, 170, 171 (left & right), 175, 178 (right), 179, 195, 198, 200 (left & right), 209, 212, 213, 214 (left & right), 215, 217, 218, 219 (bottom), 220, 224, 225, 230, 234 (top & bottom), 236, 238, 240, 247, 251, 252, 254 (top & bottom), 256, 260, 261, 262, 263, 274, 275, 276, 279, 280, 282, 283, 288, 289, 290, 291, 292, 293, 294, 296, 297, 298, 303, 305, 306, 307, 311, 322, 323, 325, 331, 332, 333, 339, 343, 344, 345, 346, 348, 349 (left & right), 350, 359, 360, 361, 363 (top & bottom), 367, 370, 371, 375, 378, 381 (top), 385, 386, 387, 388, 389, 392 (left & right), 394, 395, 400, 402, 405 (bottom), 409, 412, 415 (top & bottom), 416, 418, 419, 420, 421, 423 (bottom), 424, 449. **illustrations:** Diana Lasich—pages 30, 32 (left & right), 154, 157, 158, 159, 160; Andy Mosier, cartoonist—pages 5, 7 (bottom), 377; Kay Stephenson—title page and pages 6 (left), 8 (left), 31 (left & right), 62, 97 (left & right), 117 (left & right), 130, 204, 221 (left & right), 239, 243 (left), 266, 267, 273, 284, 285, 326, 328, 340, 341, 384, 390, 403. **major sources of historic illustrations:** *The Marvellous Country; or Three Years in Arizona and New Mexico, the Apache's Home* by Samuel Cozzens—pages 10 (left), 12, 121, 241, 299, 302, 313, 329, 334, 353, 357, 393, 422 (left); *The Exploration of the Colorado River and Its Canyons,* formerly titled *Canyons of the Colorado,* by J.W. Powell; reprinted by Dover Publications—pages 1, 27, 34 (top), 42, 47, 51, 60, 61, 71, 72, 75, 81, 82, 83, 85, 91, 107, 114, 115, 316; *Decorative Art of the Southwestern Indians* by Dorothy Smith Sides, Dover Publications—pages 104, 112, 136, 156, 246, 271, 352.

# CONTENTS

# MAPS AND CHARTS

# ABBREVIATIONS

AZ—Arizona
C.—century
CA—California
d—double
elev.—elevation

L—left
NM—New Mexico
NV—Nevada
OW—one way
pop.—population
R—right

RT—roundtrip
RV—recreational vehicle
s—single
t—triple
UT—Utah

# IS THIS BOOK OUT OF DATE?

Nothing stays the same, it seems. Although this book has been carefully researched, Arizona will continue to grow and change. New places to stay and eat will open while others change hands or close. Tours and public transportation, much needed in this state, are especially subject to last-minute alteration. Your comments and ideas to make *Arizona Traveler's Handbook* more useful to other readers will be highly valued. If you find something new or discontinued or changed, please let us know so that the information can be passed on. Perhaps a map or worthwhile place to visit has been overlooked; please bring it to our attention. The next edition of *Arizona Traveler's Handbook* should appear in 1989. All contributions (letters, maps, and photos) will be carefully saved, checked, and acknowledged. If we use your photos or artwork, you will be mentioned in the credits and receive a free copy of the book. Be aware, however, that the publisher is not responsible for unsolicited manuscripts, photos, or artwork and, in most cases, cannot undertake to return them. Send only good-quality slides or glossy black-and-white prints. Moon Publications will own the publication rights to all material submitted. Address your letters to:

Bill Weir
c/o Moon Publications
722 Wall St.
Chico, CA 95928 USA

# INTRODUCTION

Few other states have such spectacular and varied terrain as Arizona. Because most of the early travelers who crossed this land kept to the S in the hot desert valleys and plains, it is these regions that form the popular image of Arizona even today. Yet much of the northern and eastern parts of the state have extensive coniferous forests and rushing mountain streams. Volcanic activity, uplift, faulting, and erosion have given us dozens of mountain ranges and canyons. The Grand Canyon, one of the world's greatest natural wonders, ranks at the top of most visitors' lists, but many other beautiful and intriguing places remain to be discovered. *Arizona Handbook* will help you find them. Wilderness areas, early Spanish sites, Indian reservations, old mining towns, bright city lights—they're all covered. Practical information is given for every budget, especially that of the oft-neglected low-budget traveler.

## THE LAND

Though geologically complex, the land surface of Arizona can be thought of as tilting down toward the southwest. More than 90 percent of the state's drainage flows into this corner via the Colorado River and its tributaries. Mountain ranges rise in nearly every part of Arizona, but achieve their greatest heights in the north-central and eastern areas. Humphreys Peak, part of the San Francisco Peaks N of Flagstaff, crowns the state at 12,670 feet, while the Colorado River enters Mexico at an elevation of only 70 feet. Geographers divide Arizona into the high Colorado Plateau Province of the NE half, and the Basin and Range Province of the rest of the state. Average elevation statewide is about 4,000 feet. Measuring 335 miles wide and 390 miles long, Arizona is the 6th largest state in the country.

**Colorado Plateau:** This plateau, a giant uplifted landmass in Arizona's NE, also extends across much of adjacent Utah, Colorado, and New Mexico. Rivers have cut into it, forming the Grand Canyon of the Colorado and other deep gorges. Volcanos have broken through the surface, leaving hundreds of cinder cones, such as multicolored Sunset Crater, and larger composite volcanoes, like the San Francisco Peaks. Arizona's most recent burst of volcanic activity took place near Sunset Crater about 700 years ago. Elevations on the plateau range mostly from 5,000 to 8,000 feet. Sheer cliffs of the Mogollon Rim dropping to the desert mark the S boundary. To the W, the plateau ends at Grand Wash Cliffs.

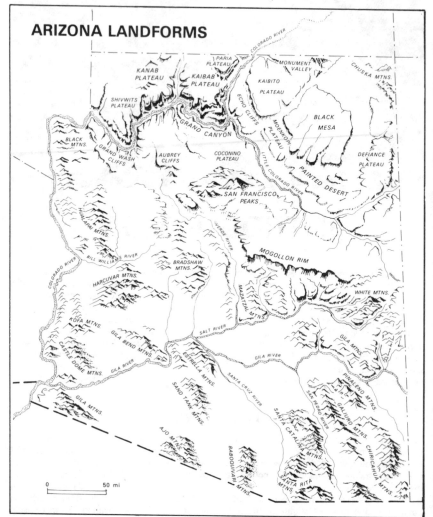

# ARIZONA LANDFORMS

0    50 mi

A layer of cloud has "filled" the Grand Canyon in this unusual shot.

**Basin and Range:** Many ranges of fault-block mountains, formed by faulting and tilting of the Earth's crust, poke through the desert plains of southern and western Arizona. Several peaks rise above 9,000 feet, creating "biological islands" inhabited by cool-climate animals and plants. Tucson-area residents can leave the Sonoran Desert behind and, within an hour, be on the high, densely wooded slopes of Mt. Lemmon.

## CLIMATE

During any season, some part of Arizona will be enjoying near-perfect weather. Sunny skies and low humidity prevail over the entire state. Average winter temperatures run in the 50s F on the low desert and the 20s to 30s in the mountains and high plateaus. Desert dwellers endure averages in the 80s and 90s in summer, when high-country residents enjoy averages in the 70s. The highest reading ever recorded in the state hit 127 F at Parker, along the Colorado River, on 7 July 1905. Even on a normal summer day in the low desert, you can expect highs in the low 100s.

**rainfall:** Precipitation corresponds roughly to elevation: the SW corner receives less than 5 inches annually, while the higher mountains and the Mogollon Rim receive about 25 inches. Most precipitation falls either in winter as gentle rains and snow, or in summer as widely scattered thundershowers. Winter moisture comes mostly in Dec. to Mar., revitalizing the desert; brilliant wildflower displays appear after a good wet season. Summer afternoon thunderclouds billow in towering formations from about mid-July to mid-September. The storms, though producing heavy rains, tend to be localized in areas less than 3 miles across. Summer thundershowers make up 60-70 percent of the annual precipitation in the low desert, and about 45 percent on the Colorado Plateau.

**caution:** Rainwater runs quickly off the rocky desert surfaces and into gullies and canyons. Flash floods can form and sweep away anything in their path, including boulders, cars, and campsites. Take care not to camp or park in potential flash-flood areas. If you come to a section of flooded roadway, a common occurrence on desert roads after storms, just wait until the water goes down, usually after only a short time. Summer lightning causes many forest and brush fires, and scares hikers foolish enough to climb mountains when storms threaten.

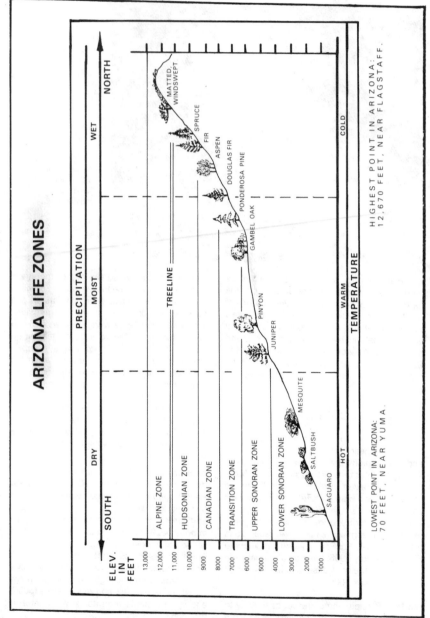

ARIZONA LIFE ZONES

# FLORA AND FAUNA

A wide variety of plants and animals find a home within Arizona's great range of elevations (more than 12,000 feet). Some plants, such as the senita cactus and elephant tree, grow only in southern Arizona and Mexico. Migratory birds often drop in. The colorful parrot-like trogon bird and more than a dozen species of hummingbirds fly up from Mexico to spend their summers in the mountains of SE Arizona. Canada geese and other northern waterfowl come to settle in for the winter on rivers and lakes in the low desert.

**protected plants:** State law prohibits collecting or destroying most cacti and other plants of the desert. Offenders can get a $500 fine and possible prison term. Cacti need time to grow (a saguaro takes 50 years to mature) and cannot survive large-scale collecting. You may, however, pick wildflowers. Although the "jumping" cactus is a myth, at least one saguaro has struck back at its oppressor—in Feb. 1982 a man N of Phoenix shot a saguaro twice with a shotgun; a 23-foot section then broke off and crushed the gunman to death.

## LIFE ZONES

To help simplify and understand the different environments of Arizona, some scientists use the Merriam system of *life zones*. Because plants rely on rainfall, which is determined largely by elevation, each life zone can be expected to occur within a certain range of elevations. The elevation ranges are not exact —south-facing mountain slopes receive more sun and lose more moisture to evaporation than north-facing slopes at the same level. Canyons and unusual rainfall patterns can also play havoc with the classifications. The life zones do give us, however, a general idea of what kind of vegetation and animal life to expect while traveling through the state.

**Lower Sonoran Zone:** This is Arizona's famed desert country of arid plains, barren mountains, and stately saguaro cacti. About one-third of the state—the S and W sections under 4,500 feet—are in this zone. The big cities and most of the state's population are here, too. With irrigation, farmers find the land good for growing vegetables, citrus, and cotton. Cacti do well: you'll see the prickly pear, cholla, and barrel, as well as the giant saguaro whose white blossoms are the state flower. The great variety of desert shrubs and small trees includes the palo verde, ocotillo, creosote, mesquite, and ironwood. Flowering plants tend to bloom either after the winter rains (the Sonoran or Mexican type), or after the summer rains (the Mojave or Californian type).

Most desert animals retreat to a den or burrow during the heat of the day, when ground temperatures can reach 150 F! Look for wildlife in early morning, late afternoon, or at night: kangaroo rat, several kinds of squirrels and mice, cottontail and jackrabbit, skunks, kit fox, ringtail cat, javelina, bighorn sheep, coyote, and the rare mountain lion. Common birds in-

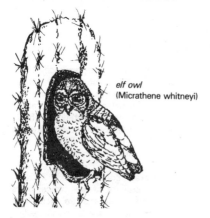

elf owl
(Micrathene whitneyi)

clude the cactus wren (state bird of Arizona), Gambel's quail, Gila woodpecker, roadrunner, hawks, eagles, owls, and common raven. Sidewinder and western diamondback rattlesnakes are occasionally seen. The rare Gila monster, identified by bead-like skin with black and yellow patterns, is the only poisonous lizard in the United States. It's slow and nonaggressive, but has powerful jaws. Also watch out for poisonous insects, especially the small "slender scorpion" whose sting is dangerous and can be fatal for children. Spiders and centipedes can inflict painful bites. It's a good idea to check for unwanted guests in shoes and other items left outside.

**Upper Sonoran Zone:**   You'll find these 4,500- to 6,500-foot elevations in central Arizona and in widely scattered areas throughout the rest of the state. Enough rain falls here to support grasslands or stunted woodlands of juniper, pinyon pine, and oak. Some chaparral-type vegetation grows here too, forming a nearly impenetrable thicket of manzanita and other bushes. Many of the same animals live here as in the Lower Sonoran Zone. You might also see black bear, desert mule deer and whitetail deer, and the antelope-like pronghorn. Rattlesnakes and other reptiles like this zone best.

**Transition Zone:**   The sweet-smelling ponderosa pine trees live in this zone—at 6,500

to 8,000 feet—where much of the winter's precipitation comes as snow. Ponderosas grow in many parts of the state, but their greatest expanse (and the largest in the country) is along the southern Colorado Plateau, from Williams in northcentral Arizona eastward into New Mexico. Gambel oak, junipers, and Douglas fir are commonly found among the ponderosa. Squirrels and chipmunks rely on the pine cones for food; other animals living here include cottontail and jackrabbit, spotted and striped skunks, red fox, coyote, mule deer, whitetail deer, elk, black bear, and mountain lion. Wild turkeys live in the woods, along with Steller's jay, screech owl, hummingbirds, juncos, and the common raven. Most snakes, such as the gopher, hognosed, and garter snakes, are harmless, but you could also come across a western diamondback rattler.

desert bighorn sheep (Ovis canadensis mexicana) at Arizona-Sonora Desert Museum, near Tucson

*javelina*
(Dicotyles tajacu)

**Canadian Zone:** Douglas fir dominate the cool, wet forests between 8,000 and 9,500 feet. Mixed in are Engelmann and blue spruce, white and subalpine fir, and quaking aspen. Little sunlight penetrates the closely spaced trees, which function as their own windbreak. Grasses and wildflowers grow in lush meadows amid the forests. Canadian Zone forests are found on the Kaibab Plateau of the Grand Canyon North Rim, the San Francisco Peaks, White Mountains, and other high peaks. You'll often see or hear squirrels as they busily gather cones to last through the long winters. Deer and elk graze in this zone, but rarely higher.

**Hudsonian Zone:** Strong winds and a growing season less than 120 days long prevent trees from reaching their full size at elevations from 9,500 to 11,500 feet. Forests receive twice as much snow as the Canadian Zone just below. Often gnarled and twisted, the dominant trees are Englemann and blue spruce,

subalpine and corkbark fir, and bristlecone pine. This zone occurs in Arizona only atop the highest mountains. On a bright summer day, the trees, grasses, and tiny flowering alpine plants are a-buzz with insects, rodents, and visiting birds, but come winter, most animals will have moved to lower and more protected areas.

**Alpine Zone:** In Arizona, this zone is found only on the San Francisco Peaks, where about 11,500 feet is the upper limit of tree growth. Freezing temperatures and snow can blast the mountain slopes even in mid-summer. About 80 species of plants, many also found in the North American arctic, manage to survive on the Peaks despite the rocky soil, wind, and cold. One species of a groundsel and a buttercup grow only here. Seasonal visitors include a dwarf shrew and 3 species of nesting birds: the Lincoln and white-crowned sparrows and the water pipit.

# HISTORY

## PREHISTORIC INDIANS

**paleo-Indians:** Arizona's first people discovered this land more than 15,000 years ago. They came from a hunting culture which extended across the Great Plains and into New Mexico and eastern Arizona. Spears in hand, tribesmen hunted bison, camel, horse, antelope, and mammoth. Smaller game and wild plant foods completed their diet. About 9,000 B.C., when the climate became drier and grasslands turned to desert, most of the large animals died off or left. Overhunting may have hastened their extinction.

**desert culture tradition:** The early tribes survived these changes by relying on seeds, berries, and nuts collected from wild plants, and by hunting smaller game such as pronghorn, deer, mountain sheep, and rabbit. Developing a precise knowledge of the land, the small bands of related families moved in seasonal migrations timed to arrive when plants of each area ripened. They traveled light, probably carrying baskets, animal skins, traps, snares, and stone tools. Most likely they sought shelter in caves or built small brush huts. Some Arizona

*A prehistoric Hopi pottery design of a Kwataka eating an animal; the Kwataka is a legendary winged monster who troubled Hopi ancestors. This fragment was excavated at Sikyatki.*

tribes continued a similar nomadic life-style until the late 1800s.

**distinct cultures emerge:** Between 2,000 and 500 B.C., cultivation skills came to the uplands of Arizona from Mexico. Indian groups, though, still kept their seasonal migrations, planting corn and squash in the spring, continuing their travels in search of wild foods, then returning to harvest their fields in autumn. Agriculture became more important about 500 B.C., when beans were introduced. The earliest pottery, to cook the beans in and to store other foods and water, was made at about the same time. The combination of beans, corn, and squash gave the people a nutritious, high-protein diet.

About A.D. 200-500, as they devoted more time to farming, the tribes began building villages of partly underground pithouses near their fields. Regional farming cultures appeared: the Hohokam of the southern deserts,

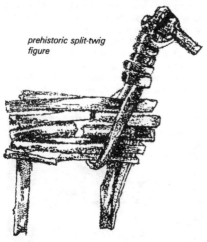

*prehistoric split-twig figure*

*petroglyph at Puerco Indian Ruin, Petrified Forest National Park*

the Mogollon of the eastern uplands, and the Anasazi of the Colorado Plateau in the north.

**growth and the great pueblos:** Villages became larger and their sites more widespread as populations increased from A.D. 500 to 1100. Above-ground pueblo dwellings began to replace the old-style pithouses. Trade among the Southwest cultures and with Mexico brought new ideas for crafts, farming, and building, along with valued items such as copper bells, parrots (prized for their feathers), and seashells and turquoise for jewelry. Cotton cultivation and weaving skills were developed. Major towns appeared between A.D. 900 and 1100, possibly acting as trade centers. Complex religious ceremonies, probably similar to those of present-day Hopi Indians, took place in kivas (ceremonial rooms) and village plazas in the uplands. Farther S in the desert, ball courts and platform mounds likely served religious and secular purposes. Desert dwellers also dug elaborate irrigation networks in the valleys of the Salt and Gila Rivers.

**decline and consolidation:** Mysteriously, people began to pack up and abandon, one by one, whole villages and regions throughout Arizona between 1100 and the arrival of the Spanish in 1540. Archaeologists try to explain their disappearance with theories of drought, soil erosion, warfare, disease, and aggression of Apache and Navajo newcomers. Refugees swelled the populations of the remaining villages during this period, then most of these too were left empty. Some of the Anasazi Indians are thought to have survived to become the modern Hopi in northeastern Arizona. The Mogollon and Hohokam disappeared completely; the modern tribes which took their place knew nothing of the people who had built the great pueblo structures.

**the Athabaskans wander in:** From west-central Canada, small bands of Athabaskan-speaking Indians slowly migrated to the Southwest. They arrived about 1300-1500 and established territories in the eastern half of present-day Arizona and adjacent New Mexico. Never a unified group, they followed a nomadic life of hunting, gathering, and raiding neighboring tribes. Some of the Athabaskans,

*Tzoe, called "Peaches" by the soldiers because of his light complexion and rosy cheeks, was a valuable Indian scout under General Crook's command in central Arizona, 1880s.*

later classified as "Navajo" on the Colorado Plateau and "Apache" farther S, learned agriculture and weaving from their pueblo neighbors.

## SPANISH EXPLORATION AND RULE

**the conquistadors:** Estevan, a Moorish slave of the Viceroy of Mexico, became the first non-Indian to enter what is now Arizona. He arrived from the S in an advance party of Fray Marcos de Niza's 1539 expedition, sent by the Viceroy to search for the supposedly treasure-laden Seven Cities of Cibola. The first of these "cities" that the party entered was a large Zuni Indian pueblo in present-day New Mexico, where they met their deaths at the hands of the Indians. When Fray Marcos heard the news, he dared view the pueblo only from a distance. Though he returned empty-handed, his glowing accounts of this city of stone encouraged a new expedition led by Francisco Vazquez de Coronado.

Coronado departed from Mexico City in 1540 with 336 soldiers, almost 1,000 Indian allies, and 1,500 horses and mules. Instead of gold, the expedition found only houses of mud inhabited by a hostile and primitive people. Despite hardships, Coronado explored the

region for 2 years, traveling as far N as Kansas. A detachment led by Garcia Lopez de Cardenas visited the Hopi mesas and the Grand Canyon rim. Another officer of the expedition, Hernando de Alarcon, explored the mouth of the Colorado River in hopes of finding a water route to resupply Coronado, but discovered the task to be impossible.

**missions and presidios:** Nearly 100 years passed after Coronado's failed quest before the Spanish reentered Arizona. A few explorers and prospectors made brief visits, but Franciscan missionaries came to stay. They opened 3 missions at the Hopi villages and had some success in gaining converts, despite strong objections from traditional Hopi. When pueblo villages in neighboring New Mexico revolted against the Spanish in 1680, the traditional Hopi joined in and killed the friars and many of their followers. Missionary efforts then shifted to southern Arizona, where the tireless Jesuit priest Eusebio Francisco Kino explored the new land and built missions from 1691 to 1711. Harsh treatment by later missionaries and land

*statue of Padre Kino, in front of Arizona Capitol*

abuses by settlers caused the Pima tribes to revolt in 1751. The Spanish then made reforms and built a presidio (military fort) at Tubac to prevent another outbreak. Similar unfair treatment by Spaniards at 2 missions on the lower Colorado River caused a revolt there in 1781; no attempt was made to reestablish them.

**Arizonac:** A fantastic silver strike during the Spanish era in 1736 drew thousands to an arroyo known by local Indians as "Arizonac," where sheets of native silver weighing 25-50 pounds each lay across the ground. The exact location is uncertain, but it was probably W of present-day Nogales. The boom soon ended, but a book published in 1850 in Spain told the amazing story. An American mine speculator picked up the tale and used it to publicize and sell mining shares. The name, shortened to Arizona, became so well known that it was later chosen for the Territory — or at least that's one theory of how Arizona got its name!

**Mexicans take over:** This land had always been on the far fringes of civilization. Politics and the Mexican fight for independence had little effect on it, so when 3 centuries of Spanish rule came to an end with Mexican independence in 1821, almost nothing changed. In the presidios, a new flag and an oath of loyalty to Mexico marked the transition. Isolation and hostile Apache continued to discourage settlement. Mission work declined as the Mexican government forced out many of the Spanish friars.

## ARRIVAL OF THE ANGLOS

**mountain men:** Early in the 19th C., adventurous traders and trappers left the comforts of civilization in the eastern states to seek a new life in the West. Sylvester Pattie and his son made the first known visit by Anglos to what's now Arizona in 1825. The younger Pattie later told of his adventures in *The Personal Narrative of James Ohio Pattie* (see "Booklist"). Although occasionally suffering attacks by hostile Indians, the Patties and later mountain men got along peacefully with the Mexicans and Indians already here. When U.S. Army explorers and surveyors first visited Arizona in the 1840s and 1850s, they relied on mountain men to show them the trails and waterholes.

**Americans take hold:** Anglo traders did an increasingly large business in the Southwest after Mexican independence — their supply route from Missouri was far shorter and more profitable than the Mexicans' long haul from Mexico City. Arizona had little importance in the Mexican War of 1847-48, ignited by American desire for Texas and California, disputes over debts owed by Mexico, and Mexican indifference to seeking a political solution. The 1848 Treaty of Guadalupe Hidalgo ceded to the United States not only the 2 desired areas, but everything in between, including Arizona and New Mexico. Arizona remained a backwater in the early American years as part of the New Mexican Territory, created by Congress in 1850. The Gadsden Purchase added what's now southern Arizona in 1854.

**new trails:** Most of the early visitors regarded Arizona as merely a place to be crossed on the way to California. The safest routes lay within

*Al Sieber, serving as an Army scout at Camp Verde in 1877*

*a fight with the Navajo, 1870s*

the Gadsden Purchase where Captain Philip Cooke had built a wagon road during the Mexican War. Many of the 49ers, headed for gold strikes in California, used Cooke's road (the Gila Trail). Hostile Indians and the difficulty of mountain crossings discouraged travel farther N, even after Edward Beale opened a rough wagon road across northern Arizona in 1857. Steamboat service on the lower Colorado River, beginning in 1852, brought cheaper and safer access to western Arizona.

**Americans settle in:** As the California Gold Rush of 1849 died down in the mid-1850s, prospectors turned eastward to Arizona. Their first big find here was a placer gold deposit near the confluence of the Colorado River and Sacramento Wash in 1857. More discoveries followed. For the first time, large numbers of people came to Arizona to seek their fortune in minerals. Farmers and ranchers followed to cash in on the market provided by the new mining camps and Army posts.

**Indian troubles and the Civil War:** Mountain men and government surveyors had maintained mostly good relations with the Indian tribes, but this changed only a few years later. Conflicts between the white man and Indian over economic, religious, and political rights, as well as over land and water, led to loss of land and autonomy for the Indian. Atrocities committed by both sides resulted as each tried to drive out the other. Army forts provided a base for troops attempting to subdue the Indians and a refuge for travelers and settlers.

Most Arizonans sided with the Confederacy during the Civil War, but quickly surrendered when large numbers of federal troops arrived. The only skirmish to take place in Arizona between the North and South occurred at Picacho Pass NW of Tucson. After a few casualties on each side, the Confederates retreated east.

## TERRITORIAL YEARS

Despite the wars and uncertainties of the early 1860s, Arizona emerged for the first time as a separate entity on 24 Feb. 1863, when President Lincoln signed the bill making it a Territory. Formerly, as part of New Mexico, Arizona had lacked representation and law and order. In 1864, Governor John Goodwin and fellow appointed officials laid out Arizona's first capital at Prescott.

**continuing Indian troubles:** The most serious problem faced by the new Territory was control of hostile Indians, especially the Apache and Navajo. Although Arizona's Indians had failed to drive out the newcomers, they did succeed in holding back development. Not until the great Apache war chief Geronimo surrendered for the last time in 1886 did white residents of the Territory feel safe.

**frontier days end:** The arrival of railroads in the 1870s and 1880s and discoveries of rich copper deposits brought increasing prosperity. Ranching and farming became important too. By 1890 most of the Army forts had outlived their usefulness. Only Fort Huachuca in SE Arizona has survived as an active military post from the Indian wars to the present.

**Mormon settlement:** Mormons in Utah, seeking new freedoms and opportunities, migrated S into Arizona. They first established Littlefield in the extreme NW corner of Arizona in 1864. A flood washed out the community in 1867 but it was rebuilt in 1877. Mormons developed other parts of the Arizona Strip in the far N, and operated Lee's Ferry across the Colorado River, just upstream from the Grand Canyon. From Lee's Ferry, settlers headed as far S as St. David (founded 1877) on the San Pedro River in Cochise County. Some settlements had to be abandoned because of land ownership problems, poor soil, or irrigation difficulties. Mormon towns prospering today include Springerville (founded 1871), Joseph City (1876), Mesa (1878), and Show Low (1890).

## STATEHOOD AND MODERN ARIZONA

It took years of political wrangling, but on 14 Feb. 1912—Valentine's Day—President William H. Taft signed the proclamation admitting Arizona as the 48th state. All of its citizens turned out for parades and wild celebrations. In Phoenix, Governor-elect George W.P. Hunt led a triumphal procession to the Capitol. Arriving in the Territory as an unemployed miner in 1881, Hunt had worked his way up to become a successful merchant, banker, territorial representative, and president of Arizona's constitutional convention. Hunt's support of labor, good roads, and other liberal causes won him 7 terms in the governor's office.

Arizona lived up to its nickname the "copper state," riding the good times when copper prices were high, as during WW I and the Roar-

*George W.P. Hunt (center) at the Constitutional Convention, 1910*

*President Taft signing Arizona Statehood Bill*

ing '20s, and suffering during economic depressions. Water—that all-important resource for farmers and cities—also preoccupied citizens. New dams across the Gila, Salt, and Verde Rivers of central Arizona ensured the state's growth. On the Colorado River, however, Arizona officials maintained a long-running feud with California and other thirsty states. Arizona pressed for its water rights from the early 1920s until 1944, even calling out the National Guard at one point to halt construction of Parker Dam, designed to supply water for Los Angeles. Wartime priorities finally forced the Arizona legislature to make peace and join the other river states in the Colorado River Compact.

**WW II and the post-war boom:** World War II brought many changes and advances. The Army Air Corps, attracted by good flying weather, came to build training bases. Army officers, including General Patton, trained their soldiers on the Arizona deserts. Aeronautical and other defense industries built factories, with the result that manufacturing income jumped from $17 million in 1940 to $85 million just 5 years later. Several POW camps were built for captured Germans and Italians. Some of the unfortunate Japanese-Americans were also interned here; in fact so many Japanese had been herded into the Poston camp (S of Parker) that for awhile it ranked as Arizona's third largest city.

The war, and the air conditioning that made the summers bearable, changed the state forever. Many of the workers and servicemen who had passed through during the hectic war years came back to live. Even some of the German POWs, it's said, liked Arizona enough to return and stay. Much of the industry and many military bases remained here as well. Retired people took a new interest in the sunny skies and warm winters of the state. Whole towns, such as Sun City (developed in 1960), grew up just for the older set. Arizona has continued to grow and diversify, yet it has retained its natural beauty and Old West heritage. The boom hasn't stopped yet.

# EVENTS

Arizona has a full schedule of rodeos, parades, art festivals, historic celebrations, gem and mineral shows, and sporting events. Activities tend to shift between southern Arizona in winter and the north in summer. Stop at a chamber of commerce to see what's coming up. The office should also have a statewide *Calendar of Events,* printed annually by the Arizona Office of Tourism.

**major holidays:** Even though not always mentioned in the text, many museums, parks, and other tourist attractions close on Thanksgiving, Christmas, and New Year's; call ahead to check.

New Year's Day: 1 January

Martin Luther King, Jr.'s Birthday: 15 January; usually observed third Mon. in January.
President's Day (honors Washington and Lincoln): third Mon. in February.
Easter Sunday: late March or early April.
Cinco de Mayo (Mexican festival celebrated in many Southwest communities): 5 May.
Memorial Day (honors veterans of all wars): last Mon. in May.
Independence Day: 4 July.
Labor Day: first Mon. in September.
Columbus Day: second Mon. in October.
Veterans Day: 11 November.
Thanksgiving Day: fourth Thurs. in November.
Christmas Day: 25 December.

# TRANSPORT

## TOURS

See your travel agent for the latest on package tours to Arizona. Within the state, local operators offer everything from city sights to rafting trips through the Grand Canyon. Gray Line has the largest selection of bus excursions, ranging from half day to 3 days; their tours leave from Phoenix, Tucson, and Flagstaff. Smaller companies offer jeep trips to scenic spots where a car wouldn't make it; you'll find jeeps at Monument Valley, Canyon de Chelly, Sedona, Phoenix, and Tucson. You can also take "flightseeing" trips from many airports; the Grand Canyon is the most popular of these. The "Transport" sections in each chapter list tour operators; also ask local chambers of commerce.

## BY CAR

Public transport serves the cities and towns but very few of the scenic, historic, and recreational areas. Unless on a tour, you really need your own transport. Most people choose cars as the most convenient and economical way to get around; they're easily rented in any sizeable town in Arizona. Phoenix and Tucson have the largest selection and also offer RV rentals. You won't normally need a 4WD vehicle unless traveling extensively on backroads. *Arizona Highways* magazine produces the best road map; almost any chamber of commerce will have one, and it's free.

**driveaways:** These are autos to be delivered to another city. If it's a place you're headed, a driveaway can be like getting a free car rental. To do it you have to be at least 21 years old and make a refundable deposit of $75-$150. There will be time and mileage limits. Ask for an economy car if that's a consideration. In a large city (Phoenix and Tucson in Arizona), look in the Yellow Pages under "Automobile Transporters & Driveaways."

**hitchhiking:** Opinions and experiences vary on hitching. It can be a great way to meet people despite the dangers and long waits. Offer to buy lunch or help with gas money to repay the driver's favor. Often rides can be arranged with fellow travelers at youth hostels. The ride boards at the University of Arizona (Tucson) and Arizona State University (Tempe, near

Phoenix) list rides both available and wanted. Highway police tolerate hitchhiking as long as it doesn't create a hazard or take place on an interstate or freeway. They do routinely check IDs, however.

## BY BUS

Greyhound and Trailways bus lines offer frequent service in Arizona on their transcontinental routes across northern and southern Arizona, and between Flagstaff and Phoenix. Arizona Central Lines specializes in the Flagstaff-Camp Verde-Phoenix-Sky Harbor Airport run, with a branch line to Prescott. Sedona Transportation Company serves Sedona, Cottonwood, Camp Verde, and Phoenix. Nava-Hopi Tours provides scheduled runs to the Grand Canyon National Park (South Rim), connecting with other lines in Flagstaff and Wil-

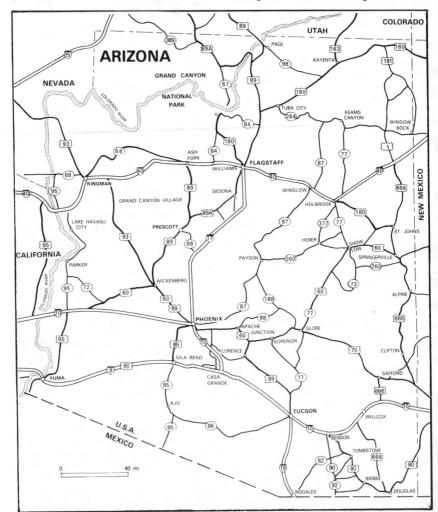

*authentic Wells Fargo stage*

liams. Citizen Auto Stage will take you from Tucson or Phoenix to Nogales, just a short walk from the cheap and colorful Mexican bus lines. Less frequent (one or 2 times a day) but useful bus services include: White Mountain Passenger Line (Phoenix to Show Low, Holbrook, and other eastern Arizona destinations); Navajo Transit System (Navajo and Hopi Indian Reservations, but doesn't connect with any other bus line in Arizona); LTR Stage Line (Phoenix to Kingman and Nevada destinations); and Sun Valley Bus Line (Phoenix to the lower Colorado River towns of Parker and Lake Havasu City, then on to Las Vegas). Some bus companies give a small discount for roundtrips. Greyhound and Trailways often offer special deals on bus passes and one-way "anywhere" tickets. Overseas residents may purchase a Greyhound Bus *Ameripass* at additional discounts outside North America.

Local bus services come in handy at the Grand Canyon National Park South Rim (summer only, free), Tucson, and Phoenix. Service in other towns is usually too infrequent for the traveler. Always have exact change ready when taking local buses.

## BY TRAIN

Amtrak features 2 luxury train lines across Arizona. Both connect Los Angeles on the W coast with New Orleans, Chicago, and other destinations to the east. On the northern route, trains run daily in each direction with stops in Arizona at Kingman, Flagstaff, and Winslow. On the southern route, they stop in Yuma, Phoenix, and Tucson, but they run only 3 times per week in each direction. Amtrak charges more than the buses for OW tickets but has far roomier seating, as well as parlor cars and sleepers. Special fares and RT discounts can often make train travel a good value. For information and reservations see a travel agent or call Amtrak toll-free (800) 872-7245 anywhere in the country. A *USA Railpass* is sold by travel agents outside North America.

## BY AIR

More than a dozen major airlines fly to Phoenix and Tucson. Fares and schedules tend to change frequently—a travel agent can help find the best flights. Big-city newspapers usually have advertisements of discount fares and tours in their Sun. travel section. You'll have the best chance of getting low fares by planning a week or more ahead.

Phoenix serves as the hub for nearly all flights within the state. Destinations from Phoenix include Tucson, Yuma, Lake Havasu City, Bullhead City, Kingman, Prescott, Sedona, Flagstaff, Page, and Winslow. The cost per mile of these short hops is high but you'll often have excellent views!

## BY BICYCLE

Touring on a bicycle is to be fully alive to the land, skies, sounds, plants, and birds of Arizona. The experiences of gliding across the desert or topping out on a mountain pass go beyond words. Some effort, a lightweight touring bicycle, and awareness of what's going on around you are all that's needed. Start with short rides if you're new to bicycle touring, then work up to longer cross-country trips. By learning to maintain and repair your steed, you'll seldom have trouble on the road. An extra-low gear of 30 inches or less will take the strain out of long mountain grades. Arizona's sunny climate offers fine year-round cycling —- just adjust your elevation for the desired temperature! As when hiking, always have rain and wind gear and carry plenty of water. Bookstores and bicycle shops have good publications on bicycle touring. *Bicyclist's Guide to Arizona* by Peter Bower contains practical information and details on short and long rides within the state.

# ACCOMMODATIONS AND FOOD

**motels and hotels:** The busiest seasons, when reservations come in handy, are: winter in the southern desert country (Phoenix, Tucson, Yuma, etc.), and summer in the high country (Prescott, Flagstaff, Payson, Grand Canyon, etc.). Rates fluctuate dramatically with seasons at the more expensive places, where off-peak prices can even be a bargain. Economy motels either keep the same rate all year or drop only slightly in the off season. For "no-frills" rooms, budget travelers can often find a Motel 6, whose rates are close to $20 year-round. The other major hotel and motel chains are well represented in Arizona, too. In the Phoenix area, a toll-free service will make reservations at more than 100 motels and hotels: tel. (800) 221-5596 in Arizona, or (800) 528-0483 out of state. Some of Arizona's restored historic hotels retain the elegance and romance of the old days. Outstanding historic places, worth a visit to the lobby even if you're not staying there, include the Hassayampa Inn (Prescott), Copper Queen Hotel (Bisbee), El Tovar (Grand Canyon), and Gadsden Hotel (Douglas).

**bed and breakfasts:** Following a long European tradition, these private homes or small inns offer a personal touch not found in the usual accommodations. Rates range from about $20 to $100 d; always call or write ahead for reservations. You'll find B&Bs in many parts of the state — in cities, resort towns, and on ranches. Usually they're not advertised; some are listed in these pages or with local chambers of commerce. More complete statewide listings are available from: Bed and Breakfast in Arizona, 4533 N. Scottsdale Rd., Suite 108, Scottsdale, AZ 85251; tel. 995-2831; and Mi Casa Su Casa, Box 950, Tempe, AZ 85281; tel. 990-0682.

**youth hostels:** The American Youth Hostels (AYH) organization offers clean and friendly accommodations for people of all ages. Hostels usually consist of dormitory rooms (separate men's and women's), kitchen, and common room. Besides being a good place for low-budget travelers, they also enable you to meet visitors from many other countries. Arizona has hostels in Phoenix, Flagstaff, Grand Canyon, Holbrook (Painted Desert Natl. Park), and Lakeside (White Mountains); more are planned. Each visitor must bring or rent sleeping sheets and be willing to pitch in to take care of the hostel. Rates run $5-$8/night for members (nonmembers usually pay a few dollars more). Reservations can be made by mail with a first night's deposit. Membership cards are sold at many of the hostels and by the national office: Box 37613, Washington, D.C. 20013-7613; tel. (202) 783-6161. A year's membership costs $10 age 17 and under, $20 age 18-59, and $10 age 60 and over. Cards are good at any hostel in the world, and foreign cards are accepted here.

**dude ranches:** These guest ranches feature horseback riding, miles of open country, excellent food, and an informal Western atmosphere. Activities include tennis, swimming, roping and riding instruction, hayrides, cookouts, square dancing, and even the real cowboy chores of working cattle. Tucson and Wickenburg are the major guest ranch centers, but other ranches are scattered around, mainly in the southern half of the state. Rates typically run $100/person per day and include all meals. Most visitors come in winter, when the desert is at its best; guest ranches often close in summer.

campgrounds: The best parts of Arizona lie outdoors, and you have a choice among hundreds of campgrounds: federal, state, or private. Federal government sites, the most common, are offered by the Forest Service, National Park Service, and Bureau of Land Management; sites commonly have tables, toilets, and drinking water; fees range from free to $7/night. Most state campgrounds additionally feature showers and hookups; they're very good value at rates of $5/vehicle per night

Hopi woman preparing fry bread

($7 w/hookups) and $1/vehicle extra for out-of-state residents. Commercial campgrounds have the most frills—showers, laundromats, hookups, stores, gamerooms, and even swimming pools at some places; rates average about $12/night; tents may or may not be accepted. Families should be aware that many of Arizona's RV parks cater to retired people —children won't be welcome. Unless otherwise stated, all campgrounds mentioned in these pages do accept families.

Other types of camping are possible too. Some Indian reservations, most notably the White Mountain Apache, offer primitive campgrounds at a small charge. You're welcome to camp almost anywhere in the National Forests. This dispersed style of camping costs nothing and for seasoned campers it gives the best outdoors experience. Since there are no facilities, the challenge is yours to leave the forest in its natural state. Be very careful with fire—try to use a campstove rather than leave a fire scar; sometimes high fire danger will close the forests in early summer. The 7 National Forests in Arizona cover vast expanses of mountain, plateau, and desert country from the state's far S to the far north. Stop at one of their offices for camping, hiking, and backroad suggestions and for maps ($1 each).

## FOOD

People debate whether or not Arizona has a native cuisine. Even if it doesn't, you'll find a wide selection. South-of-the-border food has a large following and a Mexican restaurant is never far away. Western-style restaurants will dish out cowboy food—beef, beans, and biscuits. Indian fry bread and the Navajo taco (beans, lettuce, tomatoes, and cheese on fry bread) can be sampled on and off the reservations. On the Hopi Reservation, a restaurant at the Cultural Center serves some unusual native fare. Tucson and Phoenix have the most cosmopolitan array of ethnic and fine-dining restaurants. Only a small sales tax is added to food; you're expected to leave a tip of about 15 percent for table service. Descriptions in this guide refer to price ranges for dinners (per person) as Inexpensive (to $8), Moderate ($8 to $15), and Expensive (over $15).

# MONEY, MEASUREMENTS AND COMMUNICATIONS

Prices of all services mentioned in this book were current at press time. Whenever possible, taxes have been included in the stated cost. You're sure to find seasonal and long-term price changes, however, so *please* don't use what's listed here to argue with staff at a motel, campground, museum, airline, or other office!

Foreign currency can be changed in Phoenix, Tucson, and Grand Canyon Village; anywhere else in the state involves extra delay and expense at best.

**measurements:** If you ask a rancher how many kilometers to the next town, you're out of luck. Most Arizonans haven't a clue to what the metric units mean, so visitors need to know the "olde English" system:

```
1 inch = 2.54 centimeters
   foot = .3048 meter
   mile = 1.609 kilometers
sq. mile = 2.59 sq. kilometers
   acre = .4047 hectares
pound (lb.) = .454 kilograms
```

To figure centigrade temperatures, subtract 32 from Fahrenheit (F) and divide by 1.8.

**time:** All clock times in this book use the 24-hour system, as in military time and European train timetables: 0100 is 1:00 a.m., 1200 is 12:00 noon, 1300 is 1:00 p.m., 1800 is 6:00 p.m., etc. To derive military time from regular time, just add 12 hours between noon and midnight.

Travelers in Arizona should remember that the state is on Mountain Standard Time all year, except for the Navajo Reservation which goes on Daylight Savings Time (add one hour May to Oct.) to keep up with their Utah and New Mexico sections. Note that the Hopi Reservation, completely within Arizona and surrounded by the Navajo, stays on standard time year-round with the rest of the state. In summer, Arizona is on the same time as California and Nevada, but one hour behind Utah, Colorado, and New Mexico. In winter, Arizona is one hour ahead of California and Nevada, but the same as Utah, Colorado, and New Mexico.

**postal and telephone services:** Normal post office hours are Mon. to Fri. 0830-1700 and sometimes Sat. 0830-1200. All telephone numbers within Arizona have a 602 area code (use only when calling from outside Arizona). Toll-free numbers in the U.S. have an 800 area code. To obtain a local number, dial 1-411; for a number within the state, dial 1-555-1212; and for another state, dial 1, the area code, then 555-1212. Many airlines and motel chains have a toll-free 800 number; if you don't have it, just dial 1-800-555-1212.

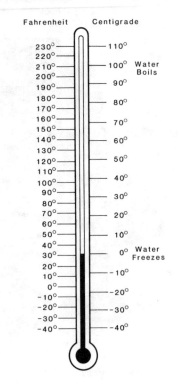

# HEALTH AND HELP

**medical services:** In emergencies, use the emergency number listed on most telephones or dial "O" for an operator. Emergency rooms of hospitals offer the quickest help, but cost more than going to a doctor's office. Hospital care is very expensive—medical insurance is recommended.

## WILDERNESS TRAVEL

**keeping the "wild" in wilderness:** As more people seek relief from the confusion and stress of urban life, the use of wilderness areas increases. Fortunately, Arizona has an abundance of this fragile and precious resource. The many designated wilderness areas have been closed to mechanized vehicles (including mountain bicycles) to protect both the environment and the experience of solitude. Most designated areas lie within National Forest lands, where you're normally free to visit anytime without a permit. Other areas, such as the National Parks and Monuments and the Bureau of Land Management's Paria and Aravaipa Canyons, require entry permits. Suggestions for backcountry travel and camping include these wilderness ethics:

✓ Check with a ranger about weather, water sources, fire danger, trail conditions, and regulations before heading into the backcountry.

✓ Tell a ranger or reliable person where you are going and when you expect to return.

✓ Travel in small groups for the best experience (group size may also be regulated).

✓ Help preserve old Indian and historic ruins.

✓ Camp at least 300 feet away from springs, creeks, and trails. State law prohibits camping

*on the Boulder Canyon Trail in the Superstition Mountains Wilderness*

within ¼ mile of a sole water source to avoid scaring away wildlife and livestock.

✔Try not to camp on meadows, as the grass is easily trampled.

✔Use a portable stove to avoid marring the land.

✔Avoid digging tent trenches or cutting vegetation.

✔Wash away from streams and springs.

✔Bring a trowel for personal sanitation; dig at least 4-6 inches deep.

✔Bring plenty of feed for horses and mules.

✔If lost, *realize it,* then find shelter, and stay in one place.

✔Take home your trash so animals can't dig up and scatter it.

**know before you go:** Some of the most spectacular and memorable hiking and camping await the prepared outdoorsperson. But because Arizona's deserts and canyons are very different from most other parts of the country, even "expert" hikers get into trouble. If you're new to these outdoors, read up on the hiking conditions and talk to rangers and local hikers. Backpacking stores are good sources of information too. Start with easy trips, then work up gradually.

**hypothermia:** Your greatest danger outdoors is one that can sneak up and kill with very little warning. Hypothermia, a lowering of the body's temperature below 95 F, causes dis-orientation, uncontrollable shivering, slurred speech, and drowsiness. The victim may not even realize what's wrong. Unless corrective action is taken immediately, hypothermia can lead to death. This is why hikers should travel with companions and always carry wind and rain protection. (Close-fitting rain gear works far better than ponchos.) Remember that temperatures can plummet rapidly in Arizona's dry climate—a drop of 40 degrees F between day and night is common. Be especially careful at high elevations, where summer sunshine can quickly change into freezing rain or a blizzard. Simply falling into a mountain stream while fishing can also lead to hypothermia and death unless proper action is taken. If cold and tired, don't waste time! Seek shelter and build a fire; also change into dry clothes and drink warm liquids. If a victim isn't fully conscious, warm him by skin-to-skin contact with another person in a sleeping bag. Try to keep the victim awake and drinking warm liquids.

## DRIVING HAZARDS

Summer heat in the low desert puts an extra strain on both cars and drivers. It's worth double checking to make sure the cooling system, engine oil, transmission fluid, fan belts, and tires are in top condition. Carry several gallons of water in case of breakdown or radiator trouble. Never leave children or pets in a parked car

Hole in radiator knocks out Larry Lipchinsky's car.

during warm weather: temperatures inside can cause fatal heat stroke in just minutes. At times the desert has *too much* water — late-summer storms frequently flood low spots in the road. Wait for the water to go down (until you can see bottom) before crossing. Dust storms also tend to be short-lived but can completely block visibility. The best thing to do then is to pull completely off the road and stop; turn off your lights so as not to confuse other drivers. Radio stations carry frequent weather updates when weather hazards exist. If you have a VHF radio (162.4 and 162.55 MHz), continuous weather forecasts can be received in the Phoenix, Tucson, Yuma, Flagstaff, and Las Vegas (NV) areas.

If stranded, whether on the desert or in mountains, stay with the vehicle unless you're *positive* of a route to help; then leave a note telling route and departure time. Airplanes can easily spot an obviously stranded car (leave hood and trunk up and tie a piece of cloth to antenna), but a person trying to walk out is difficult to see. Emergency supplies can help: blankets or sleeping bags, first-aid kit, tools and booster cables, shovel, traction mats or chains, flashlight, rain gear, water, and food (w/can opener).

## FREE INFORMATION

General tourist literature and maps are available from the Arizona Office of Tourism, 1480 E. Bethany Home Rd., Phoenix, AZ 85014; tel. 255-3618. The many chambers of commerce in the state will be happy to help; see "Information" under each place description in this book. Listed with them are National Forest offices and other government agencies that know about outdoor recreation in their area.

## VISITING INDIAN RESERVATIONS

Meeting Arizona's Native Americans affords the chance to learn about another culture. Their lands — 27 percent of the state — include some beautiful mountain, canyon, and desert country. Tribes in Arizona, from N to S, are Paiute, Navajo, Hopi, Havasupai, Hualapai,

*Hopi broad-faced* katsina *doll*

Yavapai, Apache, Mohave, Chemehuevi, Cocopah, Yaqui, Pima, and Papago. See descriptions in the individual travel sections of the reservations for museums, dances, crafts, recreation, and where to stay and eat. On any of the 21 reservations, keep in mind that you're a guest on private land. Most Indians are very private people; ask before taking their photo (you may need to pay a posing fee). The Hopi prohibit all photography, sketching, and recording in villages — don't even carry a camera there! Check to see if permits are needed before camping, hiking, or leaving the main roads. Usually a small charge applies for camping. All fishing and hunting on Indian lands require tribal permits, though you won't need Arizona state licenses. Sometimes part of a reservation will be closed to outsiders.

Tribes you might want to visit include: the Hopi for their exotic *katsina* dances and ancient pueblo villages; the Navajo for their remarkable land that includes Monument Valley, Canyon de Chelly, Painted Desert, and other natural wonders; the Havasupai for their "land of blue-green water" within the Grand Canyon; and

*Navajo jewelry for sale*

the White Mountain Apache for their forests, countless trout streams, and many fishing lakes. Indian crafts include jewelry by several tribes, Hopi *katsina* dolls and pottery, Navajo rugs and sandpaintings, Apache beadwork, and Papago basketry. Two museums of Indian culture, the Heard in Phoenix and the Museum of Northern Arizona in Flagstaff, provide a good introduction to the tribes and crafts on the reservations.

## VISITING MEXICO

Arizona has always had a close relationship with Mexico. Spanish and Mexican influences show in the state's architecture, food, language, and music. About 16 percent of Arizona's population trace their descent back to the Spanish. Visiting Mexico is easy and simple at any of the 6 border crossings. Most people in the border towns understand English,

and shopkeepers happily accept U.S. dollars. Nogales, close to Tucson, offers the best shopping and receives the most visitors. In all the border towns except Sonoita, you can park on the U.S. side and stroll across to the shops and restaurants in Mexico. Sonoita lies 2 miles beyond the boundary, and you'll probably want to drive there. See individual descriptions of the border towns within these pages.

**permits:** United States and Canadian citizens may visit the border towns for as long as 72 hours without any formalities; just announce your nationality when returning to the U.S. side. Identification should be carried (voter's registration, birth or naturalization certificate, passport, or affidavit of citizenship by a notary public). Travelers from other countries should ask for regulations about entering and returning *before* crossing over. Longer stays or travel to the interior require visitors to carry a tourist card, easily obtainable by U.S. and Canadian citizens at the border with proof of citizenship (a driver's license won't work), and usually good for 90 days.

Motorists may drive to the border towns and to Baja California without a permit. To go farther, vehicle permits must be obtained; trailers and motorbikes each need one too. For the permits, easily obtained at the border, you'll need to show proof of ownership (title, bill of sale, registration, or a notarized affidavit stating that you own the vehicle or have permission to drive it in Mexico). Some car rental agencies in Arizona will allow you to drive in Mexico, but ask them first. Most U.S. insurance policies are worthless in Mexico. Unless you have Mexican insurance, the police there might throw you in jail after an accident, even if it wasn't your fault. Purchase Mexican insurance, available by the day or longer, in Arizona border towns.

**information:** Chambers of commerce on the Arizona side (Nogales, Douglas, and Yuma) know about their neighboring towns in Mexico. With luck, you might be able to find the chambers of commerce in the Mexican towns too. Sonora, the Mexican state bordering Arizona, has a tourist office in the state capital: Secretaria de Fomento al Turismo Estado de Sonora, Blvd. Kino No. 1000, Hermosillo, Sonora, Mexico; tel. 4-73-99.

"The Grand Canyon of the Colorado is a canyon composed of many canyons. It is a composite of thousands, of tens of thousands, of gorges. In like manner, each wall of the canyon is a composite structure, a wall composed of many walls, but never a repetition. Every one of these almost innumerable gorges is a world of beauty in itself. In the Grand Canyon there are thousands of gorges like that below Niagara Falls, and there are a thousand Yosemites. Yet all these unite to form one grand canyon, the most sublime spectacle on earth...

Its colors, though many and complex at any instant, change with the ascending and declining sun; lights and shadows appear and vanish with the passing clouds, and the changing seasons mark their passage in changing colors. You cannot see the Grand Canyon in one view..."

—John Wesley Powell, from his
*The Exploration of the Colorado River and Its Canyons*

# THE GRAND CANYON AND THE ARIZONA STRIP

## INTRODUCTION

A collision of the Earth's forces—uplifting of the massive Colorado Plateau and vigorous downcutting by the Colorado River—created the awe-inspiring Grand Canyon and its many tributaries. Neither pictures nor words can fully describe them. You have to experience the Canyon by traveling along the rim, descending into the depths, and watching the continuous show of colors and patterns as the sun moves across the sky. Measurements give only a clue to the Canyon's grandeur: stretching 227 miles across northern Arizona, it averages 10 miles wide and one mile deep. Roads provide access to developed areas and viewpoints on both rims. Trails make it possible for hikers and mule riders to descend the precipitous cliffs to the Colorado River, though most of the Park remains as remote as ever, rarely visited by human beings.

Northward, between the Colorado River and the Utah border, lies the isolated Arizona Strip. This land of forests, desert grasslands, mountains, and canyons covers 14,000 square miles, yet supports only 3,200 people. The Grand Canyon presents a formidable barrier between them and the rest of the state; all highway traffic has to follow a circuitous route around the mighty chasm. Residents of Moccasin in the Arizona Strip must drive 357 miles to their Mohave County seat at Kingman, detouring through Utah and Nevada before reentering Arizona at Hoover Dam, in order to cover 140 miles as the crow flies. Historically, the Strip has far more in common with Utah, whose Mormon pioneers first settled this region. Today, it appeals to those who love wilderness. Travelers can wander the canyons, backroads, and trails here without meeting another soul. Its other attractions include fishing and boating on Lake Powell and historic Lees Ferry (15 river miles below Lake Powell), and Pipe Spring National Monument (an early Mormon ranch).

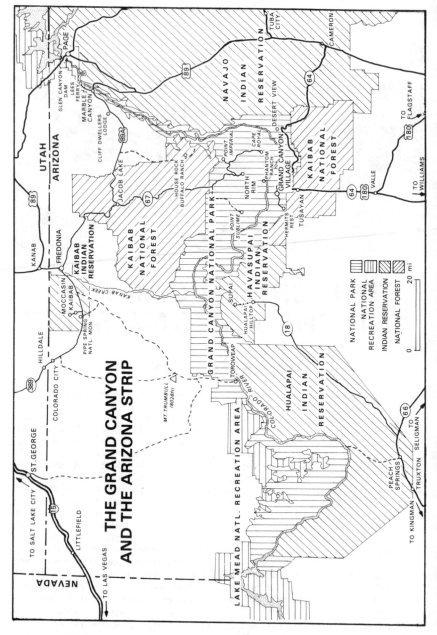

THE GRAND CANYON
AND THE ARIZONA STRIP

## THE LAND

This is a land of time. Tracing down the Grand Canyon's massive cliffs with your eyes, or walking below the rim, you see sandstones formed of ancient desert sand dunes, limestones composed of animals who lived in long-departed seas, and shales made of silt from now-vanished rivers and shores. Volcanic eruptions have left their record as layers of ash, cinders, and lava. Still farther into the Canyon lie the roots of mountain ranges, whose peaks towered over a primitive land 2 billion years ago. Time continues to flow in the Canyon with the cycles of the plants and animals that live here, and with the erosive forces of water and wind ever widening and deepening the chasm.

Geologists have a hard time telling the age of the Grand Canyon, though it is far younger than even the most recent rock layers—those on the rim, which are about 250 million years old. They were at sea level 65 million years ago when the Earth's crust began a slow uplift. Somewhere between 5 and 20 million years ago, the ancestral Colorado River took its present course and began to carve the Canyon. Gradual uplift continued, giving the waters even greater power. Today, the South Rim rises to elevations of 7,000-7,500 feet, while the North Rim towers about 1,000 feet higher. Still young, the Colorado River drops through the Canyon at an average gradient of 7.8 feet per mile, 25 times the gradient of the lower Mississippi.

**climate:** The Grand Canyon has been compared to an inverted mountain. Temperatures change with elevation as on a mountainside, but with added canyon peculiarities. In winter, the sun's low angle allows only a few hours of sunlight a day to reach the Inner Gorge, creating a cooling effect. The situation reverses during the summer, when the sun's high angle turns the canyon into an oven. At night, temperatures often drop lower than you'd expect; that's because cold, dense air on the rims pours over the edge into the depths.

In one day, a hiker can travel from the cold fir and aspen forests of the North Rim to the hot cactus country of the Canyon bottom—a

*Vista Encantadora on the North Rim*

climate change equal to that between Canada and Mexico. Summer temperatures of the Inner Gorge (elev. 2,570 feet at Phantom Ranch) soar, with average highs over 100 F; early July commonly sees the thermometer top 115. Spring and autumn offer pleasantly warm weather—the best times to visit. Winter down by the river can be fine too; even in Jan., days warm up to the 50s or low 60s and rarely see freezing weather. Only about 7 inches of precipitation make it to the bottom in an average year; snow and rain often evaporate completely while falling through the mile of warm canyon air. The South Rim has pleasant weather most of the year: summer highs in the mid-80s, cooling to highs in the upper 30s and lower 40s during winter. Winter campers will need warm sleeping bags to combat frosty nights that go down to the teens. Yearly precipitation at the South Rim's Grand Canyon Village (elev. 6,950 feet) is about 14½ inches with snow accumulations seldom exceeding 2 feet. Although averaging only 1,000 feet higher, the North Rim really gets socked in by winter storms. Snow piles up to depths of 6-10 feet in an average season, and the Park Service doesn't even try to keep the roads open from early Nov. to mid-May. Summers can be a joy in the cool fresh air; highs then run in the 60s and 70s. Bright Angel Ranger Station (elev. 8,400 feet) on the North Rim receives about 23 inches of annual precipation.

Most moisture falls in the winter months and during late summer (mid-July to mid-Sept.). Summer rains often arrive in spectacular afternoon thunderstorms, soaking one spot in the Canyon and leaving another a short distance away bone dry. The storms are fascinating to watch from the rims, but take cover away from the edge if the hair on your head stands on end or if you smell ozone. As in mountain areas, the Grand Canyon's weather can change rapidly. Always carry rain and wind gear if heading down a trail.

## FAUNA AND FLORA

The seemingly endless variations of elevation, exposure, and moisture allow for an aston-

*Kaibab squirrel* (Sciurus kaibabensis)

ishing range of plant and animal communities. The Canyon also acts as a barrier to many nonflying creatures, who live on just one side of the Colorado River or only in the Inner Gorge. Some mammals, such as the mountain lion, spotted skunk, cliff chipmunk, and common pocket gopher, have evolved into separate subspecies on each rim.

**spruce-fir forest:** You'll find dense forests of spruce and fir and groves of quaking aspen on the Kaibab Plateau of the North Rim, mostly above 8,200 feet. Common trees include Engelmann and blue spruce, Douglas, white, and subalpine fir, aspen, and mountain ash. Lush meadows, dotted with wildflowers in late summer, spread out in shallow valleys at the higher elevations. Animals of the spruce-fir forest include mule deer, mountain lion, porcupine, red and Kaibab squirrel, Uinta chipmunk, long-tailed vole, and northern pocket gopher. The shy Kaibab squirrel, easily identified by his all-white tail and tufted ears, lives only on the North Rim. He probably evolved from some Abert squirrels who crossed the Colorado River long ago, perhaps during Pleistocene time. Birds you might see are turkey, great horned owl, saw-whet owl, broad-tailed hummingbird, hairy woodpecker, hermit thrush, Clark's nutcracker, Steller's jay, and mountain bluebird.

**ponderosa pine forest:** Tall ponderosas grow extensively between elevations of 7,000 and 8,000 feet on both rims. Mature forests tend to be open, allowing in sunlight for Gambel oak, New Mexican locust, mountain mahogany, greenleaf manzanita, cliff rose, wildflowers, and grasses. Animals and birds found here include most of those of the spruce-fir forests. The Abert squirrel, though common in the Southwest, lives only on the South Rim within the Park. He has tufted ears and a body that is mostly gray with white undersides, including his tail.

**pinyon-juniper woodland:** These smaller trees take over in drier and more exposed places between elevations of 4,500 and 7,500 feet. Commonly found with them are broadleaf yucca, cliff rose, rabbitbrush, Mormon tea, sagebrush, fernbrush, serviceberry, and Apache plume. Mule deer, mountain lion, coyote, gray fox, desert cottontail, Stephen's wood rat, pinyon mouse, rock squirrel, cliff chipmunk, lizards, and snakes (including rattlesnakes) make their homes here. Birds include pinyon and scrub jay, mourning dove, plain titmouse, Bewick's wren, and black-throated gray warbler.

**desert scrub:** Except near permanent water, the low-desert country below 4,500 feet cannot support trees. You'll find such hardy plants as blackbrush, Utah agave, narrowleaf yucca, various cacti, desert thorn, Mormon tea, four-wing saltbush, and snakeweed. Animals include bighorn sheep, black-tailed jackrabbit, spotted skunk, desert woodrat, antelope ground squirrel, and canyon mouse. Most rep-

*Abert squirrel* (Sciurus aberti)

tiles hole up during the day, though lizards seem to tolerate hotter temperatures than snakes. Chuckwalla, spiny and collared lizard, common kingsnake, whipsnake, and Grand Canyon rattlesnake live in this part of the Canyon. The shy Grand Canyon or pink rattlesnake, a subspecies of the prairie rattler, lives nowhere else. Birds of the desert scrub either have to look elsewhere for nesting trees or choose a spot in cliffs or on the ground. Species you might see include the common raven, turkey vulture, golden eagle, red-tailed hawk, rock and canyon wren, and black-throated sparrow.

**riparian woodlands:** Until 1963, seasonal floods of the Colorado River ripped away all vegetation below high-water mark. When the gates of the upstream Glen Canyon Dam closed, tamarisk (an exotic species originally from the Arabian deserts) began taking over formerly barren beaches. Native cattail, coyote willow, and arrowweed now thrive too. Seeps and springs in side canyons have always supported luxuriant plant growth as well as supplying a drink for desert wildlife. Beaver, river otter, ringtail cat, raccoon, Woodhouse's toad, white-footed deermouse, tree lizard, spotted sandpiper, blue grosbeak, and Lucy's warbler make their homes near the streams. Fremont cottonwood trees in the tributaries provide welcome shade for overheated hikers. The cold, clear waters that flow from Glen Canyon dam have upset breeding patterns of the 7 native fish species, which now seek out warmer waters at the mouths of the Little Colorado River and Havasu Creek to spawn. Rainbow trout and 10 other species have been introduced.

*ringtail cat*
(Bassaricus astutus)

## HISTORY

**the first peoples:** Indians knew of this land and its canyons centuries before the white man came. At least 4,000 years ago, a hunting and gathering society stalked the plateaus and canyons of northern Arizona, leaving behind stone spearpoints and some small split-twig figures resembling deer or sheep. Preserved in caves of the Grand Canyon, these figurines have a carbon-14 age of 2,000 B.C. This culture apparently departed about 1,000 B.C., leaving the Canyon unoccupied for the next 1,500 years.

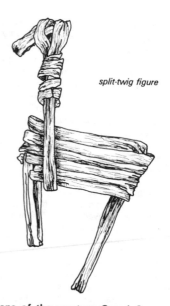

*split-twig figure*

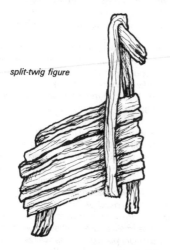

*split-twig figure*

**the next Indians:** Prehistoric Anasazi came to the Grand Canyon area about A.D. 500. Like their predecessors, they hunted deer, bighorn sheep, rabbit, and other animals, while gathering such wild plant foods as pinyon nuts and agave. The Anasazi also made fine baskets and sandals. At their peak between 1050 and 1150, they grew crops, crafted pottery, and lived in above-ground masonry villages. Drought hit the region about the end of this period, and may have caused its abandonment. By 1150 nearly all the Anasazi had departed the Grand Canyon, leaving more than 2,000 sites behind. Most likely they migrated E to the Hopi mesas.

**Indians of the western Grand Canyon:** While the Anasazi kept mostly to the eastern half of the Grand Canyon (E of today's Grand Canyon Village), another group of hunter-gatherers and farmers, the Cohonina, lived downstream between A.D. 600 and 1150. They adopted many of the agricultural, craft, and building techniques of their Anasazi neighbors. In 1300 the Cerbat, probable ancestors of the modern Havasupai and Hualapai Indians, migrated onto the Grand Canyon's South Rim from the west. They lived in caves or brush shelters and ranged as far upstream as the Little Colorado River in search of game and wild plant foods. The Cerbat also planted crops in areas of fertile soil or permanent springs. It's possible that the Cerbat had cultural ties with the earlier Cohonina. Nomadic Paiute Indians living N of the Grand Canyon made seasonal trips to the North Rim, occasionally clashing with the Cerbat when one group raided the other. The Paiute lived in brush shelters and relied almost entirely on hunting and gathering. They spent summers on the Kaibab Plateau and other high country, then moved to lower elevations for the winter. Hopi Indians knew of the Grand Canyon too, and came for religious pilgrimages and to collect salt.

**the modern tribes:** Today the Havasupai live 35 air miles NW of Grand Canyon Village in Havasu Canyon, a tributary of the Grand Canyon, and on lands atop the South Rim. The waterfalls, travertine pools, and greenery of their remote canyon have earned it fame as a "shangri-la" (see description later in this chapter). To the W of the Havasupai, the large Hualapai Reservation spreads across much of the Grand Canyon's South Rim. The only road access to the Colorado River within the Canyon goes through their lands. A small band of Paiute Indians lives on the Kaibab Reservation, just W of Fredonia in far northern Arizona.

**Spanish and American explorers:** In 1540, when Francisco Vasques de Coronado led an expedition in search of the Seven Cities of Cibola, Hopi Indians told a detachment of soldiers about a great canyon to the west. Hopi guides later took a party of Coronado's men, led by Don Lopez de Cardenas, to the South Rim but kept secret the routes into its depths. The Spaniards failed to find a way to the river and left discouraged. Looking for souls to save, the Franciscan priest Francisco Tomas Garces visited the Havasupai and Hualapai in 1776 and was well received by the Indians. Historians credit Garces with naming the Rio Colorado ("red river"). James Ohio Pattie and other American fur trappers probably came across the Grand Canyon in the late 1820s, but gave only sketchy accounts of their journeys. Lieutenant Joseph Ives led the first real exploration of the Colorado River. He chugged 350 miles upstream from the river's mouth by steamboat in 1857-58 before crashing into a rock in Black Canyon. The party continued overland to the Diamond Creek area in the western Grand Canyon. Most of the Canyon remained a dark and forbidding unknown until Major John Wesley Powell bravely led a boat expedition through it in 1869-70. On this trip and a second one in 1871-72, Powell and his men made detailed drawings and took notes on the geology, flora and fauna, and Indian ruins. As a result of these expeditions, Powell wrote *Canyons of the Colorado* (now published as *The Exploration of the Colorado River and its Canyons*) and other works.

**ranching on the Arizona Strip:** Not many pioneers took an interest in the prairie here —the ground proved nearly impossible to plow and lacked water for irrigation. Determined

*Havasupai woman with child in burden basket, late 1800s*

*Major John Wesley Powell*

Mormons began ranching in the 1860s despite the isolation and Navajo raids. They built "Windsor Castle," a fortified ranch, in 1870 as a base for a large church-owned cattle herd. Mormons also founded the towns of Fredonia, Short Creek (Colorado City), and Littlefield.

Some of these settlers had fled Utah to escape federal laws prohibiting polygamy. About 3,000 members of a polygamous, excommunicated Mormon sect still live in Colorado City and neighboring Hilldale, Utah. Federal and state officials raided Colorado City several times, the last in 1953, when 27 arrests were made (all received one-year probations). Now government policies seem to be "live and let live."

**miners and tourists:** From about 1880, prospectors entered the Grand Canyon to develop copper, asbestos, silver, and lead deposits, despite the remoteness and difficult terrain. Their trails, many following old Indian routes, are still used by modern hikers. In 1883 stage coaches began bringing tourists to see the Canyon at Diamond Creek, where J.H. Farlee opened a 4-room hotel the following year. Prospectors Peter Berry and Ralph and Niles Cameron built the Grandview Hotel in 1895 at Grandview Point and led tourists down their trail to Horseshoe Mesa. Other prospectors, such as John Hance and William Bass, also found guiding visitors to be more profitable than mining. Tourism began on a large scale soon after the railroad reached the South Rim in 1901. The Fred Harvey Company purchased

*John Hance and his burros*

the Bright Angel Lodge, built the deluxe El Tovar Hotel, and took over from the small operators. As the Canyon became better known, President Theodore Roosevelt and others pushed for greater federal protection. First a Forest Reserve in 1893, the Grand Canyon became a National Monument in 1908, then a National Park in 1919. The Park's size doubled in 1975 when legislation extended the boundaries W to Grand Wash and NE to Lees Ferry. Grand Canyon National Park now includes 1,892 square miles and receives about 3 million visitors annually.

# VISITING THE GRAND CANYON NATIONAL PARK

Most people head first to the South Rim, entering at either the South Entrance Station near Grand Canyon Village or the East Entrance Station near Desert View. A 26-mile scenic drive along the rim connects the 2 entrances. The South Rim features great views, a full range of accommodations and restaurants, and easy access (just 58 miles N of I-40 from Williams). Roads and most facilities stay open all year. Attractions include the Visitor Center, Yavapai Geology Museum, Tusayan Pueblo ruin, West Rim Drive to Hermit's Rest (8 miles), and East Rim Drive to Desert View (25 miles). The South Rim also has most of the Canyon's easily accessible viewpoints and trails. As such, large crowds of visitors, especially in summer, are the main drawback of this part of the Canyon. The Park collects an admission fee of $5/motor vehicle ($2/bus passenger or bicyclist) at the S and E entrances for the South Rim and at the main entrance for the North Rim. Except as noted, the Visitor Center, museums, programs, and trails have free admission once you're in the Park. Budget travelers can save money by stocking up on groceries and camping supplies at Flagstaff, Williams, or other towns away from the Canyon; prices within the Park run up to 25 percent higher.

Only about one in 10 visitors makes it to the North Rim's developed area at Bright Angel Point, but that visitor is rewarded with pristine forests, rolling meadows, and greater variety of wildflowers. Viewpoints here provide a perspective of the Canyon dramatically different from the lower-elevation South Rim. The North

*tourists at Grandview Hotel (first on rim), 1899*

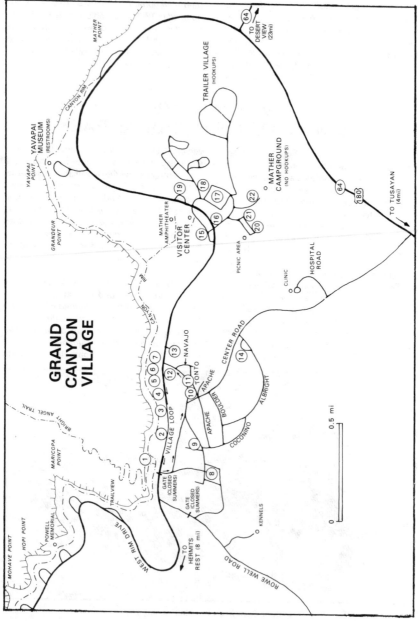

Rim offers similar lodging, restaurant, and camping facilities as the South, though on a smaller scale (no McDonalds here). Unless you want to ski in (backcountry permit required), the North Rim is open only from mid-May to Oct. or Nov., depending on the timing of the first big winter storm. Although the 2 rims stand just 10 miles apart, motorists on the S side must drive 215 miles to get here.

Adventurous travelers willing to tackle 61 miles (OW) of dirt road can head over to Toroweap Overlook on the North Rim. Here, you'll be perched a dizzying 3,000 feet directly above the Colorado River at one of the Canyon's most spectacular viewpoints. Don't expect any facilities other than the road to get you here (passable by cars in good weather) and an outhouse or two. Obtain a backcountry camping permit beforehand and bring all supplies including water. Low elevations (4,500-5,000 feet) allow year-round access, weather permitting. Check road conditions first with a ranger; tel. 638-7888. Toroweap is 91 river miles downstream from the developed areas of the Park; the road turnoff is 8 miles W of Fredonia.

## GRAND CANYON VILLAGE

1. Bright Angel Trailhead; Kolb Studio
2. Bright Angel Lodge and Restaurant
3. Thunderbird Lodge
4. Kachina Lodge
5. El Tovar Hotel and Restaurant
6. Hopi House (souvenirs)
7. Verkamp's (souvenirs)
8. Maswik Lodge and Cafeteria
9. Community Building
10. ranger office
11. youth hostel
12. historic railroad station
13. public garage
14. Albright Training Center
15. Shrine of the Ages
16. RV waste disposal station
17. Mather Center (store, post office, bank)
18. Yavapai Lodge and Cafeteria
19. service station
20. Backcountry Reservations Office
21. Camper Services (showers, laundromat, ice)
22. Sage Loop Campfire Circle

## SOUTH RIM SIGHTS

**Mather Point:** This is the first overlook you'll see when coming from the S; it's located where the S entrance road curves W to Grand Canyon Village. Stephen Mather served as the National Park Service's first director and was in office when the Grand Canyon joined the park system on 26 Feb. 1919. Below Mather Point (elev. 7,120 feet) lie Pipe Creek Canyon, the Inner Gorge of the Colorado River, and countless buttes, temples, and points eroded from the rims.

**Visitor Center:** Dioramas and other exhibits introduce you to the Park's early Indian residents, miners, explorers, early tourists, and natural history. Riverboats in the courtyard show the variety of craft that have run the Colorado. Oldest is a 1909 cataract boat used by the Stone Expedition, which put in at Green River, Wyoming, on 12 Sept. 1909, and came out 37 days and 1,300 miles later at Needles, California. Two 15-min. slide shows alternate in the auditorium, daily 0830-1930: *Grand Canyon, a Park for All Seasons,* shown on the hour, illustrates major points of interest and things to do; *Grand Canyon: Human and Natural History,* shown on the half hour, provides background on the Park. A bulletin board in the lobby lists ranger-guided rim walks, Canyon talks, and evening presentations. A ranger at the desk will answer your questions and give out maps and brochures. A bookstore offers a good selection of Canyon-related books, posters, topo maps, slides, video movies, and postcards. Open daily 0800-1700, extended in summer; tel. 638-9304 (recording of scheduled programs) or 638-7888. Located one mile E of Grand Canyon Village and 3 miles N of the South Entrance Station.

**Yavapai Museum:** Set on the brink of the Canyon, this geologic museum illustrates the Grand Canyon's long history. Panels identify the many buttes, temples, points, and tributary canyons seen through the windows. Rock samples let you compare formations from the ancient Vishnu Schist of the Inner Gorge to the youngest rocks on the rim. Fossils show life as

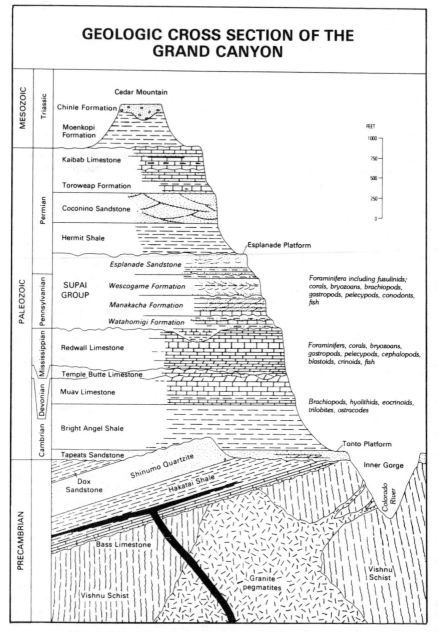

# GEOLOGIC CROSS SECTION OF THE GRAND CANYON

Edwin D. McKee, U.S. Geological Survey Professional Paper 1173; G.P.O. 1982

*view from
South Rim*

ancient as the one-billion-year-old algae in Bass Limestone. A "geologic clock" graphically ticks off the time required to form the rock layers revealed by the Colorado River. The clock takes 3 min. to complete a cycle, with each "tick" representing 11 million years. Exhibits present both Indian legends and scientific versions of the Canyon's formation. Educational video programs entertain the kids. Open daily 0900-1700, extended 0800 to sunset in summer. Books, maps, slides, video movies, and postcards can be purchased. Museum is located ¾ mile NE of the Visitor Center by road, or one mile by foot trail.

**South Rim Nature Trail:** Pick up biology and geology brochures ($.25 each) for the self-guiding trail at the Visitor Center, Yavapai Museum, or outside Verkamp's Curios (next to El Tovar Hotel). Start anywhere along the way as there are no keyed trail numbers. This is a fine hike for people of all ages. Three and a half miles of the nearly level trail have been paved, beginning at the Yavapai Museum and following the rim W past El Tovar Hotel to Maricopa Point. You'll enjoy views from many different vantage points. The South Rim Trail continues W 5 miles as a dirt path to Hermit's Rest, at the

end of West Rim Drive. Another unpaved segment heads E ½ mile from Yavapai Museum to Mather Point. The free Canyon shuttle bus (operates every 15 min. in summer) stops at 8 places near the South Rim Trail.

**West Rim Drive:** The Fred Harvey Company built this 8-mile-long road from Grand Canyon Village to Hermit's Rest in 1912. Pullouts along the way allow stopping to enjoy the views. Your map will help to pick out Canyon features: the Bright Angel Trail switchbacking down to the grove of trees at Indian Gardens; Plateau Point at the end of a short trail from Indian Gardens; the long, straight Bright Angel Canyon on the far side of the river; the many majestic temples rising to the N and E; and rapids of the Colorado River. Hermit's Rest (restrooms, giftshop, and drinking water) marks the westernmost viewpoint and end of the drive. During summer a free shuttle bus runs the length of the drive; other times you can take your own vehicle. Bicyclists enjoy this drive too, and aren't affected by the summer ban on cars.

If you've walked to Hermit's Rest on the South Rim Trail, you'll probably want to rest too. Louis Boucher, the Hermit, came to the Can-

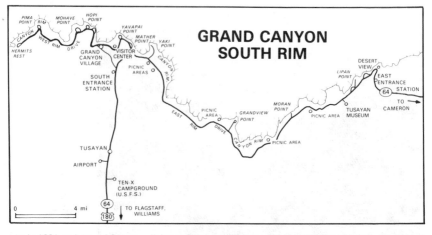

yon in 1891 and stayed 21 years, living at Dripping Springs and building the Boucher Trail to his mining claims in Boucher Canyon. Hermit Trail, built by the Fred Harvey Company after Louis Boucher had departed, begins just beyond Hermit's Rest at the end of a gravel road. The trail descends to the Tonto Trail and on to the river at Hermit Rapids. Visitors taking this trail between 1912 and 1930 could stay at a tourist camp located part way down on the Tonto Platform; only foundations remain today. A branch in the upper trail goes to Dripping Springs and Boucher Canyon.

**East Rim Drive:** Outstanding overlooks line this 26-mile drive to Desert View. Each has its own character and is worth a stop, but many people consider the aptly named Grandview Point one of the best. It's 12 miles E of Grand Canyon Village (14 miles before Desert View), then ¾ mile north. Sweeping panoramas take in much of the Grand Canyon from this commanding site above Horseshoe Mesa. The vastness and intricacies of the Canyon are especially evident here. Other major viewpoints on the East Rim Drive include Yaki Point, Moran Point, Lipan Point, and Desert View. At Lipan, by looking both up- and downcanyon, you can see the entire geologic sequence that makes up the Canyon. Hiking trails into the Canyon leave from or near each of these overlooks too (see "Inner Canyon Hiking").

**Tusayan Ruin:** Prehistoric Anasazi Indians built this pueblo about A.D. 1185. Archaeologists who excavated the site in 1930 named it "Tusayan," a Spanish term used for Hopi Indian territory. A small museum introduces the Anasazi culture with artifacts and models of dwellings; exhibits describe modern tribes of the region too. Outside, a short, self-guided trail leads to the plaza and ruins of living quarters, storage rooms, and 2 kivas. A leaflet (pick up at museum, $.25) describes how the Anasazi farmed and obtained some of their wild foods. Perhaps 30 people lived here, contending with poor soil, low rainfall, and scarce drinking water. After staying 15-20 years they moved on. The museum is open daily 0900-1630, extended in summer; may close in Jan. and February. It's on the East Rim Drive, 22 miles E of Grand Canyon Village and 4 miles W of Desert View.

**Desert View:** This overlook offers a stunning view at the end of the East Rim Drive. Although the surrounding pinyon pines and junipers suggest a lower elevation, this is the highest viewpoint on the South Rim (elev. 7,500 feet). To the E lies the multi-hued Painted Desert that gave the viewpoint its name. Below, to the N, the Colorado River flows out of Marble Canyon, then curves west. The strange-looking Desert View Watchtower uses design elements from both prehistoric and modern tribes of the Four Corners region. The Fred Harvey

Company built the 70-foot structure in 1932, using stone around a steel frame. The interior ($.25 admission) contains reproductions of a Hopi altar, wall paintings, and petroglyphs; stairs lead to windows at the top. Desert View has an information booth, snack bar, general store, service station, and campground; most services close in winter. A short nature trail loops around the point. Energetic hikers can head crosscountry to Zuni and Papago Points off the East Rim Drive, or take the long 12-mile RT route to Comanche Point N of Desert View; ask a ranger at Desert View for directions. From Desert View, AZ 64 continues E 17 miles to an overlook of the Little Colorado River Gorge on the Navajo Indian Reservation, then another 15 miles to Cameron on US 89.

## SOUTH RIM ACCOMMODATIONS

There's too much at the Grand Canyon to see in one day! In Grand Canyon Village you can stay right on the rim at Bright Angel Lodge, Thunderbird Lodge, Kachina Lodge, or El Tovar Hotel. Other lodges and and a youth hostel lie back in the woods. The town of Tusayan, just outside the Park (9 miles S from Grand Canyon Village), has additional places to stay. Reservations are essential in the busy summer season and a good idea the rest of the year.

**youth hostel:** Budget travelers will find the best bargain at Grand Canyon Youth Hostel. Only 20 beds here, so reservations (with first-night deposit) should be made: Box 270, Grand Canyon, AZ 86023. Show up promptly at 1700 if you don't have a reservation. Dormitory space costs $8/night year-round; no membership card needed. The required sleeping sheet can be rented if you don't have one. A 2-night stay limit applies from June to October. Guests may use the kitchen. Hostel is in Grand Canyon Village at 76 Tonto St. (see map); tel. 638-9018.

**Grand Canyon Village:** All the lodges here are run by Grand Canyon Park Lodges. Make reservations with them at Box 699, Grand Canyon, AZ 86023; tel. 638-2401 for advance reservations or tel. 638-2631 for same-day reservations.

One of the Grand Old Hotels of the West, El Tovar has offered the finest accommodations and food at the Canyon since 1905. The rooms have all the modern conveniences while keeping an old-fashioned ambiance; many also have canyon views; rates run $88.40-$208 s or d. Located on the rim in Grand Canyon Village. Kachina and Thunderbird Lodges, also on the

*Tusayan Ruin*

rim, offer deluxe modern rooms; $82.16-$88.40 s or d. The historic Bright Angel Lodge sits on the rim a short distance from the Bright Angel trailhead. The lobby, patio, restaurant, and lounge are popular gathering spots for hikers and other visitors. Rates for cabins range from $26 (s or d; no bath) to $140.40 (up to 6 people; w/bath). Rooms in the lodge cost $35.36 s or d. The Bright Angel History Room displays memorabilia from early tourist days and a ''geological fireplace'' in which Canyon rocks have been laid, floor to ceiling, in their proper stratigraphic sequence. The transportation desk in the lobby organizes scheduled bus service, bus and air tours, mule trips, and accommodations at Phantom Ranch (bottom of Canyon). Maswick Lodge, 2 blocks S of Bright Angel Lodge, has economy sections ($52 s or d), deluxe units ($80 s or d), and a cafeteria. Yavapai Lodge's modern rooms cost $59.28-$69.68 s or d; cabins go for $33.28 s or d; there's also a cafeteria; closed Jan. and Feb.; located near the Visitor Center, one mile E of Grand Canyon Village.

*on the brink of the Inner Gorge*

**Tusayan:** Moqui Lodge is just S of the Park entrance and one mile N of Tusayan. Rates are $50 s, $55 d from May to Sept., and $40.56 s, $45.76 d in the off season; closed Jan. and Feb.; tel. 638-2424. The Lodge has a restaurant, an information desk from which tours and horseback riding can be arranged, a gift shop, and a service station. Red Feather Inn, 9 miles S from Grand Canyon Village in Tusayan, is open all year: $55.12 s, $60.32 d from mid-Apr. to Oct., and $33.28 s, $37.44 d in winter; tel. 638-2673. Facilities include a restaurant, swimming pool, and jacuzzi. Seven Mile Lodge has rooms at $50 s, $57.20 d in summer, and $29.12 s, $34.32 d in winter; tel. 638-2291. The nearby Grand Canyon Squire Inn has deluxe rooms at $68.64 s, $74.88 d in mid-summer and during Christmas holidays; then $43.68 s, $50 d the rest of the year; tel. 638-2681. The Inn features a restaurant, swimming pool, jacuzzi, sauna, exercise room, tennis courts, bowling, and gift shop.

**Valle:** Highways US 180 from Flagstaff and AZ 64 from Williams meet at this road junction 24 miles S of Grand Canyon Village. Stay at Grand Canyon Inn, $40 s, $41.60 d year-round, though may close in mid-winter; has a restaurant; tel. 635-9203. Two small motels, closed in winter, are just S of the junction on AZ 64.

## SOUTH RIM CAMPING

Campgrounds also tend to be crowded in summer. If you don't have a reservation, it's recommended that you arrive at the Park by 1000 to look for a site. Rangers enforce the ''no camping outside designated sites'' policy with a $50 fine. Backpackers inside the Canyon need free permits from the Backcountry office (see ''Inner Canyon Hiking''). Dispersed camping in the Kaibab National Forest just S of the Park is another possibility; just don't camp along the highways. The Forest Service Office in Tusayan can make suggestions; their Kaibab Forest Map shows the backroads.

**inside the Park:** Mather Campground is conveniently located S of the Visitor Center, one mile E of Grand Canyon Village. Open early Apr. to end of Nov.; sites have drinking water but no hookups; $6/night; tel. 638-7888. Showers, laundromat, and ice are available for a small charge at Camper Services, adjacent to the campground. Reservations ($2 extra charge) can be made by mail 2-8 weeks in advance from 15 May to 1 Oct. through Ticketron, Dept. R, 401 Hackensack Ave., Hackensack, NJ 07601. Trailer Village, just to the E of Mather Campground, offers RV sites for $10.40 w/hookups (tenters may stay here when Mather is closed); open all year; make reservations with Grand Canyon Park Lodges (Box 699, Grand Canyon, AZ 86023; tel. 638-2401 for advance reservations or tel. 638-2631 for same-day reservations. Desert View Campground, near the East Entrance Station (25 miles E of Grand Canyon Village), has sites with drinking water but no hookups; open mid-May to end of Sept.; $6.

**outside the Park:** Grand Canyon Camper Village in Tusayan (9 miles S of Grand Canyon Village) has sites for tents and RVs, $10.50 ($14.70 w/hookups) and tipi tent accommodation (warmer months only; $13.65); has showers; stores and restaurants are nearby; Box 490, Grand Canyon, AZ 86023; tel. 638-2887. Ten X Campground has drinking water but no hookups; open 1 May to 31 Oct.; $6; from Tusayan go S 3 miles, then E ½ mile; tel. 638-2443. Tumbleweed RV Park is in Valle, 24 miles S of Grand Canyon Village on AZ 64/US 180; has coin showers and a store; tents or RVs without hookups $8 (RVs w/hookups $11); may close in winter; tel. 635-2118. Flintstone Bedrock City campsites in Valle cost $9.45 for tents or RVs ($12.60 w/hookups); has coin showers, store, snackbar, and amusement park; open mid-Apr. to end of Oct.; self-contained vehicles can camp in winter; tel. 635-2600.

## SOUTH RIM FOOD

**Grand Canyon Village area:** El Tovar Hotel's restaurant offers elegant dining; open daily for breakfast, lunch, and dinner (mod. to exp.); tel. 638-2631 (dinner res. recommended). Bright Angel Lodge has 2 places to eat: an informal restaurant serving breakfast, lunch, and dinner daily (mod.); and the Arizona Steakhouse, which dishes up steaks, fish, chicken, and ribs for dinner daily (mod.); tel. 638-2631. Less expensive fare is offered by cafeterias at Maswik Lodge (W end of Village; open daily for breakfast, lunch, and dinner during summer and most of winter), and at Yavapai Lodge (open daily for breakfast, lunch, and dinner from about Apr. to Dec.). Babbitt's Store (S of Visitor Center) has a deli counter and tables. Pick up fast food at Bright Angel Fountain (on the Canyon Rim behind Bright Angel Lodge; open Apr. to Oct.); and Yavapai Fast Food (Yavapai Lodge; open Apr. to Dec.). Buy groceries at Babbitt's Stores, located in Grand Canyon Village, Desert View, and Tusayan.

**Tusayan:** Moqui Lodge has a Mexican-American restaurant; open daily for breakfast and lunch only; closed Jan. and Feb.; tel. 638-2424. You'll also find restaurants at the Grand Canyon Squire Inn (tel. 638-2681) and Red Feather Inn (tel. 638-2673). The Steak House features mesquite-grilled steaks and other fare; located between Red Feather and Grand Canyon Squire Inns. We Cook Pizza, Etc. offers Italian sandwiches and dinners, as well as pizza; open daily for lunch and dinner (dinner only in winter); tel. 638-2278. There's a McDonalds in town too, but don't expect it to have the same prices as at home; the staff will happily give you a handout explaining why their costs are so high.

## SOUTH RIM SERVICES

**entertainment:** The Grand Canyon IMAX Theatre in Tusayan shows an impressive movie, *The Grand Canyon—The Hidden Secrets* on a giant screen with 6-track stereo sound. The 34-min. presentation briefly covers history, wildlife, river-running, flying, and scenic viewpoints of the Canyon. Showings take place hourly 0830-2030 every day in summer, and reduced hours the rest of the year; $4.75 adult, $3.75 seniors over 60, and $2.75 children under 12; tel. 638-2203.

For nightlife in Grand Canyon Village, try the El Tovar's cocktail lounge (often has piano music), Bright Angel Lodge's cocktail lounge (varied live music many evenings), and Yavapai

VEHICLES, ESPECIALLY MOTORHOMES, ARE FREQUENTLY THE TARGET OF THIEVES IN NATIONAL PARKS  DO NOT LEAVE VALUABLES (PURSES, CAMERAS ETC.) IN YOUR VEHICLE  REGARDLESS OF HOW WELL HIDDEN. IF YOU ARE THE VICTIM OF THEFT OR OBSERVE ANYONE TAMPERING WITH VEHICLES, CONTACT RANGERS IN YAVAPAI MUSEUM OR CALL 638-2477

Lodge's lounge (dancing with live bands or DJ; open Apr. to Dec.). Rangers present evening programs year-round; the Visitor Center can tell you what's on and where.

**shopping:** The Visitor Center has a good bookstore and sells topo maps. Babbitt's stores—at Mather Center (S of the Visitor Center), Desert View, and Tusayan—have groceries, camping and hiking supplies, clothing, books, maps, and souvenirs. Grand Canyon Trail Guides, located just W of Mather Campground, offers camping and hiking gear for sale and rent, and does repairs; closed in winter. Lookout Studio, on the rim near Bright Angel Lodge, sells beautiful rock, mineral, and fossil specimens. Indian crafts, postcards, and other souvenirs can be purchased from El Tovar Hotel, Bright Angel Lodge, Hopi House, Verkamp's Curio, Hermit's Rest, Desert View Lookout Tower, and other locations.

**other services:** Bank and post office are S across the road from the Visitor Center; the bank can cash traveler's checks, exchange foreign currency, do wire transfers, and give cash advances on Visa and MasterCard but cannot cash out-of-town checks. Grand Canyon Medical Clinic offers medical and dental services; tel. 638-2551 or 638-2469. If there's an emergency after hours; tel. 638-2477. A pharmacy is here too; tel. 638-2460 (see map for location). For an ambulance; tel. 638-2477 or 638-7888. The National Park Service provides handicapped people with wheelchairs, an access information booklet, Braille literature, sign language interpreter, and other help; ask at the Visitor Center or write ahead to the Park.

Theft has become a problem at the Canyon —be sure to keep valuables hidden or take them with you. Park rangers patrol the Park, serving as law enforcement officers and firemen; see them if you have difficulties. Pets won't be welcomed in the lodges or permitted on the inner-canyon trails, but they can stay in the kennels (see map). Camper Services, next to Mather Campground, has a laundromat and showers—a welcome sight to any traveler who's been a long time on the road or trail.

## SOUTH RIM INFORMATION

The Visitor Center has exhibits, slide shows, bookshop, bulletin board of scheduled events, and an information desk; open daily 0800-1700, extended in summer to 0800-2000; tel. 638-9304 (recording of activities and programs) or tel. 638-7888; located one mile E of Grand Canyon Village and 3 miles N of the South Entrance Station. Hearing-impaired people can get a TDD recorded message at tel. 638-7772. Stop at the Backcountry Reservation Office, next to Camper Services, for hiking information and backcountry camping permits (dayhikers don't need a permit); open daily 0700-1200 and 1300-1700 in summer, 0800-1200 and 1300-1700 the rest of the year; tel. 638-2474 (call after 1100 or you'll get just a recorded announcement). For a weather forecast and winter road conditions; tel. 638-2245. Grand Canyon Village has a public library on Village Loop Dr.; tel. 638-2718. The Park Service sells *The Guide* newspaper with the latest visitor information; $.10.

The Kaibab National Forest, though little known in the shadow of Grand Canyon National Park, offers both developed and primitive camping. Stop at the Tusayan Ranger Station for a map and information. They'll also give directions for hiking the Red Butte Trail, a 2½-mile RT climb up the prominent butte 12 miles S of Tusayan. The office is just S of Babbitt's Village Store in Tusayan; open Mon. to Fri. 0800-1200 and 1300-1700; tel. 638-2443.

## SOUTH RIM TOURS

**mule rides:** Sure-footed mules have carried prospectors and tourists in and out of the Canyon for more than a century. The large animals, a crossbreed of female horses and male donkeys, depart daily all year for day and overnight trips. Although easier than hiking, a mule ride should still be considered strenuous — you need to be able to sit in the saddle for long hours and control your mount. Daytrips go down the Bright Angel Trail to Indian Gardens and out to Plateau Point, a spectacular overlook directly above the river; the 12-mile 7-hour RT costs $59. On the overnight trip you follow the Bright Angel Trail all the way to the river, cross a suspension bridge to Phantom Ranch, spend the night in a cabin, then come out the next day via the S. Kaibab Trail; $188 ($326/2 persons) including meals and cabins. Three-day/2-night trips offered Dec. to Feb. cost $245 ($428/2 persons).

All of these trips are definitely not for those afraid of heights; if you're in doubt, Fred Harvey Movies (Box 709, Grand Canyon, AZ 86023) will send a color Super-8 movie ($12 postpaid) or videotape (VHS or Beta $16 postpaid) showing what it's like in the saddle. Requirements for riders (enforced!) include good health, weight under 200 lbs. (91 kg), fluency in English, height over 4 feet 7 inches, and ability to mount and dismount without assistance. No pregnant women are allowed. Hats (tied under chin), long pants and long shirt/sleeves, and sturdy shoes (no open-toed footwear) should be worn. No bags, purses, or backpacks allowed, but you can carry a can-

teen and a camera or binoculars. Reservations should be made 9-12 months in advance for summer and holidays. Also be sure to claim your reservation at least one hour before departure. Even without a reservation, there's a good chance of getting on by signing up for the waiting list, especially off season; register by 1000 the day before you want to go. Mules will also carry hiker's overnight gear to Phantom Ranch, $28 (30 lb. limit). For information, reservations, and standbys see the Bright Angel Transportation Desk (tel. 638-2401), or write: Grand Canyon National Park Lodges, Reservations Dept., Box 699, Grand Canyon, AZ 86023.

**horse rides:** Apache Stables offers short rides through the Kaibab National Forest ($10/one hour, $15/2 hours), 4-hour trips to the South Rim ($22), a cowboy breakfast ride, and other excursions. Season lasts Apr. to mid-Nov, depending on weather. Make reservations with Moqui Lodge (one mile N of Tusayan); tel. 638-2424.

*visitors at head of Bright Angel Trail in early 1900s; Teddy Roosevelt is in foreground*

**guided hikes:** If you'd rather go hiking or backpacking with an experienced guide, contact Grand Canyon Hiker Services. They'll make all the permit and transportation arrangements, suggest possible trips, and can even carry your gear (at extra charge). Popular guided hikes, with per-person rates based on a minimum of 4, are: Grandview Trail to Horseshoe Mesa (½ day, $21), Hermit Trail to Dripping Springs (one day, $36.75), Tanner Trail to the river (2 days, $99.75), Grand Canyon Rim to Rim (3 days, $204.75), and Havasupai Canyon (4 days, $262.50). Almost any other trip can be arranged too. Advance reservations (w/25 percent deposit) should be made if possible. Grand Canyon Trail Guides has 2 offices: next to the Backcountry Reservations office (near Camper Services) at the Park; open Apr. to Nov.; Box 735, Grand Canyon, AZ 86023; tel. 638-2391; and in Flagstaff (open all year), Box 2997, Flagstaff, AZ 86003; tel. 526-0924. Although the Grand Canyon office closes in winter, trips can still be arranged then. Any hiker may use their equipment rental and repair services.

**bus tours:** The Fred Harvey Transportation Co. will show you the sights of the South Rim with narration about the Canyon's history, geology, and wildlife. Hermit's Rest Tour visits viewpoints of the West Rim Drive (2 hours; $9.50). Desert View Tour travels along the East Rim Drive (3 hours; $15, or $18 including Hermits Rest Tour). Sunset Tour goes over to Yaki Point (1 ½ hours; $6.50; summer only). Indianlands Tour takes in the Navajo and Hopi Reservations, including Little Colorado River Gorge, Coal Canyon, Hopi Cultural Center, and a Hopi village (about 12 hours; $80). Monument Valley Expedition visits the striking landscape of buttes and sand dunes on the Navajo Indian Reservation (11-13 hours; $65). Call for departure days on the Monument Valley trip. All other tours leave daily (twice a day in summer for the Hermit's Rest and Desert View tours). Get tickets at Bright Angel, Maswik, or Yavapai Lodge transportation desks; children under 12 occupying a seat go at half price. No reservations needed, though you could make them for the Indianlands and Monument Valley tours;

Box 699, Grand Canyon, AZ 86023; tel. 638-2401.

**air tours:** Flights over the Canyon provide breath-taking views and offer a look at some of the Park's remote corners. About 40 scenic-flight companies operate helicopters or fixed-wing aircraft here. However, the 50,000-plus flights a year detract from the wilderness experience of backcountry users — Tusayan's airport is the third busiest in the state. Some restrictions on flying will likely be imposed, but flights should continue. Scenic flights depart all year from Tusayan airport, while Grand Canyon Helicopters and Madison Aviation leave right from the village of Tusayan. Transport from hotels to terminals is available. Rates listed are adults and per person; children under 12 usually fly at a discount.

Grand Canyon Airlines started flying here in 1927 with Ford Trimotors. Today they use high-wing, single- and twin-engine planes for flights over the Canyon (20 min. at $35, or 55 min. at $50) and 15-20-min. flights to the airstrip at Grand Canyon North Rim ($50 OW, $100 RT); tel. 638-2407, or (800) 528-2469 in Arizona, or (800) 528-2413 out of state. Air Grand Canyon's high-wing Cessnas offer 3 loops: a 20-min. flight over the Canyon ($35), a 45-min. trip over both rims ($50), and a 1 ½-hour tour of both Havasupai and Grand Canyons ($100); tel. 638-2686.

Grand Canyon Helicopters flies over the Canyon (20 min.; $60); to the North Rim (30 min.; $75); over Marble, Little Colorado, and Grand Canyons (45 min.; $110); and to Havasu and Grand Canyons (60 min.; $135); you can also land at Havasupai Village and visit the waterfalls ($362), or spend the night ($407); tel. 638-2419, 252-1706 in Phoenix, or (800) 528-2418 out of state.

## SOUTH RIM TRANSPORT

**shuttle services:** The Park Service runs 2 free shuttle services during the summer (Memorial Day weekend to Labor Day) to reduce vehicle traffic. The Village Loop connects the Visitor Center, Yavapai Museum, campgrounds,

*Vishnu Temple*

lodges, shops, and offices of Grand Canyon Village; service operates daily every 15 minutes from about 0545 to 2200. The West Rim Drive Shuttle leaves from the road junction in front of Bright Angel Lodge and goes to Hermit's Rest, with stops at 8 overlooks; operates daily every 15 minutes from about 0730 to 1845. Two "Hiker's Specials" leave in the morning from the Backcountry Reservations office for the S. Kaibab trailhead. Tusayan-Grand Canyon Shuttle connects Bright Angel Lodge and other places in Grand Canyon Village with Tusayan and the airport (charge); operates all year; tel. 638-2889.

**auto rentals and taxi:** Rent cars from Budget (tel. 638-9360) or Dollar Rent A Car (tel. 638-2625), both at Grand Canyon Airport. For a taxi, tel. 638-2822.

**bus:** Nava-Hopi buses go to Flagstaff (3 times daily in summer and once daily the rest of the year) and Williams (once daily); fares for either destination are $11.75 OW, $22.30 RT, or

$10.70 RT w/bus pass. See the Bright Angel Transportation Desk for schedules and tickets; no reservations needed.

**air:** Grand Canyon Airlines flies several times daily in season between the South and North Rims. Fares of $50 OW and $100 RT include ground transportation. These flights take 15-20 minutes, saving a tedious 5-hour OW drive. Reservations required; tel. 638-2407.

The only other scheduled service to Grand Canyon Airport is from Las Vegas by Scenic Airlines (tel. 638-2436 or 800-634-6801) and Air Nevada (tel. 638-2441 or 800-634-6377). Most Las Vegas to Grand Canyon trips on both airlines fly over the Canyon—an added bonus. Scenic Airlines offers 3-6 flights out daily, $109 OW, $169 RT; a "K-class" fare of $59 OW is offered on the first flights out and the last in at the Grand Canyon; make reservations at least 2 weeks ahead in summer and 2 days in winter. Air Nevada has a similar service with 3 flights daily, $109 OW, $169 RT, and $49 K-class.

*view from Bright Angel Point*

## NORTH RIM SIGHTS

"Two rims, two worlds" — the North Rim does offer a different experience from the South. Higher elevations (1,000-1,500 feet more than the South Rim) cause cooler temperatures and nearly 60 percent more precipitation. Rain and snowmelt over time have cut deeply into the North Rim, until now it is about twice as far removed from the Colorado River as the South Rim. Dramatic vistas from the N inspired early explorers to chose names like Point Sublime, Cape Royal, Angel's Window, and Point Imperial. Even away from the viewpoints, the North Rim is beautiful. Spruce, fir, pine, and aspen forests thrive in the cool air. Wildflowers bloom in blazes of color on the meadows and along the roadsides.

Visitor facilities and major trailheads are located near Bright Angel Point, a 45-mile drive S from Jacob Lake in the far N of Arizona. The road to Bright Angel Point opens in mid-May, then closes after the first big winter storm, any time from early Oct. to the end of November.

**Bright Angel Point:** At the end of the highway, near Grand Canyon Lodge, park and follow the paved foot trail to the tip of Bright Angel Point (½ mile RT). Roaring Springs Canyon on the L and Transept Canyon on the R join the long Bright Angel Canyon. John Wesley Powell's expedition camped at the bottom of this canyon and gave the name Bright Angel Creek to its crystal-clear waters. Listen for Roaring Springs far below on the L, and look to see where the springs shoot out of the cliff. A pumping station at their base generates electricity and supplies drinking water to both North and South Rims. Roaring Springs makes a good dayhike or muleback-ride destination on the N. Kaibab Trail (see "Inner Canyon Hiking"). Transept Canyon, dry much of the year, can be entered from the N. Kaibab Trail, but is best done on an overnight trip. Transept Trail (1½ miles OW) winds along the canyon rim between Grand Canyon Lodge and the campground.

**Cape Royal Scenic Drive:** Paved roads lead to some of the North Rim's most spectacular viewpoints. Point Imperial (elev. 8,803 feet) offers the highest vantage point from either rim. Views encompass the eastern end of the Park: Nankoweap Creek below, Vermillion Cliffs on the horizon to the N, rounded Navajo Mountain (in Utah) on the horizon to the NE, Painted

Desert to the E, and the Little Colorado River Canyon across to the southeast. The difficult Nankoweap Trail provides access to Nankoweap Creek and the Colorado River (see "Inner Canyon Hiking"). Point Imperial is 11 miles from Grand Canyon Lodge; go N 3 miles from the lodge, turn R 5½ miles on Cape Royal Drive, then L 2½ miles to the parking.

Cape Royal Drive continues past Point Imperial turnoff to Vista Encantadora, which overlooks an arm of Nankoweap Creek, then on to a parking area just before Cape Royal. Total driving distance from Grand Canyon Lodge is 21 miles OW. A trail continues S ⅓ mile from the parking lot to Cape Royal. On the way you'll see Angel's Window, a massive natural arch. A short side trail actually goes on top of the arch. Cape Royal is the southernmost viewpoint from the North Rim in this part of the Grand Canyon: Freya Castle lies to the SE, nearby Vishnu Temple and Creek and distant San Francisco Mountains to the S, and a branch of Clear Creek Canyon and flat-topped Wotans Throne to the southwest.

Cliff Spring Trail begins from a pullout on Cape Royal Drive ⅓ mile before road's end. The one-

*Transept Canyon from Widforss Trail*

mile RT trail to the spring goes W, descends into a forested ravine, and passes a small Indian ruin.

**Point Sublime Scenic Drive:** A 16½-mile dirt road goes to this overlook and picnic area W of Bright Angel Point. The way is bumpy and not always passable; check at the North Rim Entrance Station or the Information Desk at Grand Canyon Lodge. Views take in an impressive amount of Canyon, truly sublime. Turnoff is located ½ mile S of the Entrance Station and 14½ miles N of Grand Canyon Lodge.

**Widforss Trail:** Gently rolling terrain, fine canyon views, and a variety of forest types attract hikers of all ages. From the edge of a meadow, the trail climbs a bit, skirts the head of Transept Canyon, then runs across a plateau covered by ponderosas to an overlook near Widforss Point. The trail and point honor Swedish artist Gunnar Widforss, whose paint-

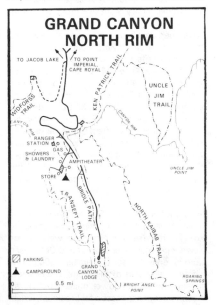

# GRAND CANYON NORTH RIM

TO JACOB LAKE

TO POINT IMPERIAL, CAPE ROYAL

KEN PATRICK TRAIL

UNCLE JIM TRAIL

WIDFORSS TRAIL

CANYON RIM

RANGER STATION

GAS

SHOWERS & LAUNDRY

AMPITHEATER

STORE

UNCLE JIM POINT

TRANSEPT TRAIL

BRIDLE PATH

NORTH KAIBAB TRAIL

PARKING

CAMPGROUND

GRAND CANYON LODGE

ROARING SPRINGS

BRIGHT ANGEL POINT

0        0.5 mi

ings depicted the national parks of the West between 1921 and 1934. Haunted Canyon lies below at trail's end, flanked by The Colonade on the R, and Manu Temple, Buddha Temple, and Schellbach Butte on the L; beyond lie countless more temples, towers, canyons, and the cliffs of the South Rim. Widforss Trail is 10 miles RT (allow 5 hours), though many people enjoy going just partway. Mule deer can often be seen along the trail. From Grand Canyon Lodge, go 2¾ miles N on the highway, then turn L one mile on a dirt road; turnoff is ¼ mile S of Cape Royal Rd. junction.

**Ken Patrick Trail:** Highlights of this rim-country trail include views of upper Bright Angel Canyon and E across the headwaters of Nankoweap Creek to Marble Canyon. From the N. Kaibab trailhead, near Bright Angel Point, the Ken Patrick winds NE, crosses Bright Angel Creek and Cape Royal Rd., then follows the rim overlooking Nankoweap Creek to Point Imperial. Parts of the trail may be overgrown. Allow 6 hours for the 12-mile hike (OW). Both the N. Kaibab and Ken Patrick trails begin from the same parking lot (2¼ miles N of Grand Canyon Lodge); Ken Patrick trail leaves from the upper end of the parking area. Point Imperial trailhead is 11 miles by road from Grand Canyon Lodge.

**Uncle Jim Trail:** The first mile follows the Ken Patrick Trail (from the N. Kaibab trailhead), then the trail turns SE to Uncle Jim Point. Allow 3 hours for the 5-mile round trip. Mules take only 2 hours! (Ask at the mule rides desk in the Lodge lobby.) Views from the point take in Roaring Springs Canyon and N. Kaibab Trail. James "Uncle Jim" Owens served as the Grand Canyon Game Reserve's first warden from 1906 until establishment of the National Park.

## NORTH RIM PRACTICALITIES

**accommodations and camping inside the Park:** Grand Canyon Lodge, overlooking Transept Canyon near Bright Angel Point, has the North Rim's only accommodation within the Park. Four types of lodging are offered: "Frontier cabins" ($41.60 s or d, $46.80 t);

"Western cabins" ($55.12 s or d, up to $70.72/5 persons); "Pioneer cabins" ($47.84/ 1-5 persons); and modern motel rooms ($51 s or d, $56.16 t, $61.36/4 persons). Open late May to mid-Oct.; reservations (w/deposit) are recommended. Contact TWA Services, Box 400, Cedar City, Utah 84720; tel. (801) 586-7686. A signboard at Jacob Lake near the turnoff for the Grand Canyon North Rim lists what services are available. The road from Jacob Lake to the Rim is usually open earlier in the spring and later in the fall than Grand Canyon Lodge, restaurants, gas station, and campground. **camping:** North Rim Campground, 1½ miles N of Grand Canyon Lodge, has drinking water but no hookups; open mid-May to mid-Oct.; $6/night. No reservations taken except for groups with sponsorship or charter (Group Reservations, North Rim, Grand Canyon, AZ 86023). Coin-operated laundromat and showers are next to the campground.

**accommodations and camping outside the Park:** Kaibab Lodge, 18½ miles N of Bright Angel Point, offers a restaurant and basic rooms ($29.40 s, $32.55 d); open June-Sept.; tel. 643-2389. Across the highway, North Rim Country Store sells groceries, camping supplies, and gas; open mid-May to mid-November. Jacob Lake Inn, open all year, is 45 miles N of the North Rim at Jacob Lake; it has an Indian crafts shop, groceries, gas, restaurant, cabins ($30.45-$44.10), and basic motel rooms ($42-$51.45); tel. 643-7232. **camping:** DeMotte Forest Camp is 18½ miles N of the North Rim; open 1 June to 30 Sept.; drinking water and showers ($.50) but no hookups; $6/night. Jacob Lake Forest Camp has drinking water but no showers or hookups; open mid-May to early Nov.; at Jacob Lake. Jacob Lake RV Park has spaces with hookups; $10/night; open mid-May to early Nov.; located ½ mile off AZ 67 just S of Jacob Lake.

**food and services:** Grand Canyon Lodge serves breakfast, lunch, and dinner (mod. to exp.) in a huge rustic dining room with Canyon views; open daily late May to mid-Oct.; reservations requested for dinner; tel. 638-2611. A cafeteria, also part of the lodge, offers faster service and slightly lower prices—but no atmosphere; open in season for breakfast, lunch,

*on the Kaibab Plateau*

and dinner. Post office and gift shop are in Grand Canyon Lodge. North Rim Pub and Game Room has indoor diversions and snacks; located next to the campground. A small general store and a service station are also near the campground. In emergencies, see a ranger or call tel. 638-2477 or 638-7888. Recorded weather forcasts; tel. 638-2245.

**information, mule rides, and transport:** Rangers staff the Information Desk in the Grand Canyon Lodge's lobby daily 0700-1900. They'll give you times of nature walks and Canyon lectures. Obtain backpacking permits and information from the Backcountry Reservation Office (Box 129, Grand Canyon, AZ 86023) either on the South Rim or at the Ranger Station on the North Rim (turnoff from the highway is  mile N of the campground). You can ride mules along the rim and into the Canyon: one-hour rim rides cost $10, 2-hour rim rides to Uncle Jim's Point are $17, ½-day trips down the N. Kaibab Trail to the tunnel are $22 (min. age 8); and the full-day rides to Roaring Springs are $48 including lunch (min. age 12); see the mule rides desk in the Lodge lobby. Requirements for riders are similar to those of

South Rim trips. Reservations for the mules are a good idea; tel. 638-2292 at the Lodge, or tel. (801) 586-7238 before June 1st. Grand Canyon Airlines has the only public transportation to the North Rim; flights are offered several times a day in season. Fares of $50 OW and $80 RT (same-day travel) include ground transportation. Reservations required; ask the Grand Canyon Lodge staff or call tel. 638-2407.

## TOROWEAP

This seldom-visited area of the North Rim lies between Kanab Canyon to the E and the Pine Mountains to the west. An overlook (elev. 4,552 feet) provides awesome Canyon views from sheer cliffs that drop nearly 3,000 feet to the river below. Toroweap, also known as "Tuweap" or "Tuweep," is 145 road miles W from the developed North Rim area. Visitors who make it here are rewarded with views, many hiking possibilities, and solitude.

**sights:** Sinyala Butte, 25 miles E from the overlook (upriver), marks the mouth of Havasu Canyon. Most of the Havasupai Indians who

view upstream from Toroweap Overlook

live on their reservation are in Supai Village, 11 miles up Havasu Canyon.

The Hualapai Indian Reservation lies directly across the Colorado River from the overlook; use binoculars to look for old hogans and a trail leading down to a spring. Lava Pinnacle, also known as Vulcan's Forge or Thor's Hammer, sits in the middle of the river directly below. This 50-foot-high lava neck is all that remains of an extinct volcano. Lava Falls, visible downstream, roars with a vengeance. Debris from Prospect Canyon of the South Rim forms the rapids, perhaps the roughest water in the Grand Canyon. Water flowing between 12,000 and 20,000 cubic feet per second drops abruptly, then explodes into foam and spray. On a scale of one to 10, river runners commonly rate this rapids a "ten." The steep Lava Falls Trail leads down to the rapids from a nearby trailhead (see "Inner Canyon Hiking").

Vulcan's Throne, the 600-foot-high rounded hill just W of the overlook, is one of the youngest volcanoes of the area. Between 30,000 and 1,200,000 years ago, eruptions of red-hot lava built about 60 volcanic cones here and even formed dams across the Colorado River. One of the dams towered nearly 500 feet, but the river has long since cut through and washed it away.

Forests cover Mount Trumbull (summit elev. 8,028 feet) to the north. Mormons used these trees to build their temple in St. George, Utah. John Wesley Powell named the rounded peak for a Connecticut senator.

Hikers can find many easy rambles across the plateau near the overlook. Vulcan's Throne would be an easy climb, while Toroweap Point is quite a challenge. Pinyon pine, juniper, cactus, and small flowering plants cover the plateau. Watch for rattlesnakes.

**practicalities:** A camping area sits close to the overlook at the end of the road; sleepwalking isn't recommended here! More sheltered camping spots can be found farther back from the rim. There's no camping charge, but you need a permit from Park Service Backcountry Reservations Office (Box 129, Grand Canyon, AZ 86023) at the South or North Rims, or from the Tuweep Ranger Station. Bring water, extra food, and camping gear.

From AZ 389, 9 miles W of Fredonia, turn S at the sign "Mt. Trumbull 53 miles." The road to Toroweap (65 dirt miles OW) is in mostly good condition when dry. Watch for livestock and take it slow through the washes. The last few miles are a bit rocky, but cautiously driven cars can make it OK. The Tuweep Ranger Station is on the L about 5½ miles before the overlook. Beyond the ranger station, Toroweap Point (summit elev. 6,393 feet) towers on the L and dumpy Vulcan's Throne (summit elev. 5,102 feet) sits on the right. You can also drive to Toroweap on a 90-mile-OW dirt road from St. George, or a 55-mile-OW primitive road from Colorado City, the roughest route. Avoid driving these roads after heavy rain or snow. Snows usually block the road from St. George between Oct. and May. No water, food, or gas is available in this backcountry. Check on road conditions before coming out; tel. 638-7888. Obtain hiking information and emergency help at the Tuweep Ranger Station (open all year).

## INNER CANYON HIKING

Hiking in the Canyon, even a short way, provides a better look and appreciation for the wonders within. Always keep in mind, however, that the Inner Canyon is a wilderness area, subject to temperature extremes, flash floods, rockslides, and other natural hazards. Careless hikers have ruined their Canyon trips by hiking without water and doing other foolish things. Always carry (and drink!) water. In summer, carry 2-3 quarts on maintained trails, and one gallon on trails with fewer water sources. All too often people will walk merrily down a trail without a canteen, then suffer terribly on the climb out.

Footgear (lightweight boots work well) should have good traction for the steep trails. Instep crampons (metal plates with small spikes) can be helpful on icy trails in winter and early spring at the higher elevations. Good fitting raingear will keep you dry during rainstorms; ponchos, on the other hand, provide little protection against wind-driven rain. Be careful if rock-scrambling — soft and fractured rock predominate in the Canyon. Don't swim in the Colorado River, its cold waters and swift currents are too dangerous.

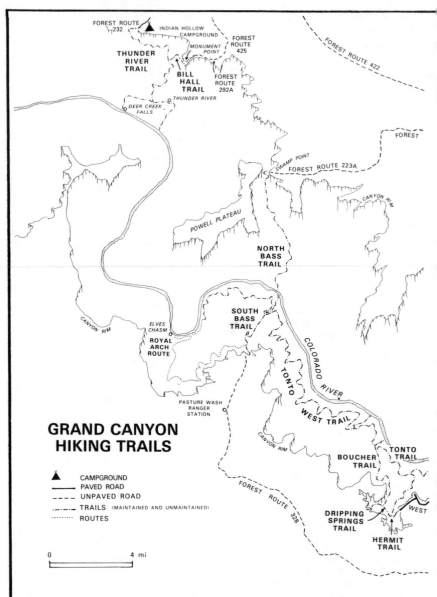

**GRAND CANYON HIKING TRAILS**

▲ CAMPGROUND
—— PAVED ROAD
---- UNPAVED ROAD
-.-.-.- TRAILS (MAINTAINED AND UNMAINTAINED)
········· ROUTES

0        4 mi

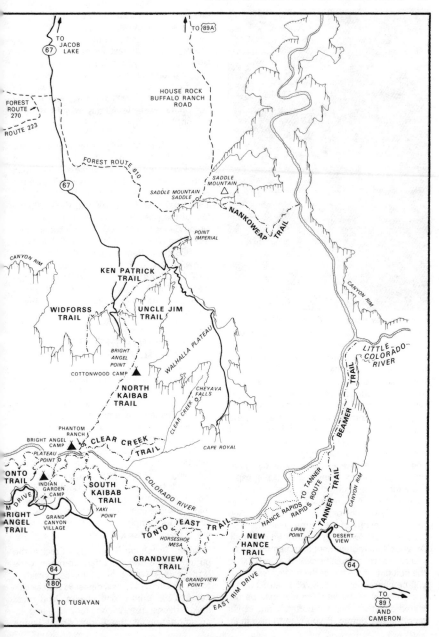

*Inner Gorge near Phantom Ranch*

**permits:** You don't need a permit if you dayhike or have reservations to stay at Phantom Ranch. Hikers planning overnight camps must get free permits from the Backcountry Reservations offices, on either the South Rim (next to Camper Services) or the North Rim (N. Rim Ranger Station). Ask for their Trip Planning Packet, which has regulations, a map, and reservation request form. The Park Service limits the number of campers in each section of the Canyon to protect the land from overuse and to provide a wilderness experience. Try to make reservations as early as possible, especially for holidays and the popular months of March to May. Reservations, which can be made only by mail or in person, are accepted for the remainder of the current year and, after 1 Oct., for the following calendar year as well. An important requirement to remember is that reserved permits *must* be picked up by 0900 on the first day of the trip or the *entire* reservation will be cancelled; tel. 638-7888 beforehand if you think you'll be late. Permits may be obtained at either rim, but normally not earlier than the day before. If you plan to hike in an

area far from the backcountry offices, such as Kanab or Nankoweap Canyons, you may request the permits to be mailed. This request should be made at least one month in advance. Don't despair if you arrive without a reservation; sign up on the waiting list as soon as the office opens on the day before you want to hike. Return by 0900 the next day to find out what's available. All this must be done in person.

**hiking information:** Several guidebooks have trail descriptions of the Canyon (see "Booklist"), but the best source of information is the Backcountry Reservations office on the South Rim; open in summer 0700-1200 and 1300-1700, then 0800-1200 and 1300-1700 the rest of the year. Visit them or write Box 129, Grand Canyon, AZ 86023. The Backcountry Information Line is open Mon. to Fri. 1100-1700; tel. 638-2474. Rangers staff the North Rim Backcountry office daily 0700-1100 and 1600-1700 from late May to mid-October. Topo maps and books are sold at the Visitor Center's bookstore and other shops in Grand Canyon Village.

## MAINTAINED TRAILS OF THE INNER CANYON

Three kinds of hikes can be taken in the Inner Canyon. You can follow maintained trails, unmaintained trails, or routes. Park Service rangers usually recommend that first-time visitors try one of the maintained trails to get the feel of Canyon hiking. These trails are wide and well signposted. Rangers and other hikers will be close at hand in case of problems. Camping in this part of the Canyon is restricted to established sites at Indian Gardens, Bright Angel, and Cottonwood. Mice and other varmints at these campgrounds have a voracious appetite for campers' food — keep yours hung out of reach or risk losing it!

Phantom Ranch, on Bright Angel Creek at the bottom of the Canyon, offers dormitory beds ($16), cabins ($48 s or d), meals (breakfast $7.25, box lunch $6, stew dinner $11, steak dinner $18.25), drinks, and snacks. You must make advance reservations for meals and accommodation at the Bright Angel Lodge

Transportation Desk, or with Grand Canyon Lodges, Box 699, Grand Canyon, AZ 86023; tel. 638-2401. If you'd rather have your gear carried, mules will do it for $28 (30-lb. limit). Mules will carry you too (see "South Rim Tours").

**Bright Angel Trail:** Havasupai Indians used this route from the South Rim to reach fields and a spring at Indian Gardens. Prospectors widened the trail in 1890 and later extended it to the Colorado River. Now it's the easiest and most used trail into the Canyon. Trailhead is just W of Bright Angel Lodge in Grand Canyon Village. Resthouses 1.5 and 3 miles below the rim have emergency telephones and usually offer water from 1 May to 30 September. Distances (OW) from the top: 4.6 miles to Indian Gardens (campground, water, and ranger station), 7.8 miles to Colorado River, and 9.3 miles to Bright Angel Creek (campground, water, ranger station, and Phantom Ranch). Allow 4-5 hours on the descent to the river and 8-10 hours coming out (elev. change 4,500 feet). Plateau Point makes a good all-day hike. You'll be 1,300 feet directly above the swirling Colorado River and enjoy a 360-degree panorama of the Canyon. Take the Bright Angel Trail to Indian Gardens, then follow signs. This is a strenuous dayhike of 12.2 miles RT; elevation change is 3,080 feet.

**River Trail:** This short, 1.7-mile trail parallels the river in the twisted rocks of the Inner Gorge. It connects the bottoms of the Bright Angel and South Kaibab Trails. Two suspension bridges cross the river to Bright Angel Creek.

**South Kaibab Trail:** Hikers on this trail enjoy sweeping views up and down the Canyon. From the trailhead near Yaki Point (4.5 miles E of Grand Canyon Village), the South Kaibab drops steeply, following Cedar Ridge toward the river and Bright Angel Creek (6.4 miles OW). An emergency telephone is at the "Tip-off," 4.4 miles below the rim, where the trail begins the descent into the Inner Gorge. Lack of shade and water and the steep grade make this trail especially difficult to climb in summer. Allow 3-4 hours for the descent and 6-8 hours coming out (elev. change 4,800 feet). Part way

down, Cedar Ridge is a good dayhiking destination—3 miles RT and an elevation change of 1,160 feet. Strong hikers also enjoy continuing down to the nearly level Tonto Trail (4.4 miles from rim), turning L 4.1 miles on the Tonto to Indian Gardens, then 4.6 miles up the Bright Angel Trail. A car shuttle would be needed for this 13.1-mile hike. Very strong hikers can make it all the way from rim to river and back in one day on the Kaibab. During summer, however, this would be grueling for *anyone* and not recommended.

**North Kaibab Trail:** Few other trails compare in the number of interesting sidetrips and variety of scenery. Hikers on this trail start in the cool forests of the North Rim, descend through the woods into Roaring Springs Canyon, then follow the rushing Bright Angel Creek all the way to the river. Trailhead is 2.3 miles N of Grand Canyon Lodge. Snows close the road from some time in Oct. or Nov. until mid-May, but the North Kaibab can be reached year-round via trails from the South Rim. A long section of trail between the rim and Roaring Springs has been cut into sheer cliffs; water-

*Kaibab Suspension Bridge*

falls cascade over in spring and after rains. A picnic ground near Roaring Springs has water; it's a good destination for dayhikers (9.4 miles RT from the North Rim; elev. change 3,160 feet).

Cottonwood Campground (6.9 miles below the rim) makes a good stopping point for the night or a base for daytrips. It has a ranger station and water in summer. Winter campers have to get water from the creek (purify first). Ribbon Falls pours into a miniature paradise of travertine and lush greenery. It's in a side canyon 1.5 miles downstream from Cottonwood Campground.

The North Kaibab Trail continues downstream along Bright Angel Creek and soon enters the dark contorted schists and other rocks of the ancient Vishnu Group. Near the bottom you'll walk through Phantom Ranch then Bright Angel Campground. Most people can go down the 14.2-mile North Kaibab in 8-9 hours of steady hiking (elev. change 5,700 feet). Climbing out can·take 10-12 hours, best done over 2 days. Fishermen often have good luck catching rainbow trout in Bright Angel Creek; winter is the best season.

## UNMAINTAINED TRAILS OF THE INNER CANYON

These trails lead to some beautiful corners of the Park. You'll find solitude and get new perspectives of the Canyon. Hikers need to be self-reliant on the unmaintained trails: they must know where water sources are, be able to use map and compass, and handle emergencies. Most trails follow prehistoric Indian routes or game trails that miners improved to pack out ore in the late 1800s. Trail conditions vary widely; some remain in excellent condition, while others have dangerous spots or require careful map reading. Although the Park Service calls the trails "unmaintained," trail work may be done if a section becomes impassible. Hermit Trail and parts of the Tonto Trail have designated camping areas that you're required to use. The following trails are listed from W to E on the South Rim, then W to E on the North Rim.

**Tonto Trail:** Hikers in a hurry will find the Tonto frustrating as they wind in and out of

*Louis Boucher (far left) at his mine*

countless canyons. This 92-mile trail contours along the Tonto Plateau, connecting most of the South Rim trails between the mouth of Red Canyon at Hance Rapids and Garnet Canyon far downstream. The Canyon panorama continually changes as you walk along, sometimes taking in spectacular views from the edge of the Inner Gorge. Most of the way is gently rolling (average elev. 3,000 feet). You might lose the trail occasionally, but with attention to rock cairns and the map, you'll soon find it again. The sun bears down relentlessly in summer, when it's best to hike elsewhere.

**South Bass Trail:** William Bass learned about this route from the Havasupai Indians in the 1880s. He then started a small tourist operation. Bass also built a trail up to the North Rim, crossing the river by boat and later by a cage suspended from a cable. No crossing exists today. The South Bass Trail is generally good and easy to follow. It drops to the Esplanade, a broad terrace, then down to the river. You'll need a high-clearance vehicle to reach the trailhead, 4 miles N of Pasture Wash Ranger Station; ask the Backcountry office for directions. Hiking the 9-mile trail to the river takes about 5 hours down and 9 hours up (elev. change 4,400 feet). No water is available before the river.

**Boucher Trail:** Louis Boucher, "the Hermit," came to the Canyon in 1891 and mined copper along Boucher Creek until 1912. Steep terrain and rock slides make the trail difficult—it's best for strong, experienced hikers with light packs. Take Hermit and Dripping Springs Trails (see below) to Boucher Trail. You'll reach the Tonto Trail just before Boucher Creek. The route down the creek to the Colorado River is an easy 1.5 miles. From the Hermit trailhead on the West Rim Drive, it's 11 miles to Boucher Creek; allow 7-8 hours down and 9-10 hours coming up (elev. change 3,800 feet). Water is available in Boucher Creek.

**Hermit Trail:** Although named for Boucher, the trail was actually built by the Fred Harvey Company for tourists about 1912. Visitors took this route to Hermit Camp, which operated until 1930. Most of Hermit Trail is in good condition; the few places covered by rock slides can

*Hermit Camp*

be easily crossed. Trailhead begins just beyond Hermits Rest, at the end of the 8-mile West Rim Drive. Water is available at Santa Maria Spring (2 miles OW) and Hermit Creek (7 miles OW). The Colorado River is an easy 1.5-mile walk down the bed of Hermit Creek. Elevation change from rim to river is 4,300 feet. Allow 5-6 hours going down and 8-10 hours climbing out.

Hermit Trail also connects with Dripping Springs Trail and Tonto Trail. Dayhikers can head to Dripping Springs, a 6-mile RT hike taking 4-6 hours (elev. change 800 feet). Descend the Hermit Trail 1.5 miles, then turn L 1.5 miles on Dripping Springs Trail. Water should be carried for the entire trip as the springs have only a tiny flow. The 22.5-mile "Hermit Loop" hike which follows the Hermit, Tonto, and Bright Angel Trails has become popular. Water is found on this loop year-round at Monument Creek and Indian Gardens, and seasonally at Salt and Horn Creeks. Hikers can easily descend the bed of Monument Creek to Granite Rapids (1.5 miles OW).

**Grandview Trail:** Dayhikers frequently use this steep but scenic trail to Horseshoe Mesa. Trailhead is at Grandview Point on the East Rim

Drive. Miners improved an old Indian route in 1892 so they could bring out high-grade copper ore from Horseshoe Mesa. Mining ceased in 1907, but mine shafts, machinery, and ruins of buildings remain. Cave of the Domes, a limestone cavern on the W side of the mesa has some good passages; look for a trail fork W of the butte atop the mesa. Three trails descend to the Tonto Trail, though the E trail is steep and hazardous. Bring water, as the springs shown on the map are either unreliable or difficult to reach. Allow 6 hours for the 6-mile RT hike to Horseshoe mesa (elev. change 2,600 feet).

**New Hance Trail:** John Hance, one of the first prospectors to get into the tourist business, built this trail down Red Canyon in 1895. The unsigned trailhead is about one mile SW of Moran Point turnoff on the East Rim Drive; get directions from a ranger. Suited for more experienced hikers, the trail descends steeply with poor footing in places to the river at Hance Rapids. Most of the way is easy to follow, especially if descending. No water is available before the river. The 8-mile trail takes about 6 hours to descend and 8-10 hours to climb out (elev. change 4,400 feet).

**Tanner Trail:** Seth Tanner improved this Indian trail in the 1880s to reach his copper and silver mines along the Colorado River. Although in good condition and easy to follow, the Tanner Trail is long (10 miles OW) and dry. It's best hiked in the cooler months. Hikers often cache water part way down for the return trip. Trailhead is about 100 yards back down the road from Lipan Point parking lot, off the East Rim Drive. Allow 6-8 hours for the descent and 8-10 hours coming out. **Beamer Trail:** This slim path begins at Tanner Canyon Rapids (lower end of Tanner Trail) and follows the river 4 miles upstream to Palisades Creek, then climbs to a high terrace for the remaining 5 miles to the Little Colorado River confluence. No camping is allowed within one mile of this spot.

**Lava Falls Trail:** The Colorado River explodes in a fury of foam and waves at Lava Falls, reached by this short but steep trail from the North Rim. Cairns mark the way down a lu-

narlike landscape of volcanic lava. Barrel cactus thrive on the dark, twisted rock. Although the trail is only 2 miles long (OW), it should be considered difficult because of the steep grades and poor footing in places. Summer temperatures get *extremely* hot (elevation at the river is only 1,700 feet). Carry water. From Toroweap Overlook (see "Toroweap" above), backtrack on the road 2.5 miles and look for a dirt track on the L; follow it 2.5 miles across Toroweap Lake (normally dry) and around the W side of Vulcan's Throne. The way may be too rough for cars. At road's end, the trail descends to a hill of red cinders about two-thirds of the way down; the last part of the descent follows a steep gulley. Lava Falls lies .25 mile downstream. Camping is possible along the river. Allow 2 hours going down and 4 hours coming out (elev. change 2,500 feet).

**Thunder River trails:** Thunder River blasts out of a cave in the Muav Limestone, cascades ½ mile, then enters Tapeats Creek. It's not only the world's shortest river but suffers the humiliation of being a tributary to a creek! Deer

*Inner Gorge*

Creek Falls, another attraction in the area, plummets more than 100 feet onto the banks of the Colorado River. Cottonwood trees, willows, and other cool greenery grace the banks of Thunder River and both creeks. Trails are generally good and easy to follow, though spring runoff and rains can make Tapeats Creek too high to cross safely.

Two trails descend from the North Rim: the Thunder River Trail from Indian Hollow Campground at the end of Forest Route 232, and the Bill Hall Trail from the E side of Monument Point at the end of Forest Route 292A. The Bill Hall Trail saves 5 miles of walking but the steep grade can be hard on the knees. Trailheads are reached by turning turning W on Forest Route 422 from AZ 67 in Demotte Park (one mile S of Kaibab Lodge and 17.5 miles N of Bright Angel Point); see the Kaibab Forest map (North Kaibab Ranger District). It's about 35 miles of dirt road from the highway to either trailhead. Cars can negotiate the roads in good weather. Winter snows bury this high country from about mid-Nov. to mid-May. Thunder River Trail and the Bill Hall shortcut both drop steeply to the Esplanade, where they meet. Thunder River Trail then switchbacks down to Surprise Valley, a giant piece of the rim that slumped thousands of feet to its present position. Surprise Valley turns into an oven in summer and lacks water. Deer Creek Trail, marked by a large cairn in the Valley, splits off to the W for Deer Creek, 3.5 miles away. A short walk down Deer Creek leads to the falls and a trail to the river just W of the falls. Thunder River Trail goes E across Surprise Valley, drops to Thunder River, and follows it to Tapeats Creek. Unless at high water, Tapeats Creek can be followed 2.5 miles upstream to its source in a cave. The Colorado River is a 2.5-mile hike downstream from the junction of Thunder River and Tapeats Creek. Camp at the designated sites near this junction, downstream on the Colorado River, or along upper Deer Creek. Good fishing attracts anglers to Tapeats Creek and may have in the past as well — prehistoric Cohonina Indians left ruins along the creek. From the Bill Hall trailhead at Monument Point to Tapeats Rapids is 12 miles OW; allow 7 hours to the upper campsite on Tapeats Creek and 9 hours all the way to Tapeats Rapids. Thunder River, 9 miles from the Bill Hall

*pinnacles of the Kaibab Formation*

trailhead, is the first source of water.

**North Bass Trail:** This difficult trail drops from Swamp Point on the North Rim into Muav Canyon, which winds down to Shinumo Creek and the Colorado River. The trail reaches the Colorado about .25 mile below where the S. Bass Trail comes down on the other side. No crossing exists today. Only experienced hikers should tackle this long and faint trail. Muav Saddle Spring, White Creek (above Redwall cliffs), and Shinumo Creek have water, and Shinumo Creek has trout as well. Shinumo can be difficult to cross in spring. Using a high-clearance vehicle, take Forest Routes 422, 270, 223, and 223A to the trailhead at Swamp Point. Allow 3-4 days for the 28-mile RT to the river (elev. change 5,300 feet).

**Clear Creek Trail:** This trail is the North Rim's version of the Tonto. Clear Creek Trail is in very good condition and easy to follow. The trail begins .3 mile N of Phantom Ranch and climbs 1,500 feet to the Tonto Plateau. It then winds in and out of canyons until dropping at the last possible chance into Clear Creek, 9 miles from Phantom Ranch. Carry water (there's no source before Clear Creek) and be prepared for very hot summer weather. The best camping sites lie scattered among the cottonwood trees where the trail meets the creek. Dayhikers enjoy the first mile or 2 of Clear Creek Trail for scenic views of the river and Inner Gorge. Strong hikers can go all the way to Clear Creek and back in a long day. Better still would be to come for several days. Cheyava Falls, highest in the Canyon, is a 6- to 8-hour RT up the long NE fork of Clear Creek. Their flow is impressive only in spring and after heavy rains. Other arms of the creek offer good hiking too; the one branching E about .5 mile downstream from the end of Clear Creek Trail has a narrow canyon in quartzite. You can also go down Clear Creek to the Colorado River, a 5-7 hour RT hike. You're soon in the dark and contorted schist and granite. A 10-foot-high waterfall .5 mile from the river can be bypassed by clambering around to the right.

**Nankoweap Trail:** Dangerous ledges on the Nankoweap Trail discourage those hikers afraid of heights. If you don't mind tiptoeing on the brink of sheer cliffs, this trail will open up a large section of Park for your exploration. Trailhead is at Saddle Mountain Saddle, 2.4 crow-flying miles NE of Point Imperial. You can't drive to the trailhead, however; it must be approached on foot: either 3 miles OW from the end of House Rock Buffalo Ranch Rd. (S from US 89A), or 3 miles OW from the end of Forest Route 610 (E off AZ 67). Both access roads are dirt, passable by cars, but the House Rock Buffalo Ranch Road lies at a lower elevation and is less likely to be snowed in. The Nankoweap Trail drops several hundred feet, then contours along a ledge all the way to Tilted Mesa before descending to Nankoweap Creek. Some care in route-finding will be needed between Tilted Mesa and the creek. Nankoweap Creek, 10

canyon wren
(Catherpes mexicanus)

miles from the trailhead, is the first source of water. The remaining 4 miles to the river are easy. Allow 3-4 days for the roundtrip. Cache water part-way down to use on the return. Elevation change is 4,800 feet.

## ROUTES OF THE INNER CANYON

The Canyon has thousands of possible routes for the experienced hiker. Harvey Butchart, who has done more off-trail hiking than anyone else, describes many routes in his 3 books (see "Booklist"). The Backcountry Reservations office can suggest interesting routes too, and give you an idea of current conditions. Also you'll probably get ideas of your own from hiking in the Canyon and studying maps. Keep in mind that much of the Canyon's exposed rock is soft or fractured—a handhold or foothold can easily break off. The Colorado River presents a major barrier, as the water is too cold, wide, and full of treacherous currents to cross easily.

**Royal Arch Loop:** This rugged trip to Royal Arch and Elves Chasm has been described as "fantastic" by experienced hikers. The route follows parts of the South Bass and Western Tonto Trails to make a long loop with the Esplanade Route and Royal Arch Canyon. Allow a minimum of 5 days for this one and be prepared for plenty of rough spots. Note that fewer than half the people who attempt this loop actually make it! Sections of the route are *very* difficult to follow. The Royal Arch-Colorado River section is very exposed and requires a 50-foot rope. An easier hike takes the Tonto Trail to its end at Garnet Canyon, descends to the Colorado, and follows the river to Elves Chasm; return is the same way. Royal Arch is just 0.5 mile upstream from Elves Chasm, but you'll need to backtrack one mile up the Colorado River to the well-trodden route used for reaching the arch. A 15-foot section of travertine takes some skill to climb, but there's often a piece of rope to help (carry your own 50-foot rope though).

**Hance Rapids to Tanner Rapids:** The Tonto Trail gives out at Hance Rapids, but you can continue upstream to Tanner Rapids and the Tanner Trail. Distance is about 11 miles.

*rafting through Marble Canyon*

## RUNNING THE COLORADO RIVER

A great adventure, running the Colorado River through the Grand Canyon provides excitement of roaring rapids and tranquility of watching Canyon walls glide by. Although explorers of 100 years ago feared this section of river and portrayed it in dark and gloomy drawings, boating the entire Grand Canyon is an enjoyable and safe experience today. Running the Colorado opens up some of the most beautiful and remote corners of the Canyon. River parties make frequent stops to explore the twisting side canyons, old mining camps, and Indian ruins along the way. Within the Grand Canyon, the Colorado River flows 280 miles, drops 2,200 feet, and thunders through 70 major rapids.

**river tours:** Twenty companies offer a wide variety of trips through the Canyon, ranging from one-day introductions to adventurous 20-day expeditions. Write the Grand Canyon National Park for a list of companies (Grand Canyon, AZ 86023) or ask at the Visitor Center.

If possible, make reservations (w/deposit) 6 months in advance with the tour operator to assure your choice of trip. All but one of the tour companies use rafts of varied sizes; the exception is Grand Canyon Dories, which uses sturdy wooden boats. Both oar-powered and motorized craft run the river. The oar- or paddle-powered trips give a more natural and quieter experience but take half again as much time. Motor-powered rafts can zip through the entire Canyon in 6 days or go from Lee's Ferry to Phantom Ranch in as few as 2 days. River-running season normally lasts from Apr. to Oct., though only oar-powered craft depart after mid-September. Most trips put in at Lee's Ferry, just upstream from the Park, and take out downstream at Diamond Creek or Lake Mead. Shorter trips can be taken by using hiking trails or helicopters. If you'd like just a taste of river running, take a one-day trip from Glen Canyon Dam to Lee's Ferry with Wilderness River Adventures based in Page (see "Page Tours"), or raft the lower Grand Canyon with Hualapai Tribal River Trips based in Peach Springs (see "Visiting the Hualapai Indian Reservation").

*lower Marble Canyon*

Typical trips and approximate costs on commercial *oar* trips are: 12 days from Lee's Ferry to Diamond Creek (226 miles; $1,150); 5 or 6 days from Lee's Ferry to Phantom Ranch (87.5 miles; $525); and 8 or 9 days from Phantom Ranch to Diamond Creek (138.5 miles; $850). Equivalent *motorized* trips are 8 days from Lee's Ferry to Diamond Creek ($800); 3 or 4 days from Lee's Ferry to Phantom Ranch ($400); and 5 days from Phantom Ranch to Diamond Creek ($500). Many other combinations are available too. Discounts may be given for groups, children under 14, early booking, and early or late in the season.

If you've children in tow, check to see if there's a minimum age; sometimes this is left up to you, other times operators require a minimum age of between 8 and 16 years. Trips usually include land transportation; most depart from Flagstaff, Page, St. George, or Las Vegas.

Food, camping gear, and waterproof bags are usually included in the price. Experienced kayakers can tag along with many of the tours and get a lower rate. You can also organize your own Canyon expedition, but you must plan far in advance and meet all the Park Service requirements; contact the River Permits office; tel. 638-7843.

**canoeing the Lower Grand Canyon:**
Canoes in the Grand Canyon? Yes, in the last 40 miles within the Park. A power boat is needed to carry the canoes from Lake Mead to Separation Canyon (mile 240 on the river). Most of the southern shore on this trip belongs to the Hualapai Indians; obtain permits from them if you plan to camp or hike on their land. David Lavender wrote an article in the Sept. 1985 *Arizona Highways* about his 5-day canoe trip from Separation Canyon to Pearce Ferry.

# HAVASUPAI AND HUALAPAI INDIAN RESERVATIONS

## VISITING HAVASU CANYON

Havasu Canyon is a land of towering cliffs, blue-green waters, breathtaking waterfalls, and lush vegetation. Havasu Creek rushes through the canyon past the Indian village of Supai before beginning its wild cascade down to meet the Colorado River. The canyon and its creek, located about 35 air miles NW of Grand Canyon Village, belong to the Havasupai Indians (*havasu* means "blue" and *pai* means "people").

Havasupai had lived here long before the first white men arrived. The tribe farmed the fertile canyon floor during the summer, then moved up to the plateau after harvest. They wintered atop the plateau, gathering the abundant wild foods and firewood. Spanish missionary Francisco Garces visited the Havasupai in 1776, reporting them to be a happy and industrious people. Though a peaceful tribe, they still suffered the usual fate of American Indians, and were confined in 1862 to a tiny canyon reservation while ranchers grabbed their plateau lands. The Havasupai protested but had to wait until 1975 for their winter homelands to be returned. The Havasupai Reservation now spans 188,077 acres; most of the 500-600 tribal members on the reservation live in Supai village.

**getting there:** The tribe wisely decided against allowing a road to invade their canyon home, so most residents and tourists arrive by mule, horse, or on foot. Another option is by helicopter from Grand Canyon airport, though the noisy machines seem out of place here. The 8-mile trail from Hualapai Hilltop to Supai is the usual way in. From Seligman on I-40, take AZ 66 NW for 28 miles, then turn R 63 miles on a signposted road, paved all the way to Hualapai Hilltop. If coming from the W, take AZ 66 NE out of Kingman for 60 miles, then L 63 miles. The road to Hualapai Hilltop climbs into forests of ponderosa pine that give way to pinyon and juniper, then desert grasslands close to the rim. Fill up with gas before leaving AZ 66; no supplies or stores are available after turning off. Hualapai Hilltop features parking areas, stables, and Arizona's worst pit toilets. Various shortcuts on dirt roads can be taken to Hualapai Hilltop, but they have poor signposting and rough surfaces.

*trail to Supai*

**hiking in:** You *must* obtain advance reservations to camp or stay in the lodge. From Hualapai Hilltop (elev. 5,200 feet) the trail descends at a moderate grade into Hualapai Canyon for the first 1.5 miles, and then levels off slightly for the remaining 6.5 miles to Supai village (elev. 3,200 feet). About 1.5 miles before the village, the trail joins the sparkling waters of Havasu Canyon. Avoid the heat of day in summer when highs can go over 100 F. Always carry drinking water. All visitors must pay a $12 entrance fee on arrival at Supai. The tribe asks you to leave pets, booze, and firearms at home. To preserve the canyon floor, no fires or charcoal may be used; campers need to bring a stove if they plan to cook.

**sights:** The famous sights of the canyon begin just downstream from Supai. Three waterfalls plunge over cliffs in a space of just 2 miles. Navajo Falls, the closest to the village, is small but pretty. It's named after a 19th C. Havasupai tribal chief who was kidnapped by Navajo Indians as an infant and raised as a Navajo. Not until he had grown to manhood did he learn of his true origin and return to the Havasupai. Spectacular Havasu Falls drops 100 feet into a beautiful turquoise-colored pool rimmed by travertine deposits. Clear inviting waters make the spot perfect for a swim or picnic.

Mooney Falls, most awe-inspiring of all, plummets 190 feet into another colorful pool. The falls take their name from a prospector who died here in 1882. Assistants were lowering him down the cliffs next to the falls when the rope jammed. After hanging helpless for 3 days, Mooney fell to his death on the rocks below when the rope broke. A rough trail descends beside the falls along the same route hacked through the travertine by miners a year after Mooney's death. You'll pass through 2 tunnels and then ease down with the aid of chains and iron stakes. At the bottom (as soon as your knees stop shaking!), you can enjoy a picnic or swim in the large pool. You'll see holes high on the canyon walls from which miners once took silver, lead, zinc, and vanadium.

Beaver Falls, 4 miles downstream from Mooney, makes a good dayhike from the campgrounds or Supai village. You'll pass countless inviting travertine pools and small cascades, of which Beaver Falls is the largest. The trail, rough in places, crosses the creek 3 times, climbs high up a cliff, then descends and crosses a 4th time below Beaver Falls. The trail continues downstream along Havasu Creek 4 more miles to the Colorado River. Travel fast and light if going to the river, as camping is prohibited below Mooney Falls. Photographing any of the falls can be a challenge; best chances for getting them in full sunlight are in May, June, and July.

**camping:** Most visitors prefer to camp, listening to the sounds of the canyon and enjoying the brilliant display of stars in the nighttime sky. Havasu Campground begins .25 mile below Havasu Falls. It has spring water, picnic tables, litter barrels, and pit toilets. What most campers don't know is that the campground extends .75 mile along Havasu Creek to the brink of Mooney Falls. You'll enjoy more solitude by walking to the far end. Navajo Campground, near Navajo Falls, is less popular because it often lacks drinking water. Camping outside these 2 areas is prohibited. Theft is a

*descending to the base of Mooney Falls*

*Havasu Creek below Beaver Falls*

serious problem in the campgrounds; don't leave valuables in tents or lying around. You must obtain advance reservations and pay $9/night per person to camp. Call tel. 448-2121 or write Havasupai Tourist Enterprise, Supai, AZ 86435. Pay on arrival at Supai. Try to make reservations far ahead, especially for holidays, weekends, and all of May, June, and July.

**accommodations and food:** In the village of Supai, you can stay in the modern Havasupai Lodge; rooms have a/c, 2 double beds, and private bath. Rates: $45 s, $50 d, $58 t; $8 each additional person. A hostel provides simple dormitory spaces and use of a kitchen for $10/person. Both the lodge and hostel require reservations: Havasupai Lodges, Supai, AZ 86435; tel. 448-2111. A cafe nearby serves breakfast, lunch, and dinner; open daily about 0700-1830. Try their Indian taco. Ice cream costs a bundle—$1 for a cone or $2.75 for a large milkshake, but other prices aren't so bad. A store across the street sells meats, groceries, and cold drinks; open daily 0700-1800.

**services:** Send your postcard home via pack train, with a postmark to prove it! The post office is open weekdays 0900-1600, next to the store. If you'd rather ride than walk, local families will take you and your gear on horses or mules from the parking lot at Hualapai Hilltop to Supai ($70 RT) or to the campgrounds ($90 RT). A sightseeing trip from Supai to the falls and back costs $35. You'll get a horse or a mule, depending on what's available. Advance reservations (at least 3 weeks) and a ½ deposit must be made with Havasupai Tourist Enterprise, Supai, AZ 86435; tel. 448-2121. Always call one day before coming to check that your animal is available. Visitors may also bring their own horses if they take along feed and pay a $15 trail fee. A health clinic in Supai can provide emergency medical care.

## VISITING THE HUALAPAI INDIAN RESERVATION

The Hualapai Indians once occupied a large area of northwestern Arizona. In language and culture, they have close ties with the Havasupai and Yavapai tribes. Early white visitors enjoyed friendly relations with the Hualapai, but land seizures and murders by the newcomers led to warfare. United States Army troops defeated the Indians and herded them S onto the Colorado River Reservation, where many died. Surviving Hualapai fled back to their traditional lands, part of which later became the Hualapai Indian Reservation. About half of the 1,400 tribal members live on their 993,000-acre reservation. Much of the lower Grand Canyon's South Rim belongs to the tribe.

**Peach Springs:** This small town, 54 miles NE of Kingman on US 66, is the only town on the reservation. Peach Springs has neither charm nor anything to see, but is the place to obtain permits for recreation and backroad use on the reservation. A river trips office organizes one- and 2-day rafting trips through the lower Grand Canyon. There's no place to stay, but nearby Truxton (9 miles SW) has 2 motels. Peach Springs does have a cafe serving basic American and Mexican food along with Indian fry bread. There's also a grocery store.

*Farlee Hotel near Diamond Creek; built in 1884, and in ruins when this picture was taken, about 1914*

**Diamond Creek Road:** This scenic 21-mile gravel road goes N from Peach Springs to the Colorado River at Diamond Creek, providing the only road access to the river within the Grand Canyon. You'll enjoy fine canyon views, though not so spectacular as the developed areas of the Grand Canyon National Park. Except for river-runners, who use the road to take out or put in their boats, few people visit this out-of-the-way spot. Yet the very first organized groups of tourists to the Canyon bounced down the road to Diamond Creek in 1883. A hotel built here and used 1884-1889 was the first at the Grand Canyon.

During dry weather, cars with good ground clearance can make it in. Summer rains (July and Aug.) necessitate use of a truck. Except for some picnic tables and an outhouse or 2, the area remains undeveloped. Hikers can explore Diamond Creek and other canyons; see Stewart Aitchison's *A Naturalist's Guide to Hiking the Grand Canyon*. Obtain sightseeing permits ($2.50/day per person) at the Hualapai Tribal River Trips office (see below). No extra charge is made for camping, but fishermen must have a tribal license ($2.50/day additional). Diamond Creek Rd. turns off US 66 beside the Health Dept. Building in town.

**river running:** Hualapai Tribal River Runners offers one-day ($150) and 2-day ($235) motorized-raft trips down the lower Colorado between Diamond Creek and Pearce Ferry on Lake Mead. The 2-day trip allows a more leisurely pace and time for hiking. Rates in-

clude food and transportation from Peach Springs. Season lasts from Apr. to Oct.; write for the schedule well in advance so reservations can be made: Box 246, Peach Springs, AZ 86434; tel. 769-2216 or 769-2347. The office is open daily in summer (May to Sept.) and Mon. to Fri. the rest of the year 0800-1630. Look for the office in the Health Dept. Bldg. next to Cash and Carry Market on the main highway.

*Colorado River above Diamond Creek Rapids*

# THE ARIZONA STRIP

Lonely and vast, the "Strip" lies N and W of the Colorado River. Phoenix and the rest of the state seem a world away, cut off by the Grand Canyon. The Arizona Strip includes some spectacular canyon and mountain country. In addition to Grand Canyon National Park, 9 designated wilderness areas totaling nearly 400,000 acres protect the most scenic and u-nique sections. Several tiny communities in the Arizona Strip offer food and accommodations for travelers. More extensive facilities lie just outside the region: Page across the river to the E, and Kanab and St. George across the Utah border to the north.

## PIPE SPRING
## NATIONAL MONUMENT

Step back to the days when cowboys and pio-neers first settled this land. Excellent exhibits in Winsor Castle, an early Mormon ranch SW of Fredonia, provide a look into frontier life. Abun-dant spring water attracted prehistoric basket-maker and pueblo Indians, who settled nearby more than 1,000 years ago, then departed. Nomadic Paiute Indians came more recently and now live on the surrounding Kaibab Indian Reservation. Mormons discovered the springs in 1858 and began ranching 5 years later, but swift Navajo raiding parties killed 2 of the men living here and stole their stock. A treaty signed in 1870 between the Mormons and Navajo ended the raids and opened the land to development.

Brigham Young, the Mormon president, then decided to locate the church's southern Utah tithing herd at Pipe Spring. A pair of 2-story stone houses, with walls connecting the ends to form a protected courtyard, went up. Workmen added gun ports "just in case," but the settlement was never attacked. The struc-ture became known as Winsor Castle after the ranch's superintendent, Anson P. Winsor, who possessed a regal bearing and was thought to be related to the English royal family. Winsor built up a sizable herd of cattle and horses and oversaw dairying and farming at the ranch. A

telegraph office, which opened in 1871 (Arizona's first), brought Utah and the rest of the world closer. Travelers frequently stopped by. In fact, so many newlyweds passed through after having been married in the St. George Temple that their route became known as the Honeymoon Trail. The Mormon Church entered a period of turmoil in the 1880s and feared that the federal government would seize church property in the dispute over polygamous marriages. Winsor Castle, which had been declining in importance to the church anyway, was sold to a non-Mormon.

President Harding proclaimed Pipe Spring a na-tional monument in 1923 "as a memorial of Western pioneer life." Park Service staff work to keep the frontier spirit alive by maintaining the ranch as it was in the 1870s. Activities such as cattle branding, gardening, weaving, spin-

*Winsor Castle*

ning, quilt-making, and baking still take place on a small scale. You can take a short tour of Winsor Castle or explore the restored rooms and outbuildings on your own. A ½-mile loop trail climbs the small ridge behind the ranch to a viewpoint; signs tell of the history and geology of the area.

**Visitor Center:** Historic exhibits are open daily 0730-1730 in summer, and 0800-1600 the rest of the year; $1/person admission; tel. 643-7105. Cowboys bring in cattle for branding, which you can see on Memorial Day weekend. Blacksmithing demonstrations take place through the summer months. Produce from the garden and goodies from the kitchen may be sold or given away. Books related to the history and flora and fauna of the region are sold. A snack bar is adjacent to the Visitor Center. The Paiute tribe operates a campground ¼ mile NE of the Monument; sites have showers and stay open all year: $5/night, or $9/night w/hookups. Nearest grocery stores, restaurants, and motels are in Fredonia. Pipe Spring National Monument is just off AZ 389, 14 miles SW of Fredonia.

# FREDONIA TO MARBLE CANYON ON US 89A

**Fredonia:** Though just a tiny town (pop. 1,220), Fredonia is the largest community on the Arizona Strip. Nearby forests supply a lumber mill operated by Kaibab Industries. Mormon pioneers, seeking refuge from discrimination against polygamy, settled here in 1885. They first called their place Hardscrabble but later chose "Fredonia," perhaps a contraction of the words "freedom" and *"dona"* (Spanish for wife).

Three modest and inexpensive motels lie along Main St.: Grand Canyon Motel (175 S. Main St.; tel. 643-7120); Baker Motel (330 S. Main St.; tel. 643-7015); and Ship Rock Motel (337 S. Main St.; tel. 643-7355). For Mexican and American food, dine at Dos Amigos, 165 N. Main St.; open Mon. to Sat. for breakfast, lunch, and dinner; tel. 643-7120. Cedar Grill is a sandwich shop at 10 N. Main St.; open Mon. to Sat. for lunch and dinner; tel. 643-7110. Post office is at 85 N. Main Street. The North Kaibab Ranger District office can tell you about hiking,

Grand Canyon viewpoints, and backroads of the National Forest N of the Grand Canyon; a N. Kaibab Forest map costs $1; open Mon. to Fri. 0730-1630; 430 S. Main St. (Box 248, Fredonia, AZ 86022); tel. 643-7395.

**Jacob Lake:** High in the pine forests (elev. 7,925 feet), this tiny village is conveniently located on US 89A at the AZ 67 turnoff for the Grand Canyon North Rim. The nearby lake honors Mormon missionary and explorer Jacob Hamblin. Jacob Lake Inn offers basic motel rooms ($42-$51.45), cabins (summer only: $30.45-$44.10), restaurant (inexp. American food for breakfast, lunch, and dinner), grocery store, Indian crafts shop, and service station; open all year; tel. 643-7232. Jacob Lake Forest Camp has sites with drinking water but no hookups; open mid-May to early Nov.; $6/night. Jacob Lake RV Park has spaces with hookups; open mid-May to early Nov.; $10/night. For advice on hiking, camping, scenic drives, and other recreation in the surrounding N. Kaibab National Forest, see the U.S. Forest Service Information Center (open daily mid-May to end of Oct.; closed in winter), next to Jacob Lake Inn; tel. 643-7298.

**San Bartolome Historic Site:** Markers tell the story of the Dominguez-Escalante Expedition, which camped near here in 1776. Led by 2 Spanish priests, the group was struggling to find a way back to Sante Fe after an unsuccessful overland attempt to California. The signposted site is on the N side of US 89A about midway between Jacob Lake and Marble Canyon.

**Cliff Dwellers Lodge:** About 1890, Anglo traders built an unusual trading post underneath a giant boulder. The old buildings can still be seen along the highway beside the modern motel. Cliff Dweller's Lodge offers rooms ($30.45 s, $34.65 d), restaurant (serving American food for breakfast, lunch, and dinner), small grocery store, and gas station; open all year; on US 89A, 33 miles E of Jacob Lake and 8 miles W of Marble Canyon; tel. 355-2228.

**Vermilion Cliffs Lodge:** You'll see the sheer Vermilion Cliffs from a pullout 11 miles E of Jacob Lake on US 89A and all the way E past

*view of Marble Canyon from Vermilion Cliffs*

Marble Canyon. The cliffs have a striking red color and appear to burst into flame during sunsets. Vermilion Cliffs Lodge has motel rooms ($18.90 s, $26.25 d), restaurant (inexp. American food), and gas station; may close in winter; on US 89A, 38 miles E of Jacob Lake and 3 miles W of Marble Canyon; tel. 355-2223.

**Marble Canyon Lodge:** John Wesley Powell named the nearby section of Colorado River canyon for its smooth marblelike appearance. US 89A crosses the river here over Navajo Bridge. The Grand Canyon National Park begins just downstream. Upriver lies Lee's Ferry, easily reached by a 6-mile paved road turning off beside Marble Canyon Lodge. The lodge offers motel rooms ($33.60 s, $39.90 d), kitchenettes ($38.85 s, $45.15 d), restaurant serving American food, store (groceries, camping supplies, and Indian crafts), post office, and gas station; tel. 355-2225.

## LEE'S FERRY

The deeply entrenched Colorado River cuts one gorge after another as it crosses the high plateaus of southern Utah and northern Arizona. Early settlers and travelers found the river a dangerous and difficult barrier until well into this century. A break in the cliffs above Marble Canyon provided one of the few places to build a road to the water's edge. Until 1929, when Navajo Bridge spanned the canyon, vehicles and passengers had to cross by ferry. Zane Grey expressed his thoughts about this crossing, known as Lee's Ferry, in *The Last of the Plainsmen* (1908): "I saw the constricted rapids, where the Colorado took its plunge into the box-like head of the Grand Canyon of Arizona; and the deep, reverberating boom of the river, at flood height, was a fearful thing to hear. I could not repress a shudder at the thought of crossing above that rapid."

The Dominguez-Escalante Expedition tried to cross at what's now known as Lee's Ferry in 1776, but without success. The river proved too cold and wide to swim safely, and winds frustrated the attempts to raft across. The Spaniards had to go 40 miles upriver into present-day Utah before finding a safe ford. About 100 years later, Mormon leaders began eyeing the Lee's Ferry crossing as the most convenient route for expanding Mormon settlements from Utah into Arizona. After Jacob Hamblin led a failed attempt at rafting in 1860, he returned 4 years later and made it across safely. Mormons built a guard post in 1869 to prevent others from taking over the strategic spot. Although Hamblin was the first to recognize the value of this crossing, it now bears the name of John D. Lee. This colorful character gained notoriety in the 1857 Mountain Meadows Massacre. One account of this unfortunate chain of events relates that Paiute Indians, allied to the Mormons, attacked an unfriendly wagon train of gentiles; Mormons then joined in the fighting until all the men and women of the wagon train lay dead.

To get Lee out of sight, the Mormon Church leaders asked him to start a regular ferry service on the Colorado River, which he began in 1872. One of Lee's wives remarked on seeing the isolated spot, "Oh, what a lonely dell!" which became the name of their place. Lee managed to establish the ferry service despite boat accidents and sometimes hostile Navajo, but his past caught up with him. In 1877, authorities took Lee back to Mountain Meadows where a firing squad and casket awaited.

Miners and farmers came to try their luck along the Colorado River and its tributaries. The ferry service continued too, though it suffered fatal accidents from time to time. The last run took place in June 1928 while the bridge was being constructed 6 miles downstream. The ferry operator on that trip lost control in strong currents and the boat capsized; all 3 persons aboard and a Model-T Ford were lost. Fifty-five years of ferryboating had come to an end. Navajo Bridge opened in Jan. 1929, an event

*Marble Canyon*

hailed by the Flagstaff *Coconino Sun* as the "Biggest News in Southwest History."

**Lee's Ferry and Lonely Dell Ranch:** Old buildings, trails, mining machinery, and a wrecked steamboat can be toured in these historic districts. A self-guiding tour booklet, available at the sites, identifies historic features and gives their backgrounds. A log cabin thought to have been built by Lee, root cellar, blacksmith shop, ranch house, orchards, and cemetery are at Lonely Dell Ranch, a short distance up the Paria River. Historic buildings near the ferry crossings include Lee's Ferry Fort (built in 1874 to protect settlers from possible Indian attack, but used as a trading post and residence), a small stone post office (used 1913-1923), structures built by the American Placer Company in the early 1900s, and some early 1900s U.S. Geological Survey buildings.

Charles Spencer, owner of the gold-mining company, brought in machinery for a sluicing operation, an amalgamator, and drilling equipment. His company first tried using mule trains in 1910 to pack coal for the operation from Warm Springs Canyon, 15 miles upstream. When this didn't work, he had a 92-foot-long steamboat, the *Charles H. Spencer,* shipped in sections from San Francisco the following year. The boat performed poorly too, using almost its entire load of coal to make just one roundtrip. It was used only 5 times. Efforts to extract the gold proved fruitless, though Spencer kept trying as late as 1965.

**Spencer Trail:** Energetic hikers climb this unmaintained trail for fine views of Marble Canyon from the rim, 1,500 feet above the river. The ingenious route switchbacks up sheer ledges E of Lee's Ferry Fort. It's a moderately difficult hike to the top, 3 miles RT. From Lee's Ferry parking lot, follow a path paralleling the river to the steamboat wreck, then take the trail leading to the cliffs.

**boating and fishing:** The Lee's Ferry area and the upstream canyon are part of the Glen Canyon National Recreation Area. The National Park Service provides 2 public boat ramps at road's end: a dirt one used by Grand Canyon river trips, and an upstream paved ramp for fishermen and boaters headed upriver. Powerboats can go 14½ miles up Glen Canyon almost to the dam. The Park Service recommends that you have a boat at least 16 feet long and a minimum 25-h.p. motor to cope with the swift currents. Boating below Lee's Ferry is prohibited without a permit from Grand Canyon National Park because rapids and currents are extremely hazardous. Rainbow and other trout flourish in the cold, clear waters released from Lake Powell through Glen Canyon Dam. Fishermen should be able to identify and must return to the river any of the endangered native fish. These species include: Colorado squawfish, bonytail chub, humpback chub, and razorback sucker.

**camping:** Sites at Lee's Ferry Campground have drinking water but no showers or hookups; $6/night. From US 89A, take the Lee's Ferry Rd. in 5 miles and turn L at the sign. The ranger station is just past the campground turnoff; obtain boating, fishing, and hiking information here; tel. 355-2234. The National Park Service requires that camping on the Colorado River above Lee's Ferry be at one of the several developed campsites. These sites lack piped water but are free. (Purify river water before drinking.)

## PARIA CANYON

The wild and twisting canyons of the Paria River and its tributaries offer a memorable experience for experienced hikers. Silt-laden waters have sculptured the colorful canyon walls, revealing 200 million years of geologic history. The name Paria means "muddy water" in the Paiute language. You enter the 2,000-foot-deep gorge of the Paria in southern Utah, then hike 35 miles downstream to Lee's Ferry, where the Paria empties into the Colorado River.

Ancient campsites show that pueblo Indians traveled the Paria more than 700 years ago. They hunted mule deer and bighorn sheep while using the broad, lower end of the canyon to grow corn, beans, and squash. The Dominguez-Escalante Expedition stopped at the mouth of the Paria in 1776 and were the first white men to see the Paria River. After John D. Lee began the Colorado River ferry

*Paria Canyon*

service in 1872, he and others farmed the lower Paria Canyon. Prospectors also came here to search for gold, uranium, and other minerals, but much of the Paria Canyon remained unexplored. In the late 1960s, the Bureau of Land Management (BLM) organized a small expedition in a study which led to the canyon becoming a primitive area. The Arizona Wilderness Act in 1984 designated the Paria Canyon a wilderness, along with parts of the Paria Plateau and Vermilion Cliffs.

Allow 4-6 days to hike the Paria Canyon because of the many river crossings and because you'll want to make sidetrips up some of the tributary canyons. The hike is considered moderately difficult. Hikers should have enough backpacking experience to be self-sufficient, as help may be days away. Flash floods can race through the canyon, especially from July to September. Rangers will close the Paria if a danger exists. Because the upper end has the narrowest passages (between Miles 4.2 and 9.0), rangers require that all hikers start here in order to have up-to-date weather information. You must have a permit, which is issued free (no more than 24 hours in advance) by the BLM ranger at the Paria Canyon Entrance Station near the trailhead (open Thur. to Mon. 0800-1100 from mid-Mar. to end of Oct.) or at the Kanab Area Office, open weekdays year-round at 320 N. 100 East in Kanab, Utah (Box 459, Kanab, UT 84741). Both offices provide weather forecasts and brochures with map and hiking info; tel. (801) 644-2672.

Best times to travel along the Paria are from about mid-Mar. to June and Oct. and November. Winter hikers often complain of painfully cold feet. Wear shoes suitable for frequent wading; canvas shoes work better than heavy leather hiking boots. You can get good drinking water from springs along the way (see the BLM hiking brochure for locations) or allow the river water to settle and then treat it. Normally the river comes up just to your ankles, but can be waist deep in a few spots in the spring or after rainy spells. During thunderstorms, it can be over 20 feet deep in the Paria Narrows, so heed weather warnings! Quicksand is more of a nuisance than a danger —usually it's just knee deep. Many hikers carry a walking stick to probe the opaque waters for good crossing places.

**Wrather Canyon Arch:** One of Arizona's largest natural arches lies about one mile up this side canyon. The massive structure has a 200-foot span. Turn R (SW) at Mile 17.9 on the Paria hike.

**trailheads:** The BLM Paria Canyon Entrance Station is in Utah, 30 miles NW from Page on US 89. It's on the S side of the highway, just E of the Paria River. Actual trailhead is 3 miles S on a dirt road at the old homestead site called White House Ruins. Exit trailhead is at Lee's Lonely Dell Ranch, one mile NW of the old ferry site.

**shuttle services:** You'll need to do a 150-mile RT car shuttle for this hike or make arrangements for someone else to do it for you, using either your car (about $55), or theirs ($125-$150). Contact: Marble Canyon Lodge, Marble Canyon, AZ 86036; tel. 355-2225; or Rona Levein Clark, Box 22, Marble Canyon, AZ 86036; tel. 355-2262. If flying in to the Page airport, see Lake Powell Air Service, Box 1385, Page, AZ 86040; tel. 645-2494.

**Buckskin Canyon:** This amazing tributary of the Paria has convoluted walls hundreds of feet high, yet it narrows to as little as 4 feet in width. In places the walls block out light to such a degree it's like walking in a cave. Be *very* careful to avoid times of flashflood danger. Hiking can be strenuous with rough terrain, deep pools of water, and log and rock jams that may need use of ropes. Conditions vary considerably from one year to the next. You can descend into Buckskin from 2 trailheads, Buckskin and Wire Pass, both reached by dirt roads. The hike from Buckskin Trailhead to the Paria River is 15.5 miles long OW and takes 12 or more hours. From Wire Pass Trailhead it's 1.3 miles to Buckskin Gulch, then 11 miles OW to the Paria. About halfway down Buckskin Gulch, you can climb out on a trail to a safe camping place. Carry water to last until the mouth of Buckskin Gulch.

# PAGE

Before 1957, only sand and desert vegetation lay atop Manson Mesa where Page now sits, 130 miles N of Flagstaff and 73 miles E of Kanab, Utah. In that year the U.S. Bureau of Reclamation decided to build a giant reservoir in Glen Canyon on the Colorado River. Glen Canyon Dam was to become one of the largest construction projects ever undertaken. The 710-foot high structure would create a lake 186 miles long with a shoreline of 1,960 miles. Workmen hastily set up prefabricated metal buildings for barracks, dining hall, and offices. Mobile homes rolled in, one serving as Page's first bank. The Bureau of Reclamation named the construction camp for John C. Page, who served as the Bureau's first commissioner from 1937 to 1943.

The remote desert spot gradually turned into a modern town as schools, businesses, and churches were established. Streets were named and grass and trees planted, and Page took on the appearance of American suburbia. The town still has a new and clean look. Though small (pop. 6,500), it's the largest community in Arizona's far N, and offers travelers a good selection of places to stay and eat. Wedged between the Arizona Strip to the W and the Navajo Reservation to the E, Page is a useful base for visiting both areas. The townsite (elev. 4,300 feet) overlooks Lake Powell and Glen Canyon Dam; the large Wahweap Resort and Marina is just 6 miles away. Unless you fly in, you'll need your own transport to get here.

**Powell Museum:** This small collection honors scientist and explorer John Wesley Powell. In 1869 he led the first expedition down the Green and Colorado River gorges, then ran the rivers a second time in 1871. It was Powell who named the most splendid section the "Grand Canyon." Old drawings and photographs illustrate his life and voyages. Fossil and mineral displays interpret the long, thick geologic section revealed by canyons of the Colorado River. Other exhibits contain pottery, baskets, weapons, and tools of Southwestern Indian tribes and memorabilia of early pioneers and the founding of Page. Travel info, one-day river trips, flight-seeing tours, and some books are available. Open daily 0900-1700 (sometimes open evenings too) from Memorial to Labor Day weekends, and Tues. to Sat. 0900-1700 the rest of the year; tel. 645-9496. The museum is in downtown Page at the corner of Lake Powell Blvd. and N. Navajo Drive.

Big Lake Trading Post, 1 miles SE on AZ 98, has a small museum of prehistoric Indian artifacts on the 2nd floor; open daily 0600-2200; free admission. The trading post sells Indian crafts, groceries, fishing supplies, and camping gear.

**accommodations:** All of Page's motels lie on or near Lake Powell Blvd., a 3-mile loop designated US 89L that branches off the main highway. Empire House Motel has a coffee shop and swimming pool; $34 s, $37 d in summer ($25.20 s, $26.25 d in winter); 107 S. Lake Powell Blvd.; tel. 645-2406. Page Boy Motel has a swimming pool; $27.30 s, $30.45 d in summer ($22 s, $24 d in winter); 150 N. Lake Powell Blvd.; tel. 645-2416. The Weston Lamplighter Motel also offers a swimming pool; $44.10 s, $49.35 d in summer ($26.25 s, $29.40 d in winter); 201 N. Lake Powell Blvd.; tel. 645-2451. Holiday Inn features a swimming pool, restaurant, and views over Lake Powell; $56.70 s, $64.05 d in summer ($31.50 s, $35.70 d in winter); 287 N. Lake Powell Blvd.; tel. 645-8851. Ramada Inn also has fine views, swimming pool, and restaurant; $63 s, $73.50 d in summer ($46.20 s, $52.50 d in winter); 716

Rim View Dr. at Lake Powell Blvd. (across from Holiday Inn); tel. 645-2466.

**food and entertainment:** Glen Canyon Steak House serves American food daily for breakfast, lunch, and dinner; specialties include steaks, seafood, ribs, and chicken; live country-rock bands perform evenings Tue. to Sun.; 201 N. Lake Powell Blvd.; tel. 645-3363. Family Tree Restaurant in the Holiday Inn offers a varied menu and is open daily for breakfast, lunch, and dinner; 287 N. Lake Powell Blvd.; tel. 645-8851. Ken's Old West Restaurant has steak, prime rib, and seafood; open daily for dinner; country-western bands provide music

*island monument in Glen Canyon*

Thur. to Sat.; 718 Vista Ave. (across from Glen Canyon Steak House); tel. 645-5160. Zapata's Mexican Restaurant is open for lunch and dinner daily except Sun.; 615 N. Navajo Dr.; tel. 645-9006. Stop for inexpensive Chinese food at Starlight Restaurant; open daily except Sun. for breakfast, lunch, and dinner; 46 S. Lake Powell Blvd.; tel. 645-3620. Pizza, spaghetti, and other Italian fare are served by: Strombolli's Pizza (open daily for lunch and dinner; 711 N. Navajo Dr.; tel. 645-2605); Village Inn Pizza Parlor (open daily for lunch and dinner; 33 S. Lake Powell Blvd.; tel. 645-3201); and Bella Napoli (may close in winter; 810 N. Navajo Dr.; tel. 645-2706). Buy groceries at Safeway in Page Plaza (corner of Lake Powell Blvd. and Elm St.), Bashas', 644 N. Navajo Dr., or at Mrs. C's Health Food Center, 32 S. Lake Powell Boulevard. Catch movies at Mesa Theatre, 32 S. Lake Powell Blvd.; tel. 645-9565. The Windy Mesa offers drinks with the sounds of country-western or rock bands many nights at 800 S. Navajo Dr.; tel. 645-2186.

**events:    January:** Wahweap Resort (tel. 645-2433) organizes a boat tour and historic presentation at Hole-in-Rock on Lake Powell, celebrating the 1880 crossing of the Colorado River by Mormon pioneers, who had to lower their wagons down canyon walls with ropes. Striper Derby continues at Lake Powell (see November, below). **February:** Striper Derby continues at Lake Powell. **May:** Four-H Horseshow. **June:** Lake Powell Open Rodeo. **July:** Fourth of July celebration with food, games, and fireworks at Page Memorial Park. Pioneer Day Parade. **August:** Mr. Burfel's Softball Tournament. **September:** The Dam Squares have a square-dance festival on Glen Canyon Dam. Northern Arizona Fall Roundup Rodeo. **November:** Fishermen compete for the biggest striped bass in the Striper Derby, lasting through Feb. at Lake Powell. Bass N' Bonanza is another fishing competion at Lake Powell. **December:** The community celebrates the holiday season with a Christmas parade in Page and a Festival of Lights at Wahweap Resort on Lake Powell. Striper Derby continues at Lake Powell.

**services:** Post office is at 615 Elm Street. Page Hospital is at the corner of Vista Ave. and N. Navajo Dr.; tel. 645-2424. For emergencies (police, fire, medical), tel. 911. Page High School has an indoor swimming pool (open all year) at the corner of S. Lake Powell Blvd. and AZ 98; tel. 645-8801. Play tennis at the courts in Page Memorial Park (corner S. Navajo Dr. and 6th Ave.) and at courts along S. Lake Powell Blvd. (Church Row). Glen Canyon Golf and Country Club has a 9-hole golf course W of town on US 89; tel. 645-2715.

**information:** Page/Lake Powell Chamber of Commerce is at 148 6th Ave., across from Page Memorial Park; (Box 727, Page, AZ 86040); open Mon. to Fri. 0900-1700; books about Lake Powell, Indians, and natural history are sold; tel. 645-2741. The public library is open daily except Sun.; corner of 697 Vista Ave. and N. Lake Powell Blvd.; tel. 645-2231.

**tours and transport:** Wilderness River Adventures offers one-day raft trips down the Colorado River from just below Glen Canyon Dam to Lee's Ferry, 15 miles of smooth-flowing water; $42 adult, $21 children under 12; the trips leave daily May to Sept. and can be arranged (5 person min.) the rest of the year, weather permitting; 50 Lake Powell Blvd. in Adkinson Mall; (Box 717, Page, AZ 86040); tel. 645-3279 (800-528-6154 outside Arizona). Blue Water Adventures runs a SCUBA dive shop and leads snorkeling, SCUBA, and camping trips on Lake Powell; 697 N. Navajo Dr.; tel. 645-3087. Lake Powell Air Service's long list of "flight-seeing" trips includes Lake Powell and Rainbow Bridge (½ hour, $41), Grand Canyon (1½ hours, $94), Monument Valley (1½ hours, $94), and Bryce (1½ hours, $94); a 2-person minimum applies to most tours; scenic flights to Phoenix, Las Vegas, Salt Lake City, and Grand Junction can also be arranged; tel. 645-2494. See "Lake Powell" below for lake tours there.

No bus service at time of writing. Rent cars from Avis (at the airport); tel. 645-2494. For a cab, call Lake Powell Taxi; tel. 645-2494. From Page's airport on the E edge of town, Sky West Airlines flies at least once daily to Flagstaff ($63 OW), Phoenix ($97 OW), St. George ($63 OW), Salt Lake City ($108 OW), Las Vegas ($100

OW), and other destinations; tel. 645-9200, (800) 453-9417 outside Utah, or (800) 662-4237 inside Utah.

## GLEN CANYON DAM

Construction workers labored from 1956 to 1964 to build this giant concrete structure. It stands 710 feet high above bedrock and its top measures 1,560 feet across. Thickness ranges from 300 feet at the base to just 25 feet at the top. As part of the Upper Colorado River Storage Project, the dam provides water storage (the main reason it was built), hydroelectricity, flood control, and the recreation provided by Lake Powell. Eight giant turbine generators churn out a total of 1,150,000 kw. at 13,800 volts. Vertigo sufferers shouldn't look down when driving across Glen Canyon Bridge, just downstream of the dam; cold, green waters of the Colorado River glide 700 feet below.

**Carl Hayden Visitor Center:** Guided tours inside the dam and generating room depart daily every hour in summer 0830-1530. You can take a self-guided tour daily 0800-1600 in summer and 0830-1600 the rest of the year. Photos and paintings in the Visitor Center show Lake Powell and construction of the dam. A Navajo rug exhibit illustrates the many different patterns used; in summer, a Navajo woman sometimes demonstrates her craft. National Park Service staff operate an information desk where you can find out about boating, fishing, camping, and hiking in the immense Glen Canyon National Recreation Area (Box 1507, Page, AZ 86040). There's also a 15-minute movie to introduce Lake Powell. On summer evenings you can watch movies on various topics at the Visitor Center or attend a campfire program at Wahweap Campground amphitheater. The Glen Canyon Natural History Association offers a variety of regional books in the rotunda. Souvenirs, snacks, and postcards can be purchased in a gift shop. The Carl Hayden Visitor Center is open daily 0800-1800 in summer, and 0830-1700 the rest of the year; tours, exhibits, and movies are free; tel. 645-2511.

## LAKE POWELL

Conservationists deplored the loss of remote and beautiful Glen Canyon beneath the lake. Today, we have only words, pictures, and memories to remind us of its wonders. On the other hand, the 186-mile-long lake now provides easy access for many people to an area most had not even known existed.

Lake Powell is the second largest man-made lake within the United States. Only Lake Mead, farther downstream, has a greater water-storage capacity. Lake Powell, however, has 3 times more shoreline — 1,960 miles — and holds enough water to cover the state of Pennsylvania a foot deep! The bays and coves offer nearly limitless opportunities for exploration by boaters. Only the lower part of Lake Powell and the ends of Labyrinth, Face, and West Canyons extend into Arizona, but Glen Canyon Dam and Wahweap Resort and Marina are here. The Carl Hayden Visitor Center, perched beside the dam, has tours of the dam, related exhibits, and an information desk for Glen Canyon National Recreation Area.

*power plant inside Glen Canyon Dam*

Ancient deserts, along with ocean and river deposits, have been changed over time into colorful layers of sandstone, siltstone, limestone, and shale in towering cliffs above the lake. Erosion has carved canyons and created delicately balanced rocks and graceful natural arches.

Summer, when temperatures rise into the 90s and 100s, is the busiest season for swimming, boating, and waterskiing. Winter temperatures drop to highs in the 40s and 50s, and freezing weather is possible. Chinook winds can blow day and night from Feb. to May. Thunderstorms in late summer bring strong, gusting winds with widely scattered rain showers. Surface levels of Lake Powell fluctuate from 3,640 to 3,700 feet in elevation.

Migrating birds, including Avocet, Canadian goose, mallard, and teal, stop by. Others, such as blue heron, snowy egret, bald eagle, and American merganser, come for the winter. Desert birds stay all year: pinyon jay, golden eagle, peregrine and prairie falcon, and the ubiquitous raven. Except right along the water, you'll find the cacti, desert scrub, and other plants of the high desert. Springs and permanent streams support lush grasses, cattails, willows, and tamarisks. Hanging gardens of water-loving plants reside in small alcoves high on the sandstone walls in Glen Canyon.

**recreation at Lake Powell:** If you don't have your own craft, Wahweap and other marinas will rent a boat for fishing or skiing or a houseboat. Boat tours visit Rainbow Bridge (the world's largest natural bridge) and other destinations. Sailboats find the steadiest breezes in Wahweap, Padre, Hall's, and Bullfrog Bays, where spring winds average 15-20 knots. Kayaks and canoes can be used in the more protected areas. All sailors need to be alert for approaching storms that can bring wind gusts up to 60 mph. Waves on open expanses of the lake are sometimes steeper than ocean waves and measure 6 feet from trough to crest. The southern 5 miles of lake lies within Arizona, where you'll need Arizona fishing permits. The rest of Lake Powell extends into Utah. Licenses and information can be obtained from marinas on the water or sporting goods stores in Page. Fishermen catch largemouth and striped bass, northern and walleye pike, catfish, and carp. Smaller fish include bluegill, perch, and sunfish. Wahweap has a swimming beach (no lifeguards), and boaters can find their own remote spots. Scuba divers step underwater to swim with the sizeable bass and to explore submerged Indian ruins, such as Moqui Fort in White Canyon. Hikers have a choice of easy daytrips or long wilderness backpacks. The canyons of the Escalante rate among America's premier hiking areas. Other

*skimming the waters of Lake Powell*

*Wahweap Marina*

places to hike include the Rainbow Bridge Trail across the Navajo Indian Reservation (see "Northeast Arizona"), Paria (described previously in this chapter), Dark Canyon, and Grand Gulch. National Park Service staff at the Carl Hayden Visitor Center can suggest trips and supply trail descriptions. Spring and fall offer the best hiking conditions, though any time of the year is possible.

**Wahweap:** "Bitter water" in the Ute Indian language. This is Lake Powell's biggest resort and marina development. Wahweap Resort and Marina offers complete boaters' services and rentals, deluxe accommodation, and fine dining. Wahweap is located 6 miles NW of Page, 4½ miles beyond the Visitor Center. Other marinas and campgrounds are upstream in Utah at Halls Crossing, Bullfrog Bay, and Hite. Dangling Rope Marina, 9 miles before Rainbow Bridge, can be reached only by boat. Make reservations (strongly recommended in summer) for all accommodations, boat rentals, and boat tours at Wahweap with Del E. Webb Recreational Properties, Box 29040, Phoenix, AZ 85038; tel. 278-8888 in Arizona, or (800) 528-6154 out of state. Wahweap Lodge offers several types of rooms starting at $57 s, $62 d in summer (15 May to 15 Oct.); $43 s, $46.50 d in spring and fall; and $34 s, $37 d in winter (1 Nov. to 31 Mar.). Guests enjoy lake views, two restaurants, and in summer, live entertainment and dancing. Lake Powell Motel has less ex-

pensive rooms nearby at US 89 and Wahweap Junction; $40 s, $43 d in summer; $30 s, $32.50 d in spring and fall; and $24 s, $26 d in winter. An RV park (has coin showers and laundry) costs $7 without hookups and $12.50 with; rates also drop off season. Wahweap Campground is operated on a first-come-first-served basis by the National Park Service; sites have drinking water but no showers or hookups (campers may use pay showers and laundry facilities at the RV park); $6. Primitive campsites (no water or fee) are located at Lone Rock, 3 miles N of Wahweap off US 89. Boaters may also camp along the lakeshore, but not within one mile of developed areas. Free picnic tables and boat ramps are located just W of Wahweap Resort. During summer (1 June to 30 Sept.), you can obtain recreation information from the Wahweap ranger station; other times see the staff at Carl Hayden Visitor Center, 4½ miles away.

The resort offers about 6 lake tours, ranging from a short, hour-long paddle-wheel cruise around Wahweap Bay ($5.50 adult, $4 children) to an all-day trip to Rainbow Bridge, 50 miles away ($44.50 adult, $22.25 children). Half-day trips to Rainbow Bridge cost $34.50 adult, $17.25 children. Boat rentals include a 14-foot Whaler with 25 h.p. motor ($44/day), an 18-foot Runabout with 125 h.p. motor ($130/day), and several sizes of houseboats starting at $576/3 nights. Fishing gear and water skis can be rented too. Rental rates drop off season.

# ARIZONA STRIP WILDERNESS AREAS

All 9 of these were designated as wilderness areas under the 1984 Arizona Wilderness Act. For hiking and access information in all but Saddle Mountain Wilderness, contact the Bureau of Land Management, 196 E. Tabernacle St., St. George, UT 84770; open Mon. to Fri. 0745-1630; tel. (801) 673-3545. The U.S. Forest Service manages Saddle Mountain and part of Kanab Creek Wilderness areas; its North Kaibab Ranger District office is at 430 S. Main St. in Fredonia (write: Box 248, Fredonia, AZ 86022); open Mon. to Fri. 0730-1630; tel. 643-7395.

**Beaver Dam Mountains Wilderness:** This 19,600-acre wilderness includes alluvial plains and rugged mountains of extreme NW Arizona and part of adjacent Utah. Desert bighorn sheep, desert tortoise, raptors, the endangered woundfin minnow, Joshua trees, and several rare plant species live here.

**Paiute Wilderness:** The jagged Virgin Mountains contain a wide variety of plant and animal life. The land ranges from desert country (elev. 2,400 feet) to pine and fir forests (elev. 8,012 atop Mt. Bangs). The 84,700-acre wilderness has several hiking trails. It's located in the extreme NW corner of Arizona.

**Grand Wash Cliffs Wilderness:** Grand Wash Cliffs mark the SW edge of the Colorado Plateau and form a major landmark of the western Grand Canyon. The wilderness protects 36,300 acres along a 12-mile section of the cliffs in an extremely remote part of Arizona. Desert bighorn sheep and raptors live in the high country, while desert tortoises can be found lower down.

**Mount Logan Wilderness:** Scenic features of this 14,600-acre volcanic region include Mt. Logan (7,866 feet), parts of the Uinkaret Mountains, and a large natural amphitheater known as "Hell's Hole." Oak, pinyon pine, and juniper woodlands cover the lower slopes. Higher and more protected areas support ponderosa pine and aspen.

**Mount Trumbull Wilderness:** Located a short distance NE of Mount Logan, this 7,900-acre wilderness protects the wooded slopes of Mt. Trumbull (8,028 feet). Geology and forests are similar to Mt. Logan. Both wilderness areas are located N of the Toroweap region of the Grand Canyon.

*Kanab Canyon, near the junction with the Colorado River*

**Cottonwood Point Wilderness:** The 6,500-acre wilderness contains multi-colored 1,000-foot cliffs, jagged pinnacles, and wooded canyons. It's on the Utah border near Colorado City, W of Fredonia.

**Kanab Creek Wilderness:** This is the largest canyon system on the Grand Canyon's North Rim. Headwaters lie 100 miles N on the Paunsaugunt Plateau in Utah. The wilderness area protects 77,100 acres along the Kanab and its tributaries. Springs in Kanab Canyon support large cottonwood trees and lush growths of desert willow, tamarisk, maidenhair fern, and grass. From Hack Canyon, a popular entry point, hikers can descend 21 miles down Kanab Creek to the Colorado River; allow 3 days for the OW trip. You'll need a Grand Canyon backcountry permit to camp below the junction with Jumpup Canyon. See Stewart

Aitchison's *A Naturalist's Guide to Hiking the Grand Canyon* for a trail description.

**Saddle Mountain Wilderness:** Much of the 40,600-acre wilderness covers the densely forested Kaibab Plateau. Mountain lion, bear, and mule deer roam the area. North Canyon Wash is noted for its pure strain of native Apache trout. Saddle Mountain (8,424 feet) is NE of the Bright Angel Point area on the Grand Canyon's North Rim.; you can see Saddle Mountain from Point Imperial viewpoint.

**Paria Canyon-Vermilion Cliffs Wilderness:** The colorful cliffs, giant natural amphitheaters, sandstone arches, and parts of the Paria Plateau are protected by this 110,000-acre wilderness. The rose-hued Vermilion Cliffs meet the Paria Canyon mouth at Lee's Ferry.

*a passage in Walpi, 1890*

# NORTHEASTERN ARIZONA

## INTRODUCTION

This is Indian country, a place made special by ancient cultural traditions of Native Americans —traditions that have survived to the present. The hard-working Hopi have been here longest; ruins occupied by their ancestors as long ago as 1,500 years lie scattered over much of NE Arizona and adjacent states. The once war-like and greatly feared Navajo are relative newcomers, having arrived perhaps 500 years ago. Visitors who respect tribal customs are welcome to the Indian lands, and will glimpse a unique way of life in a land of rare beauty.

### THE LAND

Multi-hued desert hills, broad mesas, soaring buttes, vast treeless plains, and massive mountains give an impression of boundless space. Northeast Arizona is part of the Colorado plateau; elevations range mostly between 4,500 and 7,000 feet. Several pine-forested ranges rise above the desert near the Arizona-New Mexico and Arizona-Utah borders. Navajo Mountain, just across in Utah, is the highest peak in the area at 10,388 feet. And nearby you'll find the world's highest natural stone span over water, Rainbow Bridge. The bridge can be reached by a spectacular 28-mile RT hike beginning just N of the Arizona-Utah border or easily by boat on Lake Powell. The beautiful canyons of Navajo and Canyon de Chelly National Monuments also offer excellent hiking.

**climate:** Expect warm to hot summers and moderate to cold winters. From spring to fall is the ideal time to visit, though winds in Mar. and Apr. can kick up dust and sand. The rainy months are July through September. Storms usually pass quickly, but flashfloods pose a danger in low-lying areas.

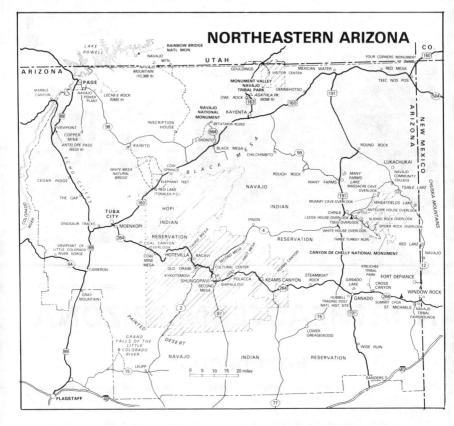

# NORTHEASTERN ARIZONA

## HISTORY

**the Hopi:** Legends and long-abandoned pueblos indicate that Indian groups have lived here for many hundreds of years. Old Oraibi, a Hopi village dating from at least A.D. 1150, is thought to be the oldest continuously in-habited settlement in the United States, and some Hopi identify even older village sites as homes of their ancestors. Indians of today recognize NE Arizona's great beauty—and probably the Ancient Ones did too—but it was of minor interest to early Europeans. Spanish explorers began to arrive in the 1500s, looking for gold and treasure, but left empty-handed. Desiring to save the Hopi's souls, Spanish

friars arrived about 1630 and had some suc-cess converting them to Christianity. But tradi-tional Hopi leaders, fearing the loss of their own culture, joined with the New Mexico pueblos in a revolt against the Spanish in 1680. Hopi killed any foreigner unable to escape, massacred many of their Christian followers, and tore down the mission buildings. During the 1800s, American frontiersmen arrived seeking mineral wealth and fertile lands, but they too usually met with disappointment. So the Hopi continued to farm in relative peace, raising their crops of corn, squash, and beans.

**the Navajo:** The semi-nomadic Navajo, relatives of the Athapascans of western Canada, wandered into the area between A.D.

1300 and 1500. This adaptable tribe learned agriculture, weaving, pottery, and other skills from their pueblo neighbors, and became skilled horsemen and sheepherders with livestock obtained from the Spanish. But the Navajo's old habits of raiding neighboring tribes and white men later almost caused their downfall. In 1863-64 the U.S. Army rounded up all the Navajo they could find, and forced the survivors on "The Long Walk" from Fort Defiance in eastern Arizona to a bleak camp at Fort Sumner in eastern New Mexico. This attempt at forced domestication failed dismally, and the Navajo were released 4 years later to return to their Arizona homeland.

In 1868 the federal government "awarded" land to the Navajo that has grown to become a giant reservation spreading from NE Arizona into adjacent New Mexico and Utah. The Navajo Nation, with 166,519 members (1981), now ranks as the largest Indian tribe in the country. About 76,000 live on the reservation in Arizona. In 1882 the federal government also recognized the Hopi's age-old land rights by setting aside land for them. The approximately 7,000 Hopi today live on a reservation completely surrounded by Navajo land. Government of-

ficials have redrawn the reservation boundaries of the Navajo and Hopi many times, but never to the satisfaction of all parties. In 1978, congressional and court decisions settled a major land dispute between the 2 tribes in favor of the Hopi. The victorious Hopi regained part of the territory previously designated as joint-use, but largely settled by Navajo. To the Hopi this was long overdue justice, while the Navajo called it "The Second Long Walk." The Navajo and Hopi Indian Relocation Commissioners have estimated that it may take until 1995 and cost $339 million to resettle families in their respective reservations.

## THE PEOPLE

The white man has always had difficulty understanding Arizona's Indians, perhaps because the Native American cultures emphasize spiritual values. The Hopi and Navajo exist in accord with nature, not against it, in adapting to the climate, plants, and animals of their land. Yet when visiting Indian villages, outsiders often see only the material side of the culture—the houses, livestock, costumes, pot-

*Navajo Fire Dance*

tery, and other crafts. One has to slow down and look much deeper to get even a small insight into Indian ways. The Hopi and Navajo arrange their settlements differently. You'll notice right away that the Hopi usually live in compact villages, even if this means a long commute to the fields or job, while the Navajo spread their houses and *hogans* across the countryside, often far from their nearest neighbor.

**ceremonies:** Religion forms a vital part of both Navajo and Hopi cultures. Navajo ceremonies are nearly always concerned with healing. If someone is sick, his family calls in a medicine man who uses sand paintings, chants, and dancing to effect a cure. Visitors should not attend these events unless invited. They aren't publicized. If you're driving

*wolf* katsina

at night and see large bonfires outside a house, it's likely there's a healing ceremony going on. Again, you should not intrude on any ceremony unless you have been invited. The Hopi have an elaborate, almost year-round schedule of dances in their village plazas and *kivas* (ceremonial rooms). Some, such as those in the kivas, are closed to outsiders, but the others can be an amazing experience. Nearly all Hopi dances act as prayers for rain and fertile crops. The elaborate, brilliant masks, the ankle bells, the drums and chanting—all are planned to get the attention of the supernatural spirits *(katsinam* or *kachinas)* who bring rain. Men perform these dances, and while they are dancing, they too are *katsinam*. At the end of the line of dancers, you might see boys who are learning; dance steps must be performed precisely. Remember while you're watching that this is a religious service. Keep clear of the performers, be quiet, and don't ask questions. Hopi ceremonies generally take place on the weekends; call or ask at the Hopi Cultural Center on Second Mesa; tel. 734-2401.

**arts and crafts:** One aspect of the strength of Navajo and Hopi cultures is evident in their excellent art and crafts. The good things are not cheap but can be fine mementos of a visit to the Indian lands. To know what the best looks like, first visit the Heard Museum in Phoenix or the Museum of Northern Arizona in Flagstaff. The established trading posts and Indian crafts shops on and off the reservations are other places to look. The Navajo are best known for their silver jewelry and woven rugs. Colorful velveteen blouses and long flowing skirts worn by the Navajo women can sometimes be purchased at trading posts. (The style was adopted during the Navajo's stay at Fort Sumner in the 1860s. It was what Army wives were then wearing!) The Hopi are famous for basketry, silverwork, pottery, and the exotic *katsina* dolls carved from cottonwood. Artists of both tribes create attractive paintings and prints with Indian motifs. Be careful when shopping; wherever there are tourists, there may be tourist junk. Indians know what their crafts are worth so bargaining is not normally done, but there's no law against it either. Prices often come down at the end of the tourist season in Sept. and October.

1. the San Francisco Peaks from atop Sunset Crater (climbing Sunset Crater is no longer permitted); 2. Lockett Meadow and the Inner Basin of the San Francisco Peaks; 3. Inner Basin of the San Francisco Peaks; 4. Hart Prairie and the San Francisco Peaks; 5. inside Tonto Natural Bridge, near Payson (all photos by B. Weir)

1. Mary Lou Gulley, owner and guide at Mystery Castle near Phoenix; 2. shopping on the Navajo Indian Reservation; 3. DeGrazia Studio, Tucson; 4. Tony Rose on the Beamer Trail, Grand Canyon National Park; 5. Melanie Bertram showing off Onyx Bridge in Petrified Forest National Park; 6. Carlos Villanueva coming down the lower Paria Canyon (all photos by B. Weir)

a Hopi family, early this century

**visiting the Indians:** Seeing and learning about Indian cultures are major rewards for visitors. It's easy to visit the reservations, and the tribes ask guests to follow only a few rules. Hordes of eager photographers besieged Hopi villages from the late 1800s until early in this century, when the Hopi cried "No more!" And that's the way it is now: photography is generally forbidden in all Hopi villages, and even the sight of a camera will upset some tribal members. The Navajo are more easy-going about having their photos taken, but you should always ask first. Expect to pay them a posing fee unless it's a public performance. Indian lands, though held in trust by the government, are private property; get permission before leaving the roadways or designated recreational areas. Don't remove anything. For example, a few feathers tied to a bush may appear to be a harmless souvenir, but they are of great religious importance to the Indian who put them there. Normal good manners, respect, and observance of posted regulations will make your visit pleasurable for both you and your hosts.

## PRACTICALITIES

**getting around:** Your own transport is by far the most convenient. Tours to the highlights of Indian country leave from major centers (see the "Transport" sections under Grand Canyon, Flagstaff, Phoenix, and Tucson). Navajo Transit System (based in Fort Defiance, tel. 729-5449) offers bus service across the Navajo and Hopi reservations from Fort Defiance and Window Rock in the E to Tuba City in the W, daily Mon. to Fri. in each direction, $13.05 OW for the whole distance. Stops on this route (E to W on AZ 264) are: Fort Defiance (PHS Hospital & 7-11 Store), Window Rock (Fed-Mart parking lot), Cross Canyon Trading Post, Ganado Post Office, Burnside Thriftway Store (near junction of US 191), Standing Rock, Steamboat Trading Post, Toyei School, AZ 77 junction, Keams Canyon Trading Post, Polacca Circle-M store, Second Mesa Trading Post, Hopi Cultural Center, Kykotsmovi turnoff, Hotevilla turnoff, Coal Mine Chapter House, and Tuba City (Shopping Center, Community Center, and PHS Hospital). Navajo Transit System also heads N from Window Rock and Fort Defiance to Kayenta, Mon. to Fri., $12.35 OW, with stops at: Fort Defiance 7-11 Store, Navajo (in New Mexico), Navajo Community College at Tsaile, Chinle (Baldwin's Market, Shopping Center, PHS Hospital), Many Farms (7-11 and Thriftway stores), Rough Rock Chapter House, Chilchinbito turnoff, Church Rock Junction, and Kayenta (7-11 store, PHS Hospital, and police station). Navajo Transit also leaves Fort Defiance and Window Rock Mon. to Fri. for the New Mexico towns of Crown Point and Gallup. You'll often see Indians hitchhiking, and you can too. Be prepared for long waits (traffic is light) and rides in the back of pick-ups.

**accommodations and food:** Because of the distances involved, visitors usually want to stay overnight on or near the reservations. Most towns have a motel or two that can easily be full in the tourist season—advance bookings are a good idea. The few trailer parks tend to fill with construction workers if a project is going on; again it's best to call or write ahead instead of counting on space. Most campgrounds are simple and have few or no facilities; only some have water. Accommodations in towns outside the reservations (Flagstaff, Winslow, Holbrook, Page, etc.) are another possibility. American and Mexican dishes are popular with the Indians, as are fast foods. Try the Navajo Taco, a giant tortilla smothered

with lettuce, ground beef, beans, tomatoes, chiles, and cheese. The Hopi Cultural Center restaurant on Second Mesa has many Indian specialties, but chances are the Hopi family at the next table will be munching on hamburgers. No alcohol is sold or permitted on the Navajo and Hopi reservations; you won't find much nightlife either.

**information:** Not always easy to get! Motels and trading posts can be helpful; tribal police located in the towns know regulations and road conditions. Visit museums run by the Navajo at Window Rock and Tsaile (Navajo Community College) and by the Hopi on Second Mesa. Local newspapers (in English) report the latest politics, sports, and social events, but not religious ceremonies. Fishing and hunting on the Navajo reservation require tribal permits from: Navajo Fish & Wildlife, Box 1480, Window Rock, AZ 86515; tel. 871-4941. Arizona Game and Fish has no jurisdiction over the reservation; you only need the tribal permits. For hiking and camping on Navajo lands, contact the Navajo Parks Dept.: Box 308, window Rock, AZ 86515; tel. 871-6647 Hopi generally won't allow hiking, fishing, or hunting by outsiders. The Hopi Tribal Headquarters can be reached at Box 123, Kykotsmovi, AZ 86039; tel. 734-2415.

**what time is it?:** This must be the question most frequently asked by visitors! While most of the United States goes on Daylight Savings Time from late Apr. to late Oct., Arizona stays on Mountain Standard Time except for the Navajo Reservation, which goes on Daylight Savings Time in order to keep in step with its New Mexico and Utah portions. But the Hopi Indians, who rarely agree with the Navajo anyway, choose to stay on Standard Time with the rest of Arizona. And then there is Indian Time, a slightly looser concept than most Americans have.

*Hopi rain symbol*

# WESTERN NAVAJO COUNTRY

## CAMERON

This trading post was built in 1916 beside the Little Colorado River, 54 miles N of Flagstaff, and named after Ralph Cameron, Arizona's last territorial delegate before statehood. Cameron's strategic location near the Grand Canyon makes it a popular stopping point. Facilities include a motel ($28.80 s, $40.20 d), RV park ($12.45 w/hookups), restaurant, grocery store, Indian crafts shop, post office, laundromat, and service station. The address for this whole operation is Box 83, Cameron, AZ 86020; tel. 679-2231. Cameron is on US 89, one mile N of the junction with AZ 64 to the Grand Canyon.

**vicinity of Cameron:** Colorful hills of the Painted Desert lie N and E of here. To the W, the high, sheer walls of the Little Colorado River Canyon make an impressive sight even with the Grand Canyon so near. The best viewpoint is 15 miles W on AZ 64, about halfway to Desert View of the Grand Canyon National Park. Besides the view, you'll also have a chance to look at Navajo jewelry here. Gray Mountain Trading Post, 10 miles S of Cameron on US 89, has Indian crafts, groceries, a restaurant, Gray Mountain Motel (Best Western; $55.12 s or d from 1 May to 15 Sept.; $26 s or $31.20 d the rest of the year; tel. 679-2214), and Whiting Brothers Motel ($29.40 s, $35.70 d in summer; $20 s, $24.15 d in winter; tel. 679-2361).

## TUBA CITY

This administrative and trade center for the western Navajo has nothing to do with tubas and is not a city. The town (pop. about 5,000) commemorates Chief Tuba of the Hopi tribe. An oasis of green lawns and shade trees, Tuba City contrasts with the surrounding desert. The springs nearby attracted Mormons, who founded a settlement in 1877. They could not get clear title to the land, however, and the U.S. Indian Agency took it over in 1903. Besides the U.S. government offices, the town has an Indian Health Hospital, schools, and a bank. Tuba City is near the junction of AZ 264 to the Hopi Mesas and US 160 to Monument Valley.

*a Navajo camp, early this century*

**practicalities:** The Tuba City Motel sits in the center of town, one mile N of the highway. Rooms cost $42 s or d; tel. 283-4545. An adjoining trading post sells Indian crafts. Either place may know of Indian dances or events, both Navajo and Hopi. The Western Navajo Fair, held in Oct., features a rodeo, arts and crafts, and dance performances. The Truck Stop Restaurant is on the highway at the turnoff for Tuba City. On the road into town are several fast-food places and some grocery stores. Pancho's Family Restaurant, next to the Tuba City Motel, serves Mexican-American food at moderate prices. Mickey's Pizza and a supermarket are in a shopping center ½ mile E on US 160.

## VICINITY OF TUBA CITY

**dinosaur tracks:** Distinct footprints can be seen 5½ miles W of Tuba City on US 160, about midway between Tuba City Junction and US 89. Look for a small sign on the N side of the highway between Mileposts 316 and 317. Some Navajo jewelry stalls will probably be here too. Scientists think carnivorous biped reptiles about 10 feet tall made these tracks, now preserved in sandstone.

**Moenkopi ("The place of running water"):** This Hopi village lies 2 miles SE of Tuba City. Prehistoric pueblo Indians built villages in the area but had abandoned them by A.D. 1300. Chief Tuba of Oraibi (50 miles SE) founded Moenkopi in the 1870s. Mormons constructed a woolen mill in 1879 with plans to use Indian labor, but the Indians apparently disliked working with machinery and the project failed. Water from springs irrigates fields, an advantage not enjoyed by other Hopi villages.

**Coal Mine Canyon:** A scenic little canyon 15 miles SE of Tuba City on AZ 264. Look for a windmill and Coal Mine Mesa Rodeo Ground on the N side of the highway (no signs), and turn in across the cattle guard. Indians have long obtained coal from the seam just below the rim.

**Elephant's Feet:** This pair of distinctive sandstone buttes stands near Red Lake, 21 miles NE of Tuba City on US 160. White Mesa Natural Bridge is 11 miles N of Red Lake; check at Red Lake Trading Post for road conditions and directions.

*dinosaur track west of Tuba City*

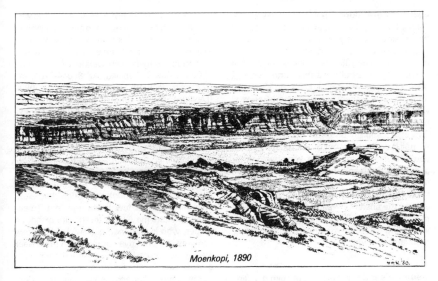

Moenkopi, 1890

# NORTHERN NAVAJO COUNTRY

## NAVAJO NATIONAL MONUMENT

The Monument preserves 3 spectacular pre-historic Indian cliff dwellings, last occupied about 700 years ago. The vanished Indians are known as Anasazi (a Navajo word for "ancient ones"), probable ancestors of the present-day Hopi. Of the 3 sites, Betatakin is the most accessible and can be seen from a viewpoint near the Visitor Center. Sandal Trail, an easy self-guiding one-mile RT walk, goes from the Visitor Center to Betatakin Point Overlook. Take binoculars along to see details of the ruins. Rangers lead groups into Betatakin during spring, summer, and fall; contact the Monument for tour times. Keet Seel, to the NE, is the largest cliff dwelling in Arizona. You get there by a 16-mile RT hike or horseback ride. Inscription House, to the W, is the smallest of the 3 ruins; it's currently closed to the public. Inscription House Trading Post should not be confused with the ruins, which are some distance away. The Monument headquarters and

Visitor Center are reached by following US 160 NE from Tuba City for 52 miles (or SW 22 miles from Kayenta), then turning N 9 miles on AZ 564 at Black Mesa Junction.

**Visitor Center:** The Anasazi left many questions behind when they abandoned this area. You can learn what is known about these people, as well as some of the mysteries, at the Monument Visitor Center. Exhibits, which show fine examples of prehistoric pottery wares and other artifacts, attempt to piece together what life was like for the Indians. An excellent 20-min. movie about the Anasazi is shown on the hour and a 5-min. slide show can be seen on request. Native plants are labeled and their uses described on Sandal Trail. Rangers will answer questions and have books and maps for sale. A gift shop offers Indian jewelry (Hopi, Navajo, and Zuni) and Navajo rugs; open mid-Apr. to mid-November. The Visitor Center is open daily 0800-1700 (later during summer) except Thanksgiving, Christmas, and New Year.

**visiting Betatakin:** Betatakin (Navajo for "ledge house") ruins are in a natural alcove on the far side of a canyon. The alcove measures 452 feet high, 370 feet across, and 135 feet deep. It contains 135 rooms and one kiva. The entire village was built and abandoned within 2 generations, between A.D. 1250 and 1300. The ruins may be visited only with park rangers, who lead trips up to 3 times a day in summer. A bus takes you to the trailhead from the Visitor Center; $1 adult, $.50 under 12. The 2½-mile RT trail is well graded but drops 700 feet, which you'll have to climb on the way back. After passing through an aspen grove on the canyon floor, the trail climbs a short distance to the ruin. Allow 4 hours for the trip and a look around the ancient dwellings. Trailhead elevation is 7,200 feet. Thin air can make the hike very tiring — people with heart or respiratory problems shouldn't go.

**visiting Keet Seel:** This isolated cliff dwelling is one of the best preserved in the Southwest. Keet Seel (Navajo for "broken pottery") has 160 rooms and 4 or 5 kivas. The site, 8 miles away by trail from the Visitor Center, may be visited from the end of May to early September. A permit is required, and there's a limit of 25 people per day. Reservations must be made at least one day in advance (but not more than 2 months) with Navajo National Monument, H.C. 71, Box 3, Tonalea, AZ 86044-9704; tel. 672-2366. Pick up your permit before 0900 (Daylight Savings Time) on the day of your hike or you lose your space. The hike's first 1½ miles runs along the rim on a dirt road to Tsegi Point. There the trail descends 1,000 feet to the canyon bottom, goes downstream a short distance, then heads upstream into Keet Seel Canyon. You may have to do some wading. Carry water — the streams are polluted by livestock. The ruins look as though they were abandoned just a few years ago, not 7 centuries! Visitors may not enter the site without a ranger, who is stationed nearby. Backpackers can stay in a primitive campground (free) near Keet Seel. You can rent horses for the trip from a local Navajo family for about $40/person. Some riding experience is advised, and riders must be at least 12 years old. Write to the Austins, c/o Horseback Reservation, Navajo National Monument, H.C. 71, Box 3, Tonalea, AZ 86044-9704.

*Betatakin Ruins*

**accommodations and food:** A free campground with water and restrooms near the Visitor Center is open mid-May to mid-October. Rangers present campfire programs in summer. Tsegi Park Motel ($27 s, $32 d) and cafe are 20 miles away on the road to Kayenta. Kayenta, another 9 miles, has 2 motels and several restaurants. Black Mesa Shopping Center, just 9 miles S at the junction of AZ 564 and US 160, has a cafe, grocery store, and service station. The road S from here goes to coal mines of the Peabody Coal Company, a major place of employment for the Navajo.

## VICINITY OF NAVAJO NATIONAL MONUMENT

**Shonto:** This Navajo settlement in a small canyon to the SW has a trading post (closed Sat. afternoon and Sun.) and a BIA (Bureau of Indian Affairs) boarding school. A shaded park in front of the trading post is a good spot for a picnic. Shonto is 10 miles from the Monument by a rough and sandy road not recommended for cars, or 33 miles via US 160 on paved roads.

**Rainbow Bridge:** A rugged 14-mile (OW) trail winds through scenic canyons to this huge natural wonder. The bridge is 309 feet high and 278 feet wide; the Capitol building in Washington, D.C. would fit neatly under the span. Easiest way to Rainbow Bridge is by boat tour on Lake Powell from Wahweap or Bullfrog marinas. But the more adventurous can hike from near Navajo Mountain Trading Post, just N across the Arizona-Utah border, and skirt the N side of Navajo Mountain to the bridge. Hikers must be experienced and self-sufficient as the route crosses a wilderness area. Bring a Navajo Mountain (Utah) topo map (15 minute) because the trail is unmaintained and poorly marked. You won't find campgrounds or supplies at Rainbow Bridge; the marina and Park Service Ranger Station are 9 miles away *by water* only. Best times to go are Apr. to early June, Sept., and October. Winter cold and snow discourage visits, while summer is hot and has hazardous flash floods. "Hiking to Rainbow Bridge" trail notes are available from

*Rainbow Bridge*

the National Park Service, Glen Canyon N.R.A., Box 1507, Page, AZ 86040; tel. 645-2471. A hiking permit (free) and camping permit ($1/person per night) should be obtained from Navajo Tribal Parks, Box 308, Window Rock, AZ 86515; tel. 871-4941. To get to the trailhead from US 160, follow Indian Route 16 N 35 miles past Inscription House Trading Post to a road fork, then turn R 6 miles to Navajo Mt. Trading Post (gas, supplies, and info usually available; tel. (602) 672-2852). Continue on the main road 6½ miles (go straight at the 4-way junction) to an earthen dam. Keep straight across the dam, take the L fork after ½ mile, then go 1.6 miles to Cha Canyon (trailhead) at the end of the road. Permission (which may not be given) is needed from Navajo Tribal Parks for hiking on the Rainbow Lodge ruin to Rainbow Bridge alternate trail, or climbing the sacred Navajo Mountain.

## KAYENTA

The "Gateway to Monument Valley" is a town of 3,400 in a bleak, windswept valley. Its name is loosely derived from the Navajo name

Teehnideeh, meaning ''boghole,'' as there were once shallow lakes here. Kayenta makes a handy spot for travelers, with 2 good motels, several restaurants, grocery stores, laundromats, and service stations.

**accommodations:** Wetherill Inn is in the center of town on US 163, one mile N of US 160. It was named after John Wetherill, an early trader and rancher of the region, who also discovered Betatakin, Mesa Verde, and other major Anasazi sites. Rooms cost $48 s, $50 d; Box 175, Kayenta, AZ 86033; tel. 697-3231. Holiday Inn is on US 160 at the turnoff for Kayenta. Rooms cost $66 s, $79 d (summer rates); Box 307, Kayenta 86033; tel. 697-3221. The Coin-Op Laundry in town has some RV spaces at $7.50/night.

**food:** The Holiday Inn's restaurant has good Navajo tacos and standard American fare. El Capitan Cafe is nearby on the other side of the highway. The Amigo Cafe (Mexican-American) is between the Kayenta turnoff and town on US 163. Golden Sands Cafe is next door to Wetherill Inn. Kayenta Trading Post has a large grocery store, located behind the Wetherill Inn. Thriftway Food Store, Circle-K, and 7-11 are near the intersection of US 160 and 163.

**shopping and services:** Look for Indian crafts at both motels, Kayenta Trading Post, and Burch's Trading Co. (near Wetherill Inn). Police, a bank, and Kayenta Community Health Service are in town. Tours in 4WD vehicles to Monument Valley and surrounding country (Crawley's Navajo Nation Tours) leave from both motels; costs start at about $24/half day or $36/full day with a 4-person minimum.

## MONUMENT VALLEY

Towering buttes, jagged pinnacles, and rippled sand dunes make this an other-worldly landscape. Changing colors and shifting shadows during the day add to the enchantment. Most of the natural monuments are sandstone rem-

*Monument Valley*

nants of land eroded by wind and water. Agathla Peak and some lesser summits are roots of ancient volcanoes, whose dark rock contrasts with the pale yellow sandstone of the other formations. The Valley lies at 5,564 feet in the Upper Sonoran Life Zone; annual rainfall averages about 8½ inches.

In 1863-64, when Kit Carson was ravaging Canyon de Chelly to round up the Navajo, Chief Hoskinini led his people to the safety and freedom of Monument Valley. Merrick Butte and Mitchell Mesa commemorate 2 miners who discovered rich silver deposits on their first trip to the Valley in 1880. On their second trip both were killed, reportedly shot by Paiute Indians. Hollywood movies made the splendor of Monument Valley known to the outside world. "Stagecoach," filmed here in 1938 and directed by John Ford, became the first in a series of Westerns that has continued to the present. John Wayne and many other movie greats rode across these sands.

The Navajo have preserved the Valley as a Tribal Park with a scenic drive, Visitor Center, and campground. From Kayenta, go 24 miles N on US 163 and turn R 3½ miles on a paved road to the Visitor Center. Or, from Mexican Hat in Utah, drive 22 miles SW on US 163 and turn L 3½ miles.

**Visitor Center:** Information desk, Indian crafts shop, and exhibits are open 0700-1900 from mid-Apr. to mid-Oct., 0800-1700 the rest of the year. A $1 entrance fee (under 12 free) is charged .

**Monument Valley Drive:** A 17-mile, self-guided scenic drive begins at the Visitor Center and loops through the heart of the Valley. Overlooks provide sweeping views from different vantage points. The dirt road is normally OK for cautiously driven cars. Avoid stopping and becoming stuck in the loose sand that sometimes blows across the road. Allow 1½ hours for the drive, open the same hours as the Visitor Center. No hiking or driving off the signposted route allowed. Water and restrooms are available only at the Visitor Center.

**valley tours:** Take one of the guided tour vehicles leaving daily (May to Sept.) from the Visitor Center to visit a hogan, cliff dwelling, and petroglyphs in areas beyond the self-guided drive. The trips last about 2-¼ hours and cost $15/person. Horseback riding costs $8/hour or $45/day, also from the Visitor Center.

**accommodations:** Mitten View Campground is near the Visitor Center, $7/night; hot showers available at an extra charge. Tenters should be prepared for winds in this exposed location. The campground closes in winter. Goulding's Lodge (see below) has the nearest, restaurant, and store. Motels are also found at Kayenta and in Utah at Bluff and Mexican Hat.

**Goulding's Lodge and Trading Post:** Harry Goulding and his wife Mike opened the trading post in 1923. It's located 2 miles W of US 163, just N of the Arizona-Utah border. The trading post has groceries, Indian crafts (some of outstanding quality), and a gas station. Rooms start at $51 s or d; open all year. Valley tours cost $20/half day, or $35/full day. Sunset tours (2 hours) leave June to Aug., $12. Children under 10 go at half price on tours. For accommodation and tour info, contact: Box 1, Monument Valley, UT 84536; tel. (801) 727-3231. The nearby Monument Valley KOA Campground costs $10.70/night and is open 1 Apr. to 15 Nov.: Box 3, Monument Valley, UT 84536; tel. (801) 727-3280. The Seventh-Day Adventist Church runs a hospital and mission near the trading post.

## FOUR CORNERS

An inlaid concrete slab marks the point where Arizona, Utah, Colorado, and New Mexico meet. It's the only spot in the United States where you can put your finger on 4 states at once. Over 2,000 people a day are said to stop at the marker in the summer season. Average stay? Seven to 10 minutes. On the other hand, 5 national parks and 18 national monuments are within a radius of 150 miles from this point!

# EASTERN NAVAJO COUNTRY

## CANYON DE CHELLY NATIONAL MONUMENT

Prehistoric Anasazi cliff dwellings and traditional Navajo ways are preserved in canyons of rare beauty. The main ones are Canyon de Chelly (pronounced "d'SHAY"), 26 miles long, and adjoining Canyon del Muerto, 35 miles long. Sheer sandstone walls rise 1,000 feet, giving the canyons a fortress-like appearance. Allow at least a full day to see some of the Monument's 83,840 acres. Rim elevations range from 5,500 feet at the Visitor Center to 7,000 feet at the end of the scenic drives. April to Oct. is the best time to visit. Winter here is cold and there may be snow. Afternoon thunderstorms arrive almost daily in late summer. Thousands of waterfalls cascade over the rims when it's raining but stop when the skies clear.

Canyon del Muerto

**the first peoples:** Nomadic tribes roamed the canyons over 2,000 years ago, collecting wild foods and hunting game. Little remains of these early visitors, but they must have found welcome shelter from the elements in the natural rock overhangs of the canyons. The Anasazi ("ancient ones" in the Navajo language), from their first appearance about A.D. 1, lived in caves during the winter and brush shelters in summer. By A.D. 500 they were cultivating permanent fields of corn, squash, and beans, and were making pottery. They lived at that time in year-round pithouses, structures partly underground and roofed with sticks and mud.

Around A.D. 700 the population began to move into cliff houses of stone masonry constructed above ground. These pueblos (Spanish for "villages") also contained underground ceremonial rooms, known as kivas, used for social as well as religious purposes. Most of the cliff houses that you now see in Canyon de Chelly date from the Anasazi golden age, A.D. 1100-1300, when an estimated 1,000 people occupied the many small villages. At the end of this period the Anasazi mysteriously vanished from these canyons, and from their other large population centers as well. Archeologists aren't sure why, but causes may include drought, overpopulation, soil erosion, and warfare. It's likely that some of the Anasazi moved to the Hopi mesas. Hopi religion, traditions, and farming practices have much in common with those of the Ancient Ones. During the next 400 years, Hopi farmers sometimes used the canyons during the growing season, but abandoned them after each harvest.

**the Navajo arrive:** First entering Canyon de Chelly about A.D. 1700, the Navajo found it an ideal base for raiding nearby Indian and Spanish settlements. In 1805 the Spanish launched a punitive expedition during which soldiers reported killing 115 Navajo, including 90 warriors. The Navajo version of the battle claimed the dead were all women, children, and old

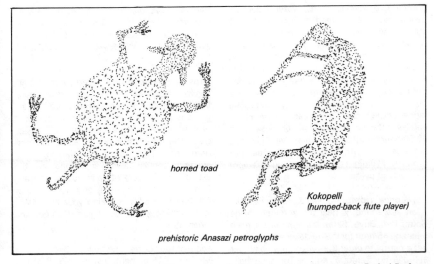

horned toad

Kokopelli
(humped-back flute player)

*prehistoric Anasazi petroglyphs*

men. The overhang where the killing took place became known as Massacre Cave. During the Mexican era raids took place in both directions; the Navajo raided for food and livestock while Mexicans came to steal women and children for slaves. Contact with Americans went badly too; settlers encroached on Navajo lands, and soldiers proved deceitful. Navajo raids finally came to an end after the winter of 1863-64, when Colonel Kit Carson led detachments of the U.S. cavalry into the canyons. The Army destroyed livestock, fruit trees, and food while skirmishing with the Indians. The starving Navajo then had no choice but to surrender and leave for a desolate reservation in eastern New Mexico. In 1868, after 4 miserable years there, they were permitted to return to their beloved canyons. Today, some of the same families continue to farm the canyon floors and graze sheep. You can see their distinctive round *hogans* (houses) next to the fields. More than 50 families live in the Monument, but most find it more convenient to spend winters on the canyon rims and to return to their fields after the spring floods have subsided.

**Visitor Center:** Exhibits show the spread of

Indian history from the Archaic Period (before A.D. 1) to the present, with many displays of artifacts. Rangers know about scheduled hikes, programs, and tours, and they'll answer your questions. Books related to the region are sold. Open 0800-1800 from 1 May to 30 Sept., and 0800-1700 the rest of the year; tel. 674-5436.

**sights:** Canyons de Chelly and del Muerto each have a paved scenic drive with viewpoints along their rims. Or you can travel inside the canyons by 4WD vehicle, horseback, or on foot. With the exception of White House Ruin Trail, *visitors must have a Navajo guide or be with a Monument ranger to enter any canyon.* This rule is enforced! It protects the ruins and the privacy of families living in the canyons. All of the land belongs to the Navajo people; the National Park Service only administers policies within the Monument boundaries.

**hiking:** White House Ruin Trail is the only hike that can be done without a guide; see description under "South Rim Drive of Canyon de Chelly" below. Rangers lead free half-day hikes in the lower canyon daily from late May to the end of September. The hiking pace is easy, but comfortable walking shoes, water, insect repellent, and hat are needed. Some wading is usually necessary — in fact, you may insist on it; under a hot summer sun, with red rocks all around you, the cool water and shade of the trees are irresistible! Meet the ranger at the Visitor Center; check departure time the day before, as hikes leave promptly. By hiring a guide you can hike almost anywhere. The ranger at the Visitor Center can help arrange it and issue the necessary permit. Guides charge $6.50/hour for up to 10 people. Overnight trips are possible with additional charges (per group) of $10/night for the guide and $20/night for the land owner.

**horseback riding:**  Justin's Horse Rentals, open year-round, is near the entrance to the South Rim Drive. Rates are $5/hour for each rider and $5/hour for the guide (one per group); get a permit to enter the canyon from a ranger at the Visitor Center. Twin Trail Tours, on the N rim of Canyon del Muerto, has 2 trips, each 12 miles RT. Both descend into the canyon; one goes upstream to Big Cave and Mummy Cave, and the other downstream to Standing Cow Ruin and Antelope House Ruin. Riders have to walk during the 700-foot descent. The starting point is 8 miles from the Visitor Center on the North Rim Drive. Tours depart Mon. to Sat. at 0900 from 15 May to 15 Oct.; cost is $35/one person, $65/2 persons, $20/each additional

person. A $5 discount is given for prepaid reservations and riders 60 and older. Overnight and group trips can be arranged. Twin Trail Tours, Box 1706, Window Rock, AZ 86515; tel. 871-4663.

**canyon driving tours:**  Jeep tours of both canyons leave the Thunderbird Lodge daily at 0900 and 1400. From mid-Nov. to early Mar., you should call ahead to make sure there will be a trip, since there's a minumum of 6 passengers. The trips, half day ($23 adult, $17 children) or full day ($39/person including lunch), are very popular. You'll enjoy unobstructed views from the back of open trucks, stopping frequently for photography and viewing ruins. Another possibility is taking your own 4WD (only) vehicle; you'll need a guide ($6/hour) and a permit.

**accommodations:**  The Thunderbird Lodge is within the Monument, just ½ mile S of the Visitor Center. The grounds have attractive landscaping with lawns and shade trees. Summer rates (1 Apr. to 31 Oct.): $48 s, $52 d; winter: $38 s, $42 d; Box 548, Chinle, AZ 86503; tel. 674-5443. Cottonwood Campground, between the Visitor Center and the Thunderbird Lodge, offers pleasant sites with many large cottonwood trees. Open all year, it has restrooms, tables, and water but no showers or hookups; free. Rangers present

*mouth of Canyon de Chelly*

jeep tours in Canyon
de Chelly

campfire programs from late May to the end of September. Canyon de Chelly Motel is in the center of Chinle on Indian Route 7, about 1½ miles W of the Monument Visitor Center; summer rates (1 Apr. to 31 Oct.): $44 s, $48 d; winter rates: $36 s, $38 d; Box 295, Chinle, AZ 86503; tel. 674-5288.

**food:**  The Thunderbird Lodge has a good cafeteria at low to moderate prices, open 0700-2030 (shorter hours and closed some days in winter). In nearby Chinle you'll find Kentucky Fried Chicken and Scooter's Drive-Inn Restaurant. Buy groceries in Chinle at the supermarket in Tseyi Shopping Center (on US 191, just N of the junction with Indian Route 7), Baldwin's 7-11, and Thriftway.

## SOUTH RIM DRIVE

**Mile 0:**  Visitor Center. The nearby canyon walls only stand about 30 feet high where the Rio de Chelly enters Chinle Wash. (All pullouts and turns are on the left.)

**Mile 2.0:**  First pullout. The canyon is about 275 feet deep here. Rangers often lead short hikes down the trail in this side canyon. Don't go hiking without a Navajo guide or ranger!

**Mile 2.3:**  Tsegi Overlook. A Navajo *hogan* and farm can be seen below. Tsegi is the Navajo word for "rock canyon," which the Spanish

pronounced "de chelle" (day shay-yay). American usage changed it to "de chelly" (d'SHAY).

**Mile 3.7:**  Junction Overlook. Here Canyon del Muerto, across the valley, joins Canyon de Chelly. Canyon depth is about 400 feet. Look for the 2 Anasazi cliff dwellings. First Ruin is in the cliff at the far side of the canyon and was the first ruin described by archaeologist Cosmos Mindeleff after his visit in 1882. The pueblo has 10 rooms and 2 kivas; it dates from the late 11th to late 13th centuries. Junction Ruin is straight across, where the 2 canyons join. It has 15 rooms and one kiva. These ruins, and nearly all others in the Monument, face S to catch the sun's warmth in winter.

**Mile 5.9:**  White House Overlook. Canyon walls rise about 550 feet at this point. White House Ruin, on the far side, is one of the largest in the Monument. The name comes from original white plaster on walls in the upper section. Portions of 60 rooms and 4 kivas remain in the 2 sections, but it's estimated there may have been 80 rooms before flood waters carried away some of the lower ruin. As many as 12 Anasazi families may have lived in this village between about A.D. 1060 and 1275. The trail to White House Ruin begins about 500 feet to the R along the rim from the overlook. Many trails connect the rim with the canyon bottom but few are as easy as this one. It's known to the Navajo as Women's Trail, who often used it to

*lower White House Ruin*

yon de Chelly, is home for Spider Woman, a benevolent Navajo deity. A darker part of her character, according to one legend, is her taste for naughty children. When Speaking Rock, the lower pinnacle, reports misbehaving children to Spider Woman, she catches and eats them. Sun-bleached "bones" are visible on top of her spire! You can see tiny cliff dwellings in the canyon walls if you look hard enough. Around to the R is Monument Canyon. Black Rock Butte (7,618 feet high), on the horizon, is the weathered heart of an extinct volcano. South Rim Drive ends here.

**Three Turkey Ruin:** Another fine Anasazi site, but located outside the Monument boundary. You'll have to drive on dirt roads to get here. From the turnoff to Face Rock and Spider Rock, continue SE on the main road 4.8 miles, turn R for 3.4 miles, then R 1.7 miles to the overlook and picnic tables.

move sheep in and out. Allow 2 hours for the 2½-mile RT and bring some water. This is the only hike in the canyon permitted without a guide; you're asked to stay on the trail. A pamphlet describing the trail can be purchased at the Visitor Center.

**Mile 12.0:** Sliding House Overlook: The ruins across the canyon on a narrow ledge are well named. Indians who constructed the village on this sloping ledge tried to brace rooms with retaining walls. Rainwater, collected in natural depressions at the overlook, is still sometimes used by the Navajo.

**Mile 14.4:** Wild Cherry Overlook. A scenic viewpoint above upper Wild Cherry Canyon.

**Mile 19.6:** Face Rock Overlook. Small cliff dwellings sit high on the rock face opposite the viewpoint. They look impossible to reach, but the Anasazi were clever at chipping foot and hand holes into the rock.

**Mile 20.6:** Spider Rock Overlook. Rock walls plummet 1,000 feet from the rim to the canyon floor. Spider Rock, the highest of the twin spires rising 800 feet from the bottom of Can-

*Canyon de Chelly*

Canyon del Muerto from Mummy Cave Overlook

## NORTH RIM DRIVE OF CANYON DEL MUERTO

**Mile 0:** Visitor Center. Cross the nearby Rio de Chelly bridge and continue NE on Indian Route 64. (All turnoffs are on the right.)

**Mile 6.2:** Ledge Ruin Overlook. The ruin, set in an opening 100 feet above the canyon floor, has 29 rooms, including 2 kivas and a 2-story structure. It dates from between A.D. 1050 and 1275. From Dekka Kiva Overlook, a short walk to the S, a solitary kiva is seen high in the cliff face. A hand- and toe-hold trail connects it with other rooms in a separate alcove to the west.

**Mile 10.2:** Antelope House Overlook. This large site had 91 rooms and a 4-story building. The village layout is clearly seen—you look almost straight down on it from the overlook. Round outlines are kivas. The square rooms were for either living or storage. Floods have damaged some of them, perhaps while the Anasazi were still living here, and the site was abandoned about A.D. 1260. The site's name comes from paintings of antelope, thought to have been done by a Navajo artist in the 1830s. The Tomb of the Weaver sits across from Antelope House in a small alcove 50 feet above the canyon floor. Here, in the 1920s, arche-

ologists found an elaborate burial of an old man. The well-preserved body was wrapped in a blanket made from what appeared to be golden eagle feathers. A cotton blanket was enclosed and the whole burial covered with cotton yarn topped with a spindle whorl. Navajo Fortress, the sandstone butte across the canyon, is seen from a viewpoint a short walk E from Antelope House Overlook. When danger threatened, the Navajo climbed up the E side using log poles as ladders. The uppermost logs were pulled up, and any attackers received a hail of rocks. The natural fortress was used from the Spanish years until Kit Carson's campaign, and hasn't been needed since.

**Mile 19.1:** Mummy Cave Overlook. The large cliff dwelling was named in the late 1800s when archeologists found 2 mummies in the talus slope below. Canyon del Muerto (Spanish for "Canyon of the Dead"), was reportedly also named after this find. Mummy Cave Ruin sits within 2 separate overhangs several hundred feet above the canyon floor. The largest section is on the E (to the L) and has 50 rooms and 3 kivas, while the western cave has 20 rooms. Between these sections is a ledge with 7 rooms, including a 3-story tower of unknown purpose. The tower dates from about A.D. 1284 and is thought to have been built by

Anasazi from Mesa Verde in Colorado.

**Mile 21.0:** Massacre Cave Overlook. In 1805, hoping to end the Navajo menace, Antonio de Narbona led an expedition of Spanish soldiers and allied Indians to these canyons. A group of fleeing Navajo managed to scale the nearly 1,000 feet to this overhang on the only route to it. Narbona's troops, however, reached the rim overlooking the cave and fired down. Narbona's account listed 115 Navajo killed and 33 taken captive. From Yucca Cave Overlook nearby, you can see a cave with at least 4 rooms and a kiva. A small cave to the L was used for food storage; the 2 alcoves were connected by a hand- and toe-hold trail. North Rim Drive ends here.

## VICINITY OF CANYON DE CHELLY NATIONAL MONUMENT

**Chinle:** This small spread-out town lies just W of Canyon de Chelly National Monument. The name Chinle is a Navajo word meaning "water outlet"—the Rio de Chelly emerges from its canyon here. A trading post opened in 1882, the first school in 1910, and the nearby Monument headquarters in 1931. Chinle has a motel, several restaurants, a supermarket, shops, laundromat, and service stations. The post office is in Tseyi Shopping Center.

**Navajo Community College (Tsaile campus):** Recognizing the need for college education, the Navajo Tribe in 1957 established a scholarship fund, financed by their royalties from oil, for education away from the reservation. But the cultural gap between the Navajo and outside worlds proved too great for many students, and they dropped out. To solve this dilemma, the tribe created Navajo Community College in 1969. Students used temporary facilities at Many Farms, Arizona until 1973, when campuses were completed here at Tsaile and at Shiprock, New Mexico. Now a 2-year program helps students prepare for university life off the reservation. They can also choose from many Navajo and Indian Studies courses: crafts, language, politics, music and dance, herbology, holistic healing, and others. The colleges offer vocational training and adult education too.

The unusual campus layout resulted from Navajo elders and medicine men getting together with the architects. Because all important Navajo activities take place within a circle, the grounds were laid out in that shape. If you know your way around inside a *hogan,* you'll find it easy getting around the campus: the library is tucked in where the medicine bundle would be kept during a ceremony, the cooking area (dining hall) is in the center, sleeping (dormitories) in the W, teaching area (classrooms) in the S, and recreation area (student union and gym) in the north. The central campus entrance, marked by the glass-walled Ned A. Hatathli Center, faces E to the rising sun.

**The Hatathli Museum:** It claims to be the "first *true* Indian museum." Managed entirely by Indians, the collection takes up 2 floors of the *hogan*-shaped Hatathli Center and inter-

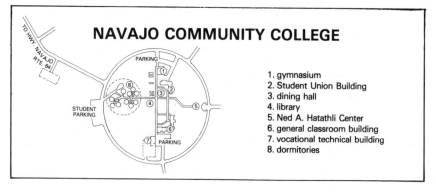

# NAVAJO COMMUNITY COLLEGE

TO HWY. NAVAJO RTE. 64

PARKING

STUDENT PARKING

PARKING

1. gymnasium
2. Student Union Building
3. dining hall
4. library
5. Ned A. Hatathli Center
6. general classroom building
7. vocational technical building
8. dormitories

prets the culture of Navajo and other tribes. The museum and adjacent sales gallery are open Mon. to Fri. 0830-1200 and 1300-1630; donation; tel. 724-6156. The library and dining hall are also open to visitors.

**Wheatfields Lake:** This large mountain lake lies in a ponderosa and pinyon pine forest E of Canyon de Chelly National Monument. Fishing and camping are popular at this pretty spot. You'll need Navajo fishing and boat permits, as on all tribal waters. Campground costs $1/person age 6 and over. A store is near the lake. Wheatfields Lake is 14 miles S of Tsaile and 42 miles N of Window Rock on Indian Route 12.

## *Lovely* WINDOW ROCK

In the early 1930s, "The Rock With a Hole in It" so impressed the Commissioner of Indian Affairs, John Collier, that he chose the site for a Navajo administration center. An octagonal Navajo Council House went up, and Window Rock became the Navajo Nation capital. The structure represents a great ceremonial hogan; murals on interior walls depict Navajo history. Tribal Council delegates meet to decide on policies and regulations for the reservation. Window Rock is a small (pop. about 3,000) but growing town at an elevation of 6,750 feet. Besides the Council Chambers and offices, there are a museum, small zoo, 2 parks, a modern motel, and a large shopping center. Window Rock's "downtown" is the shopping center at the junction of AZ 264 and Indian Route 12. Get ready for a traffic light at the corner, a rarity in Navajoland. Window Rock has the world's largest American Indian fair, held on the first Wed. through Sun. after Labor Day. The 5 days are filled with a mixture of traditional and modern festivities with singing and dancing, a parade, agricultural shows, food, crafts, concerts, rodeo, and the crowning of Miss Navajo. Write for a brochure from the Navajo Nation Fair Office, Drawer U, Window Rock, AZ 86515; tel. 871-6702 or 871-6703.

**Navajo Tribal Museum:** Exhibits introduce you to the land and early cultures of the region, then summarize the history of the Navajo peo-

*Window Rock*

ple. Examples of Navajo weaving and silversmithing show the development of the varied, distinctive styles. A large arts and crafts shop in the same building sells Navajo paintings, rugs, jewelry, jewelry-making supplies, and crafts by other Southwest tribes. Open Mon. to Fri. 0800-1645; free. Located on AZ 264, between the shopping center and Window Rock Motor Inn.

**Navajo Zoological Park:** Set beneath towering sandstone pinnacles known as the "haystacks," the zoo gives you a close look at seldom-seen animals of the Southwest. Once past the rattlesnakes near the entrance, you'll see golden eagles, hawks, bison, wolves, bobcats, mountain lions, coyotes, black bears, and other creatures. Prairie dogs, free of restricting cages, run almost everywhere. Visit daily 0800-1700; only $.50 adult. Located off AZ 264 just before the New Mexico line, ½ mile E of Window Rock Shopping Center.

**Tse Bonito Tribal Park:** This open area between the the zoo and highway has a couple of

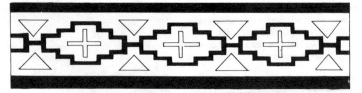

*detail from a Navajo blanket*

shaded picnic tables and restrooms, but no water. A spring, now dry, gave the place its Navajo name meaning "water between the rocks." The Navajo camped here in 1864 on the "Long Walk" to eastern New Mexico.

**Window Rock Tribal Park:** A beautiful spot shaded by juniper trees at the foot of the Window Rock. The "window" is a great hole, averaging 47 feet across, in a sandstone ridge. Loose stones just below the hole mark the site of a prehistoric Indian pueblo. You're not allowed to climb up to it, but a trail around to the L passes through wonderfully sculptured hills. The park has picnic tables, water, and restrooms. Turn E off Indian Route 12 about ½ mile N of AZ 264, then head ½ mile in, passing the Council Chambers on your L just before the park.

**accommodations and campgrounds:** Window Rock Motor Inn has a dining room, coffee shop, and swimming pool. Rooms cost $43 s, $48 d; Box 1687, Window Rock, AZ 86515; tel. 871-4108. Located on AZ 264, just E of the shopping center. Window Rock lacks trailer parks or developed campgrounds, but there's plenty of room in Tse Bonito Tribal Park, mentioned above. Camping is permitted near Window Rock Tribal Park; walk on the trail past the picnic area (check with one of the nearby tribal offices for directions). A $1/person camping fee might be charged for either park.

**food:** Just 2 restaurants in town, choose between the Motor Inn dining room, or Sirloin Steak House next door in the shopping center. East one mile across into New Mexico is a Kentucky Fried Chicken. In St. Michaels, 2 miles W, are Los Verdes Mexican Food and Tuller Cafe. Stock up on groceries at Fed Mart in the shopping center.

**services:** Visit the shopping center for the post office, bank, auto repairs, movie theater, and stores; a laundromat is across the highway.

## VICINITY OF WINDOW ROCK

**Fort Defiance:** Permanent springs in a nearby canyon attracted the Navajo who named the area Tsehotsoi, "meadow between the rocks." Colonel Edwin Vose Sumner had another name in mind in Sept. 1851, when in defiance of the Navajo, he established a fort on an overlooking hillside. Though the Navajo nearly overran Fort Defiance in 1860, the Army successfully repelled the attacks until the fort was abandoned during the Civil War. In 1863 and 1864, Colonel Kit Carson headquartered at the fort while rounding up and moving out the Navajo. After they returned, destitute, in 1868, the first Navajo Agency offices issued them sheep and supplies here. The first school on the reservation opened in 1869, and the first regular medical service in 1880. The old fort is gone now, but the town remains an administrative center with a hospital, schools, and Bureau of Indian Affairs offices.

**Navajo, New Mexico:** Trees from the extensive woodlands surrounding Navajo supply the town's large sawmill. Griswold's General Store has a cafe, supermarket, post office, and laundromat. Nearby Red Lake has fishing and primitive camping. Navajo is 17 miles N of Window Rock on Route 12, on the way to Wheatfields Lake, Tsaile, and Canyon de Chelly. This scenic, high-country road crosses pastures and forests in the foothills of the Chuska Mountains.

**St. Michaels Mission:** In the early 1900s,

Roman Catholic sisters and Franciscan friars built a school and church to serve the Navajo. The large stone church dates from 1934, when it replaced an earlier adobe structure. An historical museum focuses on mission work and includes displays of Indian history, culture, and present-day life. The museum building, originally a trading post, predates the mission. Exhibits are open in summer, Sun. to Fri. 0930-1700, other times by appointment; free. St. Michaels Mission is 2 miles W of Window Rock on AZ 264, then ½ mile S on Indian Route 12.

**Summit Campground:** Escape the summer heat by picnicking or camping among the cool ponderosa pines. Head 9 miles W of Window Rock on AZ 264 (19 miles E of Ganado) to where the road climbs over a 7,750-foot pass. Picnic tables, fireplaces, and restrooms are provided; camping charge is $1/person, age 6 and over.

## GANADO

The Spanish called this place "Pueblo Colorado" (red house) after a nearby Anasazi ruin. The name later changed to "Ganado," honoring one of the great Navajo chiefs, Ganado Mucho, or "Big Water Clansman," a signer of the treaty of June 1868 that returned the Navajo lands. A Presbyterian mission founded here in 1901 provided the Navajo with a school and hospital. The school grew into the 2-year College of Ganado, which recently closed, where students learned forestry, business administration, and general subjects.

Visit the nearby Hubbell Trading Post to experience a genuine part of the Old West. Arizona's most famous trading post has a Visitor Center and tours through Hubbell's home. Ganado is on AZ 264, 29 miles W of Window Rock, 38 miles N of Chambers on I-40, 36 miles E of Keams Canyon, and 37 miles S of Chinle.

**Ganado Lake:** Fishermen try their luck at Ganado Lake, where there's picnicking and primitive camping. The lake is 1½ miles E on

AZ 264, then N on Indian Route 27 about a mile.

**Kinlichee Navajo Tribal Park:** Anasazi Indians progressed from pit houses to pueblos while living here from A.D. 800-1300. A short trail leads to a pueblo ruin and kiva called "Kinlichee" (red house) by the Navajo, because of the red stone and clay used to construct them. A picnic area and primitive campground overlook the ruins and surrounding farmlands from a small hill. Park rangers may collect a camping fee of $1/person age 6 and over. The turnoff for the park is 8 miles E of Ganado on AZ 264 (near Milepost 455); turn N 2½ miles on a dirt road.

## HUBBELL TRADING POST NATIONAL HISTORIC SITE

John Lorenzo Hubbell began trading in 1876, a difficult time for the Navajo, who were still recovering from their traumatic internment at

*Navajo weaving at Hubbell Trading Post*

*Hubbell Trading Post today*

Fort Sumner. Born in New Mexico, Hubbell had already learned some Navajo ways and language by the time he set up business. Money rarely exchanged hands during a transaction; the Indian would bring in blankets or jewelry and receive credit. He would then point out desired items: coffee, flour, sugar, cloth, harnesses, or other manufactured items. If there was still credit left, he usually preferred silver or turquoise to money. Tribesmen bringing wool or sheep to the trading post usually received cash, however.

Hubbell distinguished himself by his honesty and closeness to the Navajo. His insistence on excellence in weaving and silverwork led to better prices for Indian craftsmen. The trading post helped bridge the Anglo and Indian cultures. Navajo often called upon Hubbell to explain government programs and to write letters to officials explaining their concerns.

**Visitor Center:** National Park Service exhibits and programs explain not only Hubbell's work, but how trading posts once linked the Navajo with the outside world. Weavers (usually women) and a silversmith (usually men) often work in the center to demonstrate their skills. Books about Indian art and culture are sold. You can take a scheduled guided tour of Hubbell's house or a self-guided tour at any time of the grounds; both are free. The house contains superb rugs, paintings, baskets, and other crafts collected by Hubbell until his death in 1930, and by the Hubbell family until 1967. And the trading post itself is still there, operating much as it always has. You can buy high-quality crafts or 'most anything else. Shelves are jammed with canned and yard goods, glass cases display pocket knives and other small items, horse collars and harnesses still hang from the ceiling, and Navajo still drop in with items for trade. A tree-shaded picnic area is next to the Visitor Center. Open daily 0800-1800 from June to Sept., and 0800-1700 the rest of the year; closed Thanksgiving, Christmas, and New Years. Located one mile W of Ganado.

# HOPI COUNTRY

For centuries the Hopi people have made their homes in villages atop 3 mesas, finger-like extensions of Black Mesa to the north. Early European visitors dubbed these extensions First Mesa, Second Mesa, and Third Mesa, counting from east to west. Arizona 264 skirts First Mesa and crosses over Second and Third Mesas on the way from Window Rock to Tuba City. The mesas have provided the Hopi with water from reliable springs, as well as protection from enemies—the 600-foot cliffs discouraged assailants. Villages remained largely autonomous until 1934, when the federal government had the tribe organize a legislative body that became the Tribal Council. Hardworking farmers, the Hopi are usually peaceable and independent. They keep closely in touch with nature and have developed a rich ceremonial life to maintain balance and harmony with their surroundings and one another.

*Hopi man spinning*

## KEAMS CANYON

Not a Hopi village, but an administrative town with a hospital and various U.S. government agencies. It's the easternmost community on the Hopi Reservation. The settlement lies at the mouth of a scenic wooded canyon named after Thomas Keam, who built a trading post here in 1875. From the town, the canyon winds NE about 8 miles, the first 3 miles of which has a road. Kit Carson engraved his name on Inscription Rock, about 2 miles beyond town. You'll pass some pleasant picnic spots on the way.

**practicalities:** Keams Canyon Motel has basic rooms ($30 s, $35 d) at the turnoff for Keams Canyon; tel. 738-2297. Keams Canyon Trailer Court has hookups and showers. There's also a campground with water. Keams Canyon Shopping Center has Indian crafts, groceries, and fast foods. A service station is next door. Post office and bank are in town.

**Awatovi:** Beginning as a small village in the 12th C., Awatovi (ah-WAHT-o-vee) had become an important Hopi town by 1540 when Spanish explorers from Coronado's expedition arrived. Franciscan friars came in 1629 and built a large church and friary using Indian labor. The mission lasted 51 years until 1680 when, fearful that their ways would be destroyed by Christianity, Hopi villages joined their New Mexico pueblo neighbors in the successful overthrow of Spanish rule, destroying the church and killing the priests. The mission was re-established in 1700, but other Hopi villages were so angered by this continued alien influence that they banded together and destroyed Awatovi. They massacred almost all the men of the 800 inhabitants, and took the women and children to other Hopi villages. A year later, in 1701, Spanish troops retaliated with little effect. Further missionary efforts among the Hopi by the Franciscans proved

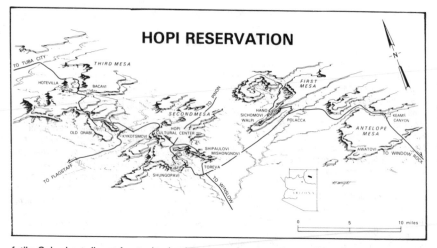

# HOPI RESERVATION

futile. Only ghosts live at Awatovi today; it was never resettled. The ruin sprawls over 23 acres with piles of rubble as high as 30 feet on the SW tip of Antelope Mesa. To visit you'll need permission (could be difficult) and a Hopi guide; ask at Hopi Tribal Headquarters, Box 123, Kykotsmovi, AZ 86039; tel. 734-2415.

## FIRST MESA

**Polacca:** With an increasing population, some Hopi have built houses in settlements below the mesas, as at Polacca (po-LAH-kah). Still, if you ask a resident of Polacca where he's from, he'll likely name one of the 3 villages on the mesa above. Christians tend to locate on lower ground; you'll rarely see churches atop a mesa. Polacca stretches for about a mile along the highway, but there's little of interest. The big thrill is a visit to the top of First Mesa. A narrow paved road climbs steeply for one mile to the crest. If you have a trailer or large vehicle, you must park it in Polacca.

**Hano:** The first village you reach *looks* Hopi, but it's really a settlement of the Tewa, a pueblo tribe from the Rio Grande region to the east. Fleeing from the Spanish after an unsuccessful revolt in 1696, some Tewa had sought refuge with Hopi living here. Hopi leaders

agreed, on the condition that the Tewa act as guards of the access path to the mesa. Despite living close to the Hopi for so long, the Tewa have kept their own language and ceremonies. Hano's fascinating history is detailed in a book by Edward P. Dozier (see "Booklist").

*Tewa Woman, 1890*

**Sichomovi:** To the visitor, Hano and the Hopi village of Sichomovi (see-CHO-mo-vee) appear as one, but residents know exactly where the line is. Sichomovi is considered a branch of Walpi, the village at the tip of the mesa.

**Walpi:** One of the most inspiring places in Arizona, Walpi (WAHL-pee) stands surrounded by sky and distant horizons. Ancient houses of yellow stone appear to grow from the mesa itself. Coming from Sichomovi, you'll see that the mesa narrows to just 15 feet before widening again at Walpi. You're free to walk around in this traditional village, but heed the signs prohibiting photography, sketching, recording, and other disturbing activities. Walpi is small (pop. about 30), and its occupants sensitive. Just beyond the village are numerous bowl-shaped depressions used to collect rainwater. Precipitous foot trails and ruins of old defenses and buildings cling to the mesa slopes far below. Walpi, inhabited for more than 300 years, is well known for its ceremonial dances. *Katsina* dolls carved by the men of Walpi and pottery made by the women are sold in the village; someone will probably ask if you want to buy. With sweeping panoramas at every turn and a determined hold on traditions, Walpi is probably the most rewarding of all the Hopi villages.

## SECOND MESA

**Second Mesa:** This junction of AZ 264 and 87 at the foot of Second Mesa is 7 miles W of Polacca and 60 miles N of Winslow. Here you'll find Secakuku Trading Post (a modern supermarket, open daily), Second Mesa Restaurant and Curio, and a post office. Second Mesa Auto Parts, service station and gas is ½ mile W at the turnoff for Shipaulovi and Mishongnovi villages.

**Shipaulovi and Mishongnovi:** These 2 traditional villages are close neighbors on a projection of Second Mesa. Dances often take place; ask at the Cultural Center for dates. Shipaulovi (shih-PAW-lo-vee) and Mishongnovi (mih-SHONG-no-vee) are reached by a short paved

*Walpi, sky village*

road climbing steeply from AZ 264, ½ mile W of the intersection with AZ 87, or by a mesa-top road (also paved) from beside the Cultural Center. Mishongnovi is the easternmost village, at the end of the mesa.

**Shungopavi:** Shungopavi (shong-O-po-vee or shih-MO-pah-vee) is the largest (pop. 742) of the 3 Second Mesa villages. Dances performed include the Butterfly Dance (a social dance), and the Snake Dance (late Aug. in even-numbered years). Buy crafts from the villagers or at Dawa's Art and Crafts on the road into the village. Shungopavi is ¾ mile S off AZ 264, midway between the junction with AZ 87 and the Cultural Center.

## HOPI CULTURAL CENTER

Proclaiming itself "At the Center of the Universe," this excellent pueblo-style museum-motel-restaurant-gift shop complex is popular with both visitors and local Hopi. It's on the W side of Second Mesa just before the road plunges down on the way to Third Mesa. For a shortcut to Chinle and Canyon de Chelly, turn N off AZ 264 beside the Cultural Center to Pinon Trading Post, 26 miles, then E 42 miles.

The museum has good exhibits of Hopi customs, ceremonies, crafts, and history; open daily 0900-1700; donation: $2 adult, $1.50 student, and $.75 children. Some religious aspects of Hopi culture are considered "secret" and won't be displayed; no one will tell you either. To learn more of Hopi mythology and customs, dig into off-reservation sources such as the NAU Special Collections or Museum of Northern Arizona libraries, both in Flagstaff.

The modern motel has rooms at $30 s, $33 d, $38 t; TV is $2 extra. Reservations are recommended: Box 67, Second Mesa, AZ 86043; tel. 734-2401. Camping and picnic grounds are next door, between the Cultural Center and Hopi Arts and Crafts shop. No water or hookups, but you can use the restrooms in the Cultural Center; free.

*Hopi Snake Dance*

The restaurant serves good but inexpensive American and Hopi dishes. This is your big chance to try *ba-duf-su-ki* (pinto bean and hominy soup), or maybe some *nok-qui-vi* (traditional stew of Hopi corn and lamb), or breakfast of blue pancakes made of the unusual Hopi corn! Open daily 0700-2100.

Three small Indian shops display a good stock of Hopi silver work, *katsina* dolls, pottery, paintings, baskets, and weavings. Hopi Arts and Crafts (Silvercrafts Cooperative Guild), a short walk across the camping area, houses an even bigger selection. You can often see Hopi silversmiths at work here.

The information desk in the Cultural Center can arrange tours and is your best source for finding out about dances on the reservation. You can also write or call the motel.

## THIRD MESA

**Kykotsmovi:** The name means "mound of ruined houses." Located near a spring at the base of Third Mesa, the settlement was founded by Hopi moving down from Old Oraibi (o-RYE-bee). Kykotsmovi (kee-KEUTS-mo-vee), also known as New Oraibi, is headquarters for the Hopi Tribal Council. Peach trees add greenery to the town. Indian Route 2 leading S to Leupp (pronounced LOOP), is paved and the shortest way to Flagstaff. RV spaces are available at Roland's Welding & Trailer Park; tel. 734-6643. Picnicking and primitive camping are at Oraibi Wash, ½ mile E of the Kykotsmovi turnoff and at a rest area overlook ½ mile W on the climb to Oraibi. Kykotsmovi Village Store has groceries and Indian crafts. Hopicrafts and Loololma Plaza craft shops are on the highway just E of the turnoff, while Pumpkin Seed Point Arts and Crafts is to the west.

**Old Oraibi:** This dusty pueblo perched on the edge of Third Mesa dates back to A.D. 1150, and is probably the oldest continuously inhabited town in the United States. The latest century has been difficult for this ancient village. In 1900 it ranked as one of the largest Hopi settlements with a population of over

*continued on page 114*

*Matilda Coxe Stevenson, anthropologist, backed up by her husband, won't take "no" for an answer when Hopi object to their prying into ceremonial secrets. (from an engraving published in the* Illustrated Police News, *6 March 1886)*

# HOPI *KATSINAM*

*Katsinam* appear to the Hopi from the winter solstice (21 Dec.) until mid-July. They dance and sing in unison, symbolizing harmony of good thought and action. This harmony is needed for rain to fall and life to be balanced. For the rest of the year the *katsinam* stay in their home in the San Francisco Peaks. A *katsina* can take 3 forms: it may be the powerful unseen spirit, it may be the dancer who is filled with the spirit, or it may be the wooden figure that represents the spirit. Dancers are always men, even when representing the female *katsinam,* as the Hopi believe that men have closer contact with the supernatural. This is balanced by gifts of *katsina* figures presented by dancers to the girls and women during ceremonies. You'll often see the spelling *"kachina,"* but *katsina* is closer to the Hopi pronunciation; there's no "ch" sound in their language.

# HOPI CALENDAR

Each village has its own style and choice of ceremonies and dances. The following is a general outline.

*Soyala* **(December):** The *Soyal katsina* staggers in from the W in the winter solstice ceremony. He has been away and idle the past 6 months and so has lost much of his strength. As the days are getting longer now, the Hopi begin planning for the upcoming planting season — thus fertility is a major concern in the ceremony.

**Kiva Dances (January):** These nighttime dances also deal with fertility, especially the need for winter moisture in the form of snow.

*Powamuya,* **the "Bean Dance" (February):** Bean sprouts have been grown in a kiva as part of a 16-day ceremony. On the final day, *katsina* dancers form in a long parade through the villages. The ogre *katsinam* appear on First and Second Mesas.

**Kiva Dances (March):** A second set of nighttime kiva dances consists of Angktiwa or "repeat dances."

**Plaza Dances (April, May, and June):** The *katsina* dancers perform in all-day ceremonies lasting from sunrise to sunset, with breaks between dances. The group, and the people watching, concentrate their thoughts in a community prayer for the spirits to bring rain for the growing crops.

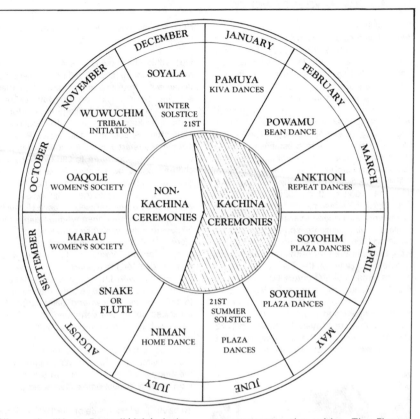

The circular calendar shows (clockwise from top):

**NON-KACHINA CEREMONIES** / **KACHINA CEREMONIES** (center)

- DECEMBER — SOYALA, WINTER SOLSTICE 21ST
- JANUARY — PAMUYA, KIVA DANCES
- FEBRUARY — POWAMU, BEAN DANCE
- MARCH — ANKTIONI, REPEAT DANCES
- APRIL — SOYOHIM, PLAZA DANCES
- MAY — SOYOHIM, PLAZA DANCES
- JUNE — 21ST SUMMER SOLSTICE, PLAZA DANCES
- JULY — NIMAN, HOME DANCE
- AUGUST — SNAKE OR FLUTE
- SEPTEMBER — MARAU, WOMEN'S SOCIETY
- OCTOBER — OAQOLE, WOMEN'S SOCIETY
- NOVEMBER — WUWUCHIM, TRIBAL INITIATION

*Niman,* the "Home Dance" (July): At the summer solstice (21 June), the plaza dances end and preparations begin for the Going Home Ceremony. In a 16-day rite, their last of the season, *katsina* dancers present the first green corn ears, then dance for rain to hasten growth of the remaining crops. Their spiritual work done, the *katsinam* return to their mountain home.

Snake and Flute Dances (August): These 2 famous ceremonies, held in alternate years, represent the clan groups and are performed for a good harvest and prosperity. The Snake Dance is held in even-numbered years at Hotevilla and Shungopavi, and in odd-numbered years at Mishongnovi. The snakes, often poisonous rattlers, act as messengers to the spirits. The Flute Ceremony takes place in odd-numbered years at Shungopavi and Walpi.

Women's Society Dances (September and October): Held in the plazas, these ceremonies celebrate the harvest with wishes for health and prosperity.

*Wuwuchim,* the Tribal Initiation (November): Young men are initiated into adulthood when they join one of 4 ceremonial societies. The society a man joins depends on his sponsor. After joining, the initiate receives instruction in Hopi creation beliefs. A new name is given him and his childhood name will not be used again.

*continued from page 111*

800, but dissension caused many to leave. The first major dispute occured in 1906 between 2 chiefs, You-ke-oma and Tawa-quap-tewa. But instead of letting bullets and arrows fly, the leaders staged a strange "push-of-war" contest. A line was cut into the mesa and the 2 groups stood on either side. They pushed against each other as hard as they could until one group, You-ke-oma's, lost. You-ke-oma and his faction then left to establish Hotevilla about 5 miles away. This event was recorded ¼ mile N of Oraibi with the line and inscription: "Well, it have *[sic]* to be done this way now, that when you pass this LINE it will be DONE, Sept. 8, 1906." A bear paw cut in the rock is the symbol of Tawa-quap-tewa and his Bear Clan, while a skull represents You-ke-oma and his Skeleton Clan. Other residents split off to join New Oraibi at the foot of the mesa. A church ruin near Old Oraibi on the S end of the mesa is all that remains of a structure built in 1901 by the Mennonite minister, H.R. Voth. Most villagers disliked having this "thing" so close to their homes and must have been elated when lightning destroyed the church in 1942. Old Oraibi is just S of the highway, about 2½ miles W of Kykotsmovi. Monongya Gallery has

*Old Oraibi, late 1800s*

Hopi art and crafts near the turnoff for Old Oraibi.

**Hotevilla:** The name Hotevilla (HOAT-vih-lah) means "skinned back." When villagers obtained water from a spring in a cave, they often scraped their backs on the low ceiling. Hotevilla is a traditional village known for its dances, basketry and other crafts. Founded in 1906 after the split from Old Oraibi, Hotevilla got a shakey start. Federal authorities demanded that the group return to Old Oraibi so that children could be enrolled in school there. Twenty-five men agreed to take their families and move back despite the continued bad feelings. But 53 others refused to leave Hotevilla. The recalcitrant men then wound up in jail for 90 days or more while their school-age children were forcibly taken to the boarding school in Keams Canyon. Women and infants of these men fended for themselves at Hotevilla that first winter, with little food and inadequate shelter. In the following year the men returned to build better houses and plant crops. Exasperated authorities continued to haul You-ke-oma off to jail for his lack of cooperation and refusal to send village children to school. Trying another tack in 1912, the federal government invited the chief to Washington for a meeting with President Taft, but the meeting didn't soften You-ke-oma's stance either.

**Bacavi:** The losing side of the 1906 split that returned to Old Oraibi was accepted back only under federal government pressure. Resentment continued to smolder between the 2 groups. At one point, when 2 of the returning women died in quick succession, cries of witchcraft went up. Finally, in Nov. 1909, tensions became unbearable. The unwelcome group packed their bags once more and settled at a new site called Bacavi (BAH-kah-vee) Spring. The name means "jointed reed," a plant found at the spring. Bacavi lies on the opposite side of the highway from Hotevilla.

# NORTHCENTRAL ARIZONA

## INTRODUCTION

The high country of northcentral Arizona offers dramatic and varied scenery. You'll see the earth's secrets in thousands of canyons, carved into the lofty land by water and time. Cinders and fiery lava, spewed out by volcanos over millions of years, have left behind unearthly landscapes. Cool pine forests cover much of northcentral Arizona, perfect country for hiking in the warmer months. Fishermen can choose among many lakes on the Colorado Plateau and rivers below it. In winter, skiers come to enjoy the downhill runs on the San Francisco Peaks (often called just "the Peaks") near Flagstaff, and the shorter runs on Bill Williams Mountain near Williams. Cross-country skiers have far more country to explore, or they can glide along groomed trails near Flagstaff.

### THE LAND

Most of northern Arizona lies atop the Colorado Plateau—a giant uplifted landmass extending into adjacent Utah, Colorado, and New Mexico. As the land rose, vigorous rivers cut deeply through the rock layers, revealing beautiful forms and colors of the Grand Canyon, awe-inspiring for its size, and of Oak Creek Canyon, whose beauties are easily accessible by car. While the rivers cut down, volcanos shot up. For millions of years, large and small volcanos have been sprouting in the San Francisco Volcanic Field around Flagstaff. The most striking volcanic features of this area include the San Francisco Peaks, whose highest point—Humphrey's Peak—at 12,670 feet is

Arizona's tallest. Sunset Crater, the state's most beautiful, is the youngster of the field. It last erupted about 700 years ago—just yesterday geologically speaking. A crater of a different sort lies E of Flagstaff: Meteor Crater formed 30,000-50,000 years ago when a speeding mass of rock smashed into the earth, displacing an estimated 300,000,000 tons of material. Northcentral Arizona's elevations drop more than 9,000 feet from the heights of Humphrey's Peak to the lower Verde and Agua Fria River valleys to the south; most of the region lies between 4,000 and 8,000 feet. Sheer cliffs of the Mogollon Rim (pronounced "MUGGY-own") mark the southern edge of the Colorado Plateau.

**climate:** Expect a cool, invigorating mountain climate over most of the region. Outdoorsmen find spring, summer, and fall temperatures ideal in the higher country, where temperatures peak in the 70s and 80s F. Lower valleys often bake in the heat then, but you can always reach the mountains in a few minutes. From early July into September, thunderstorm clouds billow into the air, dropping scattered downpours. Winter brings a battle between the sun and snow. Temperatures vary greatly from the bitter cold of storms to the warmth of bright Arizona sunshine. In Flagstaff (elev. 7,000 feet), average winter lows run in the teens, warming to highs in the lower 40s F. But almost anything's possible—from subzero to

spring-like temperatures! Though skiers enjoy the snow, not many people brave the higher elevations for camping or backpacking. Lower country experiences milder winters with only occasional snowfalls. Annual precipitation, which arrives mostly in summer and winter, varies between 10 and 30 inches, depending on elevation and rain shadows.

**flora and fauna:** The great range in elevation, together with a varied topography, provide many different habitats for wildlife. Tiny alpine plants brave strong winds and extreme cold on the highest slopes of the San Francisco Peaks, where no trees can survive. At lower elevations, dense groves of aspen, firs, and pines thrive on the mountainsides and in protected canyons. Squirrels busy themselves storing away food for the long winters here, while larger animals just visit for the summer.

Vast forests of ponderosa pine and Gambel oak cover much of the Colorado Plateau. Elk, mule deer, a few black bear, coyote, and smaller animals make these forests their home. Some of the many birds you'll likely see include the ubiquitous raven, noisy Steller's jay, and feisty hummingbird. Drier parts of northcentral Arizona support forests of juniper, pinyon pine, oak, and Arizona cypress. In other semi-arid zones, dense shrubs and stunted trees of the chaparral separate the ponderosa forests above from the desert below. Common plants of the chaparral include manzanita, silk-tassel bush, shrub live oak, catclaw acacia, and

*collared peccary*
(Tayassu tajacu)

buckbrush. Streams flowing from the Mogollon Rim attract animals from both the Rim and the desert, and often support beaver. Arizona Game and Fish Dept. stocks nonnative rainbow trout in Oak Creek and other permanent streams.

In drier country grow the grasses, yuccas, prickly pear, cholla, agave, and other plants of the desert. Coyote, gray fox, spotted skunk, blacktail jackrabbit, desert cottontail, squirrel, rattlesnake and other reptiles, Gambel's quail, and the roadrunner prefer this climate. You might see herds of pronghorn, an antelope-like creature, in the arid grasslands N of the San Francisco Volcanic Field.

Canyons create strange variations in climate: a north-facing slope may have dense growths of firs and pines while only yuccas, grasses, and sparse stunted trees can grow on the opposite slope. Or you could see juniper trees growing near the top of a canyon and Douglas firs below, a reversal of the normal order of climate zones.

## HISTORY

**native Americans:** Archaeologists have dated prehistoric Indian sites along the Little Colorado River back as far as 15,000 B.C., when now-extinct species of bison, camels, antelope, and horses roamed the land. Although some Indian groups acquired agriculture between 2,000 and 500 B.C., they maintained a seasonal migration pattern of

*black-tailed jackrabbit*
(Lepus californicus)

hunting and gathering. They planted corn, squash, and beans in the spring, continued their travels, and then returned to harvest their fields in the fall.

From about A.D. 200 to 500, as the Indians devoted more time to farming, they built clusters of pithouses, partly underground, near their fields. Regional cultures then began to form: the Anasazi of the Colorado Plateau, the Mogollon of the eastern Arizona uplands, and the Hohokam of the desert to the south. A fourth culture evolved near present-day Flagstaff between A.D. 900 and 1,000 as a blend of the 3 earlier cultures. These people are known as Sinagua (Spanish for "without water") because the region's porous volcanic soil quickly absorbs rains and snowmelt.

As the societies developed further, they started to build pueblos above ground. Villages, usually located on hilltops or in cliff overhangs with an eye to defense, became widely scattered over northcentral Arizona. By about A.D. 1100 the population had reached its peak. Inhabitants then mysteriously began to abandon villages and even whole areas. Archaeologists explain these departures by theories of drought, soil erosion, disease, and raids by the newly arrived Apache. By the 1500s, when Spanish explorers came to northern Arizona, the pueblo Indians had retreated to NE Arizona and adjacent New Mexico. Thousands of empty villages remain in northcentral Arizona, some protected in the 4 National Monuments of Wupatki (N of Flagstaff), Walnut Canyon (E of Flagstaff), Tuzigoot (S of Flagstaff), and Montezuma Castle/Montezuma Well (S of Flagstaff). You might also discover ruins while hiking through the backcountry. Sometime after about A.D. 1400, bands of Yavapai and Apache moved into the Verde Valley and Mogollon Rim areas. They did some farming, but obtained most of their food by hunting and collecting wild plants.

**white men search for gold and silver:** Antonio de Espejo, the first of several Spanish explorers, visited northcentral Arizona in 1583 seeking precious metals. Later expeditions located claims near present-day Prescott, but the Spaniards never developed them. When American prospectors rediscovered the deposits in the early 1860s, they had to work their mines in the face of attacks from Apache Indians. Fort Whipple, built by the Army in 1863, provided some protection.

**Americans settle in:** In 1864, surveyors marked out a town along Granite Creek near Fort Whipple. Carved out of the wilderness, the carefully planned community was to become Arizona's territorial capital. Arizona had just been separated from New Mexico, and President Lincoln wanted the capital a comfortable distance from the southern settlements of Tucson and Tubac, where too many Texans and other Confederate sympathizers lived. But the town's settlers didn't forget Arizona's Spanish-American heritage; they christened the settlement "Prescott" after William Hickling Prescott, author of *The History of the Conquest of Mexico.* Development farther N took longer. Captain Lorenzo Sitgreaves had brought a surveying expedition across northern Arizona in 1851, leading to the building of rough wagon roads by Beale and others, but hostile Indians and poor farming land discouraged settlement. The coming of the railroad in 1882 and success in sheep and cattle ranching opened up the region and led to the growth of railroad towns such as Flagstaff and Williams.

## TRANSPORT

You really need your own vehicle to visit the National Monuments and most of the scenic and recreation areas. Tours make brief stops at highlights of the region, but tend to be rushed (see "Flagstaff Transport"). Greyhound and Trailways provide frequent bus service across northern Arizona via Williams and Flagstaff, and between Flagstaff and Phoenix. Other bus lines connect Williams and Flagstaff with the Grand Canyon to the N, and Sedona, Prescott, and Camp Verde to the south. Amtrak runs daily trains across northern Arizona in each direction between Los Angeles (CA) and Albuquerque (NM) and beyond. Regional airlines serve Flagstaff, Sedona, and Prescott.

1. a Navajo and his sheep (Arizona Office of Tourism); 2. trekking through Paria Canyon (B. Weir); 3. Pine Country Rodeo, Flagstaff (B. Weir); 4. rafting in the Grand Canyon (Arizona Office of Tourism); 5. the Narrows of Paria Canyon (B. Weir)

1. Keet Seel Ruin, Navajo National Monument; 2. prehistoric pottery fragments; 3. Box Canyon Ruin, Wupatki National Monument; 4. Wupatki Ruin, Wupatki National Monument; 5. Betatakin Ruin, Navajo National Monument (all photos by B. Weir)

# FLAGSTAFF

Surrounded by pine forests in the center of northern Arizona, Flagstaff (pop. 40,000) has long been an important stop for ranchers, Indians, and travelers. The older downtown part of Flagstaff still has a bit of frontier feeling, expressed by its many historic buildings. But what most visitors first see of the small city is the seemingly endless line of flashing signs advertising a profusion of motels, restaurants, bars, and service stations. However there's far more to see here than Flagstaff's "auto row." To visit the distant past when the land was being uplifted, volcanos were spewing forth, and the early Indians were arriving, just head over to the Museum of Northern Arizona. To learn what the pioneers were doing here 100 years ago, drop in at the local Historical Society Museum. See work by local artists in the Art Barn, Coconino Center for the Arts, and the University Art Gallery. For an outer-worldly trip, go to Lowell Observatory where astronomers discovered Pluto, or the Astrogeology headquarters of the U.S. Geological Survey where scientists are busy mapping celestial bodies. To be outdoors, just head for the hills—Arizona's highest mountains begin at the northern boundary of town. In summer, the mountains, hills, and meadows offer pleasant forest walks and challenging climbs. Winter snows turn the countryside into some of the state's best downhill and cross-country skiing areas. As a local guidebook, *Coconino County, the Wonderland of America,* put it back in 1916, Flagstaff "offers you the advantages of any city of twice its size; it has, free for the taking, the healthiest and most invigorating of climates; its surrounding scenic beauties will fill one season, from May to November, full to overflowing with enjoyment the life of any tourist, vacationist, camper or out doors man or woman who will but come to commune with nature."

**history:** Indian groups were the first to settle near the site of present-day Flagstaff, but their villages had been long abandoned before the first white men arrived. Many ruins of old pueblos lie near town. Walnut Canyon National Monument, just E of Flagstaff, contains well-preserved cliff dwellings of the Sinagua people. Spanish explorers and missionaries knew of the Flagstaff area, but had little interest in a place that offered no valuable minerals to mine or souls to save. Beginning in the 1820s, mountain men such as Antoine Leroux became expert trappers and guides in this little-known region between Santa Fe and California. Early travelers sent out glowing reports of the climate, water, and scenery of the region, but hostile Apache, Navajo, Yavapai, and Paiute Indians nearby discouraged settlement. Despite the dangers, people in the East began to take a new interest in moving West to improve their lives.

In 1873, Samuel Cozzens, after a term as judge

*Flagstaff and the San Francisco Peaks; Northern Arizona University is in the foreground*

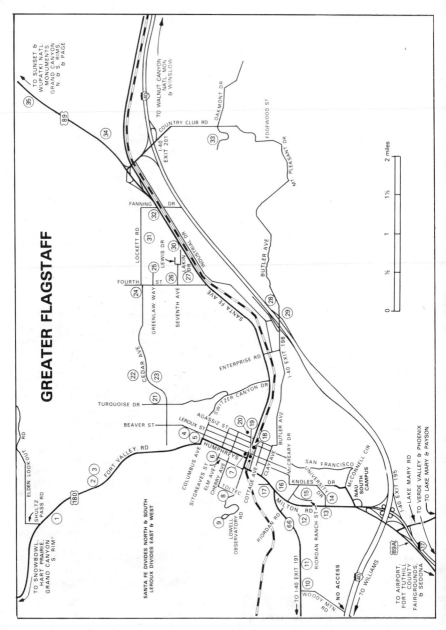

GREATER FLAGSTAFF

in Tucson and travels in the Southwest, came back East and stirred up the enthusiasm of prospective settlers with a large, well-illustrated book entitled *The Marvellous Country; or Three Years in Arizona and New Mexico, the Apache's Home.* The subtitle went on to explain: "Comprising a Description of this Wonderful Country, Its Immense Mineral Wealth, Its Magnificent Mountain Scenery, the Ruins of Ancient Towns and Cities Found Therein, With a Complete History of the Apache Tribe, and a Description of the

Author's Guide Cochise, the Great Apache War Chief, the Whole Interspersed with Strange Events and Adventures." Cozzens' book sold well in New England and soon he was busy giving talks to eager audiences. With each retelling of Arizona's wonders, his descriptions of the climate, forests, water, and mineral wealth sounded better and better. By 1875, the Arizona Colonization Company, with Cozzens as president, was established in Boston. In Feb. 1876, a group of about 50 men, each with 300 pounds of tools and clothing, set off for Arizona under the auspices of the Company. In May a 2nd group set off for the "marvelous country." All this was done without any prior visit to the proposed site along the Little Colorado River!

After 90 days of arduous travel, the 1st group arrived only to find the land already taken by Mormons, whom they distrusted. The group continued W to the San Francisco Peaks and started to build a settlement, naming it Agassiz. But finding no land suitable for farming or mining, they gave up and left for Prescott and California, even before the 2nd group arrived. The 2nd group gave up too, but not before erecting a flagpole to celebrate the 4th of July. Thomas Forsythe McMillan, who arrived from California with a herd of sheep in 1876, became Flagstaff's first permanent settler.

## GREATER FLAGSTAFF

1. Museum of Northern Arizona
2. Pioneer Historical Museum
3. Coconino Center for the Arts; Art Barn
4. Flagstaff Medical Center
5. Fort Valley Shopping Center
6. Flagstaff High School
7. Trailways Bus
8. Thorpe Park; Adult Center
9. Lowell Observatory
10. Woody Mt. Campground
11. Kit Carson RV Park
12. University Plaza Shopping Center
13. Sherwood Forest Shopping Center
14. Green Tree Village Shopping Center
15. Riordan State Historic Park
16. Northern Arizona University Campus
17. Greyhound Bus
18. Amtrak Train
19. Chamber of Commerce
20. main post office
21. Flagstaff Ice Rink
22. Buffalo Park
23. U.S. Geological Survey
24. East Flastaff Jr. High School
25. U.S. Forest Service (Supervisor's Office)
26. K-Mart Shopping Center
27. post office branch
28. Black Bart's RV Park
29. Little America
30. Kachina Square Shopping Center
31. Bushmaster Park
32. Park Santa Fe Shopping Center
33. Fairfield Continental Golf Course
34. Flagstaff Mall (enclosed)
35. KOA Campground

# DOWNTOWN FLAGSTAFF

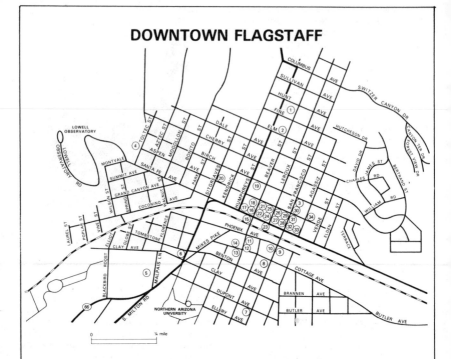

## DOWNTOWN FLAGSTAFF

1. Expeditions (river-running gear)
2. Humphrey Summit Ski (downhill and cross-country)
3. The Edge (camping, hiking, climbing, and cross-country ski)
4. Thorpe Park; Adult Center
5. Greyhound Bus
6. Imperial 400 Motel
7. El Charro
8. Milushka's Bohemian Deli and Coffee House; Morning Glory Cafe; Cosmic Cycles (bicycle and cross-country ski)
9. Lone Star Bar-B-Que
10. Downtowner Motel
11. Du Beau Motel (youth hostel)
12. Macy's Coffee House and Bakery; La Bellavia Sandwich Shoppe
13. NiMarco Pizza
14. Cottage Place
15. Chamber of Commerce
16. Trailways Bus
17. Four Winds Traders (Indian crafts); Townhouse Motel
18. Andy's Sporting Goods (fishing and hunting)
19. Cheese-A-Plenty
20. public library
21. Orpheum Theatre
22. Peace Surplus (camping gear)
23. Amtrak Train
24. Alpine Pizza
25. Weatherford Hotel (youth hostel)
26. Choi's Luncheonette
27. Hong Kong Cafe
28. Kathy's; Winnie's Natural Foods
29. Beba's Soup & Fixin's
30. Monte Vista Hotel
31. McGaugh's Newsstand
32. Cafe Espress; Martan's Burrito Palace
33. Grand Canyon Cafe
34. main post office

Other ranchers moved into the area later, for a total population of 67 in the 1880 census. On 1 Aug. 1882, the rails reached Flagstaff. Construction of the railroad brought new opportunities, new stores, restaurants, saloons, banks, and Flagstaff's first physician.

**Flagstaff's flagpoles:** It's obvious that Flagstaff was named for a flagpole, but the question is, *which* flagpole. The 1st Boston group claimed that they had put up a flagpole in Apr. or May of 1876, *before* the 4th of July celebration of the 2nd group. Both groups later claimed that "their" pole was the town's namesake. Some early settlers regarded a tall tree, trimmed of all branches, at the foot of McMillan Mesa as *the* flagstaff. But others disputed the origin, some claiming that Lt. Beale had delimbed the tree in the 1850s, and others saying it was a relic from a railroad-surveying party later on. In addition, no record exists that a flag ever flew from the tree. Another flagpole, said to have stood near Antelope Spring, did fly a flag. At any rate, citizens got together in the spring of 1881 and chose the name "Flagstaff" for their settlement.

## SIGHTS

**Northern Arizona University (NAU):** Flagstaff's character (and population!) owes much to this school located S of downtown. The University got its start in 1899 as Northern

Arizona Normal School, using a vacant reformatory building. Four young women received their diplomas and teaching certificates 2 years later. In 1925 the school began to offer a 4-year Bachelor of Education degree and took the name Northern Arizona State Teachers College. The program broadened over the years to include other degrees, a program in forestry, and graduate studies. In 1966 the institution became a university. Its sprawling campus

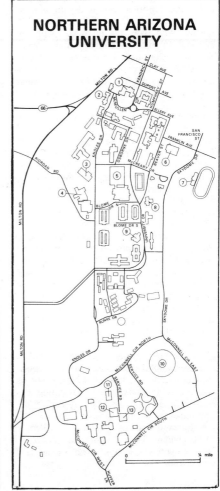

**NORTHERN ARIZONA UNIVERSITY**

1. North Union
2. Administration Building
3. main library
4. Creative Arts Building
5. University Union
6. Natatorium
7. Lumberjack Stadium
   (also parking permits)
8. bookstore and post office
9. University Dining Hall
10. Skydome
11. special collections library
12. South Campus Student Union
13. South Campus Dining Hall

now covers 686 acres, supplemented by the School of Forestry's 4,000-acre laboratory forest. A free shuttle bus makes a loop around the N and S parts of the main campus. The route follows Dupont Ave., Knowles Dr., Mc-Connell Circle, and Sky Dome Dr.; ask where the nearest stop is. The service runs about every 15 minutes during the main school terms Mon. to Fri. 0735-2155. Visitors are welcome in the University's food services, art gallery, theater and sporting events, indoor swimming pool, and libraries. Be ready for almost anything in the NAU Art Gallery, Room 231 Creative Arts Bldg. (#4 on NAU map); tel. 523-3471 to find what's going on and when. The University public information number is tel. 523-9011. To park on campus, pick up a free visitors permit from the Parking Office at Lumberjack Stadium (#7 on NAU map).

**Museum of Northern Arizona:** This active museum has excellent displays of regional natural history, archaeology, and Native American art. Contemporary Indian exhibits illustrate cultures of northern Arizona tribes and their basketry, pottery, weaving, *katsina* dolls, and ceremonies. A full-size kiva model has wall paintings from ruins at Awatovi. An art gallery features outstanding Indian and Western art. The museum's shop sells high-quality Indian crafts, including Navajo blankets, Navajo and Hopi jewelry, Hopi *katsina* dolls, and pottery by Hopi and New Mexico pueblo tribes. A bookshop offers a large selection of books and posters related to the region. You may use the library, one of the most extensive in the Southwest, located across the highway in the Research Center; open Mon. to Fri. 0900-1700. A visit to the Museum of Northern Arizona is highly recommended for anyone planning to purchase Indian crafts or to visit the Indian reservations of northern Arizona. The popular museum-sponsored Hopi and Navajo shows take place in midsummer, exhibiting the best art and crafts produced by each tribe. The museum, set beside a little canyon in a pine forest, is open daily 0900-1700; $3/adult, $1.50 children 12 and under; tel. 774-5211. From downtown Flagstaff head 3 miles NW on US 180.

**Pioneer Historical Museum:** This venerable stone building was put up in 1908 as the Coconino County Hospital for the Indigent. Townspeople also knew it as the "poor farm," because stronger patients grew vegetables in the yard. Occupants received tobacco but no alcohol. Old photos, branding irons, saddles, logging tools, and other artifacts show life in Flagstaff's pioneering days. A giant stuffed bear greets you on reaching the 2nd floor; slip by him to see more exhibits. One room displays camera gear and photos of Emery Kolb, who came to the Grand Canyon in 1902, set up a photo studio there with his brother Ellsworth, and continued taking movies and stills until 1976. Another room has memorabilia of Percival Lowell and his observatory, including a mechanical computer used from 1912 to the 1930s. Antique cars, buggies, and other large items are in the annex behind the museum. Beyond the annex are the Coconino Center for the Arts and the Art Barn. The Pioneer Historical Museum is open Mon. to Sat. 0900-1700 and Sun. 1330-1700; donation; tel. 774-6272. From downtown, the museum is on the R about 2 miles NW on US 180.

**Lowell Observatory:** Flagstaff's clean, dust-free air and usually cloudless skies attracted Dr. Percival Lowell, a rich astronomer from New England. He founded Lowell Observatory in 1894 atop Mars Hill, just W of downtown, for studying the solar system. His enthusiasm and dedication led to some controversy as well as important discoveries. For example, during long hours of observing Mars on cold Flagstaff nights, Lowell began seeing lines on the planet's surface. He thought of them as "canals," and used them as proof of life on Mars. The more Lowell peered through his telescope, the more lines he saw! Not every astronomer of the time could see these markings, and today we know from spacecraft photos that the canals were only imaginary. From studies of the orbits of Uranus and Neptune, the outermost known planets at the time, Lowell predicted in 1902 the existence of another planet farther out. Using Lowell's calculations, a worker at the observatory discovered the planet Pluto in 1930. After

twenty-four-inch Clark refractor telescope at Lowell Observatory

Jay Inge working on a map of Ganymede (a moon of Jupiter) at the U.S. Geological Survey

Lowell died in 1916, the observatory continued under his endowment and remains a prominent planetary-research center.

You're welcome to see the exhibits in the dome-topped visitors' center, open Tue. to Sat. 1000-1630 in summer, and Tue. to Sat. at 1330 the rest of the year; $1 suggested donation; tel. 774-3358. Special tours for groups can be arranged in advance. One-hour tours beginning at 1000 and 1330 illustrate the history and work of the observatory with a slide show, then visit the 1896 24-inch Clark refractor telescope. On the first of every month from 1930-2200, and Fri. nights 2000-2200 during the summer (weather permitting), the observatory presents a planetary slide show and lets visitors gaze through the telescope. The observatory is about one mile from downtown; walk or drive W on Santa Fe Ave. (don't turn with highway) to the signposted road up Mars Hill.

**astrogeology:** Many of the scientists in the Flagstaff Field Center of the U.S. Geological Survey study and map the Moon, planets, and other bodies of our solar system. At the same time they investigate landforms on Earth, such as volcanos and sand dunes, which are thought to be formed by the same processes

as the extraterrestrial features. The Apollo astronauts learned their lunar geology here, and were later guided on the Moon by scientists from the Center. There's no visitor center and regular tours are offered only to groups, but you're welcome to see exhibits in the hallways. Giant maps and spectacular color photos taken by spacecraft cover the walls. Geology of the Moon, Mercury, and Mars has been mapped in surprising detail. Even Venus is being mapped using radar images with computer-generated color. Photos include Jupiter and Saturn and their moons, remote-sensing products showing the Earth's features, and views sent back by landers on Mars and Venus. Building 1 (Astrogeology) has most of the exhibits and a specialized library that you may use. More maps and photos can be seen in the hallways of Buildings 3 and 4. You may visit Mon. to Fri. 0800-1630. Remember that the people working here are normally too busy to show visitors around. Also, don't enter offices or labs unless invited. Tours for scientific or educational groups can be arranged; call or write in advance to Branch of Astrogeology, 2255 N. Gemini Dr., Flagstaff, AZ 86001; tel. 527-7000. The U.S. Geological Survey is atop McMillan Mesa off Cedar Ave., 1½ miles NE of downtown.

*Apollo astronauts training
on a volcanic landscape
near Flagstaff*

**Riordan State Historic Park:** The Riordan brothers, Timothy and Michael, each built grand houses S of downtown Flagstaff in 1904. They joined their houses with a billiard room and christened the structure "Kinlichi" (Navajo for "red house"). Tours inside give a good idea of how well-to-do people lived in Flagstaff during the early 1900s. Tour guides explain history and architectural features. Open daily 0800-1700 from mid-May to mid-Sept. and daily 1230-1700 the rest of the year; $2 adult, free for children 18 and under. It's recommended to phone in advance to make a reservation because you may enter only in a tour group; tel. 779-4395. Now sandwiched between new condos and shopping centers, this bit of historic Flagstaff is on Riordan Ranch St. (behind Wendy's) between S. Milton Rd. and Northern Arizona University, about one mile S of downtown.

## ACCOMMODATIONS

**youth hostels:** The historic Weatherford Hotel in downtown Flagstaff offers bunkbeds in shared rooms for $7.60/members year-round. It's located close to bus and train stations at the corner of 23 N. Leroux St. and Aspen Ave.; tel. 774-2731. Nonmembers can buy a 3-day temporary membership for $3, or a one-year card for $20. Sheets cost an extra $1. A 3-day stay limit usually applies. Regular hotel rooms are available too, $18.90 s and $21 d. Hostelers have use of a kitchen or can dine downstairs in Charly's, the hotel's restaurant and pub. Musicians often perform foot-tapping bluegrass, country, or folk in the evenings here. Car rentals (Bargain Rent-a-Car) and tours to the Grand Canyon, Monument Valley, and Indian reservations can be arranged at the hostel; 4 people can rent a car (24 hours) to visit the Grand Canyon at a cost of about $10/person, cheaper than taking the bus.

J.W. Weatherford came to Flagstaff in 1887 from Texas, and stayed 47 years. He built the hotel, quite elegant in its day, in 1897. Weatherford's other projects included an opera house (now the Orpheum Theatre) and the Weatherford Road (now a hiking trail up the Peaks). The Du Beau Motel also runs a hostel (no hostel card needed) for $8.50/night

*Weatherford Youth Hostel*

including breakfast; no kitchen; 19 W. Phoenix Ave.; tel. 774-6731.

**bed & breakfasts:** In the downtown area you'll find Dierker House Bed & Breakfast ($26.25 s, $36.75 d; 423 W. Cherry; tel. 774-3249), and Du Beau Motel (bed & breakfast: $19 s, $25 d; weekly rates (no breakfast): $55 s, $65 d; 19 W. Phoenix Ave.; tel. 774-6731). Walking L Ranch, just N of town on Mt. Elden Lookout Rd., offers bed & breakfast for $26 s, $46.80 d, and your horse stays free! (Tel. 779-2219.) In the woods 2 miles S of town, Arizona Mountain Inn has bed & breakfast rooms for $55 d; housekeeping units with 1-5 bedrooms start at $60 d on weekdays and $80 on Fri. and Sat.; weekly rates begin at $320 d; costs often drop during the winter off season; 685 Lake Mary Rd.; tel. 774-8959.

**motels:** Although the youth hostels are the cheapest place for solo travelers, a party of 2 or more can often do better in a motel. Drive E on Santa Fe Ave. from downtown to look for the bargain places; the "strip" extends 3 miles. Most motels signpost their prices so just turn in where they're lowest if you want to save money. Accommodation costs fluctuate with the seasons, summer being the most expensive. Off-season, prices drop substantially at the more expensive places, while cheaper ones might shave off a couple of dollars. Rates can rise a bit during the ski season, depending on demand. The rates below apply in summer. Light sleepers should beware that many motels sit near the railroad tracks!

Places to stay downtown, besides the YH and B&Bs, include the Downtowner Motel ($17 s, $19 d; weekly rates: $63 s, $84 d; 19 S. San Francisco St.; tel. 774-8461), Imperial 400 Motel ($44.10 s, $46.20 d; 223 S. Sitgreaves St.; tel. 774-5041), Monte Vista Hotel ($47.25 s or d; 100 N. San Francisco St.; tel. 774-9086), and Townhouse Motel ($20.14 s, $24.42 d; 122 W. Santa Fe Ave.; tel. 774-5081). Most of the major motel chains are in town too. Holiday Inn (tel. 774-5221) and Travelodge University (tel. 774-3381) are on W. Hwy. 66; take I-40 Exits 191 or 195. Quality Inn (tel. 774-8771), Rodeway Inn (tel. 774-5038), Comfort Inn (tel. 774-7326), The Arizonan (tel. 774-7171), and University Inn (tel. 774-4581) are on S. Milton Rd., between downtown and I-40 Exit 195. Little America (tel. 779-2741), La Quinta (tel. 779-3614), Travelodge East (774-1821), Regal 8 (tel. 774-8756), Allstar Inns (tel. 779-6184), and Motel 6 (tel. 774-3533) are off Butler Ave. near I-40 Exit 198. On E. Santa Fe Ave., between downtown and I-40 Exit 201, you'll find Ramada Inn East (tel. 526-1399), Americana (tel. 526-2200), and Pony Soldier Motel (tel. 526-2388).

**camping:** None of the campgrounds has locations close to downtown and the bus and train connections; you really need your own vehicle to camp. The centrally located Du Beau Motel, however, allows travelers to camp on their grounds for $5 including shower and breakfast; 19 W. Phoenix Ave.; tel. 774-6731. Stay for free in the National Forest lands surrounding town; the pine forests have lots of room but no facilities. Just don't camp on private land without the owner's permission. The Coconino Forest

map comes in handy to show which is public land and where the back roads go. Carry water and be *very* careful with fire in the forests; in dry weather the Forest Service often prohibits all fires in the woods.

For developed campgrounds, all with showers, try: Fort Tuthill County Campground, open early May to late Sept., $6 for tents or RVs; a few hookups available; 5 miles S of downtown off I-17 Exit 337; tel. 774-5130. Black Barts RV park is open all year, $5.24 tents and $15.71 RVs w/hookups; 2 miles E of downtown at I-40 Butler Ave. Exit 198; tel. 774-1912. Flagstaff KOA is open all year, $14.84 tents and $15.90 RVs w/hookups; 5 miles NE of downtown on US 89 (one mile N from I-40 Exit 201); tel. 526-9926. Big Tree Campground, also open all year, is ½ mile farther N on US 89 from the KOA, $13.10 tent or RV w/hookups; tel. 526-2583. Greer's Camp Townsend is an adult RV Park for self-contained rigs (no restrooms or showers), located across the highway from Big Tree Campground; open mid-Apr. to mid-Oct.; $10.37 w/hookups; tel. 526-4977. Diamond M RV Park and Campground is 2 miles N of the KOA on US 89 (located behind J&H Windows); open all year, $10 tents or RVs w/hookups; tel. 526-1829. Kit Carson RV Park is open year-round, $9.20 tents, $14.65 RVs w/hookups; located 2 miles W of downtown on Hwy. 66 (I-40 Exits 191 or 195); tel. 774-6993. Woody Mountain Campground is ½ mile farther W from Kit Carson; open early May to end of Oct.; $10.50 tents or RVs without hookups, $14.70 w/hookups; tel. 774-7727.

# FOOD

Flagstaff, for its size, has an amazing number of places to eat. But then, it has many hungry tourists and students. Most restaurants cater to the eat-and-run crowd. You'll find the well-known chains and fast-food places on the main highways, but with a little effort you can discover some unique restaurants and cafes.

**downtown:** Come here for local atmosphere. Old-fashioned "home style" eateries abound. Charley's Pub and Restaurant, in the old Weatherford Hotel, serves good American food;

open daily for breakfast, lunch, and dinner; 23 N. Leroux St.; tel. 779-1919. Choi's Luncheonette dishes out bargain-priced breakfasts and lunches, but don't expect much decor; closed Sun.; 7 E. Aspen Avenue. Beba's Soup & Fixin's has a homey touch for her American and Continental dinners; open evenings Tue. to Sat.; 19 E. Aspen Ave.; tel. 779-5472. Cafe Espress serves home-made natural foods, including many vegetarian items; fancy coffees from the espresso bar and baked goodies from the oven are other attractions; open daily for breakfast, lunch, and dinner (except closes 1400 on Sun.); 16 N. San Francisco St.; tel. 774-0541. Kathy's is a cozy little cafe with the American standbys and a few exotic items like Aussie burgers and Navajo tacos; open daily for breakfast and lunch; dinners too on weekdays; 7 N. San Francisco St.; tel. 774-1951.

If you're looking for inexpensive Chinese-American food, and don't care about the decor, try the Grand Canyon Cafe (110 E. Santa Fe Ave.) or the Hong Kong Cafe (6 E. Santa Fe Ave.); both open Mon. to Sat. for breakfast, lunch, and dinner. Good Mexican food, again without the decor, is served at Martan's Burrito Palace (10 N. San Francisco St.) and El Charro (409 S. San Francisco St.); both closed on Sunday. The highly recommended Milushka's

Bohemian Deli and Coffee House serves great dinners, sandwiches, soups, salads, and desserts from Czech, Italian, American, and other recipes; open Tue. to Sat. for lunch and dinner; 121 S. San Francisco St.; tel. 774-8272. Morning Glory is a new cafe specializing in Thai food; open Tue. to Fri. for lunch and dinner, and Sat. for brunch; 115 S. San Francisco St.; tel. 774-9080. Homesick Texans and other barbeque fanciers will enjoy a stop at Lone Star Bar-B-Que; open Mon. to Sat. for lunch, dinner, and takeouts; 4 S. San Francisco St.; tel. 774-0984.

Macy's Coffee House and Bakery serves sandwiches, soups, crepes, quiches, and home-baked goodies with 15 different coffee brews (a coffee-hound's heaven); open daily for breakfast and lunch; 14 S. Beaver St.; tel. 774-2243. La Bellavia Sandwich Shoppe is a cozy little cafe for breakfast and lunch; open daily; 18 S. Beaver St.; tel. 774-8301. For deli sandwiches, stop at Cheese-A-Plenty at 113 W. Birch Ave.; tel. 779-5526. Pick up pizza and Italian sandwiches at NiMarco Pizza (closed Sun.; 101 S. Beaver St.; tel. 779-2691) or Alpine Pizza (open daily; 7 N. Leroux St.; tel. 779-4109). For elegant and romantic dining, make a reservation at the Cottage Place, which serves American and Continental specialties at

*Santa Fe Avenue in downtown Flagstaff*

*Arizona rose*
*(Rosa arizonica)*

moderate prices; open daily for dinner; 126 W. Cottage; tel. 774-8431.

**Northern Arizona University:** North Union (#1 on NAU map) has a cafeteria and the Timber Inn (barbecue beef). In the University Union (#5 on NAU map) you'll find the Atrium (restaurant with a garden atmosphere serving lunches of specialty sandwiches, salads, and soups), Pizzano's (pizza and pasta); Mt. Jacks (burgers, chicken, and breakfasts), The Eatery (deli sandwiches, bakery, and fast food), and Scoops (ice cream). In the center of campus, the University Dining Hall (#9 on NAU map) has a large cafeteria. South Campus Dining Hall (#13 on NAU map) has a cafeteria, while South Campus Student Union (#12 on NAU map) offers El Rancho Rojo (tacos, enchiladas, and burritos).

**other areas:** The large Mexican-American population of Flagstaff provides the town with some tasty food. In addition to those listed under "downtown," cafes include La Sierra (1066 W. Hwy. 66 near the Holiday Inn; tel. 779-0011); Kachina Restaurant (closed Sun.; 2220 E. Santa Fe Ave.; tel. 779-5790); and La Villa Bonita (closed Sun.; 4217 N. US 89, at I-40 Exit 201; tel. 526-8406). If you'd like Mexican food in a more elegant setting, try Ramona's Cantina (University Plaza, off S. Milton Rd.; tel. 774-3397) or El Chilito (1551 S. Milton Rd.; tel. 774-4666). Mama Luisa has excellent Italian

food (lunches are the best value) at Kachina Square, corner of E. Santa Fe Ave. and Steves Blvd.; tel. 526-6809 (reservations advised). Dine Chinese at Mandarin (810 W. Hwy. 66; tel. 774-2287); Hunan West (closed Tue.; University Plaza off S. Milton Rd.; tel. 779-2229); Hunan (closed Sun.; 2028 N. 4th St.; tel. 526-1009); Afton House (very pleasant decor; 3050 E. Santa Fe Ave. next to the Pony Soldier Motel; tel. 526-2545); and Mandarin Garden (Park Santa Fe Shopping Center, 3518 E. Santa Fe Ave.; tel. 526-5033).

Some popular American places include Buster's (1800 S. Milton Rd. in Green Tree Village; tel. 774-5155); Furrs Cafeteria (1200 S. Milton Rd.; tel. 779-4104); The Steak House (good Mexican food too; 914 E. Santa Fe Ave.; tel. 774-4802); Cattleman's Club (1612 E. Santa Fe Ave. in Western Hills Motel; tel. 774-6633);

Little America dining room and coffee shop (2515 E. Butler Ave.; tel. 779-2741); and Christmas Tree Restaurant (1903 N. 2nd St.; tel. 779-5888). Black Bart's Steak House serves up steaks, seafood, and other American fare; open daily for dinner; singing waiters and waitresses entertain you, and during summer there's a dinner theater; 2760 E. Butler Ave. (near I-40 Exit 198); tel. 779-3142. Many locals say the best steaks in town are served at Bob Lupo's Horsemen Lodge, which has other specialties too; open for dinner daily except Sun.; located on US 89, 8½ miles NE of downtown (3½ miles N from I-40 Exit 201); tel. 526-2655. For a splurge, take in the Sunday brunch all-you-can-eat at Little America; hours are 0900-1400, $12 adult, $8 children 6-12; 2515 E. Butler Ave.; tel. 779-2741.

**food stores:** Winnie's Natural Foods is downtown on the corner of Sante Fe Ave. and San Francisco. Young's Mini Market has groceries downtown at 1 E. Aspen Avenue. You'll find supermarkets in most of the shopping centers (see Flagstaff map).

# ENTERTAINMENT

**movies:** Catch bargain-priced movies downtown in the Orpheum Theatre, 15 W. Aspen Ave.; tel. 774-7823. To find out what's being shown on the NAU campus, call tel. 523-2391. The University Plaza Theatres (University Plaza, off S. Milton Rd.; tel. 774-4433) and Green Tree Village Theatre (1800 S. Milton Rd.; tel. 779-3202) are both S of downtown. East of downtown, see movies at Flag-East Theatre (2009 N. 4th St.; tel. 774-6992) and at Flagstaff Mall Cinema (4650 N. US 89; tel. 526-4555).

**dinner theatre:** During summer actors ham it up with melodrama, song and dance, and other vaudeville acts at Black Bart's Steak House Saloon & Old West Dinner Theatre, 2760 E. Butler Ave. near I-40 Exit 198; tel. 779-3142.

**nightlife:** For varied entertainment downtown—could be rock, country, folk, blues, or poetry reading—try Charly's (23 N. Leroux St.; tel. 779-1919) or The Monsoons (22 E. Santa Fe Ave.; tel. 774-7929). East of downtown, the Museum Club presents country, rock, blues, and reggae bands at 3404 E. Santa Fe Ave.; tel. 526-9434. The Lounge at Little America offers a dance floor and mostly Top 40 music, 2515 E. Butler Ave.; tel. 779-2741.

**culture and sports at NAU:** Northern Arizona University presents theater, opera, dance, concerts, and a variety of sports events. For information and tickets, contact NAU Central Ticket Office in the University Union (#5 on NAU map); tel. 523-2000 (recorded Hotline) and tel. 523-5661 or 523-5662 (for tickets).

**events:** Flagstaff-area people put on a variety of festivals, fairs, shows, and concerts during the year. The Chamber of Commerce will tell you what's happening; tel. 774-4505. Major annual events include—**May:** Cinco de Mayo (parade, coronation, dance, and barbeque by the Mexican-American community). **June:** Horse Show, Pine Country Rodeo and Parade,

Festival of the Arts (concerts, musicals, and plays), Festival of Native American Arts (Indian art and craft exhibitions, demonstrations, and dance performances), Fiddle Festival, and Gem

*Cowboys aim for the paydirt in rodeos throughout Arizona.*

& Mineral Show. **July:** Festival of the Arts cont., Festival of Native American Arts cont., 4th of July Fireworks, horse racing, and Lake Mary Canoe Jamboree. **August:** Festival of the Arts cont., Festival of Native American Arts cont., Festival in the Pines (arts and crafts with musical performances), and Coconino County Fair.

## RECREATION

Impress your friends by saying you went skiing and swimming on the same day in Flagstaff! Try the indoor pools at the University's Natatorium (#6 on NAU map); tel. 523-4508; or East Flagstaff Junior High School, corner of N. 4th St. and Cedar Ave.; tel. 779-4154. The pool at Flagstaff High School is open in summer, 400 W. Elm Ave.; tel. 779-4154. Play tennis at the courts in Thorpe Park (off Toltec St. in W. Flagstaff) or Bushmaster Park (off Lockett Rd. in E. Flagstaff). Joggers and strollers alike enjoy Buffalo Park, off Cedar Avenue. Ice skate from mid-Oct. to mid-Mar. at Flagstaff Ice Rink, 1850 N. Turquoise Dr.; tel. 774-1051. Play golf at Fairfield Continental Country Club's 18-hole course, 2580 N. Oakmont Dr. (take I-40 Exit 201, go S ¾ mile on Country Club Rd., then turn R on Oakmont Dr.); closed in winter; tel. 526-3211, ext. 243. The Alpineer offers instruction for rock-climbing and cross-country skiing; day and overnight ski tours can be arranged too, 317 N. Humphreys St.; tel. 774-7809.

**horseback riding:** The Flagstaff area is great horse country. If you don't have your own steed, local riding stables can provide one. Advance reservations should be made. In winter, stables usually close; their horses often head S to join the snowbirds on the desert. Hitchin' Post Stables offers guided trail rides in and near upper Walnut Canyon; $9/one hour to $35/all day; pancake breakfast, steak dinner, and haywagon rides available too; from the S edge of Flagstaff (I-40 Exit 195) take Lake Mary Rd. 5 miles SE; tel. 774-1719 or 774-7131. Ski Lift Lodge Stables leads rides near the San Francisco Peaks; $8/hour; go 7 miles NW of town on US 180; tel. 774-0729.

**downhill skiing:** Fairfield Snowbowl, on the San Francisco Peaks, has some of Arizona's best downhill action. Four chairlifts service about 32 trails ranging from novice to expert. You'll drop 2,300 feet from the top of Agassiz Chair Lift. Some runs exceed 2 miles. With sufficient snow, the season begins Thanksgiving Day and lasts through Easter; tel. 779-4577 for snow and road conditions. Be sure to call before coming out, because Flagstaff weather is notoriously unpredictable. Rentals (skis, boots, and poles/$13) are available on the mountain at the new Hart Prairie Day Lodge. An all-day lift ticket costs $18 ($22 weekends); the all-day beginner ticket is $12 ($15 weekends). The Snowbowl offers discounts for ½-day, weekdays, and for people 12 and under

*downhill at the Snowbowl*

or 65 and over. A ski school gives group and private lessons. Shuttle buses climb the 7 miles from US 180 to the ski area, $3 RT. To reach the Snowbowl, drive 7 miles NW from downtown on US 180 to the turnoff, then either take the shuttle bus or drive the remaining 7 miles. Call tel. 774-1863 for info about lifts, rentals, and instruction. Ski Lift Lodge provides the closest place to stay and a restaurant; open all year, $31.20 s or d; it's at the junction of US 180 and the Snowbowl Rd.; tel. 774-0729. Fairfield Continental Country Club offers package deals with accommodations, dinner, skiing, and transportation; tel. 526-3232 or (800) 352-5777.

**cross-country skiing:** Flagstaff Nordic Center offers 30 km of groomed trails ranging in difficulty from beginner to advanced near the San Francisco Peaks. The center is open daily from about mid-Nov. to mid-Apr. with rentals and a ski school. Trail fee is $4/person, $9/family; tel. 774-6216. A busy schedule of races, clinics, and full-moon tours fills the calendar. Flagstaff Nordic Center is in the Hochderffer Hill area near Hart Prairie; take US 180 NW 15 miles to near Milepost 232.

Hart Prairie and Wing Mountain are 2 non-developed skiing areas near the San Francisco Peaks. The rolling meadow and forest country is ideal for ski touring. Hart Prairie can be reached by driving 9½ miles NW of town on US 180, then turning R on the S end of Forest Route 151 as far as the road is clear. Parking on US 180 is prohibited. For Wing Mountain, continue on US 180 just past the Hart Prairie Rd. and turn L onto Forest Route 222B (228B on some maps). For road and skiing conditions near the Peaks, call the Coconino Forest Service office at tel. 527-7450.

The groomed trails and good snow of Mormon Lake also attract cross-country skiers. Drive 20 miles SE on Lake Mary Rd. and turn R 8 miles on Mormon Lake Loop Road. Two ski areas, open daily, offer maintained trails ($2 weekdays, $4 weekends), rental waxless ski sets ($10 complete w/trail fee), and instruction (starts at $8 for 2 hours in a small group). Trails vary from easy to challenging in both places. Mormon Lake Ski Center, in the village of Mormon Lake, has 38 km of trails running along the lakeshore and on Navajo Ridge. This is proba-

bly the best place for beginners; tel. 1-354-2240 (toll call from Flagstaff). Mormon Lake Lodge has 4 motel rooms and some cabins; tel. 774-0462 (Flagstaff) or 354-2227 (local). Montezuma Nordic Ski Center, 4 miles N of Mormon Lake village, offers 21 km of trails through the Dairy Spring Canyon area; tel. 1-354-2221 (during season). For the Mormon Lake area road and ski conditions, call the U.S. Forest Service office at tel. 527-7474.

## SHOPPING

**art galleries and Indian crafts:** Shops in downtown Flagstaff display a wealth of regional art and crafts. Indian artists produce especially distinctive work; you'll see paintings, jewelry, Navajo rugs, Hopi *katsina* dolls, pottery, and baskets. Four Winds Traders, at 118 W. Santa Fe Ave., is one of the largest and best Indian galleries; Indians themselves also shop here for stones and jewelry-making supplies; closed Sun. and Monday. Look for other shops and galleries nearby on Santa Fe Ave., N. Leroux St., N. San Francisco St., and Aspen Avenue. The Silversmith, S of downtown at 1431 S. Milton Rd., features Hopi, Navajo, and Zuni jewelry; Indian craftsmen often give demonstrations; sandpaintings and Kaibab sandstone photographs (photos printed on rock slabs) are also for sale; closed Sunday. The gift shop at the Museum of Northern Arizona, 3 miles NW on US 180, has an excellent selection of Indian art and crafts.

For limited-edition prints and paintings of the Grand Canyon and other regional subjects, visit the Franklin Gallery at 500 N. Beaver St.; tel. 774-9101. Coconino Center for the Arts displays rotating art exhibits and schedules music and dance performances; it's located behind the Pioneer Historical Museum, 2 miles NW of downtown on US 180; tel. 779-5944 to find what's on. Next door, you can see paintings (largely Western art), prints, sketches, photos, ceramics, glasswork, and other crafts in the Art Barn; tel. 774-0822. The Gallery at Northland Press features art and books about the Southwest; go 2½ miles NW from town on US 180; tel. 774-5251. Northern Arizona University's Art Gallery could have almost any kind of art in Room 231 of the Creative Arts Bldg. (#4 on NAU map); tel. 523-3471 for info and hours.

**camping supplies:** Outdoors supplies, maps, and information are available from: The Edge (also climbing gear; 106 N. San Francisco St.; tel. 774-1296); Mountain Sports (1800 S. Milton Rd.; tel. 779-5156); Peace Surplus (14 W. Santa Fe Ave.; tel. 779-4521); and Popular Surplus (901 S. Milton Rd.; tel. 774-0598). Andy's Sporting Goods specializes in hunting and fishing gear (23 N. Beaver St.; tel. 774-4401). Expeditions, Inc. carries river-running equipment, including kayaks, rafts, wet and dry suits, and river books; they also organize Grand Canyon raft trips (625 N. Beaver St.; tel. 779-3769).

**ski rentals and supplies:** You can rent cross-country gear at Flagstaff Nordic Center and the 2 Mormon Lake ski centers. Cross-country sales and rentals in town are at The Edge (106 N. San Francisco St.; tel. 774-1296) and Cosmic Cycles Bike & Ski (113 S. San Francisco St.; tel. 779-1092). You can get both cross-country and downhill rentals in town at Humphrey Summit Ski (505 N. Beaver St.; tel. 779-1308; and at the Snow Bowl turnoff; tel. 774-7852) and Mountain Sports (1800 S. Milton Rd.; tel. 779-5156).

## SERVICES

The main post office is downtown at 104 N. Agassiz St.; branches are in East Flagstaff at 2112 N. 4th St., and at the University in the basement of the bookstore (#8 on NAU map). If you need to see a doctor it's cheaper to go directly to a doctor's office than to the hospital. You'll find many offices along N. Beaver Street. Flagstaff Medical Center, the local hospital, is at 1215 N. Beaver St.; tel. 779-3366. In emergencies (police, fire, and medical) dial tel. 911. Summer jobs can often be found in Flagstaff but pay tends to be rock bottom; for job information contact the Dept. of Economic Security, 397 Malpais Lane; tel. 779-4513. The *Arizona Daily Sun* lists work possibilities.

The Adult Center hosts several clubs and offers classes in yoga, martial arts, dancing, cross-country skiing, and a wide variety of other subjects. You're sure to find something of interest if staying in town awhile. Organizations meeting here include the Flagstaff Hiking Club, Northern Arizona Paddlers Club, and Coconino Amateur Radio Club. The Adult Center is on the W edge of downtown next to Thorpe Park at 245 N. Thorpe Dr.; tel. 774-1068.

## INFORMATION

The very helpful Chamber of Commerce staff can answer your questions and tell you what's going on. The office is downtown at 101 W. Santa Fe Ave. (Flagstaff, AZ 86001); tel. 774-4505. Open Mon. to Fri. 0800-1700; also Sat. and Sun. 1000-1600 in summer. A Current Events Hotline recording has upcoming events; tel. 779-3733. The U.S. Forest Service has info about camping, hiking, and road conditions in the Coconino National Forest surrounding Flagstaff; the main office is at 2323 E. Greenlaw Ln. behind Knoles Village Shopping Center (see map); open Mon. to Fri. 0730-1630; tel. 527-7400. You can purchase any of the National Forest maps for Arizona here ($1 each). The Coconino Forest map is also available at the Chamber of Commerce and sporting goods stores.

**libraries:** A good place for a rainy day, a long bus wait, or learning more about Arizona. The main public library is downtown at the corner of 300 W. Aspen Ave. and Sitgreaves St.; open Mon. to Thur. 1000-2100, Fri. and Sat. 0900-1800, and Sun. 1300-1600; tel. 779-7670; you'll find many good regional books in the Arizona Room. The main NAU library (#3 on NAU map) not only has many books and periodicals, but a large map collection; hikers can plan trips and copy maps here; open (regular school terms) Mon. to Thur. 0730-2300, Fri. 0730-1800, Sat. 0800-1800, and Sun. 1300-2300; tel. 523-2171. The University's Special Collections Library (#11 on NAU map) contains an outstanding array of Arizona-related publications and photos; open Mon. to Fri. 0800-1700; tel. 523-5551. The Museum of Northern Arizona has an excellent regional library in the Research Center across the highway from the museum; open Mon. to Fri. 0900-1700; tel. 774-5211.

**bookstores:** McGaugh's Newsstand downtown features a good selection of newspapers, magazines, Arizona books, and general reading at 24 N. San Francisco Street. The NAU Bookstore (#8 on NAU map) also has many regional and general reading publications. The Museum of Northern Arizona sells excellent books on regional Indian cultures, archaeology, and natural history; 3 miles NW on US 180. For used books, drop into Duck's Books at 1800 S. Milton Rd. in Greentree Village, or The Bookery at 2725 E. Lakin Dr. (E. Flagstaff).

## TRANSPORT

**tours:** Nava-Hopi Tours (The Gray Line) operates regional bus tours and scheduled Grand Canyon bus service. The tours tend to show a lot in a short time. Nava-Hopi offers day trips to: Flagstaff area (Museum of Northern Arizona, Walnut Canyon, Sunset Crater, and Wupatki; $23), Grand Canyon ($25.50), Oak Creek Canyon-Sedona-Montezuma Castle-Jerome ($26), Hopi Indian Reservation ($35), and Monument Valley ($60). Except for the Grand Canyon tour, Nava-Hopi requires at least 24 hours advance notice; children under 12 go at half price; some tours don't operate in winter. Buses leave from Greyhound and other points in Flagstaff; tel. 774-5003. For an aerial perspective, fly with Alpine Air Service from the Flagstaff airport to the Grand Canyon, Meteor Crater, Sunset Crater, Oak Creek Canyon, Sedona, and and other scenic spots; tel. 779-5178.

**car rental:** A car rental allows more extensive sightseeing than public transport and costs less if several people get together. Rates fluctuate with supply and demand, competition, and the mood of the operators; call around for

*downtown Flagstaff, from Mars Hill*

the best deals. Prices for the smallest cars start at $6/day plus $.55/mile, or $30/day unlimited mileage. Insurance gets tacked on at $5/day and up. Rent cars from Avis (airport; tel. 774-8421); Bargain Rent-a-Car (Weatherford Hotel, 23 N. Leroux; tel. 526-2323); Budget (100 N. Humphreys; tel. 774-2763; and at the airport; tel. 779-0306); Hertz (airport; tel. 774-4452); Sears (100 N. Humpreys St.; tel. 774-1879); and Thrifty Rent-a-Car (500 S. Milton Rd.; tel. 779-0000. See the Yellow Pages for more agencies. For a taxi, call Alpine Cab (tel. 526-7162), Flagstaff Taxi (tel. 774-1374), or Northern Arizona Taxi (tel. 774-7329).

**long-distance bus:** Nava-Hopi buses head up to the Grand Canyon 3 times a day in summer and once a day in winter; fares for the 2-hour ride are $11.75 OW, $22.30 RT, or $10.70 RT w/bus pass; tel. 774-5003 or 774-4574. Buses leave from the Greyhound station, 399 S. Malpais Ln. (off Sitgreaves St., ½ mile S of Santa Fe Ave.); earlier pickups can be made from Amtrak and Trailways. Greyhound offers daily departures (w/sample OW fares and destinations) to: Phoenix (4X daily, $20), Prescott (1X, $14), Holbrook (5X, $18), Gallup (5X, $37), Kingman (3X, $26), Los Angeles (3X, $63), Las Vegas (2X, $50), and San Francisco (3X, $119). A small discount might be given for roundtrips. The station is ½ mile S of central downtown at 399 S. Malpais Ln.; open 0630-2300; tel. 774-4573. Trailways Bus has long-distance service and fares similar to Greyhound but fewer departures; the station is downtown at 114 W. Santa Fe Ave.; open daily about 0630-0330; tel. 774-6661 or 779-5087. Although neither bus station has a restaurant, there are plenty nearby. Arizona Central Lines connects Flagstaff with Phoenix's airport 5 times daily ($25 OW, $45 RT) and downtown Phoenix ($20 OW, $36 RT); a connecting shuttle at Cordes Junction goes to Prescott 3 times daily ($20 OW, $36 RT); call a day in advance for reservations; tel. 526-1377.

**local bus:** Pine Country Transit serves most of the city about once an hour between roughly 0900 and 1700, with an hour off for lunch; no service Sun.; tel. 779-6624 or 779-6635; pick up a schedule at the Chamber of Commerce.

**train:** Amtrak trains leave daily in the evening for Los Angeles ($70 OW), and daily in the morning for Albuquerque ($66 OW) and on to New Orleans or Chicago. Amtrak often gives substantial discounts on RT tickets. The station is downtown at 1 Santa Fe Ave; open 0515-2230; tel. (800) 872-7245 for reservations or tel. 774-8679 for the station.

**air:** Skywest Airlines flies 6 times daily S to Phoenix ($35-55 OW) and 2 times daily N to Page ($59 OW); onward connections go to Yuma, El Centro, St. George, and other destinations. Discounts apply to RT tickets purchased 7 days or more in advance; tel. (800) 453-9417 for reservations or tel. 774-4830 for the airport. America West flies 6 times daily to Phoenix ($35-55 OW) and twice daily to Las Vegas ($59-89 OW); tel. 525-1346 or (800) 247-5692. Pulliam Field, Flagstaff's airport, is 5 miles S of town; take I-17 Exit 337.

Meteor Crater

# EAST OF FLAGSTAFF

## WALNUT CANYON

Sinagua Indians chose this pretty canyon in which to build their pueblo homes more than 800 years ago. Ledges, eroded out of the limestone cliffs, provided shelter from rain and snow; the Sinagua merely had to build walls under their ready-made roof. Good farmlands, wild plant foods, and forests filled with game lay close at hand. The clear waters of Walnut Creek flowed in the canyon bottom. Sinagua occupied this site from A.D. 1120 to 1250, then decided for unknown reasons to leave. Perhaps some of their descendants now live among the modern pueblo tribes. More than 300 cliff dwellings remain from the Sinagua's stay here. Some can be seen and entered along a loop trail constructed by the National Park Service.

**Visitor Center:** A small museum displays pottery and other artifacts of the Sinagua. Exhibits also show how the Indians farmed and how they used wild plants for baskets, sandals, mats, soap, food, and medicine. A map illustrates trading routes with neighboring cultures. Rangers will try to answer your questions about the archaeology and natural history of Walnut Canyon. During the summer, they give talks several times a day. Books and maps related to the Monument and region may be purchased.

The self-guiding ¾-mile Island Trail begins behind the Visitor Center and winds past 25 cliff dwellings; buy or borrow the trail leaflet. Take some time and get a feeling of what it was like to live here as a Sinagua. The paved path descends 185 feet, which you'll have to climb on the way out. Allow 45 minutes to an hour for the Island Trail. Because of the high elevation (6,690 feet), it's not recommended for people with walking, breathing, or heart difficulties. The easier Rim Trail visits 2 scenic viewpoints and 2 reconstructed surface dwellings; allow 20-30 min. for the ½-mile loop. Vegetation changes dramatically from the pinyon and juniper forests near the rim to the tall Douglas firs clinging to the canyon ledges. Black walnut and several other kinds of deciduous trees grow at the bottom. Walnut Canyon National Monument remains open all year (except Thanksgiving and Christmas), though snows can close the trails for short periods. The Visitor Center is open in summer daily 0700-1800, and the rest of the year daily 0800-1700; Island Trail closes one hour before the Visitor Center; $3/vehicle entrance fee; tel. 526-3367. From Flagstaff, head 7 miles E on I-40 to Walnut Canyon Exit 204, then go 3 miles S on a paved road.

*Grand Falls of the Little Colorado River*

## GRAND FALLS OF THE LITTLE COLORADO RIVER

In the spring, this thundering torrent of muddy-brown water plunges 185 feet into the canyon of the Little Colorado River about 30 miles NE of Flagstaff. Best time to see the spectacle is during the spring runoff in Mar. and Apr.; in other months the river may dry up to an unimpressive trickle. A lava flow from Merriam Crater, the large cinder cone 10 miles SW, created the falls about 100,000 years ago. The tongue of lava filled the canyon, forcing the river out of its gorge, around the dam, then back over the rim into the original channel. Grand Falls of the Little Colorado River is on the SW corner of the Navajo Indian Reservation. From Flagstaff, take US 89 N 1¾ miles past Flagstaff Mall and turn R on the Camp Townsend-Winona Rd. for 8 miles, then turn L onto the Leupp (pronounced "LOOP") Rd.; follow this road NE 13 miles to the sign "Grand Falls 10 miles" and turn L. The Grand Falls road is dirt, but OK for cars. You'll see hues of the Painted Desert as the road descends to the river. Other approaches: I-40 Winona Exit 211 (7 miles E of Flagstaff), drive 2 miles on the Townsend-Winona Rd., then R on Leupp Rd. to the Grand Falls turnoff; I-40 Exit 245 (46 miles E of Flagstaff), take AZ 99 to Leupp then Leupp Rd. to Grand Falls turnoff. From Kykotsmovi, on the Hopi Indian Reservation, take paved Indian Route 2 SW 49 miles to Leupp, then Leupp Rd. to Grand Falls turnoff. Free admission, though the Navajo Tribe asks that you help keep the area clean and leash your dogs so they won't disturb livestock.

## METEOR CRATER

A speeding mass of meteoric iron smashed into the earth's crust here about 40,000 years ago. Though larger impact craters have been discovered on our planet, none have been so well preserved. The giant pit measures 570 feet deep and 4,100 feet across—enough room for 20 football fields. White men first discovered the crater in 1871, though scientists didn't agree on its meteoric origin until 1929. Apollo astronauts learned about crater geology here and practiced how to travel on lunarlike surfaces. A Visitor Center perched on the edge of Meteor Crater has exhibits on meteorites and the Apollo program. You can get a close look at a hefty 1,406-pound meteorite found nearby and hear a recorded lecture about the crater's origin and history. Apollo exhibits include a test capsule, space suit, an Astronaut Hall of Fame,

and short films. Staff at the privately owned Meteor Crater won't let you descend the hazardous trail into the crater, but you may walk the 3½-mile rim trail around it. Avoid this hike if thunderstorms threaten. Lapidary, gift, and coffee shops are in the Visitor Center. Meteor Crater is open daily 0600-1800 in summer (mid-May to mid-Sept.), 0730-1630 in winter (mid-Nov. to mid-Mar.), and 0700-1700 the rest of the year; tel. 526-7175. Admission is $4.50 adult, $3.50 senior, $2 children 13-17, and $1 children 6-12. Meteor Crater is located 40 miles E of Flagstaff and 20 miles W of Winslow; take I-40 Meteor Crater Exit 233, then head S 6 miles on a paved road.

# NORTH OF FLAGSTAFF:
# THE SAN FRANCISCO VOLCANIC FIELD

Volcanic peaks, cinder cones, and lava flows cover about 3,000 square miles around Flagstaff. The majestic San Francisco Peaks, highest of all in Arizona, soar 5,000 feet above the surrounding plateau. Eruptions beginning about 10 million years ago formed this giant volcano. Glaciers then carved deep valleys on its slopes during Pleistocene ice ages. Hundreds of small cinder cones, of which Sunset Crater is the youngest, surround "the Peaks." There's no reason to assume that the San Francisco Volcanic Field is "finished" either! The area has experienced volcanic activity, with periods of calm, all during its long history. Past eruptions have varied greatly—sometimes quiet and sometimes violent. Peaceful today, the volcanic field presents some impressive landscapes and geology. Many of the peaks and hills make good day-hike destinations.

Indians of Northern Arizona look to the San Francisco Peaks as a sacred place. The Hopi believe the Peaks to be the winter home of their *katsina* spirits, and the source of clouds that bring rain for crops. The Peaks also have a prominent place in Navajo legends and ceremonies as one of the cardinal directions. In 1984 the federal government set aside 18,200 acres of this venerable volcano for the Kachina Peaks Wilderness.

*the San Francisco Peaks*

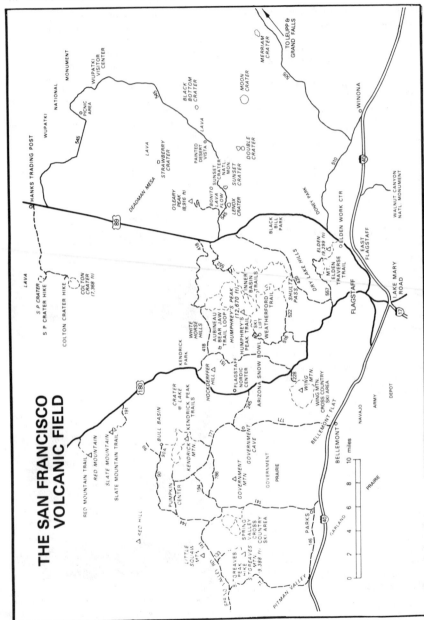

# THE SAN FRANCISCO
# VOLCANIC FIELD

## SUNSET CRATER NATIONAL MONUMENT

Sunset Crater, a beautiful black cinder cone tinged with yellows and oranges, rises 1,000 feet above jagged lava flows about 15 miles NE of Flagstaff. Although more than 700 years have passed since the last eruptions, the landscape still has a lunarlike appearance. Trees and plants struggle for a foothold. Visitor Center exhibits illustrate the forces deep within the earth and their fury during volcanic eruptions. A seismograph in the Center keeps track of the earth's movements. Film clips of Hawaiian volcanic eruptions show how Sunset Crater must have looked during its periods of activity. Rangers give varied programs, mainly during the summer, on geology, seismology, birds, and other topics. Check the bulletin board at the Visitor Center for what's on.

The self-guiding Lava Flow Trail, beginning 1 ½ miles E of the Visitor Center, loops across a lava flow at the base of Sunset Crater; allow ½ to one hour for the one-mile walk. A trail leaflet, available at the start, explains geologic features and ecology. You'll see fumaroles (gas vents), lava bubbles, squeeze-ups, and lava tubes appearing as though they had cooled only yesterday. Rangers have forbidden hiking on Sunset Crater itself since earlier climbers wore a deep gash in the soft cinder slopes. The damage has been repaired but you'll have to hike elsewhere. Lenox Crater, one mile E of the Visitor Center, provides a first-hand look at a cinder cone with a crater. It's an easy climb, taking ½ - ¾ hour to the rim and back.

Sunset Crater's first eruptions in A.D. 1064 or 1065 sent local Indian groups running for safety. Activity had subsided enough by A.D. 1110 for Sinagua and Anasazi to settle in the Wupatki Basin, 20 miles NE of Sunset Crater. Many of their ruins and a museum can be seen in Wupatki National Monument (see below); take the Sunset Crater-Wupatki Loop Road. Lava flows and smaller ash eruptions continued in the Sunset Crater area until about A.D. 1250. Back in the late 1920s some Hollywood film-makers thought Sunset Crater would make a great movie set. To get the needed special effects they planned to use dynamite, but local citizens put a stop to that. Sunset Crater became a National Monument in 1930.

Bonito Campground, across the road from the Visitor Center, is open from mid-May to mid-Nov.; $7. The campground has drinking water and restrooms but no showers. Rangers hold campfire programs in the evenings in summer. Picnic areas are near the Visitor Center, at the Lava Flow Trail, and at Painted Desert Vista

*Bonito Lava Flow and Sunset Crater*

(between Sunset Crater and Wupatki National Monuments). You can reach the Visitor Center by driving 12 miles N of the Flagstaff Mall on US 89, then 2 miles E on a signposted road; tel. 527-7042. Open all year (except Christmas and New Years Day) 0800-1700 with extended hours in summer; road and trails stay open all day; free admission.

**O'Leary Peak:** Weather permitting, the summit of this 8,965-foot lava-dome volcano provides outstanding views of Sunset Crater and other features of the area. Forest Route 545A begins ¼ mile W of Sunset Crater Visitor Center and climbs 5 miles to the fire lookout tower at the top. Stout cars can make it all the way, or you could park at the 2nd switchback and walk the last mile. Rangers from Sunset Crater sometimes lead trips up O'Leary. At the summit, you'll have the best views of the colors of Sunset Crater and the Painted Desert beyond in the late afternoon; best views of the San Francisco Peaks are in the morning.

## WUPATKI NATIONAL MONUMENT

The Sinagua, prehistoric Indian farmers, settled in small groups near the San Francisco Peaks in about A.D. 600. They lived in partly underground pit houses and tilled the soil in the few areas having sufficient moisture for their corn and other crops. The eruption of Sunset Crater in A.D. 1064 or 1065 forced many to flee, but it also improved the marginal soils: volcanic ash, blown by the wind over a large area, added minerals to the ground and enabled it to retain precious rainfall. After about A.D. 1110, the Sinagua, joined by Anasazi from NE Arizona, settled in Wupatki Basin. This valley, about 20 miles NE of Sunset Crater, became the center of a group of cosmopolitan villages. The mix of Sinagua and Anasazi cultures were influenced by Mogollon, Hohokam, and Cohonina tribes. Trade, good crop yields, and exchange of ideas gave the people a new life. Large, multistoried pueblos replaced the brush shelters and pithouses of former times. By about A.D. 1150, some villages had consolidated and built walls, which possibly indicated the strain of population pressure. During the 1200s, people began to leave the area, perhaps

because of drier conditions and declining soil fertility. By A.D. 1300 only ruins remained. Archaeologists think the inhabitants retreated S to the Verde Valley and NE to the Hopi mesas. Hopi legends trace their modern Parrot Clan to Wupatki, and their Snake Clan to nearby Wukoki. An estimated 2,000 archaeological sites lie scattered within the Monument. Some of the best have road and trail access, but most of the Monument remains closed to visitors. You'll need a permit to hike beyond the open sites. Overnight camping is not allowed, with the exception of the Crack-in-Rock hikes led by rangers in Apr. and October.

**Wupatki Visitor Center:** Pottery, tools, jewelry, and other artifacts of the early cultures are on exhibit. A Wupatki room reconstruction shows how the interior of a typical living chamber might have looked. You'll also learn a little about the present-day Navajo and Hopi tribes who live near the Monument. Insects and flowering plants of the area are displayed. You can purchase books, posters, and maps related to the region. Rangers give archaeology

*Wukoki Ruin*

*another view
of Wukoki Ruin*

talks (15 min.) and lead tours (30-45 min.) of adjacent Wupatki Ruin; programs are given mainly during summer, but groups can arrange them at other times. The nearest accommodations and supplies are in Flagstaff and Gray Mountain. Closest camping is at Sunset Crater and Flagstaff. A picnic area and scenic overlook sit between cinder cones about 3 miles NW on the loop road. Wupatki Visitor Center is open 0700-1900 in summer (Memorial to Labor Days) and 0800-1700 the rest of the year; tel. 527-7040. The Visitor Center is 14 miles E of US 89 between Flagstaff and Cameron, and 20 miles N of Sunset Crater National Monument.

**Wupatki Ruin:** At its peak, Wupatki (Hopi for "tall house") contained over 100 rooms and towered as high as 4 stories. A self-guiding trail, beginning behind the Visitor Center, explains many of the features of Wupatki; pick up a trail brochure at the start. The "ball court" at one end of the village resembles those used in Mexico for games. This is one of several found in northern Arizona, probably introduced by the Hohokam of the southern deserts. Games likely had a religious function. Archaeologists reconstructed the ball court from a wall remnant; the rest of Wupatki Ruin is only stabilized. An open-air amphitheater lies to one side of Wupatki; perhaps village meetings and ceremonies took place here. A blowhole, 100 feet E of the ball court, must have had religious importance for the people. A system of underground cracks connects this natural feature with at least 5 other blowholes in the area; air will blow out, rush in, or do nothing at all, depending on weather conditions. Cavers once tried to enter the system but couldn't get through the narrow passageways.

**Wukoki Ruin:** (Hopi for "tower house") Indians lived in this small pueblo for 3 generations. You can step inside the rooms for a closer look. From the Wupatki Visitor Center, drive ¼ mile toward Sunset Crater, then turn L 2.6 miles on a paved road.

**Citadel Ruin:** This fortress-like pueblo, perched atop a small volcanic butte, stood one or 2 stories high and contained about 50 rooms. From the top, look for some of the more than 10 other ruins nearby. On the path to the Citadel, you'll pass the pueblo of Nalakihu (Hopi for "house standing outside the village"). Nalakihu had 2 stories with 13 or 14 rooms. Both sites can be visited on a short self-guided trail; get a trail leaflet at the start. From Wupatki Visitor Center, drive 9 miles NW on the loop road.

**Lomaki Ruin:** Lomaki (Hopi for "pretty house") is one of the best preserved ruins in the Monument. Tree-ring dating of its roof timbers indicates that the occupants lived here from about A.D. 1190 to 1240. The small 2-story pueblo had at least 9 rooms. A ¼-mile

*a ruin in the backcountry of
Wupatki National Monument*

trail from the parking area also passes small ruins beside Box Canyon. The turnoff for Lomaki is 9 miles NW of Wupatki Visitor Center, ¼ mile beyond Citadel Ruin and on the opposite side of the road.

**Crack-in-Rock Ruin:** Rangers lead overnight backpacks to this dramatic ruin during Apr. and October. Crack-in-Rock sits atop an easily defended mesa with sweeping views of the Little Colorado River and distant hills. A wealth of petroglyphs has been carved around the base of the mesa and on 2 nearby mesas. You'll also see many other pueblo sites on the way in and out. The 14-mile RT ranger-guided hike is of moderate difficulty. There's a $2 charge. Call or write one or 2 months in advance to sign up for this hike: Wupatki National Monument, HC 33, Box 444A, Flagstaff, AZ 86001; tel. 527-7040.

## MOUNT ELDEN TRAVERSE HIKE

To reach the summit of Mt. Elden, the 9,299-foot peak on the N edge of Flagstaff, you can follow any of 3 good trails or drive up a road. Although not described here, Sunset Trail climbs to the top from Shultz Pass Road. Wildflowers and panoramic views are the attractions on Mt. Elden. Hiking season runs about May to Oct., longer for the drier eastern slope. Carry water. To avoid the hair-raising experience of an afternoon thunderstorm, set out early during July and Aug. when they are likely. Allow ½ day for the traverse or a RT on one trail. Elevations range from 6,900 to 9,300 feet.

**northwest approach:** The Oldham Park Trail weaves through cool forests of pine and fir to the heights. To reach the trailhead, go 3 miles NW of Flagstaff on US 180 and turn R on Schultz Pass Rd; after ½ mile, continue straight on Mt. Elden Rd. (cinder surface) where Schultz Pass Rd. makes a sharp left. At 3⅓ miles from US 180 you'll see cliffs on the R, a rock-climbing area. At 4.0 miles from US 180, look for an old road on the R blocked off with boulders—this is the Oldham Park trailhead. The trail climbs up a small valley, then switchbacks up the slope. After about 2 miles you'll reach an alpine meadow, Oldham Park. Cross the meadow to Mt. Elden Rd. and continue uphill ¾ mile to the summit. Turn L where the road forks to the Forest Service lookout tower. Climb the tower, if it's open, for the best views. You'll see much of northcentral Arizona on a clear day: Oak Creek Canyon and Mormon Lake to the S; the Painted Desert to the E; Humphrey's Peak, Sunset Crater, and other volcanos to the N; and Bill Williams Mt. to the west. Flagstaff lies directly below, spread out like a map.

**eastern route:** Elden Lookout Trail #44, about 2 miles long, connects the lookout tower with the Elden Ranger Station below. Several forks branch off the trail near the bottom; follow signs or keep to the most traveled path. The Elden Ranger Station is easy to find; it's just off US 89 near the Flagstaff Mall. This trail is steeper and more exposed than the one on the

NW side. You'll see a great difference in vegetation between the 2 sides. Climbing up the Elden Lookout Trail can be hard going in the hot summer sun, hence it's a bit easier to start the traverse from the other side.

## SAN FRANCISCO PEAKS

**Agassiz Skyride:** Hop on this chairlift for the most leisurely way to the heights. You'll be swept from 9,500 to 11,600 feet with some fantastic views. The Skyride operates daily 1000-1630 from Memorial Day weekend to Labor Day; $4 adult, $2.50 for seniors (65 or over) and children (12 or under); tel. 779-6127. From Flagstaff, drive 7 miles NW on US 180, then turn R 7 miles up the Snow Bowl Rd. to its end. You can't do any hiking from the upper chairlift station, though. The Forest Service closed Agassiz Peak to protect an alpine plant *(Senecio franciscanus),* found only on the San Francisco Peaks. Hikers headed for Humphrey's Peak must take the new Humphrey's Peak or old Weatherford trails, described below.

**Humphrey's Peak Trail:** The alpine world on the rooftop of Arizona makes a challenging dayhike destination. Get an early start, as it

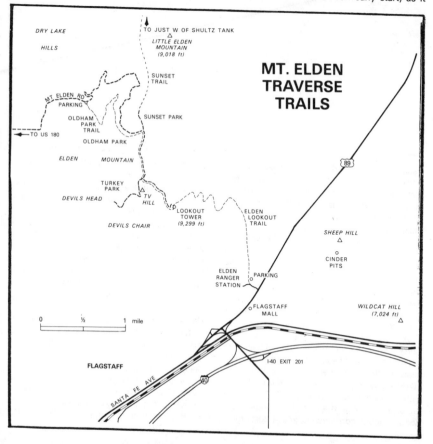

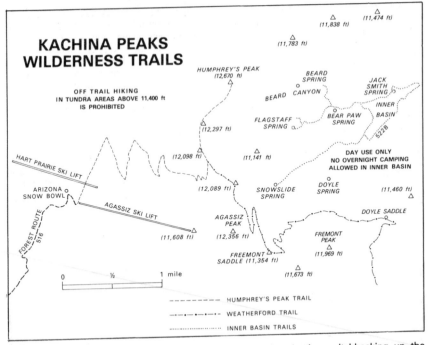

# KACHINA PEAKS WILDERNESS TRAILS

OFF TRAIL HIKING
IN TUNDRA AREAS ABOVE 11,400 ft
IS PROHIBITED

△ (11,838 ft)
△ (11,474 ft)
△ (11,783 ft)

HUMPHREY'S PEAK
(12,670 ft)
△

BEARD
SPRING
○

JACK
SMITH
SPRING ○

BEARD CANYON

FLAGSTAFF
SPRING ○

BEAR PAW
SPRING ○

INNER
BASIN

5228

△ (12,297 ft)

DAY USE ONLY
NO OVERNIGHT CAMPING
ALLOWED IN INNER BASIN

HART PRAIRIE SKI LIFT

△ (12,098 ft)

△ (11,141 ft)

ARIZONA ○
SNOW BOWL

AGASSIZ SKI LIFT

△ (12,089 ft)

SNOWSLIDE
SPRING ○

DOYLE
SPRING ○

(11,460 ft)
△

FOREST ROUTE 516

△ (11,608 ft)

AGASSIZ
PEAK
△
(12,356 ft)

DOYLE SADDLE

FREMONT
PEAK
△
(11,969 ft)

FREEMONT △
SADDLE (11,354 ft)

△ (11,673 ft)

0   ½   1 mile

– – – – – – – –   HUMPHREY'S PEAK TRAIL

– ・ – ・ – ・ –   WEATHERFORD TRAIL

・・・・・・・・・・・・・   INNER BASIN TRAILS

usually takes about 8 hours to the summit and back on the 9-mile RT trail. To protect fragile alpine tundra, the Forest Service asks that you stay on the designated trails above 11,400 feet. Snow blocks the way much of the year, so the hiking season usually lasts just from late June to September. Be prepared for bad weather by taking good rain and wind gear; getting caught in a storm near the top with just a T-shirt and shorts could be deadly. Lightning frequently zaps the Peaks, especially during July and Aug.; you'll want to stay off if storms threaten. In winter, winds and sub-zero cold can be extremely dangerous—only the most experienced groups should attempt a climb then. Carry plenty of water because you'll use more when hiking at these high elevations. The climb to the summit is strenuous, but many hikers enjoy shorter walks on the trail. A large sign marks the trailhead (elev. 9,500 feet) near the upper lodge, at the end of the Snow Bowl Road. The trail contours under the Hart Prairie

chairlift, then begins switchbacking up the mountain. You'll be in dense forests of Engelmann spruce, corkbark fir, and quaking aspen. Nearing 11,400 feet, stunted Engelmann spruce and bristlecone pine trees cling to the precarious slopes. Higher still, only tiny alpine plants survive the fierce winds and long winters. At the saddle (elev. 11,800 feet), turn L for Humphrey's Peak, following the trail along the ridge. On a clear day you'll see a lot of northern Arizona and some of southern Utah from the 12,670-foot summit.

**Weatherford Trail:** J.W. Weatherford completed this toll road into the Peaks in 1926, using only hand labor and animals. Cars could then sputter their way up to Doyle and Fremont Saddles. The road later fell into disrepair, and today is just for hikers and horseback riders; mechanized vehicles (including mountain bicycles) are prohibited. Although it's possible to reach the summit of Humphrey's Peak on the

Weatherford Trail, the long 20-mile RT discourages most dayhikers. Backpacking is possible, but high winds can make camping difficult. Leisurely dayhikes just part way up might be the best bet. Energetic hikers could head up the Weatherford Trail to Humphrey's Peak, then descend the shorter Humphrey's Peak Trail if they can arrange a car shuttle. The Weatherford Trail's gentle grade and excellent views make it a good choice for a family outing. Carry water. Easiest approach is to drive 2½ miles up the Snow Bowl Rd. from US 180, turn R on Forest Route 522 until it gets too rough for cars (about 3 miles), and continue on foot for about one mile to the Weatherford Trail. Another way is to take the Weatherford Trail from Shultz Pass Rd. near Shultz Tank; see map on page 140.

**Inner Basin hiking:** The San Francisco Peaks form a giant U-shaped valley known as the Inner Basin. Aspen, fir, and spruce thrive here. Lockett Meadow, at the Inner Basin entrance, can be reached by car from the northeast. You have to park here and continue on foot. Other roads and trails extend as far as 3½ miles up the Inner Basin, all offering wonderful hiking. Elevations range from 8,600 feet at Lockett Meadow to about 11,000 feet at Snowslide Spring. The many springs in the Inner Basin supply some of Flagstaff's water, but most have been covered and locked; it's safest to carry your own water. Aspen trees put on a magnificent golden show in late Sept. and early October. You can camp near Lockett Meadow, but not in the Inner Basin just beyond. From Flagstaff drive N on US 89 about 13 miles past the Flagstaff Mall, and turn L on Forest Route 552. The turnoff lacks signposting; look for a dirt road beside a large black cinder pit between Mileposts 431 and 432 (turnoff is ¾ mile past the Sunset Crater jct.). Follow Forest Route 552 past the cinder pit 1 mile, then turn R just before a 2nd cinder pit; Lockett Meadow is 3½ miles farther. Low-slung cars and large vehicles shouldn't attempt this road.

**Aubineau and Bear Jaw Trails:** These 2 trails climb about halfway up the N side of the San Francisco Peaks. On either path you'll enjoy cool forests of pine, fir, and aspen. Wildflowers grow in rocky alpine meadows near the top of Aubineau Trail. Both trails start near Reese Tanks. Forest Route 146, a dirt road closed to cars, connects the upper ends. With this road, Aubineau and Bear Jaw make a good 6.5-mile hiking loop. Aubineau is probably the prettier of the 2, a good choice if you don't want to do the whole loop. The trailhead is on the opposite side of the Peaks from Flagstaff. Either take US 180, Forest Route 151 (2nd turnoff), and Forest Route 418 around the W side of the Peaks; or follow US 89 and Forest Route 418 around the E slopes; see Coconino Forest map. Either route is about 26 miles long from Flagstaff. A sign on Forest Route 418 marks the turnoff for the trailhead, which is about ½ mile in. Drive in as far as you can, park, and walk up the road to a T-intersection: Bear Jaw Trail goes to the L; Aubineau to the R. Tree blazes mark both trails. Shortly after turning onto Aubineau Trail, keep R at a fork. The trail soon enters Aubineau Canyon (actually more of a valley) and stays in it all the way to Forest Route 146, 2.5 miles away. You can retrace your steps or turn L 2.1 miles on the road to the

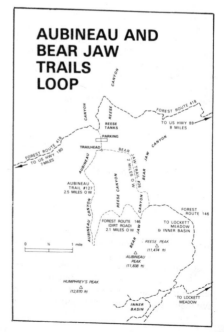

upper trailhead for Bear Jaw Trail, marked by stone cairns, tree blazes and a wide spot in the road. Bear Jaw Trail, 2 miles OW, doesn't follow a valley at all—you have to be *very* careful to look for the tree blazes. Take special care near the bottom when following a road, because the trail later turns L away from the road; this turn is easy to miss! Allow 4-5 hours for the complete loop. You'll be starting at 8,400 feet from the trailhead and reaching 10,400 feet at the upper end of Aubineau Trail. Carry water and raingear.

## SP CRATER AND COLTON CRATER

These 2 volcanic craters, about 14 miles due N of the San Francisco Peaks, offer interesting geology and good hiking. You'll get some insight into the powerful forces that created them and still lie underfoot. SP Crater's graceful shape and the black tongue of lava flowing from its base resemble the better known Sunset Crater. SP even has some reddish lava on its rim. Although climbing Sunset Crater has been forbidden, you may go up SP Crater. The near-perfect symmetry of this cinder cone has earned it a photo in many geology textbooks. Actually "SP" isn't the real name of this little volcano. Most likely prudish mapmakers got red faces on hearing what the local cowboys called it. No doubt early climbers saw the black "spatter" on the rim of the bowl-shaped crater and the "leaking" lava flow below, and said "It looks just like a shit pot." Anyway, the name stuck.

**climbing SP Crater:** The climb is moderately difficult; you'll be ascending 800 feet to the rim. Any time of the year is OK, if the weather is good. The Coconino Forest map or the 15-minute SP MTN topo map help in navigating the dirt roads, none of which have signposts. From Flagstaff, drive 27 miles N on US 89 to Hank's Trading Post (Milepost 446). Or, from the Wupatki National Monument turnoff, go N 1¼ miles to the trading post. Turn L (W) on the unsigned dirt road just S of the trading post. You'll be able to pick out SP, straight ahead, among the other volcanoes by its height and symmetry. Keep L where the road forks after

½ mile. When SP Crater is on your R, 6 miles in from the highway, you'll pass a large black water tank on the L, followed by another road fork. Keep R at the fork, then look for a vehicle track on the R after 100 yards. Take this track for ½ mile and park. People four-wheeling beyond this point have caused deep ruts on the slope. Follow the track on foot to the grassy ridgetop (SP Crater adjoins it on the R), then start up the black cinder slope of SP itself; there's no real trail—it's one step up and 2 steps sliding back on the loose cinders. Perseverance will get you onto the rim for a close look at the lava formations and a panoramic view of the San Francisco Volcanic Field. Walking around the rim is rewarding, but descending into the 360-foot-deep crater would be hazardous. The thick, blocky lava flow from SP's base extends 4 miles north. It's about 70,000 years old.

**climbing Colton Crater:** If you'd like to see another volcano, or want an easier hike, visit nearby Colton Crater. Colton is 2 miles due S of SP; take the other fork near the black water tank and go S 2 miles to an intersection with a road from the right. Park near here and head up the gentle slope to the rim, ascending about 300 feet. A gigantic explosion blew out the center of this volcano when hot basaltic magma met water-saturated rocks. Rock layers

*view of SP Crater from Colton Crater*

*inside Red Mountain*

can be seen clearly. A baby red cinder cone, only 500 feet across, sits at the bottom of Colton Crater. It's an easy walk to the crater floor, actually 260 feet lower than the land outside the crater. Or you can walk around the rim through juniper and pinyon trees, climbing about 600 higher than the lowest part of the rim.

## SLATE MOUNTAIN

A well-graded trail provides good views in all directions as you wind your way up. Kendrick Peak is to the S, the San Francisco Peaks to the SE, and Red Mountain—with its distinctive red gash—just to the north. Trail markers label many of the trees and plants. Flowers line the way from spring through fall. Early settlers mistook the fine-grained, light-gray rock of the mountain for slate, but geologists say it's rhyolite, a volcanic rock. Hiking time is about 3 hours for the 5-mile RT in which you'll climb 900 feet. The 8,215-foot summit makes a pleasant spot for a picnic. Hiking season runs about May to Oct.; carry water. To reach the trail-head, drive NW 27 miles from Flagstaff on US 180, then turn W 2 miles on Forest Route 191 (between mileposts 242 and 243 on US 180). A sign marks the trailhead.

## RED MOUNTAIN

Ever wanted to walk into the heart of a volcano? Then try Red Mountain, 33 miles NW of Flagstaff. Unusual erosion has dissected the cinder cone from the summit straight down to its base. Walk through a little canyon between towers of black cinders to enter the volcano. A 6-foot-high stone wall here is the only real climb! Ranchers built the wall to make a stock pond, but cinders have filled it in. Either clamber over this former dam or take the trail up the cinder slope to the right. Beyond the dam you'll enter a magical land of towering pinnacles and narrow canyons. It's a great place to explore; kids will love it. Trees offer shade for a picnic. Most of Red Mountain is soft volcanic tuff. Look for the rocks and minerals that weather out of it: blocks and bombs of lava, small crystals of plagioclase feldspar (transparent with striations), black glassy pyroxene and hornblende, volcanic dust, cinders, and lapilli (large cinders). A lava flow covers part of Red Mountain's SW side, about 100 feet below the summit. To reach the top (elev. 7,965 feet), take the trail back out of the crater and climb the more gentle cinder slopes on the SE side. You'll be ascending about 1,000 feet. Red Mountain is easily reached by driving 33 miles NW from Flagstaff on US 180 (or 42 miles SE from Grand Canyon National Park) to milepost 247, then turning W on the dirt road here. Red Mountain lies at the end of the road, 1½ miles in, but cars can make it only partway. You can't miss seeing the red cinders of the volcano. A less used road forks off to the L and climbs most of the way to the summit.

## KENDRICK PEAK

Although the San Francisco Peaks have higher elevations, Kendrick Peak might well have the better view. You'll get not only a splendid panorama of northern Arizona from Kendrick, but a view of the Peaks themselves. The Painted Desert, Hopi Mesas, and far-distant Navajo Mountain lie to the NE; the N rim of the Grand Canyon juts up to the N; Sitgreaves and Bill Williams Mountains poke up to the W; Oak Creek Canyon and the Mazatzals are to the S; and the magnificent San Francisco Peaks, surrounded by many smaller volcanos, rise directly to the east. Three trails, varying in length from 7.6 to 10.5 miles RT, lead to Kendrick's 10,418-foot summit. Hiking season lasts from about late June to Sept.; longer on the southern Kendrick Trail. Carry water. A Forest Service lookout tower sits atop the summit.

**Kendrick Trail #22:** This is the shortest (7.6 miles RT) and most used trail. It climbs the sunny southern slopes, making this route the best choice early or late in the season. The trail follows an old fire road the first 1½ miles before narrowing, but remains well graded and easy to follow to the top. A lookout cabin, equipped with a wood stove and 3 bare bunkbeds, sits on the ridge  mile below the summit. Hikers may use this little cabin, which has withstood the elements since 1912. To reach the trailhead, take I-40 Bellmont Exit 185 (10 miles W of Flagstaff), follow the frontage road

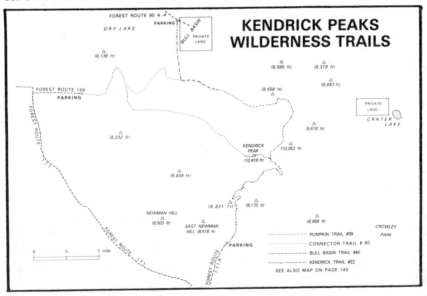

FOREST ROUTE 90 A

PARKING

DRY LAKE

BULL BASIN

PRIVATE LAND

△ (8,139 ft)

FOREST ROUTE 149
PARKING

△ (8,986 ft)    △ (8,319 ft)

△ (8,687 ft)

△ (9,558 ft)

PRIVATE LAND

CRATER LAKE

△ (8,232 ft)

△ (9,618 ft)

KENDRICK PEAK    △ (10,053 ft)

△ (10,418 ft)

△ (8,439 ft)

(8,831 ft)  △ (9,175 ft)

NEWMAN HILL
△ (8,503 ft)    EAST NEWMAN HILL (8,518 ft)

PARKING

△ (8,958 ft)

CROWLEY PARK

# KENDRICK PEAKS WILDERNESS TRAILS

PUMPKIN TRAIL #39
CONNECTOR TRAIL # 80
BULL BASIN TRAIL #40
KENDRICK TRAIL #22

SEE ALSO MAP ON PAGE 140

FOREST ROUTE 171

FOREST ROUTE 171 A

0    ½    1 mile

one mile W, drive 12 miles N on Forest Route 171, then turn R one mile on a road signposted "Kendrick Trail."

**Pumpkin Trail #39:** This longest approach (10.5 miles RT) starts W of Kendrick Peak. Pumpkin Trail has the added feature of enabling you to use the Connector Trail and part of Bull Basin Trail to make a loop. Allow a full day. To reach the trailhead, follow directions for Kendrick Trail #22, but continue on Forest Route 171 another 4½ miles, then turn R one mile at the sign for Pumpkin Trail.

**Bull Basin Trail #40:** This 8.4-mile RT route from the N may be a little difficult to follow at first. To reach the trailhead, continue 2½ miles on Forest Route 171 past the Pumpkin Trail turnoff, turn R 1½ miles on Forest Route 144, then turn R 6 miles on Forest Route 90.

## GOVERNMENT CAVE

This neat little cave is located about 4 miles S of Kendrick Peak. Maps also show the natural underground tunnel as "Lava River Cave." Red-hot lava broke through the ground near the San Francisco Peaks about 100,000 years ago, then moved westward across Hart and Government Prairies, covering the land to a thickness of more than 100 feet in places. As the outer layers of the smoking mass cooled, some of the fiery-hot interior burst through a weak spot, partly draining the lava flow. This underground river of fire eventually cooled too. A collapsed ceiling reveals the passageway. No one knows the total length of this lava-tube cave, but about ¾ mile can be easily explored. The interior remains cool year-round, so a jacket or sweater is recommended. Bring at least 2 lights to explore the cave; it would be *no fun* to have to feel your way out because your one-and-only flashlight died!

The walls and ceiling form an amazingly symmetrical tunnel. The former lava river on the floor still has all the ripple marks, cracks, and squeeze-ups of its last days. There's only one main passageway, though a small loop branch-es off to the R about ⅓ of the way through and then rejoins the main channel. The main channel is large with plenty of headroom, except for a section about ⅔ of the way through where you'll have to do some stooping. To reach Government Cave, follow directions to Kendrick Peak above, but go only 7½ miles N on Forest Route 171. Turn R ½ mile on the road signposted "171A." The cave and turnoff are shown on the Coconino and S. Kaibab Forest maps, but maps variously label this road as "171A" or "171B." A large ring of stones marks the cave entrance.

## SITGREAVES MOUNTAIN

Great views and pretty forests make the 9,388-foot summit of Sitgreaves an attractive destination. Reddish cinder cones, forested mountains, and vast prairies stretch to the distant horizon. Allow about 4 hours to hike the 4 miles to the top and back. Carry water. Hiking season for this northern approach lasts from about May to October. The route follows a valley from the trailhead to the summit ridge, then turns R up the ridge to the highest point. No established trails or signs exist on Sitgreaves but none are needed—just stay in the valley until you reach the ridge. Walking is a bit easier if you keep to the R when going up (not so many fallen trees). Beautiful groves of aspen find this cool, moist, sheltered area to their liking. Sitgreaves Mountain lies about 7 miles N of I-40, about ⅔ of the way from Flagstaff to Williams. To find the trailhead you'll need either the Coconino or S. Kaibab Forest map. Take I-40 Pittman Valley Exit 171, go N 7 miles on Forest Route 74 to its end, turn R on Forest Route 141 (Spring Valley Rd.), then look *real hard* on the R for a small road after 3 miles. The turnoff is very easy to miss and probably won't be signposted; some maps show it as Forest Route 133. Map coordinates for the turnoff: T.23N., R.3E., sec. 13. Cars can be driven in about one mile. When the road gives out, continue walking in the same direction up the valley.

# WEST OF FLAGSTAFF

## WILLIAMS

Small and friendly, Williams proclaims itself "Gateway to the Grand Canyon." The town (pop. 2,500) nestles among pine-forested hills and expansive meadows at an elevation of 6,780 feet. Downtown Williams may lack charm, but it does offer less expensive accommodation and food than the often crowded Grand Canyon Village to the north. Arizona 64, on the W edge of town, provides the shortest path (58 miles) between I-40 and the famous park. Most travelers, in a hurry to get someplace else, miss the pretty country surrounding Williams—the splendid Sycamore Canyon, small fishing lakes, high volcanos, forest drives, and hiking trails.

**history:** Charles Rodgers, the first white settler here, set up a cattle operation in 1878. The railroad and lumber town that was founded several years later took its name from Bill Williams Mountain, just to the south. The mountain in turn commemorated Ol' Bill Williams, who roamed the West as a mountain man from 1825 until his death at the hands of Ute Indians in 1849. He earned a reputation as a skilled marksman, trapper, trader, and guide —a colorful and controversial figure to the end. The Bill William's Mountain Men carry on his adventurous spirit today. The group dresses in buckskin clothing and fur hats, stages an annual 180-mile horseback ride from Williams to Phoenix, and works to keep the history of the mountain man alive. "Shady Ladies," who certainly dress the part, provide counterparts to the Mountain Men.

A more recent period of Western history came to an end in Oct. 1984, when I-40 bypassed the last section of old US Route 66. A sentimental ceremony, complete with songwriter Bobby Troup of "Route 66" fame, marked the transition. The famous highway from Chicago to Los Angeles had carried many families to a new life in Arizona and California. Its replacement, I-40, now lies in an unbroken 2,400-mile path from Durham, N.C., to Barstow, California. Although Williams lost some business when when I-40 went through, townspeople hope a proposed steam railroad from Williams to the Grand Canyon will bring more tourists.

**accommodations and camping:** Business Route I-40 divides downtown to become Bill Williams Ave. (eastbound) and Railroad Ave. (westbound). Most of William's 23 motels are along Bill Williams Avenue. Kaibab Trailer and RV Park offers space for both tents ($6) and RVs ($12.26 w/hookups); open all year and has showers; from AZ 64 on the E edge of town, take Rodeo Dr. (beside Canyon Motel), then take the first right to 81 Homestead Rd.; tel. 635-2413. Two KOA campgrounds lie a short distance from Williams: Circle Pines is 3 miles E at I-40 Exit 167; $12.60 tents, $14.20 RV w/hookups; has deluxe facilities and plans an indoor pool; open 1 Apr. to end of Dec.; tel. 635-2121. Grand Canyon KOA is 5 miles N of Williams on AZ 64 (I-40 Exit 165) on the way to the Grand Canyon; $12.08 tents, $13.65 RV w/hookups; offers an indoor pool and other amenities; open 1 Mar. to 1 Nov.; tel. 635-2307. Red Lake Campground, 10 miles N on AZ 64 from I-40 Exit 165, has showers (coin-operated) but no pool; $7.35 tents, $11 RV w/hookups; closed from 15 Jan. to 15 Feb.; tel. 635-4753.

The Forest Service has 4 campgrounds, all on small fishing lakes; camping areas have drinking water from early May to about mid-Oct. but no showers; $6 night. Kaibab, Dogtown, and White Horse Lake campgrounds also remain open in winter (free, but no water). Cataract Campground is 2 miles NW of town; head W on Railroad Ave. across I-40 to Country Club Dr. (or take I-40 Exit 161 and go N); closed mid-Oct. to early May. Kaibab Campground is 4 miles NE of town; drive E on Bill Williams Ave. across I-40 (or turn N from I-40 Exit 165) to the signposted turnoff. Dogtown Campground lies 7 miles SE of town; drive 3 miles S on 4th St. (Perkinsville Rd.), turn L on Forest Route 140, and follow signs. White Horse Lake is 19 miles

SE, near Sycamore Canyon; go 8 miles S on 4th St., turn L on Forest Route 110, and follow signs. A commercial resort on White Horse Lake offers similar camping but at lower rates ($4.20 night, no showers or hookups), cabins with cooking facilities (sleep 4 at $26.25), and a small store with groceries, fishing supplies, and rental boats; tel. 635-4357. Fishermen catch trout and catfish in White Horse Lake. In winter, visitors in the area enjoy ice fishing, cross-country skiing, and snowmobiling.

food: The Railhead on 137 W. Railroad Ave. serves barbeque beef, pork ribs, sandwiches, soups, and other fare in a Western atmosphere; open for lunch and dinner Mon. to Sat. (may close in winter); tel. 635-9316. Rod's Steak House is a fancier Western-style restaurant with good steaks, seafood, and sandwiches; open daily for lunch and dinner at 301 E. Bill Williams Ave.; tel. 635-2671. Old Smokey's Pancake House is the place to head for breakfast; it also serves sandwiches and burgers for lunch; open daily at 624 W. Bill Williams Ave.; tel. 635-2091. El Sombrero Cafe serves Mexican food at 126 W. Railroad Ave.; closed Sun. and Thur.; tel. 635-2759. Tiffany's Italian Shop, a popular local hangout, dispenses beer and pizza daily at 233 W. Bill Williams Ave.; tel. 635-2445. Other eateries include the Hot Dog Corral for fast food and ice cream at 401 W. Bill Williams Ave., and Denny's for standard American meals at 425 E. Bill Williams Avenue. Buy groceries downtown on Bill Williams Ave. at Safeway or Country Grocery. Winter Wheat stocks natural foods at 106 S. 2nd St. (just S of Bill Williams Ave.).

events: Mountain Men ride into town for the Bill Williams Rendezvous on Memorial Day weekend. Powder shoots, canoeing, roping, and cow-chip throwing contests are held along with an arts and crafts show and barbeque. Townsfolk celebrate the 4th of July with fireworks, roping events, an ice cream social, and a barbeque. Arizona Cowpuncher's Reunion and Old Timer's Rodeo brings in working cowboys for competitions, a parade, and barn dances on the first weekend of August. Bill Williams Mountain Men return on Labor Day weekend for a parade and festivities.

services: Post office is on 1st St., just S of Bill Williams Avenue. Williams Emergency Center provides medical treatment at 301 S. 7th St.; tel. 635-4441. The city park (on 6th St. one mile S of Bill Williams Ave.) is a pleasant spot for a picnic. Williams' swimming pool (open in summer) is at 603 N. 2nd St.; tel. 635-9958. Two tennis courts are near the high school; take 9th St. (opposite the Chamber of Commerce) S to Oak St. and turn R one block. Play golf from 1 May to 1 Oct. at Williams Country Club (closed Mon.); go W on Railroad Ave. across I-40 (or take I-40 Exit 171 and head N), then go one mile; tel. 635-2122. For fishing and camping supplies, stop at Pruett's Sporting Goods, 202 W. Bill Williams Avenue. Go downhill skiing on winter weekends and some holidays at the small Williams Ski Area. It's 4 miles S of town on Bill Williams Mountain. Facilities include a 1,500-foot poma lift (450 vertical feet), 700-foot rope tow for the beginners' slope, snack bar, and rental shop. Season lasts from about mid-Dec. to end of Mar.; turn S on 4th St. and follow signs; tel. 635-9216. The Forest Service has cross-country ski trails near Spring Valley; go 16 miles E on I-40 to Parks Exit 178, then head 7 miles N on Forest Route 141; pick up a ski trail map at the Forest Service office (501 W. Bill Williams Ave.).

information: The Chamber of Commerce gets so many travelers headed for the Grand Canyon that they carry maps and brochures for that area too. The helpful office is open daily 0800-1700 on the W edge of town at 820 W. Bill Williams Ave. (Box 235, Williams, AZ 86046); tel. 635-2041. To find out about hiking, camping, fishing, and road conditions in the Kaibab Forest, visit the Forest Service downtown at 501 W. Bill Williams Ave.; open Mon. to Fri. 0730-1600; tel. 635-2676. Another Forest Service office is 1½ miles W of downtown on the I-40 frontage rd.; tel. 635-2633. The S. Kaibab Forest map, showing backroads, trails, and other features may be purchased ($1) at either office. The public library is at 113 S. 1st St., just S of Bill Williams Ave.; tel. 635-2263.

transport: Public transport hub of Williams is the bus station at the corner of Bill Williams

Ave. and 3rd St.; open Mon. to Fri. 0800-1630 and shorter hours on weekends; tel. 635-9331. Greyhound offers 3 daily departures east- and westbound and once daily to Phoenix. Trailways has once-daily east- and westbound departures. Nava-Hopi runs an afternoon bus to the Grand Canyon ($11.75 OW, $22.30 RT, or $10.70 RT w/bus pass). Bargain Rent-a-Car is also based at the bus station; tel. 635-2572. Amtrak trains don't stop in Williams.

## VICINITY OF WILLIAMS

**Deer Farm:** A well-run petting zoo for children, where they can get up close to hand-feed deer, llamas, miniature donkeys, and other tame animals. The Deer Farm is open daily May to Sept., daily except Mon. and Tue. in Apr., Oct., and Nov. closed Thanksgiving to March. Admission $3 adult, $1.50 children 3-13; tel. 635-2357. It's located 8 miles E of Williams, just off I-40 at the Pittman Valley Deer Farm Exit 171.

**Bill Williams Mountain:** The summit of this 9,255-foot peak can be reached by either of 2 hiking trails or by road. On a clear day, after climbing more than 2,000 feet to the top, you'll have views of the Grand Canyon to the N, San Francisco Peaks and many smaller volcanos to the E, Sycamore Canyon and parts of the Verde Valley to the S, and vast rangelands to the west. Climb up the Forest Service lookout tower at the top for the best views, if it's open. Pine, oak, and juniper trees cover the lower mountain slopes, while dense forests of aspen, fir, and spruce grow in protected valleys and at the higher elevations. Carry water on either trail. Hiking season lasts from about June to September. By doing a car shuttle, both trails could be linked together, or a trail could be hiked just one way. The 6-mile RT Camp Clover Trail climbs the N face of Bill Williams Mountain. You'll reach the road about ½ mile from the summit; either continue on the trail across the road or turn up the road itself. Camp Clover Trailhead is beside the Williams District ranger station, 1½ miles W of town; from I-40 take Exit 171 toward Williams, then turn R (W) ¼ mile on the frontage road. The 7-mile RT

*black bear*
(Ursus americanus)

Benham Trail climbs the S and E slopes, crossing the road to the lookout tower several times. To reach the trailhead from Williams, go S 3¾ miles on 4th St., then turn R about ½ mile on Benham Ranch Road. The more gentle grade of this trail makes it good for horseback riders as well as hikers. You can also drive up; from Williams head 5 miles S on 4th St., then turn R 7 miles on Forest Route 111.

**Sycamore Canyon Point:** Though similar in beauty and size to Oak Creek Canyon to the E, Sycamore Canyon remains much as it always has, without any roads or "facilities." Elk, deer, black bear, and other animals find food and shelter on the canyon rim and within its depths. Hikers and horseback riders may visit by using a network of trails (see "Hiking in the Sedona Area"). Sycamore Canyon Point offers a breath-taking panorama 23 miles SE of Williams. From town, drive 8 miles S on 4th St./Perkinsville Rd., then turn L on Forest Route 110 to its end, 15 miles farther. The last 5 miles are single lane and may be signposted "not for low clearance vehicles," but should be OK for cautiously driven cars. No trails enter the canyon from this side, although you can spot one of the paths coming down the opposite side.

**Sycamore Trail:** This 11-mile loop overlooks parts of upper Sycamore Canyon and goes past waterfalls, an abandoned lumbermill and railroad site, lily ponds (good swimming), and pretty forest country. Stone cairns mark the trail, shown as Forest Trail #78 on the S. Kaibab Forest map. Trailhead is SE of Williams at the end of Forest Route 56; see the S. Kaibab Forest map for the many ways to get here. If you're in the mood for just a short hike, walk ⅓ mile S from the trailhead to an overlook of Sycamore Canyon. The Forest Service office in downtown Williams has a map and trail description for Sycamore Trail.

**White Horse Falls:** Two waterfalls can easily be reached near White Horse Lake. The spectacle, however, takes place only during the spring runoff and after heavy rains. (These are the same waterfalls seen along Sycamore Trail mentioned above.) From the store at White Horse Lake (see "Williams campgrounds"), cross the cattleguard in front and turn R 2 miles (N) on Forest Route 109, then turn R on a bumpy road just after crossing a concrete bridge, and go ¼ mile to a turnaround. A small waterfall is in a canyon just to the R, but walk ahead and a bit to the L to see a larger fall, 80-100 feet high.

**Perkinsville Road:** Beginning as 4th St. in downtown Williams, Perkinsville Rd. heads S through the pine forests of the Mogollon Rim, drops down to the high-desert lands of the Verde Valley, crosses the Verde River at historic Perkinsville Ranch, then climbs rugged hills to the old mining town of Jerome. The first 22 miles are paved, followed by 23 miles of dirt. Though dusty and bumpy in spots, the route is usually OK for cars except after winter snowstorms or heavy summer rains. Allow 3 hours to enjoy a OW drive, more if you'd like to drive up Bill Williams Mountain, visit White Horse Lake, go out to Sycamore Canyon Vista, or do other exploring. Stock up on gas and water before heading down this lonely road. The Prescott National Forest map covers the entire route.

## ASH FORK

Declaring itself the "Flagstone Capital of USA," Ash Fork sits in high desert grasslands, 19 miles W of Williams and 50 miles N of Prescott. The location at the junction of I-40

and US 89 makes the small community a handy stopping place for travelers. The town grew up around a railroad siding built near Ash Creek in 1882. Passengers and freight transferred to stage coaches or wagons for Prescott and Phoenix. After a long history as a railroad town, Ash Fork (pop. 650) now serves as a highway stop and a center for livestock raising and sandstone quarries.

**accommodations and camping:** As in Williams, most of the motels and other businesses lie along 2 parallel one-way streets; take I-40 Exits 144 or 146. Stagecoach Motel, 823 Park Ave., has rooms from $22.88 s, $27.04 d; tel. 637-2278. Copper State Motel, 101 E. Lewis Ave., offers basic rooms at $15.60 s, $20.80 d; tel. 637-2573. Ashfork Inn is W of downtown near I-40 Exit 144; rooms are $19.76 s, $27.04 d; tel. 637-2501. Campers can stay at KOA (has swimming pool and showers); turn in on 8th St. beside Stagecoach Motel; $10.60 tents or RVs without hookups, $12 w/hookups; tel. 637-2521. Cauthen's Hillside RV Park is on the S frontage road near I-40 Exit 144; $5 tents or RVs without hookups, $10 w/hookups; showers cost an extra $1.50; tel. 637-2300. Both campgrounds stay open all year. They're also close to the noise of I-40.

**food:** Bull Pen Restaurant, on the E side of town, stays open 24 hours; it has the standard cafe menu and a "broil your own steak," which you select from a display case. The Ranch Cafe, Lewis St., serves American breakfasts and lunches. Pattie's Place is a 24-hour cafe serving American food at the W edge of town near the Ashfork Inn.

## SELIGMAN

Another railroad town, Seligman (pop. 510) also now relies more on ranching and tourist business. The first residents arrived in 1886 and called their place "Prescott Junction" because a rail line branched S to Prescott. The Prescott line was later abandoned but the town survived. Its present name of "Seligman" honors the brothers who had connections with the railroad and owned the Hash Knife Cattle Company. Modern travelers on I-40 can take Exits 121 or 123 for the motels and restaurants in town, or head off on old Route 66. This former transcontinental highway is 19 miles longer to Kingman than I-40, but offers a change of scenery and pace, and a bit of nostalgia for the '60s TV show. Take the old highway to reach the Havasupai and Hualapai Indian Reservations (see the Grand Canyon and Arizona Strip chapter). Two motels are in Truxton, and one is at the Pearce Ferry turnoff (6 miles W of Hackberry). If approaching Seligman from the E, you can take a shortcut (saves 4 miles) on the old Route 66; turn off I-40 at Crookton Rd., Exit 139.

**accommodations and camping:** Nearly all businesses lie along Chino Avenue. Nanjo's Country Inn Motel on the E edge of town has rooms at $20 s, $25.20 d; tel. 422-3370. Canyon Shadows Motel is downtown at 114 E. Chino; $17.85 s, $25.20 d; tel. 422-3255. Romney Motel, 122 W. Chino, has rooms for $18.90 s, $21 d; tel. 422-3294. Supai Motel, 134 W. Chino, costs $15.50 s, $18.70 d; tel. 422-3663. On the W edge of town are the Navajo Motel ($19.27 s, $21.53 d; tel. 422-3312) and Motel Unique ($21.84 s or d; tel. 422-9940). The KOA, just E of Seligman, has a swimming pool and showers; $12 tent or RV w/hookups; tel. 422-3358. Northern Arizona Campground, on the W end of town, charges $6.23 for tents or RVs without hookups, and $9.86 w/hookups; tel. 422-3549.

**food:** Country Inn Restaurant is an American cafe open daily for breakfast, lunch, and dinner on the E edge of town. Aztec Cafe in down-

town serves Mexican and American food; open daily for breakfast, lunch, and dinner. The Copper Cart Restaurant offers a varied American menu; open daily for breakfast, lunch, and dinner. Get your malts, sodas, and fast food at Delgadillo's Snow Cap (take out). Seligman Sundries features an old-fashioned ice cream parlor. Mr. J's Coffee Shop is a cafe offering American breakfasts, lunches, and dinners on the W edge of town.

## GRAND CANYON CAVERNS

Large underground chambers and pretty formations of this limestone cave attract travelers on old Route 66. The caverns are 25 miles NW of Seligman, then one mile off the highway. A giant dinosaur model stands guard in front. On the 45-min. guided tours, you descend 21 stories by elevator to the caverns and walk about ¾ mile (some steps). Tours operate daily 0800-1800 in summer and 0900-1700 in winter (closed 24 and 25 Dec. and possibly the last 3 weeks in Jan.); $5.75 adult, $3.75 children 6-14. A gift shop at the entrance has a small museum of mining and ranching artifacts (free).

**practicalities:** Horseback riding may be offered in summer. A campground has drinking water but no showers or hookups; $3. A motel, restaurant, grocery store, and gas station are located back on the highway. The motel (open one week before Easter to 1 Oct.) costs $30.16 s, $33.28 d. The restaurant, open the same season as the motel, serves American breakfast, lunch, and dinner. The grocery store and gas station stay open all year. For information on cave tours or motel reservations, tel. 422-3223.

# SOUTH OF FLAGSTAFF

### LAKE AND RIM COUNTRY

More than a dozen mountain lakes lie across the pine-forested plateau country SE of Flagstaff. Fishermen, picnickers, hikers, and campers enjoy the quiet waters, rolling hills, and scenic canyons of this region. Animal life flourishes—you might spot elk, deer, turkey, maybe even a bear. Abert squirrels with long tufted ears are often seen. Best times to see wildlife are early and late in the day. Rim-country temperatures remain comfortably cool even in midsummer, and showers fall almost daily in the afternoons of July and August. Campgrounds, well-known to hot-desert dwellers, often fill up during the peak summer months. You'll find less crowded conditions early and late in the season, or anytime away from the developed sites. Nearly all the established campgrounds have been provided by the U.S. Forest Service; none have showers or hookups, and only some even have drinking water. Most campgrounds stay open from May to September. Do-it-yourself dispersed camping may be done almost anywhere in any season within the National Forests, though you're asked to avoid camping where prohibited by signs, on meadows, and within ¼ mile of springs, streams, or lakes. Boats are limited to electric motors at the smaller lakes, and 8 hp. gas motors at some of the larger ones; no restrictions apply on Upper Lake Mary.

**Upper and Lower Lake Mary:** Beginning just 8 miles from Flagstaff, these long, narrow reservoirs offer fishing, boating, and bird-watching. Walnut Creek, which was dammed to form these lakes, once continued downstream through Walnut Canyon past the many Sinagua Indian ruins there. The Riordan brothers, who built the first reservoir early in this century to supply water for their sawmill, named the lake for one of their daughters. Lower Lake Mary, the first built, now varies greatly in size depending on rainfall and water needs. Fishing is mostly for northern pike; there's a primitive boat ramp near the dam. Waterskiers zip across Upper Lake Mary in summer; it's one of the few lakes in this part of Arizona long and deep enough for the sport.

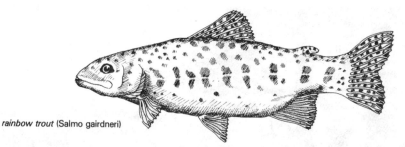

*rainbow trout* (Salmo gairdneri)

Anglers pull catfish, northern pike, walleye, sunfish, and bluegill from the waters. The best boat ramps for Upper Lake Mary are near the picnic area, just off Lake Mary Rd. (¾ mile upstream from the dam).

Lakeview Campground provides the closest camping to the lakes, but sites are too small for trailers. The campground is across the road from the "narrows" of Upper Lake Mary (14 miles SE of Flagstaff); has drinking water and $5/night charge. Lake Mary Rd. parallels the shores of both lakes; from downtown Flagstaff, head S 2 miles towards Phoenix, turn R on US 89A just before the I-40 junction, continue S one mile, then turn L on Lake Mary Road. I-40 travelers should take Exit 195B for Flagstaff, then turn S on US 89A to the Lake Mary Rd. turnoff. Driving N on I-17, take Exit 339 just before the I-40 junction. For information about recreation and road conditions in this area, stop at the Mormon Lake District Forest Service office, 4825 Lake Mary Rd. (about one mile from US 89A); tel. 527-7474.

**Walnut Canyon Hike:** This easy 6½ mile RT walk follows a section of the wooded canyon floor between Lower Lake Mary and Walnut Canyon National Monument. Wildflowers, birds, deer, varied woodlands, and rock formations await the hiker. Walnut Canyon can be visited any time of the year except when blocked by snow. In early spring there may be some wading, but this section of Walnut Creek is normally dry. The trailhead lies just off Lake Mary Rd. about 6 miles S of Flagstaff and 2 miles before Lower Lake Mary. Coming from Flagstaff, look for the well-signposted Hitchin'

Post Stables on the L, then continue ¼ mile farther to the first dirt road on the L *without* mailboxes. Turn in 300 feet, turn L again, and park after 500 feet. Rock cairns (may have fallen over) mark the start. The trail leads NE, away from Lake Mary Rd., to a small ravine, then descends into the ravine to Walnut Canyon. Turn L in the canyon (remember this junction for the trip back) and follow the dirt road. Mt. Elden can be seen ahead to the north. After 1½ miles the canyon makes a sharp bend to the R and narrows. You'll then pass 2 small sandstone caves and groves of aspen. The trail ends in a tangle of vegetation 3 miles from the start. Walnut Canyon National Monument lies about 4 miles farther downstream, but getting there involves difficult bushwhacking. Also, rangers don't like people to enter that way.

**Marshall and Vail Lakes:** These 2 small trout lakes lie to the N of Upper Lake Mary. No facilities or boat ramp. Take the signposted Marshall Lake turnoff from Lake Mary Rd. between Upper and Lower Lake Mary, and go 3 miles to Marshall Lake. To reach Vail Lake, follow the Marshall Lake Rd. ½ mile, then turn R 3 miles on Forest Route 129A.

**Ashurst Lake:** Fishermen pursue rainbow trout in this small lake. Windsurfers also find it good for their sport. Two campgrounds, both with water and $5/night fee, sit beside the lake: Ashurst Campground on the western shore and Forked Pine on the eastern side. There's a boat ramp near the entrance to Ashurst Campground. From Flagstaff, go 18 miles SE, then turn L 4 miles on paved Forest Route 82E.

Coconino Reservoir, one mile S on a dirt road, also has a good reputation for rainbow trout.

**Pine Grove Campground:** Entrance to this large campground is opposite the turnoff for Ashurst Lake, 18 miles SE of Flagstaff; turn W ¾ mile on Forest Route 651 from Lake Mary Road. Camping area has drinking water, paved roads, and a $7/night charge. Although not on a lake, Pine Grove is within a few miles of Upper Lake Mary and Ashurst and Mormon Lakes.

**Mormon Lake:** Mormon settlers arrived on the shores of this lake in 1878 and started a dairy farm. Although it's the largest natural lake in Arizona, average depth is only 10 feet. Water level fluctuates; when it's low there's not much more than a marsh. Anglers, though, have reeled in some sizable bullhead catfish and northern pike. Boats need to be hand-carried to the water. Lake Mary Rd. parallels the eastern shore and Mormon Lake Loop Rd. (Forest Route 90) circles around the W side. The Forest Service has 2 campgrounds off this loop road: Dairy Springs and Double Springs. Both have drinking water and a $5/night fee. From Flagstaff, head 20 miles SE on Lake Mary Rd. then turn R 4 miles on Mormon Lake Loop Rd. to Dairy Springs, or go 2 miles farther to Double Springs.

Lakeview Trail (2 miles RT) climbs a small hill from Double Springs Campground. For an even better view, hike 1,500 feet above Mormon Lake on the 6-mile RT Mormon Mountain Trail; start near Dairy Springs Campground. Learn more about the plants and animals of the area on a self-guided nature trail, also beginning near Dairy Springs Campground. Ledge Trail, an easy 1½ mile RT hike from Dairy Springs Campground, runs out to a ledge overlooking the lake. Evening campfire programs are offered at the Dairy Springs Campground.

Montezuma Lodge, tucked in the woods mile beyond Dairy Springs Campground, has cabins from early May to the end of Oct., $45 s or d; tel. 354-2220. Mormon Lake Lodge, on the loop road at the S end of the lake, serves as a recreational center for many visitors. The lodge offers motel rooms ($40 s or d), cabins ($40 s or d in summer, $30 in winter but no water), a cafe serving breakfast and lunch (closed weekdays in winter), Western-style steak house, saloon, grocery store with fishing and hunting supplies, boat and motor rentals, and a gas station; tel. 774-0462 (Flagstaff) or 354-2227 (local). You can rent horses in summer from Superstition Stables next door. Mormon Lake Ski Touring Center, located across the road, offers trails, rentals, and lessons for cross-country skiers (see "Flagstaff Recreation"). Munds Park, 11 miles W of the Mormon Lake Loop Rd. via unpaved Forest Route 240, has a motel, an RV campground, restaurants, and a service station. Munds Park is at I-17 Exit 322 (18 miles S of Flagstaff).

**Kinnikinick Lake:** A good fishing lake for rainbow and brown trout with an occasional catfish. Because the lake lies off the paved roads, you're more likely to find solitude here. Kinnikinick Lake has a free campground and boat ramp but there's no drinking water. From Flagstaff, go 25 miles SE on Lake Mary Rd. to just past Mormon Lake, turn L 4 miles on Forest Route 125 (dirt road), then R 4 miles on Forest Route 82.

**Stoneman Lake:** An unusual lake set in a circular depression. Geologists have not decided whether this is an old volcanic crater or a

*turkey* (Meleagris gallopavo)

sinkhole. Fishermen do agree that its waters are a hot spot for yellow perch; some state records have been landed here. Pike and sunfish are also caught. There's a boat ramp but no campground on the lake. To get here, either take the I-17 Stoneman Lake Exit 306 (34 miles S of Flagstaff) and go E 9 miles on mostly paved Forest Route 213, or go S 8 miles past Mormon Lake on Lake Mary Rd. and turn W 6 miles on Forest Route 213.

**West Clear Creek hiking:** The transparent waters of this year-round creek wind below pretty canyon walls on their way to the Verde River. Of the many canyons in the Mogollon Rim, West Clear Creek has the greatest length—40 miles. Cross-bedded patterns of ancient sand dunes in the Coconino Sandstone show up clearly on the sheer cliffs. The creek offers excellent hiking, swimming, and fishing. Fishermen, however, may find the trout difficult to entice onto a hook. Several trails into the canyon provide a choice of dayhikes and overnight trips. Adventurous hikers could spend a week making their way downstream to Bull Pen Ranch or Clear Creek Campground. The warmer months are best for a visit to the canyon. There isn't much of a trail, so you'll be wading and swimming much of the time. In spring, snowmelt can raise the stream level too high for hiking, as can very heavy rains anytime. Water is always available from the creek (purify first). Hikers should keep in mind that trails *out* can be difficult to spot. Exceptions include the Tramway Trail (marked by a steel cable across the creek), and the powerlines (2 sets of high-tension lines shown on Coconino Forest map).

A hike between these points makes a good overnight backpack, but a deep pool about 150 feet long hemmed in by cliffs must be crossed. A small inflatable boat is best for this. The pool is about ¾ mile upstream of the powerlines. Many more deep pools, including one ¼ mile long, have to be crossed if you're going downstream from the powerlines. To reach Tramway trailhead (Forest Trail 32), go 8 miles S of Happy Jack on the Lake Mary Rd., then 8 miles in on dirt Forest Routes 81 and 81E; keep straight past the turnoff for Maxwell Trail, go about 1 ½ miles, then turn L at the fork. Tramway descends steeply less than a mile into the canyon. At the powerlines downstream, a rough trail connects the creek with Forest Route 142A on the S rim. This trailhead is about 18 miles SW of Clints Well via AZ 87 and Forest Routes 142 and 142A. Roads to the trailheads may be too rough for cars after heavy rains. The Happy Jack Ranger Station, 13 miles S of Mormon Lake on Lake Mary Rd., can advise on road and trail conditions; tel. 354-2216.

**Clints Well:** Natural springs here, a rarity in the region, have long been a stopping place for travelers. They were named after Clint Wingfield, an early pioneer. Lake Mary Rd. (Forest Hwy. 3) meets AZ 87 at Clints Well; turn L for Winslow, R for Payson and Mesa. A small Forest Service campground near the end of Lake Mary Rd. is free but lacks water. Long Valley Cafe, grocery store, and service station are ½ mile S on AZ 87.

**Blue Ridge Reservoir:** Hemmed in by the canyon walls of East Clear Creek, this skinny

*beaver* (Castor canadensis)

*view from the Mogollon Rim*

lake offers good trout fishing (best in spring and fall) and great scenery. Steep terrain makes road access difficult; only hand-carried boats can be launched. Trails lead to the water's edge, but fishing is easier from a boat. Rock Crossing campground nearby has good views and ranks as one of the most popular camping spots on the Mogollon Rim. Season runs Memorial Day to Labor Day; drinking water is supplied and there's a $5/night fee. From Clints Well, go NE 5 miles on AZ 87 and turn R on Forest Route 751; campground is 3 miles in, then another 3 to the dam. The smaller Blue Ridge Campground has the same season and charge; trailers are limited to 16 feet. From Clints Well, go NE 9 miles on AZ 87, and turn R one mile on Forest Route 138. Fishermen use Blue Ridge Campground as a base for Blue Ridge Reservoir, East Clear Creek, and Long Lake. Catfish and northern pike are the most sought after in Long Lake, but the waters have trout, bass, walleye, and panfish as well. Obtain road and hiking information from Blue Ridge Ranger Station, just a mile beyond the Blue Ridge campground turnoff; tel. 477-2255.

**East Clear Creek hiking:** This canyon may not be quite as spectacular as some other places on the Rim, but the trailheads are easily reached. Deep clear pools invite swimming and solitary fishing. Rock formations, birds, flowers, and forests make for pleasant hiking. Beavers live and work along the stream, though you'd be lucky to see one of these shy nocturnal animals. Watch out for snakes; most are harmless but rattlesnakes live here too. A rough trail follows the canyon, crossing the creek at many places. Crossings shouldn't be more than knee-deep, though spring snowmelt or heavy rains anytime can make the creek too high for hiking. Long pants will protect your legs from the bramble patches. Water is always available (purify first). This creek has no relation to West Clear Creek. East Clear Creek flows NE, in the opposite direction, and joins the Little Colorado River near Winslow.

Of all the trailheads, Macks Crossing, only 2 miles from AZ 87, is the easiest to get to. From Clints Well, go 15 miles NE (4½ miles past Blue Ridge Ranger Station) and turn R on Enchanted Lane (shown as Forest Route 137 on the Coconino Forest map). After a short distance, turn R on Green Ridge Rd. and go ¾ mile. Then turn R again on Juniper which leads to Forest Route 137. The narrow, rocky road descends one mile across a cliff face (no guard rails!) to the creek. Park at the top or at several places on the way down. Near the creek and on the other side, the road is too rough for cars. From Mack's Crossing a good overnight loop hike (15 miles) can be make by going upstream on East Clear Creek to Kinder Crossing Trail, taking Kinder Crossing Trail to Forest Route 137, and following the forest road back to Macks Crossing. The section of road takes only 2-3 hours of easy walking—at least 3 times as fast as hiking in the creek. Kinder Crossing Trail also has a western trailhead on Forest Route 95, about 4½ miles S of Blue Ridge Ranger Station. The trail (#19) is marked by tree blazes down to the creek, then by stone cairns and tree blazes for ½ mile downstream along the creek before climbing the other side of the canyon to Forest Route 137. (Note that both the Coconino Forest and topo maps may incorrectly show the trail as simply crossing the creek and climbing the opposite side, instead of following the creek ½ mile.) Horse Crossing Trail #20 (see Coconino Forest map) also descends into the canyon from both sides. Trailheads for Kinder and Horse Crossing trails should be distinct and sign-posted. Horse Crossing Trail can be *very* difficult to spot while walking along the creek; careful attention to a topo map and tree blazes is necessary.

**Kehl Springs:** A small campground near the Mogollon Rim; no drinking water or charge. Aspen and oak trees give a colorful display in autumn. The Mogollon Rim and great views lie just a short hike away. From Clints Well, go SW 3 miles on AZ 87, then L on Forest Route 147 to the Rim Rd. (see Coconino Forest Map). These roads tend to be rough and dusty, but should be OK for carefully driven cars in good weather.

**Knoll Lake:** A rocky island in the middle gives the lake its name. Knoll Lake is located in Leonard Canyon, several miles N of the Mogollon Rim. A campground sits on a hill overlooking the lake. Camping season lasts from Memorial Day to Labor Day; drinking water and $5/night charge. A road and a hiking trail lead down to the boat ramp. Fishermen come mostly to seek out rainbow trout. Getting here involves about 28 miles of dirt road from either AZ 87 (between Clints Well and Strawberry) or Woods Canyon Lake off AZ 260.

**Bear Canyon Lake:** Fishermen may use only artificial lures at this trout lake. The shore is steep and tree-covered, so it's easier to use boats for fishing. You'll have to hand-carry boats to the water, however. A campground (no water or fee) is near the N end. From Woods Canyon Lake, go W 10 miles on Forest

Route 300 (the Rim Rd.), then turn N 2½ miles on Forest Route 89.

**Woods Canyon Lake:** This popular lake was one of the first of 7 lakes made on the Rim. Camp at either Aspen Campground ($7/night) or Spillway Campground ($9/night) nearer the lakeshore; both have drinking water. Season runs May to September. A store, which stays open into the fall, has groceries, boat rentals, and motors (only electrics permitted here). Rocky Point picnic area is on the S side of the lake; free but day-use only. From Payson, go E 30 miles on AZ 260 past Kohl's Ranch and on up to the top of the Rim (good views). Immediately after reaching the top, turn L 4 miles on Forest Route 300 (paved).

**Canyon Point:** This large, easily accessible campground has drinking water and is open May to September. Sites cost $6/night ($8/night for larger pull-through spaces). A trail from the beginning of Loop "B" leads to a sinkhole (1 mile RT). Canyon Point Campground lies just off AZ 260, 5 miles E of the Woods Canyon Lake turnoff. Nearby Willow Springs Lake has a boat ramp but no campground; you may, however, camp in the forest (no facilities or fee) off Forest Route 235 about one mile before the lake. To reach Willow Springs Lake from Canyon Point Campground, go W 4 miles on AZ 260, then N one mile on Forest Route 149.

**Forest Lakes Touring Center:** In winter, cross-country skiers come here to use the marked and groomed trails atop the Mogollon Rim. The Center also offers rentals, lessons, and tours. Summer visitors can rent canoes for use on the nearby Rim lakes; rentals ($15/day) include car-top carrier, paddles, and life jackets. For ski or canoe information and winter road conditions, call tel. 535-4047. Stay in cabins at the Touring Center (open all year: $51 d Fri. to Sun., $36.40 d Mon. to Thur.); tel. 535-4047. Forest Lakes Lodge has motel rooms (open all year: $45.76 s, $51 d Fri. and Sat.; $31.20 s, $41.60 d Sun. to Thur.); tel. 535-4727. Forest Lakes Touring Center is in the village of Forest Lakes on AZ 260 (6½ miles E of the Woods Canyon Lake turnoff, or 36 miles E of Payson).

*summer camp at Fern Springs on the Mogollon Rim, 1887. The woman, Mrs. Ella Mearns, was the wife of Fort Verde's surgeon.*

**Black Canyon Lake:** This small trout lake doesn't have a campground, but Black Canyon Rim and Gentry campgrounds are within a few miles. From the Woods Canyon Lake turnoff, go E 9½ miles on AZ 260, turn R 2½ miles on Forest Route 300, then L 3 miles on Forest Route 86 to Black Canyon Lake; see the Apache-Sitgreaves Forest Map.

**Chevelon Crossing:** This small campground overlooks Chevelon Creek, many miles downstream from Woods Canyon Lake. The sites remain open most of the year (elev. 6,200 feet); no water or fee. Parking is tight; small vehicles will have an easier time. Best fishing is in the large pools upstream that harbor rainbow trout. There are 3 routes to this out-of-the-way campground: Forest Route 504 is the usual way in; turn off AZ 260 one mile W of Heber. Or take AZ 99 S from Winslow and turn L on Forest Route 504. Or you can take Forest Route 169 by turning N from Forest Route 300 (the Rim Rd.) W of Woods Canyon Lake.

**Chevelon Canyon Lake:** This long skinny reservoir is 12 miles upstream from Chevelon Crossing via Forest Routes 169 and 169B. See the Apache-Sitgreaves Forest Map for other ways of getting here. It's one of the larger lakes on the Mogollon Rim with 208 surface acres. Fishing is mostly for rainbow trout. A primitive campground (elev. 6,400 ft.; no water or fee) is near the northern end.

# SEDONA AND THE
# RED ROCK COUNTRY

Drifting clouds, towering pinnacles, and sheer canyon walls create a magical setting for Sedona. Monoliths of vivid red sandstone appear to be cast adrift from the Mogollon Rim. Oak Creek, which carved this landscape, glides gracefully through Sedona. A ribbon of green along the creek contrasts sharply with the red land.

**history:** The prehistoric Hohokam and Sinagua Indians tilled the soil along Oak Creek for their corn, beans, and squash long before the white men came. American settlers first arrived in the late 1800s to farm and run cattle in the valley. The town dates from 1902, when Theodore Schnebly opened a post office and named it "Sedona" after his wife. Schnebly also built a wagon road up the rim in the same

year to haul vegetables and fruit to Flagstaff and lumber back to Sedona; his trips took about 11 hours each way.

**modern times:** From a tiny agricultural community just 20 years ago, Sedona has developed into a major tourist destination and art center. The present population of more than 11,000 includes many retired people, artists, and nature lovers. Sunny skies and pleasant temperatures prevail. At an elevation of 4,300 feet, Sedona avoids the extremes found in the low desert and high mountains. The community lies 28 miles S of Flagstaff, and sprawls haphazardly around the junction of US 89A and AZ 179. You'll hear residents refer to this junction as the "Y" when giving directions.

## SIGHTS

Besides the surrounding scenery, attractions include outstanding art galleries, elegant restaurants, and luxurious resorts. The showiest place in town is Tlaquepaque (t'lah-kay-PAH-kay), a recreated village reminiscent of a suburb of Guadalajara, Mexico. Among the tiled courtyards and fountains you'll find restaurants and a great variety of art galleries and crafts shops. South of town, the Chapel of the Holy Cross presents a striking sight atop a sandstone ridge; you're welcome to visit 0900-1800 daily; drive 3 miles S on AZ 179 to Chapel Rd. and turn L one mile.

Probably the prettiest sights belong to nature herself. Oak Creek Canyon, just upstream from Sedona, is the best known and easily reached. A 16-mile drive N on US 89A toward Flagstaff takes you through this canyon, past dramatic rock formations and dense forests. In autumn (mid-Oct. to mid-Nov.), turning leaves add to the rich hues of the sculptured canyon walls. Some of the best panoramas of the Sedona area are seen from Schnebly Hill Rd.; take the signposted turnoff from AZ 179 (½ mile S of the US 89A jct.); you'll soon leave the pave-ment and wind high up the cliffs of the Mogollon Rim, reaching Exit 320 of I-17 11½ miles later (20 miles S of Flagstaff). Cautiously driven cars can usually make this trip in good weather (call the Sedona National Forest office for road conditions; tel. 282-4119). Hikers can head into wilderness to explore the West Fork of Oak Creek, Wilson Mountain, Pumphouse Wash, and hundreds of other areas.

## ACCOMMODATIONS

Be sure to have reservations if you're coming for the weekend—the popular places fill up fast during the Apr. to Nov. peak season. Prices in Sedona tend to run on the high side then, but often drop substantially in winter. Campers headed for Oak Creek Canyon on a summer weekend should plan to arrive Fri. morning. The 5 Forest Service campgrounds here are expensive, and they stay open only for the summer. The Cottonwood and Camp Verde areas to the S offer less expensive motels and year-round camping.

**motels:** In town, moderately priced places ($25-$50) include Canyon Portal Motel (210 N. US 89A; tel. 282-7125); Cedars Resort (20 N.

*Chapel of the Holy Cross*

US 89A; tel. 282-7010); Sunset Inn Sedona (2545 W. US 89A; tel. 282-1520); La Vista Motel (500 N. US 89A; tel. 282-7301); Matterhorn Motor Lodge (301 N. US 89A; tel. 282-7176); Quality Inn/King's Ransom (¾ mile S on AZ 179 from US 89A; tel. 282-7151 or 800-228-5151); Sedona Motel (one block S on AZ 179;

tel. 282-7187); Sky Ranch Lodge (on Airport Rd.; tel. 282-6400); and Star Motel (295 Jordan Rd. off N. US 89A; tel. 282-3641).

**bed and breakfasts:** Keyes' Bed and Breakfast is in West Sedona; $40 ($45 weekends) s or d; tel. 282-6008. Graham's Bed

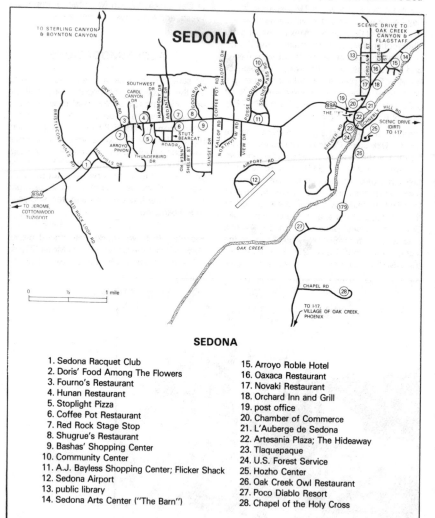

## SEDONA

1. Sedona Racquet Club
2. Doris' Food Among The Flowers
3. Fourno's Restaurant
4. Hunan Restaurant
5. Stoplight Pizza
6. Coffee Pot Restaurant
7. Red Rock Stage Stop
8. Shugrue's Restaurant
9. Bashas' Shopping Center
10. Community Center
11. A.J. Bayless Shopping Center; Flicker Shack
12. Sedona Airport
13. public library
14. Sedona Arts Center ("The Barn")
15. Arroyo Roble Hotel
16. Oaxaca Restaurant
17. Novaki Restaurant
18. Orchard Inn and Grill
19. post office
20. Chamber of Commerce
21. L'Auberge de Sedona
22. Artesania Plaza; The Hideaway
23. Tlaquepaque
24. U.S. Forest Service
25. Hozho Center
26. Oak Creek Owl Restaurant
27. Poco Diablo Resort
28. Chapel of the Holy Cross

and Breakfast is in the Village of Oak Creek, 6 miles S on AZ 179; $65-$85 s or d; tel. 284-1425. Singing Hills Ranch is out in the country near Page Springs; go 10 miles SW on US 89A (from the "Y") then turn L 2½ miles on Page Springs Rd.; $30 s, $40 d; tel. 634-4734. The Sedona-Oak Creek Canyon Chamber of Commerce (tel. 282-7722), Bed and Breakfast in Arizona, Inc. (Phoenix tel. 995-2831), and Mi Casa Su Casa (Tempe tel. 990-0682) have additional listings.

**Sedona resorts:** Poco Diablo ("Little Devil") Resort features all the amenities: fireplaces, a top-notch restaurant, swimming pools, jacuzzis, tennis and racquetball courts, 9-hole golf course, etc.; rates start at $78 s or d. Poco Diablo is 2 miles S on AZ 179 from AZ 179; tel. (800) 352-5710 in Arizona or tel. (800) 528-4275 out of state. The Orchards Inn & Grill has 2 swimming pools and a jacuzzi; rooms are $89.25 d from Sun. to Thur. ($99.75 Fri. & Sat.) in season; located just N of the "Y"; tel. 282-7131. L'Auberge de Sedona offers luxurious cottages in a French country inn atmosphere; rates of $180 d ($192 Fri. & Sat.) include breakfast and 5-course French dinners; located beside Oak Creek at 301 Little Lane (off N. US 89A one block N of AZ 179); tel. 282-1661. The Best Western Arroyo Roble Hotel has a swimming pool, jacuzzi, and views from private balconies; rates start at $67.60 s or d; 400 N. US 89A; tel. 282-4001.

**Oak Creek Canyon resorts:** You'll find rustic cabins and plush lodges tucked back in the woods within Oak Creek Canyon. These resorts stay open all year except as noted. Lomacasi Cottages (open 1 Apr. to 1 Dec.; $40-$55; tel. 282-7912) and Red Rock Lodge ($28-$49; tel. 282-3591) lie just beyond Sedona on N. US 89A. Briar Patch Resort ($75 s or d; tel. 282-2342) and Terracotta Resort ($45-$78 s or d; tel. 282-7723) have a variety of cottages 3 miles N on US 89A. Oak Creek Terrace Resort, 4½ miles N of Sedona on US 89A, has motel rooms ($50-$65) and cabins ($65-$125); tel. 282-3562. Slide Rock Lodge is 6 miles N of Sedona on US 89A, just S of the famous Slide Rock swimming area; rooms start at $38 s or d; tel. 282-3531. Garland's Oak Creek Lodge is 8

miles N of town on US 89A; open 1 Apr. to mid-Nov.; rates include family-style meals (breakfast and dinner): $70 s or $90 d for a small cabin, $88 s or $108 d for a large cabin; tel. 282-3343. You can also come to Garland's just for a memorable dinner, but reserve first. Junipine Resort features modern and spacious accommodations 8 miles N of Sedona on US 89A; $125-$150 (4 people); tel. 282-3375 or (800) 842-2121 in Arizona. Don Hoel's Cabins are 9½ miles N of town on US 89A; closed Jan.; the rustic cabins start at $35 s or d; tel. 282-3560.

**campgrounds:** Some of the prettiest places lie N of town in Oak Creek Canyon. The Forest Service maintains 5 campgrounds here: Manzanita (6 miles N on US 89A), Banjo Bill (8 miles N on US 89A), Bootlegger (8¾ miles N on US 89A), Cave Spring (11½ miles N on US 89A), and Pine Flat (12½ miles N on US 89A). All but Bootlegger Campground have drinking water and a $7/night charge; Bootlegger costs $4/night. Trailers and large RVs have adequate room only in Cave Spring and Pine Flat Campgrounds. None of the camping areas have hookups or showers. Unfortunately, the campgrounds remain open only from about Memorial Day to Labor Day, though the season is sometimes extended. The rest of the year, tenters looking for established campgrounds have to head S to Dead Horse Ranch State Park near Cottonwood or Forest Service campgrounds near Camp Verde. Dispersed camping is forbidden in Oak Creek Canyon, but you could find a spot in the National Forests elsewhere. The Sedona Ranger Station can tell you about camping and hiking in the area; tel. 282-4119.

RVs may stay year-round in Sedona at: Shady Rest RV Park (next to Tlaquepaque) ¼ mile S on AZ 179 from US 89A; $12.36 w/hookups; tel. 282-9938. Rancho Sedona Mobilodge (near Schnebly Hill Rd. turnoff), ½ mile S on AZ 179 from US 89A; $16.60 w/hookups; tel. 282-7255. Oak Creek Mobilodge is one mile S on AZ 179 from US 89A; $12 w/hookups; tel. 282-7701. Near Sedona on N. US 89A is the Hawkeye RV Park. Open all year, it costs $15.60 RV w/hookups and $10.40 tents; tel. 282-3449.

# FOOD

**American and Continental:** You can enjoy some of Arizona's finest dining in Sedona. Reservations are advised at the more expensive places. The Oak Creek Owl features American and Continental cuisine in an elegant atmosphere with excellent service; open daily for lunch and dinner (mod. to exp.); ½ mile S on AZ 179 from US 89A; tel. 282-3532. Rene at Tlaquepaque serves outstanding American and Continental cuisine in a French Provincial atmosphere; open for lunch and dinner daily except Tue. (mod.); in Tlaquepaque, ¼ mile S on AZ 179 from US 89A; tel. 282-9225. L'Auberge de Sedona is an elegant French restaurant; open daily for breakfast, lunch, and dinner (exp.); 301 Little Lane (off N. US 89A one block N of AZ 179); tel. 282-1661. The Willows dining room in Poco Diablo Resort serves American and Continental dishes daily for breakfast, lunch, and dinner (mod.); there's a daily buffet, but the Sunday brunch buffet ranks as the ultimate in overwhelming choices (open 1030-1430; $16.80 adult); located 2 miles S on AZ 179 from US 89A. Shugrue's features steak and seafood among their other specialties; open daily for breakfast (except Mon.), lunch, and dinner (mod. to exp.); 2250 W. US 89A; tel. 282-2943. Fournos offers a varied Continental and seafood menu; open Thur. to Sat. for lunch and dinner, Sun. for brunch (mod.); 3000 W. US 89A; tel. 282-3331. For something different in fine dining, try the Orchards Grill; they describe their food as "the new light American cuisine"; the menu lists everything from sushi to pizza; open daily for breakfast, lunch, and dinner (mod.); 254 N. US 89A; tel. 282-7131.

**American cafes:** If you're looking for a good inexpensive meal, try the Coffee Pot Restaurant; open daily for breakfast, lunch, and dinner; 2445 W. US 89A; tel. 282-6626. Doris' Food Among the Flowers serves natural foods (vegetarian); open daily except Mon. for breakfast and lunch (inexp.); 3006 W. US 89A; tel. 282-2334. The Novaki, despite its Hopi Indian name, serves standard American breakfasts and lunches daily (inexp.); N. US 89A at Jordan Rd.; tel. 282-1666.

**Mexican:** El Rincon, in Tlaquepaque, specializes in Mexican food; open Tue. to Sat. for lunch and dinner, and Sun. for lunch (inexp.-mod.); tel. 282-4648. The Oaxaca offers Mexican and American dining; open daily for breakfast, lunch, and dinner (inexp.-mod.); 231 N. US 89A; tel. 282-4179. At both El Rincon and the Oaxaca you can enjoy the Mexican atmosphere inside or dine outdoors on a patio.

**Italian:** The Hideaway, overlooking Oak Creek, has good Italian food—spaghetti, fettuccini, manicotti, pizza, etc.; open daily for lunch and dinner (inexp.) in Country Square shopping center (on AZ 179, ¼ mile S of US 89A); tel. 282-4204. Stoplight Pizza dishes up pizza and subs daily except Sun. for lunch and dinner (inexp.); 2701 W. US 89A; tel. 282-2099.

**Chinese:** Dine Chinese at Hunan, open for lunch and dinner daily except Mon. (inexp.-mod.); 55 Sinagua Dr. (go 3 miles W on US 89A from the "Y" and follow signs); tel. 282-3118.

**groceries:** Buy them at A.J. Bayless or Bashas' supermarkets on W. US 89A.

**out-of-town dining:** The Village of Oak Creek, on AZ 179 about midway between Sedona and I-17, has several good places to eat: The Happy Cooker cafe is open daily for breakfast and lunch and claims to have the "best hamburger in Sedona"; Castle Rock Plaza; tel. 284-2240. Serrano's Mexican Food, also in Castle Rock Plaza, is open for lunch and dinner daily except Sun.; tel. 284-2151. Buy baked goodies, breakfast, and sandwiches at Sedona Bakery (closed Sun. and Mon.), Castle Rock Plaza. Sedona Yacht Harbour Restaurant is open for dinner Wed. to Sun., but the only way to get your yacht here is on a trailer; this fine dining establishment offers steaks, seafood, veal, chicken and other dishes at moderate prices; located N of Castle Rock Plaza; tel. 284-1510.

The Western-style Page Springs Restaurant overlooks Oak Creek downstream from Sedona; steak, seafood, and chicken dominate the menu (inexp.-mod.); open daily for lunch and dinner; go 10 miles SW on US 89A (from the "Y") then turn L 2½ miles on Page Springs Rd.; tel. 634-9954. During the day (0800-1600) you may visit the fish hatchery across the road.

Vince's Little Star is a cozy family-run Italian restaurant in downtown Cornville; open daily except Mon. for dinner (inexp.-mod.); from the Page Springs Restaurant, continue 4 miles to the end of the road, then turn R one mile (or take the I-17 Cornville exit and go NW 9 miles); tel. 634-4063.

## OTHER PRACTICALITIES

**entertainment:** See the latest flicks at the Flicker Shack, located in the A.J. Bayless shopping center on W. US 89A (1 ½ miles W of the "Y"); tel. 282-3777. You might catch a concert or play at the Sedona Arts Center ("the Barn") at N. US 89A and Art Barn Rd. on the N edge of town; tel. 282-3809. Red Rock Stage Stop jumps to live rock, blues, or country-rock bands Thur. to Sat. nights; a DJ spins the music on Tue. and Wed.; barbequed ribs and other foods are served daily, 2468 W. US 89A; tel. 282-6082. Shugrue's Restaurant and Lounge also has varied live music Thur. to Sat., 2250 W. US 89A; tel. 282-2943. To get the latest on Sedona's music, events, and nightlife, check the weekly *Sedona Times* newspaper.

**recreation:** Slide Rock, 6½ miles N of Sedona in Oak Creek Canyon, attracts many swimmers; the fun is in sliding through a natural chute (wear jeans, as this is hard on the seat!). Try to avoid summer weekends when the spot becomes too crowded. Arizona State Parks recently took over Slide Rock and plans to improve parking and facilities. Grasshopper Point is another natural swimming hole, 2 miles N of town. The Sedona public swimming pool at the Community Center (Posse Ground Rd. in West Sedona) is open in summer; tel. 282-5629. Tennis courts at the Sedona Racquet Club are open to the public for a fee, W. US 89A (3¾ miles from the "Y"); tel. 282-4197. Play golf at Poco Diablo Resort's 9-hole course (2 miles S on AZ 179; tel. 282-7333, ext. 135); or Village of Oak Creek Country Club's 18-hole course (6½ miles S on AZ 179, then R on Bell Rock Rd.; tel. 284-1660). Fishermen can pull rainbow trout from Oak Creek. Rainbow Trout Farm offers easier fishing but has a charge; equipment is supplied and no license is needed; located 3 miles N of Sedona in Oak Creek Canyon; open daily 0730-1730 all year; tel. 282-3379. Kachina Riding Stables offers trail rides year-round in the red rock country around Sedona; the stables are 6 miles SW of town off Red Rock Loop Rd.; $10/1 hour, $18/2 hours, then $7/each additional hour; tel. 282-7252.

*Slide Rock in Oak Creek Canyon*

**events:** Sedona goes Irish every March for a St. Patrick's Day parade, said to be the largest in the West. Clowns, bands, and floats march through town in a noisy celebration. A Queen of the Green receives her crown in a gala coronation ball prior to the big day. Other annual Sedona events celebrate music and the arts: Spring Festival of the Arts at Tlaquepaque in May; Fiesta des Los Artes in June; Call of the Canyon Festival of the Arts in Sept.; Jazz on the Rocks Festival in Sept.; and Fiesta del Tlaquepaque in October. More than 5,000 candle-lit luminarias brighten Tlaquepaque during the Festival of Lights in December.

**shopping:** What Sedona lacks in size as an art center, compared with Santa Fe or Scottsdale, it strives to make up for in higher quality. Its 25 or so art galleries display an impressive range of original art. Southwestern themes run through much of the work — in colors, forms, Indian motifs, and cowboy legends. Most of the art galleries lie along the first half-mile of AZ 179 S from the "Y," and in "Old Town," the first half-mile of US 89A N from the "Y." Tlaquepaque (¼ mile S on AZ 179 from US 89A) makes a good starting point for a trip into

*a courtyard in Tlaquepaque*

Sedona's art world. Fountains, sycamore-shaded courtyards, and the Spanish-Colonial architecture create a delightful atmosphere. Even nonshoppers will enjoy exploring the many shops and galleries here, no two alike.

Many of Sedona's cultural activities center around the Sedona Arts Center, on the N edge of town at N. US 89A and Art Barn Road. Changing art exhibits can be seen Tue. to Sat. 1030-1630 and Sun. 1330-1630 (closed last week of Dec. and first week of Jan.); free. A gift shop offers work by local artists. Sedona Arts Center often schedules concerts, plays, and other evening events; tel. 282-3809.

**services:** The post office is conveniently located on US 89A just W of the "Y." Nearest hospital is the Marcus Lawrence Hospital at 202 S. Willard in Cottonwood, 19 miles SW of Sedona; tel. 634-2251. For emergencies (fire, police, ambulance) call tel. 911.

**information:** Sedona-Oak Creek Canyon Chamber of Commerce has a good supply of literature and can tell you of coming events; open Mon. to Fri. 0900-1700 and Sat. 0930-1500; located at the corner of N. US 89A and Forest Rd., just N of the "Y" (Box 478, Sedona, AZ 86336); tel. 282-7722. The Forest Service office can tell you of camping, hiking, and road conditions in the National Forests surrounding Sedona; open Mon. to Fri. 0730-1630; located at 225 Brewer Rd. (take the street opposite the post office on W. US 89A); Box 300, Sedona, AZ 86336; tel. 282-4119. Sedona Public Library is open Mon. to Sat. (call for hours); located on Jordan Rd. off N. US 89A; tel. 282-7714. The latest on dining, nightlife, art exhibits, events, and local news will be listed in the *Sedona Times,* a lively weekly newspaper.

**tours:** Three companies offer jeep trips into the rugged backcountry. Time Expeditions specializes in trips to prehistoric Indian ruins; a 2½ hour tour to a well-preserved cliff dwelling costs $35/person (other trips can be arranged too); tel. 282-2137. Pink Jeep Tours (tel. 282-5000), and Sedona Red Rock Jeep Tours (tel. 282-2026) offer a variety of scenic trips at similar prices. For the best views, take a flight

*art in Tlaquepaque galleries*

with Sedona Air Center; short local tours cost $10-$20/person (min. 2); longer flights take in the Grand Canyon and Havasupai at $60/person (min. 2), or the Grand Canyon plus Havasupai, Meteor Crater, Canyon de Chelly, Monument Valley, and Lake Powell at $120/person (min. 3); tel. 282-7935.

**transport:** A trolley service connects the shopping areas, motels, and RV parks in Sedona, taking 1 hours for a round trip; operates daily except Mon. from mid-Mar. to late Oct.; RT fares: $1.50 adult, $.50 children; pick up a schedule from the Chamber of Commerce. Rent cars from Budget (at the airport; tel. 282-4602); Bargain Rent-a-Car (tel. 282-4162); Cheap Wheels (tel. 282-2140); or Sedona Motors (tel. 282-2199). Sedona Shuttle Service runs twice daily to Phoenix ($25 OW), stopping at Trailways Bus station and Sky Harbor Airport; the shuttle leaves Sedona from Sedona Mobil station near the "Y"; tel. 282-2066. Sedona's airport sits atop a mesa SW of town;

take Airport Rd. from W. US 89A. Golden Pacific flies to Phoenix once or twice daily ($56 OW), and to Prescott ($21 OW), Kingman ($72 OW), and Winslow ($76 OW); tel. 282-1515 or (800) 352-3281. Air Sedona flies 4 times daily to Phoenix ($48 OW; senior citizens $40 OW); stops can be arranged for Cottonwood, Camp Verde, Scottsdale, and Deer Valley; tel. 282-7935 or (800) 228-7654 in Arizona.

## HIKING IN THE SEDONA AREA

Rugged canyons, delicate natural arches, and solitude await those who venture into the backcountry. Much of this land remains unchanged from prehistoric times. Hiking possibilities have almost no limit—you can venture on easy dayhikes or chart a week-long trek across the wilderness. Spring and autumn have the most pleasant temperatures, but hiking is possible all year. Summer visitors can avoid the 100-plus F temperatures in the desert by getting an early start and heading for the higher country; winter hikers keep to the desert and canyon areas when snow blocks trails in the ponderosa pine forests above. Best source of information for backcountry travel is the U.S Forest Service office in Sedona (225 Brewer Rd.; tel. 282-4119). Their Coconino Forest map

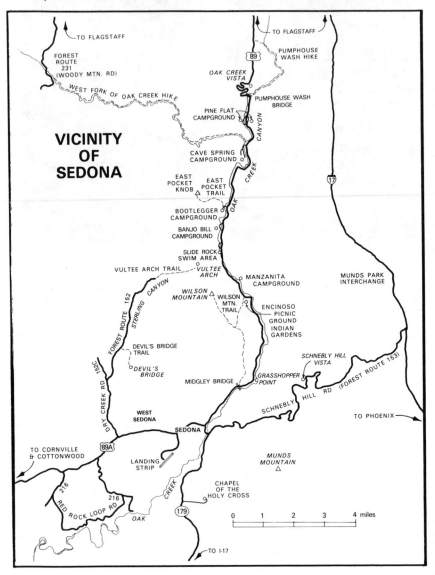

**VICINITY OF SEDONA**

TO FLAGSTAFF

FOREST ROUTE 231 (WOODY MTN. RD)

WEST FORK OF OAK CREEK HIKE

TO FLAGSTAFF

89

PUMPHOUSE WASH HIKE

*OAK CREEK VISTA*

PUMPHOUSE WASH BRIDGE

PINE FLAT CAMPGROUND

*OAK CREEK CANYON*

CAVE SPRING CAMPGROUND

17

EAST POCKET KNOB

EAST POCKET TRAIL

BOOTLEGGER CAMPGROUND

BANJO BILL CAMPGROUND

SLIDE ROCK SWIM AREA

VULTEE ARCH TRAIL

*VULTEE ARCH*

MANZANITA CAMPGROUND

MUNDS PARK INTERCHANGE

*STERLING CANYON*

*WILSON MOUNTAIN*

WILSON MTN. TRAIL

ENCINOSO PICNIC GROUND INDIAN GARDENS

FOREST ROUTE 152

DEVIL'S BRIDGE TRAIL

*DEVIL'S BRIDGE*

SCHNEBLY HILL VISTA

*GRASSHOPPER POINT*

SCHNEBLY HILL RD (FOREST ROUTE 153)

MIDGLEY BRIDGE

FOREST ROUTE 152C

DRY CREEK RD

**WEST SEDONA**

SCHNEBLY HILL RD

TO PHOENIX

TO CORNVILLE & COTTONWOOD

89A

**SEDONA**

LANDING STRIP

*MUNDS MOUNTAIN*

216

216

RED ROCK LOOP RD

*OAK CREEK*

179

CHAPEL OF THE HOLY CROSS

0  1  2  3  4 miles

TO I-17

($1) shows back roads and many of the trails. Look in libraries for *Oak Creek Canyon and the Red Rock Country of Arizona* by Stewart Aitchison; this handy-sized guide has a good introduction and descriptions of hiking trails and back roads. The following 6 hikes will acquaint you with this colorful land. The first 5 lie within the Red Rock/Secret Mountain Wilderness area; no mechanized vehicles allowed.

**Devil's Bridge Trail #120:** From the trailhead (elev. 4,600 feet), a well-graded path climbs steadily through juniper, pinyon pine, Arizona cypress, and manzanita to the base of a long natural arch. You can't see the bridge until you're almost there, but when you arrive, the majestic sweep of the arch and fine views of distant canyons and mountains reward your effort. The 1.8-mile RT hike has an elevation gain of 400 feet. A smaller trail forks off to the R about 330 feet before the bridge and climbs steeply to the top of the arch. Devil's Bridge lies NW of Sedona on the other side of a ridge. From the "Y" in Sedona, head W 3.1 miles on US 89A, turn R 2.1 miles on paved Dry Creek Rd. (Forest Route 152C), then turn R 1.2 miles on dirt Sterling Canyon Rd. (Forest Route 152). Sterling Canyon Rd. is not recommended during wet weather; other times it's OK for cars. The trailhead should be signposted. The first part of the trail follows a badly eroded jeep road, passable by car for only a short distance.

**Vultee Arch Trail #22:** This hike follows Sterling Canyon upstream to a small natural bridge, visible in the sandstone to the north. Though the canyon is dry most of the time, Arizona cypress, sycamore, ponderosa pine, and other trees and plants find it to their liking. Trailhead elevation is 4,800 feet, and you'll be climbing 400 feet higher on the 3.4-mile RT trail. Carry some water, especially if it's a hot day. The arch and a bronze plaque at the end of the trail commemorate aircraft designer Gerard Vultee and his wife Sylvia, who died when their plane hit East Pocket Mesa to the N during a snowstorm on 29 Jan. 1938. Adventurous hikers can find a trail E across the pass to Oak Creek Canyon, coming out near Manzanita Campground. Trailhead for Vultee Arch is at the end of Sterling Canyon Rd.; follow directions for

*Oak Creek near Sedona*

Devil's Bridge Trail, but continue 3 miles past that turnoff to road's end.

**Wilson Mountain Trail #10:** Energetic hikers will enjoy this trail from the bottom of Oak Creek Canyon to the top of Wilson Mountain. A stiff 2,300-foot climb is followed by a long level stretch extending to the N edge of the flat-topped mountain. Total trail length is 9 miles RT, or 6 miles RT if you turn around where the trail levels off on the summit plateau. Two very different trails, South Wilson and North Wilson, start from the bottom (elev. 4,600 feet), meet part way up on First Bench, then continue as one trail to the top. South Wilson Trail begins from the N end of Midgley Bridge (1.9 miles N of the "Y" on US 89A) and switchbacks through Arizona cypress, juniper, pinyon pine, agave, yucca, and other sun-loving plants. Higher up, manzanita, shrub live oak, and other chaparral-zone plants become more common. North Wilson Trail, on the other hand, climbs steeply through a cool canyon filled with tall ponderosa pine and Douglas fir; trailhead begins on US 89A just N of Encinoso picnic area (5.3 miles N of the "Y"). A stone cairn marks the junction where the trails meet at First Bench.

This large level area dates from long ago, when a piece of Wilson Mountain's summit broke off and slid part way down. More climbing takes you to the rim of Wilson Mountain; keep R where the trail forks and follow the path N to some spectacular viewpoints. From the northernmost overlook, tiny Vultee Arch can be seen far below across Sterling Canyon. Beyond, on the horizon, stand the San Francisco Peaks. Small meadows and forests of ponderosa pine and Gambel oak cover the large summit expanse of Wilson Mountain. Carry 2-3 quarts of water. Ignore old trail descriptions that tell of South Wilson Trail heading up Wilson Canyon; the new route leaves the canyon directly from the trailhead near Midgley Bridge. Wilson Canyon and Mountain get their names from Richard Wilson, a bear hunter who lost to a grizzly in June 1885. Wilson's bear gun was being repaired on the day he spotted grizzly tracks in Oak Creek Canyon, but he set out after the bear anyway with a smaller rifle. Nine days later, horsemen found Wilson's badly mauled body up what's now Wilson Canyon.

**East Pocket (A.B. Young) Trail #100:** This well-graded trail climbs out of Oak Creek Canyon to East Pocket Mesa, located N of Wilson Mountain. The trail makes more than 30 switchbacks to reach the ponderosa pine-forested rim, a 1,600-foot climb and 3.2 miles RT. From the rim, the trail climbs gently to East Pocket Knob Lookout Tower, another 0.8 mile and 400 feet higher. You can enjoy the good views of Oak Creek Canyon on the way up, from the rim, and atop the lookout tower (open during the fire season). The trailhead (elev. 5,200 feet) is across Oak Creek from Bootlegger Campground (just N of Milepost 383 on US 89A, 8.75 miles N of Sedona). Wade or hop stones across the creek (don't cross if flooded) to a dirt road paralleling the bank, and look for a well-used trail climbing the slope. After leaving the woodlands along Oak Creek, the trail ascends through chaparral vegetation. Allow 3-4 hours and carry 1-2 quarts of water. Cattlemen built the trail in the 1880s to bring their herds to pasture. The Civilian Conserva-

tion Corps under A.B. Young improved it in the 1930s.

**West Fork Trail #108:** An easy, almost level trail extends about 2.5 miles upstream through the narrow canyon of West Fork, a major tributary of Oak Creek. Sheer canyon walls rising hundreds of feet, luxuriant vegetation, and the clear stream make this an idyllic spot. Because of the numbers and diversity of plant and animal species here, the lower 6 miles of the canyon has a "Research Natural Area" designation. The stream, which you'll be crossing many times, is usually only ankle-deep for several miles. Carry water and plenty of film. Don't camp or build fires in the Natural Area. Finding the trailhead takes some effort, but it's there. Look for 2 large wood posts with a heavy chain between them on the W side of US 89A midway between Mileposts 384 and 385 (10 miles N of Sedona). A day-use parking area is 0.15 mile N of the entrance. An old asphalt-paved trail descends to Oak Creek, then a dirt trail continues past the ruins of Mayhew's Lodge and into West Fork Canyon.

Although most visitors come for a leisurely dayhike, strong hikers can travel the entire 14-mile length of West Fork canyon in one day if they have an early start and a car shuttle. If doing the 14-mile trip, start at the upstream trailhead. This is where Forest Route 231 (Woody Mountain Rd.) crosses West Fork. (Woody Mountain Rd. begins as a turnoff from Business I-40, about 2 miles W of Flagstaff.) Only the lower end of the canyon has a trail; in other parts you'll be walking in the streambed or clambering over boulders. The first 6 miles from the upper trailhead are usually dry, but this stretch is followed by a series of deep pools that may require swimming. You should avoid any hiking in the canyon after heavy rains, because of possible flooding. The rough terrain and deep pools make backpacking difficult, so most people do the trip as a long dayhike.

**Lower Pumphouse Wash:** Some boulder-hopping and wading here will take you through a beautiful pristine canyon. Though millions of motorists have crossed the Pumphouse Wash

Bridge on their drive through Oak Creek Canyon, hardly any have ventured into this little tributary canyon. The 3.5-mile OW hike is best done from May to Oct., after the spring snowmelt is over. You'll want to choose a warm sunny day to enjoy the nifty swimming holes on the way. There's no trail in the canyon; the route involves walking over boulders, wading, and possibly some swimming. Allow 4 hours for the trip—more if you'll be playing in the water a lot. The lower trailhead is Pumphouse Wash Bridge at the bottom of the switchbacks on US 89A (13.5 miles N of Sedona); upper trailhead is an unsigned pulloff on the E side of US 89A about 100 yards S of Milepost 391 (16.5 miles N of Sedona). From the upper trailhead, go E ½ mile away from the highway (no trail; climb over the fence) and descend the moderate slope into Pumphouse Wash. Be alert for rattlesnakes on the rim, though they're rarely seen in the canyon. At the bottom, turn R (downstream) until you come to the highway bridge, a total descent of 800 feet. Look for signs of beaver houses dug into the streambanks. You'll recognize the Coconino Sandstone that forms the canyon's cliffs by its long, graceful crossbeds; this rock was once sand dunes in a long-ago desert.

## SYCAMORE CANYON

Imagine Oak Creek Canyon without the highway, resorts, campgrounds, and town of Sedona. That's what Sycamore Canyon is, a twisting slash in the earth 21 miles long and up to 7 miles wide. As the crow flies, Sycamore Canyon is about 15 miles W of Oak Creek Canyon. A wilderness designation protects the canyon; only hikers and horseback riders may descend into its depths. Several trails wind down to Sycamore Creek, mostly from the E side, but not a single road! Motorists may enjoy the sweeping view from Sycamore Point on the W rim, approached from Williams (see "Vicinity of Williams"). Sycamore Canyon Wilderness falls under the confusing jurisdiction of 3 different National Forests: Coconino, Kaibab, and Prescott. The ranger station in Sedona (Coconino National Forest) is your best source of information for trail conditions, trailhead access, and water sources; 225 Brewer Rd.; tel. 282-4119. The May 1985 issue of *Arizona Highways* magazine has a story of a Sycamore Canyon hike and beautiful photos.

*Sycamore Canyon from Sycamore Point*

# ALONG THE VERDE RIVER

Below the cream- and red-colored cliffs of the Mogollon Rim, the Verde River (Spanish for 'green') brings life to its broad desert valley. The waters come from narrow canyons of Oak Creek, Wet and Dry Beaver Creeks, West Clear Creek, Sycamore Creek, and other streams. Prehistoric Indians made camps in the area, finding a great variety of wild plant foods and game between the 3000-foot elevations of the lower valley and the Rim country 4,000 feet higher. From about A.D. 600 to 700, groups began cultivating the Verde Valley, taking advantage of the good climate, fertile lands, and abundant water. Trade and contacts with the Hohokam culture to the S also aided development of the region. Hohokam people probably migrated into the Verde Valley too, though archaeologists have difficulty determining whether the early farming communities were actually Hohokam or just influenced by their culture. The Verde's inhabitants learned to grow cotton, weave cloth, make pottery, and build ball courts. Sinagua from the Flagstaff area arrived between A.D.1125 to 1200 and gradually absorbed the cultures already here. Villages then started to consolidate. Large multi-storied pueblos replaced the small pit houses of earlier times. Two of these pueblos, Montezuma Castle and Tuzigoot, are now Na-

tional Monuments and easily visited. Archaeologists don't know why, but the Verde Valley's population had departed from the area by A.D. 1425. The elaborate Hohokam culture, based in the Gila and Salt River Valleys to the S. also disappeared about this time. Perhaps part of the Sinagua migrated NE, eventually arriving at the Hopi and Zuni pueblos.

Early Spanish explorers, arriving a century and a half later, found small bands of nomadic Tonto Apache and Yavapai Indians roaming the valley. In language and culture, the Tonto Apache had ties with Apache and Navajo tribes to the E, while the Yavapai shared cultural traits with the Hualapai and Havasupai to the northwest. Anglos and Mexicans poured into the valley during a gold rush at the Hassayampa River and Lynx Creek in 1863. Farmers and ranchers followed, taking for themselves the best agricultural lands along the Verde. The displaced Indians attacked the settlements, but failed to drive off the newcomers. Soon the Army came in to make patrols and build Camp Lincoln (later Camp Verde). General George Crook successfully subdued the tribes by clever campaigning and the enlisting of Indian scouts from other Apache groups. The Tonto Apache and Yavapai Indians received the Rio

*posed photo of Apache Indian scouts, late 1800s*

*mule litter of the U.S. Army Medical Corps, Fort Verde in 1880s*

Verde Reservation in 1873, but the federal government took it away 2 years later and ordered them to leave for San Carlos Reservation, 150 miles away. In the cold of Feb. 1875, the Indians started the 2-week journey; of the 1,451 who started on foot, at least 90 died from exposure, were killed by infighting, or escaped. Early in this century some Apache and Yavapai received permission to return to their Verde River homelands. What were once thousands of Indians occupying millions of acres now number less than 1,000 people on a few remnants of their former lands on the Camp Verde, Prescott, and Fort McDowell Reservations.

Anglo farmers in the Verde Valley prospered after the Indian wars ended. Cottonwood, founded in 1879, became the valley's main trading center. Copper mining succeeded on a large scale at Jerome, which sprang to life in 1882 high on a mountainside. Mine company officials located a giant smelter below Jerome in 1910 and laid out the town of Clarkdale. However, ore bodies were depleted in the early 1950s, forcing many residents of Jerome and Clarkdale to seek jobs elsewhere. Today the Verde Valley dozes on with some industry and farming, and as a popular area with tourists and retirees.

## CAMP VERDE

Early in 1865, 19 men set out from Prescott to start a farming settlement in the Verde Valley. They knew the mining camps around Arizona's new capital would pay well for fresh food. The eager farmers chose lands where West Clear Creek joins the Verde, about 5 miles downstream from the modern town of Camp Verde. After planting fields, digging an irrigation system, and building a fort, they saw their hopes nearly come to an end when Indian raids destroyed much of the crops and livestock. Army troops then marched in and built Camp Lincoln one mile N of the present townsite. As too many places were then commemorating the former president, the Army later had to rename the post "Camp Verde." Untamed Indians kept the cavalry and infantry busy during the late 1860s and early 1870s. Infantry also built a road, later known as the General Crook Trail, W to Fort Whipple (near Prescott) and E along the Mogollon Rim to Fort Apache. In 1871 the post moved one mile S to its current location, where more than 20 buildings were neatly laid out around a parade field. The name changed to "Fort Verde" in 1879, but the Indian wars were almost over. A battle in 1882 at

*Dr. Edgar A. Mearns, post surgeon at Fort Verde 1884-88, spent much of his spare time excavating prehistoric Indian sites in the Verde Valley.*

Big Dry Wash marked the last large engagement between soldiers and Indians in Arizona. Having served its purpose, Fort Verde closed in 1891. Land and buildings were then turned over to the civilian community. Today exhibits and the 4 surviving fort buildings at Fort Verde State Historic Park give a feeling of what life was like for the enlisted men, officers, and wives who lived here. Other attractions near town include the multi-storied cliff dwelling of Montezuma Castle, the unusual springs at Montezuma Well, camping, hiking, and rafting the Verde River.

## SIGHTS

**Fort Verde State Historic Park:** Like most posts of the period, Fort Verde never had a protective wall around it, nor did Indians ever attack. Army patrols used Fort Verde as a supply post and staging area. The 10-acre park preserves the administration building, commanding officer's house, bachelors' quarters, the doctor's quarters, and part of the old parade field. Begin your visit at the adobe administration building, used by General George Crook during his winter campaign of 1872-1873 that largely ended Indian raids in this region. Exhibits illustrate life of the soldiers and their families, Apache Army scouts, settlers, and prospectors who came through here more than 100 years ago. You'll see old photos, maps, letters, rifles, uniforms, pack saddles, a map of the Army's heliograph communications network, and Indian crafts. The 3 adobe buildings of "Officers' Row" have been restored and furnished as they were in the 1880s. Fort Verde State Historic Park is open daily 0800-1700; $1 adult, children under 18 free; tel. 567-3275. From Main St. in Camp Verde (2 miles E of I-17 Exit 285), turn N one block on Lane Street.

**Montezuma Castle National Monument:** This towering cliff dwelling so impressed early visitors that they thought it was a castle built by the famous Aztec ruler of Mexico. Actually,

*Montezuma Castle*

*Montezuma Well*

this pueblo was neither a castle nor part of Montezuma's empire. Sinagua Indians built it in the 12th and 13th centuries, toward the end of their stay in the Verde Valley. The 5-story stone and mortar structure contains 20 rooms tucked back under a cliff 100 feet above Beaver Creek. The overhang shielded the village from rain, snow, and the hot summer sun but allowed the low winter sun's rays to warm the dwellings. The well-preserved ruins, once occupied by about 50 people, are too fragile to be entered; you have to view them from below. An even larger pueblo once stood against the base of the cliff; "Castle A" had 6 stories and about 45 rooms, but little remains today. The Visitor Center displays artifacts of the Sinagua and has exhibits depicting their everyday life. Other exhibits describe plant and animal life and geology of the Verde Valley. Related books are sold. A level ⅓-mile trail loops below Montezuma Castle to foundations of Castle "A." Giant Arizona sycamore trees shade a picnic area beside the creek. Montezuma Castle National Monument is open daily from 0800-1700 in winter, extended to 0800-1800 in spring and autumn, and 0700-1900 in summer (Memorial Day to Labor Day); $3/vehicle; tel. 567-3322. Take I-17 Exit 289 and follow signs 2 miles; from Camp Verde, drive N 3 miles on Montezuma Castle Rd., then turn R 2 miles at the sign.

**Montezuma Well:** This natural sinkhole and lake, 11 miles NE of Montezuma Castle, is worth visiting both for its scenic beauty as a desert oasis and for the Indian ruins here. A ⅓-mile self-guiding loop trail climbs to the rim. Other trails wind down to the lake and to the outlet where water enters an ancient irrigation ditch. The sinkhole measures 470 feet across and is only partly filled by a 55-foot-deep lake. Cool, clear waters of the lake attract ducks, coots, and other birds. The Sinagua built pueblos here between A.D. 1125 and 1400 and used the water to irrigate their crops. Parts of their villages and irrigation canals can still be seen. Modern farmers continue to use the water, which flows at 1,100 gallons/minute. Look for the Hohokam pithouse exhibit beside the road on the L ¼ mile before Montezuma Well. Timbers that once held up the walls and roof have long since rotted away, but distinct outlines remain of the supporting poles, walls, entrance, and firepit. A tree-shaded picnic area is located ½ mile before Montezuma Well. Montezuma Well is part of Montezuma Castle National Monument and is open during the same hours. No Visitor Center or admission charge. From Camp Verde or Montezuma Castle, take I-17 N to Exit 293 and follow signs 5 miles; another approach is to take I-17 Sedona Exit 298 and head S 4½ miles on a gravel road.

# PRACTICALITIES

**accommodations and camping:** In Camp Verde, stay at the Copper Canyon Inn ($22 s, $26.25 d; tel. 567-9564) or Fort Verde Motel ($24 s, $27 d; tel. 567-3486), both downtown on Main Street. Beaver Creek Inn ($36.40 s, $41.60 d; tel. 567-4475) is N in the planned community of Lake Montezuma (near Montezuma Well; take I-17 Exit 293). Yavapai-Apache RV Park is 3 miles N of town at the junction of I-17 Exit 289 and Middle Verde Rd. (Montezuma Castle Exit); $4 tent, $11 RVs w/hookups; open all year and has showers; check in at the Short Stop Grocery; tel. 567-3109. The Forest Service runs Clear Creek Campground (6 miles SE on Main St./General Crook Hwy.) and Beaver Creek Campground (take I-17 N to Sedona Exit 298 and turn S 2 miles on Forest Route 618). Sites have drinking water and a $3 fee from mid-Mar. to the end of Oct.; in winter they stay open but have no water or fee.

**food:** At Valley View Restaurant, you can choose from seafood, steak, chicken, veal, and pork dishes, as well as a long list of sandwiches, while enjoying views of the Verde Valley; open daily except Mon. for lunch and dinner (breakfast too on Sat. and Sun.); located on the N edge of downtown; tel. 567-3592. An old-style atmosphere graces the turn-of-the-century Montezuma Inn Cafe and Deli; open daily except Sun. for breakfast, lunch, and dinner on Main St.; tel. 567-6209. Carrie's Country Kitchen is a cafe serving standard American fare; open daily for breakfast, lunch, and dinner (except closed Tue. afternoon) on Main St.; tel. 567-9943. Custard's Last Stand mixes a bakery with a fast-food cafe; open daily for breakfast, lunch, and dinner on Main St.; tel. 567-9900. Vivianos Mexican Restaurant is open daily except Mon. for lunch and dinner on the S edge of town (S. Access Rd.); tel. 567-9966. Stop for pizza at Babe's Round Up on Montezuma Castle Rd. at the N edge of town; tel. 567-9903; or Crusty's Pizza in Fort Verde Shopping Center off N. Main St.; tel. 567-6444. The Quail's Nest Restaurant, beside Beaver Creek golf course at Lake Montezuma (near Montezuma Well), offers a wide range of food; dinner specialties include steaks, prime rib, and seafood; open daily for breakfast, lunch, and dinner; tel. 567-4492. Buy groceries at Fairway in Fort Verde Shopping Center (off N. Main St.), natural foods at Growing Health (Arnold and 3rd Sts.; one block W past Valley View Restaurant).

**events, shopping, and services:** During Fort Verde Days on the 2nd weekend in Oct., the community brings back the old days with cavalry parades and drills, a barbeque, mule race, roping events, art shows, games, and a dance. White Hills Indian Arts on Main St. offers a good selection of jewelry and other work by Indians of Arizona and New Mexico; tel. 567-3490. The post office is just W of downtown on Finney Flats Rd. (AZ 279). Play golf at Beaver Creek's 18-hole course at Lake Montezuma (near Montezuma Well); tel. 567-4487.

**information:** The Yavapai-Apache Visitor Center is just off I-17 at Middle Verde Rd. Exit 289 for Camp Verde and Montezuma Castle. Stop here for slide programs and exhibits on nearby sights, regional information, and shopping for Indian crafts. The building itself, designed by Hopi architect Dennis Numkena, is worth a visit. Elements of Hopi legends fit into the design: the ladder-shaped tower in the center represents a rise into the 4th world—the most perfect one; the whirlwind or eternity symbol appears at many places inside and out; and a well-like structure inside symbolizes the *Sipapu,* where the Hopi emerged into the world. Open daily 0800-1700 with extended hours in summer; free; tel. 567-5276. The Camp Verde Chamber of Commerce will also help you; it's in *The Journal* office across from the Chevron station on N. Main St. (Box 1665, Camp Verde, AZ 86322); tel. 567-9294. The U.S. Forest Service office has information on camping, hiking, road conditions, and running the Verde River; open weekdays 0800-1630; head SE one mile from downtown on Main St./General Crook Hwy. (HC 62, Box 1100, Camp Verde, AZ 86322); tel. 567-4121. Beaver Creek Ranger District office is helpful too; it's located N of Camp Verde near Beaver Creek Campground—take I-17 N to Sedona Exit 298, and turn S 2 miles on Forest Route 618 (Rimrock, AZ 86335); tel. 567-4501.

## VICINITY OF CAMP VERDE

**General Crook National Recreation Trail:** This historic trail dates back to 1871, when General George Crook led a small group of cavalry to survey the route from Fort Apache in eastern Arizona to the territorial capital in Prescott. The Army needed a trail to supply their forts and secure the region from hostile Apache. Work began in 1872, and 2 years later the first wagon trains covered the 200-mile distance. The route had long been abandoned when groups of Boy Scouts and others cleared and marked the old path for a bicentennial project. About 138 miles are now open to hikers and horseback riders. From Camp Verde, the western section stretches 21 miles through Copper Canyon to Cherry Road. The long east-ern section of trail climbs from Camp Verde to the pine-forested Mogollon Rim and follows it 114 miles to a point W of Show Low. Much of the way appears as the old Army cavalry knew it. Some mileposts, carved on boulders or trees, can still be seen. Spring and autumn are the best times to hike; cross-country skiers can tour the higher elevations in winter. For trail information, obtain *A Guide to the General Crook Trail* by Eldon Bowman, published by the Museum of Northern Arizona and the Boy Scouts of America in 1978, or contact the U.S. Forest Service. The July 1982 issue of *Arizona Highways* has good photos and historical articles on the General Crook Trail.

**Pine Mountain Wilderness:** Pine Mountain (6,814 feet) crowns the Verde Rim S of Camp Verde. The wilderness is small, about 20,000 acres, but offers solitude and natural beauty far from towns and highways. Chaparral, juniper and pinyon woodlands, and majestic ponder-

*General George Crook on his mule "Apache"; Indian scout Chief Alchesay stands on right, late 1870s*

osa pine forests cover the rough terrain. You might see mule or whitetail deer, javelina, bear, or mountain lion. To reach the trailhead, take I-17 Exit 268 (Dugas Rd.) located 18 miles S of Camp Verde and 6 miles N of Cordes Junction; then head E 22 miles on dirt Forest Route 68 to the Salt Grounds (¼ mile before Nelson Place). This road is best driven by cars only in good weather. From the parking area there's a one-mile walk to the wilderness boundary. An 8-mile RT loop can be done to the top of Pine Mountain using Forest Trails 159, 14, 161, and 12. Allow 6 hours for this trip and carry water. Elevation gain is about 1,600 feet. See the Prescott, Tonto, or Coconino Forest maps and the Tule Mesa (7½ minute) topo map. The Verde Ranger District office in Camp Verde can tell you the road and trail conditions.

**river running on the Verde:** Experienced boaters in kayaks or rafts can venture down-river from Camp Verde toward Sheep Bridge (near Horseshoe Reservoir), 59 miles away. People are just beginning to discover this wild and scenic stretch of river. You're likely to see well-preserved Indian ruins and abundant wildlife along the way. An area of shoreline along the river may be closed Dec. to Apr. to protect a bald eagle nesting site. The main river-running season lasts from Jan. to early Apr. during spring run-off, but inflatable kayaks can negotiate the sometimes-shallow waters year-round. The ice-cold water in winter and spring necessitates use of full or partial wet suits. With time for rest stops and scouting rapids, rafts typically average 2 miles per hour. The stretch between Beasley Flats and Childs has the wildest water. Canoeists often have trouble negotiating the rapids here and wind up with a smashed boat. Unless you really know what you're doing in whitewater, it's best to avoid this potentially dangerous section. The Forest Service has a free *River Runners Guide to the Verde River;* contact the Verde or Beaver Creek Ranger Districts (see "Camp Verde Information") or the Tonto National Forest office at 2324 E. McDowell Rd. in Phoenix; tel. 225-5200. You can join commercial trips down the Verde led by World Wide Explorations (Box 686, Flagstaff, AZ 86002; tel. 774-6462) from about Feb. to May. Another possibility is canoeing or tubing the leisurely section of river between Cottonwood and Camp Verde. Adventures Unlimited (H.C., Box 518, Camp Verde, AZ 86322; tel. 567-9222) will supply canoes with paddles, life jackets, and a drop-off service for $30; in summer they also rent tubes.

# COTTONWOOD

Named for the trees along the Verde River, Cottonwood provides a handy base for visiting the old mining town of Jerome, the prehistoric Tuzigoot ruins, and other attractions of the Verde Valley. The town is located 16 miles NW of Camp Verde, 19 miles SW of Sedona, and 41 miles NE across Mingus Mt. from Prescott. Actually Cottonwood has 2 downtowns—a new section along US 89A, and the original "Old Town," now bypassed by the highway. Clarkdale, just 2 miles NW of Cottonwood, has many old houses and businesses dating from its years as a smelter town. Although a lot of residents lost their jobs when the smelter shut down in 1952, others were glad to be rid of its heavy black smoke. A newer industry, the Phoenix Cement Company, supplied the cement used in building Glen Canyon Dam on the Colorado River near Page.

**Tuzigoot National Monument:** Sinagua Indians built and lived in this hilltop pueblo from A.D. 1125 to 1425. Tuzigoot ("TOO-zee-goot") stood 2 stories high in places and contained about 92 rooms. At its peak, the pueblo housed 250 people. The large size of the ruin is thought to be the result of a drought in the 1200s, which forced many dry-land farmers to resettle at Tuzigoot and other villages near the Verde River. Most rooms lacked doorways—a ladder through a hatchway in the roof permitted entry. The original roofs, now gone, were pine and sycamore beams covered by willow branches and sealed with mud. While excavating the site in 1933-1934, University of Arizona researchers found a wide variety of artifacts, including the grave offerings contained in 450 burials. A Visitor Center next to the ruins displays some of the finds: stone axes and tools, projectile points, pottery, turquoise and shell jewelry, and religious objects. Other exhibits illustrate what's known about the Sinagua's agriculture, weaving, building tech-

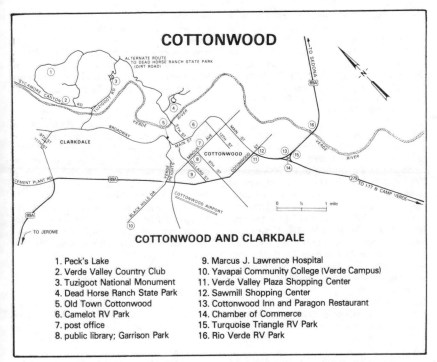

# COTTONWOOD

## COTTONWOOD AND CLARKDALE

1. Peck's Lake
2. Verde Valley Country Club
3. Tuzigoot National Monument
4. Dead Horse Ranch State Park
5. Old Town Cottonwood
6. Camelot RV Park
7. post office
8. public library; Garrison Park
9. Marcus J. Lawrence Hospital
10. Yavapai Community College (Verde Campus)
11. Verde Valley Plaza Shopping Center
12. Sawmill Shopping Center
13. Cottonwood Inn and Paragon Restaurant
14. Chamber of Commerce
15. Turquoise Triangle RV Park
16. Rio Verde RV Park

niques, and burials. A reconstruction shows how one of Tuzigoot's rooms might have looked when the Sinagua lived here. Outside, a ¼-mile trail loops through the maze of ruins. You can climb up to a 2nd story lookout at the summit. The Apache name "Tuzigoot" was chosen for this site because the word had a nice ring to it; originally the name referred to nearby Peck's Lake and meant "crooked water." Tuzigoot National Monument is open daily 0800-1700, extended to 0800-1900 in summer (Memorial Day to Labor Day); $3/vehicle admission; tel. 634-5564. Take the old road (Broadway) running between Cottonwood and Clarkdale, then turn E 1⅓ miles on Tuzigoot Rd. to the ruins.

## PRACTICALITIES

**accommodations:** In Old Town Cottonwood stay at Hopi Motel ($22.35 s, $25.65 d; 218 E. Main St.; tel. 634-7771) or Sundial Motel ($23 s, $25 d; 1034 N. Main St.; tel. 634-8031). In the newer part of town try: Little Daisy Motel ($22 s, $24 d; 34 S. Main St.; tel. 634-7865); View Motel with swimming pool and spa ($23 s, $25 d, $34 d kitchenettes; 818 S. US 89A; tel. 634-7581); Las Campanas Hotel ($36.38 s, $42.80 d; 302 S. US 89A; tel. 634-4287); Willow Tree Inn ($29.40 s, $31.50 d; 1089 AZ 279 near junction with US 89A; tel. 634-3678), or the Best Western Cottonwood Inn with swimming pool, spa, and restaurant ($44 s, $50.40 d; 993 S. Main St. at corner of US 89A and AZ 279; tel. 634-5575 or tel. 800-528-1234).

**campgrounds:** Dead Horse Ranch State Park offers pleasant camping along the Verde River. The park stays open all year and has showers. Day use costs $2/vehicle, campsites for tents or RVs run $5 (or $7 w/hookups); out-of-state people pay $1/vehicle extra; tel. 634-5283. From E. Main St. in Cottonwood, turn N ¾ mile on 5th St. and cross a river ford; if high water closes the road, take the alternate way from Tuzigoot Road. Turquoise Triangle RV Park has showers and is open all year; $8 tents or RVs ($11 w/hookups); tel. 634-5294; located on US 89A, mile E of the junction with AZ 279. Rio Verde RV Park has showers and is open all year; $8 tents or RVs ($10.40 w/hookups); tel. 634-5990; go one mile E on US 89A from the junction with AZ 279. Camelot RV Park is in town at 858 E. Main St.; $10.60 RV w/hookups (no tents); tel. 634-3559.

**food:** The Paragon Restaurant offers a varied menu and pleasant atmosphere; open daily for breakfast, lunch, and dinner at the Cottonwood Inn, at the junction of US 89A and AZ 279; tel. 634-7650. White Horse Inn features steaks, seafood, prime rib, and a good salad bar; open daily for dinner and weekdays for lunch; go one mile E on US 89A from the junction with AZ 279; tel. 634-9970. Little Acorn Family Restaurant serves breakfast and lunch daily, dinner on Fri. and Sat.; 315 S. Main St.; tel. 634-9952. The Menu Tree specializes in breakfasts; open daily for breakfast and lunch; Verde Valley Plaza (junction of US 89A and Cottonwood St.); tel. 634-7920. For Cantonese dining, stop at House of Chin; open daily except Mon. for breakfast, lunch, and dinner at E. Main and 12th Sts.; tel. 634-8702. El Chaparral, a Mexican cafe, is open daily except Wed. for lunch and dinner; on US 89A just E of the AZ 279 junction; tel. 634-2771. Vic's Fine Mexican Food is another cafe serving south-of-the-border food, open daily except Sun. for lunch and dinner; 157 S. Main; tel. 634-3721. Pick up pizza and Italian sandwiches at Verde Pizzeria (open daily), 140 S. Main St.; tel. 634-5000. JR's Black Hills Restaurant features steaks, seafood, barbeque ribs, build-your-own sandwiches, and other items; open daily except Mon. for lunch and dinner; 910 Main St. in Clarkdale; tel. 634-9792. Buy groceries at Safeway in Sawmill Shopping Center or at Bashas' in Verde Valley Plaza, on opposite sides of US 89A at the intersection with Cottonwood Street. Mount Hope Natural Foods is on the W edge of Old Town Cottonwood at 104 Main Street.

**entertainment and events:** Catch movies at the Old Town Palace, 914 N. Main St. in Old Town Cottonwood; tel. 634-7167. Major annual events include the Verde Valley Fair in Apr., Verde Valley Gem and Mineral Show in May, Peck's Lake Barbeque and Fireworks on July 4th, and a Christmas Parade in December.

**services:** Post office is at 700 E. Mingus Avenue. Medical services are provided by the Marcus J. Lawrence Hospital, 202 S. Willard St.; tel. 634-2251. A swimming pool (open in summer; tel. 634-7468) and tennis courts are at Garrison Park, near the corner of E. Mingus Ave. and 6th Street. Play golf at Verde Valley Country Club's 9-hole course; turn E on Tuzigoot Rd. from Broadway (between Cottonwood and Clarkdale), cross the Verde River, then turn L on Sycamore Canyon Rd.; tel. 634-5491.

**information:** The Verde Valley Chamber of Commerce will tell you about the sights, events, and facilities in the area; open daily (except holidays) 0900-1700. The office is in an adobe-style building conveniently located at the intersection of US 89A and AZ 279 (1010 S. Main St., Cottonwood, AZ 86326); tel. 634-7593. Cottonwood's public library is at 401 E. Mingus Ave.; tel. 634-7559.

**transport:** Sedona Transportation Company operates twice daily between Sedona and Phoenix with a stop at Cottonwood; area tours can be arranged too; tel. 282-2066. Verde Valley Transit runs buses from Cottonwood to Jerome several times daily except weekends; tel. 634-7943.

## JEROME

Jerome, clinging to the slopes of Cleopatra Hill above the Verde Valley, might be Arizona's most unusual town. For more than 70 years its

*Jerome smelter about 1890; main stack towered 160 feet and measured 22 feet in diameter. Miners' houses cling to hillside in background.*

booming mines produced copper, gold, and silver. Most residents departed after 1953 when the mines closed, but Jerome survived. Museums, art galleries, antique shops, and restaurants have brought the hillside town back to life. Old-fashioned buildings—some restored, others abandoned but still standing—add to the atmosphere. Walking Jerome's winding streets is like touring a museum of early 20th C. American architecture. From almost any point in town, you can enjoy expansive views across the Verde Valley to the Sedona Red Rock Country, Sycamore Canyon, the Mogollon Rim, and the pointed San Francisco Peaks. Three very different museums will introduce you to the mining history of the area and the people who lived here.

**history:** Prehistoric Indians came long ago to dig the brilliant blue azurite and other copper minerals for use as paint and jewelry. Spanish explorers, shown the diggings by Indian guides, failed to see any worth in the place. In 1876, several American prospectors staked claims to the rich copper deposits, but lacked the resources to develop them. Eugene Jerome, a wealthy lawyer and financier, saw a profit to be made and offered money to mine the ore. A surveyor laying out the townsite named it in honor of the Jerome family, though Eugene Jerome never visited the area. From the time the United Verde Copper Company began operating in 1882, the town's economy went on a wild roller coaster ride dependent on copper prices. Mines closed for brief periods, then rebounded. So many saloons, gambling

William A. Clark (1839-1925), owner of United Verde Mine in Jerome and founder of Clarkdale.

Dr. James "Rawhide Jimmy" Douglas, Jr.; he purchased the Little Daisy Mine in 1912 then built the mansion now used as Jerome State Historic Park.

dens, and brothels thrived in Jerome that a New York newspaper called it the "wickedest town in the West." Fires roared through the frame houses and businesses 3 times between 1897 and 1899, yet Jerome rose to be Arizona's 5th largest city. Floods and underground blasting shook the earth so much that buildings keeled over; the town's famous sliding jail took off across the street and down the hillside, where it can be seen today. Banks refused to take the average Jerome house or business as collateral. The community experienced its greatest prosperity during the roaring twenties, when Jerome's population hit 15,000. The stock market crash and ensuing depression spelled disaster for the copper industry; mines and smelter shut down and the population plummeted to less than 5,000. World War II brought Jerome's last period of prosperity before the mines shut down for good in 1953. Many people thought Jerome would become a ghost town when the population shrank to only 50 souls. But beginning in the late 1960s, ar-

tists, shop owners, tourists, retirees, and others rediscovered Jerome's unique character and setting.

## SIGHTS

**Jerome State Historic Park:** The Douglas Mansion, built in 1917 by James "Rawhide Jimmy" Douglas, sits on a hill overlooking the Little Daisy Mine. Today, the old mansion abounds with Jerome's mining lore. Outside you can see a giant stamp mill and the more primitive *arrastre* and Chilean wheels once used to pulverize ore. Signs at viewpoints identify some of Jerome's historic buildings. Indoors, a video presentation illustrates the many changes Jerome has seen. An assay office, the Douglas library, old photos, mining tools, smelter models, and mineral displays show different aspects of the effort expended to gain metals from the earth. Upstairs, a neat 3-dimensional model shows Jerome's mine

*underground in the United Verde Mine, Jerome, 1940s*

*underground in the United Verde Mine, Jerome, 1940s*

interior of the power room of the United Verde Mine, 1911

shafts, underground work areas, and geologic features. Jerome State Historic Park is open daily 0800-1700; $1 adult, children under 18 free; tel. 634-5381. A small picnic area beside the mansion has expansive views of the Verde Valley. Turn off US 89A at Milepost 345 at the lower end of Jerome (8 miles W of Cottonwood), then follow the narrow paved road one mile.

**Jerome Historical Society Mine Museum:** Look for the 2 large half-wheels at the corner of Main St. (US 89A) and Jerome Avenue. Paintings, photos, stock certificates, mining tools, and ore samples illustrate Jerome's development. Open daily 0830-1630; $.50 adult, children under 12 free.

**Gold King Mine Museum:** If you're fascinated by old machinery, or if you've ever wanted to poke around a ghost town site, this collection just might satisfy your curiosity. Among the hoists, pumps, engines, and ore cars, look for a short mine shaft replica, which may be entered, and an assay office complete with a stuffed miner. A small petting zoo at-

tracts the kids. The museum has some nice touches like doors that read "mens," "womens," and "others"; or the outdoor bathtub with a sign "baths 5 cents." Enter through the gift shop, which sells mining memorabilia and other souvenirs. Open daily 1000-1700; $2 adult, $1 children 6-17; may close in winter. Overnight camping here costs $5/vehicle; showers but no hookups. From the upper switchback on US 89A in Jerome, turn NW one mile on the Perkinsville Rd.; on the way you'll pass a large open-pit mine on the L, where Jerome's smelter was located at the turn of the century.

## PRACTICALITIES

**accommodations:** Modern motels have yet to hit town; if that's what you're looking for, stay in Cottonwood, 8 miles below. Jerome does offer 2 hotels, very old-fashioned by today's standards, but well kept. Reservations should be made for weekends. The Connor Hotel at 168 Main St. has rooms ranging from $22 s or d (bath down the hall) to $49 s or d (larger room with shower); light sleepers should choose rooms away from the downstairs bar; tel. 634-5792. The Miner's Roost Hotel, 311 Main St., features Victorian-style rooms, some with private bath, at $54.75 s or d including breakfast; tel. 634-5094. Nancy Russell's Bed and Breakfast is in an old miner's house, $40 s, $45 d; Box 791, Jerome, AZ 86331; tel. 634-3270.

camping: Gold King Mine has the only close-in campground; sites have little grass or trees, but where else can you camp on historic mine tailings? The $5/vehicle charge includes use of showers (no hookups); from the upper switch-back on US 89A in Jerome, turn NW one mile on the Perkinsville Road. In winter, Dead Horse Ranch State Park and RV parks in Cottonwood would be more comfortable places to camp. Come summer, the coolest spots are the 2 Forest Service campgrounds on Mingus Mountain. Neither has drinking water or fee; season runs about early May to early Nov.:

Potato Patch is 7½ miles SW on US 89A (on the R near Milepost 337); Mingus Mountain Campground is 8 miles SW on US 89A, then L 3 miles on Forest Route 104.

food and entertainment: The House of Joy certainly has a reputation. In the old days, its painted ladies operated a lively business in the house. Present owners have kept the red lights and other brothel decor while offering excellent continental cuisine at moderate prices. This popular dining spot is open only for dinner on Sat. and Sun.; make reservations well in advance by calling after 0900 on Sat. or Sun.; tel. 634-5339. House of Joy is on the R on Hull St., just after the beginning of the uphill one-way section of US 89A. Macy's European Coffeehouse and Bakery serves sandwiches, baked goodies, fancy coffees, and other refreshments; open daily in morning and afternoon at 416 Main St. at Hull Ave.; tel. 634-2733 (this Macy's is an offshoot of the one in Flagstaff). Betty's Ore House, 309 Main St., offers sand-

*the blast furnace of Jerome's first smelter, 1880s*

*Jerome's sliding jail*

wiches and other fare; open daily. The adjacent Miner's Roost dining room features steak, barbequed ribs, seafood, and chicken; open only for dinner on Fri. and Sat.; tel. 634-5094. Maude's Downstairs Cafe (closed Tue. and Wed.), 115 Jerome Ave., prepares home-made breakfasts, lunches, and baked goods. English Kitchen, 119 Jerome Ave., is an old-style cafe serving breakfast, lunch, and dinner; open daily. For entertainment, locals hang out in the Spirit Room of the Connor Hotel and at Paul & Jerry's Saloon, both on upper Main Street.

**events:** The Jerome Home Tour visits historic houses and buildings not normally open to the public (3rd weekend of May). Jerome Arts and Crafts Festival takes place over the 4th of July weekend. Local people display their heirlooms and explain the history behind them during the Jerome Theme and Memorabilia Show in August. Out-of-town dealers stage the Antique Show and Sale on Labor Day weekend.

**shopping, services, and information:** Shops up and down Main St. display a wide variety of art work, crafts, antiques, jewelry, and clothing. Post Office is at 134 Main Street. Obtain free maps and brochures at the Chamber of Commerce in the Arizona Discoveries shop, 317 Main St.; tel. 634-5716. Jerome Public Library at 109 Jerome Ave. is open only a few days a week. Verde Valley Transit has a bus service between Jerome and Cottonwood several times daily except Sun.; tel. 634-6462 or 634-8963.

# PRESCOTT

That's "Prescutt," pardner. Unlike most Western towns that boomed haphazardly into existence, Prescott was carefully laid out to plan. The mile-high town rests in a mountain basin ringed by the pine-forested Bradshaws, towering Thumb Butte, jumbled mass of Granite Mountain, boulder-strewn Granite Dells, and vast grasslands of Chino and Lonesome Valleys. Downtown, the Doric-columned courthouse sits in a spacious grassy plaza surrounded by tall elm trees. The equestrian statue in front commemorates the spirit of William "Bucky" O'Neill, a former newspaperman, sheriff, mayor, adventurer, and Spanish-American War hero. He led a company of Theodore Roosevelt's Rough Riders to Cuba, where an enemy bullet cut him down. The Palace Bar, on Montezuma St. opposite the courthouse, carries on the tradition of "Whiskey Row," where more than 20 saloons went full-blast day and night at the turn of the century. The Sharlot Hall Museum, 2 blocks W, preserves Prescott's past with early buildings and excellent historic collections. On the other side of town, the Smoki (SMOKE-eye) Museum has a wealth of artifacts from American Indian cultures. About 100 Yavapai Indians live in the Prescott area, mostly on their 1,400-acre reservation just N of town. Though Prescott is small (pop. 25,000), it has several art galleries, an active artists' community, 2 colleges, and an aeronautical university. Just outside town you'll discover the area's beautiful forests, fishing lakes, mountains, and remote ghost towns.

**history:** Soon after Congress carved the Territory of Arizona from New Mexico in 1863, Governor John Goodwin and a party of appointed officials set off from Washington. Their arduous 3-month journey took them to the rich mineral districts in central Arizona, a promising new land that was relatively free from Confederate sympathizers, who lived mostly in the southern towns of Tucson and Tubac. The party first set up a temporary capital at Fort Whipple in Chino Valley. Then, to be closer to mining activities and timbered

land, both the government and fort moved 17 miles S to a site along Granite Creek. Fort Whipple then served as a center for campaigns against hostile Tonto Apache and Yavapai Indians during the 1860s and 1870s. Sentries had to be constantly alert against Indian attacks as workmen felled trees to build the Capitol and Governor's Mansion. Early citizens named their settlement after William Hickling Prescott, an historian noted for his writings about Mexico. Unlike towns to the S that had adobe buildings and a strong Spanish-Mexican flavor, Prescott took its character from settlers of New England and the Midwest. Plentiful forests provided timber for log cabins and later frame buildings.

In 1867 the legislature had a change of heart and moved down to Tucson. Prescott's future looked bleak, as Apache attacks and high transportation costs threatened further mining or agricultural development. Then improved mining techniques and new gold strikes in the 1870s brought the region back to life. The legislature even returned in 1877 before going to Phoenix for good in 1889. By then Prescott had become a thriving city and no longer needed the politicians' business. Mining, ranching, and trade prospered. Even a disastrous fire in 1900, which wiped out Prescott's entire business district including Whiskey Row, couldn't destroy community spirit. Undaunted, the saloon keepers moved their salvaged stock across the street and continued serving libations as the fires blazed. Within days townsfolk began rebuilding, creating the downtown you see today. Agriculture and a bit of mining continue in the Prescott area, but it's the ambience of the place that draws most people. Part of its charm lies in the many historic buildings lining Prescott's tree-shaded streets, the clean pine-scented air, and agreeable 4-season climate.

## SIGHTS

**Sharlot Hall Museum:** Not one, but a dozen buildings make up this excellent historical museum. Start anywhere you like. Open Tue.

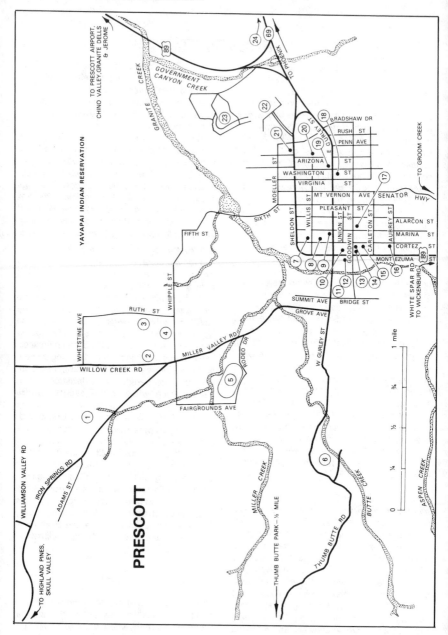

to Sat. 0900-1700, Sun. 1300-1700, closed Mon. (unless a national holiday). All exhibits have free admission (donations accepted). The complex is at 415 W. Gurley St., 2 blocks W from the Plaza. Offices, research library, conservation laboratory, and rotating exhibits are in the modern solar-heated Museum Center; tel. 445-3122. Sharlot Hall founded the museum in 1928 by displaying her own collection in the Governor's Mansion. Herself a pioneer, she arrived in Arizona in 1882 by wagon train at the age of 12. She developed an interest in the land and people of Arizona and then shared her thoughts in writings and poems. From 1909 to 1911 she was the territory's first historian, traveling Arizona's primitive roads to collect information and stories first hand.

The 2-story Governor's Mansion, built from logs on this site in 1864, looks too primitive for a "mansion" by our standards, but in those days most people lived in tents or lean-tos. Governor John Goodwin and Territorial Secretary Richard McCormick occupied opposite ends. The territorial legislature met here for their first session while waiting for the capitol to be finished. One room pays tribute to Sharlot Hall by displaying many of her personal belongings. The rest of the mansion has been restored and furnished as it was during the early years.

Sharlot Hall Building (built 1934) houses most of the Indian and pioneer displays. Well-done exhibits show military life at Fort Whipple, ranching, saloons, stores, recreation, and Prescott heros. An Indian room displays many fine examples of Indian pottery, basketry, jewelry, and other crafts from both prehistoric and modern tribes of the Southwest.

The Fremont House was built in 1875 and moved to this site in 1972. It contains furnishings typical of a well-to-do family in the late 1870s. John Fremont, Arizona's 5th territorial governor, rented the house from 1878 to 1881. He had earned fame as an explorer of the West during the 1840s, but failed miserably in Arizona politics. Fremont didn't care for Prescott's climate and spent long periods back East or in Tucson. Public pressure forced his resignation after 3 years in office. The Bashford House (built in 1877 and moved here in 1974) contains a gift shop. Books on Arizona history, Papago Indian baskets, other crafts, and souvenirs can be purchased. William Bashford purchased the house and remodeled it during the 1880s in an ornate late-Victorian style.

The museum complex also includes smaller buildings. The Ranch House is a little log cabin with branding irons, saddles, harnesses, and other cowboy gear. Fort Misery, one of Prescott's earliest buildings, dates from 1864 when it was a general store. Later Judge John Howard took it over and dispensed "misery" to lawbreakers; the cabin appears as when he lived in it. The School House is a replica of the territory's first public school, built near Granite Creek in 1864. A blacksmith shop sees use in restoration projects, such as the museum's

---

## PRESCOTT

1. Ponderosa Plaza Shopping Center
2. Yavapai Regional Medical Center
3. Prescott High School
4. Y.M.C.A.
5. Yavapai County Fairgrounds
6. Plaza Shopping Center
7. Murphy's Restaurant
8. Head Hotel
9. Hassayampa Inn
10. courthouse and plaza
11. Sharlot Hall Museum
12. Whiskey Row; Bead Museum
13. Chamber of Commerce
14. post office
15. Hotel Vendome
16. U.S. Forest Service
    (Supervisor's Office)
17. public library
18. Arizona Central Lines
19. Ken Lindley Field
20. Smoki Museum
21. Greyhound Bus
22. Yavapai Community College
23. Fort Whipple (now a V.A. Hospital)
24. U.S. Forest Service
    (Bradshaw Mt. District)

1887 Porter locomotive. Each of the more than 350 flowers in the rose garden commemorates an outstanding Arizona woman.

**Smoki Museum:** From a split-twig figure 3,000-4,000 years old to baskets and pottery of modern tribes, this collection preserves a wide variety of Southwest Indian artifacts. A kiva floorplan duplicates one at Oraibi on the Hopi reservation. A Zuni Shalako (spirit of the rain clouds) towers 10 feet high. Some of the pottery and stone tools come from prehistoric pithouses excavated in nearby Chino Valley. Open 1000-1630 daily except Mon. from 1 June to 1 Sept.; other times groups can visit by appointment (see Chamber of Commerce; tel. 445-2000). Admission is $1 adult, children under 12 free. The pueblo-style museum building is at 100 N. Arizona St., one block N off E. Gurley Street.

The Smoki "tribe" was organized in 1921 by white members of the community. Their original purpose was to entertain visitors with Indian dances at the annual Frontier Days celebration. Later the group took a more serious interest in collecting rituals, dances, and artifacts. Members of the semi-secret organization can be identified by a 4-dot tattoo on the side of their left hands. The Smoki have come under heavy fire from Hopi and other Indian tribes who find the dances offensive and who object to "secret" religious items in the museum. But the Smoki continue their spectacular annual performance, which always includes the Smoki Snake Dance with live bull snakes. The Smoki ceremonials take place on the first or second Sat. evening in August.

**The Bead Museum:** A *bead* museum? Yes, this collection contains beads and personal adornments from the far corners of the world and from many ages. Open 0900-1700 Mon. to Sat.; free. Beads are also for sale. The Bead Museum is in Liese Artifacts and Worldly Goods on Whiskey Row, 140 S. Montezuma St.; tel. 445-2431.

**Phippen Museum of Western Art:** Paintings, sketches, and bronzes by outstanding artists celebrate Western heritage and art. Promising new artists receive attention too. The museum honors George Phippen, a well-known Western artist who founded Cowboy Artists of America and was their first president. A gift shop sells cards, jewelry, crafts, and artworks. Open in summer (15 May to 15 Sept.) Mon. and Wed. to Sat. 1000-1700, Sun. 1300-1700; open the rest of the year daily except Tue. 1300-1600; $2 adult, $1 children and students; tel. 778-1385. The museum is in a ranch-style building 6 miles N of Prescott on US 89 (one mile N of the US 89A turnoff).

**Fort Whipple:** This historic Army fort dates from 1863. It honors Brig. General Amiel Weeks Whipple, who served with the Army's Corps of Topographical Engineers until he was killed in the Civil War. The post played a major role during the Indian Wars and was maintained until 1912. Ten years later it became a Veterans Administration hospital. Many of the former barracks, officers quarters, and other military buildings dating from the turn of the century remain. You're welcome to visit the hospital grounds, though there's no museum or Visitor Center. Fort Whipple is on the NE edge of town off US 89.

# ACCOMMODATIONS

Prescott has a good selection of places to stay. Try to have a reservation for weekends during the warmer months, as lots of desert refugees come up then. Rates often drop a bit in winter (summer rates shown below). Book way in advance for Frontier Days, held around July 4th, and expect to pay more.

**historic:** Prescott's old hotels, dating from the early 1900s, offer a real experience. The Hassayampa Inn stood as the town's grand hotel in 1927 and still does today, thanks to a recent renovation. The plush lobby has a painted ceiling, old piano, and other antiques. All rooms now have private baths and a/c; rates start at $34 s, $40 d. The hotel's Peacock Room offers elegant dining. Located at 122 E. Gurley St.; tel. 778-9434 (or Phoenix tel. 257-8884). Hotel Vendome (built 1917) also offers attractively restored rooms with private baths, $47.70 s ($58.30 Fri. & Sat.), $74.20 d ($84.80 Fri. & Sat.); 230 S. Cortez St.; tel. 776-0900. The

Head Hotel (built 1898-1903) has been restored on a more modest scale; rooms, some with private bath, cost $26.13 s, $31.36 d; weekly rates run $69.42 s or d without bath, or $83.10 s or d with bath; 129 N. Cortez St.; tel. 778-1776. Highland Hotel (built 1903) used to be a brothel where the girls scouted potential customers from the bay windows. The hotel has not been much restored, but then neither have the prices; rooms (bath down hall) cost $13.25 s, $17 d; weekly rates are $56 s, $69 d; located on Whiskey Row at 154 S. Montezuma St.; tel. 445-9059. Prescott also has the historic Hotel St. Michael at the corner of Montezuma and Gurley Sts., but it was closed at this writing.

**bed and breakfast:** Prescott Pines Bed and Breakfast has rooms starting at $47.70 s or d on the S edge of town, 901 S. White Spar Rd. (S. US 89); tel. 445-7270. Other B&Bs are listed with Bed and Breakfast of Arizona (4533 N. Scottsdale Rd., Suite 108, Scottsdale, AZ 85251; tel. 995-2831) and Mi Casa Su Casa (Box 950, Tempe, AZ 85281; tel. 990-0682).

**motels:** Motels in Prescott (with basic summer rates) include: Wheel Inn Motel ($27.56 s, $29.68 d; close to downtown at 333 S. Montezuma St.; tel. 778-7346); Sierra Motel ($27.56 s, $35 d; 809 White Spar Rd.; tel. 445-1250); Comfort Inn ($35 s, $41.34 d; 1290 White Spar Rd.; tel. 778-5770); Motel 6 ($19 s, $23.27 d; 1111 E. Sheldon St.; tel. 778-0200); Apache Lodge Motel ($34 s, $40.28 d; 1130 E. Gurley St.; tel. 445-1422); Colony Inn ($31.80 s, $40.28 d; 1225 E. Gurley St.; tel. 445-7057); and Best Western Prescottonian Motel ($42.40 s, $50.88 d; 1317 E. Gurley St.; tel. 445-3096). Airport Centre Inn is near the airport and Antelope Hills golf course at the corner of US 89 and Willow Creek Rd.; $37.10 s, $42.40 d; tel. 778-6000.

**camping:** White Spar Campground, 2½ miles S of downtown on US 89, has drinking water from mid-May to end of Sept. but no showers or hookups; $5; some sites stay open in winter (no water or fee). Indian Creek Campground is 4 miles S on US 89, then L ½ mile on Forest

*Granite Basin Lake*

Route 97; open mid-May to end of Sept. (no water or fee). Lynx Lake and nearby Hilltop Campgrounds sit above a pretty lake containing trout and catfish. These 2 campsites are open early Apr. to mid-Nov.; drinking water but no showers or hookups, $6; picnickers may use tables near the boat ramp free of charge. To reach Lynx Lake, head E 3 miles on AZ 69 (from N. US 89), then turn S 2½ miles on Walker Rd.; Hilltop campground is one mile farther. A cafe, store, and boat rentals are at the N end of Lynx Lake. Granite Basin campground lies near a small lake at the base of Granite Mountain, NW of town; open all year but no drinking water or charge; from W. Gurley St., turn NW 4 miles on Grove Ave./Miller Valley Rd./Iron Springs Rd., then turn N 3½ miles on Forest Route 374. Lower Wolf Creek Campground (S of town) tends to be less crowded on busy summer weekends than other Prescott camping areas; open mid-May to mid-Nov.; no drinking water or fee; take Senator Hwy. (Forest Route 52) S 7½ miles, then turn W one mile on Forest Route 97. Watson Lake Park, beside Granite Dells, is open all year and has showers; $6.36 tents, $8.48 RV w/hookups, no charge for day use; tel. 778-4338; head 4 miles N of town on US 89. Point of Rocks RV Camp (just N of Watson Lake Park) is open all year with RV sites at $10.48 w/hookups (no tents); tel. 445-9018. Willow Lake Camping Resort features a swimming pool, fishing, store, and showers; $8.40 tents, $11 RV w/hookups; tel. 445-6311; located 5 miles N of town off Willow Springs Road. Powell Springs campground, near the village of Cherry between I-17 and Prescott, stays open all year and has spring water (no charge); from the turnoff on AZ 169 (5 miles W of I-17 and 25 miles E of Prescott) turn N 4 miles on Forest Route 372.

# FOOD

**American and Continental cuisine:** Murphy's serves sandwiches, steak, prime rib, seafood, and other dishes in an old mercantile building dating from 1890; dim lighting, antiques, and greenery add to the romantic setting; open daily for lunch and dinner (mod. prices) at 201 N. Cortez St.; tel. 445-4044. The Peacock Room of the Hassayampa Inn has an old-fashioned atmosphere for its varied menu of American and Continental specialties; open for Sun. brunch and daily for breakfast, lunch, and dinner (mod.); 122 E. Gurley St.; tel. 778-0780. The Bronze Saddle, part of Sunset Hills Restaurant, offers steak, prime rib, seafood and other fare; open daily for dinner (mod.); 1109 E. Gurley St.; tel. 445-2031. Prescott Mining Company features steak, prime rib, seafood, chicken, and veal in a rustic atmosphere; open daily for dinner, Mon. to Sat. for lunch, and Sun. for brunch (inexp. to mod.); 155 Plaza Dr. (behind Plaza Shopping Center); tel. 445-1991. The Pine Cone Inn's menu lists steaks, seafood, and other American cuisine; open daily for lunch and dinner (mod.); live dinner music is featured many nights; 1245 White Spar Rd.; tel. 445-2970. Mario's serves Italian dinners, pizza, and sandwiches; open daily for lunch and dinner (inexp.); 107 S. Cortez St.; tel. 445-1122. Roman Deli Italian Restaurant features pasta dishes, veal, and seafood; open daily except Sun. for lunch and dinner (inexp. to mod.); 623 Miller Valley Rd.; tel. 778-0740.

**inexpensive American:** Family Affair Cafeteria is open on weekdays for breakfast, lunch, and dinner, Sun. for breakfast and lunch; 128 N. Cortez St.; tel. 445-8270. Greens & Things offers omelettes, Belgian waffles, bagels, sandwiches, and fruit drinks; open daily except Sun. for breakfast and lunch; 106 W. Gurley St.; tel. 445-3234. Berry's Pie Pantry & Restaurant, in an old Victorian house, has mostly American food; open daily for breakfast, lunch and dinner; 111 Grove Ave. (just off Gurley St.); tel. 778-3038. K-Bob's Steak House cooks up mesquite-broiled steaks, fried chicken, kabobs, and sandwiches; open daily for lunch and dinner (inexp. to mod.); 1355 Iron Springs Rd.; tel. 778-0866. C.J.'s Eggcetera specializes in breakfasts and lunches; 434 W. Goodwin St.; tel. 778-5749. In the Dog House, you can get 11 different kinds of hot dogs (other sandwiches too); open daily except Sun. for lunch; 126 S. Montezuma St.; tel. 445-7962. One of Prescott's many American cafes, the Prospector's Skillet stays open 24 hours, 1301 E. Gurley St. (N. US 89).

**other cuisines:** El Charro, an inexpensive Mexican cafe, is open Mon. to Sat. for lunch and dinner; 120 N. Montezuma St.; tel. 445-7130. Dine Chinese at the Canton Cafe; open daily for lunch and dinner (inexp. to mod.); 1102 Willow Creek Rd.; tel. 445-0070. The China Jade Restaurant specializes in Mandarin-style cuisine; open Sun. for dinner, Mon. to Sat. for lunch and dinner (inexp. to mod.); 1459 W. Gurley St. (Plaza Shopping Center); tel. 445-4072.

Lighting and Christmas Parade.

## OTHER PRACTICALITIES

**entertainment:** There's something happening many summer nights on the Plaza—could be a concert, dance, or speech. Catch movies at the Marina Theatres (205 N. Marina and Willis Sts.; tel. 445-1010) or Plaza West Cinemas (Fry's Shopping Center at 1509 W. Gurley St.; tel. 778-0207). The bars along Whiskey Row (Montezuma St.) sometimes have live bands. The Pine Cone Inn (1245 White Spar Rd.; tel. 445-2970) offers more sedate live dinner music (usually from the '40s). Softball fans have a good chance of seeing a game in season—Prescott bills itself the "Softball Capital of the World." Local newspapers *The Prescott Sun* and *The Prescott Courier* list what's going on in town.

**events:** Prescott's major annual events include: **May:** Zonta Home Tour (visits to about 5 outstanding Prescott homes, both historic and modern). Prescott Downs thoroughbred and quarter horse race season begins (held at the county fairgrounds most weekends and holidays from Memorial Day to Labor Day). George Phippen Memorial Western Art Show & Sale. Whiskey Row Marathon. **June:** Sharlot Hall Folk Art Fair celebrates pioneer skills: costumed participants demonstrate blacksmithing, horseshoeing, woodworking, spinning, weaving, churning, cowboy cooking, and other crafts. On the same weekend, Territorial Prescott Days features games, art shows, music, and dancing. Square Dance Festival. **July:** Frontier Days Rodeo and Parade (over 4th of July holiday) draw spectators from all over Arizona and beyond for the "world's oldest rodeo" (since 1888), Western art show, entertainment, dances, and fireworks. Bluegrass Festival. **August:** Antique Auto Show. Soroptimist Antique Show. Smoki Ceremonials (recreated Indian dances by white men). Mountain Artists Arts & Craft Show. **September:** Yavapai County Fair and Horse Show. **December:** Courthouse Christmas

**services:** The post office is at the corner of Goodwin and Cortez Sts., across from the Plaza. Yavapai Regional Medical Center provides hospital services at 1003 Willow Creek Rd.; tel. 445-2700. Go swimming at the YMCA outdoor pool in summer, 750 Whipple St.; tel. 445-7221. Or swim year-round at the indoor Yavapai College pool (turn N onto the campus from 1100 E. Sheldon St.; the swimming pool is in the first building on the L); tel. 445-7300 ext. 257. Play tennis at Yavapai College, Prescott High School (on Ruth St.), or next to Ken Lindley Field (E. Gurley St. at Arizona St.). Granite Mountain Stables offers trail rides, cookouts, and haywagon rides year-round; rates run from $8 (one hour) to $35 (all day); located off Williamson Valley Rd. (go NW on Grove Ave./Miller Valley Rd./Iron Springs Rd. to Williamson Rd., then turn R 5 miles to the sign); tel. 778-6092. Play golf on 18-hole courses either at Antelope Hills (next to the airport, 7 miles N of town on US 89; tel. 445-0583) or at Prescott Country Club (14 miles E on AZ 69; tel. 772-8984).

**information:** The Chamber of Commerce will help you find what you're looking for and tell you about upcoming events. Open Mon. to Fri. 0900-1700; tel. 445-2000 (or tel. 253-5988 in Phoenix). At other times call for a telephone recording of local sights and events. Office is at 117 W. Goodwin St. opposite the Plaza (or write Box 1147, Prescott, AZ 86302). The Forest Service has maps and information about hiking, camping, and back roads in their vast lands. The supervisor's office (344 S. Cortez St.; tel. 445-1762) has literature, but you'll get the best first-hand information from rangers at the Bradshaw District office on AZ 69, one mile E of town (or write Holiday Hills Box 3451, Prescott, AZ 86301). Open Mon. to Fri. 0800-1630, also Sat. and Sun. during the summer; tel. 445-7253. Prescott's excellent public library includes a Southwest collection; open daily except Sun. at 215 Goodwin St.; tel.

445-8110. Yavapai College also has a fine library, open daily during school terms; turn N onto the campus from 1100 E. Sheldon St.; tel. 445-7300. The Worm Bookstore stocks topo maps and books about Arizona, 128 S. Montezuma St.; tel. 445-0361. The Book Nook, 324 W. Gurley St., buys and sells used books; tel. 778-2130.

**transport:** Greyhound has one bus daily to Phoenix ($16.45 OW) and Williams ($12.65 OW), with connecting service to the Grand Canyon ($24.40 OW); open weekdays 0900-1630 and Sat. 1200-1600; 820 E. Sheldon St.; tel. 445-5470. Arizona Central Lines offers twice-daily service to Flagstaff ($20 OW) and Phoenix ($20 OW to downtown or airport); make reservations one day ahead; 619 E. Gurley St.; tel. 445-1131. For a taxi, call Ace at tel. 445-5510. Rent cars from Airport Centre (airport; 7 miles N on US 89; tel. 778-6000); Ugly Duckling (620 S. Montezuma; tel. 445-4102; also at the airport; tel. 445-8320); or Thrifty (at Skatetown, 546 1st St.; tel. 445-8444). North-Aire operates 2½-hour scenic flights from the airport to the Grand Canyon; tel. 445-8320. Golden Pacific Airlines flies about 10 times daily to Phoenix ($45 OW), and usually at least once daily to Sedona ($20 OW), Kingman ($39), and Las Vegas ($74); local office is at the airport; tel. 757-3214 or (800) 352-3281.

# VICINITY OF PRESCOTT

**Granite Dells:** With their giant boulders that have weathered into delicately balanced forms and fanciful shapes, the scenic Dells are a good place for a picnic or hike. Rock climbers like to tackle the challenging granite formations. Indians used to hide out here, and some ruins and artifacts have been discovered. From the 1920s to the '50s, Granite Dells Resort attracted crowds of vacationers; a large dance pavillion survives from that era. Watson Lake Park (camping and free day use) lies at the S edge of the Dells, 4 miles N of town on US 89.

**Thumb Butte Trail:** This popular loop hike begins just W of town and climbs Thumb Butte

Saddle (elev. 6,300 feet) for good views of Prescott and the surrounding countryside. The trail winds through a valley of dense ponderosa pines, then crosses windswept ridges where pinyon, juniper, oak, and prickly pear grow. Two short spur trails lead to vista points from which you can see the city, Granite Dells, Chino Valley, and seemingly countless mountains, including the distant San Francisco Peaks. Reaching the fractured granite summit of Thumb Butte takes some effort and skill; this last 200-foot ascent is best left to rock climbers. The trail itself is a moderately easy outing, 1¾ miles RT with an elevation gain of 600 feet; allow 2½ hours. Signs identify many of the plants along the way. Local people like to come up for the sunset. Hiking season lasts from about Apr. to Nov., or whenever trails are not blocked by snow. From downtown, head W 3½ miles on Gurley St./Thumb Butte Rd. to Thumb Butte Park; signposted trailhead is on the L side of the road.

**Granite Mountain:** On a daytrip, hikers can explore the rugged Granite Mountain Wilderness and enjoy fine views from an

*Thumb Butte*

overlook (elev. 7,125 feet). Rock climbers come to challenge the granite cliffs that offer a nearly complete range of difficulties. Five trails allow many hiking combinations, but only Granite Mt. Trail #261 climbs to the heights. This trail ascends gently 1⅓ miles to a trail junction at Blair Pass, then turns R and switchbacks another 1⅓ miles to a saddle on Granite Mt.; from here the trail turns SE and climbs a bit more along the next mile to a viewpoint. Ponderosa pines grow at the trailhead and on top of Granite Mt., though much of the trail passes through manzanita, mountain mahogany, pinyon, agave, and other plants of the chaparral. Average hiking time for the 7½-mile RT hike is 6 hours. It's a moderately difficult trip with an elevation gain of 1,500 feet; carry water. Season lasts from about May to October. The area is covered by the Iron Springs and Jerome Canyon 7½ minute topo maps. From W. Gurley St. in Prescott, turn NW 4 miles on Grove Ave./Miller Valley Rd./Iron Springs Rd., then turn R 5 miles on Forest Route 374 past the campground and lake turnoffs.

**other hikes:** Dozens of trails wind through the rugged Bradshaw and Mingus Mountains near Prescott. See the Forest Service rangers for trail descriptions, maps, and backroad information; their Bradshaw District office is on AZ 69, one mile E of town; tel. 445-7253. Probably the most unusual trail is the 1,200-foot Groom Creek School Nature Trail, built especially for blind people by the Sunrise Lions Club of Prescott. Trail pamphlets (obtain from the Bradshaw office) in both Braille and print explain natural features and processes. You'll find the trail just past the village of Groom Creek, 6 miles S of town on the Senator Highway.

**Crown King and vicinity:** Old mines, ghost towns, and wilderness surround this rustic village 55 miles SE of Prescott. Prospectors discovered gold at the Crowned King Mine in the 1870s, but mine owners had to wait until the late 1880s before the ore could be processed profitably. A branch line of the Prescott and Eastern Railroad reached the site in 1904. Legal battles closed mine operations in the early 1900s, and today the mining camp attracts retired people and serves as an escape from

summer heat. The Crown King Saloon goes way back to 1898, when it was built at Oro Belle camp, 5 miles southwest. Pack mules hauled it piece by piece to Crown King in 1910.

Rough roads discourage the average tourist, but the region can be explored with maps, determination and, preferably, a high-clearance vehicle. Easiest way in is from Cleator on Forest Route 259, which can be reached from the I-17 Bumble Bee or Cordes exits. You'll be following the twisting path of the old railroad on the drive up. Cautiously driven cars can make it OK. Rougher roads approach Crown King from Prescott and Mayer. The Prescott National Forest map, $1 from Forest Service offices, shows backroads and most trails. You can get meals at the saloon or a restaurant, and there's a general store. No motels or RV parks here, but you can camp in the Forest Service campgrounds at Horsethief Basin Recreation Site, 7 miles to the southeast. Usual season for Kentuck Springs and Hazlett Hollow Campgrounds (elev. 6,000 feet) is 1 May to 30 Nov.; both are free. Hazlett Hollow and Turney Gulch (res. group area) have drinking water. Castle Creek Wilderness, E of the campgrounds, has very steep and rocky terrain; vegetation varies from chaparral to ponderosa pine. The staff at Crown King Work Center, up the hill from town, can tell you about trails and roads. They are mostly local people, who know the area well. *Arizona's Best Ghost Towns* by Phillip Varney contains good information on this historic and very scenic part of Arizona.

# ARCOSANTI

The vision of Paolo Soleri, Italian laureate designer, can be seen under construction in the high desert country between Flagstaff and Phoenix. The vision is a joining of architecture and ecology which Soleri has dubbed "arcology." The city, designed to make the best use of energy and land, will grow vertically, using pedestrian walkways and elevators instead of freeways. Arcosanti's strangely shaped buildings make efficient use of the sun's energy. Construction began in 1970, but it progresses slowly as funds come in. When

*craft studios at Arcosanti*

finished, the city will house 3,500 people. The public is welcome to visit this project, the first of its kind, open daily 0900-1700 all year. Tours, lasting about one hour, take visitors through some of the buildings and explain Soleri's goals; $4 adult, under 10 free. The Visitor Center (free admission) has a model of Arcosanti, architectural exhibits, books by Soleri, and crafts. The famous Cosanti bronze and clay windbells make attractive gifts and help finance the project. A cafe and bakery (open daily) serve good breakfasts and lunches. Arcosanti schedules festivals and frequently

hosts concerts. Seminars and workshops allow interested people to participate in construction. For information on seminars, workshops, music classes, and events, write Arcosanti, HC 74, Box 4136, Mayer, AZ 86333; or call tel. 632-7135. Hotel accommodations cost $15 s, $20 d, and $25 d (reservation suggested), or you may park overnight for $3. Arcosanti is easily reached from I-17 (34 miles SE of Prescott and 65 miles N of Phoenix); take Cordes Jct. Exit 262A, then follow signs 2½ miles on a dirt road. A motel, cafes, RV park and gas stations are near the interchange.

# WESTERN ARIZONA

## INTRODUCTION

Few other landlocked states can boast more than 1,000 miles of shoreline. The Colorado River, after its wild run through the Grand Canyon, begins a new life. Tamed by massive dams and irrigation projects, the Colorado now flows placidly toward the Gulf of California. The deep blue waters of the river and the lakes it forms make up Arizona's western boundary, separating the state from California and Nevada. Boaters and fishermen are beginning to discover this watery paradise, whether breezing along on water-skis or seeking a quiet backwater for some fishing. But once you step away from the life-giving waters, you're in desert country, the real desert, where legends have been made by those who lived here — the Indian tribes, hardy prospectors, determined pioneer families, and even a U.S. Army camel corps.

### THE LAND

Numerous small ranges of rocky hills break up the monotonous desert plains of western Arizona, much of which lies at elevations under 2,000 feet. The valley of the Colorado River, where most of western Arizona's population lives, drops from about 1,220 feet when leaving the Grand Canyon to just 70 feet at the Mexican border. A few mountain ranges in the N rise high enough to support forests of manzanita, oak, pinyon and ponderosa pine, and even some fir and aspen. Highest and most notable of these "biological islands" are the Hualapai Mountains, easily reached by road from Kingman. Hualapai Peak (8,417 feet) crowns the range. Old mines and ghost towns dot the mineral-rich Cerbat and Black Mountains, also in the north. The Kofa and Castle Dome Mountains in the S make up the Kofa National Wildlife Refuge, a home for desert bighorn sheep, mule deer, desert tortoise, Gambel's quail, rare native palm trees, and other life. Along the Colorado River, 3 other national wildlife refuges, Havasu, Cibola, and Imperial, protect migratory and native birds, plants, and animals.

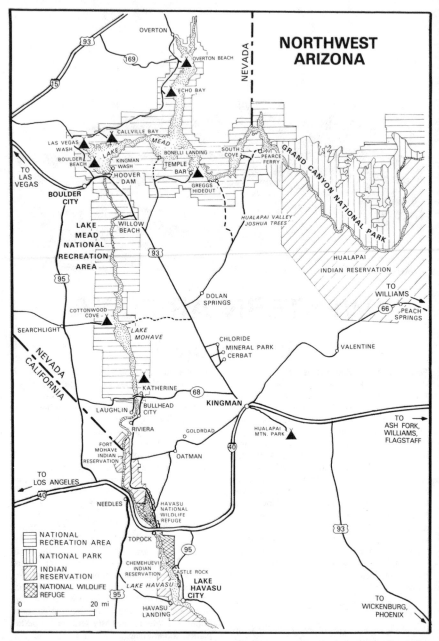

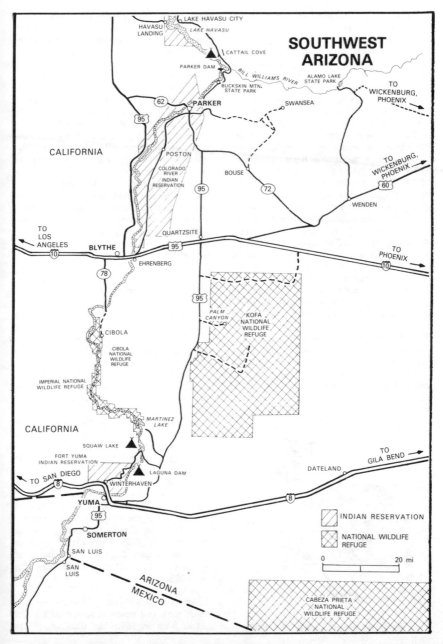

## SOUTHWEST ARIZONA

LAKE HAVASU CITY
HAVASU LANDING
*LAKE HAVASU*
CATTAIL COVE
PARKER DAM
*BILL WILLIAMS RIVER*
ALAMO LAKE STATE PARK
TO WICKENBURG, PHOENIX
BUCKSKIN MTN. STATE PARK
(62)
(95)
**PARKER**
SWANSEA

CALIFORNIA

POSTON
COLORADO RIVER INDIAN RESERVATION
BOUSE
(95)
(72)
TO WICKENBURG, PHOENIX
(60)
WENDEN

TO LOS ANGELES
(10)
**BLYTHE**
QUARTZSITE
(95)
TO PHOENIX
(10)

(78)
EHRENBERG

CIBOLA
CIBOLA NATIONAL WILDLIFE REFUGE

(95)
*PALM CANYON*
KOFA NATIONAL WILDLIFE REFUGE

IMPERIAL NATIONAL WILDLIFE REFUGE

*MARTINEZ LAKE*

CALIFORNIA

SQUAW LAKE
FORT YUMA INDIAN RESERVATION
TO SAN DIEGO
(8)
WINTERHAVEN
LAGUNA DAM

TO GILA BEND
DATELAND
(8)

**YUMA**
(95)

**SOMERTON**

SAN LUIS
SAN LUIS

INDIAN RESERVATION

NATIONAL WILDLIFE REFUGE

0        20 mi

ARIZONA
MEXICO

CABEZA PRIETA NATIONAL WILDLIFE REFUGE

**climate:** The sun shines down from the azure skies nearly every day; few places in the United States receive more sunshine than western Arizona. In winter, thousands of "snowbirds" descend on the desert from northern climes to enjoy the sun and fresh air. Winter nights can be frosty, but daytime temperatures usually warm to the 60s or 70s F. Spring and fall often have perfect weather—wildflowers too, in the early spring. By May the snowbirds are gone —Arizona towns along the Colorado River often make the news as the hottest spot in the country, where midsummer highs can exceed 120 F. Parker holds the record for Arizona of 127 F on one day in 1905. Yet despite average highs that exceed 100 F from June to Sept., many visitors do come in summer to play in the water, cooling off by boating, water-skiing, swimming, and tubing. So western Arizona actually has 2 seasons: a winter which attracts many retirees and others who enjoy fishing, exploring ghost towns, prospecting, and hikes in the desert, and a summer season of more active water sports. Annual rainfall varies from about 10 inches in the higher country to less than 3 inches in the S near Yuma.

**flora and fauna:** For most of the year, plant and animal life in the desert appears very sparse. Actually it's there—a great variety of plants, reptiles, amphibians, mammals, and birds—but awaiting the right conditions to come out. With good winter or summer rains, dormant seeds will spring to life, quickly bloom

*desert kangaroo rat* (Dipodomys deserti)

and produce new seeds; seemingly "dead sticks" sprout leaves and flowers. Cactus and other succulents rapidly absorb precious rain for the long dry spells ahead. Most animals, large and small, hide out during the daytime in caves, burrows, or bushes. The small pocket mice and kangaroo rats do not even require drinking water; they feed mainly on seeds and manufacture their own water! Larger animals include western spotted skunk, kit and gray fox, badger, ringtail, bobcat, mountain lion, mule deer, and desert bighorn sheep. Your best chance of seeing desert critters is in early morning and late afternoon; binoculars come in handy. Birds flock to the wetlands along the Colorado River in great numbers, especially in spring and fall. Canadian geese and many species of ducks winter here. Nesters include the great blue heron, great egret, green heron, least bittern, white-winged dove, and Yuma clapper rail.

## HISTORY

**native Americans:** Indians lived along the Colorado River's shores long before the first white men arrived. Frequent wars between the tribes, lasting into the mid-19th C., forced the Maricopa Indians to migrate up the Gila River to what is now southcentral Arizona. The victorious Mohave, Quechan, and Cocopa tribes still live along the lower Colorado, and were joined in the early 1800s by a nomadic Paiute group, the Chemehuevi. All the lower Colorado tribes followed a simple life of living in brush-and-mud shelters, farming, hunting, and gathering wild plant foods from the desert. Surprisingly, some Hopi and Navajo from NE Arizona also live on the Colorado River Reservation (established in 1865), in addition to Mohave and Chemehuevi. This voluntary resettlement of the Hopi and Navajo began in 1945, made possible by the original intent of the Colorado River Reservation to serve "Indians of said river and its tributaries" and by permission of the Colorado River Tribal Council.

**Spanish explorations:** Spanish explorers made their first tentative forays up the Colorado River in 1540, but didn't stay. The

*Mohave Indian chief, 1800s*

tireless Jesuit priest Eusebio Francisco Kino explored the lower Colorado in 1700-1702, collecting information for the mapmakers of the day. During the 1760s, fear of Russian expansion down the coast of California caused the Spanish to build coastal settlements there, and open a land route from Mexico. In 1780, Spanish troops and missionaries built 2 missions on the Colorado River, La Purisima Conception (opposite where Yuma is today) and nearby San Pedro y San Pablo de Bicuner. Abuses by the foreigners infuriated the local Quechan Indians, who revolted the following year. Father Francisco Garces and most of the male Spaniards were killed, while women and children were taken captive. Spanish troops ransomed the captives but made no more attempts to settle along the Colorado River.

**Americans arrive:** Rugged mountain men like James Ohio Pattie, who later wrote an account of his travels (see "Booklist"), explored the Colorado River area in search of beaver skins and adventure during the early 1800s. Camp Yuma (later Fort Yuma) was established in 1851 at the river crossing of the Southern Overland Trail (Cooke's Road) to assist Americans headed W for California goldfields. Ten years later, troops built Fort Mohave upstream on the Colorado River to protect travelers taking the Beale Wagon Road across northern Arizona. Government surveyors explored much of the lower Colorado during the 1850s, but maps still showed the NW corner of the territory as "unexplored." It wasn't until 1869 that John Wesley Powell filled the last big gap on his epic boat voyage down the Colorado from Green River, Wyoming, to Callville, Nevada (now under Lake Mead).

Although Spanish miners had worked gold deposits in western Arizona before Mexican independence in 1821, large-scale mining in the region didn't begin until the 1860s. Gold discovered in 1858 at Gila City, 20 miles upstream from Yuma, had attracted 1,200 miners by 1861. Yet 3 years later the gold played out; a traveler reported that "the promising Metropolis of Arizona consisted of 3 chimneys and a coyote." Prospectors later found many other gold and silver deposits up and down western Arizona, hastening development of the region. Lead-zinc and copper mines opened too. Most of the old workings lie abandoned now, marked by piles of tailings, foundations, and decaying walls.

Steamboats plied the Colorado River after 1852, providing faster and safer transport than wagon trains. For more than 50 years they served the forts and mining camps along the shores. Some of the giant riverboats stood 3

*dry-crushing mill at Goldroad, 1903*

decks high and were 140 feet long, yet drew only 2 feet of water. These giant sternwheelers took on their cargos from ocean ships at Port Isabel on the Gulf of California, then headed upstream as far as 600 miles. Boat traffic declined when the Southern Pacific Railroad went through Yuma in 1877, then virtually ended in 1909 when the Laguna Dam was built.

Farmers in southern California had been eyeing Colorado River water, and began diverting it in 1901 to their fields around the Salton Sink. Four years later, however, a flood destroyed controlling gates and the entire Colorado River roared down the canal, flooding the Imperial Valley. Frantic rockfilling by the railroad finally returned the river to its normal seaward course in 1907, but left a new body of water behind —the 35-mile-long Salton Sea. More canals and dams have been built on the Colorado since, until today it is one of the most useful and used rivers in the world.

## INDIAN TRIBES

Six tribes now live along the lower Colorado between the W end of the Grand Canyon and the Gulf of California. The 3 Yuman-speaking tribes, Mohave, Quechan, and Cocopa, have been here since prehistoric times. Later they were joined by Uto-Aztecan-speaking Cheme-huevi, followed by some Hopi and Navajo of NE Arizona.

**Mohave:** Northernmost of the Yuman tribes, the Mohave formerly lived in loosely organized bands, uniting only for warfare or defense. They farmed the bottomlands, hunted, and gathered wild foods. Crafts included finely made baskets, pottery, and beadwork. Ceremonial dances and long funeral wakes were important in their social life. Even today, the Mohave and Quechan cremate their dead—a rare practice among American Indian tribes. Mohave live on the Fort Mohave Reservation near Needles, Calif., and in a larger group on the Colorado River Reservation near Parker, Arizona. You can learn more about the tribe and see their crafts at the tribal museum just S of Parker.

**Quechan:** Formerly known as the "Yuma," the tribe prefers to be called "Quechan." In the 19th C. their territory ran up and down much of the lower Colorado and about 25 miles up the Gila River. Federal government actions trimmed their land considerably during the late 19th and early 20th centuries. Today the tribe lives in California on the Fort Yuma Reservation opposite Yuma, Arizona. They have a museum

*Mohave squaws and children, 1880s*

*Quechan Indian family, 1884*

in an historic building once part of Camp Yuma.

**Cocopa:** The Cocopa lived downstream from the Quechan in the Colorado River delta area, once one of the most fertile areas in the Southwest. Their population, like that of other Colorado River tribes, was greatly reduced by European-introduced diseases. Today they live on 2 tiny reservations S of Yuma and in the Mexican states of Sonora and Baja California.

**Chemehuevi:** This group of Paiute Indians once roamed the eastern Mohave Desert in a nomadic hunting and gathering pattern. They settled in the Chemehuevi Valley of the Colorado River in the early 1800s and took up the agricultural practices of their Mojave neighbors. The U.S. Government gave the Chemehuevi a reservation in 1907, but Lake Havasu inundated much of their farmland in 1938. The tribe now lives on the Chemehuevi Reservation opposite Lake Havasu City and on the Colorado River Reservation near Parker.

## TRANSPORT

Regional airports in Yuma, Blythe (CA), Lake Havasu City, Bullhead City, and Kingman have connections to Phoenix, southern California, and Las Vegas. Greyhound, Trailways, and Amtrak serve Kingman on their routes across northern Arizona, and Yuma on their southern Arizona routes. Sun Valley Bus stops at Needles (CA), Lake Havasu City, and Parker on its route between Las Vegas and Phoenix. LTR Bus connects Kingman with Las Vegas and Phoenix on a more direct route, bypassing the Colorado River towns. Boat cruises visit nearby points of interest from marinas at Katherine Landing and Boulder Beach in the Lake Mead National Recreation Area, and go through the scenic Topock Gorge between Lake Havasu City and Laughlin, Nevada. Cheapest trips of all are the free 24-hour ferries across the river between Bullhead City and the gambling casinos at Laughlin. Having your own car (or boat!) allows you to explore the quiet and scenic backcountry of western Arizona.

*Mohave camp, late 1800s*

*Kingman, about 1899*

# THE NORTHWEST CORNER

## KINGMAN

Kingman sits in high desert country (elev. 3,325 feet) between the Cerbat, Hualapai, and Black Mountains. Lewis Kingman came through the area in 1880 while surveying a right-of-way for the Atlantic and Pacific Railroad between Albuquerque, New Mexico, and Needles, California. The railroad camp that took his name soon grew into a major mining and transportation center for NW Arizona. A county election in 1866 declared the county seat should move from Mineral Park to Kingman, but residents of Mineral Park balked at turning over county records. Kingmanites then sneaked over to Mineral Park in the dead of night to snatch the records and bring them to Kingman, where they've stayed ever since. Mining has declined since WW II, with the last major operation (Duval's Mineral Park copper mine) shutting down in 1981. Kingman is small (pop. 10,100), but serves many motorists on their way across the country on I-40 or to Las Vegas or Phoenix. Kingman's boosters proclaim the town's 1,400 rooms and 50 restaurants as fit for a king. At-

tractions in the vicinity that you might want to visit include Hoover Dam and the Lake Mead National Recreation Area, ghost towns and old townsites like Oatman and Chloride, cool forests of Hualapai Mt. Park, London Bridge in Lake Havasu City, and glittering casinos in Laughlin and Las Vegas.

**Mohave Museum of History and Arts:** This museum's varied collection will give you a feeling for the history of NW Arizona. Ten dioramas, a mural, and many artifacts show development from prehistoric times to the present. The Hualapai Indian Room contains a full-size *wickiup* (brush shelter), pottery, baskets, cradleboard, and other crafts. You can try your hand at grinding mesquite beans with the Indian *mano* and *metate*. Other things to see include paintings, sculpture, and crafts in the art gallery, photos showing construction of Hoover Dam, carved turquoise mined from the Kingman area, memorabilia of movie star Andy Devine, and the outdoor mining exhibits. The museum even has a pipe organ, often used in concerts here. History buffs will appreciate the museum's library. A gift shop sells books on the region and Indian crafts. Open Mon. to Fri. 1000-1700, Sat. and Sun. 1300-1700; closed major holidays; donation; tel. 753-3195. Located at 400 W. Beale St.; take I-40 Exit 48 and go ¼ mile on Beale Street.

**wagon tracks:** Wagons creaking down the hill into Kingman from the 1870s to 1912 carved deep ruts into the soft volcanic bedrock here. Another road bypassed this spot in 1912, leaving the old road in its original condition. Evenly spaced holes beside the road have stirred up some debate: some people think wagonmasters used long poles in them for braking; other theories say the local Board of Supervisors planned to dynamite the road for use by automobiles. The site lies near a pretty canyon just a short drive from town. From the museum, take Grandview Ave. N .4 mile from Beale St., then turn R .6 mile on Lead Street. Look for a wooden footbridge on the R and follow the path across it to the old wagon road.

**Bonelli House:** This historic house of native tufa stone reflects the lifestyle and taste of a prominent Kingman family early in this century. The Bonellis built it in 1915 using both American and European design features to replace an earlier residence lost to fire. Thick walls insulate the interior from the temperature extremes of Kingman's desert climate. The Bonelli family lived here until 1974, when the city of Kingman purchased the house to restore as a bicentennial project. Ask at the Chamber of Commerce or Mohave Museum for times of tours (donation).

**accommodations:** Most of Kingman's motels and restaurants line E. Andy Devine Ave. (AZ 66/US 93) between I-40 Exits 44 and 53, and along W. Beale St. (US 93) off I-40 Exit 48. You'll find about 23 motels on Andy Devine, then another 5 on Beale Street. Rates start from about $14 in winter, going up several dollars in summer.

The historic Beale Hotel, built in 1906 and now being restored, served for many years as the social center for ranchers and miners of the area. Rates now run $15-$25, depending on size and whether the room has a private bath or

*wagon tracks*

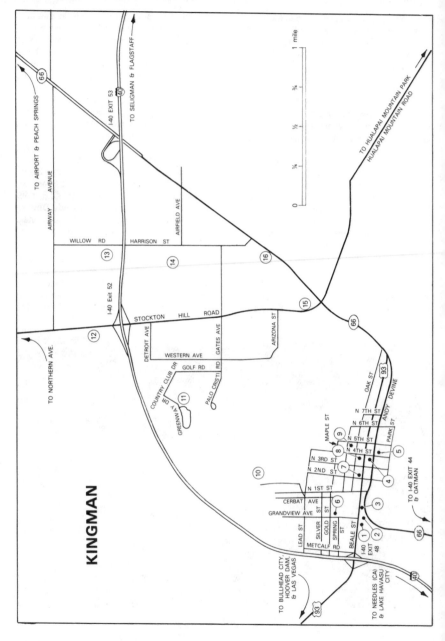

KINGMAN

not. A home-style restaurant is planned for the lobby. The Beale Hotel sits on the corner of 325 Andy Devine Ave. at 4th St.; tel. 753-2297.

**camping:** The Kingman KOA costs $10.75 tents, $14.75 RV w/hookups; take I-40 Exit 53 (Andy Devine) and go NE on AZ 66 for one mile, then L on Airway one mile, and R on Roosevelt to the campground; tel. 757-4397. Circle S Campground offers spaces for tents ($8) and RVs ($9.50 w/hookups) at 2360 Airway; tel. 757-3235. RVs can also stay at King's Rest RV Park, $12 w/hookups, 3131 McDonald; tel. 753-2277; and Golden Glory Trailer Park, $9.45 w/hookups, 5847 E. AZ 66 (2 miles NE of airport); tel. 757-2923. Hualapai Mt. Park, 14 miles SE of town, offers tent and RV sites in cool pine forests, see "Vicinity of Kingman."

**food and entertainment:** You'll find all the popular chain and fast-food places among the motels on Andy Devine. For more local atmosphere, try City Cafe ("home cooking"; 1929 E. Andy Devine; tel. 753-3550); Barbara's (2890 E. Andy Devine; tel. 753-2711); Golden Corral (steaks; 3157 Stockton Hill — I-40 Exit 52; tel. 753-1501); Mortons Freight Stop (24 hours; 3300 E. Andy Devine — I-40 Exit 53; tel. 757-3585); and Union 76 (24 hours; 946 W. Beale — I-40 Exit 48; tel. 753-7600). Get pizza and Italian food at Buccilli's Pizza (2775

---

### KINGMAN

1. Mohave Museum of History and Arts
2. Chamber of Commerce
3. Locomotive Park
4. Beale Hotel
5. Amtrak Train
6. swimming pool
7. bus station
8. library; post office branch
9. Bonelli House
10. wagon wheel tracks
11. Kingman Municipal Golf Course
12. Kingman Regional Hospital
13. Centennial Park
14. Mohave County Fairgrounds
15. main post office
16. Lewis Kingman Park

---

Northern; tel. 757-7279); and Pizza Hut (3395 E. Andy Devine; tel. 757-3292). Mexican food is served at Poblanita (1921 Club Ave.; tel. 753-5087); Carter's Rodeway (401 W. Beale; tel. 753-5707); and La Posada (1420 E. Andy Devine; tel. 753-6337). Dine Chinese at House of Chan (960 W. Beale; tel. 753-3232; closed Sun.); Jade Restaurant (3370 Stockton Hill; tel. 757-3207); and Golden China Restaurant (4135 Stockton Hill; tel. 757-5265). For nightlife try the Long Branch Saloon with live or DJ country and Western music and dancing nightly, 2255 Airway Ave.; tel. 757-8756. Catch movies at The Movies, 4055 Stockton Hill; tel. 757-7985.

**services:** The main post office is at 1901 Johnson, though the downtown branch on N. 4th St. (next to the library) can be more convenient. Kingman Regional Hospital is at 3269 Stockton Hill Rd. (just N from I-40 Exit 52); tel. 757-2101. Swimming pools are found at the corner of Grandview Ave. and Gold St.; tel. 753-5636; and in Centennial Park at 3333 Harrison; tel. 757-7910. Centennial Park also has tennis and racquetball courts, ballfields, and picnicking. Kingman Municipal golf course has 9 holes; 1001 E. Gates (W off Stockton Hill Rd.); tel. 753-6593. Valle Vista offers an 18-hole course; 9886 Concho Dr. (14 miles NE on AZ 66); tel. 757-8744.

**information:** The Chamber of Commerce can help you explore this corner of Arizona. Open daily 0800-1700; tel. 753-6106; downtown at 333 W. Andy Devine (Box 1150, Kingman, AZ 86402). The public library is in Kingman's original one-room schoolhouse, built in 1896, 219 N. 4th (N off Andy Devine and Beale); tel. 753-5730.

**transport:** All 3 bus lines, Greyhound, Trailways, and LTR, stop at the 203 E. Beale terminal downtown; tel. 753-2522 (Greyhound and LTR), and tel. 753-6350 (Trailways). The station, open daily 0800-1900 and 2200-0400, has a cafeteria and lockers. Some sample bus destinations and OW fares are: Flagstaff $26, Phoenix $20, Tucson $37, Bullhead City $6.35, Las Vegas $22, and Los Angeles $49. Amtrak has passenger train service daily W to Los Angeles and E to Flagstaff, Albuquerque, and beyond; tel. (800) 872-7245 for info and reservations. The Amtrak terminal is downtown at the corner of 4th St. and Andy Devine; tel. 753-6886. Golden Pacific Airlines flies daily from the airport 4 miles NE of town to: Las Vegas $45, Phoenix $53, Prescott $39, and Sedona $59; tel. 757-3214, or (800) 352-3281 in Arizona, or (800) 528-7146 outside Arizona. Rent cars from Rucker Motors, 4195 Stockton Hill; tel. 757-4041; Hertz, 2364 Kingman Ave.; tel. 753-5588; and Kinsel Motors, 3505 Stockton Hill; tel. 757-3131. For a taxi call Kingman Cab; tel. 753-3624.

## VICINITY OF KINGMAN

**Hualapai Mountain Park:** The Hualapai Indians, whose name means "pine-tree folk," lived in these mountains until being relocated northward by the military in the 1870s. Now a county park, the mountains are easily reached by a 14-mile paved road running SE from Kingman. The park offers dense forests, scenic views, hiking trails, picnicking, camping, and rustic cabins. Elevations range 5,000-8,417 feet, attracting animals and birds rarely seen elsewhere in NW Arizona. The forested slopes contain groves of manzanita, scrub and Gambel oak, pinyon and ponderosa pine, white fir, and aspen. Mule deer, elk, mountain lion, fox, raccoon, and other animals roam the forests. The park office has checklists of plants, animals, and birds found here. Hiking trails wind through the mountains, visiting overlooks and climbing Aspen and Hayden Peaks.

Campsites have drinking water (except in winter) but no showers, $3/night. A small RV area offers hookups for $7/night. Cabins, with cooking and bath facilities, cost $15-$40 d. on Fri., Sat., and Sun., then $5 less per night on weekdays. You can visit the park any time of year, though heavy winter snowstorms may require chains or 4WD. For information and reservations at the campground, RV park, or cabins, visit or call the Mohave County Parks Dept. (open Mon. to Fri. 0800-1700), 303 Oak St. (Box 390, Kingman, AZ 86402); tel. 753-9141, ext. 215. The Hualapai Ranger Station is near the park's entrance; tel. 757-3859. Hualapai Mountain Park might change ownership in the near future—plans are afoot to

transfer it to the state park system.

The nearby Hualapai Mt. Lodge offers a motel, RV park, restaurant, swimming pool, horseback riding, and store. Some of the well-preserved buildings date to the 1930s, when they were part of a Civilian Conservation Corps camp. The motel ($36.75 for 1-4 persons) and restaurant (serving American breakfast, lunch, and dinner) are open Wed. to Sun. from Easter to 31 Dec., and Fri. to Sun. the rest of the year. Self-contained RVs can stay year-round, $10/night w/hookups. The grocery store is open summer only (May to mid-Sept.). From Kingman, drive to the county park, then turn L one mile at the fork just past the ranger station; tel. 757-3545.

The Bureau of Land Management operates Wild Cow Springs Campground (free; no water) in a ponderosa pine and oak forest; from Hualapai Mt. Park, continue S 5 miles on unpaved BLM Rd. 2123.

**Burro Creek Campground:** A perennial

*headframe of the Golden Gem Mine*

*Golden Gem Mill*

stream flows through this scenic canyon area, 70 miles SE of Kingman on US 93. Picnicking, birdwatching, swimming, and rock hounding for agates are popular. The BLM campground here has drinking water but no showers; $2 night.

**Cerbat:** Gold and silver deposits in the Cerbat Mountains, N of present-day Kingman, attracted miners in the late 1860s. They founded the town of Cerbat and worked such mines as the Esmeralda, Golden Gem, and Vanderbilt. Cerbat became the Mohave County seat in 1871, but lost the honor 2 years later to nearby Mineral Park. By 1912 Cerbat's post office had closed. The Golden Gem's mill and headframe still stand, structures that rarely survive in other ghost towns. You'll also see stone foundations and several buildings. The turnoff for Cerbat is 9 miles NW of Kingman on US 93, near Milepost 62; head E ¾ mile on a good dirt road, turn L ½ mile, then turn R 2 miles to the site. Keep L when passing a group of modern buildings just before old Cerbat.

**Mineral Park:** During most of the 1870s and 1880s Mineral Park reigned as the county seat and most important town in the area, but it lost those distinctions in 1887 to Kingman. By 1912 Mineral Park had even lost its post office. Very little remains to be seen today except the modern Duval copper mine, which shut down in 1981. The turnoff for Mineral Park is 14 miles NW of Kingman on US 93, between Mileposts 58 and 59; turn E 5 miles on a paved road to the site.

**Chloride:** After discovering silver chloride ore here in the early 1860s, prospectors founded this town—the oldest mining camp in NW Arizona. Hualapai Indians made life precarious during Chloride's first years until Army troops subdued the tribe. Several buildings survive from the town's long period of mining activity, which lasted into the 1940s. A few hundred people, including many retirees, now live here.

An old miner's shack has been restored and furnished; ask to see it at Sheps store on 2nd St. (1 ½ blocks S of the post office). The Silver Bells, a group of women dedicated to preserving Chloride's history, make and sell antique-styled clothing at Sheps store.

Artist Roy Purcell painted giant, brightly colored murals in 1966 and 1975 on cliffs 2 miles SE of town. He titled his work "The Journey—images from an inward search for self." Indian petroglyphs can also be found in the area. From Chloride, take Tennessee Ave. (the main road into town) past the post office and Tennessee Mine, then follow signs; the road may be too rough for low-slung cars.

A few basic motel rooms are available behind Sheps store; $15 and up; tel. 565-3643 or 565-3619. RVs may park overnight in town (ask first at Sheps). Frank's Chloride Tavern serves

*detail from Roy Purcell's "The Journey"*

breakfasts and Mexican food, Tennessee Ave. and 2nd Street. Chloride General Store, next to the post office, offers fast food and groceries. Townspeople dress up in old-style clothing for Old Miners' Day, the last Sat. in June, for a parade, barbeque, games, and shootouts. The turnoff for Chloride is 20 miles NW of Kingman on US 93 at Grasshopper Junction; go E 3 miles on a paved road.

**Oatman:** The weathered old gold-mining town of Oatman sits on the western foothills of the Black Mountains, 28 miles SW of Kingman. Elephant's Tooth, the gleaming white quartz pinnacle E of town, beckoned prospectors, who knew that gold and silver often occur with quartz. Gold mining began in 1904, attracting hordes of miners and business people, who soon founded a town. They named it in memory of the Oatman family, victims of an Apache attack in 1851. The town prospered with many new businesses, 7 hotels, 20 saloons, and even a stock exchange. Area mines produced nearly 2 million ounces of gold

before declining in the 1930s. Oatman, which once had over 12,000 citizens, began to fade away. It might have disappeared altogether had it not become a travelers' stop on Route 66. Oatman lost the highway traffic in 1952, when engineers rerouted the road to the south. A few hundred citizens hang on today, relying largely on tourist business.

Many old buildings survive, some now in use as gift shops and cafes. The Oatman Hotel, a 2-story adobe structure built in the 1920s, has exhibits upstairs of life in the boom days. Pick up a self-guiding tour sheet at one of the shops to learn more about Oatman's history. You're almost sure to meet the town's wild burros, which wander the streets looking for handouts from visitors. Oatman celebrates Gold Camp Days on Labor Day weekend with shootouts, costume parade, and dancing. Shootouts, usually just in fun, also take place every Sat. and Sun. on Main Street.

The Old Trails Saloon and Cafe serves Mexican and American food, or you could try the Ragged Ass Miner's Saloon for hamburgers, fried chicken, steaks, and other items. Both saloons feature live bands and dancing on Sat. and Sun. afternoons. RVs can stay at the Oatman Plaza on Main St.; hookups (water and elect. only) cost $5/night.

**Goldroad:** This picturesque ghost town is about 3 miles NE of Oatman on the way to Kingman. Goldroad thronged with life after the discovery of gold around 1901, but later faded away. By the early 1940s it was inhabited only by weeds and desert critters. Foundations and crumbling adobe walls remain. Mine

*an Oatman burro*

*Oatman*

shafts and tailings cover surrounding hillsides. Take care when exploring the site; walls and mine shafts are liable to collapse.

## BULLHEAD CITY

Don't expect a *city*—this small town on the Colorado River is more a get-away-from-it-all place for fishermen and boaters. The site lay empty and remote in the 1940s, when construction workers arrived to build Davis Dam. With completion of the dam in 1953, everyone thought the construction camp called Bullhead City would fold up. But instead it became a center for outdoor recreation. In addition to the Colorado River at the town's doorstep, there are 240 square miles of deep blue water in Lake Mohave, beginning just 6 miles N at Katherine's Landing. The "bullhead" rock formation that gave the place its name did disappear—under the waters of the lake. Bullhead City lies 35 miles W of Kingman via AZ 68, and 25 miles N of Needles, CA on AZ 95. Bright lights of gambling casinos in Laughlin, Nevada, beckon from across the river.

**it's hot!:** Even the Chamber of Commerce admits the town gets hot in summer. In 1984 Bullhead City "won" the distinction for being the hottest spot in the nation, with 71 days of national highs. Not everyone likes having the National Weather Service in town; in 1981, after being told Bullhead City was the nation's 1980 hot spot, about 100 local merchants signed a petition protesting the nationwide coverage given to their hot weather. But life goes on. Air conditioning, low humidity, and the cool waters of the Colorado keep most residents and visitors from complaining.

**accommodations and camping:** Bullhead City, and its subdivision of Riviera just to the S, have about 20 motels. More places to stay lie across the river at the casinos in Laughlin. Try to have reservations for motels and RV parks, especially if arriving on a weekend. Most RV parks prefer guests staying a week or longer, but the following will also accept overnighters. KOA Kampground offers full facilities at Hwy. 95 and Merrill Ave. (S of downtown); $11.88 tent or RV w/hookups; tel. 763-2179. Ridgeview Park RV Resort is at 2751 Locust Blvd. (on the N edge of town just past the airport); $14 RV w/hookups; tel. 754-2595. Clark County (NV) has a campground beside the water near Davis Dam; sites cost $4; drinking water but no showers; located near the turnoff to Laughlin from NV 163. Many RVers just park for the night on the vast casino parking lots in Laughlin. You'll also find a motel, RV park, and campground 6 miles N at Katherine Landing.

*Davis Camp, the original
Bullhead City*

**food:** For dining in Bullhead City, try Gerard's at Silver Creek Inn for Continental cuisine (1120 Hwy. 95; tel. 763-8181); the Rib Ranch's ribs and other meat dishes (closed Sun., 135 Hwy. 95; tel. 754-3349); D'Angelo's for Italian foods (2141 Clearwater, S in Riviera; tel. 758-1878); Valdo's for Mexican dining, (1768 Hwy. 95; tel. 763-3101); and China Szechuan for Mandarin and Szechuan styles, (1490 Hwy. 95; tel. 763-2610). Some of your best eating deals will be on the Nevada side; all seven casinos have restaurants with enticing prices like $1.49 breakfasts, $2.75 dinners, and $4.95 seafood buffets.

**services and recreation:** Bullhead Community Hospital is at 2735 Silver Creek Rd.; tel. 763-2273. One of the best fishing areas along the Colorado River lies right in front of Bullhead City. The cold and swift waters from Davis Dam harbor large rainbow trout, channel catfish, and, during late spring and early summer, giant striped bass weighing in at 20 pounds and more. Golfers can head 5 miles S for a round on the 9-hole Chaparral Golf Course, 1260 E. Mohave Dr.; tel. 758-3939.

**information:** The Chamber of Commerce will tell you about the area; open Mon. to Fri. 0800-1700, Sun. 0900-1500; the office is on the S side of Bullhead Community Park (or write Box 66, Bullhead City, AZ 86430); tel. 754-3891. Laughlin Chamber of Commerce can make hotel reservations and answer questions about the casinos there, Box 2280, Laughlin, NV 89029; tel. (702) 298-2214, or for toll-free reservations: tel. (800) 227-5245. There's a public library S in Riviera at 1130 E. Hancock Rd.; tel. 758-6867.

**transport:** Rent cars from Hill Brothers (171 Hwy. 95; tel. 754-3201). Greyhound Bus goes 3 times daily E to Kingman and beyond, and 3 times daily W to Needles and Los Angeles; open daily 0500-2230; station is in a convenience store downtown across from Hill Brothers RV Land; tel. 754-4655. Havasu Airlines will take you to Las Vegas $42-$55 OW, Lake Havasu City $30 ($20 standby), and Phoenix $69; tel. 754-2292.

**Laughlin:** The 7 casinos on the Nevada side of the river will happily accept your money in any of the usual gambling games of the state. Cheap bus tours from Arizona and southern California cities bring people by the thousands. Laughlin's casinos have a more casual, and some say more friendly, atmosphere than the bigger gambling centers of Las Vegas and Reno. Besides the games of chance, you could check out the movies, live shows, hotel rooms, swimming pools, and cheap restaurant deals offered by many of the casinos. From Bullhead City you can drive 8 miles to Laughlin via Davis Dam, but it's more fun to take one of the free passenger ferries, leaving frequently 24 hours a day from the shore N of downtown Bullhead City. A free shuttle-bus service connects the casinos.

# LAKE MEAD
# NATIONAL RECREATION AREA

The Colorado River forms 2 long lakes as it winds more than 240 miles through Lake Mead National Recreation Area. From Grand Canyon National Park, the deep blue waters flow around the extreme NW corner of Arizona past black volcanic rocks, stark hillsides, and white sandy beaches. Striking desert scenery and inviting waters make the area a paradise for boating, fishing, water-skiing, swimming, and scuba diving. Visitors often sight bighorn sheep on the canyon cliffs and feral burros in the more level areas. Adventurous hikers can explore the hills and canyons of this wild country, knowing that it rarely sees human visitors. To get the most out of a visit to Lake Mohave and Lake Mead, you really need a boat; roads approach only at a few points. If you don't have your own, marinas offer rentals from humble fishing craft to luxurious houseboats. Boat tours take in some of the scenery of Lake Mead (from Lake Mead Marina), the Black Canyon (below Hoover Dam), and Lake Mohave (from Katherine's Landing). The National Park Service provides free boat ramps, campgrounds ($5/night; no showers or hookups), and ranger stations at most of the places accessible by car. Rangers patrol the Recreation Area and answer visitors' questions. Park Service people also staff the Alan Bible Visitor Center at the turnoff for Boulder Beach, 4 miles W of Hoover Dam. The boating and camping season lasts all year at the lakes, with spring and fall the ideal times to visit. Most people come in summer, and though it's hot, swimmers and water-skiers best appreciate the water then. In winter, you wouldn't want to hop in without a wetsuit, though topside temperatures are usually pleasant during the day.

**fishing:** Both Lake Mohave and Lake Mead offer excellent fishing year-round. In either lake you'll find largemouth and striped bass, rainbow and cutthroat trout, channel catfish, crappie, and bluegill. Lake Mohave's upper reaches have an especially good reputation for rainbow trout, while Lake Mead has hot fishing for striped bass—some specimens top 50 pounds. Most marinas sell licenses and tackle. Marinas and ranger stations can advise on the current fishing regulations and the best spots to fish. Shore fishermen only need a license from the state they're in. If you fish from a boat, you'll need a license from one state and a special-use stamp from the other.

*rainbow trout at Willow Beach Fish Hatchery*

## LAKE MOHAVE

Heading upstream from Bullhead City, you'll first come to Lake Mohave. Squeezed between hills and canyon walls, the lake appears like a calmer Colorado River. Though 67 miles long, Mohave spreads only 4 miles at its widest. Davis Dam, which holds back the lake, is open daily 0730-1545 MST for self-guided tours. Katherine Landing, nicknamed "Katy's Gulch" by some people, is 6 miles N of Bullhead City. Besides offering the lake's only public swimming beach, Katherine Landing has a boat ramp, campground, marina with boat rentals, RV park, motel, restaurant, and store. Boat tours depart daily for a 1½-hour cruise downstream to Davis Dam and upstream to some pretty coves; $6.50 adult, $4.50 children 5-11. For accommodation and boat rentals (including houseboats), contact Lake Mohave Resort, Bullhead City, AZ 86430; tel. 754-3245.

Cottonwood Cove is about halfway upstream on the main body of water on the Nevada side. If driving there, turn off US 95 at Searchlight, and go E 14 miles on NV 164. You might enjoy a stop at Searchlight's small museum of river artifacts. Cottonwood Cove has a motel, RV park, campground, restaurant, and marina with rentals (including houseboats); contact Forever Resorts, 1000 Nevada Hwy., Suite 207, Boulder City, NV 89005; tel. (702) 297-1464 or (800) 255-5561. Northward, the lake narrows at El Dorado Canyon and becomes a river again. Trout and trout fishermen hang out in the cold river currents upstream. A road (NV 165) approaches Eldorado Canyon from the Nevada side but there's no campground or resort.

About a dozen river miles before Hoover Dam you'll reach Willow Beach on the Arizona shore. It's only a 4-mile detour from US 93 if coming by car. No Park Service campground here, but Willow Beach has an RV park, motel, restaurant, and a marina with boat rentals at Willow Beach Resort, Box 187, Boulder City, NV 89005; tel. (602) 767-3311. The "Wall of Fame" in the resort cafe and store has photos of fishermen and their trophy trout catches. Willow Beach National Fish Hatchery, ½ mile upstream by road, raises large numbers of rainbow trout for stocking the Colorado and lakes. The hatchery also studies and propagates endangered native species—Colorado River squawfish, razorback suckers, and humpback chub. You're welcome to visit the raceways outside (open daily 0700-dark) and the inside displays (open daily 0800-1600).

A popular canoe trip begins below Hoover Dam and follows the swift Colorado beneath sheer 1,500-foot cliffs of the Black Canyon to Willow Beach. Hot springs at the base of the cliffs make an enjoyable stop. Obtain permission to launch your canoe for this trip from the Bureau of Reclamation Warehouse, Box 299, Boulder City, NV 89005; tel. (702) 293-8356 or (702) 293-8286. Raft tours do this trip year-round for $50 adult and $25 children under 12, including 3 hours on the river, lunch, and transport from the Gold Strike Inn (between Boulder City and Hoover Dam); tel. (702) 293-3776 or (702) 293-6379.

**Arizona Hot Springs Hike:** This 6-mile RT hike follows a canyon through layers of volcanic rock to hot springs near the Colorado River, downstream from Hoover Dam. The

*Katherine Landing*

*Hoover Dam under construction*

highly mineralized spring water surfaces in a side canyon at temperatures ranging from 113-142 F. Allow 5 hours for the hike down and back, plus time to soak in the hot springs. You'll be descending 800 feet to the river, then climbing out the same way. Hiking is best in fall, winter, and spring; summer temperatures can become hazardous. As in any desert hike of this length, bring water (one gallon/person) and wear a sun hat; also be alert for rattlesnakes and flashfloods. Don't hike if thunderstorms threaten. Check trail conditions with a ranger beforehand—the way might be difficult to follow in spots. From Hoover Dam, drive 4.4 miles SE on US 93 to a dirt parking area on the R at the head of White Rock Canyon. Follow the canyon on foot down to the Colorado River, then walk ¼ mile downstream along the river to the side canyon with the hot springs. Climb a 20-foot ladder to reach the best springs.

## HOOVER DAM

Completed in 1935, this immense concrete structure stood as one of the greatest engineering feats of its day. It remains almost as impressive today, especially when considering the mind-numbing statistics: 3,250,000 cubic

*Hoover Dam*

*Winged Figure of the Republic*

yards of concrete used, a height of 726 feet above bedrock, production of 4 billion kilowatt-hours of energy annually, and 96 lives lost during construction. With all these numbers coming at you, it's easy to miss the beauty of the dam's form and decoration. Look for the graceful curves, Winged Figures of the Republic sculptures, art deco embellishments, terrazzo floor designs, and other touches. Guided tours leave frequently every day 0730-1915 Memorial Day weekend through Labor Day, and 0900-1615 the rest of the year (Nevada time); $1 adult, 15 and under free. There's also a free exhibit room with a relief map of the Colorado River, a model of a generating unit, and memorabilia from construction of the dam. Park on the Nevada side.

# LAKE MEAD

Lake Mead, held back by Hoover Dam, ranks as the largest artificial lake in the United States. The reservoir holds the equivalent of 2 years flow of the Colorado River. In the shape of a rough "Y," one arm of Lake Mead reaches N to the Virgin River, while the longer eastern arm stretches up the Colorado River into the Grand Canyon. Boaters have lots of room on the lake's 115-mile length. Countless little beaches and coves provide hideaways for camping and swimming. Largemouth black bass, striped bass, rainbow and cutthroat trout, channel catfish, bluegill, and crappie swim in the waters.

**Alan Bible Visitor Center:** Park Service exhibits introduce Lake Mead National Recreation Area's fishing, boating, other water sports, wildlife, and desert travel. A 15-min. movie, "Experiencing the Lake Mead Area," is shown every half hour. A botanical garden outside helps identify local flora. Books on the history, geology, plants, and wildlife may be purchased. Nautical and topo maps are sold too. Rangers have handouts and can tell you about backcountry camping, roads, and trails. Evening programs are presented on weekends from May to October. The Visitor Center is open daily 0830-1630; tel. (702) 293-4041. It's located on US 93 at the turnoff for Boulder Beach, 4 miles W of Hoover Dam.

**Boulder Basin:** Above Hoover Dam the lake opens into broad Boulder Basin. Campgrounds and marinas are located at Boulder Beach, Las Vegas Wash, and Callville Bay. Boulder Beach, just a few miles by car from Hoover Dam, has good swimming and a lifeguard in summer. Lake Mead Resort at Boulder Beach has a motel, restaurant, and boat rentals (including houseboats), 322 Lakeshore Rd., Boulder City, NV 89005; tel. (702) 293-3484 or (800) 752-9669. Tour boats leave the marina for 1-hour cruises on the lake to Hoover Dam; $6.50 adult, $4 children under 12. RVs can stay at Boulder Beach in Lakeshore Trailer Village, 268 Lakeshore Rd., Boulder City, NV 89005; tel. (702) 293-2540. Las Vegas Boat Harbor, at Las Vegas Wash, has a restaurant, store, and marina (fishing and ski boat rentals), Box 771, Henderson, NV 89015; tel. (702) 565-9111. Callville Bay Resort & Marina offers an RV park, restaurant, and boat rentals (including houseboats), 1000 Nevada Hwy., Suite 207, Boulder City, NV 89005; tel. (702) 565-8958 or (800) 255-5561. Kingman Wash, on the Arizona shore near Hoover Dam, has only a primitive boat ramp and camping.

cactus wren
(Campylorhynchus
brunneicapillus)

ment, has a motel, RV park, restaurant, and boat rentals (including houseboats), Temple Bar, AZ 86443; tel. 767-3400. There's also a Park Service campground. From Hoover Dam, go SE 19 miles on US 93, then turn L 28 miles on a paved road. Bonelli Landing, a primitive boat ramp and campground on the Arizona shore, is reached by dirt road off the route to Temple Bar.

**South Cove:** Upstream the lake narrows in Virgin Canyon before opening into South Cove, the last large open-water area of Lake Mead. There's a boat ramp on the Arizona side but no campground or resort. By car, South Cove is reached on a paved 45-mile road branching off US 93 between Hoover Dam and Kingman. You'll pass through Dolan Springs (small motel, RV parks, restaurants, and stores) and an area with tall Joshua trees. These trees look like a strange cactus but really belong to the lily family. They grow to heights of 25 feet. Primitive boat ramps and camping are located downstream of South Cove at Gregg's Hideout and upstream at Pearce Ferry both reached by dirt roads.

**Virgin Basin:** Upstream from Boulder Basin you'll pass through 6-mile-long Boulder Canyon before emerging into Virgin Basin, the largest and most dramatic part of Lake Mead. Rock formations with names like Napoleon's Tomb, the Haystacks, and Temple Bar provide scenic landmarks. Many narrow coves snake far back into the mountains. Two resorts lie along the giant Overton Arm, branching N to the Virgin River. Echo Bay Resort has a motel, RV park, restaurant, and boat rentals (including houseboats), Overton, NV 89040-0545; tel. (702) 394-4000 or (800) 752-9669). Overton Beach Resort, farther N, offers a RV park, restaurant, and marina with boat rentals, Overton, NV 89040; tel. (702) 394-4040). Both Echo Bay and Overton Beach areas have Park Service campgrounds as well. Valley of Fire State Park, several miles W of Overton Beach, is noted for its impressive rock formations of red Jurassic sandstone; open all year and has campsites; tel. (702) 394-2388. Indian artifacts from Pueblo Grande de Nevada are displayed in the Lost City Museum in the town of Overton, 11 miles N of Overton Beach. The Indian villages, now mostly under Lake Mead, date from the 1st C. A.D.

Temple Bar Resort, Arizona's main develop-

*desert bighorn sheep*
(Ovis canadensis
mexicana)

*London Bridge*

# WESTCENTRAL ARIZONA

## LAKE HAVASU CITY

The late Robert McCulloch founded Lake Havasu City in 1964 to provide facilities for new factories and a healthful environment for his employees to live in. The planned city grew up on the eastern shore of Lake Havasu, 19 miles S of I-40 and 73 miles N of I-10, both major crosscountry routes. Lake Havasu City might have become another ho-hum town had it not been for a brainstorm by McCulloch and his town planner, Disney man C.V. Wood. They decided to purchase London Bridge! Back in London the 136-year-old bridge had been slowly sinking into the Thames. No longer able to handle busy city traffic, the famous London landmark was put up for sale in 1967. McCulloch snapped it up for the bargain price of $2,460,000, then spent more than twice that amount to have all 10,276 granite blocks shipped to Long Beach, California, trucked to Lake Havasu City, and painstakingly reassembled. After 2 years of construction, the bridge was up in its new home. The Lord Mayor of London graciously came over in Oct. 1971 to preside at the bridge's dedication, much as King William IV and Queen Adelaide had at-

tended the original dedication in 1831. London Bridge may be one of the stranger sights on the Arizona desert, but it put Lake Havasu City on the map!

More has been added since — an "English Village" complete with British pub, City of London Arms Restaurant, a variety of shops and galleries, a London taxicab, and even a bright-red English telephone booth. Nearby London Bridge Resort adds more English-theme atmosphere. At first, the bridge spanned only dry land. Workers later dug a water channel underneath, cutting off Pittsburgh Point. Now you walk or drive across London Bridge to reach the campground, beach, marina, airport and other facilities on the new island, still known as Pittsburgh Point. As in other Colorado River towns, fun on the water draws many visitors. Lake Havasu, 45 miles long and 3 miles wide, is great for boating, water-skiing, and sailing. Boat rentals, boat tours, swimming beaches, tennis, and golf courses are readily available too. Present population of Lake Havasu City is more than 18,500.

**accommodations:** You have a choice of about 23 motels and resorts. London Bridge Resort, close to London Bridge and the water, has a 9-hole golf course, tennis, swimming pools, and elegant decor; rooms start at $81 ($97.20 overlooking the water). It's worth stepping inside the plush lobby to see the world's only replica of the ornate Gold State Coach. The original, built in 1762, has carried every British monarch since George III to their coronations at Westminster Abbey. London Bridge Resort is at 1477 Queen's Bay Rd.; tel. 855-0888. Nautical Inn, on the water across London Bridge, offers an 18-hole golf course, tennis, and swimming pool; rooms start at

$51.84; 1000 McCulloch Blvd.; tel. 855-2141. Less expensive places ($20-$30) include: Shakespeare Inn (2190 McCulloch Blvd.; tel. 855-4157); E-Z 8 Motel (41 S. Acoma Blvd.; tel. 855-4023); Havasu Motel (all (kitchenettes, 2035 Acoma Blvd.; tel. 855-2311); and Windsor Inn Motel (451 London Bridge Rd.; tel. 855-4135). See the Chamber of Commerce (in English Village beside London Bridge) for other places to stay.

**camping:** Lake Havasu State Park has 45

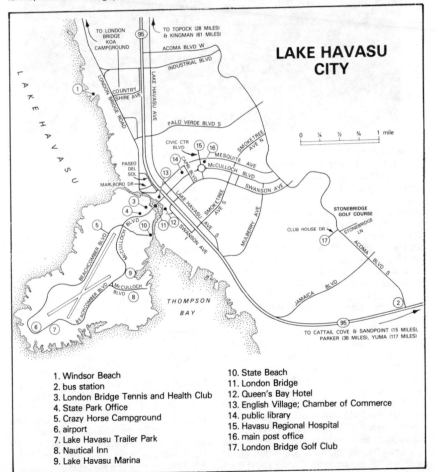

1. Windsor Beach
2. bus station
3. London Bridge Tennis and Health Club
4. State Park Office
5. Crazy Horse Campground
6. airport
7. Lake Havasu Trailer Park
8. Nautical Inn
9. Lake Havasu Marina
10. State Beach
11. London Bridge
12. Queen's Bay Hotel
13. English Village; Chamber of Commerce
14. public library
15. Havasu Regional Hospital
16. main post office
17. London Bridge Golf Club

**THE CITY OF LONDON ARMS**

BUILT BY THE CITY OF LONDON
ON THIS ACRE OF LAND GENEROUSLY PRESENTED BY
McCULLOCH PROPERTIES Inc.

OPENED BY
THE Rt. Hon. THE LORD MAYOR OF LONDON
ALDERMAN SIR PETER STUDD G.B.E. M.A. D.Sc.
9TH OCTOBER. 1971.

miles of shoreline, covering most of the Arizona side of the lake. Besides the state and concession-run campgrounds, boaters can choose among 225 primitive camping sites accessible by water only. Crazy Horse Campground, ½ mile across London Bridge on the island, offers primitive tent camping ($5) and RV sites ($10.50 w/hookups); showers, store, and snack bar; 1534 Beachcomber Blvd.; tel. 855-2127. Lake Havasu Trailer Park, 2 miles SW at the far end of the island, has RV sites only ($13 w/hookups); 601 Beachcomber Blvd.; tel. 855-2322. Cattail Cove, 15 miles S on AZ 95, offers picnicking, camping for tents ($5) and RVs ($7 w/hookups), showers, and a boat ramp; tel. 855-7851. Sandpoint Marina is nearby (take the Cattail Cove turnoff), offering RV sites ($10.50 w/hookups), store, and marina (fishing, ski, patio, and houseboat rentals); tel. 855-0549. London Bridge KOA Kampground, 4 miles N of downtown, has spaces for tents ($9.50) and RV's ($14); 3405 London Bridge Rd.; tel. 764-3500. Park Moabi, on the California side near the I-40 Colorado River bridge, offers spaces for RVs ($10 w/hookups) and tents ($6 and $10) with showers, boat ramp, marina with rentals, and store; tel. (619) 326-3831 (park office) or (619) 326-4777 (marina). Also in California, Havasu Landing Resort has spots for both tents ($5) and RVs ($8 and $10); directly across the lake from Lake Havasu City (ferry service is available from English Village); tel. (619) 858-4593.

**food:** King's Retreat Restaurant in London Bridge Resort has a long list of Continental, English, and American specialties at moderate prices; open daily for breakfast, lunch, and dinner; tel. 855-0888. *Cuisine francaise* and other Continental fare are offered by the Versailles Restaurant (open Mon. to Sat. for dinner; 2134 McCulloch Blvd.; tel. 855-4800). Dine Chinese at New Peking (2010 McCulloch Blvd.; tel. 855-4441), or Kun Yen Restaurant (357 S. Lake Havasu Ave.; tel. 855-1208). For seafood and steaks try Chelsea's Fish House (open daily for dinner; 460 El Camino Way; tel. 855-1177); Captain's Table (open daily for breakfast, lunch, and dinner; 1000 McCulloch Blvd.; tel. 855-2141); and London Broiler (350 London Bridge Rd.; tel. 855-9501). For pizza and other Italian dishes you have a choice of Alice's Pizza (86 S. Smoketree Ave.; tel. 855-3484); Arturo's Pizza (Havasu Plaza Shopping Center; tel. 855-9558); J.J.'s Pizza Place (3524 McCulloch Blvd.; tel. 855-7475); Petrossi's Pizza (344 London Bridge Rd.; tel. 855-9468); and Pizza Hut (1543 Marlboro Dr.; tel. 855-6071). Colarusso's serves Italian dinners (34 Scott Dr.; tel. 855-2929). For Mexican food try Casa de Miguel (1550 S. Palo Verde; tel. 453-1550), or Taco Hacienda (2200 Mesquite Ave.; tel. 855-8932). Golden Horseshoe Steakhouse offers steaks and other American favorites, 4501 London Bridge Rd. (5 miles N of town); tel. 764-3121.

**entertainment:** For movies drop in at the Cinema Theatre (2130 McCulloch Blvd.; tel. 855-3111) or London Bridge Theater (English Village; tel. 453-5454). Nightspots include The Bonadventure (2061 Swanson; tel. 855-9555); Herm Degan's (1515 Marlboro Dr.; tel. 855-9540); Nautical Inn (1000 McCulloch Blvd.; tel. 855-2141); and Pioneer Hotel & Dance Hall (271 S. Lake Havasu Ave.; tel. 855-1111).

**events:** Sailing or powerboat races are held on many weekends: cruising sailboat regattas in Jan., March, and Dec., London Bridge Regatta in Apr. (said to be the largest inland sailboat race in the country), Hobie Cat Regatta in Apr., Sailboard Regatta in Oct., and Havasu Classic Outboard World Championships in November. The Spring Art Festival in Apr. features work of regional artists. Fireworks light up the sky on July 4th. London Bridge Days celebrates the dedication of the famous structure in Oct. with a Grande Parade, triathlon, contests, games, live entertainment, and food. A Square Dance Festival also livens the scene in October. The Gem and Mineral Show takes place in November. A Christmas Boat Parade of Lights brightens December. Check with the Chamber of Commerce for dates and details.

**services:** The main post office is on the corner of 80 Civic Center and Mesquite. Havasu Regional Hospital is at 101 Civic Center; tel. 855-8185. For swimming, head ½ mile across London Bridge to State Beach; free. Windsor Beach, another park with beach and a boat ramp, is 1½ miles N of London Bridge on the mainland. London Bridge Tennis & Health Club has 11 tennis courts at 1401 McCulloch Blvd. (on the R just after crossing the bridge); tel. 855-6274. London Bridge Golf Club has two

*The City of London Arms (English Village)*

18-hole courses, 2400 Club House Dr. (off S. Acoma Blvd.); tel. 855-2719. A third 18-hole course is at Nautical Inn, 1000 McCulloch Blvd. (one mile across London Bridge); tel. 855-2141. Fishermen discovered the lake well before any developer. Fishing was good (and still is!) for largemouth bass, crappie, and channel catfish. Saltwater striped bass, introduced in the early '60s as an experiment, thrived. With weights up to 60 lbs., the landlocked fish is now the hottest thing in the lake. The stripers feed in spring and summer below Davis Dam, eating thread-fin shad and other fish churned up by water flowing out the turbines. During fall and winter they return to the lake and are sought out by thousands of eager fishermen. Pick up a local fishing booklet for striper techniques. Fun Center, on the water next to English Village, rents canoes, pedal boats, jet skis, wet bikes, and sailboats; tel. 453-4386 or 855-7032. The Nautical Inn, on the island, offers para sailing rides; tel. 855-2141. Lake Havasu Marina, 1100 McCulloch Blvd. (¾ mile across London Bridge) rents fishing, pontoon, and ski boats; tel. 855-2159. You can rent houseboats across the lake at Havasu Landing Resort from Lake Havasu Houseboat Vacations; tel. (602) 855-3282 or (619) 858-4613. Sandpoint Marina, 14 miles S on the AZ side (take the Cattail Cove turnoff), offers fishing, ski, patio, and houseboat rentals; tel. 855-0549. Park Moabi, in California near the I-40 Colorado River bridge, also has a boat ramp and marina with rentals; tel. (619) 326-4777.

**information:** The Chamber of Commerce has 2 offices, both well stocked with literature. The one in the English Village is easier to find; it's open daily 0900-1700; tel. 855-5655. The main office is at 1930 Mesquite Ave., #3, Lake Havasu City, AZ 86403; open Mon. to Fri. 0900-1700; tel. 855-4115. The Lake Havasu State Park rangers can tell you about their recreation areas, including boat camping; the office is just across London Bridge on the R; tel. 855-7851. The public library is at 1787 McCulloch Blvd.; tel. 855-2140.

**transport:** A ferry and several boat tours leave from the shore at English Village. On Fri., Sat., and Sun. passenger ferries cross the lake to Havasu Landing Resort on the Chemehuevi Indian Reservation, a 3½ mile trip; OW fares: $2

adult, $1 children 6-12. You can take a narrated 45-min. tour of the area from Lake Havasu Boat Tours; $4 adult, $2 children 5-12. Blue River Safaris Tours offers daily 2-hour trips upstream into the spectacular Topock Gorge; $15 adult, $5 children 5-11; an all-day cruise goes to Laughlin, 4 hours upstream, spends 4-5 hours there, then returns; $40 adult RT fare includes a buffet and "fun package"; tel. 453-5848. The gambling casinos in Laughlin offer free bus rides, free food, and other inducements to get you (and your money) there; call Tony's Tour (tel. 855-4233), All Seasons Tours (tel. 855-6661), or Holiday Tour Club (tel. 855-3977). Havasu Airlines will fly you there and back for just $20; tel. 855-5011. Rent cars from Avis (1690 Industrial Blvd.; tel. 855-5082); Hertz (airport; tel. 855-4500); and Rent-a-Dent (airport; tel. 453-3368). Sun Valley Bus Lines has 2 buses daily to Las Vegas via Needles (CA) and Searchlight (NV), and to Phoenix via Parker and Wickenburg, leaving from the Terrible Herbst gas station at AZ 95 and S. Acoma Blvd.; tel. 855-4028. Havasu Airlines flies to Bullhead City, Las Vegas, and Phoenix from the airport terminal across London Bridge at the far end of the island; tel. 855-5011.

## VICINITY OF LAKE HAVASU CITY

**Topock Gorge by canoe:** A perfect one-day outing on the cool waters of the Colorado River above Lake Havasu. The usual put-in point is Park Moabi (CA) where I-40 crosses the river. Here swift currents speed canoeists on their way without rapids or serious turbulence. Take-out is at Castle Rock on the upper end of Lake Havasu, about 7 hours and 17 river miles later. Topock Gorge is in the Havasu National Wildlife Refuge, where hundreds of bird species have been spotted. Look for the mud nests of swallows clinging to the cliffs. Herons, ducks, geese, long-billed prospectors, and red-winged blackbirds are easily identified visitors to the canyon. If you're lucky, you may even spot a desert bighorn sheep on the steep slopes. Indian petroglyphs cover Picture Rock, a huge dark mass about halfway between Devil's Elbow and Blankenship Bend. Sandy beaches make good stopping places for a walk or picnic, but no fires or camping are permitted.

Summer temperatures can get uncomfortable but a hop in the river will always cool you off. Bring a hat and sunscreen to protect yourself from the Arizona sun. Other kinds of boats besides canoes can make the trip. Rafts need a little more time, while powerboat skippers need to watch for sandbars. Topo maps (1:24,000 scale) for the area are "Topock, Ariz.-Calif." and "Castle Rock, Calif.-Ariz." If you don't have a canoe, contact Trowbridge Recreation (Box 144, Lake Havasu City, AZ 86403; tel. 855-3506), or Fun Center (285 S. Lake Havasu Ave., Lake Havasu City, AZ 86403; tel. 855-6481 or 855-7032); both provide canoes with life jackets ($16.50 one day rental), and can arrange transportation ($9/canoe with a $45 minimum) to Topock or Park Moabi. Many other canoe trips can be taken; for example, Trowbridge will drop you off at Needles for a 2-day trip or at Bullhead City for a 3- or 4-day canoe excursion.

**Havasu National Wildlife Refuge:** The marshes, open water, and adjacent desert of the Refuge support many types of animals and birds. The main part of the Refuge includes Topock Marsh near Needles (CA) and extends southward to just N of Lake Havasu City. Another part protects the delta area of Bill Williams River S of Lake Havasu City. Most of the more than 40,000 acres lie on the Arizona side. In winter, the Refuge is home for the snow goose, Canada goose, and other waterfowl. Boating, fishing, and other water sports are permitted except where signposted. No camping is allowed in Topock Marsh (except at the concession), Topock Gorge, or Mesquite Bay; you may boat camp on the Arizona shoreline below the S entrance to Topock Gorge. For a map and regulations, contact Havasu National Wildlife Refuge, Box A, Needles, CA 92362; tel. (714) 326-3853.

## PARKER AND THE PARKER STRIP

From 1871 to 1908, Parker was just a post office on the Colorado River Indian Reservation. But when a railroad line came through, the town began to grow as a trading center for the reservation and nearby mining operations. Mining later declined, but agriculture and

tourism thrived with the building of 2 dams upstream. The Headgate Rock Dam, finished in 1941, formed Lake Moovalya, whose waters irrigated farmlands of the reservation. Workers completed Parker Dam in 1938, which created Lake Havasu, to supply water and electrical power to southern California. Resorts and parks lining both shores of the river and Lake Moovalya draw visitors year-round. Better known as the "Parker Strip," this 11-mile stretch of scenic waterway begins several miles N of Parker and extends to Parker Dam. Despite hot summer temperatures that rival the nation's highs, many people come to enjoy the excellent boating and water-skiing from around Easter through Labor Day. In Sept. the scene calms and the temperature cools. Winter visitors, many of whom are retired, enjoy fishing, hunting, hiking, rock-hounding, and exploring ghost towns.

**accommodations:** You have a choice of staying in town or upstream along the Parker Strip. The 8 or so motels in town are easy to find along Parker's 2 major streets, California Ave. and Agency Rd./Riverside Drive. Heading N about 5 miles on AZ 95, you'll see a long line of RV parks, resorts, restaurants, bars, and marinas of the Parker Strip. Places to stay (with distances from the N edge of Parker) include: Arizona Shores Resort Motel (5½ miles; tel. 667-2685); Branson's Resort (7½ miles; tel. 667-3346); Riverfront Resort (13 miles; tel. 667-2322); Casa del Rio Resort (15 miles; tel. 667-2727); and Havasu Springs Resort on Lake Havasu (16 miles; tel. 667-3361). You'll also find places on the California shore opposite the Parker Strip (distances from Parker): River Shore Resort (7 miles; tel. 619-665-2572); Big Bend Resort (12 miles; tel. 619-663-3755); River Lodge (14 miles; tel. 619-663-3056); and Black Meadow Landing on Lake Havasu (25 miles; tel. 619-663-4901).

**camping:** RVs can stay at Lazy D Mobile Home Park in Parker, $8 night; located at the end of 15th St. (off California Ave.); tel. 669-8408. More than 3 dozen trailer parks and campgrounds line the waters along the Parker Strip. The Parker Chamber of Commerce will give you a list and map. La Paz County Park

# Notice to Shippers!

---

THE COLORADO STEAM
NAVIGATION CO'S
STEAMERS

## Newbern and Montana

*Leave San Francisco
for Mexican Ports and Mouth
of Colorado River*

covers a long section of riverbank about 8 miles N of Parker; the park offers picnicking, tent and RV camping, hookups, showers, tennis, golf driving range, swimming beach, and boat ramp; day-use fee $1 person, camping $6 car (2 persons), RV w/hookups $8 (2 persons); tel. 667-2069. Buckskin Mountain State Park, 11 miles N of Parker, sits on a secluded section of grassy shoreline backed by low cliffs; a concession runs a snack bar, marina, inner-tube rental, boat ramp, and store; tel. 667-3210. A short hiking trail begins opposite the highway turnoff; picnic sites and a campground (all with hookups but no showers) are near the water; $2 day use, $7 camping; nonresidents add $1/vehicle; tel. 667-3231. A 2nd part of Buckskin Mt. State Park lies 2 miles farther upstream; this smaller "River Island Unit" offers picnicking, camping (showers but no hookups), swimming beach, and boat ramp; $2 day use, $5 camping; nonresidents add $1/vehicle; tel. 667-3386. Empire Landing, 8 miles from Parker on the California side, offers a beach, picnicking, and camping (no showers or hookups); free day use, camping costs $4/vehicle; tel. (602) 855-8017.

**food:** Look for American fare at the County Seat (Arizona and Kofa Aves.; tel. 669-9474); Coffee Ern's (24 hours; 1707 California Ave.; tel. 669-8145); Turtle Barn (1500 California Ave.; tel. 669-2543); and Sunrise Cafe (908 Agency Rd.; tel. 669-8842). The Fireside Inn features fine dining of American and Italian specialties (401 California Ave.; tel. 669-8080). Los Arcos serves Mexican food (closed Mon.; 1200 California Ave.; tel. 669-9904). Canton Restaurant offers Chinese meals (closed Mon.; 621 Riverside Dr.; tel. 669-2361). For pizza try La Piazza (801 11th St.; tel. 669-2441) or Toby's Pizza Parlor (1317 Joshua Ave.; tel. 669-9388). A variety of other restaurants lies along the Parker Strip N of town.

**entertainment and events:** Catch movies at Parker Theatre, 1007 Arizona Ave.; tel. 669-2211. Annual events include: Parker Score 400 for off-road vehicles in Feb.; International Water Ski Race in Feb.; Lions Club Donkey Basketball (teams battle for victory while riding donkeys) in Feb.; La Paz County Fair in March; Parker Enduro boat race (9 hours of nonstop action) in March; National Jet Boat Assoc. races March to May and Sept. to Nov.; Southern California Sailing Club races in May; Water Ski shows on Wed. evenings in May, June, and July; Innertube Race in June; 4th of July Fireworks; Indian Day Celebration in Sept.; Parker Rodeo in Oct.; Southwest Art Rendezvous in Nov.; Southern California Sailing Regatta in Nov.; Holiday Lighted Boat Parade in Nov.; All Indian Rodeo in Dec.; and Christmas Lighted Boat Parade in December.

**services:** The main post office is at the corner of Joshua Ave. and 14th Street. Parker Community Hospital is on Mohave Rd. in the S side of town; tel. 669-9201. The public swimming pool is at 1317 9th St.; tel. 669-5678. Play golf at Havasu Spring's 9-hole course, 16 miles N of Parker; tel. 667-3361. Nobody offers boat tours in the area, but rentals are readily available from marinas along the Parker Strip. Camp-a-Float, at Havasu Springs Resort, has a new idea in houseboats—just put your RV on their special outboard-powered trailer floaters and take off across Lake Havasu; tel. 667-2901. Fishermen head for the river below Headgate Rock Dam for large and smallmouth bass, striped bass, catfish, crappie, and bluegill.

Boaters and water-skiers discourage some fishermen from Lake Moovalya, but the fish are there. You'll need reservation fishing permits to fish in lower Lake Moovalya and the Colorado River downstream. Tubers enjoy leisurely trips downriver; a popular trip is the 7-mile, 3-hour float from Parker to Big River Park on the California side.

**information:** The Parker Chamber of Commerce will help you find the resort or other facilities you're looking for, and tell you what's going on. The office is open Mon. to Fri. 0900-1700; located at 1217 California Ave. (Box 627 Parker, AZ 85344); tel. 669-2174. The public library is at the corner of 1001 Navajo Ave. and Agency Rd.; tel. 669-2622.

**transport:** Sun Valley Bus goes twice daily to Phoenix and to Las Vegas from the stop at 913 Fiesta; tel. 669-2807. For a cab, call Parker Taxi; tel. 669-2811.

## VICINITY OF PARKER

**Colorado River Indian Reservation:** President Lincoln signed the bill establishing this reservation in 1865. The 268,691 acres, most of which lie in Arizona, are the home of Mojave, Chemehuevi, Hopi, and Navajo Indians. Don't expect any picturesque Indian villages, as the 6,000-plus inhabitants live in modern houses and work at their farms or jobs like anyone else along the Colorado River. To learn about the tribes and others who've passed this way, visit the Colorado River Indian Tribes Museum 2 miles S of Parker. You'll see artifacts from prehistoric Anasazi, Hohokam, and Patayan cultures, models showing traditional shelters of the 4 modern tribes, and a large collection of baskets and other crafts. Old photos and artifacts show early reservation life, Anglo explorations, mining, and ranching. A library houses an extensive collection of books, manuscripts, photographs, and tapes relating to various tribes. Baskets, beadwork, and other Indian-made crafts are sold in the gift shop. The museum is open Mon. to Fri. 0800-1700, and Sat. 1000-1500, closed Sun. and some holidays; donation; tel. 669-9211 ext. 213. The nearby Irataba Snack Bar serves Indian fry bread, stew, and other fare for lunch on weekdays. From downtown Parker, head SW 2 miles on either Agency or Mohave Roads.

**Parker Dam:** The world's deepest dam lies about 15 miles upriver from its namesake, the town of Parker. When building the dam, workers had to dig down 236 feet through sand and gravel of riverbed before hitting bedrock needed to secure the foundation. Lake Havasu,

*Mohave Indians playing ring-toss game, 1850s*

the reservoir behind the dam, has a storage capacity of about 211 billion gallons. One billion gallons a day is pumped into the Colorado River Aqueduct for southern California destinations. You're welcome to take a free self-guided tour of the dam and power plant, open daily 0800-1700.

**Quartzsite:** Like swallows returning to Capistrano, thousands of "snowbirds" flock to this tiny desert town in winter. From an estimated 600-1,000 summer residents, the population jumps to, about 6,000. Charles Tyson settled here in 1856, building a fort to fend off Indian attacks. Tyson's Wells soon became an important stage stop on the run from Ehrenburg to Prescott. Later the place was renamed "Quartzite," after the mineral, but the post office added a "s" for "Quartzsite." Hadji Ali lies under a pyramid-shaped marker in the local cemetery. He was one of several camel drivers imported from the Middle East along with about 80 camels in 1856 and 1857 by the U.S. Army. The Army hoped that the large, hardy beasts would improve transportation and communication in the Southwest deserts. Although the camels showed promise, the Army abandoned the experiment during the Civil War. Most of the camels were turned loose on the desert, terrorizing stock and wild animals for many years. The homesick camel drivers, except for Hadji Ali, went back to their own lands. Hadji Ali, whose name soldiers changed to "Hi Jolly," stayed in Arizona and took up prospecting.

Quartzsite is 35 miles S of Parker and 20 miles E of Blythe (CA) at the junction of I-10 and AZ 95. A couple of motels, some RV parks, and several restaurants serve passing motorists and the winter community. Most RVers, though, prefer the open freedom of the desert and head for La Posa Recreation Site just S of town. La Posa lacks any facilities but is free for stays of 14 days or less; long-term visitors pay $25 for the season. The giant Quartzsite Pow Wow Gem & Rock Show hits Quartzsite in early February. More than 100,000 people attend the 10-day flea market to buy and sell rocks, minerals, gems, lapidary supplies, crafts, antiques, and other treasures.

**Alamo Lake State Park:** This Alamo lies far from where Davey Crockett and his friends fought it out with the Mexicans. *Alamo* means "cottonwood tree" in Spanish. The lake is on the Bill Williams River at an elevation of 1,146 feet. When Alamo Lake began to fill in the

Hi Jolly monument in
Quartzsite

mid-'60s, the cottonwood, mesquite, and palo verde trees were flooded and became the home of small fish. Hungry bass and catfish fed on the small bluegill, sunfish, and red shiners. Fishermen then moved in to feed on the bass and catfish. A marina provides groceries, fishing supplies, and rental boats. The State Park has picnic tables, campgrounds with showers and hookups, and boat ramp; $2 day use, $4 primitive camping, $5 developed sites, and $7 w/hookups; tel. 669-2088. Spring and fall are the most popular times for a visit to this remote 3,500-acre desert lake. To get here, drive to Wendon (60 miles SE of Parker or 108 miles NW of Phoenix), then go 35 miles N on a paved road. An alternate route from Phoenix is the graded dirt road that takes off 23 miles NW of Wickenburg; the sometimes bumpy backway is about 20 miles shorter that the paved route.

**Swansea:** Of the ghost towns near Parker, Swansea is the best preserved. Ruins of a large brick smelter, mine, and over a dozen buildings remain. The Clara Consolidated Gold and Copper Mining Co. built the smelter in the early 1900s to process their ore locally, instead of sending it to faraway places like Swansea, Wales. Clara Consolidated closed the smelter in 1912, but mining continued by other companies until 1924. A high-clearance vehicle should be used to navigate the dirt roads to the site. From Bouse, 27 miles SE of Parker, take the road N across the RR tracks and go 13 miles to the site of Midway, take the L fork (crossing under the power lines after about ⅓ mile) and go NW 18½ miles to a road junction, then turn R 6 miles to Swansea. Another approach is on roads E from Parker. Local advice and good maps should be obtained; see the U.S.G.S. "Swansea" 15-minute topo map.

# THE SOUTHWEST CORNER

## YUMA AND VICINITY

Yuma's rich historical background and sunny subtropical climate make the small city (population 48,500) an attractive destination. In winter, an estimated 40,000 "snowbirds" fill the many trailer parks in town, along the river, and out on the desert. Boaters and fishermen can explore countless lakes and quiet backwaters on the Colorado River. Date palm groves, citrus trees, and vegetables grow on extensive farmlands surrounding Yuma. The Mexican city of San Luis offers shopping and another culture just 25 miles south.

**Yuma's beginnings:** The long recorded history of Yuma begins in 1540, nearly 70 years before the founding of Jamestown. Captain Hernando de Alarcon led a Spanish naval expedition along the western coast of Mexico and then a short way up the Colorado River, becoming the first white man to visit the area. He hoped to meet and resupply Francisco Vasquez de Coronado's expedition to the Seven Cities of Cibola farther E, but the 2 groups never met. First contacts between the Spanish and native Quechan Indians went well, but

resentment and hostility flared in later years. While searching for a land route between Mexico and California, Spanish explorers discovered that the best crossing on the lower Colorado River was just below the confluence of the Gila River. Soldiers and missionaries built a fort and missions here, across from present-day Yuma, but angry Quechan destroyed the settlements during a violent uprising in 1781, ending Spanish domination of Yuma Crossing.

Although small bands of American mountain men started drifting through in the early 1800s, little attention was paid to the area until the Mexican War. Kit Carson with Colonel Stephen Kearny and 100 soldiers marched across in 1846 while securing former Mexican lands between Santa Fe and San Diego. Colonel Philip Cooke followed with the Mormon Battalion and supply wagons, blazing the first transcontinental road across the Southwest. Crowds of 49ers, seeking gold in the Sierra Nevada of California, pushed westward along "Cooke's Road" a few years later. In 1851 the Army built Camp Yuma atop a hill on the California side to secure Yuma Crossing from Indian attacks. Nearby mining successes, the coming of steamboats, and road improvements en-

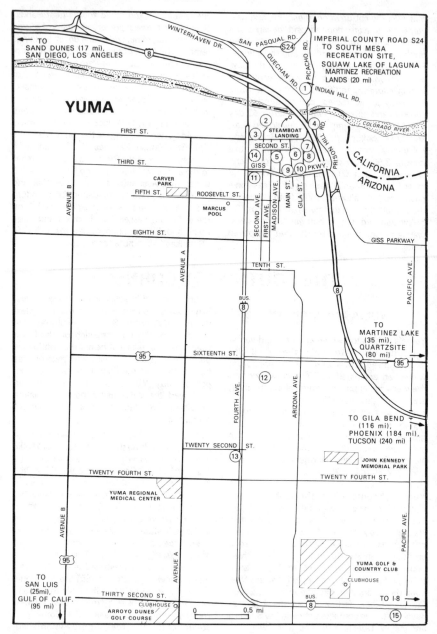

*Yuma Territorial Prison in its heyday*

couraged the founding of Colorado City on the Arizona side in 1854. When a disastrous flood wiped out the settlement 8 years later, residents rebuilt it on higher ground with the new name Arizona City. Later they decided on the present name of Yuma. Yuma Territorial Prison, the town's first major construction project, boosted the economy in 1876. Laguna Dam ended the riverboat era in 1909, but guaranteed water for the fertile desert valleys. Today Yuma ranks as one of Arizona's most important cities and the center of a rich agricultural area.

## YUMA

1. Quechan Indian Museum; St. Thomas Mission
2. Customhouse Museum
3. U.S. Fish and Wildlife Service
4. Yuma Territorial Prison
5. Century House Museum
6. Lute's Casino
7. Yuma Art Center
8. Amtrak Train
9. post office branch
10. Chamber of Commerce
11. public library
12. Greyhound Bus
13. main post office
14. Trailways Bus
15. airport

## SIGHTS

**Yuma Territorial Prison:** In 1875 the territorial legislature was about to award $30,000 to Phoenix for construction of a major prison. But Yuma's representative, Jose Maria Redondo, did some fast talking and got the project for his hometown, and the "Hell-hole of Arizona" was born. Righteous citizens of the Territory were fed up with murders, robberies, and other lawless acts of the frontier. They wanted bad characters behind bars. Niceties of reform and rehabilitation didn't concern them. Yuma was the ideal place for a prison, surrounded by hostile deserts and treacherous currents of the Colorado River. Prisoners endured searing 120 F summer temperatures, and if that wasn't

the prison today

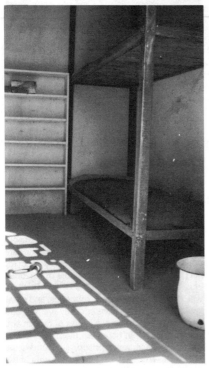

a cell in the prison

enough, recalcitrant inmates faced the darkness of a scorpion-infested dungeon. Most of the stone and adobe walls had to be built by the prisoners themselves, as money and labor were scarce.

Over the 33 years of prison operation, 3,040 men and 29 women paced the floors and gazed between iron bars. The prison, having withstood the toughest outlaws of frontier Arizona's wildest years, outgrew its site and closed in 1909. The remaining 40 prisoners were marched in shackles down Prison Hill to a train waiting to take them to a new prison in Florence. High school students in Yuma attended classes at the prison from 1910 to 1914 after their school burned. Even today the Yuma High School sports teams call themselves the "Criminals." You can step inside the prison, now a State Park, and imagine how it once was. Photos show faces of men and women imprisoned here. Read the stories about the inmates, guards, riots, and escape attempts. You'll learn about "Heartless" Pearl Hart and see her Colt 45 "Peacemaker." A Quechan Indian exhibit contains artifacts and old photos. Outside, you can explore the cellblocks, climb the main watchtower for views, and visit the prison graveyard. Yuma Territorial Prison is open daily 0800-1700; $1 adult, 17 and under free; tel. 783-4771. Take Prison Hill Rd. off Giss Parkway.

**Century House Museum:** Century House, one of Yuma's oldest buildings, was once home for the influential businessman E.F. Sanguinetti. Exhibits inside relate the history and cultures of Yuma Crossing—the Indians, explorers, missionaries, soldiers, miners, riverboat captains, and early settlers. The garden out back is aflame with bougainvillea and alive with chattering parakeets, a talking myna bird, colorful parrots, and other birds. Open Tue. to Sat. 1000-1600 all year, and Sun. 1200-1600 from Oct. to Apr.; free; tel. 782-1841. Adobe Annex, next to Century House, sells historical, Indian, and gold mining books and local crafts. Century House is in the N part of town at 240 S. Madison Avenue.

**U.S. Army Quartermaster Depot:** Another good place to get a feel for Yuma's history. The former depot and customhouse, overlooking the waterfront, is thought to be the oldest American-built structure in Yuma. The Army used it during the 1870s as a supply depot for the Indian Wars. Later the Custom Service took it over as an office and residence. Period rooms, old photos, and letters tell the story of this historic building. A steam locomotive and giant freight wagon sit outside. Open Tue. to Sat. 1000-1600; tel. 343-2500. Located at the N end of 2nd Ave. behind City Hall.

**Quechan Indian Museum:** Located on the hill just across the Colorado River from Yuma, the museum building dates from 1855, when it was part of Camp Yuma. Later, at the outbreak of the Civil War in 1861, the post's name changed to Fort Yuma. The site overlooks Yuma Crossing, the only ford in the area. Fort Yuma now belongs to the Quechan Indians, who have their museum and tribal offices here. Museum exhibits illustrate the arrival of the Spanish and missionary Father Francisco Garces, the Quechan Revolt in which Garces was clubbed to death, history of Fort Yuma, and Quechan Indian life. Artifacts include clay figurines, flutes, gourd rattles, headdresses, bows and arrows, and war clubs. Open Mon. to Fri. 0800-1200 and 1300-1700; $.50; tel. 572-0661. The nearby St. Thomas Mission occupies the site of Concepcion Mission where Indians murdered Father Garces in 1781. Take Indian Hill Rd. off Picacho Rd. (see map).

**Yuma Art Center:** Inside the old Southern Pacific RR Depot you'll see contemporary work by many Arizonans. Anglo, Indian, and Hispanic artists interpret their cultures and feelings in the paintings, prints, sculptures, and crafts. Some works are for sale. Open Tue. to Sat. 1000-1700 and Sun. 1300-1700; closed 16 June to 31 Aug.; free; tel. 783-2314. Located at 281 Gila St. in the NE corner of town.

## PRACTICALITIES

**accommodations:** Yuma, located midway between Phoenix and San Diego, makes a handy travelers' stop. Most of the 2 dozen motels in town lie along Business I-8 (old US 80) on 32nd St. and 4th Avenue. Costs for some go up as much as $10 during the popular winter and spring seasons, but the less expensive places have little or no seasonal increase. The more deluxe motels include the Chilton Motor Inn (300 E. 32nd St.; tel. 344-1050); Days Inn Suite Hotel (2600 S. 4th Ave.; tel. 726-4830); Royal Motor Inn (2941 S. 4th Ave.; tel. 344-0550); Shilo Inn Yuma (1550 S. Castle Dome Rd., off I-8 16th St. exit; tel. 782-9511); Stardust Resort Motor Inn (2350 S. 4th Ave.; tel. 783-8861); and Yuma InnSuites (1460 S. Castle Dome Rd.; tel. 783-8341). For lower budget accommodation ($20-$30), try Caravan Oasis Motel (10574 Fortuna Rd.; tel. 342-1292); El Cortez Motel (124 1st Ave.; tel. 783-4456); El Rancho Motel (2201 S. 4th Ave.; tel. 783-4481); Motel 6 (2730 S. 4th Ave.; tel. 344-3550; and 1640 S. Arizona Ave.; tel. 782-2873); Navajo Lodge (2801 S. 4th Ave.; tel. 344-1270); and Sixpence Inn of Yuma (1445 E. 16th St.; tel. 782-9521).

**campgrounds:** The more than 100 RV parks in and around Yuma cater mostly to retired people. Only a few parks welcome families with children, and usually just in the slow season (summer and fall). Some of the RV parks in town which also accept tenters include A Shady Tree (1210 W. 3rd St.; tel. 783-4742); Blew-In (1290 W. 3rd St.; tel. 343-1641); Blue Sky (10247 E. I-8 Frontage Rd.; tel. 342-1444); First Street Trailer Park (1850 W. 1st St.; tel. 782-0090); and Lucky Park del Sur (5790 W. 8th St.; tel. 783-7201). Dateland Farm Plaza, 65 miles E on I-8 (Exit 67), offers RV and tent camping, (families welcome); tel. 454-2227. Ask the Yuma Chamber of Commerce for a longer RV park list.

Some of the best camping lies upstream on the Colorado River. Laguna Martinez National Recreation Lands, 20 miles N on the California side, are perfect for families and anyone wanting to enjoy desert walks, fishing, or boating. Cross the river to Winterhaven (CA) then turn N on Imperial County Road S-24 and follow signs. The "Long-Term Visitor Areas," such as Quail Hill and Cripple Creek, are for self-contained vehicles only, as the sites lack improvements; free up to 14 days, then a $25 season pass is needed. South Mesa Recreation Site has water, restrooms, outside showers; free up to 14 days, then you'll need the $25 season pass. Squaw Lake, at the end of the road, offers water, restrooms, outside showers, paved parking, and a boat ramp; $4/night. An easy 2-mile nature trail winds through river vegetation and desert hills from the N end of the parking lot. The Bureau of Land Management maintains Laguna Martinez; tel. 344-2262. Martinez Lake is reached on the Arizona side farther upstream, about 35 miles N of Yuma; go N on US 95, then turn L on Martinez Lake Road. Fisher's Landing has tent and RV camping ($2, or $4 w/electric), restaurant, store, and marina (but no boat rentals); tel. 783-6513. Nearby Martinez Lake Resort offers motel rooms (from $35), RV park ($12.50 w/hookups), restaurant, and marina with boat rentals; tel. 783-9589.

**food:** For American food, try Bobby's (2497 S. 4th Ave.; tel. 726-1825); Brownie's Restaurant (1145 S. 4th Ave.; tel. 783-7911); Chester's Chuckwagon (2256 S. 4th Ave.; tel. 782-4125); Golden Corral Family Steak House (2401 S. 4th Ave.; tel. 344-9936); or Hungry Hunter Restaurant (2355 S. 4th Ave.; tel. 782-3637).

Good places for Mexican dining include Beto's Mexican Food (812 E. 21st St.; tel. 782-6551); Chretin's (485 15th Ave.; tel. 782-1291); and El Charro (601 W. 8th St.; tel. 783-9790).

Dine Chinese at Gene's (771 S. 4th Ave.; tel. 783-0080); Imperial China (195 S. 4th Ave.; tel. 783-4306); or Mandarin Palace (350 E. 32nd St.; tel. 344-2805).

Places for pizza include Domino's (741 S. 4th Ave.; tel. 782-7561; and 710 E. 32nd St.; tel. 344-0555); Lujano's Pizza (2255 S. 4th Ave.; tel. 782-2581; and 995 W. 8th St.; tel. 783-0167); Rocky's New York Style Pizzeria (2601 S. 4th Ave.; tel. 344-4260); and Village Inn Pizza Parlor (2630 S. 4th Ave.; tel. 344-3300; and 41 E. 16th St.; tel. 783-8353). You'll find supermarkets and many other restaurants along S. 4th Ave. and E. 32nd St. (Business I-8).

**entertainment:**   Catch movies at Plaza 5 Theatres, 1560 S. 4th Ave.; tel. 782-9292. For local color visit Lute's Casino; play dominos, pinball, or pool; a snack bar serves beer, burgers, and tacos; 221 S. Main St.; tel. 782-2192. Nightspots include the Back Room

Squaw Lake

& Saddle Club (rock 'n roll or country; 2020 S. 3rd Ave.; tel. 783-9870), Chilton Best Western (various groups; 300 E. 32nd St.; tel. 344-1050), and Sky Chief (various groups; 1530 E. 32nd St.; tel. 726-0847). For the latest info on dining and dancing, concerts, plays, and art exhibits, see ¿*Que Pasa?*, a magazine supplement to the Sat. Yuma Daily Sun.

Some annual events you might want to catch:
**Jan.:** Gem and Mineral Show, All States Picnic (a big "snowbird" get-together), and a Fiddler's Contest.

**Feb.:** Yuma Crossing Day (pioneer craft demonstrations, Indian dances, and art exhibits), and Silver Spur Rodeo and Parade.

**March:** San Diego Padres' Spring Training, Military Appreciation Days (airshow and static displays at the local Marine base), Roadrunner Marathon, Senior Citizens Craft Show and Sale, and Square and Round Dance Festival.

**Apr.:** Yuma County Fair.

**July:** 4th of July Community Celebration.

**Aug.:** World Championship Raft Race (8 mile course on the Colorado River).

**Oct.:** Horse Racing.

**Nov.:** Arizona City Days (celebration of Yuma's pioneer days with music, art, and special museum exhibits), Mexicali Exposition (held at Civic Center in Yuma), Greyhound Dog Racing (lasts through Mar.), and Gold Rock Ranch Roundup.

**Dec.:** AKC All Breed Dog Show.

**services:** The main post office is at 2222 S. 4th Ave.; a branch is downtown at 370 S. Main St. (across from the Chamber of Commerce).

Yuma Regional Medical Center is at 2400 S. Ave. "A"; tel. 344-2000. Jump in one of the public swimming pools (tel. 783-1271): Carver, corner 5th St. and 13th Ave.; Kennedy, corner 24th St. and Kennedy Ln.; and Marcus, corner 5th St. and 5th Avenue. Hit tennis balls at one of the 9 Desert Sun Courts near the Convention Center, 35th St. and "A" Ave.; tel. 783-1271. Play golf on the 18-hole courses at Arroyo Dunes (32nd St. & Ave. "A"; tel. 726-5622); Desert Hills Municipal (1245 Desert Hills Dr.; tel. 344-4653); Mesa del Sol (10583 Camino del Sol; tel. 342-1283); and Yuma Golf and Country Club (32nd St. & Fortuna Ave.; tel. 726-1104).

Dogs head for the finish line at Yuma Greyhound Park from Nov. to Mar.; 4000 S. 4th Ave.; tel. 726-4655.

Fishermen on the Colorado River and lakes catch largemouth black bass, striped bass, channel catfish, tilapia, bluegill, crappie, and others. Check fishing regulations with Arizona Game and Fish (tel. 344-3436), BLM (tel. 344-2262), and the Quechan Indian Fish and Game (tel. 572-0544). The Chamber of Commerce will give you a fishing info sheet.

Go rockhounding in the hills for agate, jasper, petrified wood, fossils, and other treasures; pick up a free rockhounding pamphlet from the Chamber of Commerce to find out where to go.

**information:** The Chamber of Commerce knows what's going on and where things are. They also have many useful handouts. Open Mon. to Thur. 0830-1700 and Fri. 0900-1700; a drive-in window is open on Sat. 1000-1600 from Nov. to March. Write: Box 230, Yuma, AZ 85364; tel. 782-2567. Their office is downtown at the corner of Giss Parkway and Main St.; take I-8 Exit 1. The U.S. Fish and Wildlife Service has information about the Cabeza Prieta, Kofa, Imperial, and Cibola National Wildlife Refuges; their office is downtown near the river at 356 W. 1st St.; open Mon. to Fri. 0800-1700; tel. 783-7861. To enter Cabeza Prieta, you must have a permit (obtain here or in Ajo) and suitable vehicle. Yuma's large and attractive library is at 350 S. 3rd Ave.; open Mon. to Thur. 0900-2100, Fri. and Sat. 0900-1700; tel. 782-1871.

**transport:** For a taxi call City Cab (tel. 343-1131); Desert Cab (783-7713); or Yuma Taxi Service (tel. 782-4768). Rent cars from Avis (airport; tel. 726-5737); Budget (2090 E. 32nd St.; tel. 344-1822); Hertz (airport; tel. 726-5160); National (airport; tel. 726-0611); or Ugly Duckling (1350 S. 4th Ave.; tel. 782-7810).

Greyhound Bus goes daily to Phoenix (3X; $33 OW), Tucson (3X; $35 OW), Los Angeles (4X; $40 OW), San Diego (4X; $37 OW), and other destinations. Station is open Mon. to Fri. 0700-2100, Sat. & Sun. 0800-1300; tel. 783-4403; it's at 170 E. 17th Pl. (off 16th St. behind Fed-Mart, and 2 blocks E of 4th Ave.). Trailways has 2 buses daily to Tucson, Los Angeles, San Diego, and other destinations at similar fares; buses leave from the station at 4th Ave. and 2nd St.; tel. 783-7341.

Amtrak trains run 3 times a week to Phoenix ($36 OW), Los Angeles ($50 OW), New Orleans ($200 OW), and other places; tel. (800) 872-7245. The depot at 291 Gila Street in the NE corner of downtown.

Yuma International Airport is conveniently located on the S side of town, off 32nd Street. Three airlines offer frequent daily service to Phoenix and Los Angeles with onward connections: Sky West (tel. 800-453-9417); America West (tel. 800-247-5692); and American Eagle (tel. 800-433-7300). Fares can vary widely depending on seat availability and competition, but run about $55 OW to Phoenix and $94 OW to Los Angeles. The airport has a travel agency, restaurant, and car rentals.

## VICINITY OF YUMA

**San Luis (Mexico):** A different culture lies a mere 25 miles to the south. Shopping attracts many visitors, who simply park on the Arizona side and walk across the border. More than a dozen shops are within a few blocks of the crossing. Many local craftsmen work with leather; you'll probably see them turning out belts, bags, saddles, and other items in the shops. Other crafts come from all over Mexico —including clothing, blankets, pottery, carved onyx chess sets, glassware, and musical instruments. San Luis Rio Colorado, its full name, was founded by farmers in 1906. The current population of about 130,000 makes it the largest city along the Arizona-Mexico border. A spacious park with welcome greenery and flowers marks the downtown area.

*ceramic cowpoke factory in San Luis*

The nearby bus station, corner of Av. Juarez and Calle Quinta, has 3 bus lines to such places as Tijuana, Mexicali, Ensenada, San Felipe, Santa Rosalia, Hermosillo, Mazatlan, Guadalajara, and Mexico City. White sandy beaches, fishing, and swimming on the Gulf of California draw many sun lovers. El Golfo de Santa Clara, a small fishing village 70 miles S, and the larger town of San Felipe 125 miles SW are both reached by paved roads.

U.S. citizens may visit San Luis, El Golfo, San Felipe, and Mexicali without formalities as long as 72 hours. You'll need a tourist card for longer stays or more distant destinations; obtain cards at the border or from a Mexican consulate or Mexican tourist office. The cards are free, but you need to show proof of citizenship (passport, birth or naturalization certificate, voting registration card, or notarizied affadavit of citizenship). Motorists also need a permit for their vehicles, except for border areas and Baja California; obtain at border by showing proof of ownership or a notarized affidavit by the owner authorizing the driver to take the car into Mexico. To avoid a stay in jail if there's an accident, purchase Mexican insurance beforehand; Overland International sells insurance in Yuma at 1000 16th St.; tel. 782-1638. Visitors from countries who need a U.S. visa can usually make a border-town visit without formalities, but check first with U.S. Immigration. For a longer visit, a multiple entry or new visa will likely be needed to return to the United States. Hermosillo and other major Mexican cities have U.S. consulates.

**Sand Dunes:** Though not typical of the Sonoran Desert, barren sand dunes lie about 17 miles W of Yuma on I-8. Movie producers have used the "Great American Sahara" for scenes in *Star Wars* and *Beau-Geste*-type films. Dune-buggie drivers like to play here too. A rest area off I-8 in the middle of the dunes provides a place to stop and park. From 1915 to 1926, motorists crossed the dunes on a road made from wooden planks strapped together. Remnants of this road can still be seen.

**Cabeza Prieta National Wildlife Refuge:** The 860,000 acres of desert valleys and small rocky ranges remain as wild as ever. You won't

*Gambel's quail* (Callipepla gambelii)

find any paved roads, so 4WD vehicles are recommended. In the Refuge, there's just the desert: very hot in summer, but beautiful with wildflowers in spring if some rain has fallen. Endangered Sonoran pronghorn, desert mule deer, and desert bighorn live here. Because the military sometimes uses the skies for gunnery and missle tests, be sure to get a permit before entering. Obtain permits from the U.S. Fish and Wildlife offices in Yuma or Ajo. The Refuge Visitor Center is in Ajo. See "Southern Arizona" chapter.

**Imperial National Wildlife Refuge:** Plants and animals of the Colorado River receive protection within this long, narrow refuge. Birds are the most conspicuous wildlife, especially in spring and fall when many water and land species visit. The refuge includes the river, backwater lakes, ponds, marshland, riverbottom land, and desert. Fishing, canoeing, and birding are popular activities, though some areas may be signposted against entry. No camping is permitted in the refuge, but waterskiers may use 2 portions of the Refuge. Martinez Lake Resort and Fisher's Landing (see "Yuma camping") offer camping, motel, restaurants, and marinas just downstream from the refuge. For a bird list and more info on Imperial, visit the refuge headquarters on the N side of Martinez Lake, or write Box 72217, Martinez Lake, AZ 85365; tel. 783-3371. The refuge is located about 40 miles N of Yuma; head N on US 95 and turn L onto Martinez Lake Road.

**Cibola National Wildlife Refuge:** Cibola lies along the Colorado River just upstream from Imperial Refuge. Habitats and wildlife are similar to Imperial. You're welcome to hike, boat, or fish, but camping is prohibited. For map and info, write Box AP, Blythe, CA 92226; tel. (602) 857-3253. Access to Cibola is best from the California side, off CA 78. Refuge Headquarters, in Arizona, are reached by CA 78/Farmer's Bridge Exit from I-10 (2 miles W of Blythe, CA) then S to Farmer's Bridge over the Colorado River; pavement ends here and it's 3½ miles farther to the headquarters.

**Kofa National Wildlife Refuge:** Desert critters such as coyote, cottontail, bobcat, fox, desert mule deer, and desert bighorn sheep live in the dry, rugged Castle Dome and Kofa Mountain ranges. Gambel's quail scurry into the brush while falcons and golden eagles soar above. Rare stands of native palm trees grow in Palm Canyon, reached by a short hike. Gold, discovered in 1896, led to development of the King of Arizona mine, from which the Kofa Mountains got their name. Some mining claims remain today, and may be signposted against trespassers. Several roads penetrate the scenic mountains and canyons, but these routes tend to be rough and best suited to 4WD vehicles. Hikers can more extensively explore this rugged country. The refuge covers 660,000 acres of wilderness, totally lacking in visitors' facilities—you must carry water and all supplies. A short hike up Palm Canyon reveals tall California Fan Palms *(Washingtonia filifera)* tucked into tiny side canyons. To reach the trailhead, go N 62 miles on US 95 from Yuma (or S 18 miles from Quartzsite) and turn E onto Palm Canyon Rd. between Mileposts 85 and 86. The road is dirt but OK for cars. At road's end, 9 miles later, follow the trail into Palm Canyon for about ½ mile. You'll see the tower-

*Palm Canyon*

ing palms in clefts on the N side of the main canyon. Take care if climbing up to the palms because of sheer cliffs and loose rock. The trail pretty much ends here but it's possible to rock scramble another ½ mile up the main canyon (watch for rattlesnakes) to a large natural ampitheater (no palm trees). Allow one hour from the trailhead to see the palms and return, or 3 hours to go all the way to the ampitheater and back. Other areas of the Kofas are better for long hikes; ask a Refuge employee for suggestions. For info on the Kofa Refuge, visit the Kofa National Wildlife Refuge in Yuma at 356 1st St.; or write Box 6290, Yuma, AZ 85364; tel. 783-7861.

# SOUTHCENTRAL ARIZONA

## INTRODUCTION

Nowhere else in Arizona do you find such a contrast between city and wilderness as in the southcentral part. Over half the state's population lives in the urban sprawl centered on Phoenix in the Valley of the Sun. Yet just beyond its borders you'll find craggy mountains, vast woodlands, and seemingly endless desert. Man tends to keep close to the rivers, where he can find water to nourish his crops and cities. But a different kind of thirst—for gold and silver—lured many pioneers into the rugged mountains of southcentral Arizona. Most of the towns they founded have faded into memories; only those communities with copper, tourists, or other resources survive.

**the land:** None of the mountains in this region achieves great heights; most summit elevations range only from 3,000 to 8,000 feet. But what they lack in size is more than made up in their challenging terrain—off-trail travel can be very difficult. The major ranges, all with good hiking and a chance to experience wilderness,

lie to the N and E of Phoenix. They include the Bradshaws, Mazatzals, Sierra Anchas, Superstitions, and Pinal Mountains. South and W from Phoenix you'll find a very different sort of country—the often harsh desert most people associate with Arizona, plains of rock and sand with small craggy ranges breaking through here and there. Springs and streams are nearly nonexistent; only hardy desert plants and wildlife can make it here.

**getting there and around:** Phoenix's Sky Harbor Airport has by far the best connections in Arizona. You also have a good choice of rental cars and long-distance bus connections from the city. Amtrak has train service across southern Arizona, stopping at Phoenix, Tucson, and a few other places, but only 3 times a week in each direction.

**climate:** Because most of southcentral Arizona sits at elevations under 4,500 feet, temperatures stay on the warm side. This is

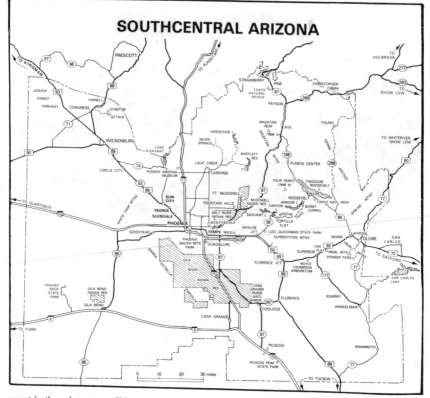

# SOUTHCENTRAL ARIZONA

great in the winter—you'll be enjoying spring-like weather while people in the North are digging out from snowstorms. Spring and fall warm up to just where you like it. Higher country becomes very pleasant then, and it's a good time to be outdoors. In summer, though, the sun turns most of the region into a giant oven—highs over 100 F become commonplace. Drink plenty of liquids and wear a sun hat if out in this season's heat. Annual rainfall varies from about 5 inches in the lowest desert to over 20 inches in the highest mountains. Most moisture arrives in 2 seasons: gentle winter rains between Dec. and Mar., then as violent thundershowers during July and August. These summer storms can kick up huge clouds of dust, cause flash floods, and start lightning-ignited brush fires.

**flora and fauna:** The cacti feel right at home across most of this region: prickly pear, cholla, barrel cactus, the giant saguaro, and many more. Small plants and low trees also thrive. Good rainfalls prompt spectacular floral displays in early spring, and a smaller show after the summer rains. Learn more about desert flora at the Desert Botanical Gardens in Phoenix and the Boyce Thompson Arboretum near Superior. Most animals hole up during the day, though lizards seem to enjoy sitting on hot rocks. In the larger mountain ranges you might meet mountain lion, black bear, bighorn sheep, javelina, pronghorn, or deer. Always watch where you put hands and feet in the desert so you don't disturb any rattlesnakes, gila monsters, scorpions, or poisonous spiders.

## INDIANS

**Hohokam:** Nomadic groups roamed across Arizona in seasonal cycles for thousands of years before learning to cultivate the land. Around 200-300 B.C. Indians we know as the Hohokam settled in the Gila and Salt River Valleys, growing crops in fields irrigated by canals or runoff from storms. They also continued to gather many wild plants and hunt for game. For most of their history the Hohokam lived in pit houses, built of brush and mud over shallow pits. Later some lived in square adobe houses. Larger towns had ballcourts and hundreds of houses. Hardy, drought-resistant corn was their main food, supplemented by beans, squash, and wild foods. The Hohokam made pottery, clay figurines, stone bowls, shell jewelry, paint palettes of slate, and cotton cloth. They were industrious agriculturalists, and their network of irrigation canals exceeded 300 miles in the Salt River Valley alone. The larger canals were more than 15 feet wide and 10 feet deep. Where the Hohokam came from and where they went remain mysteries, as they disappeared around A.D. 1450.

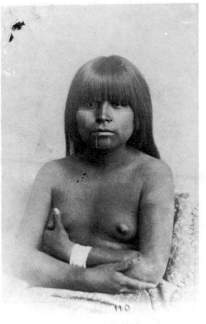

*Pima woman, late 1800s*

**the Pima and Maricopa appear:** The Pima Indians who followed the Hohokam have much in common and may be related. Living along the valleys of the Gila and Salt Rivers, the Pima used the farming methods of their predecessors, but suffered greatly when white men built dams upstream early in this century. Today the Pima farm, raise cattle, work in small industries, and do traditional handicrafts.

*pronghorn* (Antilocapra americana)

Maricopa Indians, who originally lived along the Colorado River, migrated up the Gila River to escape the more agressive Mohave and Yuman tribes. Pima and Maricopa Indians now share the same reservations. The tribes maintain a museum, gift shop, and restaurant on the Gila River Reservation about 30 miles SE of Phoenix.

**the Apache resist:** While the Pima and Maricopa got along peacefully with the white men, Apache groups strongly opposed the newcomers. Though nothing could stop men hungry for gold and land, the Apache certainly *discouraged* them. Apache resistance slowed the development of Arizona's towns and industries until late in the 19th century. Today the Apache live on the White Mountain and San Carlos Reservations in eastern Arizona, several small reservations in northcentral Arizona, and with the Mohave Indians on Fort McDowell Reservation NE of Phoenix.

# PHOENIX AND THE VALLEY OF THE SUN

Hub of the sprawling Valley of the Sun, Phoenix has a larger population, bigger businesses, and greater clout than any other city in Arizona. Here the state laws are made and the big corporate deals signed. The Phoenix area is also a cultural and sports center, often in keen competition with Tucson down the road. Many retired people choose to live in the Valley of the Sun, and whole towns are planned just for them. A Western sense of informality and leisure slows the pace of Phoenix a bit, a relaxed style quickly picked up by newcomers. And there have been a lot of them—Phoenix is now the 9th largest city in the country and one of the fastest growing. The city's population is over three-quarters of a million and totals one-and-a-half million when the surrounding cities are added. You'll frequently hear people call the Phoenix area the "Valley of the Sun" but rarely see this name on a map. Still, it accurately reflects the 300 days of sunshine the area receives on average and the "Valley's" pleasant winters.

**the mountains:** Desert mountains form the skyline of the Valley everywhere you look. Some, like Squaw Peak, even poke up in the middle of Phoenix, rewarding hikers with a panorama of the city. Camelback Mountain provides another Phoenix landmark NE of downtown. The bulky South Mountains offer nearly 15,000 acres for hiking, horseback riding, and picnicking—they're the world's largest city park. More remote are the Sierra Estrellas to the SW and the White Tank Mountains to the west. The highest peaks of the area are NE in the Mazatzals, crowned by 7,894-foot Mazatzal Peak. But the most famous range of all would have to be the Superstitions to the east. Stories of Jacob Waltz's "lost" gold mine, that's supposed to exist somewhere in these jagged mountains, still excite the imagination.

**climate:** The city lies at an elevation of roughly 1,100 feet in the desert, where you can expect average summer highs to go *over* 100 F, dropping to the 70s or 80s at night. The Valley comes into its own from Oct. to May, when flocks of "snowbirds" migrate from the northern states and provinces. Even in midwinter, daytime temperatures range in the 60s or low 70s. You won't need a snow shovel. Average rainfall is only 7.05 inches a year.

## HISTORY

**Why Phoenix?:** It's the water. Hohokam Indians tamed the Salt River in the Valley as early as 300 B.C., channelling its waters through intricate networks of canals to fields of beans, corn, squash, and cotton. At their peak, around A.D. 1100, the Hohokam settlements had grown to a population of 50,000 to 100,000. Their culture may have been the most sophisticated ever developed N of Mexico in prehistoric times. Hohokam cities had multistory adobe buildings and ballcourts (large walled fields made for playing a game with rubber balls). They introduced cotton and weaving to the Southwest. For at least 1,700 years the Hohokam tilled the soils until mysteriously disappearing about A.D. 1450. You can see some of their ruins, canals, and artifacts at Pueblo Grande Museum. The Pima Indians who later settled here referred to their predecessors as "Hohokam," meaning "all used up" or "departed." American pioneers

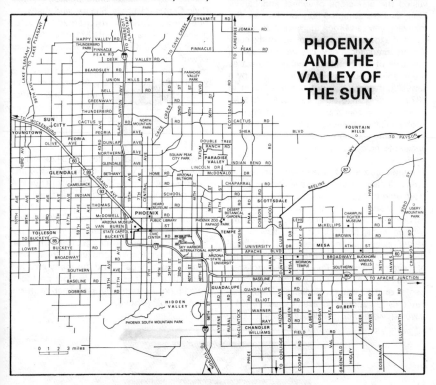

PHOENIX AND THE VALLEY OF THE SUN

discovered the canal system in the 1860s and soon put it back to work for their farms.

**Americans finally arrive:** Spanish and early American explorers overlooked the area. It wasn't until after the Civil War that stories of gold in Prescott and other areas of central Arizona attracted streams of fortune-hunters into this wild land. Pinal and Tonto Apache continued to discourage outsiders, but in Sept. 1865 the Army arrived to build Camp McDowell. Ranching and businesses soon followed as the region became safe. But it was Jack Swilling, a former Confederate soldier-turned-prospector, who first took advantage of the Valley's farming potential. He formed a company in 1867 with $400, 8 mules, and 16 unemployed miners to dig out the Hohokam canals. By the summer of 1868 they had harvested the first crops of wheat and barley. Their success attracted 30 more farmers the following year, and soon there were the beginnings of a town. Darrel Duppa, one of the early settlers, predicted a new city would rise from the ruins of the Hohokam civilization, just as the mythical phoenix bird arose from its own ashes. Surveyors laid out the new town in 1870, marking off lots that sold for $20 to $140 apiece. Wood was scarce in early Phoenix, so adobe buildings went up; they looked, according to some accounts, much like those in the ancient Hohokam villages.

**Phoenix comes of age:** With increasing prosperity and a nearby railroad line, residents built ornate Victorian houses, planted trees, put in sidewalks, opened an ice plant, and made other improvements; it soon looked like a town transplanted from the Midwest. By 1889 Phoenix had enough energy and political muscle to claim the state capital from Prescott. Not even 20 years old, Phoenix had established itself as the business, political and agricultural center of the territory. Roosevelt Dam, dedicated by Theodore Roosevelt himself in 1911, assured water for continued growth. East-

erners sought out the glamorous West, now that it was safe, and flocked to dude ranches. Here they could dress like cowboys, ride the range, and eat mesquite-grilled steaks. World War II jerked Phoenix awake with urgent new industries and aviation training. Growth has been frantic since, helped by the availability of air conditioning that makes the summers bearable. Major manufacturing and service industries now dominate Phoenix's economic scene, but agriculture is still important. Farmers raise crops of citrus, cotton, melons, sugar beets, and vegetables.

## GETTING AROUND

Downtown Phoenix remains the heart of the Valley. You'll find the State Capitol, Phoenix Civic Center, Heritage Square, and many offices here. Streets are named for U.S. presidents—Van Buren, Monroe, Adams, Washington, Jefferson, and others. A newer downtown, or "midtown," has grown up a mile N on Central Avenue. Along this strip you'll find the Main Library, Art Museum, Little Theatre, Heard Museum, and still more office buildings. Central Ave., which runs N-S, connects and neatly divides downtown and midtown. Parallel roads W of Central are called "avenues," and those E are "streets."

Phoenix Transit System; tel. 257-8426, will get you around the Valley with an extensive and low-cost bus service—if you're not in a hurry. A little planning and phoning before taking trips in this area will save a lot of time, as distances can be great and traffic slow. City planners have long talked about a freeway system but little has been done. Traffic gets very thick during rush hour; there's certainly no "rush" to it. Smoke from industry and the many cars has created a serious air pollution problem, something not normally associated with the blue skies of Arizona.

1. San Xavier Mission, near Tucson; 2. Pima County Courthouse, Tucson; 3. Desert View Watchtower, Grand Canyon National Park; 4. Ned A. Hatathli Center at Navajo Community College, Tsaile; 5. Tumacacori National Monument, south of Tucson (all photos by B. Weir)

**THE GRAND CANYON**
1. from Desert View on the South Rim; 2. on the Bright Angel Trail; 3. view from near Grandeur Point on the South Rim ; 4. Angel's Window at Cape Royal on the North Rim; 5. the Colorado River from Desert View (all photos by B. Weir)

# SIGHTS

You'll find dozens of museums in the Valley: historical, archaeological, religious, art, and some unusual collections. The Heard Museum (Southwest Indian) ranks as the most outstanding; it's a good choice if you have time to see only one museum in Phoenix. Foreign visitors are amused to discover that Arizonans regard early 20th C. buildings as "very old." Because the Phoenix area is so large, you'll need a city map to find your way around (purchase from a book store or service station).

## DOWNTOWN PHOENIX

**Arizona State Capitol:** The old state capitol, with its shiny copper dome, was completed in 1901, some 11 years before statehood. The Arizona legislature outgrew this structure 25 years ago and moved into new quarters just behind it. The old capitol became a museum, carefully restored to its 1912 appearance when Arizona was a brand-new state. You'll see a lifelike statue of then-governor George W.P. Hunt sitting behind his desk, and hear a recording telling of Hunt's long career in public office. The Senate and House chambers and other rooms are full of Arizona history — photos, tales of frontier days, a bugle from the USS *Arizona*, Indian crafts, and other memorabilia. Guided tours leave at 1000 and 1400, or you can take a self-guided one. To dig deeper into the state's past, drop into the research library, Room 300. The Capitol is open Mon. to Fri. 0800-1700; free; tel. 255-4581. It's at 1700 W. Washington (free parking across the street in front; turn in from Adams St.).

**The Arizona Museum:** Curators have packed the 2 rooms of this small museum with Indian crafts, pioneer memorabilia, and very odd oddities. Arizona's Indians are represented by baskets, pottery, Hopi *katsina* dolls, a war club, and other artifacts. You can see a large model of the battleship *Arizona* (launched in 1915 and sunk at Pearl Harbor on Dec. 7th, 1941), an ostrich egg from the old ostrich farm near Phoenix, tools used to build the State Capitol,

*Arizona State Capitol*

an 1883 steam engine that powered one of the first motorcycles (a high-wheeler!), a rifle collection, a portable spittoon, and much more! Two steam locomotives from early mining operations sit outside. The Arizona Museum is open Wed. to Sun. 1100-1600; free; tel. 253-2734. It's on the corner of Van Buren and 10th Avenue.

**Arizona Hall of Fame:** Historic exhibits honor people who have made outstanding contributions to the state. Open Mon. to Fri. 0800-1700; free; tel. 255-2110. Located downtown at 1101 W. Washington.

**Galleria:** The Arizona Bank has changing art exhibits at the 101 N. 1st Ave. and Adams St. office. Open Mon. to Thur. 0900-1500, and Fri. 0900-1700; free; tel. 262-2209.

**Arizona History Room:** First Interstate Bank has rotating exhibits of Western art, mining, and culture downstairs in their office at 100 W. Washington St. and 1st Avenue. Open Mon. to Fri. 1000-1500; free; tel. 271-6879.

**Arizona Museum of Science and Technology:** Kids especially will have lots of fun in this hands-on museum. You get to operate com-

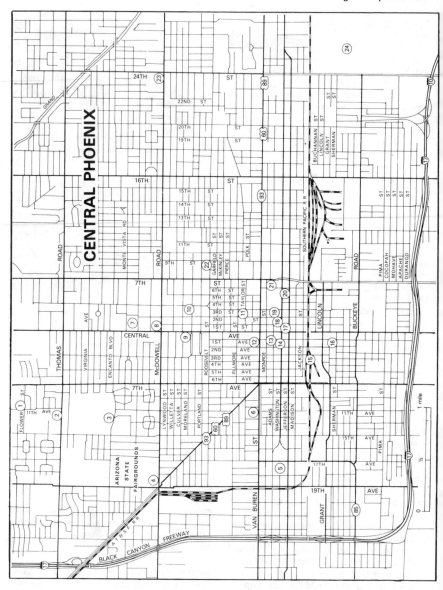

puters, see your own thermal image, walk into an infinity chamber, generate electricity, step into a camera obscura, and experience many other science-related displays. The museum also has a small gift shop and an ice-cream parlor. Open Mon. to Sat 0900-1700, and Sun. 1300-1700; $2.50 adult, and $1.50 children 4-12; tel. 256-9388. Located at the corner of Adams and 2nd Sts. (across from Phoenix Civic Plaza).

**Rosson House and Heritage Square:** The Victorian-style Rosson House, built in 1895, dominates this block of historic buildings. Meticulous restoration has returned the Rosson House to its turn-of-the-century appearance, when it was one of Phoenix's most elegant. You can tour the interior and learn about its construction and people who lived here; open Wed. to Sat. 1000-1530, and Sun.

---

### CENTRAL PHOENIX

1. Judaica Museum
2. Phoenix College Theatre
3. Encanto Park Bandshell
4. Arizona Mineral Museum
5. State Capitol
6. Arizona Museum
7. Heard Museum
8. Phoenix Art Museum; main public library; Phoenix Little Theatre
9. Central Arizona Museum
10. Phoenix Performing Arts Theatre
11. Visitors Bureau (Phoenix and Valley of the Sun)
12. Y.M.C.A.
13. Galleria (Arizona Bank art exhibits)
14. Arizona History Room (First Interstate Bank)
15. Amtrak Train
16. Duppa-Montgomery Homestead
17. Phoenix Transit (local bus)
18. Arizona Museum of Science and Technology
19. Symphony Hall
20. Greyhound Bus
21. Rosson House and Heritage Square
22. youth hostel
23. Tonto National Forest (main office)
24. Sky Harbor Airport

---

1200-1530; $2 adult, $.50 children 7-13; tel. 262-5071. Tours start next door at the Burgess Carriage House, built in a Colonial Williamsburg style of architecture rarely seen this far west. Originally at 2nd St. and Taylor, it's the only structure to have been moved to Heritage Square. Burgess Carriage House now contains a gift shop.

The other buildings on Heritage Square, all with free admission, are representative of early Phoenix: the Duplex (1923) is now used for offices; the Stevens House (1901) has rotating exhibits sponsored by ASU (Arizona State University); the Stevens-Haustgen House (turn of the century) exhibits varied products of the Craftsmen's Co-op Gallery; the Bouvier-Teeter House (1899) is now a dining room for the Duck and Decanter Restaurant; the Silva House (1900) has Salt River Project exhibits; and a second Carriage House (about 1900) now houses the Duck and Decanter kitchen (offering sandwiches, soups, quiches, and salads daily from 0730 to 2100). The Lath House Pavilion dates only from 1980 but is typical of early Phoenix architecture. Heritage Square is at 6th and Monroe Sts., one block E of Civic Plaza.

**Duppa-Montgomery Homestead:** Historians credit the English adventurer and scholar Darrel Duppa with naming both Phoenix and Tempe. Duppa's adobe house dates from 1870, and is probably the oldest building in Phoenix. An old bar and other historic artifacts are displayed inside. Open Sun. 1400-1700 from Nov. to May; free; tel. 253-5557 or 255-4470. Located at 116 W. Sherman St. (7 blocks S of Washington).

## CENTRAL AVENUE CORRIDOR

**Central Arizona Museum:** Inside the 1917 Ellis-Shackelford mansion you'll find an early 1900s drug store, a general store, a 1905 air cooler (that used a 75-lb. block of ice), and an exhibit about reservoirs and canals of the Salt River Project. You can also learn why Phoenix was once the ostrich capital of the world. The museum sells books about Arizona's history and has a small research library. Open Tue. to

Sat. 1000-1600; free; tel. 255-4470. Located at 1242 N. Central Avenue.

**Phoenix Art Museum:** A varied collection of more than 11,000 works of art spans the 15th through 20th centuries. Particularly strong are the 18th C. French painting exhibits, and the Oriental, Contemporary, Mexican, and Western Art collections. Visiting exhibitions also occupy a large area. The museum often schedules tours. Kids will enjoy touching, exploring, and even creating their own art in the Junior Museum downstairs. The museum's reference library is also downstairs. You'll find art souvenirs just inside the entrance in the museum store. Open Tue. to Sat. 1000-1700 ('til 2100 on Wed.) and Sun. 1300-1700; $2 adult, $1 student and senior citizen, children 12 and under free; tel. 257-1880 or 257-1222 (recording of local art events). Located at 1625 N. Central Ave. at McDowell.

**Heard Museum:** The Heard features the best exhibits on Southwest Indians you're likely to see *anywhere*. The collection is large enough to give a good overview of regional Indian cultures, but small enough that it won't overwhelm you. Indians talk about their culture in "Our Voices Our Land," an audiovisual program with beautiful photography and native music. See exhibits of the Southwest—land and people—from the earliest prehistoric times to the present. Clothing, tools, weapons, and even a Navajo hogan all demonstrate the resourcefulness of the tribes. Large displays show superb Indian jewelry from Navajo, Hopi, and Zuni craftsmen. A *katsina* collection from the Hopi and Zuni tribes fills an entire room. The Heard Museum also has large collections of Southwest pottery, weavings, basketry, and paintings.

Its Primitive Art Gallery exhibits work from the world's far corners of South America, Africa, the Pacific, and Asia. Two other galleries have visiting shows. For deeper research, you can visit the anthropology library. The museum's sizeable shop sells Indian art and crafts and books on Indian cultures. Open Mon. to Sat. 1000-1645, and Sun. 1300-1645, but closed holidays; $3 adult, $1 student and children; tel.

252-8840. It's in a Spanish Colonial-style building at 22 E. Monte Vista Rd. (3 blocks N on Central Ave. from McDowell, then one block E on Monte Vista).

# NORTH PHOENIX

**Arizona Mineral Museum:** Many of Arizona's pioneers came in search of the glitter of gold and silver, or the brilliant colors signifying copper minerals. Here you'll see these and many more. Most eye-catching are the beautiful specimens of copper ore—azurite, malachite, chrysocolla, cuprite, chalcanthite, and turquoise. Old mining tools, lamps, assay kits, photos, and models show how miners did their work. A fluorescent room demonstrates the effect of 2 different wavelengths of ultraviolet light. Lapidary exhibits display the art of gem cutting and polishing. The museum staff can tell you of upcoming rock & mineral shows (most are held over the winter months) and put you in touch with local shops and clubs. A gift shop sells specimens, gold pans, and books. Open Mon. to Fri., 0800-1700, and Sat. 1300-1700; free; tel. 255-3791. It's on the SW corner of the State Fairgrounds at the corner of McDowell and 19th Ave.; enter fairgrounds on 17th Ave. from McDowell.

**Judaica Museum:** Learn about the Jewish ceremonies and religious holidays at Temple Beth Israel's museum. It displays many ancient artifacts from the Holy Land. Open Tue. to Thur. 0900-1400, and Sun. 0900-1200; closed in summer; free; tel. 264-4428. Located at 3310 N. 10th Ave. (approach from Osborn Rd. off either 7th or 19th Aves.).

**Cave Creek Museum:** This small collection features prehistoric Indian artifacts, a pithouse replica, mining displays, and ranching history of the area. The museum is open Thur. to Sun. 1330-1630 (closed June to Sept.); free; tel. 488-2764 or 488-3183. Cave Creek lies among foothills about 30 miles N of downtown Phoenix. Drive N on Cave Creek Rd. or head E from I-17 on AZ 74 (Exit 223). Turn S on Basin Rd. to Skyline Drive.

miner's cabin
(reconstruction) at
Pioneer Arizona

**Pioneer Arizona:** The frontier comes back to life in this museum of living history. You'll see how residents of the territory lived from the mid-1800s to statehood in 1912. Hop on a wagon for a free narrated tour of the village. Or walk around to see historic exhibits and craftsmen at work. Many of the 30 or so buildings are authentic, having been brought from other sites. The nearly complete little town has a school, church, sheriff's office, bank, blacksmith shop, woodworking shop, opera house, cabins, and houses (including the John Sears mansion, thought to be Phoenix's first frame house). Pioneer Arizona emphasizes historical accuracy, setting it apart from most other "western villages" based more on Hollywood fiction than fact. Mountain men, cavalry, gunfighters, and special exhibits enliven the community on the weekend nearest its birthday (15 Feb.) and weekends in November. On weekends from Oct. to May you might catch a frontier melodrama in the opera house; call for times. The Whiskey-Road-to-Ruin restaurant, named after an 1881 saloon in Gila Bend, serves home-style lunches Wed. to Sun. and a fish-fry dinner on Friday. Pioneer Arizona is open Wed. to Sun. 0900-1600; summer hours (June to Sept.) change to Wed. to Fri. 0900-1300, Sat. and Sun. 0900-1600; $3 adult, $2 student and senior, $1 children 6-12; tel.

993-0212. It's set among rocky desert foothills about 30 miles N of downtown Phoenix. Take I-17 N to Pioneer Rd. (Exit 225) and follow signs.

## WEST PHOENIX

**Wildlife World Zoo:** This collection of exotic wildlife began as a breeding farm for rare and endangered species in 1974, and opened to the public 10 years later. You'll meet the patas monkey, fastest of all primates, which can run dog-like across the ground at 35 miles per hour. Larger animals include the scimitar-horned oryx, dama gazelle, addax (an antelope of the Sahara Desert), kangaroo, zebra, and camel. The zoo really shines in its bird collection—pheasants, toucans, cockatoos, macaws, currasows, ostrichs (all 5 of the world's species), and some birds not displayed anywhere else in the country. A large walk-in aviary contains Palawan peacock pheasants of the Phillipines, Eyton's tree ducks of Australia, crowned pigeons of Papua New Guinea, and other unusual birds. Open daily 0900-1700 (except mid-June to mid-Sept. when it's open Mon. to Fri. 0800-1200, Sat. and Sun. 0800-1800); $4 adult, $2.50 children 2-12; tel.

935-WILD. The zoo is about 18 miles W of I-17 on Northern Ave. (3 miles W of Litchfield Rd.), just past Luke A.F.B.

## SOUTH PHOENIX

**Mystery Castle:** Boyce Luther Gulley dreamed of building his own castle, so one day in 1927 he left his wife and daughter and disappeared. His whereabouts and this castle remained unknown until after his death in 1945. The daughter, Mary Lou Gulley, now lives in the castle and leads tours through the imaginative rooms. Everything from Stutz-Bearcat wheels to discarded bricks have gone into this strange mixture of American West and scrapyard. Tours are short (about 20 min.) but anyone who has dreamed of castles should enjoy it. Open Tue. to Sun. 1100-1700 from 1 Oct. to 4 July; closed the rest of the year; $2.50 adult, $.50 children 5-14; tel. 268-1581. Mystery Castle is 7 miles S of Phoenix near the entrance to South Mountain Park. Drive S on Central Ave. then L ½ mile on Mineral Road.

*Mystery Castle*

## EAST PHOENIX

**Pueblo Grande Museum:** Good exhibits show how archaeologists dig and analyze their finds. Scientists have been able to reconstruct the prehistoric Hohokam society and environment using pollen, plant and animal remains, artifacts, and burials. They know, for example, that the average Hohokam man stood 5 feet, 4 inches tall, weighed 130-140 pounds, and had a 40-year life span. You can see Hohokam crafts, stone tools, and illustrations of their pithouses, pueblos, canals, and ballcourts. After looking at the indoor exhibits, you'll better appreciate the ruin outside. The Hohokam began construction of Pueblo Grande about A.D. 1200 on an artificial hill overlooking the Salt River, and occupied the site for 200 years. From the ruins you can see ancient canal banks and an oval-shaped depression thought to be a ballcourt. A trail guide describes features of Pueblo Grande's construction. Open Mon. to Sat., 0900-1645, and Sun., 1300-1645; $ .50; tel. 275-3452. The museum and ruins are 5 miles E of downtown at 4619 E. Washington Street.

**Arizona Military Museum:** The museum tells the story of Arizona's military history from Spanish days to the present. Old maps, photos, weapons, uniforms, and other memorabilia illustrate each period. The museum building was headquarters during WW II for a prison camp holding German submariners. Open Sat. and Sun. 1300-1600; free; tel. 267-2676. The museum is in the Arizona National Guard complex at 5636 E. McDowell Rd., about 7 miles E of downtown; stop to check in at the entrance gate.

**Desert Botanical Gardens:** If you've been curious about all those strange cacti and other desert plants of Arizona, this is the place to find out what they are. A ¼-mile trail in the gardens winds past more than 50 species. Signs list their names and the trail guide tells more. The gardens display exotic plants from other regions too, representing more than half of all

*Military authorities thought the desert near Phoenix a perfect place to hold captured German submariners. These prisoners escaped by tunneling. All were recaptured, though 2 made it as far as Mexico.*

cactus species in the world. If you're lucky enough to be here in the spring, you'll see many plants in bloom. A Wildflower Hotline operating during Mar. and Apr. tells you where wildflowers can be seen in Arizona; tel. 941-1239. The gift shop sells natural history books, souvenirs, and cactus specimens. Open daily from 0900 (0700 in July and Aug.) until sunset; $2.50 adult, $2 age 60 and over, and $ .50 children 5-12; tel. 941-1217 or 941-1225. The Desert Botanical Gardens are off Galvin Parkway in Papago Park (enter from either 6400 E. McDowell Rd. or 5800 E. Van Buren Street).

**Phoenix Zoo:** Animals and birds from Arizona and all over the world inhabit 125 acres of roll-ing hills. The zoo uses moats and steep inclines, when possible, to give the animals an open and natural setting. Tropical rainforests, mountains, grasslands, temperate woodlands, and deserts recreate appropriate habitats for the more than 1,000 zoo residents. You'll see bighorn sheep from Arizona, oryx from the Arabian deserts, tigers from India, gorillas from Africa, wallabies from Papua New Guinea, and many others. Children will enjoy meeting the farm animals in the "Petting Zoo." If a lot of walking doesn't appeal, just hop on the "Safari Train" for a narrated tour of the grounds; $1. The Phoenix Zoo is open daily 0900-1700 (0800-1700 from June to Aug.); $5 adult, $2 children 4-14 (with adult); tel. 273-1341. It's off Galvin Parkway in Papago Park (enter from

*Shand Mason Steamer (circa 1873), Hall of Flame*

either 6400 E. McDowell Rd. or 5800 E. Van Buren St.).

**Hall of Flame:** Being a volunteer fireman in the old days carried great prestige. Men eagerly joined the local fire brigade, which also acted as a social club. Firemen competed in drills and marched in parades with their glistening machines. The museum houses what may be the world's largest display of firefighting gear. Equipment in this amazing collection comes from all over the world. Many items are works of art in themselves. The first gallery contains hand- and horse-drawn pumpers, hose carriers, and hook-and-ladder wagons from the 18th and 19th centuries. A second gallery displays antique motorized fire trucks. Old prints show firefighters in action. Open Mon. to Sat. 0900-1700; $3 adult, $1 students 6-17; tel. "ASK-FIRE." The Hall of Flame is opposite Papago Park at 6101 E. Van Buren St. (turn S ¼ mile on Project Drive).

**Salt River Project History Center:** The Salt River Project displays feature both the Hohokam and modern canal systems, Indian artifacts, construction of Theodore Roosevelt Dam, and electric power history. Open Mon. to

Fri. 0830-1600; free; tel. 236-2208. The Center is at 1521 Project Dr., across from the Hall of Flame.

# SCOTTSDALE

Sometimes billing itself as "The West's Most Western Town," Scottsdale has porch-fronted shops that sell Western clothing, Western art, and Indian crafts. Chaplain Winfield Scott, the first resident, fell in love with the Valley and homesteaded here in the 1880s. During his frequent travels, he promoted the land as "unequalled in greater fertility or richer promise." A small close-knit community soon formed at Brown Ave. and Main Street. But the little village has grown up—115,000 people live here now. Both residents and visitors enjoy the top-notch specialty shops, art galleries, cultural events, restaurants, resort hotels, and beautiful landscaping. Scottsdale, just E of Phoenix and just N of Tempe, makes an ideal base for a stay in the Valley, though it's a little more expensive than Phoenix.

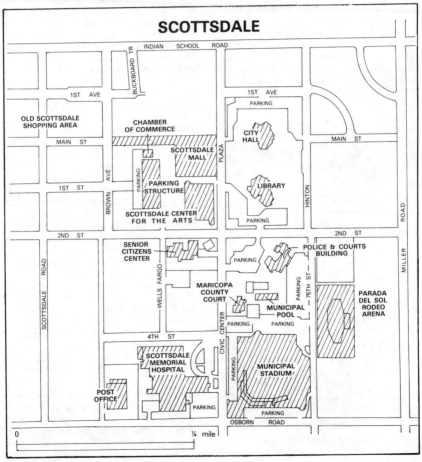

## SIGHTS

**The Little Red Schoolhouse:** Scottsdale was so small in 1909, when this schoolhouse was built, that all the town's children could fit into the 2 classrooms. From the 1920s until the 1960s, Mexican agricultural workers used it as a schoolhouse and community center. The Mexican barrio and the cottonfields where they worked have disappeared, but The Little Red Schoolhouse has been preserved as a reminder of the town's past. Located near the center of the original Scottsdale, the schoolhouse makes a good place to begin a visit of the modern city. Scottsdale's Chamber of Commerce occupies the building today. They'll give you a pamphlet for a self-guided walking tour of Old-Town Scottsdale and answer questions about sights, shopping, restaurants, and places to stay. Ask for a

*frolicking in front of City Hall*

Scottsdale Trolley schedule. The Chamber is open Mon. to Fri., 0830-1700; tel. 945-8481. The schoolhouse is in the Civic Center Complex, just E of the intersection of Brown Ave. and Main Street.

**Scottsdale Center for the Arts:** Scottsdale's residents have always had a keen interest in the arts. This city-owned facility contains a large gallery of contemporary art, a gallery gift shop, a 790-seat performing theater, and a cinema. Admission to the art gallery is free, but there's a charge for performances and movies. Call tel. 994-ARTS to find out what's coming up. The Center is open Tue. to Fri. 1000-2000, Sat., 1200-2000, Sun. 1200-1700. Part of the Civic Center Complex, it's located between The Little Red Schoolhouse and the Library.

**Cosanti Foundation:** Italian-born Paolo Soleri first came to Scottsdale in 1947 to study architecture with Frank Lloyd Wright. In 1956 Soleri started Cosanti, his own foundation, with the goal of designing energy- and space-efficient cities. Still striving for those ideals, Soleri feels that urban sprawl, of which the Valley is a prime example, wastes agricultural land and harms society. He uses the word *arcology,* a combination of "architecture" and "ecology," to describe his work. At Cosanti Foundation you can see some of Soleri's unique structures and learn about his ideas for making the world better to live in. Books, drawings, sculpture, and Soleri's famous windbells purchased in the gallery/giftshop help finance the Foundation. To see *arcology* in action, visit Arcosanti—Soleri's city-in-the-making 65 miles N of Phoenix (see end of "Northcentral Arizona" chapter). The Cosanti Foundation is open daily 0900-1700; $1 donation; tel. 948-6145. It's at 6433 Doubletree Rd.; from central Scottsdale go 5 miles N on Scottsdale Rd., then turn L one mile on Doubletree Road.

**Taliesin West:** The renowned architect Frank Lloyd Wright didn't just design buildings according to a plan; he let them "grow" from the inside out. His idea for training student architects was similar. Apprentices had to grow and develop far beyond the learning of facts and formulas. Taliesin West began in 1938 as a winter home for Wright's Wisconsin school, opened 6 years earlier. Students at Taliesin West lived then in tents and simple shelters and now, nearly 50 years later, still do! Most stay 3-5 years, living in close contact with one another, the faculty, and the surrounding desert. Wright died in 1959, but the Frank Lloyd Wright School of Architecture and Taliesin Associated Architects carry on his high standards. Students lead daily walking tours from mid-Oct. to mid-May, beginning every half-hour 1000-1600 and lasting about 45 minutes. There's a limited tour schedule in summer; call for times. Besides touring some of the grounds, you'll see highlights of Wright's work in models, photos, and a slide presentation. Most visitors with a feeling for architecture and design find the tour worthwhile, despite the high $5 charge ($2 children under 12). Taliesin West is set in the western foothills of the McDowell Mountains NE of Scottsdale. It's recommended to call first before going out, as tours are occasionally cancelled; tel. 860-8810 or 860-2700. From central Scottsdale, go N 10 miles on Scottsdale Rd., turn R 4.3 miles on Shea Blvd., turn L on Via Linda, then L on 108th St. and follow signs.

**Rawhide:** A replica of an 1880s Old West town with about 25 buildings containing shops, Western exhibits, a museum, saloon, Golden Belle Restaurant (steaks, chicken, ribs), burro rides for the kids, and stagecoach rides. The museum displays such Western curiosities as Tom Mix's boots, Wyatt Earp's gun, and a pair of Geronimo's moccasins. Rawhide has free admission but there are plenty of places inside to spend your money. Open Mon. to Fri. 1700-2400, Sat. and Sun. 1200-2200, though shops close at 2100; tel. 563-5111. From central Scottsdale, go N about 13 miles to 23023 N. Scottsdale Road.

**Fountain Hills:** The world's highest fountain shoots 560 feet into the skies of this community 18 miles NE of Scottsdale. A 15-minute display takes place daily on the hour from 1000-2100. The surrounding park is a fine place for a picnic or stroll. From Scottsdale go N 6 miles on Scottsdale Rd. and turn R 12 miles on Shea Boulevard.

# TEMPE

An enterprising merchant—Charles Trumbull Hayden—arrived here in 1872 to set up a trading post. He chose this spot on the south bank of the Salt River because it was the safest place to cross with his freight wagons. Hayden also found it a good location for a flour mill and a ferry service. Darrel Duppa came over from Phoenix to visit Hayden's Ferry one day, and remarked that the Salt River Valley reminded him of the Vale of Tempe between Mt. Olympus and Mt. Ossa in Thessaly, Greece. Hayden liked the name and it stuck. Farmers settled in Tempe (pronounced "tem-PEE"), raising livestock, dairying, and growing a variety of crops. In 1885 the territorial legislature established Arizona State Teachers College nearby, which has grown into one of the largest universities in the country. Many of Tempe's original buildings have survived; you'll see Hayden's home, his flour mill (rebuilt in 1918 after a fire), and other old buildings along Mill Avenue. Sandwiched between Phoenix to the W and Mesa to the E, Tempe lies just S of Scottsdale.

**Tempe Historical Museum:** Pioneering days are remembered in the museum's collection of agricultural tools, an old post office, a covered wagon, home furnishings, and a 1919 Model-T firetruck. Open Tue. to Sat. 1000-1630; free; tel. 731-8377. It's located in the Tempe Community Center at the SW corner of 3500 S. Rural Rd. and Southern Avenue.

**Niels Peterson House:** Built in 1892, this Queen Anne/Victorian-style house uses a clever ventilation system to keep the interior liveable in summer. You can tour the inside, partly restored to its 1930s appearance, Mon. to Fri. 1000-1400; free; tel. 829-1392 or 731-8377. The house is on the NW corner of 1414 W. Southern Ave. and Priest Drive.

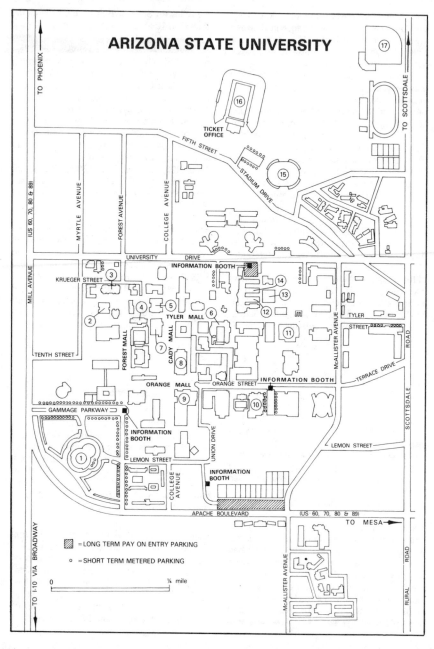

ARIZONA STATE UNIVERSITY

⬛ = LONG TERM PAY ON ENTRY PARKING

○ = SHORT TERM METERED PARKING

0 _____ ¼ mile

**Tempe Arts Center:** Contemporary artists display their paintings, sculpture, photography, even food. Exhibits, which change monthly, are free. Most work is for sale. The Sculpture Garden outside contains many modern pieces. "Happenings" (performances) take place occasionally, for which there might be a charge. Open Tue. to Sun. 1200-1700; tel. 968-0888. The center is in Tempe Beach Park along the Salt River at the corner of Mill Ave. and First Street.

## ARIZONA STATE UNIVERSITY

Broad lawns, stately palms, and flowering subtropical trees grace the 600-acre campus of Arizona's largest university. Just recently ASU celebrated its first centenary. Classes originally met in a single 4-room red-brick structure set on 20 acres of cow pasture. Growth has been spectacular within the last 25 years, when most of the campus buildings have gone up. The school now has more than 40,000 students and a teaching faculty of about 1,400. Undergraduates have 92 fields to choose from, while graduate students can earn a Master's in 68 areas of interest or a Doctorate in 42. Attractions on campus include the striking Gammage

### ARIZONA STATE UNIVERSITY

1. Grady Gammage Auditorium
2. Harry Wood Gallery (Art Building)
3. Gallery of Design (College of Architecture)
4. Northlight Gallery (Matthews Hall)
5. Anthropology Museum
6. Zoology Display (Life Sciences Center)
7. University Art Collection (Matthews Center)
8. Hayden Library
9. Memorial Union
10. ASU Bookstore
11. Daniel E. Noble Science Library
12. Planetarium (Physical Sciences Center)
13. Geology Museum
14. Center for Meteorite Studies (Physical Sciences Center)
15. University Activity Center
16. Sun Devil Stadium
17. Packard Baseball Stadium

Auditorium, several art galleries, and a variety of small museums. The well-landscaped campus is a pleasant place for stroll. Activity slows down in summer (it's hot!) but most of the galleries and museums stay open, except as noted below.

**getting around:** Parking is tight, as you might expect with so many students (many of whom commute), but you can use the parking meters ($ .50 for 50 minutes), 2 pay lots ($1.50/day) on campus, or look for a spot on a side street off campus. See map for campus parking areas. Most of the central campus is closed to motor traffic. Phoenix Transit; tel. 257-8426, connects the university with the rest of the Valley while the Tempe Trolley; tel. 831-0043, has service in town. The open-air University Tram cruises the outer areas of campus.

**Memorial Union:** This social center of the university is a good place to start a visit. The Information Desk on the main floor can tell you about the latest concerts, movies, theatre, art showings, and sporting events. It's open 0800-2300 (shorter hours in summer and breaks) or you can call tel. 965-5728. Across from the desk you'll find a bulletin board of apartments for rent and "for sales." Around the corner is a Ride Board, if you're looking for someone going your way. Memorial Union Art Gallery, at the other end of the building, often has visiting shows. But you might not make it that far, because you'll have to pass 9 tempting eateries on the way: a deli, pizza place, grill—everything from a Pasta Express to a Cafe Ole. Stop in "The Club" for regular cafeteria meals. Relax downstairs in a lounge or patio, go bowling ($ .75/game and $ .35/shoes), play a game of billiards ($1.50/hour per table), or see a movie ($2/nonstudents).

**Grady Gammage Auditorium:** You'll see this circular structure, which commemorates one of the ASU presidents, on the SW corner of campus. Dedicated in 1964, it was Frank Lloyd Wright's last major design. You can take a free ½-hour tour inside, usually on Tue., Thur., and Sat. afternoons; call tel. 965-3434 for tour times and concert information.

*Grady Gammage Auditorium detail*

The Gammage Auditorium is easy to spot, set into a curve of the Phoenix-Mesa highway (US 60/70/80/89).

**University Art Collection:** A varied display of paintings, prints, sculpture, and crafts by artists from the United States, Latin America, and other parts of the world. Visiting art exhibits appear too. Open Mon. to Fri. 0800-1700, and Sun. 1300-1700; free; tel. 965-2874. The collection is on the 2nd floor in Matthews Center.

**Northlight Gallery:** Photographic exhibits, both historic and modern, are featured. Open Sun. to Thur. 1030-1630 (closed in summer); free; tel. 965-5667. Located in Matthews Hall (behind Matthews Center).

**Anthropology Museum:** Displays illustrate prehistoric Hohokam and modern Indian cultures, archaeological techniques, and concepts of anthropology. Open Mon. to Fri. 0800-1700; free; tel. 965-6213. It's in the Anthropology Building, next to Matthews Center.

**Harry Wood Gallery:** See student exhibitions of paintings, photography, or sculpture. Open Mon. to Fri. 0800-1700 (closed in summer); free; tel. 965-3468. Located in the School of Arts building.

**Gallery of Design:** Learn the latest architectural techniques, illustrated by drawings and scale models. Open Mon. to Fri. 0800-1700; free; tel. 965-3216. The Gallery of Design, along with the Howe Library of Architecture, Planning, and Design Services, is in the College of Architecture and Environmental Design.

**Zoology Display:** Meet the university's live rattlesnakes, gila monsters, and other reptiles. More lovable are a family of kit foxes kept in a courtyard. Open Mon. to Fri. 0800-1700; free; tel. 965-3571. Located in the Life Sciences Building (east wing).

**Planetarium:** Watch programs about the heavens; usually Tue. and Thur. evenings during the main Sept. to May school terms; $1 admission; call tel. 965-6891 for times. Located in Room B-350 of the Physical Sciences Center.

**Center for Meteorite Studies:** See visitors from outer space in Room C-139 of the Physical Sciences Center. Open Mon. to Fri. 0800-1630; free; tel. 965-6511.

**Geology Museum:** You can check the 6-story Foucault Pendulum to see if the Earth is still spinning, or watch the seismograph to learn if it is shaking. Exhibits identify rocks, minerals, and fossils. Open Mon. to Fri. 1000-1300 (closed summer); free; tel. 965-5081. Located in "F" Wing of the Physical Sciences Center.

**Daniel E. Noble Science Library:** Here you'll find the books used by the surrounding science and engineering departments; tel. 965-7133. Hikers can plan their trips with the map collection and make needed photocopies. Hours for the map collection, during regular and summer terms, are Mon. to Thur., 0800-2000, Fri. 0800-1700, (closed Sat.), and Sun. 1300-1700; tel. 965-3582.

**Hayden Library:** The University's main library

also has the Arizona, Chicano, East Asian, and Government Documents special collections. Open Mon. to Thur., 0700-2400, Fri. 0700-2200, Sat., 0900-1700, and Sun., 1000-2400; tel. 965-3106. Shorter hours during summer and breaks, and for the special collections.

**ASU Bookstore:** A good selection of general interest books as well as textbooks, supplies, and maps. You can pick out a Sun Devils T-shirt or other souvenirs. Open Mon. to Thur. 0800-1800 (Fri. 'til 1700).

**sports:** ASU, as sports crazy as any other large university, has fielded some top teams. You can see their trophies, clippings, and photos at the Sports Hall of Fame, located in the circular corridor of the Activity Center; open Mon. to Fri. 0800-1700. Football takes place in the giant 70,000-seat Sun Devils Stadium; basketball in the 14,000-seat Activity Center, and baseball in the 8,000-seat Packard Stadium. Sun Devils Athletic Ticket Office sells tickets to the games; tel. 965-2381.

*ASU Campus*

# MESA

Mesa typifies middle America. Houses with neatly trimmed lawns line the broad streets. In Sept. of 1877, however, when Mesa's Mormon settlers began their long journey from Idaho, this land was only desert with a thin strip of greenery along the Salt River. The eager families, loaded with supplies and driving their cattle, arrived 5 months later. They immediately began to rebuild the old Hohokam irrigation canals, hoping to turn the desert green and make a prosperous new life under the warm Arizona sun. Because the land reminded them of a table top, they named their settlement "Mesa." From the 80 Mormon pioneers, Mesa has grown to be Arizona's 3rd largest city with a population of over 210,000. More people arrive in winter to enjoy the sunny climate, the lakes, and the Superstition Mountains close at hand. Mesa, next door to Tempe and 15 miles E of Phoenix, is easily reached by the Superstition Freeway. The Mesa Chamber of Commerce sponsors free "Tag-Along" tours from Nov. to April. You drive your own car, following a leader, to visit orchards, Granite Reef Dam, Champlin Fighter Museum, and other area attractions. Call the Chamber office for a schedule; tel. 969-1307.

## SIGHTS

**Arizona Temple:** Rising from beautifully landscaped gardens, the Mormon Church's Arizona Temple is Mesa's most notable landmark. The structure was completed in 1927 from a plan based on classical Greek architecture. Friezes at the top 4 corners of the exterior represent the gathering of the house of Israel from the 4 corners of the Earth. Marriages and other sacred ceremonies take place inside. The interior is closed to non-Mormons, but you're welcome to wander among the exotic plants in the gardens and take a free tour within the Visitor Center, the building just N of the temple. Tours present the basic doctrines of the Church of Latter-Day Saints, or Mormons, through a series of movies and animated dio-

ramas. The presentation explains the importance of temples and shows slides of the Arizona Temple's interior. The one-hour tours begin on the hour and half hour daily from 0900-2100. If you'd like to know more about the Mormon religion, ask to see their other movies and video tapes. The Arizona Temple is at 525 E. Main St., just E of downtown; tel. 964-7164.

**Buckhorn Mineral Wells:** One of the Valley's more unusual attractions. In 1939, hot underground water was discovered and developed into a health spa. You hop into your own tub (106 degrees F) for $10 and get a rejuvenating massage for another $15. A sign lists the water's mineral content. You can also visit their museum of over 400 stuffed animals, most of which are native to Arizona. Birds hang from the rafters, javelinas glare from the walls, a coyote snarls from behind a couch, etc.; $2 adult, $1 children under 12. The museum and baths are open Tue. to Sat. 0900-1700; tel. 832-1111. You can also stay here; cottages start at $16.05 s, $26.75 d. Buckhorn is 7 miles E of downtown Mesa at 5900 E. Main St. (at corner of Recker Rd.).

*javelina at Buckhorn Mineral Wells*

*Messerschmitt Bf-109E3 at Champlin Fighter Museum*

**Mesa Museum:** Recreated cave and village displays will give you an idea of how early Indians lived. Petroglyphs and a variety of Salado and Hohokam pottery can also be seen, as well as a stagecoach, a 1908 autobus, and an adobe schoolhouse. Kids will enjoy visiting the authentic jail or trying to crack the big safe. Another project is deciphering the "secret" stone maps of the Lost Dutchman Mine. Outside you can grab a gold pan and try panning some gravel from the stream. There's a gift shop with books and souvenirs. Open Tue. to Sat. 1000-1700, and Sun. 1300-1700; free. In Dec. the museum has an animated Christmas display and stays open 'til 2000. Located downtown at 53 N. McDonald near the corner of W. 1st St.; tel. 834-2230.

**Champlin Fighter Museum:** The excitement of viewing the world's hottest aircraft from WW I and WW II draws visitors to this unique collection. Here you'll also learn about the men who flew them. Autographed photos accompany stories of the fighter aces who fought in conflicts from WW I to Vietnam. Realistic paintings show aircraft in action. Then there're the planes, housed in 2 giant hangars. You'll see a replica of the Mercedes-powered Rumpler Taube — the world's first combat aircraft (1911), using only hand-thrown bombs; a Fokker Dr-I Triplane, the type flown by the "Red Baron" ace, Manfred von Richthofen of Germany; a British Sopwith Camel, one of which finally downed the "Red Baron"; the extremely rare German Messerschmitt 109 and Focke Wulf 190 so successful in WW II; the Supermarine Spitfire that helped save the day in the Battle of Britain; the American P-51D Mustang, reputed to be the finest fighter of WW II; and dozens of other beautifully preserved planes. Famous aircraft engines include the 1941 rocket engine used in Messerschmitt 163 Komets, and one of the 8 engines used on Howard Hughes' "Spruce Goose" on its first and only flight. You can peek into the restoration area where mechanics keep these antique craft in flying condition. In a video presentation, you'll hear aces telling how they flew and fought, and see actual combat footage taken during WW II, and in Korea and Vietnam. A gift shop sells aircraft models, posters, and books. You can visit Champlin Fighter Museum's "Aircraft of the Aces" daily 1000-1700; $4 adult, $2 children 4-14; tel. 830-4540. It's at Falcon Field (off McKellips Rd.) on the NE edge of Mesa about 7 miles from downtown.

# VALLEY OF THE SUN ACCOMMODATIONS

**youth hostel:** Valley of the Sun International Hostel is at 1026 N. 9th St. (between Portland and Roosevelt Sts.), Phoenix, AZ 85006; tel. 262-9439. Cost is $7 ($8 winter) for members, $2 extra for nonmembers; fans but no a/c. Probably the best choice for low-budget travelers. Located in a residential area 1 ½ miles NE of downtown. You can walk to many of Phoenix's sights from here, rent a bicycle ($3/day) from the hostel, or take a city bus. Facilities include kitchen, laundry, ping pong, dart board, games, TV, and info-packed bulletin boards. The house parents sell YH passes and sometimes organize tours. The hostel is rarely full, but you can make reservations (w/advance payment). A 3-night stay limit applies if the hostel is crowded. Check-in opens at 1700. From the downtown Phoenix Transit terminal (near Greyhound Bus) at 1st St. and Washington, take Bus #10 and get off at the corner of Roosevelt and 10th Street.

**Y.M.C.A.:** A central, inexpensive place for both men and women, located downtown at 350 N. 1st Ave., Phoenix, AZ 85003; tel. 253-6181. Has a swimming pool and cafeteria (open weekdays for breakfast and lunch). Rooms, all singles, cost $15/day or $60/week.

**bed & breakfasts:** These are private homes open to travelers in the European tradition. The degree of luxury varies, but the hosts offer a personal touch not found in the usual motels. Advance reservations are requested.

Bed and Breakfast in Arizona, Inc., 4533 N. Scottsdale Rd., Suite 108, Scottsdale, AZ 85251; tel. 995-2831. Their list of 240 Arizona homes includes many in the Valley. Prices range $20-90 s, $30-110 d.

Mi Casa Su Casa, Box 950, Tempe, AZ 85281; tel. 990-0682. The name is Spanish for "My house is your house." You'll find one of their listings in almost any part of the Valley or state. Prices range $30-100 s, $35-125 d.

## HOTELS AND MOTELS

Nowhere else in Arizona do you find such a wide selection and price range as in the Phoenix area. The luxury hotels can be a bargain in summer—prices plummet as the mercury soars. Seasonal savings decrease with lower-priced accommodation, but competition helps keep prices reasonable. It's easy to find a place to stay, thanks to the local Visitors Bureau. You can use its toll-free number to make reservations for over 100 places in the Valley; tel. (800) 221-5596 in Arizona, or (800) 528-0483 out of state. At the airport you can use the free phones next to the hotel map near baggage claim. For the lowest-priced motels you're on your own, as they won't be listed by these services. Good places to look for them are along Grand Ave. between I-17 and Van Buren St., and along E. Van Buren St. between downtown and 40th St.; this was the old highway route and still has many motels, new and old, in the $10-$30 range. The following are just a few of the accommodations available in the Valley; for a more complete list see the free *Visitors Guide* put out by the Phoenix & Valley of the Sun Convention & Visitors Bureau, or the telephone book's Yellow Pages. The rates listed apply in summer; add up to $10 in winter.

**Phoenix:** For a deluxe hotel in the heart of downtown, try Hotel San Carlos, 202 N. Central Ave., 85001; tel. 253-4121; $51.36 s, $62.06 d. On the N side of Phoenix near I-17 there are the International Villa Motor Inn (all kitchenettes) at 4526 N. Black Canyon Hwy. (between Indian School and Camelback Rds.), 85017; tel. 242-7088; $23.45 s or d; and the Regal 8 Inn at 8152 N. Black Canyon Hwy. (near Northern Ave.), 85021; tel. 995-7592 or (800) 851-8888; $25.55 s, $30.40 d. Heading E across town from I-17 you'll come to the Budget Lodge Motel at 402 W. Van Buren St., 85003; tel.

254-7247; $21.31 s, $25.59 d; and the E-Z-In Motel (some kitchenettes) at 2450 Grand Ave., 85009; tel. 252-2801; $36 s or d. On the E edge of downtown there's the Downtown Chalet Motor Inn (some kitchenettes) at 938 E. Van Buren St., 85006; tel. 252-3447; $29.96 s or d. Near the airport 2 miles E of downtown is a Motel 6 at 2323 E. Van Buren St., 85006; tel. 267-1397; $19.21 s, $23.49 d. Three miles E of downtown are the Sands Motel at 3320 E. Van Buren St., 85008; tel. 275-7848; $26.75 s or d; and the Phoenix 6 Motel at 3644 E. Van Buren St., 85008; tel. 275-7661; $25.70 s or d. Near Papago Park 6 miles E of downtown is another Motel 6, 5315 E. Van Buren St., 85008; tel. 267-8553; $19.21 s, $23.49 d.

**Scottsdale:** In the cooler months you'll have trouble finding a place under $50. An exception is Motel 6 at 6848 Camelback Rd., 85251; tel. 947-7321; $19.21 s, $23.49 d. Papago Inn (Best Western) is on 7017 E. McDowell Rd., 85257; tel. 947-7335; $42.80 s, $47.08 d.

**Tempe:** Close to I-10 on the W side of town are the Regal 8 Motel at 1720 S. Priest Dr., 85281; tel 968-4401; $22.97 s, $28.22 d; and the All Star Inn at 513 W. Broadway, 85282; tel. 967-8696; $27.25 s, $30.40 d. Convenient to both Tempe and Scottsdale is the All Star Inn at 1612 N. Scottsdale Rd., 85281; tel. 945-9506; $27.25 s, $30.40 d. If you want to stay near the ASU campus, there's the Holiday Inn at 915 E. Apache Blvd., 85281; tel. 968-3451 or (800) 238-8000; $46.20 s, $54.60 d.

**Mesa:** Just W of downtown is All Star Inn at 630 W. Main St., 85201; tel. 969-8111; $28.25 s, $31.40 d. On the S side near the Superstition Freeway is a Motel 6 at 336 W. Hampton Ave. (off Country Club Dr.), 85202; tel. 898-9467; $19.85 s, $24.05 d.

## RESORTS

The Arizona Biltmore, built in 1929, is easily the most famous of the Valley's many resorts. Frank Lloyd Wright had a hand in the design and use of novel molded-concrete blocks. The Biltmore soon gained fame for its dramatic architecture, high standards, and lavish gardens. Nancy and Ronald Reagan checked in for their honeymoon on 5 Mar., 1952. Facilities include almost everything you can think of — 18 tennis courts, 2 golf courses (18-hole), 3 swimming pools, croquet, spas, gym, shops, restaurants, live entertainment, etc. Rates from 8 Sept. to 25 May start at $149.80 s, $165.85 d, but drop to $69.55 s, $80.25 d in summer. The Biltmore is 8 miles NE of downtown at 24th St. and Missouri Ave., 85016; tel. 955-6600 or (800) 528-3696 (outside Arizona).

Recently built, The Pointe has more than 1000 luxurious suites with all kinds of recreational facilities and restaurants. Rates are similar to the Biltmore. The Pointe has 3 units: Squaw Peak at 7677 N. 16th St., 85020; the nearby Tapatio Cliffs, 11111 N. 7th St., 85020; and South Mountain, 7777 S. Pointe Parkway, 85044. All can be reached at tel. (800) 528-0428. You'll find many other plush resorts in the Valley; contact the Visitors Bureau for a list or reservations.

## CAMPGROUNDS AND RV PARKS

Many of the Valley's trailer parks cater to retired people; children won't be welcome. The following accept families except as noted:

**Phoenix:** North Phoenix KOA is the most central campground accepting both tenters and RVs, 2550 W. Louise Dr. (17 miles N of downtown, just off I-17 Deer Valley Rd. Exit 215), 85027; tel. 869-8189; $13.91 tent, $18.73 RV w/hookups. The nearby Desert's Edge RV Park accepts adults only, 22623 N. Black Canyon Hwy. (take I-17 Deer Valley Rd. Exit 215 then ½ mile N on frontage road), 85027; tel. 869-7021; $13.38 RV w/hookups. Closer to downtown are the Trailer Corral (adults only) at 4040 W. Van Buren St. (2 miles W of I-17), 85009; tel. 278-6628; $10.60 RV w/hookups; the Green Acres RV Park at 2605 W. Van Buren St. (just W of I-17), 85009; tel. 272-7863; $13.66 RV w/hookups; and the Michigan Trailer Park (adults only) at 3140 W. Osborn at Grand Ave, 85017; tel. 269-0122; $15 RV w/hookups.

**Tempe:** In the SE corner of town is Casa Fiesta Travel Trailer Resort (adults only Nov. to Apr.) at 750 W. Baseline Rd. (one mile E of I-10), 85283; tel. 839-1052; $15.71 RV w/hookups. One mile E of ASU campus is Tempe Travel Trailer Villa: 1831 E. Apache Blvd., 85281; tel. 968-1411; $12.60 RV w/hookups.

**Mesa:** Four miles E of downtown is Goodlife Travel Trailer Resort (adults only) at 3403 E. Main St., 85203; tel. 832-4990; $15.71 RV w/hookups. Farther out is Mesa Regal RV Resort (adults only) at 4700 E. Main St., 85205; tel. 830-2821; $15.71 RV w/hookups.

**Apache Junction:** Both tenters and RVs can stay at Apache Trail KOA, 1540 S. Tomahawk Rd. (1½ miles SE on US 60/89 from junction with AZ 88), 85220; tel. 982-4015; $12.19 tent, $15.37 RV w/hookups; and Lost Dutchman State Park, 6 miles NE on AZ 88, Box 1651, 85220; tel. 982-4485; $5 ($6 nonresidents).

*broad-tailed hummingbird*
(*Selasphorus platycercus*)

Right in town is the Lost Dutchman Travel Trailer Resort (adults only) at 400 N. Plaza Dr. (¼ mile NE on AZ 88), 85220; tel. 982-4173; $15.71 RV w/hookups.

**North of Phoenix:** Forty-six miles N of Phoenix is the Black Canyon City KOA, take I-17 Exit 242; Box 569, Black Canyon City AZ 85324; tel. 374-5318; $11.96 tents, $15.04 RV w/hookups. Lake Pleasant County Park has a variety of campsites and picnic areas along both the lower and upper lakes. Frog Tanks Campground has hookups and showers near the lower lake, $6. Dirty Shirt Campground, 4 miles N near the upper lake, lacks hookups and showers, $2. You also have to pay a $4/day park entrance fee per vehicle. Take I-17 Exit 223 (26 miles N of Phoenix), then W 11 miles on AZ 74; tel. 583-8405. Another place to camp is at Black Canyon Shooting Range ($3 primitive sites, $6 w/hookups) just W of I-17 at Exit 223; tel. 582-8313.

Cave Creek and Seven Springs campgrounds are in the Tonto National Forest just N of the Valley; large sycamore and ash trees provide shade; sites have picnic tables and pit toilets but no drinking water or fee; from the town of Cave Creek go 7 miles E on Cave Creek Rd. to a junction and keep L on Forest Route 24; the road becomes dirt after 2 miles, then it's another 11 miles to Seven Springs. Cave Creek Campground, which is a mile farther, is a group fee area and requires advance reservations.

Bartlett Lake is an irrigation reservoir on the Verde River with primitive camping (pit toilets but no drinking water), an unsurfaced boat ramp, and fishing for bass, crappie, catfish, and bluegill; the Mazatzal Mountains soar into the sky across the lake; from the town of Cave Creek go 7 miles E on Cave Creek Rd., turn R 6 miles on Forest Route 205, then continue 8 miles on Forest Route 19 (dirt) to the lake. Horseshoe Lake, upstream from Bartlett, has primitive camping near the dam (pit toilets but no drinking water); fishing varies with the lake level and you'll have to hand-carry boats to the water (no boat ramp); follow directions to Bartlett except turn L at the intersection of Forest Routes 19 and 205. Take Forest Route 205 all the way to the dam. Camping at both lakes is free; tel. 488-3441 for more information.

**other areas:** Maricopa County parks ring the Valley, offering camping in McDowell Mt. Regional Park to the NE, Usery Mt. Park to the E, Estrella Mt. Park to the SW, and White Tank

Mt. Park to the west. Except for Estrella, camping areas in these parks close in summer. See "Recreation" below.

# VALLEY OF THE SUN RESTAURANTS

The Valley has an amazing number of restaurants and range of cuisines—enough to fill a guidebook in themselves. And there *is* such a book, entitled *100 Best Restaurants in the Valley of the Sun* by John and Joan Bogert, revised annually. Its detailed info would be handy for diners staying awhile in the Phoenix area. The *Visitors Guide,* put out free by the Visitors Bureau, also has a long restaurant listing. Another good source is the monthly *Phoenix Magazine.* Make reservations at the more expensive places; also check to see if coat and tie are required for the men. The following list has only a small selection of dining possibilities in the Valley.

Restaurants are marked: ★ = Bargain; ★★ = Moderate; ★★★ = Expensive.

## AMERICAN

★★**The American Grill:** Offers a varied menu from grilled seafood and chowders to cheese grits casserole. Hilton Village, 6113 N. Scottsdale Rd., Scottsdale; tel. 948-9907. Open daily for lunch and dinner.

★**Furr's:** Popular cafeteria chain with a wide choice of food. Open daily for lunch and dinner. In Phoenix at 3030 E. Thomas Rd.; tel. 956-8650; and 8114 N. Black Canyon Hwy.; tel. 995-1588. In Glendale at 4303 W. Peoria Ave.; tel. 931-2438. In Sun City at 10415 W. Grand Ave.; tel. 974-3639.

★**Good Earth:** Delicious natural food served in attractive settings. In Phoenix at 4102 E. Thomas Rd.; tel. 956-1716; and at 10223 N. Metro Parkway E.; tel. 943-4573. In Tempe at 801 S. Mill Ave.; tel. 968-3444. In Mesa at 1261 W. Southern Ave.; tel. 890-0440. Open daily for breakfast, lunch, and dinner.

★★ to ★★★**Oscar Taylor:** Good solid food with Chicago prohibition-era decor. Biltmore Fashion Park, 2420 E. Camelback Rd., Phoenix;

tel. 956-5705. Open daily for lunch and dinner.

★★ to ★★★**The Other Place:** Generous servings in an early Arizona setting. In Scottsdale at 7101 E. Lincoln Dr.; tel. 948-7910. In Tempe at Fiesta Inn, 2100 S. Priest Dr. (near Broadway); tel. 967-8721. In Mesa at 1644 S. Dobson Rd.; tel. 831-8877. Open Mon. to Fri. for lunch and dinner; Sat. and Sun. for dinner only.

★**Piccadilly:** Cafeteria with varied selections. In Phoenix at 1501 W. Bethany Home Rd.; tel. 249-1172; and 7611 W. Thomas Rd.; tel. 849-6163. In Scottsdale at 4571 E. Thomas Rd.; tel. 840-4670. In Tempe at 3300 S. Price Rd.; tel. 839-1537. Open daily for lunch and dinner.

★★★**Rick's Cafe Americana:** Seafood, steaks, and other offerings in an exotic Casablanca atmosphere with nightly entertainment. In Mercado del Lago on McCormick

*Gila woodpecker (Melanerpes uropygialis)*

Ranch, 8320 N. Hayden Rd., Scottsdale; tel. 991-2233. Open Mon. to Sat. for lunch, and daily for dinner.

★ **Sugar Bowl:** An old-fashioned ice cream parlor offering a myriad of temptations for sweet tooths. It also serve home-style meals daily for lunch and dinner. In Old Scottsdale at the corner of 4005 N. Scottsdale Rd. and 1st Ave.; tel. 946-0051.

## CHINESE

★ ★ **China Doll:** Very large selection of Cantonese specialties, including Dim Sum (weekend lunches), 3336 N. 7th Ave., Phoenix; tel. 264-0538. Open daily for lunch and dinner.

★ ★ **Golden Phoenix:** Mandarin cuisine, 6048 N. 16th St., Phoenix; tel. 263-8049. Open Sun. to Fri. for lunch and daily for dinner.

★ ★ **Sesame Inn:** Top Szechuan, Mandarin, and Hunan cuisine, 3912 E. Camelback Rd., Phoenix; tel. 957-3993. Open Mon. to Fri. for lunch and dinner; Sat. and Sun. for dinner only.

★ **Szechuan Inn:** Szechuan and Mandarin dining, 1617 E. Thomas Rd., Phoenix; tel. 274-7051. Open Mon. to Fri. for lunch and dinner; Sat. and Sun. for dinner only.

## CONTINENTAL
### (reservations requested)

★ ★ ★ **Avanti:** Italian cuisine dominates the varied menu, 2728 E. Thomas Rd., Phoenix; tel. 956-0900; and in Scottsdale at 3102 N. Scottsdale Rd.; tel. 949-8333. Open Mon. to Fri. for lunch and dinner; Sat. and Sun. for dinner only.

★ ★ ★ **The Compass:** Glide high above the city in the Hyatt Regency's revolving restaurant, 122 N. 2nd St. in downtown Phoenix; tel. 252-1234. Open Mon. to Fri. for lunch and dinner; Sat. for dinner only; Sun. for brunch and dinner.

★ ★ ★ **Gold Room:** The main dining room of the Arizona Biltmore Resort has the high standards you'd expect. Sunday brunch here ranks as one of Phoenix's great splurges, Missouri Ave. and 24th St.; tel. 954-2504. Open daily for

breakfast, lunch, and dinner (dinner served only Fri. and Sat. in summer).

★ ★ ★ **La Champagne:** Sophisticated food and service. Registry Resort, 7171 N. Scottsdale Rd.; tel. 991-3800. Open daily except Mon. for dinner only.

★ ★ ★ **Mancuso's:** Outstanding Northern Italian and continental cuisine. The Borgata shopping center, 6166 N. Scottsdale Rd., Scottsdale; tel. 948-9988. Open daily for dinner only.

★ ★ ★ **Orangerie:** Fine food and service. Arizona Biltmore Resort, Missouri Ave. and 24th St.; tel. 954-2507. Open daily for lunch and dinner.

## DELIS

★ **Duck and Decanter:** In Phoenix at 622 E. Adams St. (Heritage Square); tel. 253-0759; and 1651 E. Camelback Rd.; tel. 274-5429. In Scottsdale at 6900 E. Camelback Rd.; tel. 941-3896. Open daily for lunch and dinner.

★ **Katz:** 5144 N. Central Ave., Phoenix; tel. 277-8814. Open Sun. and Mon. for breakfast and lunch; Tue. to Sat. for breakfast, lunch, and dinner.

★ **Miracle Mile:** A kosher-style cafeteria with good portions of excellent food, 9 Park Central Mall, Phoenix; tel. 277-4783; and in West Phoenix at Chris-Town Store, 1733 W. Bethany Home Rd.; tel. 249-2904. Open Mon. to Sat. for breakfast, lunch, and dinner (closes 1730 on Sat.).

## FRENCH

★ **Cafe Casino:** An inexpensive French cafeteria and bakery. In Phoenix at 4824 N. 24th St. (at Camelback); tel. 955-3430; and Scottsdale at 1312 N. Scottsdale Rd.; tel. 947-1987. Open daily for breakfast, lunch, and dinner.

★ ★ ★ **Etienne's Different Pointe of View:** Perhaps the Valley's ultimate in sophisticated dining with a dazzling view of Phoenix. For a feast, check out the Sunday brunch. Pointe

Resort at Tapatio Cliffs, 11111 N. 7th St., Phoenix; tel. 863-0912. Open Mon. to Sat. for dinner only; Sun. for brunch only.

★ ★ **French Corner:** Good food with informal service at 50 E. Camelback Rd., Phoenix; tel. 234-0245. Open Mon. to Sat. for breakfast, lunch, and dinner.

★ ★ ★ **La Chaumiere:** Excellent food in one of Scottsdale's older houses, 6910 Main St., Scottsdale; tel. 946-5115. Open Mon. to Sat. for lunch and dinner; may close in summer.

★ ★ ★ **Voltaire:** Superb food and friendly atmosphere, 8340 E. McDonald Dr., Scottsdale; tel. 948-1005. Open Tue. to Sun. for dinner only; may close in summer.

## GERMAN

★ ★ **Felsen Haus:** Authentic food and beer with lively polka music, 1008 E. Camelback Rd., Phoenix; tel. 277-1119. Open Mon. to Sat. for lunch and dinner; Sun. for dinner only.

## GREEK

★ ★ **Demetra's Kitchen:** Great food and service, 4110 N. 49th St., Scottsdale; tel. 840-5646. Open daily except Mon. for dinner only.

★ to ★ ★ **Greekfest:** Tasty food at family prices, 1219 E. Glendale Ave., Phoenix; tel. 265-2990. Open Mon. to Sat. for lunch and dinner.

## INDIAN

★ ★ **Gourmet of India:** Both meat (chicken *tandoori,* mutton *biriyani,* etc.) and vegetarian dinners are offered, 3001 E. Thomas Rd., Phoenix; tel. 952-9311. Open daily except Sun. for dinner; also lunch in winter.

## ITALIAN

★ ★ **Prego Ristorante:** A more casual restaurant than Avanti, but run by the same people, 5816 N. 16th St., Phoenix; tel.

241-0288. Open Mon. to Fri. for lunch and dinner; Sat. and Sun. for dinner only.

★ ★ **Risorante Pronto:** Features Italian-Swiss cuisine, 3950 E. Campbell Ave., Phoenix; tel. 956-4049. Open Mon. to Fri. for lunch and dinner; Sat. and Sun. for dinner only.

★ ★ **Tomaso's:** Northern Italian dining, 3225 E. Camelback Rd., Phoenix; tel. 956-0836. Open Mon. to Fri. for lunch and dinner; Sat. and Sun. for dinner only.

## JAPANESE

★ ★ to ★ ★ ★ **Ayako of Tokyo:** Chefs offer teppanyaki table-top cooking, deep-fried tempura bar, and a sushi bar, 2564 E. Camelback Rd., Phoenix; tel. 955-7007. Open Mon. to Fri. for lunch and dinner; Sat. and Sun. for dinner only.

★ ★ to ★ ★ ★ **Osome:** Waitresses dressed in kimonos serve attractively prepared food in either the Japanese Tatami Room or a Western dining room. There's also a sushi bar. At 619 W. Osborn Rd., Phoenix; tel. 264-6578. Open Tue. to Fri. for lunch and dinner; Sat. and Sun. for dinner only.

★ **Tokyo Express:** Inexpensive but good food, 3517 E. Thomas Rd., Phoenix; tel. 955-1051. Open Mon. to Sat. for lunch and dinner.

## MEXICAN

★ to ★ ★ **Aunt Chilada's:** In a century-old former general store. Pointe Resort at Squaw Peak, 7330 N. Dreamy Draw Dr., Phoenix; tel. 861-5985. Open daily for lunch and dinner.

★ **Garcia's:** This popular restaurant has grown into a chain across 11 states. In Phoenix at 2212 N. 35th Ave.; tel. 272-5584; 4420 E. Camelback Rd.; tel. 952-8031; and at 3301 W. Peoria Ave. (near Metrocenter); tel. 866-1850. Also in Scottsdale at 7633 E. Indian School Rd.; tel. 945-1647. In Tempe, Garcia's is at 1604 E. Southern Ave.; tel. 820-0400. All are open daily for lunch and dinner.

★ **Tee Pee:** Daily specials, 4144 E. Indian

School Rd., Phoenix; tel. 956-0178; open Mon. to Sat. for lunch and dinner.

## MIDDLE EASTERN

★ ★ to ★ ★ ★ **Armenia Steak and Kabob Restaurant:** Exotically spiced shish kabobs and other specialties, 7055 E. Indian School Rd., Scottsdale; tel. 994-4717. Open Mon. to Fri. for lunch and dinner; Sat. and Sun. for dinner only.

★ ★ **Bagdad:** Belly and folk dancing enliven the dining, 4015 N. 16th St., Phoenix; tel. 266-9747. Open Mon. to Sat. for dinner only.

★ **Haji-Baba:** Excellent inexpensive meals. Also Middle Eastern groceries, magazines, records, and musical instruments; 1513 E. Apache Blvd., Tempe; tel. 894-1905. Open Mon. to Sat. for lunch and dinner (closes Sat. at 1800).

★ **Mediterranean House:** The cafe's owner has an Israeli and Yemeni background. 1588 E. Bethany Home Rd., Phoenix; tel. 285-1773. Open Mon. to Sat. for lunch and dinner.

## PIZZA

★ **Organ Stop:** Part of the attraction here is music from a giant Wurlitzer theatre organ, 5330 N. 7th St.; tel. 263-0716. Open Mon. to Thur. for dinner only; Fri. to Sun for lunch and dinner.

★ **Pizzafarro's:** One of the Valley's best, 4225 E. Camelback Rd., Phoenix; tel. 840-7990. Open daily except Mon. for dinner only.

★ **Tommy's Pizza:** In Phoenix at 518 E. Dunlap Ave.; tel. 997-7578; 5341 N. 7th Ave.; tel. 274-8815; 17039 N. 19th Ave.; tel. 993-1320; and 2301 W. Glendale Ave.; tel. 246-0050. Open daily for lunch and dinner.

## POLYNESIAN

★ ★ to ★ ★ ★ **Trader Vic's:** Outstanding cuisines from the far corners of the world. Exotic South Seas decor, 7111 Fifth Ave., Scotts-

dale; tel. 945-6341. Open Mon. to Sat. for lunch and dinner; Sun. for dinner only.

## SEAFOOD

★ ★ **Famous Pacific Fish Company:** A good place to come for fresh seafood in a nautical setting. Many items are broiled over mesquite charcoal, 4321 N. Scottsdale Rd., Scottsdale; tel. 941-0602. Open Mon. to Sat. for lunch and dinner; Sun. for dinner only.

★ ★ ★ **Rusty Pelican:** Decor and food will convince you that you're beside the ocean. Near the Metrocenter at 9801-A N. Black Canyon Hwy., Phoenix; tel. 944-9646. Open Mon. to Fri. for lunch and dinner; Sat. and Sun. for dinner only.

## SOUL FOOD

★ **Lucille's:** Good cookin', 1202 E. Washington St., Phoenix; tel. 262-9835. Open Mon. to Fri. for breakfast, lunch, and dinner (closes 1800).

★ **Mrs. White's Golden Rule Cafe:** More good cookin', 808 E. Jefferson St., Phoenix; tel. 262-9256. Open Mon. to Fri. for breakfast, lunch, and dinner.

## THAI

★ to ★ ★ **Char's:** Authentic and fiery cuisine in the restaurant that introduced Thai food to the Valley. In Phoenix at 7810 N. 12th St.; tel. 246-1077. In Tempe at 927 E. University Dr.; tel. 967-6013. In Mesa at 45 W. Broadway Rd.; tel. 833-9894. Open Tue. to Sat. for lunch and dinner, Sun. for dinner only.

★ **Daa's Thai Room:** Great food with pleasant surroundings. Don't ask for "hot" spices unless you can take it *very* hot! 7419 E. Indian Plaza (near corner of Scottsdale and Camelback Rds.), Scottsdale; tel. 941-9015. Open Mon. to Fri. for lunch and dinner; Sat. and Sun. for dinner only.

★**Thai Rama:** Inexpensive Thai food on a varied menu. 1702 W. Camelback Rd., Phoenix; tel. 246-8622. Open daily for lunch and dinner.

## VIETNAMESE

★**Saigon House:** A chance to try another spicy Asian cuisine, 10423 N. 19th Ave. at Peoria Ave., Phoenix; tel. 997-4712. Open Tue. to Fri. for lunch and dinner, Sat. and Sun. for dinner only.

## WESTERN

★★**Don & Charlie's American Rib and Chop House:** Topnotch steaks and barbeque, 7501 E. Camelback Rd., Scottsdale; tel. 990-0900. Open daily for dinner only.

★★**Mining Camp:** Great Western grub, much of it all-you-can-eat, in a replica of an old mining camp cook shanty. Great for the kids. Located 4 miles NE of Apache Junction on AZ 88 in the E end of the Valley; tel. 982-3181. Open Sun. for lunch and dinner; Tue. to Sat. for dinner only.

★★★**Pinnacle Peak Patio:** Country music and perhaps even a mock gunfight every night. Strictly cowboy-Western atmosphere. If you wear a tie inside, it'll be snipped off and added to the large collection on the rafters! Located in the foothills of the McDowell Mts. about 20 miles NE of Scottsdale, via Scottsdale and Pinnacle Peak Rds. at 10426 W. Jomax Rd.; tel. 949-7311. Open daily for dinner only.

★★**Rustler's Rooste:** Country music and huge portions. Pointe Resort at South Mountain, 7777 Pointe Parkway, Phoenix; tel. 231-9111. Open daily for lunch and dinner.

★★**Waterin' Hole Chuckwagon 'n' Saloon:** Cowgirls bring your steaks, ribs, chicken, or seafood in the rustic dining room. Pointe Resort at Tapatio Cliffs, 11111 N. 7th St., Phoenix; tel. 944-4451. Open Mon. to Sat. for lunch; Sun. for dinner only.

★**Real Texas Bar-B-Que:** The decor isn't much, but the ribs are great and you couldn't beat the prices, 2415 W. Bethany Home Rd., Phoenix; tel. 249-9985. Open Tue. to Sat. for lunch and dinner.

## SPECIALTY FOOD STORES

**Italian:** DeFalco's Italian Groceries, 2724 N. 68th St., Scottsdale; tel. 990-8660. Filippo's Italian Grocery & Liquor Wheel, 3445 E. McDowell Rd., Phoenix; tel. 275-1113.

**Kosher:** Norman's Kosher Star Market, 4128 N. 19th Ave., Phoenix; tel. 265-3762.

**Mexican:** Azteca Bakery & Tortilla Shop, 1407 S. 16th St., Phoenix; tel. 252-5457. El Molino Tamales, 117 S. 22nd St., Phoenix; tel. 244-0364.

**Middle East:** Ararat Foods, 4119 N. 19th Ave., Phoenix; tel. 277-3517. Middle Eastern Bakery and Deli, Inc., 3052 N. 16th St., Phoenix; tel. 277-4927.

**Natural:** Gentle Strength Cooperative, 234 W. University Dr., Tempe; tel 968-4831.

**Oriental:** Lee Hing Oriental Food Center (Chinese and SE Asian), 1510 W. McDowell Rd., Phoenix; tel. 254-9444. Oriental Food Center (Chinese, Japanese, and Philippine) 3920 Grand Ave., Phoenix; tel. 841-6215.

# ENTERTAINMENT

**movies:** Newspapers list the latest flicks. For old movie classics and other special films, call the Valley Art Theatre, 509 S. Mill Ave. in Tempe; tel. 967-6664, or Scottsdale Center for the Arts, 7383 Scottsdale Mall in Scottsdale; tel. 994-2787. The Union Cinema, lower level of the Memorial Union on the ASU campus, shows current movies during the school year for only $2 nonstudents; free travelogues and other programs are presented during the summer; tel. 965-5728.

## THEATER AND CONCERTS

To find out what's happening in the Valley, call the Visitor Hotline; tel. 252-5588 (24 hours) or the Arts Council; tel. 271-9052. Newspapers, especially the 2 weeklies, *New Times* and *City Life* (both free at newsstands), review the entertainment scene.

**Phoenix:** The Phoenix Performing Arts Theatre presents a varied program of theater, music, and dance from Sept. to May at 1202 N. 3rd and Moreland Sts.; tel. 256-3341. Arizona Theatre Company performs plays and musicals from late Nov. to June at Phoenix College Theatre, 1202 W. Thomas Rd. and other locations; tel. 279-0534. Symphony Hall frequently hosts performances by the Phoenix Symphony and other groups. It's in downtown Phoenix's Civic Plaza at 225 E. Adams St.; tel. 262-7272. Phoenix Little Theatre, opened in 1920, ranks as the theater with the longest continuous run in the country; it's in the Phoenix Civic Center (behind the Phoenix Art Museum) near the corner of Central Ave. and McDowell Rd.; tel. 254-2151. (Note that the Civic Plaza and Civic Center are 2 different places.) The city of Phoenix presents free concerts Apr. to Oct. in Encanto Park's band shell, featuring band, jazz, and dance groups; on the NE corner of 15th Ave. and Encanto Blvd.; tel. 262-4634.

**Scottsdale:** The Scottsdale Center for the Arts has diverse musical and theatrical offerings at 7383 Scottsdale Mall (one block S of Indian School Rd.); tel. 994-ARTS. The Louise Lincoln Kerr Cultural Center hosts soloists and small musical groups at 6110 N. Scottsdale Rd. (S of the Borgata shopping center and behind the Cottonwoods Resort); tel. 948-6424. Actors Lab Arizona maintains regular (Oct. to May) productions, touring shows, and a one-year school for professional actors at Miller Plaza, Suite 114, 7624 E. Indian School Rd.; tel. 990-1731.

**Tempe:** The Gammage Center for the Performing Arts, on the ASU campus, offers a varied program of theater, concerts, and dance in its distinctive rotund structure. The Center can also tell you of other events on campus; tel. 965-3434. **Mesa:** Mesa Little Theatre offers productions from Oct. to Apr. at the Gaslight Theatre in Mesa Activity Center, 155 N. Center; tel. 834-9500. **Sun City:** The Sundome Center for the Performing Arts frequently hosts big-name performers at 19403 R.H. Johnson Blvd. in Sun City West; tel. 975-1900.

**dinner theater:** The Copper State Players perform at Max's Dinner Theatre, 6727 N. 47th Ave. in Glendale; tel. 937-1671.

## SOCIAL SPOTS

See the weeklies *New Times* and *City Life* for the complete list of the places to go. Call first for times and to check dress codes. **Phoenix:** Back Stage presents contemporary music performers nightly (no cover) in an off-Broadway atmosphere at 4321 N. Central Ave.; tel. 265-2505 (also in Scottsdale at 7373 Scottsdale Mall; tel. 949-1697; and in Tempe at 530 W. Broadway Rd.; tel. 829-1177). Eye of the Tiger takes you into the jungle with contemporary, jazz, African, and reggae hits, Tue. to Sat. (no cover), 4343 N. 7th Ave.; tel. 264-6415. Finney Bones presents local and national comedians in its search for the "funniest person in the world," open Mon. to Sat. (cover), 4821 N. 20th St.; tel. 955-0606. Graham Central Station gives you rock, country, and other music, both live and DJ, in the Valley's largest nightclub, open nightly (cover), 4029 N. 33rd Ave.; tel. 279-3800. Mr. Lucky's offers you a choice of a rock or country band upstairs and a Top-40 DJ downstairs; Fri. nights also feature an all-you-can-eat fish fry (other nights there's a chuckwagon buffet); open nightly (sometimes a cover), 3660 Grand Ave.; tel. 246-0686. Pony Express keeps the dance floor galloping with DJ rock'n'roll, open Mon. to Sat. (sometimes a cover), 3905 E. Thomas Rd.; tel. 244-2694. Timothy's hosts live jazz nightly (no cover) at 6335 N. 16th St.; tel. 277-7634. Warsaw Wally's has blues music nightly (cover Fri. and Sat.) at 2547 E. Indian School Rd.; tel. 955-0881.

**Scottsdale:** Anderson's Fifth Estate has entertainment by comedians, band, or DJ; open nightly (cover), 6820 5th Ave.; tel. 994-4168. Rick's Cafe Americana has Top-40 bands, open nightly (no cover), 8220 N. Hayden Rd.; tel. 991-2233. Tiffany Lounge, in the Scottsdale Hilton, entertains with contemporary groups nightly (no cover), 6333 N. Scottsdale Rd.; tel. 948-7750.

## SPORTING EVENTS

The Arizona State University Sun Devils battle their opponents in an active program of football, baseball, basketball, swimming, gymnastics, archery, and other sports. To find out what's going on, call Sun Devil Sports; tel. 965-6592. The ASU Sun Devil football stadium hosts the annual Fiesta Bowl, the country's 5th biggest NCAA bowl game, played on New Year's Day. The Phoenix Giants, a minor-league baseball team, play ball at Phoenix Municipal Stadium, 56th and E. Van Buren Sts. (Apr. to Aug.); tel. 275-4488. Several major league teams visit the Valley for spring training in Mar. and Apr.: the Oakland A's at Phoenix Municipal Stadium, the San Francisco Giants at Scottsdale Stadium, the Seattle Mariners at Tempe's Diablos Stadium, the Chicago Cubs at Hohokam Stadium in Mesa, and the Milwau-

*coyote* (Canis latrans)

*saguaro*
(Cereus gigantus)

kee Brewers at Sun City Stadium. The NBA Phoenix Suns basketball team's season runs Oct. to Apr.; home games are played at Arizona Veterans Memorial Coliseum, 1826 W. McDowell Rd.; tel. 263-SUNS. The Phoenix Open attracts big-name professional golfers each Jan. to the Phoenix Country Club at N. 7th St. and Thomas Rd.; tel. 263-0757.

Engines roar as cars strain for the finish line Feb. to Nov. at Manzanita Speedway, 35th Ave. and West Broadway; tel. 276-9401 or 276-7575. Phoenix International Raceway holds 4 major events each year at S. 115th Ave. and Baseline Rd.; tel. 932-0777 or 246-7777. Arizona Desert Racing is for off-road vehicles all year at various locations (usually free admission); tel. 252-1900. Dogs hit the track at Phoenix Greyhound Park every night except Mon. and Tue.; you'll stay cool in the a/c grandstands ($1 admission), E. Washington and 40th Sts.; tel. 273-7181. Thoroughbred and quarter horses go for it at Turf Paradise from Oct. to May; $2 grandstands admission, 1501 W. Bell Rd. and 19th Ave.; tel. 942-1101.

# RECREATION

Valleyites take their sports seriously—the recreational facilities seem limitless. You can play golf, tennis or raquetball, go horseback riding, jump in the pool, tube the Salt River, and even go surfing! Phoenix Parks and Recreation Dept. has some excellent parks and a variety of educational and recreation programs for children, adults, and seniors; tel. 262-6861 or 262-6711. Several large county parks ring the Valley, giving additional opportunities to escape city life; for info call the Maricopa County Parks and Recreation Dept.; tel. 262-3711. Two active outdoors groups, Central Arizona Hiking Club and Arizona Bicycle Club, can be reached through American Youth Hostels, 1026 N. 9th St., Phoenix, AZ 85006.

## SPORTS

**golf and tennis:** Both are extremely popular in the Valley, and played year-round. Enthusiasts often spend their entire vacation at resorts offering top-notch facilities and professional instructors. Four Phoenix city parks have golf courses and 22 parks have tennis courts; tel. 262-6861 or 262-6711. You'll find a list of both public and private golf courses and tennis courts in the Visitors Bureau's free *Visitors Guide.*

**swimming:** Phoenix alone has 23 public pools; see the Phoenix telephone book Yellow Pages under "swimming pools." If you're looking for waves and water slides, try Big Surf in Tempe or Oasis Family Water Park in Glendale.

**Big Surf:** It's all here—surf, sun, sand, and pretty girls! Artificial waves 3-5 feet high come

*water slides at Oasis Family Water Park*

crashing onto the broad sandy beach. You can rent surfboards and rafts or bring your own. For added thrills try the 300-foot Surf Slide and whiz down at speeds up to 15 miles per hour. Small children have a shallow pool to play in. The season runs mid-Mar. to the end of Sept. (call for hours), closed Mon.; $5 age 8 to adult, $3 age 7 and under. Big Surf is in northern Tempe at 1500 N. Hayden Rd. (S of McKellips Rd.); tel. 947-SURF or 947-2478.

**The Oasis:** Water slides and a wave pool provide the excitement. Body surfing and raft rental but no surfboarding. Small children have their own small pools. Open May to mid-Oct. (call for hours); $8 age 9 to adult, $7 children 4-8, children under 4 free. Rates go down in the evening after 1700. From downtown Phoenix take I-17 N 17 miles to Pinnacle Peak Rd. (Exit 217), then W 2 miles on Pinnacle Peak Rd.; tel. 266-5200.

**tubing the Lower Salt River:** Cool off in the summer on a leisurely float down the Salt River E of Mesa. Salt River Recreation rents inner tubes and provides shuttle bus service back to the starting point for only $5.25/person, or just a shuttle pass for $2.10; tel. 984-3305. Season runs from early May to the end of September. The shuttle bus serves 5 points along the river, giving a choice of floats from 1½ hours to all day. An extra tube will carry your cooler of cold drinks (don't bring glass containers). Weekends often see large crowds, when the Salt becomes one big party. Beware of the sun—hats, long-sleeved shirts, pants, and sun-block lotion should be used. Wear tennis shoes to protect your feet when walking out into the river. Life jackets are a good idea and a necessity if you bring the kids along. Don't tie your tubes together, rather lock your feet into each other's tubes. Below Granite Reef Dam the Salt River is a river no more—the waters get channeled into canals, leaving only a dry riverbed downstream most of the year. No camping is allowed on the lower Salt River (Stewart Mt. Dam. to Granite Reef Dam) from 1 Apr. to 31 October. From the eastern edge of Mesa, take Bush Hwy. N to the Salt River.

**horseback riding:** The Phoenix area has

*tubing the Salt*

miles of scenic trails suitable for horses. Maricopa County Parks sponsors monthly rides from Oct. to Apr.; tel. 262-3711. Many of the stables can arrange lessons, breakfast rides, steak cookouts, hayrides, overnight trips, and boarding. For rides into South Mountain Park, see: All Western Stables (10220 S. Central Ave.; tel. 276-5862), Ponderosa Stables (10215 S. Central Ave.; tel 268-1261), or South Mountain Stables (10005 S. Central Ave.; tel. 276-8131). Carefree Ranch Stables, Pima Rd. in Carefree, has rides into the desert foothills in the northern part of the Valley; tel. 488-3944. One or 2-hour guided trips into Phoenix Mountain Preserve leave from Hole-in-the-Wall Stables at the Pointe Resort, 7677 N. 16th St. in Phoenix; tel. 997-1466. Near Papago Park, you can ride from Papago Riding Stable, 400 N. Scottsdale Rd. in Tempe; tel. 966-9793, or Weldon's Riding Stables, 1029 N. 52nd St. (off Van Buren) in Phoenix; tel. 244-2388. In Scottsdale, you have a choice of: Indian Trails Horse Country Club (9001 E. Indian Bend Rd.; tel. 948-8120), Mountain View Stables (9990 E. Cactus Rd.; tel. 948-6684), and Old MacDonald's Farm (26540 N. Scottsdale Rd.; tel. 585-0239). For guided all-day and overnight pack trips into the wild Superstition Mountains, see: Superstition/Peralta Stables at 2151

N. Warner Rd. (off N. Meridian Rd.) in Apache Junction; tel. 982-6353; or O.K. Corral Stables, 1 ½ miles NE of Apache Jct. on AZ 88 then L at the sign; tel. 982-4040. Riding season is Oct. to May.

**ice skating:** Hit the ice at Ice Palace, 3853 E. Thomas Rd. in Phoenix; tel. 267-0591; Metro Ice Palace, Metrocenter in Phoenix, I-17 and Peoria Ave.; tel. 997-6158; and Oceanside Ice Arena (next to Big Surf), 1520 N. Hayden Rd. in Tempe; tel. 947-2470.

**roller skating:** Roll at Rollero, 7318 W. Indian School Rd., Phoenix; tel. 846-1510; Skate World, 4451 E. Oak St., Phoenix; tel. 267-7116; and The Great Skate, 10054 N. 43rd Ave., Glendale; tel. 842-1181.

## PARKS

**Encanto Park:** A 222-acre oasis of lakes, picnic areas, 2 golf courses (9 and 18 holes), tennis courts, and swimming pool. You can check out sports equipment from the Recreation Building located S of the swimming pool. Concerts often take place in the band shell. Encanto Park is just 2 miles N of downtown Phoenix at N. 15th Ave. and Encanto Boulevard.

**Papago Park:** This large area on the E edge of Phoenix was once declared a national monument because of its desert flora and Indian history. Today it's a city park with numerous attractions, including the Phoenix Zoo, Desert Botanical Gardens, an 18-hole golf course, and Phoenix Municipal Stadium. The Park also offers picnicking, hiking, a bike trail, horseback riding (rental stables are nearby), and a small lake where children 15 and under may fish without a license. George W.P. Hunt, 7 times governor of Arizona, now occupies the prominent pyramid tomb on a small hill. Enter Papago Park at 60th St. from Van Buren St. or 54th St. from McDowell Road.

**Squaw Peak Park:** Squaw Peak crowns a group of desert hills 9 miles NE of downtown Phoenix. It's a place for hiking, picnicking, and horseback riding in a natural setting. Saguaro cactus, palo verde, creosote bush, barrel cactus, cholla, and other desert plants thrive on the hillsides. The hike to the summit of 2,608-foot Squaw Peak makes a good half-day's outing. The trail climbs steeply in places, rising 1,200 feet in 1 miles, but is easy to follow. On Sun. the Peak hosts a remarkable crowd of teenagers, families, little old ladies, joggers wearing headsets, etc., all puffing along. You can bring a dog with you if it's on a leash. Be sure to carry water and get an early start in the warmer months. For an easier hike, try the gentle trail from the end of the road.

*atop Squaw Peak*

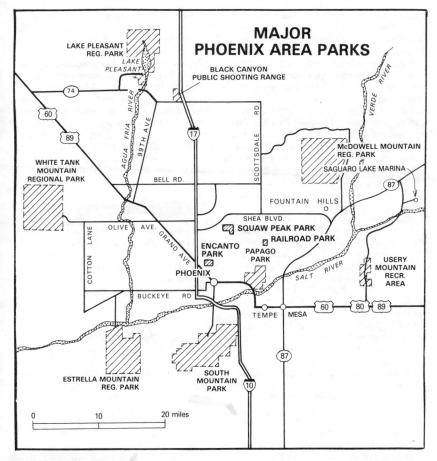

## MAJOR PHOENIX AREA PARKS

LAKE PLEASANT REG. PARK

LAKE PLEASANT

BLACK CANYON PUBLIC SHOOTING RANGE

74

60

89

AGUA FRIA RIVER

99TH AVE

17

SCOTTSDALE RD

VERDE RIVER

McDOWELL MOUNTAIN REG. PARK

SAGUARO LAKE MARINA

WHITE TANK MOUNTAIN REGIONAL PARK

BELL RD.

FOUNTAIN HILLS

87

COTTON LANE

OLIVE AVE.

GRAND AVE

SHEA BLVD.

SQUAW PEAK PARK

RAILROAD PARK

ENCANTO PARK

PAPAGO PARK

PHOENIX

SALT RIVER

USERY MOUNTAIN RECR. AREA

BUCKEYE RD.

TEMPE MESA

60 80 89

87

ESTRELLA MOUNTAIN REG. PARK

SOUTH MOUNTAIN PARK

10

0          10          20 miles

**South Mountain Park:** This is the world's largest city park, with 15,728 acres of desert mountain country. A paved road winds to the top for some great views of the Valley. On the way you'll pass several picnic areas and a children's playground. Forty miles of hiking and horseback trails lead through the backcountry. Stables, just before the Park's entrance, rent horses. Hikers will enjoy Hidden Valley, a half-day trip through a landscape of giant granite boulders and stately saguaro. To reach the trailhead, go 2 miles past the Park entrance gate and turn L onto the Summit Rd., following it 4 miles; keep R past the turnoffs for 2 lookout points, then stay L at the next fork (don't go toward the TV towers). At the road's end, a sign "Hidden Valley 1 ¾ miles" marks the trailhead. The first mile follows a ridge with good views before gently dropping into a valley. After a mile or so, some large slick rocks have to be negotiated before entering the wide, bowl-shaped Hidden Valley. Near the lower end of the little valley you'll pass through a natural tunnel about 50 feet long. This makes a good turn-around point, or you can explore more of the valley and surrounding hills. In summer carry extra water and avoid the heat of the day. South Mountain Park is 7 miles S of downtown Phoenix on Central Avenue.

**McCormick Railroad Park:** Rail buffs of all ages will want to hop on the 5/12-scale trains for a ride around the Park's grassy acres. Two old railway stations house shops with model train supplies, railroad books, and souvenirs. Outside, a standard-gauge, Mogul-type Baldwin Steam Engine and some cars are on display. On Sun. afternoons you can visit several model railroad clubs, each running a different scale train. McCormick Railroad Park and train rides are open daily. Rides operate 1100 to 1730 in winter (extended to about 1930 the rest of the year); $.50/person fare. This unusual park is in Scottsdale at 7301 E. Indian Bend Rd. just E of Scottsdale Rd.; tel. 994-2312.

**Saguaro Lake:** Scenery, fishing, and boating attract people year-round. The 10-mile-long lake within the Tonto National Forest is the last in the chain of lakes on the Salt River, and the closest to Phoenix. Saguaro Lake Marina has a snack bar, boating supplies, and fishing and ski boat rentals; tel. 986-0969. Lakeshore Inn serves breakfast, lunch, and dinner daily at moderate prices (closes 1630 on Mon.); tel. 984-5311. Boat tours make an 11-mile scenic loop from Oct. to April. The Forest Service provides boat ramps and picnic areas. Boaters can reach Bagley Flat Campground (tables, pit toilets, but no water; free) about 4 miles from the marina. Dispersed camping is also permitted, but again you'll need a boat. Picnic and boating areas almost always fill up on Sundays, and sometimes Sat., from mid-spring to mid-summer; try to arrive by early morning then. Get to Saguaro Lake via the Bush Hwy., either from eastern Mesa or off AZ 87.

**Black Canyon Shooting Range and Recreation Area:** Shooters and archers can practice at this fine facility. Visitors also enjoy picnicking and camping ($6 w/hookups, $3 primitive site; showers available). The range operates Wed. to Sun. and the trap and skeet range is lighted for night use. It's located 25 miles N of Phoenix, just off I-17 (Exit 223); tel. 582-8313 for rifle and pistol range; tel. 582-5296 for trap & skeet and archery.

**Lake Pleasant Regional Park:** The large lake has paved boat ramps, a marina, snackbar (closed Mon.), and Dirty Shirt Campground (no hookups or showers; $2). You can rent small sailboats, windsurfs, and rowboats from the marina. The lakes' open waters provide fine conditions for sailing. The Arizona Yacht Club sponsors races. Fishermen seek out largemouth bass, white bass, catfish, bluegill, and crappie. The park charges a $4/vehicle fee per day. Lake Pleasant is about 30 miles NW of Phoenix; take I-17 N to AZ 74 (Exit 223), then go W 10 miles. From Sun City you can go N 15 miles on 99th Ave.; tel. 566-0405.

**McDowell Mt. Regional Park:** A wide variety of desert plants grows in the eastern McDowells, 15 miles NE of Scottsdale. Elevations range 1,500-3,100 feet. The Park attracts nature lovers, picnickers, hikers, and horseback riders. There's a campground with drinking water ($6; closed in summer). Access is from Fountain Hills on the S side of the park via Fountain Hills Blvd. to McDowell Mt. Road.

**Usery Mt. Recreation Area:** You'll have good views of the Salt River Valley and the Superstition Mts. from the pass between Pass Mt. and Usery Mt. Range, 12 miles NE of Mesa. Picnicking, hiking, horseback riding, and archery practice are other attractions. There's a campground ($6 w/hookups; closed in summer). From Apache Blvd. (US 60/89) in Apache Jct., turn N on Ellsworth Rd. which turns into Usery Pass Road.

**Estrella Mt. Regional Park:** Spanish explorers named the range Estrella ("star") after the pattern of deeply carved canyons radiating from the summit. Sierra Estrella Golf Course, in the NW corner of the Park, has 18 holes, pro shop; tel. 932-3714, and a snack bar. The recreation area offers picnicking, primitive camping ($2; all year), hiking, and horseback trails. The park's water is a bit salty; you might want to bring your own. From downtown Phoenix, take AZ 85 about 20 miles W to just

1. Red Rock Crossing, near Sedona; 2. Devil's Bridge, near Sedona; 3. below Havasu Falls, Havasupai Indian Reservation; 4. along the Echo Canyon Trail, Chiricahua National Monument; 5. on Desert View Trail, Organ Pipe Cactus National Monument (all photos by B. Weir)

1. desert paintbrush; 2. teddy bear cholla cactus; 3. ocotillo blossoms; 4. prickly pear cactus;
5. saguaro cactus; 6. beavertail cactus (all photos by B. Weir)

*Saguaro Lake*

past Avondale, then turn S 3 miles on Bullard Ave.; tel. 932-3811.

**White Tank Mt. Regional Park:** Extensive trails for hikers and horseback riders lead through this range on the W side of the Valley.

You might see petroglyphs and pottery shards left by Hohokam Indians. Picnic and camping areas are provided but no drinking water. Campsites cost $2 but close for summer. From Peoria, NW of Phoenix, take Olive Ave. W for 15 miles.

# OTHER VALLEY OF THE SUN PRACTICALITIES

## SHOPPING

The Valley has thousands of shops eager to sell you something. Glittering department stores and boutiques display the latest in high fashions. Or you can visit rustic porch-fronted shops and be outfitted in Western duds from boots to bola ties. Western and Indian art make distinctive purchases. Anglo and Hispanic artists recall the frontier days in their paintings and sculpture, while Indian artists reveal their own heritage in art forms and crafts. Mexican import shops represent skilled craftsmen from south of the border.

**Old Scottsdale:** Arts, crafts, clothing, and restaurants abound in the area centered around Brown St., just W of Scottsdale's Civic Center. More shops line Main St. W across Scottsdale Rd. to 69th Street. **Fifth Ave.:** Scottsdale's biggest shopping area lies along this curving street between Scottsdale Rd. and Indian School Road. Local businessmen promote the selection of over 350 shops here as "Arizona's ultimate shopping experience." Fifth Ave. is located 4 blocks N of Old Scottsdale.

**The Borgata:** An elegant shopping center modeled after the Italian village of San Gimignano, N of Rome. It's complete with cobblestone paths, courtyards, and medieval towers and archways. Your credit cards will take a beating in most of the shops, but window shopping is fun. The Borgata is at 6166 N. Scottsdale Rd., 2 miles N of Old Scottsdale.

*The Borgata*

**El Tianguis:** An Aztec word for "marketplace," this Mexican-style *mercado* houses inexpensive Mexican cafes and shops offering high-quality crafts from Mexico and other countries. It's operated by the Mexican-American and Yaqui Indian community of Guadalupe. From I-10 near Tempe, exit E at Baseline Rd. then turn R on Avenida del Yaqui to Calle Guadalupe.

**other shopping malls:** Biltmore Fashion Park, Camelback Rd. and 24th St., Phoenix, has several restaurants and about 50 luxury shops with names like Saks Fifth Avenue, Polo/Ralph Lauren, Gucci, and I. Magnin; tel. 955-8400. Chris-Town Shopping Center, 1703 W. Bethany Home Rd., Phoenix, offers 4 large department stores, 27 places to eat, 11 movie theaters, a post office, and dozens of shops; tel. 242-9070. Los Arcos Mall, Scottsdale and McDowell Rds., Scottsdale, contains 2 depart-

ment stores, 14 restaurants, 66 shops, and 2 cinemas; tel. 945-6376. Metrocenter (exit W at Peoria or Dunlap Aves. from I-17) in Phoenix, is *big:* 5 department stores, 37 restaurants, 17 movie theaters, banks, hotels, miniature golf, ice-skating rink, etc.; tel. 997-2641. Park Central, Central Ave. and Osborn Rd., Phoenix, has a selection of 70 shops and 10 restaurants; a giant 1,600-pound statue of an Indian sun worshipper greets visitors at the entrance; tel. 264-5575. You'll find many more shopping centers listed in the Yellow Pages.

**art galleries:** Scottsdale has most of the many galleries in the Valley. For a list of galleries and what's being shown, see the weekly newspaper *New Times*. **Indian music:** Canyon Records and Indian Arts stocks more than 400 albums of Indian music from many American tribes, 4143 N. 16th St., Phoenix; tel. 266-4823.

## SERVICES

Phoenix's main post office is at 1441 E. Buckeye Rd.; tel. 261-4011. Other main post offices include Scottsdale's at 7242 E. Osborn Rd.; Tempe's at 233 E. Southern Ave.; and Mesa's at 135 N. Center.

Exchange foreign currency at First Interstate Bank, 100 W. Washington St., Phoenix (or any branch office); International Banking; tel. 271-6143; or at United Bank of Arizona, 3300 N. Central Ave., Phoenix (or most branch offices); International Div.; tel. 263-7227.

Need a doctor? Maricopa County Medical Society will refer you; tel. 252-6094.

Down and out? Job Service (Arizona Dept. of Economic Security), 438 W. Adams St., Phoenix, offers free services; tel. 252-7771.

## EVENTS

Concerts, festivals, shows, and other special events happen nearly every day in the Valley, and the Visitors Bureau can tell you what's going on. Pick up their *Calendar of Events* brochure or call the Visitors Hotline; tel. 252-5588. These are some of the best-known annual happenings:

**January:** The Fiesta Bowl kicks off on New Year's Day at Arizona State University's Sun Devil Stadium. Top PGA golfers compete in the Phoenix Open, a 50-year-old tournament. Rockhounds display their beautiful specimens in Rockazona, a large rock and gem show near Sun City.

**February:** Parada del Sol in Scottsdale features the world's longest horse-drawn parade and a big rodeo. The horsey set enjoys Scottsdale's All-Arabian Horse Show and Phoenix's Aid to Zoo Horse Show. Indians put on the *O'Odham Tash* Indian Pow Wow near the city of Casa Grande, 45 miles S of Phoenix, with a parade, rodeo, dances, and crowning of the *O'Odham* queen.

**March:** Valley Shakespeare Festival presents the Bard's best at Scottsdale Center for the Arts. Hello Phoenix celebrates the Valley's history with music, dancing, ethnic food, and arts and crafts. Phoenix's Rodeo of Rodeos presents a parade, Western Hoe-Down Festival, and competition among top-ranked cowboys. Scotland comes to Phoenix for the Arizona Highland Games, with bagpipe bands, highland dancing, and competitions. Mesa celebrates Mesa Day with a miniature parade (everything's hand drawn) and arts and crafts displays.

**April:** Old Town Tempe Spring Festival exhibits work by some of the Southwest's best artists and craftsmen, along with food treats, and live performances; action takes place along Mill Ave. at 4th, 5th, and 6th Streets.

**May:** Mexican music, dancing, and food mark Cinco de Mayo (May 5th), the anniversary of Mexico's 1863 victory over France.

**June to September:** It's too hot! Valley residents head for the nearest swimming pool or drive to the high country.

**October:** The Arizona State Fair in Phoenix features exhibits of the state's best in agriculture, livestock, and home crafts, along with concerts, rides, and games. Phoenix Art Museum puts on a Cowboy Artists of America Exhibition.

**November:** The American Graduate School of International Management in Glendale sponsors the Thunderbird Balloon Race & Gas Classic, a world-class event with both hot-air and gas balloons. Old Town Tempe Fall Festival of the Arts repeats the activities of the April Spring Festival.

**December:** At the end of the month, the Valley gets ready for the Fiesta Bowl with an impressive parade and a big marathon.

**phone numbers:**
Emergencies (police, fire, medical): tel. 911.
Police: tel. 262-6151 (Phoenix).
Fire and Paramedics: tel. 253-1191 (Phoenix).
Maricopa County Sheriff: tel. 256-1011 or (800) 352-4553.
Road Conditions (statewide): tel. 262-8261.
Community Information & Referral Services: tel. 263-8856.
Community Legal Service (Legal Aid): tel. 258-3434.
Lawyers' Referral (County Bar Assoc.): tel. 263-0886.
Doctors' Referral (Maricopa County Medical Society): tel. 252-6094.
Phoenix Transit: tel. 257-8426.
Visitor Hotline (Valley events): 252-5588.
Phoenix & Valley of the Sun Convention & Visitors Bureau: tel. 254-6500.
Valley Reservation System: tel. (800) 221-5596 (in Arizona) or (800) 528-0483 (outside Arizona).
Arizona Office of Tourism (statewide): tel. 255-3618.
ASU Gammage Center: tel. 965-3434.
ASU Sun Devil Ticket Office: tel. 965-2381.
Sportsline (latest sports scores): tel. 258-1212.
Civic Plaza Box Office: tel. 262-7272.
Forest Facts (U.S. Forest Service): tel. 225-5296.
Weather (state & local): tel. 957-8700.

# INFORMATION

**tourist offices:** Phoenix & Valley of the Sun Convention & Visitors Bureau has free *Visitors Guides* and many brochures at 505 N. 2nd St. (Suite 300) in Phoenix (85004); tel. 254-6500; open Mon. to Fri. 0830-1700. The Visitors Bureau has branch offices downtown in the Hyatt Regency at the NW corner of Adams and 2nd Sts. (open Mon. to Fri. 0900-1500), and at terminals 2 and 3 of Sky Harbor Airport (open Mon. to Fri. 0900-2100, Sat. & Sun. 0900-1700). Other helpful chambers of commerce in the Valley include: Scottsdale, 7333 Scottsdale Mall (Box 129, Scottsdale, AZ 85252); tel. 945-8481; open Mon. to Fri. 0830-1700. Tempe, 504 E. Southern Ave. (85282); tel. 967-7891; open Mon. to Fri. 0830-1700. Mesa, 10 W. 1st St. (85201); tel. 969-1307; open Mon. to Fri. 0800-1700. Apache Junction, near City Hall complex at 1001 N. Idaho Rd. and University (Box 1747, Apache Junction, AZ 85220); tel. 982-3141; open Mon. to Fri. 0900-1700. The Arizona Office of Tourism has info about all regions of the state, 1480 E. Bethany Home Rd., Phoenix, AZ 85014; tel. 255-3618; open Mon. to Fri. 0800-1700.

**Tonto National Forest:** Find out about hiking and camping in their 2,900,000 acres of forests and cactus located N and E of the Valley. Their land includes the Superstition and Mazatzal ranges and the lakes along the Verde and Salt rivers. Maps of the Forest and of the wilderness areas are sold ($1 each). Main office is at 2324 E. McDowell Rd. in Phoenix (85038); tel. 225-5200; open Mon. to Fri. 0745-1630.

**libraries:** The main Phoenix library is at 12 E. McDowell Rd. and Central Ave.; tel. 262-6451.

It's open Mon. to Thur. 0900-2100, Fri. and Sat. 0900-1800, and Sun., 1300-1700. Nine branch libraries lie scattered around town. Scottsdale's main library is at 3839 Civic Center Plaza; tel. 994-2476; open Mon. to Fri., 1000-2100, Sat., 1000-1800, and Sun. (Sept. to May) 1200-1700. Tempe's library is at the SW corner of 3500 S. Rural Rd. and Southern Ave.; tel. 968-8231; open Mon. to Thur. 1000-2100, Fri. and Sat., 1000-1730, and Sun. 1330-1730. Mesa's library is downtown at 64 E. 1st St.; tel. 890-3100; open Mon. to Thur. 0930-2100, Fri. and Sat. 0930-1730, and Sun. (Sept. to May) 1330-1730. The State Capitol has a research library and map collection in Room 300, 1700 W. Washington; tel. 255-4035; open Mon. to Fri. 0800-1700. You can also use the libraries on the ASU campus (see "Tempe").

**newspapers and magazines:** *Arizona Republic* comes out every morning and has a big Sunday edition; its sister paper, *The Phoenix Gazette,* is published evenings Mon. to Saturday. For local news and happenings, also look for the weekly *New Times*, free at newsstands. *Phoenix Magazine* comes out monthly with news and useful information about the Valley. Scottsdale has its own magazines too, the monthly *Scottsdale Scene* and the quarterly *Scottsdale Magazine.*

*The U.S. Forest Service can tell you about recreation on the Salt River (pictured) and other areas of the Tonto National Forest.*

**bookstores:** Al's Family Book Store claims to have over 500,000 books, new and used, paperback and hardback, at 1454 E. Van Buren St. in Phoenix; tel. 253-6922. Bob and Faye's Paper Book Exchange specializes in used books: in Phoenix at 1827 E. Indian School Rd.; tel. 264-6698; and in Tempe at 2043 E. University Dr.; tel. 966-2065. Shopping malls have the popular book chains.

**maps:** For Arizona and other places see A Wide World of Maps, Inc. in Phoenix (2626 W. Indian School Rd.; tel. 279-2323); in Tempe (1526 N. Scottsdale Rd.; tel. 949-1012); and in Mesa (1440 S. Country Club Dr.; tel. 844-1134). Topo maps are also sold by REI (1405 W. Southern Ave. in Tempe; tel. 967-5494); Arizona Hiking Shack (11645 N. Cave Creek Rd. in Phoenix; tel. 944-7723); and The North Face, 3925 E. Indian School Rd. in Phoenix; tel. 955-3391).

*hiking on Squaw Peak*

## TRANSPORT

**tours:** The Gray Line has daily tours of the Phoenix area ($12), and longer day trips to the Superstitions and Apache Trail ($29), Tucson ($46), Nogales ($30), Sedona ($25), and the Grand Canyon ($40); 2- and 3-day trips visit the Grand Canyon ($76-$218), Lake Powell ($199-$295), and Monument Valley ($189--$246); Box 2471, Phoenix, AZ 85002; tel. 254-4550. Sonoran Stage runs day and overnight excursions to even more places than Gray Line at similar rates, but not as frequently; Box 923, Phoenix, AZ 85001; tel. 253-4808.

To see some of Arizona's real backcountry, take a 4-wheel-drive tour with: Back Road Tours (1725 E. Pebble Beach, Tempe, AZ 85282; tel. 838-7965); Big Red Jeep Tours (Box 34564, Phoenix, AZ 85067; tel. 241-6050); Arizona Awareness (2422 N. 72nd Place, Scottsdale, AZ 85257; tel. 947-7852); or Arizona Desert Jeep Adventures (10640 E. Clinton St., Scottsdale, AZ 85259; tel. 948-9192). Take a Hike leads dayhikes in the desert, 8528 E. Sutton Dr., Scottsdale, AZ 85260; tel. 991-1231. Fly high over the Valley in a hot-air balloon during the cooler months with Pegasus (tel. 893-9454), Rainbow Balloon (993-0875), or Unicorn Balloon (tel. 991-3666). The Visitors Bureau's *Visitors Guide* lists many more tour operators. Sunday's *Arizona Republic* "Travel" section often advertises special travel deals. Las Vegas anyone?

**local bus:** Phoenix Transit will take you to the parks, shopping areas, most of the sights, and the airport for just $ .65 to $1.30, depending on distance; transfers are free. All-day passes cost only $2.50 (purchase at the terminal) and you get a brochure of suggested tours. The downtown terminal, at 1st St. and Washington, has timetables and a difficult-to-read route map; or call tel. 257-8426. Most buses head for home between 1900 and 2000, staying in bed completely on Sun. and major holidays. On those days you can use Dial-A-Ride; tel. 271-4545.

*horned lizard* (Phrynosoma)

They operate about 0700-1830; call at least 30 min. before you want to be picked up; fares start at $1.75, depending on distance.

**long-distance bus:** The Greyhound terminal is downtown at 525 E. Washington St.; tel. 248-4040. Lockers and a Burger King restaurant are available. You'll find other Greyhound stations in Tempe (502 S. College Ave.; tel. 967-4030); Mesa (522 N. Country Club Dr.; tel. 834-3360); and Sun City (10795 Grand Ave.; tel. 933-5716. Some destinations and OW fares to: Los Angeles (7 x daily), $30; San Diego (3 x daily), $30; El Paso (7 x daily), $30; Tucson (8 x daily), $15 local or $17 express; Flagstaff (4 x daily), $22.75; Globe (4 x daily), $19.15; Wickenburg (2 x daily), $6.60; Yuma (3 x daily), $26.55. Roundtrip fares may have a small discount. Two buses daily make the run to Sky Harbor Airport.

Trailways Bus has moved its main terminal to northern Phoenix, 5 miles from downtown, at I-17 and Camelback Rd.; tel. 246-4341. Lockers and vending machines are available. Trailways also stops in Tempe (822 S. Mill Ave.; tel. 968-2376); Mesa (522 N. Country Club Dr.; tel. 834-3315); and Sun City (10777 Grand Ave.; tel. 977-4289). Some destinations and OW fares to: Los Angeles (4 x daily), $30; El Paso (3 x daily), $30; Tucson (3 x daily), $15; Flagstaff (3 x daily),

$20; Wickenburg (2 x daily), $10. Roundtrip fares may have a small discount.

LTR Stage Line leaves the Phoenix Greyhound and Trailways terminals twice daily for Kingman ($10.75), Las Vegas ($53.70), and other destinations; tel. 273-6842. Sun Valley Bus Line also leaves the Phoenix Greyhound and Trailways terminals for Las Vegas, but goes via Parker and Lake Havasu City; tel. 254-4888. If you're headed for Flagstaff, Arizona Central Lines leaves from Sky Harbor Airport 5 times daily with stops at the Phoenix Hilton, Amtrak station, Cordes Jct. (connections to Prescott 3 times daily), and Camp Verde; fares to Flagstaff are $25 OW ($45 RT) from the airport and $20 OW ($36 RT) from downtown Phoenix; tel. 241-9191.

**auto rentals:** The Valley moves on wheels; if you need some, check the Yellow Pages or the Visitors Bureau's *Visitors Guide*. Rental companies offer many different plans; most have offices at the airport or make free pick-ups. You can rent RVs too. Prices for autos start at $10.50/day for local use only (50 free miles) at places like Cheap Wheels; tel. 275-8222.

**driveaways:** These are autos that need delivering to another city. If it's a place you're headed, a driveaway can be like getting a free car rental. To do it you have to be at least 21 years old and make a deposit of $75-$150. There will also be time and mileage limits. Ask for an economy car if that's a consideration. Travelers have recommended American Auto Shippers, 7140 N. 16th St., Phoenix; tel. 870-9300. Others are listed in the Yellow Pages under ''Automobile Transporters & Driveaways.''

**taxis:** Ace Taxi; tel. 956-1009, has lower than average rates. Other companies include Arizona Taxi; tel. 253-8294, Checker Cab; tel. 257-1818, and Yellow Cab; tel. 252-5071.

**train:** Amtrak has 3 eastbound and 3 westbound departures every week. Terminal is downtown at 401 W. Harrison St. and 4th Ave.; tel. 253-0121. For reservations and info; tel.

(800) 872-7245. Westbound departs in the evening for Yuma and other points, arriving in Los Angeles the next morning (9 hours, $70 OW). Eastbound leaves in the morning for Tucson (2½ hours, $22 OW), and on to either New Orleans (1½ days, $212) or Chicago (2 days, $233). Amtrak gives generous discounts on RT fares, making them more competitive with the bus and plane.

**air:** Commercial flights to the Valley land at Sky Harbor Airport, just 3 miles E of downtown Phoenix. See the Yellow Pages for the airlines,

charters, and ticket agencies. Sky Harbor has 3 separate terminals, connected by a free 24-hour shuttle bus. The busy airport is well organized but you'll have to do some walking. The Visitors Bureau staffs information desks in Terminals 2 and 3 (Mon. to Fri. 0900-2100, Sat. and Sun. 0900-1700). Free telephones connect many Valley hotels and motels. Taxis outside have widely varying fares—you might want to shop around. Phoenix Transit Bus #17 is the cheapest way into town. It leaves the airport Mon. to Fri. every 30 min. about 0600-1840 and Sat. hourly about 0730-1730; tel. 257-8426.

# NORTHEAST OF PHOENIX

## PAYSON AND THE COUNTRY BELOW THE RIM

When the Valley bakes under the summer sun, many Phoenix-area residents drop everything and drive NE to the cool pine forests around Payson. This might be the reason why the road to Payson, AZ 87, has the nickname "Beeline Highway." From Mesa, the Beeline Hwy. crosses the 2 Indian reservations of Salt River and Fort McDowell, then climbs over a pass in the Mazatzal Range before turning N to Payson. In Payson, 78 miles from Mesa, you're at an elevation of 5,000 feet and in almost the exact center of Arizona. Sheer cliffs of the Mogollon Rim tower 2,000 feet higher in the north. Novelist Zane Grey fell in love with this country and built a lodge at the foot of the Rim. Here he wrote many of his books and set off on "hunting expeditions" to secure both ideas for stories and trophies for his walls. (See below for more details.) Today, sportsmen come in season to stalk elk, deer, turkey, and other game. Anglers are lured by trout-filled streams and stocked reservoirs. Hikers enjoy walks in the forest or more ambitious treks in the Mazatzal or Sierra Ancha Ranges. Although Payson has no "sights" itself, the town makes a good base for exploring the surrounding countryside.

**history:** It wasn't the cooler weather and pretty scenery that brought Payson's first set-

tlers—it was the glitter of gold. Miners set up camp in 1881, but ranching and lumbering soon took over as more rewarding occupations. A fort provided protection against Apache raids in the precarious early years. The town's name honors Senator Louis Edwin Payson, who had nothing to do with the community and never came here! Frank C. Hise, the postmaster, assigned the name to repay a political favor.

**accommodations:** You have a choice of motels in town or secluded cabins in the sur-

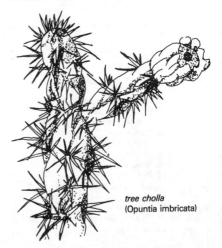

*tree cholla*
(Opuntia imbricata)

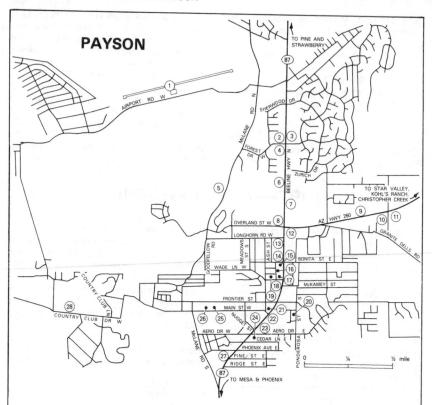

## PAYSON

1. Payson Municipal Airport
2. Swiss Village Bakery
3. Swiss Village Lodge and Restaurant
4. Black Forest Inn
5. Rumsey Park; rodeo grounds
6. Aunt Alices
7. Highline Motel
8. Safeway
9. Mario's Villa
10. 260 Cafe
11. U.S. Forest Service
12. Fairway
13. El Rancho Restaurant
14. Diamond Dart Motel
15. Molly Brown's Cafe
16. Bit and Bridle BBQ
17. Pedro Wong's Drive-in
18. Vicki's Kitchen; Beeline Bus Agency
19. Nana's Pizzeria
20. Pyle Memorial Hospital
21. Chamber of Commerce
22. Corner Deli
23. Trails End Motel; Beeline Cafe; La Casa Pequena
24. Paysonglo Motel; Knotty Pine Cafe
25. public library
26. post office
27. Super 8 Motel
28. Payson Country Club

rounding forests, as well as campgrounds and RV parks. Make reservations for the weekend rush, especially in summer. In town, beginning from the south, you'll find: Super 8 Motel (Beeline Hwy. and W. Phoenix; tel. 474-4526 or 800-843-1991); Paysonglo Lodge (1005 S. Beeline Hwy.; tel. 474-2382); Trails End Motel (811 S. Beeline Hwy.; tel. 474-2283); Diamond Dart Motel (302 S. Beeline Hwy.; tel. 474-2201); Highline Motel (301 N. Beeline Hwy.; tel. 474-6402); and Swiss Village Lodge (801 N. Beeline Hwy.; tel. 474-3241 or Phoenix toll-free tel. 255-0170).

Heading E on AZ 260 outside of town are the: Lazy D Ranch Motel (4 miles E of Payson; tel. 474-2442); Star Valley Resort Motel (4 miles E of Payson; tel. 474-5182); Diamond Point Shadows Motel & Restaurant (6 miles E of Payson; tel. 474-9986); Kohl's Ranch Resort (motel, cabins, restaurant located 17 miles E of Payson; tel. 478-4211 or Phoenix toll-free tel. 271-9731); and Christopher Creek Lodge (motel, cabins, restaurant, located 22 miles E of Payson in the resort village of Christopher Creek; tel. 478-4300). Also in Christopher Creek are Creekside Mountain Cabins and Steakhouse (tel. 478-4389) and Grey Hackle Lodge (tel. 478-4392).

**campgrounds:** The Forest Service (tel. 474-2269) maintains several campgrounds E of Payson on AZ 260, all open Apr. to Sept., with drinking water but no showers: Ponderosa (13 miles E; $5; also a group campground nearby); Tonto Creek Upper and Lower (17 miles E; $4); and Christopher Creek (22 miles E; $5). Payson Pines RV Resort is just ½ mile E on AZ 260 from the Beeline Hwy.; has showers, coin laundry, and recreation room; $10.60 tents, $15.90 RV w/hookups; tel. 474-2300. For RV and trailer parks, try also: Ox Bow Estates RV Park (3 miles S on the Beeline Hwy.; tel. 474-2042) and the adults-only Roblos Roost RV Park (17 miles N on the Beeline Hwy. in Strawberry; tel. 476-4531).

**food:** Swiss Village Lodge, 807 N. Beeline Hwy., has a restaurant featuring both Continental and American specialties; there's also a less expensive coffee shop; tel. 474-5800.

Black Forest Inn and the nearby Swiss Village Bakery turn out great pastries and inexpensive meals, across from Swiss Village Lodge, 614 N. Beeline Hwy.; tel. 474-2307. "Home cooking" is featured at: Knotty Pine Cafe (1001 S. Beeline Hwy.; tel. 474-9927); Beeline Cafe (815 S. Beeline Hwy.; tel. 474-9960); Vicki's Kitchen (602 S. Beeline Hwy.; open 24 hours; tel. 474-9958); Molly Brown's Cafe (402 S. Beeline Hwy.; tel. 474-3198); 260 Cafe (803 E. Hwy. 260; tel. 474-9932); and Aunt Alices (512 N. Beeline Hwy.; tel. 474-4720).

Dine Mexican at El Rancho (200 S. Beeline Hwy.; tel. 474-3111) and La Casa Pequena (911 S. Beeline Hwy.; tel. 474-6329). If you've always hankered after Chinese-Mexican food, head over to Pedro Wong's Drive In (closed Wed.), 510 S. Beeline Hwy.; tel. 474-2305. For Italian-American dining, try Mario's Villa, 600 E. Hwy. 260; tel. 474-5429. Pick up pizza at Nana's Pizzeria (closed Sun.), W. Wade and Beeline Hwy.; tel. 474-2165. You'll get good sandwiches at the Corner Deli, Main St. and Beeline Highway. Bit and Bridle features BBQ broiled on a mesquite fire, 430 S. Beeline Hwy.; tel. 474-2074. You'll find McDonalds, Burger King, Pizza Hut, and Kentucky Fried Chicken near the center of Payson. For groceries visit Safeway or Fairway, both at the corners of Hwy. 260 and Beeline Highway.

**entertainment and events:** Payson Picture Show plays the current flicks, in Payson Plaza, one block E on Bonita off Beeline Hwy.; tel. 474-3918. Nightspots for lively country and western, rock, or requests include Winchester Saloon (615 W. Main St.); tel. 474-9953, La Casa 'Pequena (911 S. Beeline Hwy.); tel. 474-6329, Swiss Village Lodge (807 N. Beeline Hwy.); tel. 474-5800, and Pete's Place (Star Valley, 4 miles E on Hwy. 260); tel. 474-9963. Major community events include an Arts & Crafts Show in May; a Country Music Festival in June; Firecracker Softball Tournament, Junior Rodeo, and Loggers Festival in July; the "World's Oldest Continuous Rodeo" (since 1884) and the Art Fest in Aug.; and the Fiddlers Festival in September.

**services:** The post office is on W. Main St. (off Beeline Hwy.). Payson's hospital is at 807 S.

Ponderosa St.; tel. 474-3222. You'll find a swimming pool, tennis courts, ballfields, and picnic grounds in Rumsey Park on N. McLane Rd. (from the junction of Beeline and Hwy. 260, go W on Overland and Longhorn Rds. then R ½ mile on McLane); tel. 474-4628. Play golf on the 18-hole Payson Golf Course, 1504 W. Country Club; tel. 474-2273. Rent horses for trail rides from Longhorn Ranch, 4000 E. Granite Dells Rd. (4 miles E of town); tel. 474-2257; Kohl's Ranch Stables, 17 miles E on AZ 260; tel. 478-4226; or OK Corral Stables, 15 miles N on Beeline Hwy. in Pine; tel. 476-4303. For camping, fishing, and hunting supplies and info see: Big Jeff's Sporting Goods (111 E. Cedar; tel. 474-4186), Payson Sport Shop (805 S. Beeline Hwy.; tel. 474-6655), Paysons's Country Store (709 S. Beeline Hwy.; tel. 474-3366), or Yellow Front (Beeline and Hwy. 260; tel. 474-3867).

**information:** The Payson Chamber of Commerce sits on the corner of Beeline Hwy. and Main St. (P.O. Drawer A, Payson, AZ 85547); open Mon. to Sat. 0800-1700, Sun. 1000-1600; tel. 474-4515. For camping and hiking info see the U.S. Forest Service office, one mile E on AZ 260 (Box 100, Payson, AZ 85541); tel. 474-2269. Payson Public Library is at 510 W. Main; tel. 747-2585.

**transport:** For a taxi, call Payson Cab; tel. 474-5647.

## VICINITY OF PAYSON
3/92

**Tonto Natural Bridge:** Deposits left by mineral springs have created the world's largest natural travertine bridge. The springs still flow, as they have for about a million years, building the massive arch even larger and watering lush vegetation. You might not even realize you're standing on top when you arrive—the bridge measures 400 feet wide and spans a 150-foot-wide canyon. Graceful travertine formations underneath look like those inside a limestone cave. A small waterfall cascades over the top of the arch, forming

jewel-like droplets of water that sparkle in the sun and create pretty rainbows. A precipitous but safe trail winds down to the canyon floor 183 feet below. To explore the underground tunnel you'll need shoes suitable for clambering over wet and muddy rocks. Less surefooted visitors can admire the bridge from viewpoints at the top overlooking each side of the arch. The site is open daily all year; $2.50 adult (less for children). You can have a picnic, use the volleyball court, or cool off in a spring-fed swimming pool (no lifeguard; $1.25 adult, $.75 age 7-17). A lodge has rooms for $38 s, $48 d ($36 s, $44 d without bath), and serves breakfast and dinner. A campground with showers costs $7.50. From Payson go 11 miles N on AZ 87 then turn L at the sign onto a 3-mile gravel road; Box 45, Pine, AZ 85544; tel. 476-3440.

**Strawberry:** This tiny village sits just below the Mogollon Rim, 19 miles N of Payson. Wild strawberries grow here but they're hard to find

*Tonto Natural Bridge*

*Strawberry Schoolhouse*

nowadays. Turn W 1½ miles at Strawberry Lodge to see Arizona's oldest schoolhouse. Pioneers built the one-room log structure in 1885. You can step in to see the restored interior during the summer; other times by appointment; ask at Strawberry Lodge. The road continues past Fossil Creek (good hiking) to Camp Verde, but is hard going for cars. A better route to Camp Verde is AZ 87 N up onto the Rim 8 miles, then L on the paved George Crook Trail. Rooms in Strawberry Lodge range $28-$36, the more expensive having fireplaces and balconies; reservations for weekends should be made a couple of weeks in advance; tel. 476-3333. Dine at Strawberry Lodge or the Strawberry Shortcake Cafe.

**Zane Grey's Lodge:** The canyons, great forests, and expansive views of the Rim country inspired author Zane Grey to build a hunting cabin here about 1920. He made many stays over the next 9 years, enjoying the wilderness while working on novels about the American West. You'll see the same sweeping views

from his lodge today. Exhibits inside display original furniture, manuscripts, and first editions. Open daily in Mar. 1000-1600, Apr. to Oct. 0900-1700, and Nov. 1000-1600; closed Dec. to Feb.; $1 adult, under 12 free; tel. 478-4243. From Payson head E on AZ 260 for 17 miles and turn L at the sign just past Kohl's Ranch; then go 4¾ miles in on a partly paved road (not recommended for large rigs). You can also visit Tonto Fish Hatchery, just E of Zane Grey's Lodge, where rainbow and brown trout grow to catchable size; open daily except winter 0800-1700.

**The Mazatzal Wilderness:** The Yavapai Indians knew this vast country of desert and mountains as *mazatzal,* "land of the deer." The name still fits well, only scattered ruins remain of the Indians, pioneers, and miners who tried to live here. The Wilderness, commonly pronounced "ma-ta-ZEL" but more correctly "MAH-zat-zall," covers over 250,500 acres in a strip beginning 8 miles W of Payson that extends S for 30 miles and is as wide as 15 miles.

The climate zones vary from Lower Sonoran Desert, with saguaro and palo verde (2,200-4,000 feet), up through dry grasslands, oaks, pinyons, and junipers of the Upper Sonoran Desert (4,000-7,000 feet), to the Transition Zone, with ponderosa pines and a few pockets of firs on the upper slopes (7,000-7,888 feet). You might meet deer, javelina, black bear, or even a mountain lion. Hikers in this big country need to be self-sufficient with maps, compass, and water; springs and streams cannot be counted on during the summer.

Best times for a visit are spring and fall; summer is OK if you're prepared for possible 100-plus temperatures and late-season thunderstorms; winter is fine at the lower elevations but severe snow storms can hit the high country. You won't need any permits to hike or horseback in the Wilderness. Of the 14 trailheads, the Barnhardt is the most popular: from just S of the Rye Creek bridge (14½ miles S of Payson on AZ 87), go W 4.8 miles on Forest Route 419 to the end of the road. You have a choice of 3 trails here. A popular 19-mile, 2-day backpack loop encircles Mazatzal Peak via the Barnhardt, Mazatzal Divide, and Y Bar Basin (Shake Tree) Trails. For detailed hiking info see the Forest Service people at Payson; tel. 474-2269, Phoenix; tel. 225-5200, or Carefree; tel. 488-3441. They'll give you free trail literature on hiking, and sell a Mazatzal Wilderness topo map for $1. *Arizona Trails* by David Mazel describes 10 hikes ranging from one to 6 days. Francois Leydet tells of his 6-day journey by horseback in the Mazatzals in the Feb. 1974 *National Geographic.*

## YOUNG

Remote and off the tourist track, Young has been called one of Arizona's last "cow towns." To get here you have to take largely unpaved roads: either S 24 miles on Forest Highway 12 from the Mogollon Rim (turn off AZ 260 at Milepost 284, about 33 miles E of Payson); or N 47 miles on AZ 288 (32 miles of dirt road) from near Roosevelt Lake (off AZ 88 between Roosevelt Dam and Globe). Roads to Young are best avoided in winter and just after heavy rains.

In the late 1800s one of Arizona's bloodiest and most savage feuds took place in Pleasant Valley, between the Rim and Young. The trouble started when the Tewksbury Clan gave protection to a band of sheep brought into the area in 1887. Cattlemen led by the Graham Clan wouldn't stand for competition from the "woolies" and attacked, killing a Navajo sheepherder, and destroying or driving away the animals. The Tewksburys retaliated and the war was on. The fighting didn't end until all the Grahams had been killed. All efforts by lawmen to restore order failed, and at least 19 people died during the 5 years of terror. History buffs can search out many of the battle sites near Young. The town's cemetery has marked graves belonging to 5 members of the Graham faction: Harry Middleton, Al Rose, Charles Blevin, William Graham, and John Graham. You'll find Young Cemetery behind Young Baptist Church on the main road, ½ mile E of Moon's Saloon.

*one of Young's watering holes*

downtown Young

Historians still debate details of the feud. Accounts of the tragedy are given in *Arizona's Dark and Bloody Ground* by Earle Forrest, and in *Globe, Arizona* by Clara Woody and Milton Schwartz. Zane Grey dramatized the events in his novel *To the Last Man.* Grey obtained his material during hunting trips in Pleasant Valley. Today, a very independent breed of people inhabit Young. These folks, many of whom are retired ranchers and miners, don't like authority or development. Even the Forest Service office (Young's biggest employer) represents too much government control for some residents.

**practicalities:** Young doesn't have any motels, but you'll find plenty of places to camp in the surrounding Tonto National Forest. Young's social life revolves around the Antler Bar and Cafe; tel. 462-3423, and Moon's Saloon Bar and Cafe (no relation to *Moon Publications!*). Townspeople occasionally have cabins for rent; try asking around at the Antler Cafe or Moons's Saloon. Both serve inexpensive breakfasts, lunches, and dinners daily. The Antler has a bonus of a free "museum" — everything from old saddles and mining gear to an Electrolux vacuum cleaner and a tuba; dusty bears and mountain lions also grace the walls. For fishing, hiking, and camping info, contact the Forest Service office in Young; open Mon. to Fri. 0745-1145 and 1230-1630; tel. 462-3311 (turn off the main road ¼ mile E of Moon's Saloon).

## VICINITY OF YOUNG

**north of Young:** The unfortunate Navajo sheepherder who fell as the first victim of the Pleasant Valley War lies in a lonely grave N of Young; a white cross, pile of stones, and sign mark the spot; from the main road, 4 miles N of Young and 20 miles S of AZ 260, turn W one mile on Forest Route 200. Valentine Ridge Campground is 18 miles N of Young and 6 miles S of EZ 260, then ½ mile E on Forest Route 188. Colcord Campground (no water or charge) is just E of the main road on Forest Route 33, about 3 miles S of AZ 260 and 21 miles N of Young. Canyon Creek Campground (no water or charge) and Canyon Creek Fish Hatchery lie just below the Rim at an elevation of 6,600 feet; follow Forest Route 33 in 5 miles. The fish hatchery has a self-guided tour, open daily 0800-1700. Fishermen can try their luck in Canyon Creek for rainbow and some brown trout; use flies and artificial lures only. Colcord Lookout (elev. 7,513 feet) has a sweeping panorama of the Young area and the Mogollon Rim; turn W off the main road onto Forest Route 291 (opposite the Forest Route 33 turnoff), and go in 3 miles.

**south of Young:** Workman Creek Waterfall takes a 200-foot plunge S of Young; to get there, go S on the main road from town for 21 miles and turn L 3½ miles on Forest Route 487;

*vicinity of Young*

park at the cattleguard and sign "Primitive Road, Unsuited for Public Use," then walk ¼ mile to the falls. This pretty valley supports dense stands of Douglas fir, white fir, and smaller numbers of Arizona sycamore and the relatively rare Arizona maple. You'll see several places to camp (no facilities) along the road to the falls. Swimmers can cool off in the "Bathtubs," natural pools in Workman Creek; from the Workman Creek bridge (AZ 288) follow the trail downstream 1/8 mile. Rose Creek Campground (elev. 5,400 feet) is off the main road 23 miles S of Young; drinking water and pit toilets but no charge.

**wilderness areas near Young:** The Sierra Ancha Wilderness contains 20,850 acres lying 15 miles S of Young and 36 miles N of Globe. Lack of good roads and rugged terrain discourage most visitors—precipitous box canyons and sheer cliffs make travel difficult. Elevations range 3,200-7,600 feet. Spring-fed creeks in the eastern part have carved several short but deep box canyons, including Pueblo, Cold Springs, and Devil's Chasm. Prehistoric Salado Indians built cliff dwellings in these canyons, then departed. Forest Route 203 (Cherry Creek Rd.) loops around the E side of the Sierra Anchas, providing views into these spectacular canyons. You'll need a 4WD vehicle for this trip; the northern part of the road is particularly rough; allow 3½ hours for the drive. For hiking info and a wilderness map contact the Forest Service office in Young; tel. 462-3311, or offices in Payson, Roosevelt, Globe, Carefree, Mesa, or Phoenix. Salome Wilderness, 15 miles SW of Young, protects the Salome and lower Workman Creek watersheds. Hell's Gate Wilderness, 13 miles NW of Young, preserves parts of Tonto, Haigler, Marsh, and Houston Creeks. Sheer cliffs rising above Tonto Creek form the "Hell's Gate"; good fishing here but only the most adventurous fishermen make it in (Forest Trail #37).

# EAST OF PHOENIX:
# THE APACHE TRAIL LOOP

Driving E through Phoenix, Tempe, Mesa, then Apache Junction, you might think the "city" will never end. But as soon as you turn onto AZ 88 in Apache Junction, the shopping centers, gas stations, and hamburger stands fade away... you're left with just the desert, lakes, and mountains. Here begins a 200-mile loop through some of the West's most rugged country. Allow 6 hours just for driving this circuit around the rugged Superstition Mountains, taking AZ 88 to Globe, then returning to Apache Junction via US 60/70. The big attractions, besides the wild scenery, are hiking and horseback riding in the Superstition Wilderness, boating on a chain of lakes along the Salt River, stepping inside prehistoric pueblo Indian dwellings in Tonto National Monument, seeing copper mining operations near Globe, Miami, and Superior, and finally the Boyce Thompson Arboretum—an amazing collection of plants from all over the world.

## SUPERSTITION WILDERNESS

The 159,700-acre wilderness lies S of the Salt River and Apache Trail, about 40 miles E of Phoenix. You'll find some of the Southwest's best desert hiking in the canyons and mountains of the Superstitions. Elevations vary from about 2,000 feet along the western boundary to over 6,000 feet in the eastern uplands. Desert vegetation dominates, but a few pockets of ponderosa pine hang onto the highest slopes. Wildflowers put on colorful extravaganzas in early spring and following summer rains.

**gold fever:** You can really believe the lost gold mine legends while gazing into these mysterious mountains. One set of stories tells how Don Miguel Peralta discovered fantastic amounts of gold somewhere among the Super-

*riding in the Superstitions*

stitions in 1845, but later he and his group of miners met their death at the hands of Apache Indians. The location of his "Sombrero Mine" remains a mystery. At least one of Peralta's party did survive the massacre and, 30 years later, revealed the mine's location to a German immigrant, Jacob Waltz. Locally known as the "Dutchman," Waltz worked the mine without ever revealing its location. Those who tried to follow him into the Superstitions either became lost in the maze of canyons or were later found murdered. The power of the "Lost Dutchman's Mine" legend has intensified since the prospector's death in 1891. That no rich gold deposits have ever been found—and that geologists say the Superstitions are an unlikely location for gold—have done little to diminish the legends.

**climate:** Spring and fall bring the most pleasant weather for a visit to the Superstitions. Winter is often fine too, at lower elevations; snow and cold can hit the higher areas. Summer, which lasts from May to Oct., gets unbearably hot. Temperatures exceed 115 F in the shade at times, and there's precious little shade! You can venture into the Superstitions in the summer by making a crack-of-dawn departure and getting out again by late morning when the heat hits. Carry plenty of water, especially in summer when springs and creeks are likely to dry up.

**hiking:** Twelve trailheads and 180 miles of trail provide all kinds of possibilities. Being so close to Phoenix, the Superstitions get unusually heavy traffic for a wilderness area. The western half receives the most use, especially near Peralta and First Water Trailheads. You're more likely to see javelina, desert mule deer, mountain lion, black bear, and other wildlife in the eastern half of the range. You don't need a permit to hike or camp in the Superstitions; you're asked only to leave the area as you found it, and limit groups to 15 people and stays to 14 days. Horses may be brought in too. Prospecting involving any kind of surface disturbance or the filing of new claims is now prohibited. The U.S. Forest Service manages the Superstition Wilderness as part of the giant Tonto National Forest. They can give advice on

travel here in their offices in Phoenix (2324 E. McDowell Rd. or Box 5348; 85010; tel. 225-5200), Mesa (26 N. MacDonald St.; 85201; tel. 261-6446), and Roosevelt (Box 647; 85545; tel. 467-2236). They have a Superstition Wilderness topo map with background, trailhead, and trail info which costs $1. *Arizona Trails* by David Mazel has the best trail descriptions and maps of any source; 23 hikes receive detailed coverage.

## FOUR PEAKS WILDERNESS

This new wilderness covers 60,700 acres in the southern Mazatzal Mountains, lying to the N of Apache Lake, opposite the Superstition Wilderness. Four Peaks are visible over a large section of central Arizona; they've been a major landmark since Indian times. From their deeply incised lower slopes along Canyon and Apache Lakes at an elevation of 1,600 feet, the mountains top off at Brown Peak, northernmost of

*Hiking Boulder Canyon Trail in the Superstitions*

the 4, at 7,657 feet. Vegetation runs the whole range from saguaro cactus at the base to ponderosa pine, Douglas fir, and aspen near the top. Javelina, deer, black bear, mountain lion, and smaller animals inhabit the slopes. Black bear here are thought to make up one of the highest concentrations in Arizona; wise campers try to hang food out of reach at night. The Forest Service has a free pamphlet of hikes in the Four Peaks area, available from the Phoenix, Mesa, and Roosevelt offices. Trailheads can be reached from AZ 87 to the W (NE of Mesa), or from AZ 188 to the E (NW of Roosevelt Dam).

## APACHE JUNCTION TO ROOSEVELT DAM: THE APACHE TRAIL

Once a raiding route for Apaches, the Apache Trail is now safe, but the surrounding country remains as primitive as ever. Jagged ridges, towering cliffs, and the desert itself remind man of his limitations and small scale. The road twists and climbs as it tries to find a way through the rugged land. Weaver's Needle, the 4,535-foot landmark for gold seekers in the Superstition Wilderness, can be glimpsed to the south. Ten to one the stories about Jacob Waltz and his "Lost Dutchman's Gold Mine" are just tall tales. Despite the efforts of thousands of gold-crazed prospectors, no major finds have been confirmed. Geologists have studied the mountains and found them to be remnants of volcanic calderas—an unlikely place for rich veins of the precious metal. More likely, perhaps, the crafty "Dutchman" worked as a fence for gold thieves employed in the Vulture Mine near Wickenburg. Miners stealing nuggets wouldn't be able to sell their loot in Wickenburg, so Waltz may have run a "gold-laundering" operation by caching the Vulture gold in the Superstitions. If so, he still has a lot of people fooled about his "mine" even after 100 years!

**Mile 0.0:** Beginning of AZ 88 in Apache Junction.

**Mile 1.5:** O.K. Corral Stables, 2½ miles L at the sign. The stables offer a variety of guided and unguided horse rides in the Superstition

and Goldfield Mountains; overnight pack trips can be arranged too; tel. 982-4040.

**Mile 4.2:** Mining Camp Restaurant on R has Western fare in a replica of an old mining camp cook shanty. Open Sun. for lunch and dinner; Tue. to Sat. for dinner only; tel. 982-3181.

**Mile 4.8:** Site of Goldfield on the L; Goldfield boomed in the 1890s with the discovery of gold but became a ghost town when mining yields dwindled in 1915. People still mine gold in this area at times, and you'll see prominent "No Trespassing" signs when they do.

**Mile 5.4:** Lost Dutchman State Park on the R; picnicking, dayhiking, and camping at the base of the Superstition Mountains; cost per vehicle: $2 day use, $5 camping (no hookups); nonresidents add $1; tel. 982-4485.

**Mile 5.7:** First Water Trailhead on R; 3 bumpy miles takes you to a popular trailhead for hikes in the Superstition Wilderness. Many people camp along this road (no facilities) in the cooler months.

**Mile 7.3:** Needle Vista Viewpoint on R; Weaver's Needle, the striking high pinnacle rising among the Superstitions, has often figured in lost gold mine legends. The name honors frontier scout Pauline Weaver (a man). Local Indians had a different name—referring to a certain part of a stallion's anatomy! Climb a nearby hill for a better view.

**Mile 12.4:** Overlook on R for Canyon Lake, 950 surface acres. The series of lakes along the Salt River provides fishing and boating for visitors and precious water for Phoenix. Canyon Lake was created by Mormon Flat Dam, completed in 1925. After the viewpoint, the road sweeps down from the heights to the lakeshore.

**Mile 14.5:** Acacia Picnic Site on L (swimming and fishing).

**Mile 14.8:** Palo Verde Boating Site on L (boat launch); Boulder Picnic Site on R (swimming and fishing).

**Mile 15.2:** Canyon Lake Marina on L; Boulder Canyon Trailhead on right. Facilities at the marina include boat rental and storage, fishing

*the "Narrows" of La Barge Creek in
the Superstitions*

supplies, a snack bar, picnicking, and a camp-ground; tel. 986-5546. Another camping area, The Point, can be reached only by boaters; it's on the L, 3 miles upstream from the marina. A tour boat takes visitors on a scenic 1½ hour cruise; tel. 827-9144 for times. Fishermen have hooked large-mouthed and yellow bass, trout, catfish, bluegill, carp, walleye, and crappie. During the busy mid-spring to mid-summer season, Sunday crowds often fill all available parking in the Canyon Lake area; try to arrive early. Boulder Canyon Trail #103 begins across the highway, climbing up the ridge with spectacular views into the Superstitions and back over the Canyon Lake area. The trail continues on through La Barge and Boulder Canyons, linking with several other trails in the Superstition Wilderness.

**Mile 15.6:** Laguna Boating Site on L (boat launch).

**Mile 17.3:** Tortilla Campground on L; Tortilla Flat (cafe, hotel, curio shop) on right. The campground is open Nov. to Apr.; water sup-ply is questionable for drinking—it's better to bring your own; $5/night. Tortilla Flat, "pop. 6," the only town along this section of road, looks like it came straight from a movie set. The tiny community has been a popular traveler's stop ever since the road went through. A hungry pioneer, who saw the sur-rounding flat boulders as stacks of tortillas, gave the place its name. The cafe serves inex-pensive American and Mexican meals. Souve-nirs and even a few hotel rooms are available; Box 34, Tortilla Flat, AZ 85290 (no tel.). Lots of old mining and farming relics lie around; look to see if the dummy "outlaw" is still swinging in the breeze from a rope.

**Mile 22.9:** Pavement ends. The next 22 miles to Roosevelt Dam are graded dirt road.

**Mile 24.4:** Beginning of descent down Fish Creek Hill with spectacular views of the canyon below. Fish Creek Hill is the Apache Trail's most exciting part, especially for the driver, who must negotiate sharp bends as the road traverses a cliff face and drops 1,500 feet in 3 miles. Fish Creek, near the bottom of the de-scent, occasionally has a trickle of water but no fish. Hikers can head up Fish Creek Canyon.

**Mile 30.1:** Forest Route 212 on R to Reavis Trailhead, 3 bumpy miles. Reavis Ranch Trail #109 crosses the eastern part of the Superstition Wilderness. Elisha Reavis lived a hermit's life on his ranch from 1872 until he died in 1896.

**Mile 30.2:** Apache Lake Vista, from which the lake comes into view in the canyon below. Held back by Horse Mesa Dam, Apache Lake's 2,600 surface acres reach nearly to Roosevelt Lake—a distance of 18 miles.

**Mile 32.1:** Turnoff on the L for Apache Lake Recreation Area. Apache Lake Marina and Resort have a boat ramp, boat rentals (fishing, ski, and houseboats), boat storage, fishing and camping supplies, restaurant, tent and RV campground ($9.45 w/hookups and showers), and a motel w/kitchettes, $40-$50; Box 23, Tor-tilla Flat AZ 85290; tel. 467-2511. The Forest Service has a campground (no water, free) next to the marina and allows dispersed camping along the lakeshore. Fishermen can catch small- and large-mouth bass, yellow bass, crap-pie, catfish, sunfish, and walleye.

**Mile 39.0:** Burnt Corral Campground and boat ramp on L; the Forest Service camping area is free but lacks drinking water.

**Mile 44.3:** Theodore Roosevelt Dam; keep R for southern Roosevelt Lake and Globe; turn L across the dam (no vehicles over 30 feet) for northern Roosevelt Lake and Payson. Roosevelt Dam marks the end of the dirt section. Workers built the dam with stone blocks between 1905 and 1911. An engineering feat of its day, the 280-foot-high structure is still the world's highest masonry dam. President Teddy Roosevelt motored over the Apache Trail in 1911 to dedicate the dam later named after him.

## ROOSEVELT LAKE

Roosevelt Lake, fed by Tonto Creek from the N and the Salt River from the E, stretches 23 miles and is as much as 2 miles wide. With 17,335 surface acres, it's the largest of the 4 Salt River Lakes. Most of the shoreline has a gentle slope, good for both camping and boat launching. Summers at Roosevelt's 2,100-foot elevation are only slightly cooler than the Valley's; nonetheless water skiing and boating attract many visitors. Fishermen enjoy the rest of the year, when it's not so hot. Known as a good bass and crappie lake, Roosevelt also contains catfish and sunfish. A flock of Great Basin Canadian Geese take up residence during the winter at Bermuda Flat on the northern arm. The southern half of this area is closed to the public from 15 Nov. to 15 Feb., but you can view the geese from the highway.

**accommodations and food:** The Forest Service has many free recreation sites both N and S of the dam. Camping is mostly primitive with pit toilets, boat ramps, and one RV sewage-disposal site as the only improvements. Roosevelt Marina, 2 miles SE of the dam, has boat rentals (fishing and pontoon), wet and dry boat storage, a paved boat ramp, a

*Theodore Roosevelt Dam*

snack bar, gasoline for boats and autos, and a store; tel. 467-2245. Lakeview Trailer Park, across the highway, has spaces with hookups ($10); no tents; tel. 467-2203. Roosevelt Lake Resort offers a motel ($27.30 s, $29.40 d), trailer park ($7.80 RV w/hookups), restaurant, boat storage, and service station; 12 miles E of the dam (20 miles NW of Globe); tel. 467-2276. Spring Creek Store, ½ mile NW of the resort turnoff, has groceries, camping and fishing supplies, and gasoline. Rockhouse Store, 6 miles N on the Young Highway (AZ 288), has groceries, gasoline, and a trailer park ($5 RV w/hookups); tel. 467-9306. Punkin Center, a village 22 miles N of Roosevelt on AZ 188, has Punkin Center Lodge; tel. 479-2229, restaurants, stores, and gasoline.

**information:** The Forest Service office puts out a recreation map of Roosevelt and Apache Lakes for $1. Rangers will tell you about camping, fishing, hiking, and boating in the area; Box 647, Roosevelt, AZ 85545; tel. 467-2236. The office is ½ mile E of Roosevelt Lake Marina on AZ 88.

## TONTO NATIONAL MONUMENT

Two well-preserved cliff dwellings of the prehistoric Salado Indians overlook the blue waters of Roosevelt Lake. The Salado (Spanish for "salt") lived in this part of the Salt River Valley about A.D. 1150-1400. Skillful farmers, they dug irrigation canals to water their corn, squash, beans, grain amaranth, and cotton. They also roamed the desert hills for cactus fruits, mesquite beans, deer, pronghorn, and many other wild foods. Crafts included beautiful polychrome pottery and intricately woven cotton cloth. At first they built small scattered pueblos along the river, but about 1250 some of the Salado began living on more defensible ridgetops. Finally, from 1300 until their mysterious departure soon after 1400, part of the population moved into caves like those in the Monument.

**Visitor Center and ruins:** Exhibits show how the Salado lived and what we know of their history. Stone tools, pottery, cotton cloth, and other artifacts demonstrate their artistry. A self-guided trail behind the Visitor Center climbs the hillside to the Lower Ruin, which you can enter. Originally the cave had 19 rooms, with another 12 in the Annex outside, but the elements have worn away those exposed. Allow one hour for the trip; you'll be climbing 350 feet higher on a well-graded path. The Upper Ruin, reached by a different trail, is about twice the size of the Lower, but it's farther away and takes advance planning—you

*Lower Ruin at Tonto National Monument*

must call or write at least 2 days in advance to arrange a visit. Ranger-guided tours for the Upper Ruin leave at 0900 (allow 3 hours for the 3-mile RT hike); there's no extra charge. A nature trail near the Visitor Center identifies many desert plants. The Monument is open daily 0800-1700 but the ruin trail closes at 1600; Box 707, Roosevelt, AZ 85545; tel. 467-2241. The Visitor Center is one mile off AZ 88, 2 miles SE of Roosevelt and 28 miles NW of Globe; $3/vehicle admission. If you're driving the Apache Trail Loop, this is the half-way point time-wise; Apache Junction is 3 hours away by either the 80-mile Apache Trail or the 120-mile route via Globe.

## GLOBE

Globe, tucked into a narrow valley between the Apache Mountains to the NE and the Pinal Mountains to the S and W, is a handy stopping place for travelers. The town's 3,500-foot elevation gives it a pleasant climate most of the year. Though its years of glory as a big copper-mining center have passed, Globe still has a lot of character. On a drive down Broad St. you can visit the museum, see ruins of the Old Dominion Copper Mine, and look at the many buildings dating from the early 1900s. The Chamber of Commerce, also on Broad St., has a walking tour that gives you the history of these old structures.

**history:** Prospectors scouring the hills of the western part of San Carlos Apache Indian Reservation in 1875 struck silver. Their most remarkable find was a globe-shaped silver nugget, said to have rough outlines of the continents scarred on its surface. Miners converged on the area, setting up camp on the E bank of Pinal Creek. The problem of this being Indian land was soon resolved by officially slicing it off the reservation. That didn't go over well with the Apache, who menaced the camp until Geronimo's surrender in 1886. Silver began to give out after only 4 years, but by then rich copper deposits had been discovered under the silver lodes. The Old Dominion Copper Company moved in and grew to be one of the greatest copper mines in the world during the early 1900s. Globe prospered too—its 50

restaurants and saloons never closed, and about 150 "working women" lived in neat little shacks along N. Broad Street. George W.P. Hunt arrived in 1881 as a young man and worked his way up to become a leading merchant and banker of Globe before going on to serve as Arizona's first governor. Labor troubles and declining yields began to eat into mining profits, and the Depression shut down the Old Dominion completely in 1931. Copper mining shifted to nearby Miami, leaving Globe to doze on as a quiet county seat.

## SIGHTS

**Gila County Historical Museum:** This small but varied collection represents the Indian, pioneer, and mining heritages of the area. Prehistoric Indian artifacts came from Besh-ba-gowah Pueblo right in town, and from other sites near Globe. Displays also show crafts of present-day Indians. Period rooms recreate pioneer days with a kitchen, bedroom, and doctor's office. A "mine" gives an idea how underground mining was done in the old days. Ore cars and large machinery sit outside. Open Mon. to Fri. 0900-1630 and Sat. 1000-1600; donation; tel. 425-7385. Located opposite the Old Dominion Copper Co. Mine at 1330 N. Broad Street.

**Cobre Valley Center for the Arts:** Local artists recently banded together and opened an

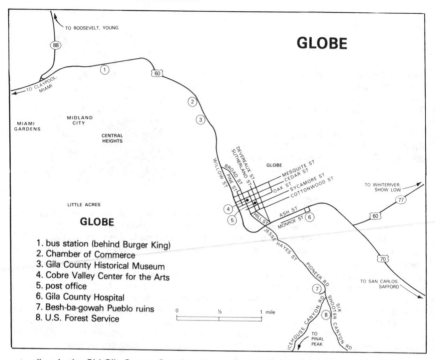

**GLOBE**

1. bus station (behind Burger King)
2. Chamber of Commerce
3. Gila County Historical Museum
4. Cobre Valley Center for the Arts
5. post office
6. Gila County Hospital
7. Besh-ba-gowah Pueblo ruins
8. U.S. Forest Service

art gallery in the Old Gila County Courthouse, built 1906-1907. Doing much of the restoration themselves, the artists have also added a theater and historical exhibits. They schedule art classes and art auctions. There's a bookstore downstairs. Open daily; call for hours; free. Located downtown at the corner of Broad and Oak Sts.; tel. 425-0884.

**Besh-ba-gowah:** Salado Indian villages lined both sides of Pinal Creek about 600 years ago. Besh-ba-gowah, exposed to the elements and man, is in poor condition compared with cliff dwellings like those at Tonto National Monument, but the extensive foundations and few remaining walls testify to its original size. Archaeologists count 200 rooms at Besh-ba-gowah, built and inhabited between 1225 and 1400. Its name comes from an Apache word meaning "metal camp." The ruin is 1½ miles S

of downtown Globe; follow S. Broad St. to its end, then turn R across the bridge, turn L on Jess Hayes Rd./Ice House Canyon Rd. one mile, then make a sharp R to "Globe Community Center." Besh-ba-gowah is across from the Center next to a ballfield.

**Pinal Peak:** A good dirt road winds up the timber-clad slopes to the summit, elev. 7,812 feet. Weather permitting, you'll enjoy great views, hiking, picnicking, and 2 of the coolest campgrounds in the Tonto National Forest. For the 18-mile drive from Globe, follow Jess Hayes Rd. SE (turn L after crossing the bridge from the end of S. Broad St.) to the junction of Ice House Canyon and Six Shooter Canyon Rds., turn R 2½ miles on Ice House Canyon Rd., turn R 3 miles on Forest Route 55 (pavement ends), then L 12½ miles on Forest Route 651 to the summit.

## PRACTICALITIES

**accommodations:** You'll find Globe's motels either downtown on Broad St. or along US 60, which bypasses downtown. Coming in from the N or W, you'll pass: Motel Villa (US 60 and Manor Dr.; tel. 425-4425); Willow Motel (US 60 at 792 N. Willow St.; tel. 425-4573); Belle-Aire Motel (1600 N. Broad St.; tel. 425-4406); and Ember Motel (1105 N. Broad St.; tel. 425-5736). Pioneer Hotel is the oldest and cheapest place in town, 189 N. Broad St.; tel. 425-8515. Also try Apache Land Motel (US 60 at 351 Ash St.; tel. 425-9888); Copper Manor Motel (US 60 at 637 Ash St.; tel 425-7124); El Rey Motel (US 60 at 1201 Ash St.; tel 425-4427); and El Rancho Motel (US 60 at 1302 Ash St.; tel. 425-5757). RV's have overnight parking with hookups at Casa de Monti, E of Globe near the junction of US 60 and US 70; tel. 425-6574. Tent campers and small RVs can head S about 18 miles into the Pinal Mountains. The Forest Service has free campgrounds open Apr. to Dec. on Forest Route 651 at Sulfide del Rey (no water), and Pinal (water from May to Oct.).; and on Forest Route 112 at Pioneer Pass (water from May to Oct.); see the Tonto Forest Map or call the Forest Service in Globe (tel. 425-7189).

**food:** Globe has some neat little cafes downtown: El Rey Cafe at 999 N. Broad St., and La Casita at 470 N. Broad St. serve Mexican food; La Luz del Dia is a Mexican bakery and coffee shop at 304 N. Broad St.; Su Il's Oriental Kitchen has Chinese fare downstairs in the Pioneer Hotel at 189 N. Broad St.; Larry's Fountain is the place for shakes and burgers at 109 S. Broad St.; and Peg's Kitchen dishes up Mexican and American food at 247 S. Broad Street. For steaks try the Crestline Steak House, about one mile E on US 60. More restaurants, including the fast-food chains, are located on the outskirts at both ends of Globe on US 60.

**entertainment and events:** Globe Theatre screens current movies at 141 N. Broad St.; tel. 425-5581. Some of Globe's major events are: the Gila County Gem & Mineral Show in January or February; Copper Dust Stampede Rodeo, dance, and parade in April; Mining Country Arts and Crafts Fair in April; old fashioned 4th of July celebration; Old Time Fiddlers Contest in August; Mexican Independence Day Fiesta in September; Gila County Fair in September; horse races in October; Bustle & Boots Square Dance Festival in October; and Copper Valley Marathon and 10,000-meter races also in October.

**services:** The main post office is downtown at Sycamore and Hill Streets. Gila County Hospital is in eastern Globe at 1100 Monroe St.; tel. 425-5721. Globe Community Center has a swimming pool, picnic areas, and ballfields (see directions for Besh-ba-gowah). Cobre Valle Country Club is open to the public with a 9-hole golf course, swimming pool, tennis, and raquetball courts; located just N on AZ 88 between Globe and Miami; tel. 473-2731. Cook Circle C Ranch offers trail rides in the Pinal Mountains from their stables in Ice House Canyon (Rt. 1, Box 25C, Globe, AZ 85501); tel. 425-4532.

**information:** Globe Chamber of Commerce is very helpful; open Mon. to Fri., 0800-1700, Sat., 0800-1400, and sometimes on Sunday. The office is at 1450 N. Broad St. (one block NW of the historical museum); Box 2539, Globe AZ 85502; tel. 425-4495. The Forest Service has maps and literature about the hiking trails (which tend to be steep) and camping of the area. Their office is on Six-Shooter Canyon Rd., 2 miles S of downtown; open Mon. to Fri. 0745-1145 and 1230-1630; Rt. 1, Box 33, Globe, AZ 85501; tel. 425-7189. The main public library is 6 miles W in Miami at 1052 Adonis Ave.; tel. 473-2621.

**transport:** Greyhound Bus stops at the station behind Burger King, on US 60 about 2 miles NW of downtown. Greyhound has 4 westbound and 4 eastbound departures daily. The bus station is open Mon. to Fri. 0800-1700 and Sat. 0800-1300; tel. 425-2301.

*Apache village*

## VICINITY OF GLOBE

**Miami and Claypool:** The strangeness of the man-made landscape is striking as you approach these 2 towns W of Globe. Many-tiered terraces of barren, buff-colored mine tailings from the crushers and dark slag dumps from the furnaces dominate the view. Miami and Claypool stretch along Bloody Tanks Wash, named for a massacre of Apache in 1864 by a band of whites and allied Maricopa Indians. Developers arrived in 1907 to lay out a townsite, calling it after the town of Miami, Ohio. Giant copper-ore reduction plants built by the Miami Copper and Inspiration Companies earned the title "Concentrator City" for the new town. Miami has had its ups and downs since, depending on copper prices. Currently prices are down, as you might guess from the appearance of downtown, but copper production continues. Miami has half a dozen historic buildings, described in a walking-tour leaflet available from Globe Chamber of Commerce. There are 2 motels and several restaurants in Miami.

## VICINITY OF GLOBE
## SUPERIOR

Opening of the rich Silver King Mine in 1875, followed by the Silver Queen, brought streams of fortune hunters into this mineral-laden region. As in Globe, miners found rich deposits of copper when the surface silver began to play out. Superior lies just W of scenic Queen Creek Canyon in a valley surrounded by the rugged Pinal Mountains. North of town you'll see machinery and extensive tailings of the Magma Copper Mine, whose shafts plunge 3,500 feet underground. A couple of motels and several restaurants are in town. Oak Flat Campground (elev. 4,200 feet), has free Forest Service sites with picnic tables, grills, and pit toilets but no water; open all year; 4 miles E of Superior (13 miles W of Miami) on US 60; turn S onto Magma Mine Rd. near Milepost 231.

**vicinity of Superior:** The highway from Globe and Miami wends its way past spires and balanced rocks of Queen Creek Canyon. Apache Tear Caves, 2 miles W of town, contain shiny black stones. Legends say they came as tears from 75 Apaches who leaped to their deaths off a nearby cliff in the 1870s, rather than surrender to the U.S. Cavalry; geologists say the stones are a form of volcanic glass. Either way you can collect them for a small fee or visit the rock shop, open daily, 0700-1630 (0800-1200, June to Aug.); take the Apache Tears Rd. S one mile, midway between Superior and Boyce Thompson Arboretum.

**Boyce Thompson Southwestern Arboretum:** You can see more than 1,500 different desert plants in this large plant museum. Short trails lead through yuccas and agaves, a cactus garden, native desert vegetation, riparian (stream bank) natives, exotic plants, palms, pines, and eucalyptus. More than 174 bird and 72 animal species have been spotted. Greenhouses contain cactus and succulents that wouldn't otherwise survive winter cold. Elevations range from 2,400 feet at the gardens to 4,400 feet atop nearby Picket Post Mountain. A heliograph station, which used mirrors to flash sun's rays, operated atop the peak during the Apache wars. The Visitor Center has some exhibits and a gift shop offering books, prints, posters, and seed packets. There's often a large selection of cactus and other plants for sale. Today both the University of Arizona and the State Parks Board have a part in the Arboretum. Open daily (except Christmas) 0800-1700; $1.50 adult, $.75 children 5-17; tel. 689-2811. Copper mining magnate

William Boyce Thompson founded the Arboretum in 1927 for botanical research and teaching. His 26-room mansion, Picket Post House, overlooks the grounds and can be visited on tours daily 1000-1700; $3 (entrance is separate from the Arboretum); tel. 689-2845. The Arboretum, just off US 60, is located 3 miles W of Superior, 60 miles SE of Phoenix, and 98 miles N of Tucson.

## FLORENCE JUNCTION TO APACHE JUNCTION

**Florence Junction:** Not a town at all—just a junction. If you're interested in turquoise, drop into the Hardy Turquoise store just E of the junction; open Mon. to Fri. 0800-1600; tel. 463-2371. The town of Florence, which has the very good Pinal County Historical Museum, is 16 miles S on US 89 (see below).

**Peralta Trailhead:** One of the most popular trailheads for the Superstition Wilderness turns off US 60/89 about 9 miles NW of Florence Junction (8 miles SE of Apache Junction). Follow the graded-dirt Forest Route 77 in for 7 miles. You'll also see the Dons Camp on the L just before the trailhead. The Dons Club, an organization devoted to teaching legend and lore of the Southwest, throws a big one-day bash here, usually in Mar., when thousands of people descend on the Superstitions in an all-for-fun search for the Lost Dutchman's Mine. If

*Weaver's Needle from Fremont Saddle in the Superstitions*

you've heard the stories about this gold mine, you know that it "lies" in the shadow of Weaver's Needle. Since the famous landmark is only a short hike from Peralta Trailhead, you've come to the right place to search for the end of rainbows. Actually, there's good hiking here—3 trails branch off into the wilderness. Peralta Trail #102 goes up Peralta Canyon to Freemont Saddle, where you get a great view of Weaver's Needle and beyond. It's 4 miles RT and a 1,400-foot climb to the pass; carry water and avoid the heat of a summer day. Peralta Trail continues down the other side past the base of Weaver's Needle and connects with other trails in the Superstitions.

# SOUTH OF PHOENIX

On the drive between Phoenix and Tucson you cross desert plains with views of rugged mountain ranges. Desert flora blooms in bright colors in spring. Several places are worth stopping for whether you take the old Pinal Pioneer Parkway (US 89) or the speedier I-10.

## FLORENCE

Florence, one of the oldest white settlements in Arizona, dates back to the arrival of Levi Ruggles in 1866. Ruggles noted a safe fording place on the Gila River nearby and thought the valley suitable for farming. He laid out a townsite that soon became a trade center and stage stop for surrounding army camps. Some people advocated Florence as the Arizona territorial capital, but the town had to settle for becoming the Pinal County seat. The first county courthouse went up in 1878, constructed of adobe blocks like most buildings of the time. The courthouse survives and is now McFarland State Historic Park. The second county courthouse was completed in 1891; its ornate cupola stands out as Florence's chief landmark. Not everybody comes to Florence by choice—the Arizona State Prison sits just outside town. Convicts completed the prison in 1909 to replace the Territorial Prison at Yuma. Florence has 2 museums and a number of historic buildings; you can pick up a visitor's guide at the tourist office or Pinal County Historical Museum.

**Pinal County Historical Museum:** You'll see a lot of history in this diverse collection. Indian pottery, baskets, and stone tools come from prehistoric and modern tribes of the area. An 1880 horse-drawn opera coach shows that the early pioneers did enjoy a bit of elegance. Also displayed are tools, mining gear, household items, and clothing of early settlers. News clippings describe the tragic death of silent-screen hero Tom Mix in a car accident nearby. Bullet aficionados will be thrilled to see hundreds of different types in a big display. The prison exhibits are sobering: hangman's nooses (the actual ones used) framing photos of their victims, a hanging board, gas-chamber chair, massive prison registers from Yuma and Florence, and the story of murderess Eva Dugan—hung (and at the same time accidentally decapitated) in 1930. The museum is open Wed. to Sun. 1300-1700 (closed 15 July to 1 Sept.); donation; 715 S. Main St.; tel. 868-4382.

**McFarland State Historic Park:** This adobe building served as Pinal County's first courthouse, sheriff's office, and jail from 1878 to 1891, then functioned for 50 years as the county hospital. In 1883 an angry Florence mob took 2 murder suspects from the jail and strung them up in a corridor. Most exhibits and artifacts relate to the life of Ernest McFarland (1894-1984), who started his political career as Pinal County Attorney in 1925, and later rose to serve as a U.S. Senator, Arizona Governor, and Chief Justice of the State Supreme Court. Unless you have a special interest in McFarland or in the courthouse itself, you could skip this museum. Open Thur. to Mon. 0800-1700; $1 (age 17 and under free with adult); tel. 868-5216; located near the N end of Main St. at Ruggles Street.

**Tom Mix Monument:** October 12th, 1940, was a sad day for fans of movie hero Tom Mix.

Speeding N from Tucson in his big Cord, he lost control and rolled over in a ditch, now called Tom Mix Wash. A roadside monument, topped by a riderless horse, marks the spot, 17 miles S of Florence on US 89.

**Poston's Butte:** Charles Poston explored and mined in what's now Arizona from 1853 to 1861, but his greatest achievement was successfully lobbying in Washington D.C. for a territorial government. He went on to become the first superintendent of Indian affairs in Arizona and one of the first Arizona delegates to Congress. His congressional term finished, he traveled to India and became a "fire worshipper." Upon returning to Arizona in 1878, he built a continuous fire as a temple of the sun atop this hill, naming it "Parsee Hill." The flames died out several months later, ending a project that others called "Poston's Folly." He lies buried on the hill, renamed Poston's Butte, located NW from Florence across the Gila River.

**practicalities:** Florence is just a small place, population 5,800. Stay at Blue Mist Motel, junction of US 89 and AZ 287; tel. 868-5875. RVs can park at Chase's Shady Rest Trailer Villa (850 S. Main St.; tel. 868-4341) and Caliente Casa de Sol (4 miles N on US 89; tel. 868-5520). You'll find several restaurants on Main Street. For more information about the Florence area, see the Pinal County Visitor Center, 912 Pinal St. (E. 2 blocks on 8th St. from Main); open Mon. to Fri. 0800-1700 (1000-1400 in summer); Box 967, Florence, AZ 85232; tel. 868-4331.

## CASA GRANDE RUINS NATIONAL MONUMENT

A short turn-off from AZ 87 just N of Coolidge leads to Arizona's biggest and most perplexing prehistoric building. The rectangular structure stands 4 stories high and contains 11 rooms above an earthen platform. An estimated 2,800 tons of mud went into the project, whose walls vary in thickness from 4½ feet at the base to 1¾ feet near the top. Archaeologists don't know the purpose of Casa Grande, but some speculate that it was used for ceremonies or

*Casa Grande (south side)*

astronomical observations; certain holes in the walls appear to line up with the sun on the summer solstice and possibly with the moon during certain lunar events. Smaller structures and a wall, remnants of which still stand, surround the main building. Hohokam Indians, who had been farming the Gila Valley since about 200-300 B.C., built Casa Grande around A.D. 1350. It has little resemblance to other Hohokam pueblos; Mexican cultures may have influenced its construction. By about 1450, after just a few generations of use, the Hohokam abandoned it along with all their other villages. The Jesuit priest Eusebio Kino recorded the site in 1694, giving it the Spanish name for "big house."

**Visitor Center:** Exhibits introduce you to the Hohokam—their irrigation canals, farming tools, jewelry, ball courts, and Mexican connections. Conjectures are raised as to the disappearance of the Hohokam culture. Rangers lead tours of Casa Grande or you can take the self-guided trail. Signs also identify cactus

*Casa Grande (east side)*

and other desert plants. Books on Arizona's Indians, settlers, and natural history are sold. The Monument is open daily 0700-1800; $3/vehicle. It's located one mile N of Coolidge off AZ 87; the modern town of Casa Grande is about 20 miles away.

## GILA RIVER ARTS AND CRAFTS CENTER

To learn about the Pima and Maricopa Indians, or just to take a break from freeway driving, stop at this cultural center on the Gila River Reservation. The inexpensive restaurant offers Indian fry bread and Mexican and American foods. Crafts in the gift shop include Maricopa pottery, Papago baskets, Hopi *katsina* dolls, Navajo rugs, and pottery from the New Mexican pueblos. Jewelry, paintings, and prints come from many tribes. An exhibit room gives the history of the Pima and Maricopa and displays their artifacts. The Heritage Park outside contains traditional structures of the Hohokam, Pima, Maricopa, Papago, and Apache tribes.

Signs describe the culture of each group. Gila River Arts and Crafts Center is open daily except holidays 0900-1700; admission is free to the inside exhibits, but you'll need to buy a $1 token from the gift shop to enter the Heritage Park. Take I-10 Exit 175, 30 miles SE of Phoenix (90 miles NW of Tucson), and go W ½ mile to the large white building.

## PICACHO PEAK STATE PARK

Picacho Peak has been a landmark for Indians, Spanish explorers, American frontiersmen, and modern-day motorists. The Battle of Picacho Pass, on 15 Apr. 1862, was the westernmost conflict of the Civil War and the only one to take place in Arizona. Confederate forces killed Lt. James Barrett, leader of the Union detachment, and 2 privates, while losing 2 men themselves. Aware that Union reinforcements would soon arrive, the Confederates then retreated eastward. The battle site is thought to be just outside the State Park boundary, toward the freeway. Inside the Park, you can hike to the top of 3,370-foot Picacho Peak or try easier trails. The Park also has several picnic areas and a campground with showers and hookups.

**hiking trails:** Hunter Trail climbs 1,400 feet to the summit, a 4-mile RT taking 4-5 hours. Be careful on the back side where the trail crosses some loose rock. An easier hike, also with expansive views, goes as far as the saddle, a 2-mile RT hike taking 1½ hours. Easier still is the Calloway Trail to a low pass between Bugler's and Picacho Peaks, 1½ miles RT, taking an hour. A nature trail loop introduces desert plants; allow 30 minutes. **practicalities:** Costs to visit are $2 for day use, $5 for camping, and $7 for an RV w/hookups; nonresidents add $1; tel. 466-3183. Take I-10 Exit 219.

# SOUTHWEST OF PHOENIX

## GILA BEND

The town (pop. 1,800) sits near the Gila River 68 miles SW of Phoenix. Father Kino, who came through in 1699, found a prosperous Maricopa Indian village here whose irrigated fields yielded 2 harvests annually. The Butterfield stagecoaches first rolled through in the early 1850s and a settlement later grew around one of their stations. Today the small town serves as an agricultural center and a travelers' stop. Surrounding farms raise cotton, wheat, barley, and other crops. San Lucy, a Papago Indian village, lies just N of town. On Business Loop I-8 you'll find 7 motels, an RV park, and a variety of restaurants.

**vicinity of Gila Bend:** Heading S on AZ 85 to Ajo and Organ Pipe Cactus National Monument, you'll pass through a small group of jagged volcanic mountains known as "Crater Range." Painted Rocks State Park, 25 miles NW of Gila Bend, is in 2 parts: a group of boulders covered with Indian petroglyphs, and a recreation lake. Dark desert varnish (a natural manganese and iron-oxide stain) on the rocks provided an excellent working surface for

*petroglyphs at Painted Rock State Park*

prehistoric Indians, who pecked out symbols and figures of people and animals. You can picnic or camp here but there's no water. The lake, a 4-mile drive N, has drinking water and is better for camping; no hookups, but showers are planned. Large-mouth bass, channel catfish, bluegill, crappie and other fish live in the waters; however, tests have shown high DDT levels in them. Ask a ranger for the latest news. An odd feature of the lake is that it's *down-stream* of the dam! Earth scooped out here to build Painted Rock Dam has since filled with water. The reservoir that is behind the dam is used for flood control; its level fluctuates too much for recreational use. The usual state park fees apply at both the historic and lake units, except that no extra fee is charged for nonresidents at the lake; tel. 683-2151. The area is used mostly in the cooler months—it gets too hot (over 100 F) in summer.

# NORTHWEST OF PHOENIX

## WICKENBURG

You still get a sense of the Old West in easy-going Wickenburg. Western-style buildings line the downtown streets, and horses are a common sight. Even a bit of gold fever lingers, still drawing prospectors to mine-scarred hills in search of the "mother lode." Cowboys continue to work the range, though now joined by guests from local dude ranches. The picturesque rocky hills around Wickenburg offer ideal horseback riding. Wickenburg's cool and sunny weather lasts from November to May. Summers at the town's 2,100-foot elevation often bring very hot weather. Located 58 miles NW of Phoenix, you can get here from Phoenix via US 60/89 (Grand Ave.) or the longer but less congested route past Lake Pleasant on AZ 74.

history: Henry Wickenburg had been roaming the hills of Arizona for a year in search of gold before striking it rich at the Vulture Mine in 1863. According to some legends, he noticed the shiny nuggets when reaching down to pick up a vulture he'd just shot; others claim he noticed them when picking up a rock to throw at his burro. Either way, Wickenburg set off a frenzied gold rush. The Vulture Mine lacked water needed for processing, so miners hauled the ore 14 miles NE to the Hassayampa River. The town that grew up around the mills became Arizona's 3rd largest city in just a few years. It missed being the territorial capital in 1866 by just 2 votes. Prospectors located other gold deposits in the Wickenburg area until more than 80 mines operated at the height of the gold rush. Mining still continues today for gold and other minerals, but on a small scale—many people consider it just a hobby.

## SIGHTS

Desert Caballeros Western Museum: This fine museum takes you back to Wickenburg's Wild West days. Dioramas illustrate the history of Vulture Mine and the early mining community, the triumphs and tragedies. Period rooms and a street scene show how Wickenburg actually looked. An Indian Room displays a varied collection of prehistoric and modern crafts, including *katsina* dolls, pottery, baskets, and stone tools. Dazzling minerals and even giant fish scales from the Loch Ness monster can be seen in the Mineral Room. A large art gallery features outstanding Western paintings and sculpture by Remington, Russell, and other inspired artists. The museum and art gallery are open Tue. to Sat., 1000-1600, and Sun., 1300-1600; $1.50 adult, children free. Located at 20 N. Frontier St. (one block W of the downtown highway junction); tel. 684-2272.

Hassayampa River: Normally you'll see just a dry streambed. Its Apache name means "river that runs upside down," because its waters flow beneath the sandy surface. A wishing well and sign at the W end of the highway bridge tell the story that anyone drinking from the stream will never tell the truth again. Old Jail Tree: The town lacked a jail in the early days, so prisoners were shackled to this old mesquite tree. The tree stands behind the Circle-K store at the highway junction downtown.

## PRACTICALITIES

**guest ranches:** Wickenburg prides itself as the "Guest Ranch Capital of the World." The degree of luxury varies, but all 5 guest ranches offer horseback riding and a swimming pool. Basic high-season rates are listed here; add up to 15% service charge and 5% tax. Flying E Ranch is open 15 Nov. to 1 May; rates include meals: $83 s, $130 d.; 4 miles W on US 60, then one mile S; Box EEE, Wickenburg, AZ 85358;

tel. 684-2690. Kay El Bar Ranch has been around so long that it's on the National Historic Register; open 15 Oct. to 1 May; rates include meals: $75 s, $135 d; go 3 miles N on US 89; Box 2480, Wickenburg, AZ 85358; tel. 684-7593. Rancho Casitas is also 3 miles N off US 89; $750 one month (minimum stay); Box A-3, Wickenburg, AZ 85358; tel. 684-2628. Wickenburg Inn emphasizes tennis with 11 courts, pro shop, and lessons; located 7 miles N off US 89; open all year; rates include meals: $100 s, $140 d; Box P, Wickenburg, AZ 85358;

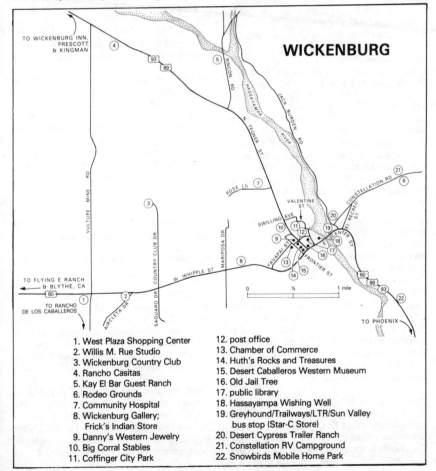

1. West Plaza Shopping Center
2. Willis M. Rue Studio
3. Wickenburg Country Club
4. Rancho Casitas
5. Kay El Bar Guest Ranch
6. Rodeo Grounds
7. Community Hospital
8. Wickenburg Gallery; Frick's Indian Store
9. Danny's Western Jewelry
10. Big Corral Stables
11. Coffinger City Park
12. post office
13. Chamber of Commerce
14. Huth's Rocks and Treasures
15. Desert Caballeros Western Museum
16. Old Jail Tree
17. public library
18. Hassayampa Wishing Well
19. Greyhound/Trailways/LTR/Sun Valley bus stop (Star-C Store)
20. Desert Cypress Trailer Ranch
21. Constellation RV Campground
22. Snowbirds Mobile Home Park

tel. 684-7811. Rancho de los Caballeros is the most elegant of the group; open early Oct. to early May; guests have a pool, tennis courts, and an 18-hole golf course; rates include meals: $110 s, $168 d; go 3½ miles W on US 60, then 2½ miles S; Box 1148, Wickenburg, AZ 85358; tel. 684-5484.

**motels:** You'll find all the motels in town along US 60, which becomes Center, then Whipple Street. From E to W: La Siesta Motel (510 E. Center; $29.40 s, $35.70 d; tel. 684-2826), Best Western Rancho Grande (293 E. Center; $35.70 s, $38.85 d; tel. 684-5445), Mecca Motel (162 E. Center; $24.68 s, $27.83 d; tel. 684-2753), Double J Motel (510 W. Whipple; $14.70 s, $27.30 d; tel. 684-2471), Wagon Wheel Motel (573-½ W. Whipple; $21 s, $23 d; tel. 684-2531), Westerner Motel (680 W. Whipple; $22 s, $28.35 d; tel. 684-2493), and Circle JR Motel (741 W. Whipple; $26.25 s or d; tel. 684-2661). For something different, check out the Garden City Motel on a hill 8 miles SE of town; the lonely spot offers quiet, good views of surrounding mountains, and a chance to see wildlife; no restaurant but some rooms have kitchenettes; $31.50 s, $34 d; Box 70, Wickenburg, 85358; tel. 684-2334; look for the signs between Mileposts 118 and 119 on US 60/89.

**camping:** Wickenburg-Circle City Kampground, 12 miles SE on US 60/89 has the only full-service facilities for both tents ($10.50) and RVs ($14 w/hookups); tel. 388-2431. Closer in, RVs can stay at Snowbirds Mobile Home Park (adults only, one mile SE on US 60/89; tel. 684-2044); Desert Cypress Trailer Ranch (adults only, behind McDonalds at 434 Constellation Rd.; $12 w/hookups; tel. 684-2153); or Constellation Park (only $2 but no water or facilities, one mile NE on Constellation Road). Another possibility for both tents and RVs is camping out in the desert; avoid washes and be sure you're on public land.

**food:** Frontier Inn (closed Mon.) has great Western-style BBQ, steaks, and seafood at 466 E. Center Street. La Casa Alegre serves Mexican and American food at 540 E. Center Street. For standard American fare try: Kelly's Cafe,

530 E. Center St.; Gold Nugget Restaurant, 222 E. Center St.; Horseshoe Cafe, 207 E. Center St.; Rancho Bar 7 Restaurant, 111 E. Center St.; Cock 'N' Bull Restaurant, 445 N. Tegner St. (US 89 N); or Charley's Steakhouse, 1101 W. Whipple Street. Pick up pizza at Sangini's, 107 E. Center St. or Pizza Hut, 515 W. Whipple Street. Western Deli, 683 W. Whipple St., has sandwiches and a full menu. For fast food stop at Blake's Lotaburger, 1051 W. Whipple St.; or McDonald's, 424 E. Center Street. Buffets and a la carte offerings for lunch and dinner are offered at 2 of the guest ranches: Rancho de los Caballeros (tel. 684-5484) and Wickenburg Inn (tel. 684-7811); reservations needed at both. You'll find Safeway and other stores in West Plaza Shopping Center on the W edge of town.

**entertainment:** Saguaro Movie Theater screens the current films at 176 E. Center St.; tel. 684-7189. Gold Rush Days celebrates Wickenburg's Western heritage with a shoot-out, parade, rodeo, concerts, "mellerdramas," gold-panning contest, and other activities, usually the 2nd weekend in February. The 4th of July has fireworks and a watermelon feed. The Wickenburg Bluegrass Festival brings foot-tapping music and dancing to town in the fall, usually the 2nd weekend in November.

**shopping:** Huth's Rocks and Treasures has many rocks and minerals for sale, rough and polished, as well as topo maps and mineral books for amateur prospectors, 128 N. Frontier St. (closed in Aug.). View Western art at the Wickenburg Gallery (open Tue. to Sat. 1100-1700, 1100-1500 in summer), 662 W. Whipple St.; and Willis M. Rue Studio (open daily 1000-1500), W. Whipple St. at Aircleta Drive. For Indian jewelry and other crafts see Frick's Indian Store (may close in summer), 642 W. Whipple St.; and Danny's Western Jewelry, 163 N. Tegner Street.

**services:** Post office is at 55 E. Yavapai St. between N. Tegner and N. Frontier Streets. The Community Hospital is at 111 Rose Lane, ¾ mile N off Tegner St.; tel. 684-5421. Coffinger City Park offers picnicking, a swimming pool, tennis courts, and ballfields; off N.

Tegner St., just across the Sols Wash bridge. Play golf year-round at the 9-hole Wickenburg Country Club course, 2 miles W on US 60 then N on Country Club Rd.; tel. 684-2011. You might also be able to use the 18-hole course at Rancho de los Caballeros; tel. 684-2704. Big Corral rents horses by the hour, half day, or full day; lessons and hayrides available too; closed in summer; located off N. Tegner St., just before the bridge over Sols Wash; tel. 684-2809.

**information:** The very helpful Wickenburg Chamber of Commerce is in the old railroad depot on N. Frontier St. (one block W of N. Tegner St.); open Mon. to Fri. 0900-1700; Box CC, Wickenburg, AZ 85358; tel. 684-5479. The public library is at 164 Apache St. (one block N of Center St. and just W of the river); tel. 684-2665.

**transport:** Greyhound, Trailways, LTR, and Sun Valley buses stop at the Star-C store, 444 E. Center St.; tel. 684-2601. Greyhound and

Trailways have one or 2 departures daily E to Phoenix and W to California. LTR and Sun Valley each have 2 departures daily to Phoenix and Las Vegas; LTR goes to Las Vegas via Kingman, while Sun Valley goes via Parker and Lake Havasu City.

## VICINITY OF WICKENBURG

It's fun to search out some of the old gold mines and ghost towns surrounding Wickenburg. Caution is needed on the dirt roads to the sites; get local advice on conditions and avoid traveling after heavy rains. The Vulture Mine would be worth seeing but has been closed to visitors. Stanton, a ghost town NW of Wickenburg, is open and well worth visiting.

**Stanton:** Originally called Antelope Station, the settlement was started in 1863 when prospectors found placer gold in Antelope Creek. Just 5 years later the population had reached 3,500. Three buildings remain from the old

*view of opera house from hotel porch, Stanton*

days: the stage stop, hotel, and opera house. A 4th building, the bath house, dates from only 1980. The gold began to play out by the early 1900s and Stanton started fading away. Gold mining continues in Antelope Creek by members of the Lost Dutchman's Mining Association, though it's just for fun. Ask permission to look around the old site; no charge, though you could make a donation. From Wickenburg follow US 89 N for 18 miles (2 miles past Congress) and turn R on a graded dirt road signposted for Stanton and Octave. You'll see old shacks, mine tailings, rusting machinery, and some new operations along this road. After entering Stanton, 6½ miles later, turn L through the Lost Dutchman's Mining Assn. gate. The main road continues another mile to Octave townsite (signposted "No Trespassing"), then becomes too rough for cars. On

Rich Hill, between Stanton and Octave, prospectors picked up gold nuggets the size of potatoes just lying on the ground. Another road turns off at Stanton and goes up the valley to Yarnell.

**Yarnell Hill Lookout:** Stop at the view tower for a sweeping scene of the desert and distant mountains below. The lookout is 25 miles N of Wickenburg on US 89, just before Yarnell. Because the lookout is on the southbound lane only, northbound travelers will have to do a U-turn at Yarnell and backtrack ½ mile.

**Joshua forest:** Joshua trees *(Yucca brevifolia)* line US 93 beginning about 22 miles NW of Wickenburg and continuing for 16 miles. Large clusters of pale-green flowers appear from early Feb. to early April.

## CASA GRANDE ARTIFACTS

*shell finger ring*

*stone ax*

*copper bells*

*stone ax*

# EASTERN ARIZONA

## INTRODUCTION

Eastern Arizona will surprise you. Instead of the arid desert country you might expect, you'll find 2,000 square miles of forested peaks, placid lakes, and sparkling streams of the White Mountains! The mountains' cool summer climate, abundant trout-filled waters, and winter sports are the big attractions for visitors. Mount Baldy, a peak sacred to the Apache Indians, crowns the range at 11,590 feet and is Arizona's 2nd highest mountain. Sunrise Ski Resort, several miles N, has some of the Southwest's most challenging downhill runs. Cross-country skiers and summer hikers can find solitude almost anywhere in these mountains. For a wildly scenic, high-country drive, try the Coronado Trail between Springerville and Clifton; slow and winding, the route offers almost unlimited picnicking, hiking, and camping possibilities. Over to the W, another highway offers a different surprise—you're driving along SW of Show Low, when suddenly the road begins to descend into a magnificent chasm. It's the Salt River Canyon, a smaller but equally colorful version of the Grand Canyon.

Traveling N from the White Mountains, you'll notice the scenery changing from mountain firs and pines to junipers and vast rangelands of lower, more arid country, and then to the multihued, barren hills of the Painted Desert. You can have a closer look at this striking desert country and its famous fossilized wood at Petrified Forest National Park. Southward from the White Mountains, the drop in elevation is even greater—you'll be in cotton-growing country along the Gila River. "Islands" of high mountains, such as Mt. Graham (10,717 feet) near Safford, break up the often-monotonous, low-desert country. A paved road runs nearly to the top of Mt. Graham, taking you from the Lower Sonoran Life Zone to the Canadian. The Galiuro Mountains to the W are a roadless wilderness with several peaks over 7,000 feet in elevation.

**getting there and around:** Eastern Arizona almost requires private transportation. Only limited bus, train, and air connections service the area. Greyhound and Trailways buses stop in Winslow and Holbrook on their runs across

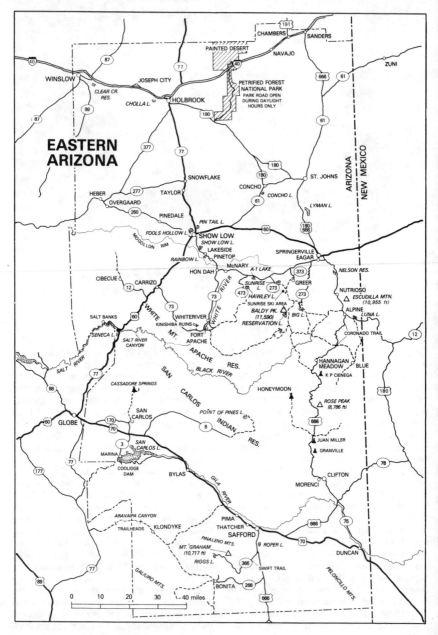

northern Arizona. Greyhound also stops at Globe and Safford on a southern route between Phoenix and New Mexico. Winslow is the only town served by Amtrak train. Golden Pacific Airlines connects Winslow with Sedona, Phoenix, and other cities.

**climate:** The high country provides welcome relief in summer from the searing heat of the deserts. Most eastern Arizona resort areas are at elevations of 6,000-7,000 feet, where average summer temperatures run in the 60s and 70s F, and highs rarely exceed the mid-80s. Afternoon thunderstorms drench the forests almost daily from mid-July to early Sept., bringing about ⅓ of the area's 15 or so inches of annual precipitation. Early summer is the driest time of year. Camping above 6,000 feet is difficult in winter, as heavy snowfalls and lows in the teens are common. Most winter days are bright and sunny, though, and highs often reach the mid-40s F. Skiers enjoy this weather, and even some fishermen will be out, chopping holes in the lake ice to get at that elusive trout. The high-desert country to the N, around Petrified Forest Natl. Park, can be cold in winter and hot in summer but is usually snow-free. The low desert S of the White Mountains has mild winters and rarely gets snow. As in the rest of eastern Arizona, late summer is the rainiest time.

*Alchesay, Apache Chief and U.S. Army scout*

## THE APACHE

**arrival:** Close relatives of the Navajo, the Apache have similar language and customs. Groups of Apache are thought to have migrated from Canada, arriving in Texas and New Mexico in the 16th century. A few moved W, forming the tribes that now live on the White Mountain and San Carlos Reservations in eastern Arizona and 3 small reservations in central Arizona. The early Apache lived a nomadic life—the men hunted game while the women searched out wild plant foods. They had few material possessions, and their homes were probably small conical huts covered with animal skins. Cultivation of corn, beans, and squash, learned from either the pueblo or Navajo Indians, later supplemented hunting and gathering. Horses obtained from the Spanish gave the Apache great mobility, and by the mid-18th C. their raiding routes stretched from the Hopi mesas in the N to central Sonora in Mexico. Their predatory habits did not endear them to their neighbors—in fact, the name "Apache" may have come from a Zuni Indian word for "enemy."

**troubles with the white man:** The Apache vigorously defended their lands from encroaching settlers, and they soon earned a reputation as the fiercest tribe in the Southwest. Attempts to exterminate them by the Spanish, the Mexicans, and finally the Americans caused the tribe to retaliate with a murderous vengeance. By 1870 it was finally realized that a military solution wasn't going to work.

**reservation life:** The federal government then initiated a "Peace Policy," which placed all Indians on reservations and taught them to farm and raise livestock. The San Carlos Reservation, just S of the White Mountains, was created in 1871 as a home for various tribes — Mojave, Yavapai, Yuma, and several different Apache groups. Officials thought the Indians would be easier to control if centralized on one reservation, but the plan worked poorly and may even have extended the Apache wars. Quarrels developed between the different groups, attempts at farming went poorly, and government agents frequently cheated the Indians. Geronimo and other war chiefs escaped at times to lead raids against settlements in southern Arizona and northern Mexico. By the time Geronimo surrendered in 1886, the federal government recognized that the San Carlos Reservation had failed and removed all tribes except the San Carlos Apache. Meanwhile, many of the White Mountain and Cibeque Apache had succeeded in holding onto part of their own territory to the N, which became a reservation in 1897.

In a ranching program in 1918, 5 head of cattle were issued to each of 80 Apache families. Although the program almost failed, the herds on the Fort Apache Reservation grew to 20,000 by 1931. Still, it wasn't until 1936 that the white men finally removed the last of their own cattle from the reservations. Recognizing the recreational value of their lands, in the 1950s the White Mountain Apache began to build access roads, reservoirs, campgrounds, marinas, motels, and restaurants. They also own and operate a large lumber industry. During this development, the tribe has taken care to preserve the great natural beauty of the reservation. San Carlos Apache have developed their lakes and streams for visitors as well, but on a smaller scale.

**traditions:** Driving through the Apache homeland, you might think that their culture is gone — you see members of the tribe living in modern houses, going to the shopping center, and working at regular jobs. But the Apache continue to use their own language and to preserve some old traditions. Boys still study under medicine men to learn the prayers, rituals, and medicinal plants used in healing ceremonies. Elaborate coming-of-age ceremonials still mark the passage into adulthood of young women. Known as "Sunrise Dances," these rites usually take place during summer; ask for dates at the tribal offices in Whiteriver and San Carlos.

**crafts:** Frequently on the move in pre-reservation days, the Apache had only a few utilitarian crafts. The products of 2 of these — baskets and cradleboards — are made and sold today. Look for them at trading posts on the reservations. Buckskin dresses, worn by women before the introduction of calico, are occasionally seen at Sunrise Dances. Attractive designs in beadwork decorate necklaces, bolo ties, and other adornments. Woodcarvers have recently begun fashioning realistic dolls depicting dance movements of the Apache Spirit Dancers. Craftsmen on the San Carlos Reservation set peridot, a transparent yellow-green gemstone, in bolo ties, necklaces, earrings, and other jewelry.

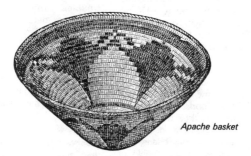

*Apache basket*

# THE HIGH DESERT

## WINSLOW

Starting as a railroad terminal in 1882, the town commemorates Gen. Edward Francis Winslow, a president of the Atlantic and Pacific Railroad. Ranchers turned the community into a major stock-raising center and shipping point. Located 58 miles E of Flagstaff, Winslow (pop. 8,635) is a handy stopover for travelers.

**Homolovi ruins:** You can visit nearby pueblo Indian ruins constructed by the Anasazi. The 6 Homolovi sites date from about A.D. 1250 to 1500, after which it's believed the inhabitants migrated to the Hopi mesas. The Hopi hold these ruins sacred and still visit to leave *pahos* (prayer feathers) for the spirits. Serious archaeological work has only recently begun. Homolovi II, or "place of the mounds," is the largest site. It and the other 5 sites have become the Homolovi Ruins State Park. As many as 3,000 Anasazi may have lived in Homolovi II, which had an estimated 800 rooms and 3 plazas. Though badly weathered, the ruins show what a prehistoric site looks like before extensive excavation or reconstruction. Look for the petroglyphs along the base of the mesa on which the ruins sit. Visitors are welcome, but they mustn't remove or disturb anything. From I-40, just E of Winslow, take AZ 87 (Exit 257) mile N and turn L 5 miles on the first dirt road. About half way you'll pass Homolovi I on the R, a smaller site that may also be visited. The Winslow Chamber of Commerce has a brochure on the ruins and can give directions to other sites.

The Little Painted Desert County Park, 13 miles NE on AZ 87 (I-40 Exit 257), is noted for beautiful sunsets. Facilities include a 2-mile scenic rim drive overlooking colorful desert hills, a hiking trail, picnic tables, and restrooms.

Hood Park, on the banks of the Clear Creek Reservoir, is a popular spot for swimming, picnicking, fishing, and boating. A campground is planned. Fishermen catch trout, bass, and catfish. Boaters may use the boat ramp and head 2½ miles upstream into a canyon with 200-foot cliffs. The park is open all year. It's 5 miles SE of Winslow off AZ 99; tel. 289-4629.

From Winslow, Meteor Crater is 25 miles W, the Hopi and Navajo Reservations are just to the N, Petrified Forest Natl. Park is 50 miles E, and the Mogollon Rim forest and lake country are 40 miles south.

**accommodations and food:** Winslow has 19 motels and 14 restaurants, mostly along US 66 (Bus. I-40) between I-40 Exits 252 and 257. The highway splits downtown into 3rd St. (westbound) and 2nd St. (eastbound). RVs can park at Cox's North Park Service, 2001 N. Park Dr. (N from I-40 Exit 253); tel. 289-4361; and Sonoma Trailer Park on W. US 66 (I-40 Exit 252); tel. 289-4312.

**shopping and services:** For Indian crafts and jewelry, check Bruchman's Curio Stores at 1501 E. 2nd St. and at 1220 E. 3rd St., and Silver Nugget at 106 E. 2nd Street. Post office is at 223 Williamson Ave. between 2nd and 3rd Streets. Winslow Memorial Hospital is on the N edge of town at 1501 Williamson Ave. (take I-40 Exit 253); tel. 289-4691. The Winslow City Park, at the corner of Colorado Ave. and Cherry St., has indoor and outdoor pools, tennis, and racquetball courts; tel. 289-4792. Play golf at the 9-hole Hospitality Golf Course, on N. Park Dr.; tel. 289-4915.

**information:** The Winslow Chamber of Commerce is just N of I-40 Exit 253; look for the giant Indian totem. Or write Box 460, Winslow, AZ 86047. The staff have a map and info on sights and facilities in the area; tel. 289-2434. An exhibit room introduces the land and people of NE Arizona. The office is open in summer daily 0800-1700, and the rest of the year Mon. to Sat. 0800-1700. The county library, 420 W. Gilmore, has a good collection of books on Arizona and the Southwest; tel. 289-4982.

**transport:** Greyhound Bus is downtown at 111 Warren Ave.; tel. 289-2171; and Trailways is nearby at 100 Warren Ave.; tel. 289-2936. Amtrak has rail service but there's no agent in town; tel. (800) 872-7245 for schedule and ticket information. Golden Pacific has daily air service to Phoenix; tel. 289-5551.

**Joseph City:** Mormons established the farming community of Allen's Camp in 1876 under great difficulties. Attempts to dam the Little Colorado for irrigation failed repeatedly, leaving the crops to wither away. Although 4 other Mormon settlements along the Little Colorado were abandoned, the town, renamed Joseph City, persevered. It is the oldest community in Navajo County.

## HOLBROOK

The railroad reached this site in 1881 and named it for one of their engineers. Eastern investors recognized the surrounding rangelands as prime cattle country, and wasted no time in seeking grazing rights. Within 2 years, the Aztec Land and Cattle Company, based near Joseph City, had 60,000 head of cattle on the land. The Aztec, better known as the "Hashknife" outfit for the shape of its brand, became the 3rd largest cattle empire in the United States—its cowboys worked the longhorns across one million acres. On holidays, the cowpokes, looking for a good time, rode into Holbrook with guns blazing. Rustling and poor management troubled the Hashknife operation until it shut down about 1900, but Holbrook (pop. 5,960) remains a ranching center. You can see some early history in the museum, located downtown in the old (1898) county courthouse. Travelers often use Holbrook as a base for visiting the nearby Petrified Forest National Park and the Navajo and Hopi Indian Reservations.

**accommodations and food:** Holbrook's 17 motels and 18 restaurants are along Navajo Blvd. (N and S from I-40 Exit 286) and W. Hopi Dr. (I-40 Exit 285); the 2 streets meet in the center of town. The youth hostel, in a former motel, is the choice of budget travelers. Rates are only $5.25/person in summer, $6.25 in winter; nonmembers add $2. The hostel is next to Tom's Rock Shop, just S of downtown, at the corner of Apache Dr. and 57 Tovar St.; tel. 524-6770. From the bus station go to the nearest main intersection and turn L, cross the train tracks and go one block, then turn R one block to the hostel. The owner, Mrs. Lloyd Taylor, has been in Holbrook since the 1930s and can tell you many tales.

*Holbrook, Arizona* Dec 1st 1899

Mr. *L B Berryhill*

You are hereby cordially invited to attend the hanging of one

### George Smiley, Murderer.

His soul will be swung into eternity on Dec 8, 1899, at 2 o'clock, p. m., sharp.

Latest improved methods in the art of scientific strangulation will be employed and everything possible will be done to make the proceedings cheerful and the execution a success.

**E. J. WATTRON,**
*Sheriff of Navajo County.*

*Invitation to a hanging; this wording brought a letter of condemnation from President William McKinley to Territorial Governor Nathan Oakes Murphy. Governor Murphy issued a one-month stay of execution and chastised Sheriff Wattron. The hanging took place 8 Jan. 1900.*

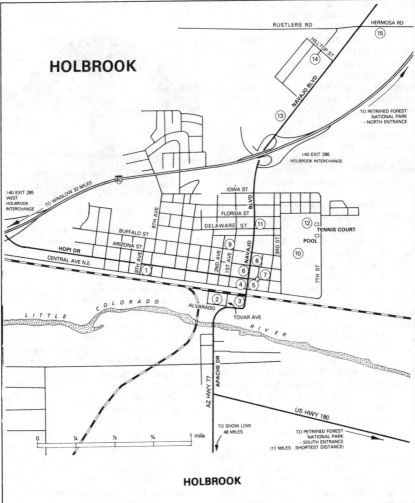

## HOLBROOK

1. Farr West Trading Co.
2. youth hostel; Tom's Rock Shop
3. Jim Gray's Rock Shop
4. Julien's (Indian jewelry)
5. bus station; L&L Trading Post
6. Tate Ford (car rental)
7. post office
8. Navajo County Historical Museum; Chamber of Commerce
9. public library
10. Navajo County Fairgrounds
11. Pow Wow Trading Post
12. Hunt Park
13. Holbrook Plaza Shopping Center
14. Heward Motors (car rental)
15. KOA Campground

**campgrounds:** The KOA campground is one mile NE on Hermosa Dr. off Navajo Blvd.; $10/night; take I-40 Exit 286 or 289. Cholla Lake County Park is also open all year and has drinking water, camping, fishing, and boating. Fishermen can catch bass, bluegill, and catfish in the 360-acre lake. Camping costs $6/night or $8 w/hookups. The park is 10 miles W of Holbrook; take I-40 Exit #277 and follow signs for 2 miles.

**events:** The Pony Express rides again every year in Jan. or Feb., when riders carry the mail from Holbrook to Scottsdale. (You can send your letter along too, by putting the usual stamp on and marking the lower left corner "Via Pony Express." Enclose it in a 2nd envelope addressed to Postmaster, Holbrook AZ 86025.) Local firefighters show off on Firemen's Fun and Games Day, 1st Sat. in May, with entertainment and training games. The Hispanic community celebrates Cinco de Mayo (5 May) with a beauty pageant, dances, food, and games. Old West Days, the last week in June, features a parade, arts and crafts exhibits, roping events, a cowchip-throwing contest, horseshoe tournament, and a street dance. Fireworks and "the state's best barbeque" mark the 4th of July. Hear foot-stomping music at the Old Time Fiddlers Contest the 1st week in August. The Navajo County Fair, with horseraces, is held in September. The Arizona All-Indian Fair, Pow Wow, and Rodeo, on the last weekend in Sept., presents a parade, championship finals rodeo, livestock, dances, and arts and crafts. A Christmas parade brightens winter on the 1st Sat. in December.

**shopping:** You're forbidden to remove anything from the Petrified Forest National Park, but you can shop in Holbrook for the appealing wood-turned-to-stone. Small pieces cost just pennies; larger polished specimens run from a few dollars to thousands. Turquoise, geodes, and other natural treasures are available too. Try Jim Gray's Rock Shop (2 blocks S on Navajo Blvd. from Hopi Dr.), and Tom's Rock Shop (one block W of Jim Gray's). For Indian crafts, look into Julien's at the corner of Hopi Dr. and Navajo Blvd., L&L Trading Post (one block S of Julien's), Farr West

*Hashknife brand*

Trading at 905 W. Hopi Dr., Pow Wow Trading Post at 752 Navajo Blvd., and Lewis Traders (4 miles E, across from Holbrook Truck Plaza, I-40 Exit 292).

**services and information:** Holbrook's Hunt Park has a swimming pool and tennis courts; from Navajo Blvd., turn E on Florida St.; tel. 524-3331. The 9-hole Hidden Cove Golf Course is about 3 miles W of town; take I-40 Exit 283 (Perkins Valley Rd.); tel. 524-3097. The helpful Chamber of Commerce office is in the old county courthouse, on the corner of Navajo Blvd. and Arizona St. (324 Navajo Blvd., Holbrook, AZ 86025); tel. 524-6558. The office and historical museum hours from 1 June to 15 Oct. are: Mon. to Fri. 0700-1900, Sat. 0800-1700, and Sun. 1000-1400; open the rest of the year Mon. to Fri. 0800-1700 and Sat. 1000-1600. The public library is at the corner of 1st Ave. and Buffalo St.; tel. 524-3732.

**transport:** Holbrook's bus station is on the corner of Hopi Dr. and Navajo Blvd., where Greyhound (tel. 524-3832) and Trailways (tel. 524-3750) congregate. The station closes Sat. afternoons and all day Sunday, but buses still stop. You can rent cars from Tate Ford; tel. 524-6268, and from Heward Motors; tel. 524-2266. Roy Baker offers tours of Petrified Forest National Park; 503 W. Arizona St., Holbrook, AZ; tel. 524-6535.

# PETRIFIED FOREST NATIONAL PARK

The Petrified Forest National Park, like the Grand Canyon, is an open book to the earth's past. The Park's barren, multi-colored hills, part of a widespread geologic formation called the Chinle, provide a world-famous source of petrified wood and related fossils. The hills' delicately tinted bands of reds, grays, oranges, and whites have eroded to reveal life, frozen in stone, from 225 million years ago. This land would be unrecognizable to its inhabitants then: primitive fish, massive amphibians, and fearsome reptiles. Rivers carried fallen trees from distant mountains and buried them in low-lying plains. Before their fall, some of the giant trees had towered 200 feet into the air. Water-borne minerals transformed the logs, replacing wood cells and filling spaces between them with brightly colored quartz and jasper crystals. Some of the strange animals that once crawled or swam here have also been preserved; you'll see their fossilized remains in Park exhibits. But it has been the trees that have traditionally attracted the most attention. In the late 1800s, much of the petrified wood was lost to collectors, who carted away the best logs for souvenirs or dynamited them for their crystals. The battle for preservation was won in 1906, when President Theodore Roosevelt signed a bill establishing the Petrified Forest National Monument. A 1958 act of Congress, followed by acquisition of new lands, changed the status to a National Park in 1962.

**flora and fauna:** A surprising amount of life exists in the Park, despite the meager 9-inch annual rainfall and lack of permanent water. Prickly pear and cholla cacti are widespread. Desert primrose, Indian paintbrush, mariposa lily, sunflowers, and other plants bloom when they've received sufficient moisture. Also common are buckwheat (a shrub which turns orange-brown in the fall) and saltbush (named for the tiny salt crystals formed on its leaves to conserve moisture). The most frequently seen animals in the Park are birds, small mammals, and lizards. Birds include the raven, rock wren, and horned lark. You're most likely to spot prairie dogs, jackrabbits, and cottontails, but pronghorn, coyotes, and bobcats live here too.

*Petrified Forest
National Park*

*petroglyph at Puerco Indian Ruin*

**the three parts:** The southern section, with some of the finest petrified wood specimens in the world, was the original National Monument. The central section has the greatest number of prehistoric Indian sites. During their stay from about A.D. 300-1400, the Anasazi, Sinagua, and Mogollon tribes progressed from semi-nomadic hunters and gatherers to farmers who lived in permanent pueblos and had a complex ceremonial life. Scientists are trying to decode the numerous petroglyphs, and have just recently discovered that some were used as solar calendars. The northern section of the Park encompasses part of the Painted Desert, famed for its landscape of ever-changing colors (the effect of the sun playing on rocks stained by iron, manganese, and other minerals). Colors become most vivid near sunset and sunrise, fading towards midday. Added in 1932, this northern section is the largest in the Park.

**visiting the Park:** Sightseeing in the Park (average elevation 5,400 feet) can be good at any time of year; just protect yourself from the sun in the warmer months. You can begin the 28.6-mile scenic drive through the Park at either end. Coming from the W, you'll find it more convenient to use the S entrance off US 180 from Holbrook. After visiting the Park, continue on I-40 from the N entrance. Coming from the E, the N entrance is more practical. The drive is open daily in winter from 0800-1700, extended in summer to 0600-1900. Winter snow or ice storms occasionally close the road. An early start is recommended; you can easily use a full day enjoying all the walks, views, and exhibits. Admission is $5/car or $2/bus passenger. Near both entrances are visitor centers with exhibits of geology, fossils, ecology, and human history of the Park. Books, postcards, posters, and maps are sold. You can also talk with a ranger and obtain backcountry permits. Don't remove any petrified wood or other objects from the Park. Rangers estimate that people taking one "harmless little souvenir" results in the loss of tons of wood every year!

**services:** No campgrounds or lodging are located within the Park; you'll have to go W to Holbrook or E to the smaller communities of Navajo or Chambers. Picnic fixings come in handy, as there is only one restaurant (near the N entrance) and a snack bar (across from Rainbow Forest Museum, inside the S entrance). Only the developed areas have water; you'll probably want to carry something to drink. Shops sell souvenirs at 3 locations—outside the Park near the S entrance and inside the Park at the Rainbow Forest complex (near the S entrance) and next to the Visitor Center at the N entrance station.

**backcountry travel:** Hikers may explore the 2 areas designated as wilderness (see below). The backcountry remains relatively undiscovered; it's been estimated that only one out of a thousand Park visitors strays more than a short distance from his vehicle. Travel is usually cross-country, easy to do with plenty of landmarks and open terrain—you're free to roam. Water must be carried (no springs) and you'll need a hat and long-sleeved shirt for sun protection. Rangers can give advice and a hiking leaflet. They also issue the free permits required for overnight trips. Horseback riding and pack animals are permitted too; there's a limit of 6 animals per party and you'll need to carry feed and water. All backcountry users should note rules against campfires, pets (OK elsewhere in the park if on a leash), and firearms. Rainbow Forest Wilderness (7,240 acres) has grassland, badlands, abundant petrified wood, and traces of Indian inhabitants. It's in the southern half of the Park, reached from the Flattops trailhead. Painted Desert Wilderness in the N is much larger (43,020 acres)—a colorful land of mesas, buttes, and badlands. Indian sites and their petroglyphs can be visited; ask a ranger for directions. Onyx Bridge, a 50-foot-long petrified tree in the Black Forest, is a popular destination. It's about 4 miles RT from the Kachina Point trailhead. Pilot Rock (6,295 feet), about 7 miles to the NW from the trailhead, is the highest point in the Park.

## SCENIC DRIVE

Description is from S to N, but the road can be driven in either direction. Mileages are along the drive only and don't include side trips:

**Mile 0:** Beginning of scenic drive from US 180.

**Mile 0.1:** Souvenir store and gas station, with a sign for MUSEUM (not connected with the national park). Here you'll see a dazzling collection of polished petrified wood, including giant log cross-sections and carved pieces, most of which are for sale. You can also buy unpolished petrified wood and other minerals, rocks, and fossils.

**Mile 0.2:** Entering Petrified Forest National Park. A ranger collects $5/car and gives you a map. If you've brought in unpolished wood or other objects, ask the ranger to mark or bag them to avoid any misunderstandings about their source, as it's against the law to take *anything* from the Park.

**Mile 2.4:** Rainbow Forest Museum and Visitor Center. Learn how the trees became petrified and study the different types found in the Park. Microphotographs show intricate cell details of some petrified wood specimens. Fossils and illustrations of cycads, ferns, fish, amphibians, reptiles, and other early life give you a look back to far distant times. Geologic exhibits show how the land has changed from a low, swampy plain to a high, arid plateau. See artifacts of the prehistoric Indians, now vanished, who lived here for more than 1,000 years. A "Conscience Wood" exhibit is full of stolen petrified wood, returned with apologetic and remorseful letters. The Giant Logs Trail begins behind the Visitor Center and winds in a ½-mile loop past monster-sized logs—a rainbow of reds, yellows, grays, whites, blacks, pinks, and oranges. The base of one fallen tree stands higher than a man. Across the road from the Visitor Center is Fred Harvey's Curios and Fountain (snack bar); it may be closed in winter.

*Agate House*

**Mile 2.5:** Picnic area.

**Mile 2.6:** Long Logs Nature Trail and Agate House Turnoff (½ mile to parking). The self-guiding nature trail is an easy ½-mile walk, a good opportunity to have a close look at the ancient trees. Buy or borrow a trailguide brochure at the start of the loop. The jumble of logs here is thought to have been a logjam, buried in mud, sand, and volcanic ash. Many logs measure over 100 feet long. Agate House, on a short side trail, is a pueblo occupied about 700 years ago. The Indians built the unusual structure entirely with chunks of colorful petrified wood! Two of its 7 rooms have been reconstructed to show their original size.

**Mile 5.2:** The Flattops. This is the trailhead for day-hiking and overnight backcountry trips in the Rainbow Forest Wilderness. Overnight trips require a permit. Camping must be within the wilderness area and more than ½ mile from the road.

**Mile 8.1:** Crystal Forest Nature Trail. Some of the prettiest and most concentrated petrified wood in the Park lies along this paved ¾-mile trail.

**Mile 9.9:** Jasper Forest Turnoff (½ mile to parking). There's a great view to the W and N from the overlook. Below you can see pieces of petrified wood eroded from the hillsides.

**Mile 10.1:** Agate Bridge. Erosion has carved out a gully beneath a large log, leaving it as a bridge. In years past, one of the Hashknife cowboys rode his horse across the log on a $10 bet. Rangers won't let you do this today, though! It's unsafe. Because of cracking, the log was braced with a concrete beam in 1934.

**Mile 12.9:** Blue Mesa Turnoff (2½ miles to parking). Blue Mesa has several panoramic overlooks and a ¾-mile loop nature trail. The trail is a good introduction to the Chinle Formation and its badlands topography, showing how they were formed and are now eroding. Buy or borrow a trail brochure at the start.

**Mile 14.5:** The Tepees. From the overlook, notice symmetrical, cone-shaped hills.

**Mile 16.5:** Newspaper Rock Turnoff (⅓ mile to parking). This is an impressive collection of ancient petroglyphs on a cliff face. The drawings have not yet been interpreted, but seem to represent animals, spiritual figures, and perhaps some doodling.

**Mile 17.4:** Puerco Indian Ruin. Before A.D. 1100, local Indians lived in small scattered settlements. Their building of larger pueblos, such as Puerco, shows a change to an agricultural lifestyle requiring greater pooling of efforts. The broad, meandering Puerco River not only provided reliable water all year, but its floodplain had rich soil for farming. The river also attracted birds, pronghorn, and other game. Indians built a one-story pueblo with about 76 rooms and at least 2 kivas (ceremonial rooms) around a rectangular plaza. You can see the foundations of these rooms and one of the kivas. Archaeologists think that this site was occupied between A.D. 1100 and 1200 and again from about 1300 to 1400. The last occupants appear to have packed up and left peaceably, perhaps over a period of years. Buy or borrow a brochure about the pueblo and its inhabitants. Many fine petroglyphs cover the boulders below the village. Though more scattered, they are comparable to those at the better-known Newspaper Rock. One of the Puerco petroglyphs was found to mark the summer solstice, and rangers may have a demonstration program here from about 14 to 28 June; ask at the visitor centers. About 14 sites with solar markings have been discovered in the Park.

**Mile 17.7:** Puerco River bridge. The scene was probably far different when Indians occupied the pueblo. Records indicate that cottonwood trees grew along the floodplain as late as the 19th century. Ranchers took advantage of the abundant grasslands in the late 1880s by increasing their herds, but drought from 1891-94 dried up the grasses, and gross overstocking destroyed the range. Runoff carried high concentrations of salts into the river, killing less salt-resistant plants. Floods have worked their toll, scouring and widening the river and leaving loads of silt in their wake. Now the river is dry during much of the year.

**Mile 18.3:** Railroad Historical Marker. The Petrified Forest first gained national attention with the completion of the Atlantic and Pacific Railroad (later the Santa Fe) across northern Arizona. Train travelers disembarked at the

*author on Giant
Logs Trail*

nearby Adamana Station, now abandoned, to visit the "trees turned to stone."

**Mile 23.6:** Lacey Pcint Overlook of the Painted Desert.

**Mile 24.1:** Whipple Point Overlook of the Painted Desert. Lieutenant A.W. Whipple was one of the first whites to visit the Petrified Forest, in 1853.

**Mile 24.3:** Nizhoni Point Overlook of the Painted Desert. The hillside below appears to be covered with shards of glass shining in the sun. Actually these are natural pieces of selenite gypsum, a very soft mineral that can be scratched with your fingernail.

**Mile 25.4:** Pintado Point Overlook of the Painted Desert. You are now on a volcanic lava flow, which covers the entire rim and protects the underlying, softer Chinle Formation from erosion.

**Mile 26.0:** Chinle Point Picnic Area Turnoff (¼ mile). Tables are provided for picnicking. Water and restrooms are available in the warmer months.

**Mile 26.2:** Painted Desert Inn and Kachina Point Overlook. The original inn was built in 1924 by Herbert Lore, who used Indian labor and local material. Travelers bumping their way across Arizona on Route 66 stopped for meals and to shop for Indian crafts. The Park Service purchased the inn and surrounding land in 1936 to add to the then national monument. The inn was reconstructed and enlarged as a park concession and information station, but its 4 sleeping rooms were not used after WW II. The structure was closed when the Painted Desert Headquarters complex opened in 1962. Plans were made for its demolition, but enough people recognized its unique Southwestern architecture, a mixture of Spanish and Indian pueblo styles, that it was saved. Budget permitting, it's now open in summers as a Park museum. The trailhead for Painted Desert Wilderness (Onyx Bridge, Black Forest, etc.) begins near Kachina Point, behind the inn.

**Mile 26.7:** Tawa Point Overlook of the Painted Desert.

**Mile 27.5:** Tiponi Point Overlook of the Painted Desert.

**Mile 28.1:** Visitor Center and N entrance station. A 17-min. movie is shown on the hour and half hour, illustrating the Park's features and formation of the petrified wood. Exhibits show plant and animal fossils, and you can see a "Conscience Wood" display. A ranger will answer your questions and issue backcountry permits. Next door, Fred Harvey Painted Desert Oasis offers a cafeteria, curio shop, and gas station, open daily.

**Mile 28.6:** Junction with I-40.

# THE WHITE MOUNTAINS

## SHOW LOW

With so many recreational opportunities in the nearby White Mountains, Show Low has become an important center for sportsmen, tourists, and desert dwellers escaping summer heat. Attractions include excellent trout fishing, hiking, camping, horseback riding, golf, scenic drives through the forests and along the Mogollon Rim, and big-game hunting. Show Low took its name from a winner-take-all poker game played in 1876. Croyden Cooley, a noted Indian scout, and his partner Marion Clark, had established a 100,000-acre ranch here in 1870, but found the place wasn't big enough for both of them. Agreeing to settle their differences with a game of cards, they sat down at the kitchen table in Cooley's house for a session of "seven-up." The two played through the night until they were down to their last hand. Clark said, "Show low and you win." Cooley pulled out an unbeatable deuce of clubs and took the ranch. Several years later, the property was bought and settled by the Mormon Church. The site where the game was played is now occupied by the town's Church of the Latter-Day Saints. Show Low's main street took its name "Deuce of Clubs" after the winning card. The town of 4,870 sits on the pine-forested Mogollon Rim at an elevation of about 6,400 feet.

**sights:** Fool's Hollow Lake has 140 acres stocked with brown trout, bass, and catfish. It's just 3 miles NW of Show Low (see the Apache-Sitgreaves Forest Map). The free campground on the W shore is open mid-Apr. to mid-Oct.; no drinking water.

You never know what kind of fish you're going to catch at Show Low Lake: rainbow or brown trout, largemouth bass, walleye, or catfish. A boat ramp and boat rentals are available; limit of 8 hp. for motors. The Navajo County campground on the W side is open early May to the end of Sept. and costs $4/site (water but no hookups). The lake is about 5 miles S of Show Low; go S 4 miles on AZ 260 and turn E on Show Low Lake Road.

Pin Tail Lake is an unusual waterfowl area N of Show Low created between 1977 and 1979. Workers filled a natural volcanic depression with treated sewage effluent and built artificial islands for nesting sites. The marshland was an instant success with ducks and other wildlife. A trail, interpretive signs, and parking are provided for bird watchers. Go N 3½ miles on AZ 77 and turn R onto Pintail Lake Road.

Mogollon Rim Overlook and Nature Trail is an easy 1½ mile walk with signs describing the area's forests, medicinal plants, and history. You have good views from the overlooks of forested valleys and ridges below. The trailhead is 7 miles S of Show Low on AZ 260, between Mileposts 347 and 348.

*elk* (Cervus canadensis)

**accommodations and food:** About 12 motels are stretched out along Deuce of Clubs. You can park your RV at Camptown (tel. 537-2578) or Country Lane Trailer Park (tel. 537-4783). Both tenters and RVs can head to campgrounds at Fool's Hollow Lake and Show Low Lake (both described above). Look for restaurants along Deuce of Clubs. You can find Western food at Paint Pony Steakhouse and Branding Iron Steak House (open as a deli at lunchtime). For Mexican dinners try Maxwell House, Guayos's, La Casita, Gavino's, or White Mountain Restaurant. Chinese food is served by Asia Garden and Hong Kong Cafe. Pick up pizza at Pizza Hut (Pineway Center), Pizza Palace, or Pat's Place. Other restaurants and the usual fast-food places are in town too. Get groceries at Safeway in the Show Low Plaza, in the center of town.

**entertainment and events:** The local hangout is Bill's Bar—Western music bands nightly except Sun. and Monday. The Tulip Festival on Easter weekend features arts and crafts shows and musical entertainment. The 4th of July is celebrated with a big parade, a rodeo, and week-long entertainment. You can loosen up at the Square Dance Festival on the 2nd weekend in July. Show Low Shootout in August is a folklore festival with cavalry demonstrations and arts and crafts. All through Dec., the town dresses up in bright lights to celebrate the holidays.

**services and information:** Navapache Hospital is between Show Low and Lakeside; tel. 537-4375. The city park has picnicking, tennis, and handball courts. Play golf at Show Low Golf and Country Club's 18-hole course; tel. 537-4354. The Chamber of Commerce can help you find accommodations and other services in town. Their office is open Mon. to Fri. 0900-1700; W. Deuce of Clubs at S. 8th Ave. (Box 1083, Show Low, AZ 85901); tel. 537-2326. The public library is at the corner of S. 2nd Dr. and E. McNeil St.; tel. 537-2447.

## LAKESIDE AND PINETOP

Their names well describe the countryside of lakes and pine forests. The twin towns lie near the edge of the Mogollon Rim 8 miles SE of Show Low. Lakeside was originally named "Fairview" at its founding in 1880 by Mormon pioneers, but took on the present name when Rainbow Lake, the first of a series of reservoirs, was finished. Several smaller lakes have been added too, and the town seems to have as much water area as land. Soldiers making the long climb up the Mogollon Rim from Fort Apache in the 1870s stopped to rest at a place thay called "Pinetop"; Mormon ranchers founded a settlement here in 1878. Now Lakeside (elev. 6,745 feet) and Pinetop (elev. 7,279 feet) are major resort centers with countless summer cabins and resorts. The area's year-round population of about 8,000 jumps to 25,000 in summer. Though starting as separate communities, the 2 towns have expanded outward along the highway and now appear as one.

**sights:** Rainbow Lake is an 80-acre reservoir in Lakeside just W of AZ 260. Rainbow trout (what else?) are stocked along with brown trout and some bass and catfish. You can fish from the bank (near the dam) or rent a boat. Lakeside Campground ($6 and $7/sites), is open mid-May to late-September.

Scott Reservoir is a smaller fishing lake about 3 miles NE of Lakeside on Forest Route 45. It has a boat ramp and campground (no drinking water or charge). Only electric motors are permitted.

Woodland Reservoir is a small (18-acre) lure-only lake stocked with rainbow trout and some largemouth bass, catfish, and green sunfish. Fishing is best in spring and fall. Electric boat motors only. There's picnicking but no camping. The lake is one mile W of Pinetop on Forest Route 316.

The U.S. Forest Service office (across the highway from Lakeside Campground) has 2 self-guided auto tours of the woodlands, wildlife, and history of the National Forest; cassette tapes and players are loaned free. The Porter Mountain tour is 33 miles long and takes about 2 hours. Lake Mountain tour follows a 45-mile course; allow 4 hours.

Blue Ridge Trail (Forest Trail 107) is a popular 9-mile loop for hikers and horseback riders. Trailhead is near Lakeside off Forest Route 187, just past Springer Mountain Lookout. The Forest Service office can give you a map.

Forest Route 300 follows the Mogollon Rim from Pinetop W nearly all the way to Camp Verde, with many panoramic views along the way. Most of the road is dirt—check conditions first with the Forest Service. A 113-mile hiking and horseback trail also follows the rim for most of this distance on the old General Crook Trail. Army troops constructed the wagon road between 1872 and 1874 to move military supplies and troops between Camp Verde and Fort Apache. Ask at a U.S. Forest Service office about trail conditions and trailheads, or see *A Guide to the General Crook Trail* by Eldon Bowman, published by Museum of Northern Arizona and Boy Scouts of America in 1978.

**accommodations and camping:** Since this is the largest resort area in the White Mountains, you have a choice of about 2 dozen motels and resorts, and there's even a youth hostel. The Pinetop-Lakeside Chamber of Commerce has a list of places to stay and will help find what you're looking for. Prices range from about $5 to $150, depending on degree of luxury and the season. All the resorts are nestled in cool pine forests. Lake of the Woods Resort, in Lakeside, also has its own fishing lake. The White Mountain Youth Hostel is 1½ miles off the highway; turn N at Lakeside Baptist Church, go to end of road, turn R to a stop sign, turn L across a creek, turn R up a hill, pass 3 roads, then turn R to end of road, turn R again, after 100 yards turn L on a dirt road to a red barn. The hostel is small (8 beds) and would like you to call ahead; tel. 367-4036; or write Rt. 1, Box 210K, Lakeside AZ 85929. Rates are $4.25 in summer, $5.25 in winter.

RVers can choose from about 10 trailer parks. Tenters and RVers can stay at the Lakeside Campground in town or at Show Low Lake several miles north. Another possibility is just to head for the woods—you can camp free almost anywhere in the National Forest. The Lakeside Ranger Office can suggest areas.

**food:** Restaurants are surprisingly good for such small communities. Try the Brass Stag or The Christmas Tree, both in Lakeside, for American food. In Pinetop, choices include American cuisine at The Chalet Restaurant, The Fireside, and Roundhouse Resort; steaks at Charlie Clark's Steak House and Moonridge Steak House; Italian at Ozzie's; and Mexican at La Casa Moya and El Rancho. Pinetop also has G.J.'s Pizza and a variety of fast-food places.

**events:** Sunrise Ski Area hosts ski races and games in early March. Artists and collectors display their crafts at the Pinetop-Lakeside Art & Antique Festival in June. Parades, arts, and crafts mark the end of summer in the Fall Festival held in September.

**shopping and services:** You can buy fishing, hunting, and camping supplies at The Squire's

*kit fox* (Vulpes macrotis)

Sports Den, Yellow Front, and White Mountains Sporting Goods stores in Pinetop. Ski rentals and sales are provided by several shops in Pinetop. Sports Village Athletic Club in Pinetop has a swimming pool, tennis and racquetball courts, and other facilities open to the public; tel. 368-3333. You can go horseback riding from about May to Oct. with Hansen's Riding Stables in Lakeside (tel. 368-6254) and Pinetop Lakes Riding in Pinetop (tel. 369-0505). Pinetop Lakes Golf & Country Club has an 18-hole course open to the public; tel. 369-4184.

**information:** See the Pinetop-Lakeside Chamber of Commerce to get the latest on services and what's going on. Their office is centrally located in an A-frame cabin between Moonridge Lodge and Skier's Edge on the main highway (Box 266, Pinetop, AZ 85935); tel. 367-4290. The Lakeside Ranger Station can inform you about camping, hiking, driving, and cross-country skiing in the Apache-Sitgreaves National Forest; their office is across the highway from Lakeside Campground (or write Rt. 3, Box 3001, Lakeside, AZ 85929); tel. 368-5111. Get fishing and hunting licenses and info from Arizona Game and Fish, on the S edge of Pinetop; tel. 367-4281. The public library and senior center are in Lakeside, tel. 368-6688.

**transport:** A ski shuttle makes the run to Sunrise Ski Area on Fri., Sat., and Sun. during the season; tel. 368-6834.

## WHITE MOUNTAIN APACHE INDIAN RESERVATION

Some of Arizona's best outdoor recreation is found on the more than 1½ million acres belonging to the White Mountain Apache. Your only problem will be choosing among their fishing streams, lakes, ski runs, hiking possibilities, and over 1,000 campsites. Much of the credit is due to the farsighted planning and development of the tribe. Though tribal permits are required for almost any activity, their costs are reasonable. You don't need

*illustration from Samuel Cozzen's 1873 book,* The Marvellous Country

state licenses for fishing, boating, or hunting, however, just the tribal permits. Some areas, such as sacred Baldy Peak, are closed or require a special-use permit. The best source of information is the Game and Fish Dept., Box 220, Whiteriver, AZ 85941; tel. 338-4385. Their office is next to the White Mountain Apache Motel in Whiteriver. You can also get permits at Carrizo, Hon Dah, Hawley Lake, A-1 Lake, and Sunrise Lake.

Use caution on the Reservation's many back roads; sometimes they are too rough for cars, especially after rains or snowmelt. The Game and Fish people can advise you on road conditions. The Apache and the federal government disagree on the name of the reservation; government officials tend to use the term "Fort Apache," while the Indians understandably prefer "White Mountain Apache." But either way, it's the same place.

**fishing:** You have 400 miles of mountain

# WHITE MOUNTAIN APACHE INDIAN RESERVATION

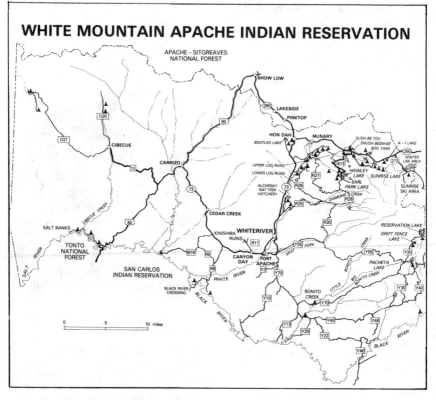

streams and more than 25 lakes to cast your line in. The waters are stocked with fighting rainbow and brown trout from fish hatcheries at Williams Creek and Alchesay Springs. If you use a boat, you'll need a permit ($1/day or $10/year). Sunrise is the only lake where large motors are allowed; everywhere else you're limited to electrics. Fishing goes on year-round, though some lakes are closed in winter. Where permitted, fishermen have enjoyed success in winter with ice-fishing.

Fishing licenses cost $4.50/day; children get a discount. Season fees are $35/summer season, $25/winter season, or $50/calendar year. An agreement with the San Carlos Apache Tribe honors the fishing permits from either tribe along both banks of the Black and Salt Rivers where the reservations border, though a special-use permit will be needed.

**hunting:** Plentiful big and small game roam the reservation. The tribe holds regular seasons for elk, mountain lion, javelina, and antelope. You'll need a guide for hunting elk, lion, bear, and pronghorn. Also lots of money! The guided hunts can cost $1,000 a day, but have a high success rate. Smaller animals and birds are more easily hunted; fees are $40 for either a javelina or small game license, and you aren't required to have a guide.

**others:** You'll need a permit ($4/family) to have a picnic on the reservation unless you already have a current tribal permit for camping, fishing, or other activity. Camping facilities are basic, usually just picnic tables, fireplaces, and toilets; some campsites have drinking water. Backpacking is also permitted, but be sure to have the proper special-use permit. Camping fees must be paid in advance at one of the places where permits are sold. Costs for a campsite are $5/day, $70/1st month, $60/2nd month, and $50/3rd month. Kayakers and rafters can challenge the waters of the White, Black, and Salt Rivers on the reservation. Best times are usually during the winter snow melt in April and May. A special-use permit is required. Sunrise Ski Area, with its many downhill runs, becomes a busy place in winter, but the tribe has also made cross-country ski trails nearby. Yet another area near Sunrise is set aside for snowmobilers. Ski and snowmobile passes must be purchased.

## SALT RIVER CANYON

Father Eusebio Francisco Kino visited this colorful canyon in 1698 and called it "Salado," for the salt springs in the area. You get great views of the canyon from US 60 as the highway swoops down to the bridge 48 miles SW of Show Low. More of the area is easily explored by driving on the dirt road that parallels the river. The route is highly scenic with towering cliffs above and the river below. Take the turnoff just N of the highway bridge until you come to a fork. At the fork, you have a choice of turning L and driving under the bridge ½ mile upriver to Apache Falls, or bearing R on the road downstream to Cibecue Creek (4 miles) and the Salt Banks, another 3½ miles. The road is rough in spots but should be OK for a cautiously driven car. The desert country here at 3,000 feet contrasts sharply with the White Mountains, a short drive north. Saguaro cacti grow on the slopes to the R after the ford on Cibecue Creek. Don't cross if the water is fast-flowing and muddy.

To visit the Salt Banks, continue 3 miles past Cibecue Creek, turn L at the fork, and drive ½ mile to a parking area. Walk a little way downstream to the Salt Banks, a long series of salt springs that have deposited massive travertine formations. Minerals and algae color the springs with oranges, reds, and dark greens. This site has been sacred to the Apache who came to get salt and to perform religious ceremonies. Cliff dwellings and petroglyphs date from the 13th century. The ruins can be visited just downstream from the Salt Banks.

After the Salt Banks turnoff, the road begins a steep climb and becomes too rough for cars. The White Mountain Apache have several primitive campsites (no drinking water) along the Salt River between the highway bridge and the Salt Banks. You'll need a camping permit; nearest place to get one is Carrizo, 24 miles north. Fishing in the Salt River is mostly for channel catfish and some small-mouth bass and bluegill.

## CIBECUE

This small town in the western part of the reservation is the center for the Cibecue Apache, a

*Salt River Canyon*

group distinct from the White Mountain and San Carlos Apache. But for administration (and recreation permits), the Cibecue area is considered part of the White Mountain Reservation. Visitors can enjoy camping and good fishing for rainbow and brown trout in the upper 15 miles of Cibecue Creek nearby. The fishing and camping spots begin 5 miles N of town on the dirt road paralleling the creek. Elevations average about 6,000 feet. Apache Traders in Cibecue has gas and supplies. To reach Cibecue, turn NW on Indian Route 12 from US 60, 8 miles S of Carrizo.

In the winter of 1880, a Cibecue medicine man named Noch-ay-del-klinne began teaching a new religion that predicted the expulsion of all white men. His enthusiastic following grew rapidly, worrying officers at Fort Apache. In the following August, they dispatched troops and 23 Apache scouts to arrest the medicine man. Fighting broke out upon their arrival at Cibecue, and soldiers killed the medicine man. The scouts then mutinied and joined the attack on the troops. Angry Apache pursued the survivors the entire 40 miles back to the fort. Captain Hentig and 6 other soldiers died in what is said to be the only revolt by Apache scouts in their 75 years with the Army.

## WHITERIVER

The administrative center of the White Mountain Apache started as an Army fort in 1870, located between 2 forks of the White River. First known as Fort Ord, the name was changed to Camp Mogollon, Camp Thomas, and Camp Apache — all within one year! Troops and Apache scouts rode out to subdue rebellious Apache in the Tonto Basin (1872-73), and then to fight Victorio (1879) and Geronimo (1881-86). The last major action was the Mexican Campaign (1916-17). In 1922 the U.S. Indian Service converted the fort into a school, naming it in honor of President Theodore Roosevelt. Surprisingly, most of the first students were Navajo, but local Apache enrolled later. Whiteriver sits in a valley at 5,000 feet, surrounded by high forested hills. Just downriver from town you'll find dry grasslands with sparse juniper trees. It's easy to confuse the name of the town with that of the river flowing beside it, but the town is spelled as one word. Whiteriver has a trading post, motel, restaurants, Indian Health Service Hospital, and tribal offices.

*"officers' row" at Fort Apache*

**Fort Apache Museum:** You can see Apache crafts, games, and even a *wickiup,* their traditional brush shelter. Many old photos and artifacts show the history of the scouts and soldiers who manned the fort. One of the most prominent Apache scouts was Alchesay, whose name you see so often in the reservation. Known for his honesty and dedication to both the Army and his people, Alchesay helped put down rebellions of hostile tribes and assisted General Crook in making peace with Geronimo in 1886. The museum is open Mon. to Fri. 0800-1700 and on summer weekends 0900-1600; tel. 338-4625. A few crafts and books on the Apache are for sale. Go 4 miles SW on the highway from Whiteriver and turn L across the river; the museum is ahead on the L atop the small hill.

**Kinishba Ruins:** Kinishba is Apache for "brown house." Prehistoric Indians built 2 large pueblos and smaller buildings between A.D. 1232 and 1320 on both sides of a ravine. The mixed population came from areas of the Little Colorado, central Gila, and Salt Rivers. Residents abandoned the village around 1350, possibly because of insufficient water. A University of Arizona team excavated the ruins from 1931 to 1939 and found 14 types of pottery and a great wealth of shell jewelry in the more than 700 rooms. Only one of the large structures has survived. Because it has not been stabilized, entry is prohibited, but you can see the ruins by walking around outside. To reach the site from Whiteriver, go 6 miles SW on the highway, then turn R on a dirt road; ruins are 2 miles in (keep L at the fork).

**Alchesay National Fish Hatchery:** This hatchery, along with Williams Creek Fish Hatchery (SE of McNary), keeps the streams and lakes of the reservation stocked with trout. Visitors are welcome on weekdays 0700-1530, and they can use the picnic area. The turnoff for Alchesay Hatchery is 4 miles N of Whiteriver. A paved road (signposted) goes NE 5 miles to the site.

**practicalities:** White Mountain Apache Shopping Center, just S of the town's center, has a movie theater, swimming pool, super-

*Kinishba Ruins*

market, and stores. White Mountain Apache Motel, beyond the shopping center, has modern rooms ($30 s or d), restaurant, and gift shop. Get information and permits next door at the tribal Game and Fish Department; open Mon. to Fri. 0800-1200 and 1300-1700 (until 1900 on Fri.); in summer they're also open weekends 0800-1600, and stay open for lunch. You can reach them at Box 220, Whiteriver AZ 85941; tel. 338-4385 or 338-4386. White Mountain Line buses run between Show Low and Whiteriver Garage; tel. 338-4501.

## CAMPING AND FISHING SPOTS EAST OF WHITERIVER

**Little and Big Bonito Creeks:** *Bonito* is Spanish for "pretty." These streams have rainbow and brown trout, though some sections need special-use permits. Take the highway SW 4 miles out of Whiteriver and turn L on the road past Fort Apache. Two miles farther, turn R on a dirt road signposted "Tonto Lake-

*group of Apaches*

Pacheta Lake-Maverick-Drift Fence-Hurricane Lake-Reservation Lake''; the creeks and campgrounds are another 16 miles.

**East Fork of the White River:** The stream has rainbow and some brown trout. Upper reaches may be closed (signposted) to fishing. From Fort Apache, continue E 8 miles to the campground.

**Pacheta Lake:** Best campsites are on the E side of this 68-acre lake (elev. 8,170 feet). Drinking water is available. Fishermen catch rainbow and brown trout. People say the name came from 2 cowboys playing cards around the turn of the century; both were caught cheating and called ''pair-of-cheaters,'' a name that later became Pacheta. To get here, either follow the signs from Fort Apache (41 miles), or take the better roads (AZ 273 and Forest Route 116) from AZ 260 past Sunrise and Reservation Lakes.

**Drift Fence Lake:** A 16-acre lake at 8,900 feet between Pacheta and Reservation Lakes. There are small campsites at each end of the lake, but large vehicles will have more room at the N end. The lake was named by cowboys during cattle roundups, when remaining stock drifted along the fence on the W side of the lake to lower pastures.

**Reservation Lake:** This 280-acre lake, the 2nd largest on the reservation, offers good fishing for rainbow, brown, and brook trout. Aspen, fir, and spruce forests grow at the 9,000-foot elevation. Rental boats, supplies, and permits are available from late May to early September. Several campgrounds surround the lake. The easiest way in is from the north: From McNary, take AZ 260 E 16 miles to AZ 273 (road to Sunrise Lake); head SE on AZ 273 for 14 miles, turn S 10 miles on Forest Route 116, then turn R and cross a cattle guard to the lake. From Fort Apache you can take Apache Route Y-70, a 47-mile drive.

## CAMPING AND FISHING NORTH OF WHITERIVER

**Diamond Creek:** You can choose among several campgrounds along the creek, whose waters are stocked with rainbow and a few brown, brook, and native trout. Take the turn-off for Alchesay Fish Hatchery 4 miles N of Whiteriver, and turn R onto Apache Route R-25. A small campground sits near the confluence of Diamond Creek and the North Fork of White River. More spots on Diamond Creek are reached upstream on Apache Route R-25.

**North Fork of the White River:** Rainbow and brown trout are stocked, and you might catch a few brook and cutthroat. Campgrounds and fishing spots along this stream are reached via Log Road, which parallels it. Take the Williams Creek Hatchery turnoff (Log Rd.), 15 miles N of Whiteriver (4 miles S of Hon Dah).

**Bootleg Lake:** At one time you could get illegal booze here, but now your best chance is for rainbow trout or channel catfish. Elevation of the 10-acre lake and small campground is 6,800 feet. Turn W off AZ 73 about 3 miles S of Hon Dah, and go in 3 miles.

**Cooley Lake:** A small campground and 11-acre lake at an elevation of 7,100 feet near Bootleg Lake. Fishermen catch channel catfish, with some rainbow trout and largemouth bass. Corydon E. Cooley came to the White Mountains in 1869, liked them, married the daughter of an Apache chief, and settled down. He was the winner who "showed low" in the poker game that gave Show Low its name. The turnoff is one mile S of Hon Dah, then about ½ mile in.

## HON DAH

The Apache name for this travelers' stop means "Be my guest." Strategically located 19 miles N of Whiteriver at the intersection of AZ Hwys. 260 and 73, the complex includes a motel ($25.50 s or d), cabins with kitchens ($27.50 and up), restaurant (open Mon. to Sat.

0600-2100 and Sun. 0600-1400), grocery store, and service station. Purchase reservation permits and fishing gear at the Hon Dah store. Motel address is Box 597, McNary, AZ 85930; tel. 369-4311.

## McNARY

This old lumber town has an unusual history, though there's not much to see. Back in 1916, an energetic businessman in Flagstaff named Tom Pollock chose this as the spot for a new lumber enterprise. He leased the land from the Apache, had a railroad line run to the site, and named it Cooley (after Corydon E. Cooley of the famous Show Low card game). Meanwhile, 1,000 miles E in McNary, Louisiana, the W.M. Cady Lumber Co. was running out of timbered land. To solve the problem, they bought out Pollock's Apache Lumber Co., and moved practically their whole town westward to Cooley in 1924. Renamed McNary, the town became known for its harmonious mixture of blacks, whites, Mexican-Americans, and Indians. When fire destroyed the sawmill in 1979, it was rebuilt 40 miles E near Eagar.

*Apache warrior wearing owl-feather medicine hat*

## CAMPING AND FISHING SPOTS
## EAST OF McNARY

**Bog Creek:** A camping area sits next to Bog Creek, named after difficulties experienced by wagon trains in the pioneer days. In the last century it took 6 days—if the weather was good—to make the 60-mile trip by wagon from Fort Apache to Springerville. With rain, the wagons sunk to their axles in the gooey mud of this creek. Now the waters are stocked with rainbow, brown, and brook trout. From McNary, go E 6½ miles on AZ 260.

**Shush Be Zahze Lake:** If you can't pronounce the Apache words, just call it "Little Bear." The 15-acre lake, at an elevation of 7,900 feet, has a small campground. You can try for rainbow, brown, and brook trout. Go 7 miles E of McNary on AZ 260 and turn N one mile (keep L at the fork).

**Shush Be Tou:** The name is Apache for "Big Bear." The 18-acre lake has a campground and fishing similar to nearby Shush Be Zahze. Directions are the same, except take the R fork.

**Hawley Lake:** Trout swim in the waters of this 260-acre lake. In winter you can fish through the ice. Constructed in 1959, this was the first lake on the reservation designed for recreation. Facilities include a boat dock with rentals, service station, grocery store, campground, trailer park, cabins, and horseback riding stables; tel. 335-7511. Permits for fishing, camping, and other activities can be purchased in the store. From AZ 260, 7½ miles E of McNary, turn S 8 miles on AZ 473. Despite the 8,175-foot elevation, the road in is kept open year-round. Earl Park Lake (47 acres), ½ mile SE of Hawley Lake, also offers fishing.

**Bog Tank:** This 12-acre lake (elev. 8,100 feet) is stocked with rainbow, brown, and brook trout. Bog Tank and a small campground are 10 miles E of McNary on AZ 260, then ¼ mile north. Horseshoe Lake, one mile S, has groceries, fishing supplies, and permits.

**Horseshoe Lake:** You can fish on this 121-acre lake (elev. 8,100 feet) for rainbow, brown, and brook trout. Information, camping, supplies, rentals, and permits are available at the boat dock and store, open May to September. The road is cleared in winter for ice fishermen. Go 10 miles E of McNary on AZ 260, turn S, and follow the road across the dam for ¾ mile to the S side of the lake. **A-1 Lake:** A 24-acre lake stocked with rainbow and brook trout. It's 13 miles E of McNary on AZ 260 on the S side of the highway.

## SUNRISE RESORT AND SKI AREA

**Sunrise Lake:** Fishermen know the 879-acre lake (elev. 9,000 feet) for its big rainbow trout. This is the only place on the reservation where you can use gas motors (limit 7½ horsepower). The campground is one mile S of the lake. A store sells groceries, gas, supplies, and permits. You can rent boats, canoes, and sailboards from the marina near the lodge. Sunrise Resort Lodge has a restaurant, indoor pool, sauna, whirlpool spa, volleyball and other games, and horseback riding. The lodge closes for about 6 weeks at the end of the ski season in April, then reopens for summer visitors from Memorial Day to Labor Day. Summer rates are $40 s or d.

**Sunrise Ski Area:** Forty-two ski runs radiate downward through pine and aspen forests of the White Mountains. The cluster of 3 peaks—Sunrise, Apache, and Cyclone Circle—is served by 3 triple chairlifts, 3 double chairlifts, and 4 surface lifts. Snow-making machines add to the natural snowpack for a season from Nov. to April. Lift rates are $15/half day ($8 for 12 and under) and $20/full day ($12 for 12 and under). You can go night skiing on some weekends, $10. Rentals ($11/day for skis, boots, poles), group lessons ($16/half day or $24/day including practice lifts), and private lessons ($24/hour with $10/hour per additional person) are available. Shops sell and repair ski gear. Nonskiers can also enjoy the heights from the day lodge (meals available) atop Apache Peak; take the enclosed and heated snow cat that departs from Sunrise Day Lodge at the bottom.

For the latest accommodation and skiing info, contact Sunrise Ski Resort, Box 217, McNary AZ 85930; toll-free tel. (800) 772-SNOW in Arizona, or (800) 882-7669 outside Arizona. Sunrise Ski Resort offers package deals including room, breakfasts, and lift tickets. Room-only rates start at $40/night s or d, but jump to $80 s or d on Fri. and Sat. during the peak ski season (21 Dec. to 2 Mar.); toll-free tel. (800) 55-HOTEL in Arizona; tel. (800) 882-7669 outside Arizona. To reach the resort, go 15 miles E of McNary on AZ 260 (or 18 miles W of Springerville) and turn S 4 miles on AZ 273. Ski lifts and Sunrise Day Lodge are another 4 miles from the hotel, connected by shuttle bus about every half hour. Accommodations get tight during the ski season and many skiers stay instead at Pinetop or Lakeside, 30 miles west.

# EAST OF THE WHITE MOUNTAIN APACHE INDIAN RESERVATION

## GREER

This pretty valley, high in the mountains at 8,500 feet, was first settled in 1879. Later it was named for Americus Vespucius Greer, a prominent Mormon pioneer. The community comes to life in the summer, when visitors enjoy the fishing, forest walks, or just the cool mountain air. Winter is the next busiest season—snow worshippers flock to the slopes of nearby Sunrise Ski Area, or put on their "skinny skis" to glide along the miles of marked cross-country ski trails at Greer. The quietest times are mid-Apr. to early May, when the first signs of spring appear, and fall—crisp days and aspens turning gold. You can fish the waters of the 3 Greer lakes, just N of town, and the Little Colorado River—all stocked with trout. Nestled in the foot of the White Mountains, Greer is 18 miles E of Sunrise Ski Area, 16 miles W of Springerville, and 225 miles NE of Phoenix. From AZ 260, turn 5 miles S on AZ 373.

**accommodations and food:** Greer's 15 or so resorts have rustic cabins, usually with a kitchen and cozy fireplace. Molly Butler Lodge, founded in 1910, claims to be the oldest guest lodge in Arizona. It's open all year and has rooms ($26 s or d), cabins ($57.20 s or d), restaurant (dinner only), and saloon; tel. 735-7226. Greer Lodge is famed for its relaxing atmosphere, generous family-style meals (breakfast and dinner), Greenhouse Bar, and private trout pond. Lodge rooms cost $55/adult including breakfast and dinner; open all year; tel. 735-7515. Greer Mountain Resort has cabins, RV park, restaurant (breakfast, lunch and dinner), and weekend entertainment; tel. 735-7560. Pappy's Diner, next to the post office, has a breakfast menu and pizza dinners.

**campgrounds:** You'll pass 2 National Forest campgrounds on the way in to Greer: Benny Creek ($4; no drinking water) on the L and Rolfe C. Hoyer ($7; drinking water) on the right.

**services and information:** Obtain fishing gear, camping supplies, and cross-country ski rentals and tours from: Circle B Market (tel. 735-7540), Lee Valley Mercantile (tel. 735-7300), and Greer Ski and Outdoor Shop (tel. 735-7555). The Greer Chamber of Commerce will give you a business directory of resorts and services of the community. They also have maps of cross-country ski trails. Write—Box 242, Greer, AZ 85927; tel. 735-7230.

## MOUNT BALDY WILDERNESS

The pristine forests and alpine meadows of 11,403-foot Mount Baldy present a rare opportunity to visit a subalpine vegetation zone. You'll see magnificent forests untouched by commercial logging. Engelmann and blue spruce dominate, but the slopes are also covered by quaking aspen, white fir, corkbark fir, Douglas fir, southwestern white pine, and ponderosa pine. You might catch a glimpse of elk, mule or whitetailed deer, black bear, beaver, wild turkey, blue grouse, or other wildlife. Mount Baldy is an extinct volcano, 8 or 9 million years old and worn down by 3 periods of glaciation.

West Fork (#94) and East Fork (#95) Trails follow the respective branches of the Little Colorado River up the NE slopes of Mount Baldy. The 2 trails, each 7 miles long, meet just before the grassy summit. The last ½ mile of trail crosses White Mountain Apache land, which might be closed to outsiders, so first contact their Game and Fish Office in Whiteriver; tel. 338-4385. Apache Indians still make pilgrimages to their sacred peak. Hiking season lasts June to Oct., but plan to be off the summit by early afternoon in July and Aug., when severe thunderstorms are likely. The trailheads (elev. 9,000 feet) are 4 miles apart on Forest Route 113 (AZ 273), easily reached from Greer, Sunrise, or Big Lake. In fact, both trails also go N to Greer, about 7 miles away. Horseback riders are welcome on the trails and may use small corrals near Phelps Cabin at the East Fork trailhead. No permits are needed in the Mount Baldy Wilderness, but the Forest Service asks visitors to limit camping groups to 5 persons or members of an immediate family. A map of the wilderness is sold ($1) at Forest Service offices.

## BIG LAKE

Top-rated for trout by many fishermen, Big Lake (elev. 9,000 feet) is surrounded by rolling hills of mountain meadows and forests of spruce and fir trees. Marinas with boat ramps, rental boats, motors, fishing supplies, and limited groceries are at Big Lake (575 acres) and nearby Crescent Lake (197 acres). Get information at the Visitor Center on the main road between the 2 lakes. You have a choice of 4 campgrounds at Big Lake—all have drinking water and charge $6-$8.50/night—Rainbow, Grayling, Brookchar (tenters only), and Cutthroat. Camping season lasts mid-May to mid-September. Big Lake is on AZ 273 about 23 miles S from AZ 260; the turnoff from AZ 260 is

7 miles E of the Greer junction (or 4 miles W of Springerville). You might want to try your luck with rainbow trout on the way at Mexican Hay Lake (bring your own boat; no facilities).

**vicinity of Big Lake:** Lee Valley Lake (35-acres) has brook trout (best early and late in the season) and great scenery. Elevation is 9,400 feet. The lake is just outside the Mount Baldy Wilderness, between Big Lake and Sunrise. Winn Campground is at the end of Forest Route 554, 2 miles in from Forest Route 113 (AZ 273). Greer, Lee Valley Lake, Sunrise Lake, Big Lake, and Crescent Lake are all within a 10-mile radius. Camping season at the 8,800-foot elevation is mid-May to the end of Sept.; sites have drinking water and $5 fee.

East Fork of the Black River offers fishing for rainbow trout; stay at Diamond Rock or Aspen Campgrounds (no drinking water; free). Season runs early May to the end of October. The area is 9 miles SE of Big Lake and 10 to 14 miles SW of Alpine.

East Fork of the Black River has fishing for rainbow and brown trout. West Fork Campground is beside the stream (no drinking water; free). You could do an 8-mile day or overnight hike downstream from the crossing of Forest Route 116 to West Fork Campground or vice versa. The Apache-Sitgreaves National Forest map shows the back roads in this area.

## SPRINGERVILLE AND EAGAR

Since Henry Springer's Trading Post opened in 1879, Springerville has grown to be an important trade, ranching, and lumbering center. The Madonna of the Trail, an 18-foot statue in the middle of town, commemorates the hardy pioneer women of the covered wagon days. Springerville and the adjacent town of Eagar lie in Round Valley beside the Little Colorado River. Rolling grass-covered hills surround the valley. Springerville has little to see but is a handy stop for travelers.

**accommodations and camping:** The 7 or so motels are along Main St. (US 60) in downtown Springerville. KOA campground is one mile

*Madonna of the Trail, Springerville; inscription reads: "A tribute to the pioneers of Arizona and the Southwest who trod this ground and braved the dangers of the Apaches and other warrior tribes."*

NW on US 60; open all year; $10.50/2 persons; tel. 333-4632. Nearby Becker Lake offers trout fishing.

**food:** Besides the motel restaurants, try Merrill's (Mexican-American), Spanish Inn (Mexican-American, dancing; closed Sun.), Safire Restaurant (American) or Pinon Tree Restaurant (American)—all on Main Street. Round Valley Plaza, just S of downtown on S. Mountain Ave., has a Safeway supermarket and other stores.

**shopping and services:** Pick up fishing, hunting, and camping supplies at the Sports Shack on E. Main Street. White Mountain Communities Hospital is in downtown Springerville; tel. 333-4368. Eagar has a public swimming pool; tel. 333-2238.

**information:** The White Mountain Chamber of Commerce in downtown Springerville can tell you about the area and facilities; tel. 333-2123; or write Box 181, Springerville AZ 85938. For latest info on recreation, road conditions, and maps of the Apache-Sitgreaves National Forest, visit the U.S. Forest Service on S. Mountain Ave., just S of Round Valley Plaza; tel. 333-4372; or write Box 640, Springerville, AZ 85938. Springerville's public library is downtown; tel. 333-4694.

## VICINITY OF SPRINGERVILLE

**Lyman Lake State Park:** Rain and snowmelt from the White Mountains fill this 1,400-acre lake. Though it's cold here in winter due to the 6,000-foot elevation, fishermen will be out year-round. You're most likely to catch blue and channel catfish, largemouth bass, walleye, and northern pike. The lake is large enough for water skiing (no motor restrictions) and sailing. Excellent campground facilities include restrooms, showers, hookups, grocery store, and snack bar. The marina has a boat ramp and boat rentals. Charges (per vehicle) are $2 day use, $5 camping, or $7 w/hookups; out-of-state residents add $1. Campers should be prepared for strong winds on the open terrain. The park is 17 miles N of Springerville on US 180/666; tel. 337-4441. Look for a herd of buffalo near the entrance.

**St. Johns:** Sol Barth founded this town in 1874, after reportedly just winning a few thousand dollars and several thousand head of sheep from local Mexicans in a card game. He named the community "San Juan" after its first female resident, Senora Maria San Juan de Padilla de Baca. Mormon settlers who arrived in 1879 anglicized the name. You can learn more about the area's history in the Apache County Museum and Library on Main St.; open Mon. to Fri. 1000-1600, closed holidays; $ .50 adult admission; tel. 337-4737. St. Johns is 29 miles N of Springerville.

**Kolhuwalawa:** Arizona's 23rd Indian reservation was created in 1985 to give the Zuni (ZOO-nee) tribe back their "heaven." The 1,400 acres, located 14 miles N of St. Johns, is thought by the Zuni to be the place where the human spirit goes after death. Anthropologists think that Zuni religious leaders have held sacred dances and ceremonies here since at least A.D. 900, when ancestors of the tribe began migrating from pueblos in Arizona to New Mexico. The Zuni people, like the Hopi, still live in pueblos and maintain many of their old traditions. You can visit Zuni village, one of the fabled Seven Cities of Cibola sought by Coronado in 1540. Zuni is 58 miles NE of St. Johns, across the New Mexico border.

**Concho Lake:** Fish for rainbow and brook trout in this 60-acre lake, located about 16 miles W of St. Johns. The lake has a boat ramp and restrooms.

**South Fork:** Three resorts and a National Forest campground are near the South Fork of the Little Colorado River (elev. 7,700 feet), 5 miles W of Springerville. The campground, 2½ miles S of AZ 260 on Forest Route 560, is on both sides of the stream. Camping season lasts mid-May to end of Sept. (no drinking water; free). A hiking trail follows the South Fork several miles upstream. Resorts include South Fork Guest Ranch (tel. 333-4455), Canyon Cove (tel. 333-4602), and White Mountain Resort (tel. 333-4602).

## THE CORONADO TRAIL

Seeking treasures of the legendary Seven Cities of Cibola in 1540, Francisco Vasquez de Coronado and his men struggled through the rugged mountains of Eastern Arizona. Though the Spaniard's quest failed, the name of this scenic highway honors his effort. You'll dis-

*mountain lion* (Felis concolor)

cover the *real* wealth on a drive over Coronado's old route—the scenery of rugged mountains, clad in majestic forests, rolling in blue waves towards the horizon. The blazing gold of aspen in the fall is matched only by the dazzling display of summer wildflowers. The 123 miles of paved highway between Springerville and Clifton twist over country little changed from Coronado's time. Hikers, fishermen, and cross-country skiers will be far from the crowds when exploring this region. Allow enough time for the journey through this high country—even a nonstop drive will take 3½ hours. But you'll probably want to stop many times to enjoy the views, do some walking, or perhaps have a picnic. Drivers should stock up on groceries and gas before venturing on the 95 miles from Alpine to Clifton/Morenci; no towns are along this stretch. Winter snows can close the highway from Alpine to just N of Morenci between mid-Dec. and mid-Mar., but the section from Springerville to Alpine is kept open. Miles of good cross-country ski trails attract winter visitors to the forests surrounding Alpine.

**Nelson Reservoir:** Rainbow, brown, and brook trout live in this 60-acre lake located 10 miles S of Springerville. Picnic tables, restrooms, and a boat ramp are provided, but there's no camping. Escudilla Mountain, the large rounded peak to the S, is Arizona's 3rd highest peak.

**Escudilla Mountain:** Coronado undoubtedly spotted the 10,955-foot summit of this ancient volcano in 1540. Perhaps it was a homesick member of his expedition who named the mountain after an *escudilla*, a soup bowl used in his native Spain. In 1951 a disastrous fire burned the forests on the entire north face of Escudilla. Aspen trees then took over where mighty conifers once stood—the normal sequence after a mountain fire. Raspberries, snowberries, currants, elderberries, strawberries, and gooseberries flourished too. The forests of spruce, fir, and pine on top escaped the fire. Lower down you'll find surviving woodlands of aspen, Rocky Mountain maple, ponderosa pine, and Gambel oak. Elk, deer, black bear, and smaller animals roam the hillsides. Escudilla was once grizzly territory, but the last one was killed in the 1920s or '30s.

Now a wilderness area of 5,200 acres, Escudilla offers some good hiking. Outstanding views from the fire lookout on top reward those who make the climb. Two trails lead towards the summit: Escudilla National Recreation Trail, a well-graded 3-mile trail from Terry Flat to Escudilla Lookout; and Government Trail, a steep 2-mile ascent beginning about one mile E of Hulsey Lake and meeting the Escudilla Trail on the summit ridge. The Escudilla Trail is the better one but isn't shown on all maps. Turn E off the highway onto Forest Route 56 about 21 miles S of Springerville (6 miles N of Alpine); stay on Forest Route 56 about 4 miles to the Escudilla trailhead, or turn L onto Forest Route 57A for the Government Trail.

## ALPINE

Mormon settlers founded this town in 1879, naming it Frisco for the nearby San Francisco River. Later, thinking their mountains resembled the Alps, they renamed the community "Alpine." The setting is pretty — Alpine nestles in a high mountain valley (elev. 8,046 feet) surrounded by extensive woodlands. But the Alps it's not! Alpine (pop. 525) is an excellent base for outdoor activities — hiking, fishing, hunting, horseback riding, golfing, scenic drives, and the winter sports of cross-country skiing, sledding, and snowmobiling.

**accommodations:** Sportsman Lodge, on the highway, has motel rooms and kitchenettes starting at $19 s, $21 d.; tel. 339-4576. Alpine Cabins, in town next to the M&J Corral Restaurant, has kitchenettes; $28 (up to 4 people) but drops to $18/day for longer stays; tel. 339-4610. Mountain Hi Lodge, ½ mile E on Main St., has similar facilities at $21 s or d; tel. 339-4311. Tal-Wi-Wi Lodge, 3 miles N of Alpine, has motel rooms ($26 for up to 4 persons), and a restaurant serving 3 meals daily; tel. 339-4319. Judd's Ranch, one mile N of Alpine, has cabins with kitchenettes and a fishing lake. Open late Apr. to Oct., $28 s or d; tel. 339-4326.

*Couch's spadefoot toad* (Scaphiopus couchi)

**camping:** Alpine Divide Campground, set in a forest of ponderosa pine and Gambel oak 4 miles N of Alpine, has great views. The sites, with drinking water, are maintained mid-May to mid-Sept. and cost $3/night; the rest of the year camping is on a "pack-in pack-out basis," free. Luna Lake Campground, 4 miles E of Alpine on US 180 near the New Mexico border, is surrounding by fir- and spruce-covered mountains. Luna Lake (75 acres) has a boat launch, boat rentals, and a store with limited supplies. Fishermen will be after trout nearly all year — even out on the ice in winter. The campground has drinking water; it's open mid-May to mid-Sept.; $4/night. RVs can also stay at Alpine Village Trailer Park (tel. 339-4476), and Mayse Corral Trailer Park near Luna Lake (tel. 339-4450). Mayse Corral may also have trailers for rent at low cost.

**food:** The Sportsman and M&J Corral restaurants in town serve a variety of American and Mexican foods. The Alpine Country Club serves dinners Thur. to Sat.; tel. 339-4574 (reservations suggested).

**services:** Alpine Hardware and Master's Auto Parts have camping, fishing, and hunting supplies. Judd's Ranch has horseback riding; tel. 339-4326. Alpine Adventures, at the junction of US 666 and 180, offers trail rides and backcountry hiking, fishing, and hunting trips. They also have cross-country ski and snowmobile rentals and instruction; Box 349, Alpine, 85920; tel. 339-4574. See how far you can hit a golf ball through the thin mountain air at Alpine Country Club. Their 18-hole course has rental carts and clubs and a restaurant. The course is 4 miles E of town; tel. 339-4574.

**information:** The Alpine Chamber of Commerce has a list of accommodations and services; write Box 410, Alpine AZ 85920. The National Forest's Alpine ranger office is very helpful with info on hiking, cross-country ski trails, fishing, camping, and scenic drives. Their district covers the N half of the Coronado Trail, including Escudilla Mountain and most of the Blue Range Primitive Area. The office is at the junction of US 666 and 180; tel. 339-4633 and 339-4384; or write Box 469, Alpine AZ 85920.

## BLUE RANGE PRIMITIVE AREA

This rugged wilderness country lies S of Alpine along the Arizona-New Mexico border. South-flowing Blue River, fed by several perennial streams, neatly divides the Blue Range Primitive Area in two. The Mogollon Rim, whose high cliffs form the southern boundary of the Colorado Plateau, crosses the area from west to east. All this geologic uplifting and downcutting has created spectacular rock formations and rough, steep canyons. Elevations range from 9,100 feet near Hannagan Meadow to 4,500 feet in the lower Blue River. Hiking down from the rim, you'll find the spruce, fir and pine forests giving way to pinyon pine and juniper in the lower valleys. Wildlife you might run across include Rocky Mountain elk, Coues whitetailed deer, mule deer, black bear, mountain lion, javelina, and bobcat. You may also see such rare and endangered birds as the southern bald eagle, spotted owl, American peregrine falcon, aplomado falcon, Arizona woodpecker, black-eared bushtit, and olive warbler. The upper Blue River and some of its tributaries harbor small numbers of trout.

**hiking:** Best weather is usually from Apr. to early July, and Sept. to late October. Violent thunderstorms lash the mountains in July and August. Snow covers much of the land from Nov. to March. Many day hikes and backpacking trips are possible on Forest Service trails. You can hike from trailheads along the Coronado Trail (US 666) or from Forest Route 281 (running S from Luna Lake along the Blue River). Forest Route 567 (Red Hill Rd.) connects the 2 roads along the N boundary of the primitive area. Other trailheads are to the E in New Mexico and to the S off Forest Route 475. The Forest Service office in Alpine has maps and trail descriptions. The book *Arizona Trails* by David Mazel also has detailed info and maps.

## HANNAGAN MEADOW

The splendid high country around Hannagan Meadow, 23 miles S of Alpine, is great for hiking — several trails lead into the adjacent Blue Range Primitive Area. Forests of aspen, spruce, and fir surround the tiny village (elev. 9,100 feet). You'll find some of the best cross-country skiing and snowmobiling in Arizona, though the area remains relatively unknown. The road from Alpine is normally kept open in winter, but storms occasionally close it for a few days.

**Hannagan Meadow Lodge:** The rustic cabins, dining room, and trailer park of this remote region offer comfortable accommodations. Cross-country skiers can glide along marked trails during the late Nov. to late Mar. season, but they'll have to bring their own equipment. Hunting trips can be organized from the lodge. Cabins, which start at $35/night, and the lodge dining room stay open all year. The trailer park has hookups and is open only during summer. A small store, open June to Dec., sells Indian crafts, groceries, and gasoline. Write Hannagan Meadow Lodge at Box 335, Alpine AZ 85920 or tel. 339-4370. If heading S, this is your very last chance to get gas or supplies until Clifton-Morenci, 70 miles away.

**Hannagan Meadow Campground:** This National Forest campground stays open mid-May

*view near K.P.
Cienega
Campground*

to mid-Sept.; no drinking water or fee; located ¼ mile S of the Lodge.

**vicinity of Hannagan Meadow:** K.P. Cienega Campground overlooks a large meadow (*"cienega"* is Spanish for meadow) and a sparkling stream. Sites in this idyllic spot have spring water; free. Turn off the Coronado Trail 5 miles S of Hannagan Meadow and drive 1½ miles on a dirt road to the meadow. K.P. Trail (#70) into the Blue Range Primitive Area begins here, too.

Blue Vista overlook and nature trail sit on the very edge of the Mogollon Rim, 7 miles S of Hannagan Meadow. Turn ¼ mile SW to parking and picnic tables, but don't take this turnoff with a trailer or large vehicle! In clear weather you can see countless ridges rolling away to the horizon from this 9,184-foot vantage point. Learn more about the great variety of trees and plants by taking the ¼-mile nature trail to another viewpoint and picnic table. Mount Graham (10,717 feet) is the highest peak of the Pinaleno Range to the S (70 miles away).

## BELOW THE RIM

Strayhorse Campground has spring water; free. It's located 4 miles (and 1,600 feet!) below Blue Vista, and 64 miles N of Clifton. Raspberry

Creek Trail (#35) leads E to Blue River in the Blue Range Primitive Area, 10½ miles and a drop of 2,500 feet. Highline Trail (#47) goes W 14½ miles, linking with several other trails. This area, W of Strayhorse Campground, tends to be less used, and trails harder to follow.

**Rose Peak:** At an elevation of 8,700 feet, Rose Peak has great views. It's also a good place for bird-watching. The turnoff is near Milepost 207, about 17 miles S of Blue Vista and 51 miles N of Clifton. You can reach the forest lookout tower by a ½-mile trail or by driving up a steep, narrow, one-mile road (unless the gate's locked).

**Juan Miller Campgrounds:** Season runs about Apr. to Oct.; no drinking water or fee. Head E one mile from the Coronado Trail on Forest Route 475. The turnoff is near Milepost 189, 35 miles S of Blue Vista and 33 miles N of Clifton. Forest Route 475 continues E to Blue River, another 15 miles, passing many small canyons and ridges good for day-hiking.

**Honeymoon Campground:** A secluded spot at the end of a 22-mile dirt road. You can fish for trout in Eagle Creek, stocked May to September. No drinking water or fee, and you're asked to carry out trash. Turn W onto Forest

Route 217 near Milepost 188 of the Coronado Trail. Many of the ranches on the way date back to the late 1800s.

**Granville Campground:** This campground, and nearby Cherry Lodge picnic area, make a pleasant place to stop. Sites have drinking water from May to Sept.; free. They're on opposite sides of the road about 20 miles N of Clifton between Mileposts 178 and 179.

**Morenci Open Pit Mine:** From the overlook, 10 miles N of Clifton, you can gaze into one of the biggest man-made holes in the world! Trains and trucks appear like toys laboring to haul copper ore out of the ever-deepening pit. Most of old Morenci town lies buried under debris somewhere in the pit; when the town got in the way of the mining, Phelps Dodge built a new community and destroyed the old one. The "move," completed in 1969, was easily made since Phelps Dodge owned the town as well as the mine. From the mine overlook, the road drops to modern Morenci (elev. 4,080 feet), then switchbacks down to Clifton (elev. 3,502 feet). You'll pass a giant smelter, now closed, on the way.

## CLIFTON

Coronado's expedition marched through this area in 1540, unaware of gold deposits within the hills. Mexican miners, though, discovered the gold in 1867 and began small-scale placer operations. As the gold played out, Eastern prospectors took note of the copper deposits. They registered claims, and by 1872 had staked out the town of Clifton. The nearby mining towns of Joy's Camp (later renamed Morenci) and Metcalf were also founded at this time. Miners faced great difficulties at first—the nearest railhead was in Colorado, and Apache raids harassed operations. In 1878, Arizona's first railroad connected the smelter in Clifton with the Longfellow Mine at Metcalf, 9 miles north. Instead of a locomotive, mules pulled the empty ore cars uphill to the mine; on the way back down, the mules got a free ride. Three tiny locomotives, one on display in Clifton, later replaced the mules.

Both Metcalf and old Morenci are gone now—Metcalf abandoned and destroyed, and old Morenci deeply buried in tailings. The new Morenci lacks the character of an old mining town. Clifton, however, still has its old buildings, the "Copper Head" locomotive (built in the 1880s), and an unusual jail. Booze joints and brothels, where desperados engaged in frequent shootings, once lined Chase Creek Street. Today Chase Creek Street is quiet and the old jail empty, but Clifton remains one of Arizona's more distinctive towns.

**sights:** Strolling along Chase Creek St., you

*Copper Head locomotive*

Chase Creek Street

can imagine how it once was—when the boisterous miners of old came looking for a good time. The street parallels US 666 on the Morenci side of town. Clifton's old jail, beside the Valley National Bank, was built in 1881 by blasting and hacking a hole into the hillside. The jail's first occupant was the man who built it, Margarito Verala. After doing a fine job, Verala received his pay, got drunk on mescal, and proceeded to shoot up the town until he was arrested. You're welcome to step inside the gloomy interior. If the gate's locked, check at the city hall or police station for the key. The "Copper Head" locomotive sits next to the jail. Contact Phelps Dodge if you'd like to see some of their operations; free tours lasting 2-3 hours take you through the open pit mine, crushers, and concentrators; tel. 865-4521.

**accommodations and food:** Rode Inn Motel ($25 s, $30 d) is on the S side of Clifton; tel. 865-4536. Morenci Motel, 6 miles up the highway from Clifton, costs $27 s, $31 d, and has a restaurant; tel. 865-4111. Another Morenci restaurant—the Kopper Kettle—is in the shopping center. In Clifton you have a choice of several fast-food places along the highway, or Cole's Pizza Parlor (pizza, steaks, and seafood) on Ward's Canyon in S side of town, and Vozza's Steak House on Frisco Ave. in the N side.

**shopping and services:** Stock up on groceries at the Morenci Shopping Center, especially if headed N, as no supplies or gas are available for the next 70 miles. Morenci has a hospital (tel. 865-4511), and a swimming pool (tel. 865-2003). Clifton has a swimming pool too, on Park Ave.; tel. 865-9934. The Greenlee County Fair takes place during the first weekend of October.

**information:** The Greenlee County Chamber of Commerce has information about the history, sights, and facilities of the area. You can see old photos of Morenci, taken before it disappeared, and of Clifton in its busier days. Rockhounds can get directions to several agate digs. The Chamber, 251 Chase Creek St., is open weekdays, 0800-1700; tel. 865-3313. Or write Box 1237, Clifton AZ 85533. Clifton had a historical museum but it closed after a big flood; the Chamber people will know if it's reopened. For hiking and camping info on the southern half of the Coronado Trail, see the U.S. Forest Service office in Clifton (Box 698, Clifton, AZ 85533), at the W end of town shortly before the highway climbs towards Morenci; tel. 865-2432. A public library is in the Morenci shopping center; tel. 865-2775.

*cotton harvesting in the low desert*

# THE LOW DESERT

## SAFFORD

Surrounded by the rugged Pinaleno, Gila, and Peloncillo Mountain ranges, Safford lies in the low (2,900-foot) Gila River Valley. Ancient Hohokam, Mogollon, and Anasazi sites go back at least 2,000 years. The Apache arrived about 1700 and managed to discourage European settlers until 1874. Then 4 Civil War veterans founded a town and named it after Anson P. Safford, territorial Arizona's 3rd governor.

Though small (pop. 8,190), Safford serves as the main center for a large area of SE Arizona. Cotton is king in the valley, but the irrigated river-bottom land also supports sorghum, barley, alfalfa, and other crops. Highlights for visitors include the drive to the 10,000-foot level of Mt. Graham (hiking and camping), the Galiuro Wilderness (for adventurous hikers), the Museum of Anthropology in Thatcher, and the Aravaipa Canyon Primitive Area.

**accommodations and campgrounds:** Safford's 7 motels are along US 70, also signposted as 5th St. and Thatcher Boulevard. Each motel has a/c, and the more expensive ones also have swimming pools—you may want both in summer when highs push 100 degrees. Roper Lake State Park, 6 miles S of downtown, has pleasant campsites on the S shore of a small lake. It's open all year and has showers; $2 day use or $5 camping (non-residents add $1); tel. 428-6760 (see "Vicinity of Safford"). Several National Forest campgrounds are on the Mt. Graham Drive (see "Vicinity of Safford"). RVs can stay at Tower Mobile Court, 1½ miles E on US 70; tel. 428-6997; and Ivanho Mobile Home Park, 3 miles E on US 70; tel. 428-3828.

**food:** Western-style dinners (steaks, BBQ'd chicken and ribs, etc.) are served by the Branding Iron about 2½ miles N of downtown; go N on 8th Ave., then L on River Rd.; tel. 428-6252. For Chinese cuisine try New China Inn (Mt. Graham Shopping Center); tel. 428-5662; or

The Tiki (Desert Inn Motel); tel. 428-0521. Dine Mexican at Casa Manana (corner US 70 and 1st Ave.); tel. 428-3170, Pioneer Restaurant (Pioneer Motel); tel. 428-0734, El Charro (628 Main St.); tel. 428-4234, or El Coronado (409 Main St.); tel. 428-7755. Supermarkets and chain restaurants are in Mt. Graham and Gila Valley Shopping Centers W of downtown.

**services:** Post office is on the corner of US 70 and 5th Avenue. Mount Graham Community Hospital is SW of town at 1600 20th Ave.; tel. 428-1171. A public swimming pool (open Memorial Day to Labor Day) is in Firth Park behind the Chamber of Commerce; tel. 428-9987. Tennis players can use the lighted courts at Graham County Park, 2 miles S on US 666, or at the junior high school, 520 11th Street. The Graham County Park also offers raquetball, basketball, ballfields, jogging track, and picnicking; all but the track are lighted for night use. Play golf at the 18-hole Mount Graham course, SW of town; tel. 428-1260. Feeling run down with too many aches and pains? If so, you might want to "take the waters" at one of the hotsprings spas S of Safford: Kachina Health Spa; tel. 428-2711; or Lebanon Hot Mineral Baths; tel. 428-3299. Hikers can purchase topo maps at Consolidated Title, 605 Main St.; tel. 428-0180.

**information:** The Safford-Graham County Chamber of Commerce is very helpful and well stocked with literature and maps; open Mon. to Sat., 0900-1700, shorter hours on Sundays. The office is easy to find on the main highway just W of downtown; tel. 428-2511; or write 1111 Thatcher Blvd., Safford AZ 85546. The Forest Service office has hiking and camping info on the Pinaleno Mountains (Mt. Graham) and Galiuro Wilderness. You'll find it on the 3rd floor of the post office downtown on the corner of US 70 and 5th Ave., open weekdays, 0730-1600; tel. 428-4150; or write Box 709, Safford, AZ 85546. If you plan to visit Aravaipa Canyon, you'll need a permit from the Bureau of Land Management (BLM) office. Rockhounds can pick up brochures here telling where fire agates and other stones can be collected. The BLM office is at 425 E. 4th St., Safford AZ 85546 (one block N of US 70, behind Bill McGlocklin Ford dealership). Open week-

days, 0745-1615; tel. 428-4040. You can also get permits and info by mail. The public library and Graham County Historical Museum (Indian artifacts and pioneer memorabilia) are at 808 8th Ave.; tel. 428-1531. The museum is open very limited hours—call first.

**transport:** Greyhound stops several times a day in each direction on its route between Phoenix and El Paso, Texas. The station is at 836 Thatcher Blvd. (W. 70); tel. 428-2150. Local tours are arranged by Allen Weech, Box 9, Pima AZ 85543; tel. 485-2288.

# VICINITY OF SAFFORD

**Museum of Anthropology:** Thatcher, just 3 miles NW of Safford, is home for Eastern Arizona College, a 2-year school. Its museum has an excellent collection of excavated Indian pottery, axes, arrowheads, and jewelry. Visit the museum's small library to learn more about archaeology and anthropology. Kids have special displays too: hands-on exhibits of fire-making, shell-jewelry crafting, and arrowhead-chipping. Hours are Mon. to Fri. 0900-1200, and 1300-1700 during the school year (early Sept. to mid-May); free. The museum is near the corner of Main St. (US 70) and College Avenue.

**Roper Lake State Park:** The shores of this pretty lake offer camping, picnicking, swimming, and fishing. Fishermen can launch their boats (electric motors OK) and try for catfish, bass, bluegill and crappie. Hedonists can hop in the hot tub, fed by a natural spring, but the water may be only lukewarm. Learn about desert plants on the short nature trail beginning near the hot tub. Roper Lake is 6 miles S of Safford off US 666. Dankworth Ponds day-use area also has good picnicking and fishing; it's several miles farther S on US 666. Charges for either area of the park are $2 for day use or $5 for camping (Roper Lake); nonresidents add $1. Open all year; tel. 428-6760.

**Mount Graham Drive:** Mt. Graham (10,717 feet), in the Pinaleno Mountains, rises nearly 7,000 feet into the air above Safford. A good road, called the Swift Trail, ascends the eastern slopes through a remarkable range of vegeta-

*Pinaleno Range from Roper Lake State Park*

tion and animal life. Leaving the cactus, creosote bush, and mesquite at the start, you'll soon be among small juniper, oak, and pinyon pine. Higher on the twisting road, you'll enter forests of ponderosa pine, Douglas fir, aspen, white fir, and other trees. Thick stands of Englemann spruce dominate the highest ridges. Besides the sweeping views, you can enjoy a picnic or hiking.

To drive the 35-mile-long Swift Trail, go 7 miles S from Safford on US 666 (or 26 miles N from I-10) and turn W at the sign. The first 28 miles are paved, followed by 7 of gravel. Winter snows close the higher parts of the road from about early Nov. to mid-May. The drive from Safford and back takes about 4½ hours, not including stops. Stock up on gas and supplies before leaving town. A road guide to the features of the Swift Trail and a Coronado Forest Map (Pinaleno Range) are available from the Safford Chamber of Commerce or U.S. Forest Service in Safford. Hikers have many trails but should be prepared for steep sections; pick up a leaflet of campground and trail descriptions in the Safford Forest Service of-

fice. The 5 developed campgrounds all have drinking water and stay open May to mid-Oct.; fees are $4 or $5. Campground elevations range from 6,700 feet at Arcadia to 9,300 feet at Soldier Creek. Anglers can try for trout in Riggs Lake, near the end of the Swift Trail.

**Galiuro Wilderness:** Rugged and brush-covered, the Galiuro Mountains rise in 2 parallel ranges above the desert. The terrain is so rough and steep that you'll have to keep mostly to the network of trails. You're not likely to see many other hikers in this little-known range. The Galiuros are SW of Safford, on the other side of the Pinalenos, and NW of Willcox. The main trailheads are on the E slopes: Ash Creek, High Creek, and Deer Creek. The 10 trails total 95 miles. Prominent peaks along the E ridge are Bassett (7,671 feet), Kennedy (7,540 feet), and Sunset (7,094 feet); along the W ridge stand Rhodes (7,116 feet), Maverick (6,990 feet), and Kielburg (6,880 feet).

Vegetation varies with elevation and slope orientation: S and W slopes have dense growths of manzanita, live oak, and other brush, with juniper, pinyon, and oak trees higher up; the higher canyons and N-facing slopes are wooded with Arizona cypress, ponderosa pine, Chihuahua pine, Mexican white pine, Douglas fir, and some white fir. Sycamore, alder, aspen, and other deciduous trees grow along stream banks. Mule deer, whitetail deer, black bear, javelina, and mountain lion roam the rugged hillsides and canyons. The old Power's cabin ruin (built 1910), mine shafts, and ore-milling machinery can be seen in Rattlesnake Canyon (Galiuro Corridor). Power's Garden cabin, also in Rattlesnake Canyon, may be open for use by hikers. Streams usually dry up during late spring and early summer. The more reliable springs (purify first) are Power's Garden, Mud, Corral, Holdout, Cedar, and Jackson Cabin. See the Forest Service office in Safford for latest water, trail, and road conditions.

**Aravaipa Canyon:** A jewel in the desert, Aravaipa Canyon is renowned for its scenery and variety of wildlife. Waters of the Aravaipa

*in Aravaipa Canyon*

Creek flow all year, a rare occurrence in the desert, providing an oasis for birds and other animals. Giant ash, sycamore and willow trees shade the canyon floor. Rocky hillsides, dotted with saguaro cactus and other desert plants, lie only a few steps from the lush vegetation of the creekbed. Birders have sighted more than 200 species in the canyon, including the bald eagle and peregrine falcon. Mule deer, javelina, and coyote frequent the area, and you might even see a mountain lion or bighorn sheep. Also keep an eye out for any of the several species of rattlesnakes.

Although there's no established trail, hiking is easy. Tributary canyons invite side trips—Hell Hole Canyon is especially enchanting, despite its name. Tennis shoes work well as you'll be wading across the creek frequently. Camping spots are plentiful on grassy terraces. To visit the 11-mile canyon, *even for day hikes,* you must get a permit from the BLM office in Safford (see "Safford Information"). Advance reservations are needed for weekends in spring and fall, the best hiking seasons. Permits may

*natural arch in Hell-Hole Canyon, a tributary of Aravaipa Canyon*

also be available from rangers stationed near each end of the canyon, but call first to check. BLM has a 2-night (3-day) stay limit. Horseback riders may visit on day trips only, and not more than 5 per group. Pets are prohibited.

Trailheads, though only 11 trail miles apart, require 160 miles of driving from one end to the other. The East Trailhead is reached by the Klondyke Rd. (turn off US 70 about 15 miles NW of Safford) or the Fort Grant Rd. (turn off US 666 either 19 miles S of Safford or 17 miles N of I-10). Follow signs to Aravaipa Canyon Wilderness; don't go to the settlement called "Aravaipa." A ranger is stationed in Klondyke, 10 miles before the trailhead. Fourmile Campground (drinking water; free) is nearby; turn L just after Klondyke. You can also camp along Turkey Creek Canyon (no facilities), a pretty tributary of the Aravaipa Creek near the trailhead. The West Trailhead is much closer to Phoenix and Tucson but has no place to camp. From AZ 77, about midway between Winkelman and Mammoth, turn E 13 miles on Aravaipa Rd. to the ranger station and trailhead.

saguaro cacti in Aravaipa Canyon

# SAN CARLOS
# APACHE INDIAN RESERVATION

San Carlos Reservation has climates and scenery for everyone: cool pine forests in the NE, grasslands and wooded ridges (pinyon and juniper) in the center, and cactus-studded desert surrounding San Carlos Lake in the southwest. The Black and Salt Rivers form the natural boundary with the White Mountain Apache Reservation to the north. Much of the land is fine cattle-grazing country and supports large tribal herds. You can reach San Carlos Lake and Seneca Lake by paved highways, but roads to other recreation areas may be too rough for cars, especially after rains or snow melt. You'll need an access permit ($5.50) to venture onto the reservation's back roads or trails.

**San Carlos:** This small community is very much a government town in appearance. Neat rows of office buildings and apartments line the main street. Here you'll find the tribal offices, post office, grocery store, San Carlos Cafe, and a service station.

Stop at Peridot Trading Post 3 miles S of San Carlos to look at Apache crafts. You can purchase baskets, beadwork, cradleboards, and peridot jewelry. Peridot is a deep yellow-green transparent olivine mineral. The cut stones, sold mounted and loose, resemble emeralds.

**San Carlos Lake:** The 19,500-acre lake measures 23 miles long by 2 miles wide, making it the largest lake completely within Arizona. All this is held back by 880-foot-high Coolidge Dam, dedicated by President Coolidge himself in 1930. Obtain information, permits, fishing supplies, boat rentals, groceries, snacks, and gasoline at San Carlos Lake Marina, 2 miles N of the dam. A trailer park with hookups is next to the marina. Soda Canyon Point Campground (drinking water) is also nearby. Several other campgrounds are on both the N and S sides of the lake. Though famed mostly for its prolific bass population, San Carlos Lake has produced state-record specimens of catfish, crappie, and bluegill. The

miles are paved; it's recommended to check road conditions first. **Seneca Park:** Located in the NW corner of the reservation just off US 60/AZ 77, 33 miles N of Globe and 5 miles S of the Salt River Canyon bridge. A campground with drinking water is on 27-acre Seneca Lake.

**fishing and hunting:** Fishing is the big attraction for most visitors—San Carlos Lake is known as Arizona's hottest bass spot. Farther N you can catch trout, catfish, and smallmouth bass in the Black River, Point of Pines Lake, Seneca Lake, and over 100 stock ponds. Licenses cost $4/day or $40/year; boat permits are $1.50/day or $25/year. Some areas such as the Black and Salt Rivers need a special-use permit for fishing, hiking, or camping ($7/day) in addition to the regular permits. You may fish on both sides of the Black and Salt Rivers with

*When the Warm Springs Apache were moved to San Carlos in 1877, Chief Victorio and a small band escaped. He led a savage campaign against Americans and Mexicans in 1879-80, killing nearly 1,000 people before being shot by a Mexican bounty hunter.*

lake and marina are 13 miles S from the town of San Carlos.

**camping and picnicking:** In winter you'll probably want to stick to the low country around San Carlos Lake (elev. 2,425 feet), then head for the hills in summer. Campsites are generally open all year. Camping and picnicking permits ($6/day) must be bought beforehand; see "fishing and hunting" below. Backcountry driving, hiking, river running, and boating also require tribal permits.

**Cassadore Springs:** This small picnic area and campground has spring water; it's about 12 miles N from the town of San Carlos. **Point of Pines:** The 35-acre lake and campground (no drinking water) are in the eastern part of the reservation; from US 70, 5 miles E of Peridot, turn NE 55 miles on Indian Route 8 (Geronimo Trail) to the campground. Only the first 20

*"Patchy" Slaughter, an Indian baby captured in a raid on an Apache camp by John H. Slaughter, scout for a troop of 7th Cavalry, who took her to his home. She later died from accidental burns at about the age of six.*

either San Carlos or White Mountain permits, but permits of the 2 reservations are otherwise not interchangeable. Certain areas may be closed. Purchase permits at the tribal game and fish office in San Carlos (open Mon. to Fri. 0800-1630, across from Valley National Bank), Noline's Country Store (on US 70 near San Carlos Lake turnoff), San Carlos Lake Marina, Talley & Son (Safford), Sportsmen Shack Pima), and in Globe at the Circle-K and Dixon's Exxon station.

Hunters can pursue big and small game. Fees vary depending on what you're hunting and whether you're an Arizona resident. They range from $50 for small game to more than $1000 for an elk. Contact the tribal game and fish office in San Carlos (tel. 475-2361) for latest regulations and scheduled hunts.

**events:** Look for Apache dances, crafts, foods, and cowboys showing off their riding skills at the San Carlos Rodeo in late April, and at the Tribal Fair in late Oct. or early November. Traditional dances are also held during the summer; call the tribal office for dates and places; tel. 475-2361. The Sunrise Ceremony occurs most frequently, marking the coming of age for young women with blessings and a strengthening of tribal ties.

**information:** Permits are needed for most activities on the reservation, including picnicking. For the latest regulations, facilities, fees, and road conditions, contact the San Carlos Tribal Office, Box O, San Carlos, AZ 85550; tel. 475-2361 (ask for Game and Fish).

*San Carlos Apache
basket design*

# SOUTHERN ARIZONA

## INTRODUCTION

Southern Arizona is a sea of desert and grasslands from which mountains soar like islands. Giant saguaro and other hardy plants cover the Sonoran Desert from Tucson westward toward the Colorado River Valley, while desert grasslands fill most of the valleys eastward. Four ranges have peaks over 9,000 feet where you could be up to your neck in snow during the winter—the Santa Catalinas, Santa Ritas, Huachucas, and Chiricahuas. Mount Lemmon, in the Santa Catalinas near Tucson, has downhill ski runs. Climate varies dramatically with elevation. Expect mild winters and very hot summers on the desert, slightly cooler and wetter weather on the grasslands. Astonishing varieties of birds, animals, and plants find a niche in southern Arizona's varied topography. Some species, such as the "whiskered" senita cactus and the colorful trogon bird, have come from Mexico and are rarely seen elsewhere in the United States.

When the Spanish entered this region about 1539, they found several groups of natives, most notably the warlike, nomadic Apache and the more settled and peaceful Papago and Pima. Most of the Spanish, Pima, and Apache have left southern Arizona, but their legacy in culture, place names, and legends remains strong. The Old West lives on as well—in the dozens of abandoned mining camps, on the ranches where cowboys still work vast ranges, and on the streets of Tombstone where the Earps and Doc Holliday shot it out with the Clanton gang. Allow time to explore southern Arizona. It's a big land with much to discover.

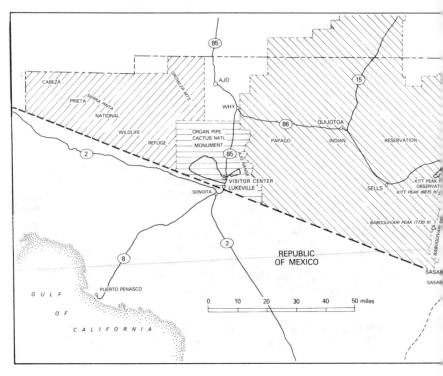

# TUCSON

Though the "Old Pueblo," as it's known locally, is modern and lively, its Old West heritage
will surprise you. Tucson (pronounced "TOO-
sawn") has some of the best cultural offerings
in Arizona—a large university, historic sites,
and a great variety of restaurants and nightlife.
Yet it remains on a human scale—you can *walk*
this city to see most of the sights. Set in a
desert valley at an elevation of 2,400 feet, Tucson ranks as the state's 2nd largest city (metro
population 625,000). Summers are warm but
not as hot as those in Phoenix or Yuma. And
Mt. Lemmon, at 9,157 feet, is just an hour's
drive away. Temperatures peak in June and
July with highs generally near 98 F and lows
near 70. Even in Dec. & Jan. it's spring-like with
average highs in the mid-60s and lows in the
upper 30s. Of the 11 or so inches of annual rainfall, over half falls in the July to Sept. rainy

season. Desert vegetation, with palo verde,
cottonwood, and mesquite trees, is surprisingly lush. Many varieties of cacti display
brilliant flowers from Apr. to late May. The
mountains ringing Tucson offer skiing in the
winter, and great hiking almost anytime. In just
minutes, hikers can get out of town W to the
Tucson Mts., NE to the Santa Catalinas, or E to
the Rincons.

## HISTORY

Hohokam Indians farmed the valley floor at
least as far back as A.D. 100. Pima and other Indian tribes had replaced the Hohokam long
before the first Spanish arrived in the 1500s.
The first Spanish visitors to this area found a
Pima Indian village, Chuk-son (*chuck* means

"dark mountain;" *son* means "foot of"), at the foot of Sentinel Peak (the hill with the big "A" now painted on it). The name was changed by the Spanish to "Tucson" when the Presidio of San Augustin del Tucson was laid out in 1775. Attacks by roving Apaches made fortifications necessary, so adobe walls 12 feet high and 750 feet long were built to enclose the new settlement. Mexico inherited Tucson from Spain after the 1821 revolution, but little changed except the flag.

**Americans take hold:** Tucson came under the wing of the United States with the Gadsden purchase in June 1854, but 21 months of boundary-marking and bureaucratic delays passed before the arrival of American officialdom in the form of the Army's First Dragoons. Although Apaches continued to menace settlers and travelers in the area, Anglo-Americans began to arrive, and the Butterfield Overland Stagecoach opened service to Tucson. To cope with the desert climate, the Anglos adopted much of the food, building techniques, and other traditions that the Mexicans had developed. The results of these practices, as well as of Anglo-Mexican intermarriage, are seen today in Tucson's cultural mix.

**wars and the Wild West:** Confederate cavalry under the command of Captain Sherrod Hunter captured Tucson in Feb. 1862. Union troops led by Colonel James Carleton marched in from California and clashed in Apr. with the Confederates at Picacho Pass, about 42 miles NW of Tucson. After this battle, the most westerly of the Civil War, the outnumbered Confederates retreated. The 1860s were Tucson's Wild West days. Shootouts were frequent and men rarely ventured onto the dusty streets unarmed. Still, the town prospered after the war and was the territorial capital from 1867 to 1877. By 1880, when the

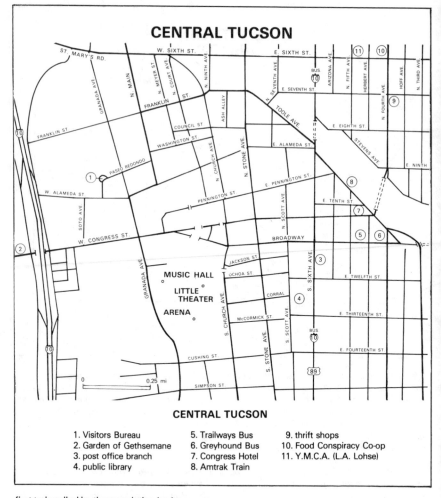

# CENTRAL TUCSON

## CENTRAL TUCSON

1. Visitors Bureau
2. Garden of Gethsemane
3. post office branch
4. public library

5. Trailways Bus
6. Greyhound Bus
7. Congress Hotel
8. Amtrak Train

9. thrift shops
10. Food Conspiracy Co-op
11. Y.M.C.A. (L.A. Lohse)

first train rolled in, the population had grown to over 7,000. The Arizona Territorial University opened its doors in 1891 on land donated by a saloonkeeper and a pair of gamblers. Davis-Monthan Field brought Tucson into the Air Age and was an important training base during WW II. Many of the airmen and others passing through the city during those hectic years returned to settle here. With its new post-war industries and growth of tourism, the "Old Pueblo" has been booming ever since.

## WALKING TOUR

**northern portion:** The historic walking tour is a good way to see the Spanish and Mexican legacies of Tucson. A convenient place to start is the **Metropolitan Tucson Convention & Visitors Bureau,** located in the restored Manning House on Paseo Redondo (on the W edge of downtown). Colonel Levi Howell Manning, a former mayor of the city, built the house in

1907. Pick up a visitors' guide and get the latest on cultural happenings, sights, recreation, restaurants, and motels. The office is open Mon. to Fri. 0830-1700; tel. 624-1817. It's closed on weekends but literature is placed outside.

Next, stop at the **Edward Nye Fish House.** Built by a rich businessman in 1868, it has 15-foot ceilings and solid adobe walls more than 2½ feet thick. The Fish House now contains the Tucson Museum of Art Library. Its extensive collection of art books, magazines, and slides is open to the public Mon. to Fri. 1000-1500 (closed in Aug.). Ask to see the Fish Room, restored to its 1870's appearance. The old family photo album can be viewed. Next door to the Fish House on the N side is the **Stevens House,** part of which dates from 1856. Hiram Sanford Stevens was a good friend of Edward Fish, and much of Tucson's social life centered around their homes. The Stevens House is now the Janos Restaurant. The **Tucson Museum of Art,** behind the Stevens House, is noted for Spanish colonial paintings and furnishings and for pre-Columbian artifacts from Latin America, all in the permanent collection. Special exhibitions frequently appear too. The gift shop sells books, cards, and local crafts. Open Tue. to Sat. 1000-1700, Sun. 1300-1700, closed Mon.; admission is $2 adult, $1 children age 12-17.

Of adobe construction, **La Casa Cordova** is one of the oldest houses in the area, dating from about 1848. Enter the courtyard from the back. Interior exhibits show life in the 1850s. It's maintained by the adjacent Tucson Museum of Art and open the same hours; free. Next is **Old Town Artisans,** a shop displaying art and crafts by more than 150 artists representing Western, Indian, and Mexican styles. The sculptures, paintings, prints, and crafts are worth a look even if you're not buying. The front 2 rooms were built between 1862 and 1875 with adobe walls and saguaro-rib ceilings. Open Mon. to Sat. 1000-1700, Sun. 1200-1700. The Courtyard Cafe serves soups, salads, and sandwiches. Lunch is also served in the Barrel Stave Room (closed Sun.). You can find cheesecake and other goodies in the Old Town Bake Shop.

Across the street is the **Romero House.** Built in the 1860s and modified many times since, the house is now used by the Tucson Museum of Art School. It's located on the site of part of the original Presidio wall. A plaque marks the NW corner of this wall at the corner of Washington St. and Main Ave., one block W of Romero House. Across Washington is the **Sam Hughes House.** Hughes came to Tucson for his health in 1858, joining the handful of Anglos here, and became an important businessman and developer of early Tucson. He moved into this house with his bride in 1864, but had to expand it considerably over the years for his 15 children. He and his wife lived to celebrate their 50th wedding anniversary here. The house is now a series of garden apartments.

The **Steinfeld Mansion** is a Spanish mission-style brick and stucco house dating from the turn of the century. It's known for having one of Tucson's first bathtubs with piped-in water. The mansion has been restored and is now used for offices. Heading 2 blocks E to Court Ave., you'll find the house built by French stonemason Jules le Flein, now the **El Charro** Mexican restaurant. Le Flein came to Tucson in the late 1800s to remodel the St. Augustine Cathedral. In 1900 he built this house for his family with volcanic stone from Sentinel Peak. Next, if you're planning on exploring more of Arizona, the Southwest Parks and Monuments Association Bookshop is a worthwhile stop. It has publications on the Southwest's history,

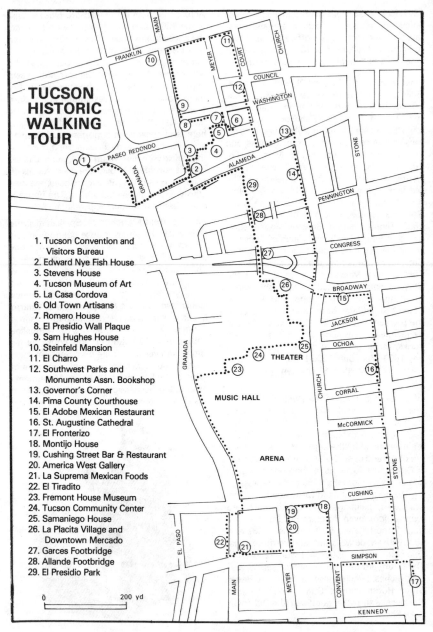

# TUCSON HISTORIC WALKING TOUR

1. Tucson Convention and Visitors Bureau
2. Edward Nye Fish House
3. Stevens House
4. Tucson Museum of Art
5. La Casa Cordova
6. Old Town Artisans
7. Romero House
8. El Presidio Wall Plaque
9. Sam Hughes House
10. Steinfeld Mansion
11. El Charro
12. Southwest Parks and Monuments Assn. Bookshop
13. Governor's Corner
14. Pima County Courthouse
15. El Adobe Mexican Restaurant
16. St. Augustine Cathedral
17. El Fronterizo
18. Montijo House
19. Cushing Street Bar & Restaurant
20. America West Gallery
21. La Suprema Mexican Foods
22. El Tiradito
23. Fremont House Museum
24. Tucson Community Center
25. Samaniego House
26. La Placita Village and Downtown Mercado
27. Garces Footbridge
28. Allande Footbridge
29. El Presidio Park

0    200 yd

Indians, wildlife, flora, hiking trails, and other topics. Open Tues. to Fri. 1130-1730 and Sat. 1000-1600. The bookshop is in the old Stork's Nest building, built in 1883 and converted to a maternity center in 1922.

Turning L on Alameda, you'll come to **Governor's Corner.** Louis C. Hughes, Territorial Governor in 1893-1896, had an adobe house on this site. The Valley National Bank building here now has a painting of this street corner as it appeared in 1893. Visitors are welcome to come in and see it during office hours. **Pima County Courthouse,** a colorful building constructed in 1928, replaced earlier structures of 1868 and 1881. The present courthouse is a mix of Southwest, Spanish, and Moorish architecture. Upstairs, a portion of the original Presidio wall is preserved in a glass case—find it in the S wing of the 2nd floor, just before the Justice Courts.

**southern portion:** Go S 2½ blocks for **El Adobe Mexican Restaurant and Old Adobe Patio.** The restaurant and several small

*St. Augustine Cathedral*

shops occupy the Charles O. Brown House. Brown owned the Congress Hall Saloon, a popular watering hole and gambling spot for politicians of the day. The oldest part of the house (on Jackson St.) dates from about 1858. Between 1868 and 1877 Brown built on Broadway (then Camp St.) and connected the two sections with an attractive patio and garden. Continuing 2 blocks down Stone, you'll come to **St. Augustine Cathedral,** constructed in 1896. Its impressive sandstone facade, fashioned after the Cathedral of Queretaro in Mexico, was added in the late 1920s, as were the stained-glass windows. A bronze statue of St. Augustine stands watch above the doorway with a saguaro, yucca, horned toad and other symbols of the desert.

Four more blocks down Stone is the former newspaper office **El Fronterizo.** Carlos Y. Velasco began publishing a Spanish-language newspaper here about 1878. Around on Cushing St. is **Montijo House,** which has preserved the name of the well-known Mexican ranching family that once owned it. The house was completed during the Civil War and remodeled in the 1890s in an ornate Victorian style. The **Cushing Street Bar and Restaurant** has an attractive 1880's decor. Joseph Ferrin operated a general store and lived here about 100 years ago. Next door is **America West Gallery,** the home of rancher Francisco Carrillo in the 1860s. The well-preserved house contains exotic antiques and primitive art from many countries. The patio has a collection of Mexican millstones. Around the corner on Main is La Suprema Mexican Foods. Pick up fresh tortillas or just watch them being made.

**El Tiradito,** or "Wishing Shrine," commemorates a tragic love triangle. The story has many versions, but one account tells of a love affair between young Juan Olivera and his mother-in-law. Juan was caught and killed by his father-in-law on this spot in 1880. Because he had sinned, the dead Juan could not be taken to the church cemetery, and was buried where he fell. Pious people lit candles and prayed for his soul at the site. Later, parents prayed for their errant daughters at the shrine. The custom then developed that anyone could light a candle on the grave and make a wish. If the candle burned to its base, the wish would

*El Tiradito*

be granted. The shrine is said to be the only one in North America dedicated to a sinner.

The **Fremont House Museum,** an adobe house constructed by the Jose Maria Soza family in the 1850s, was saved in 1969 when surrounding houses were torn down to make room for the new Tucson Community Center. The old structure was named for the 5th Territorial Governor, John C. Fremont, who lived here in 1881. Fremont received his post as a political favor from President Hayes in 1878, but showed more interest in mining ventures and traveling back East than in dealing with the Arizona legislature. Mounting protests by irate citizens forced his resignation in 1881. Inside you can see how a wealthy Tucson family lived in the 1880s. Tour guides point out and explain the architectural features of the house. Four different types of ceiling are used: saguaro rib, ocotillo, painted cloth, and wood paneling. Open Wed. to Sat. 1000-1600; donation; 151 S. Granada Ave.; tel. 622-0956. A guided tour of El Presidio Historic District is led by the Fremont House Museum on Sat. mornings, Nov. to Mar., lasting about 2 hours; $2. Call for reservations and time.

The building on the R as you leave the Fremont House is the Tucson Community Center Music Hall. Walk up the steps alongside it into an oasis of gardens, trees, and fountains. The small building ahead (E) is the Little Theatre. To the R is the giant Arena where sporting events are held. Just beyond the Little Theatre is **Samaniego House,** built in the 1840s. Around 1880 it was purchased by Mariano G. Samaniego, a stage-line owner, rancher, and local politician. His well-preserved house, with adobe walls and saguaro-ribbed ceilings, is now a restaurant.

Follow the map around through **La Placita Village,** a modern group of offices and shops designed to resemble a Mexican marketplace. On Fridays from 0900-1500, La Placita Village becomes an open-air market offering produce, flowers, handicrafts, and food stalls. Continue on the **Garcés Footbridge** across Congress St., then the **Allande Footbridge** across Pennington St. to **El Presidio Park.** These modern bridges honor early Spaniards. Francisco Garcés, an explorer and Franciscan priest, was the first missionary to visit the Pima Indian village at the base of Sentinel Peak. Pedro Allande, first resident commander of the Tucson Presidio, once led a spirited defense against 600 warring Apaches. Despite a severe leg wound, he continued to direct his 20 presidial soldiers and saved the settlement. El Presidio Park was Plaza de Las Armas of the original Presidio. Around 200 years ago, soldiers drilled on this spot and held holiday fiestas. The soldiers have gone but residents still have fiestas. The park is a quiet spot to rest and enjoy the sculptures and fountains. The Visitors Bureau is just a short walk away, returning you to your starting point.

**other sights near downtown:** When Felix Lucero lay wounded on a WW I battlefield, he made a vow to create religious statues if he recovered. He did, and life-size sculptures of the Last Supper and other subjects can be seen at the Garden of Gethsemane, on the NE corner of W. Congress St. and Bonita Ave. near I-10. Open 0900-1600 daily; free.

You can't miss "A" Mountain, a small peak just W of downtown. In earlier days it was a

*Felix Lucero's Garden of Gethsemane*

lookout point for hostile Indians, which explains its original name—Sentinel Peak. The giant "A" dates from 23 Oct. 1915, when the local university football team beat Cal State Pomona in a 7-3 victory. Sports fans then headed over to paint on the "A." It became a tradition, and every year the freshman students whitewash the giant letter (and themselves) for all to see. To enjoy the panorama from the top, drive W on Congress St. and turn L at the sign to Sentinel Peak Road.

## UNIVERSITY OF ARIZONA

In 1885, the 13th Territorial Legislature awarded Tucson $25,000 to establish Arizona's first university. Most townspeople didn't think much of the idea. They wanted to have the territorial capital (awarded to Prescott), or at least the territorial insane asylum (awarded to Phoenix and worth $100,000). It was left to a handful of determined citizens to get the school built. The walls started to go up after land was donated a mile from town by a saloonkeeper and 2 gamblers, but money ran out before the roof was finished. A federal loan put the roof on, and the university opened in 1891. Classrooms, library, offices, and dorms were all in one lone university building, today known as Old Main. The first year saw 6 faculty and 32 students, nearly all of whom were in the Preparatory School. (Like many other parts of the U.S. at the time, Arizona suffered from a lack of secondary as well as higher education.) The university has expanded to a present population of over 36,000 students and a faculty of about 2,100. Hundreds of programs are offered by 13 colleges and 6 schools. Visitors can enjoy theater and concert performances, the Flandrau Planetarium, sporting events, and several museums. For information, call the University switchboard; tel. 621-2211. The U. of A. campus is about a mile E of downtown; take Sun Tran Bus #1.

**Student Union:** This building, in the center of the campus, is the best place to meet students and see what's going on. You'll find cafeterias, a variety of cafes, student services, and recreation areas here. In the basement, the Cellar is often jumping to live music during lunch hour. Sam's Place is busy with students playing pocket billiards, table tennis, and other games. Travelers might want to check the Ride Board to see if someone is going their way. The Hiking Center has a good stock of topo maps for local trails. Mail home a card at the post office, or pick up film at the Photo Shop. The first floor has several places to eat, an Information Desk, and local art in Union Gallery. A cafeteria and the Cactus Lounge—a comfortable place to relax despite its name—are on the 2nd floor. Union Club, on the 3rd floor, has a fancier restaurant (lunch only) and sweeping views of the campus and mountains. Gallagher Theatre, on the E end of the building, shows popular

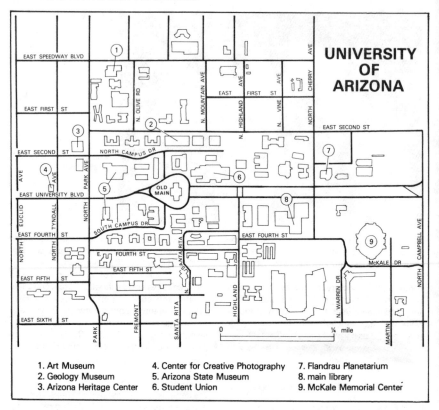

# UNIVERSITY OF ARIZONA

1. Art Museum
2. Geology Museum
3. Arizona Heritage Center
4. Center for Creative Photography
5. Arizona State Museum
6. Student Union
7. Flandrau Planetarium
8. main library
9. McKale Memorial Center

movies nightly. On the W end is the Campus Bookstore, well stocked with textbooks, general reading, school supplies, and U. of A. clothing.

**Arizona Historical Society Museum:** If you can visit only one of the dozens of historical museums in the state, make it this one! Beginning with prehistoric Indians, the Museum takes you through all the periods of Arizona's early history: Spanish, Mexican, Mountain Men, Territorial, and Early Statehood. Displays are well illustrated and full of artifacts. Visitors of all ages enjoy the early 1900's copper mine exhibit, where they walk through a realistic mine complete with sound effects, and then come out to a giant ore stamper and other processing machinery. Period rooms and special exhibits are also carefully prepared. A gift shop

has a good selection of books and crafts. The headquarters of the Arizona Historical Society is here, with a research library open to the public. Open Mon. to Sat. 1000-1600, Sun. 1200-1600 (library closes at 1300 on Sat. and all day Sun.); donation. The Museum is located at 929 E. 2nd St. and Park Ave; tel. 628-5774.

**Arizona State Museum:** A good place to learn about archaeology and Arizona's Indians, both prehistoric and modern. There's also a variety of natural history displays. The gift shop sells related books and Indian crafts. Open Mon. to Sat. 0900-1700, Sun. 1400-1700; free; tel. 621-6302. Located on campus at the corner of E. University Blvd. and N. Park Ave. The museum is in 2 buildings—exhibits are in the S one; library and offices in the N, across E. University Boulevard.

the "Cellar" at the
Student/Union

**Flandrau Planetarium:** Tucson has earned the title "Astronomy Capital of the World." With 45 telescopes operating in the city and surrounding peaks, astronomy is a major industry here—worth $40 million annually. Planetarium exhibit halls display astrolabes and early telescopes, meteorites, lunar specimens, video excerpts from Apollo lunar programs, and photos of planets, the moon, stars, and nebula. A 16-inch telescope is available for stargazing on clear evenings. Dramatic planetarium shows are held most afternoons and evenings. Call for program; tel. 621-4556. Open Mon. 1300-1600, Tue. to Fri. 1000-1600 & 1900-2100, Sat. & Sun. 1300-1700 & 1900-2100. Exhibits free; shows $3.50 adult, $2.75 students, U of A staff, seniors, and children 3-18 (no one under 3 allowed). A gift shop sells books, posters, and souvenirs related to astronomy. Located on campus at the corner of N. Cherry Ave. and E. University Blvd.; parking is available across E. University Blvd. (reach from N. Campbell Ave.).

**Geological Museum:** See rare and wondrous minerals, some very delicate with unbelievable colors. Much of the collection comes from Arizona mines. There are fossils, too: giant mastodon skulls, dinosaur tracks, flying reptiles, fish, and birds. Open Mon. to Fri. 0830-1700 when school is in session; free. Located in the Geology/Mineralogy Building on E. 2nd St. (NW of the Student Union) on campus.

**University Art Museum:** The diverse collection spans the years from the Middle Ages through the Renaissance to the present. Changing exhibitions come from the University or other institutions. A gift shop sells books, magazines, posters, and cards. Open during school year Mon. to Sat. 0900-1700, Sun. 1200-1700; and in summer (1 June to 15 Aug.) Mon. to Sat. 1000-1530, Sun. 1200-1600; free. Located on campus at E. Speedway Blvd. (near N. Park Ave.).

a burned-out building near the University

# WEST OF DOWNTOWN

**Arizona-Sonora Desert Museum:** This is a world-famous living museum of the animals and plants native to the Sonoran Desert of Arizona, the Mexican state of Sonora, and the Gulf of California. Meet rattlesnakes, gila monsters, scorpions, and other desert dwellers face to face (with glass separating you and them, of course). Watch frolicking otters and busy beavers through underwater panels. Try to spot the birds in the walk-in aviary—not as easy as you'd expect—desert birds often blend well with their surroundings. Mountain lions, bighorn sheep, javelina, and over 200 other types of animals dwell in almost-natural sur-

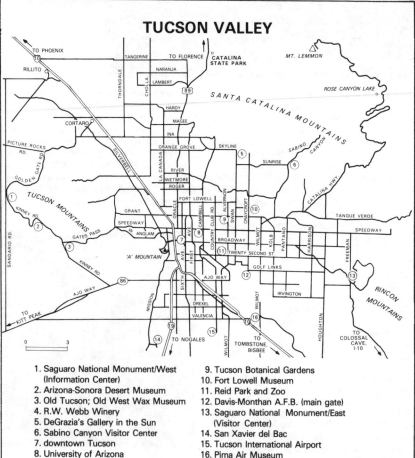

**TUCSON VALLEY**

1. Saguaro National Monument/West (Information Center)
2. Arizona-Sonora Desert Museum
3. Old Tucson; Old West Wax Museum
4. R.W. Webb Winery
5. DeGrazia's Gallery in the Sun
6. Sabino Canyon Visitor Center
7. downtown Tucson
8. University of Arizona
9. Tucson Botanical Gardens
10. Fort Lowell Museum
11. Reid Park and Zoo
12. Davis-Monthan A.F.B. (main gate)
13. Saguaro National Monument/East (Visitor Center)
14. San Xavier del Bac
15. Tucson International Airport
16. Pima Air Museum

roundings. Desert flora are well represented and labeled in the gardens. A realistic limestone cave and earth science exhibits take you deep underground and far back in time.

Bring a sunhat and good walking shoes — you'll need half a day to see all the exhibits. Animals are more active in the morning, making it a good time to visit. Special programs are scheduled daily to introduce you to some of the creatures living here. The setting is superb, with great views over the Avra Valley. Visible to the SW are Baboquivari Peak (7,730 feet), sacred to the Papago Indians, and the nearer Kitt Peak (6,875 feet), site of important astronomical observatories. A gift shop and snack bar are near the entrance. A picnic area is ¼ mile away. The Desert Museum is open daily 0830-sunset (0700-sunset in summer); $6 adult, $1 ages 6-12; tel. 883-2702. No pets. The museum is located in Tucson Mountain Park, 14 miles W of Tucson. Take Speedway Blvd. west across Gates Pass. Large RVs and trailer-rigs should take Ajo and Kinney roads.

**Saguaro National Monument/West:** This half of the Monument is smaller but has denser and more vigorous stands of saguaro (pronounced sah-WAH-roe) than the E half (on the other side of Tucson). Stop at the small Information Center for maps and hiking info. A short (100-yard) nature trail beside the Center introduces the unique saguaro and other plants of the Sonoran Desert. The 9-mile Bajada Loop Drive takes in some of the scenic countryside. Or go day hiking on some of the 16 miles of trails. Wasson Peak (4,687 feet) is a popular day hike via the King Canyon Trail. Park Service rangers lead weekend hikes in the cooler months. The Information Center is open daily 0800-1700; tel. 883-6366. To reach the Monument from Tucson, continue 2 miles past the Arizona-Sonora Desert Museum described above.

**Old Tucson:** The West was won many times over at this famous movie studio. It started back in 1939 as the setting for the Columbia Pictures film "Arizona." More than 100 features have been filmed here, including "Dirty Dingus McGee," "Rio Lobo," and "Death of a Gunfighter." The well-known TV shows "Bonanza," "Gunsmoke," "Little House on the

*desert bighorn sheep stands guard at Arizona-Sonora Desert Museum*

*Old Tucson*

Prairie," and others were shot here too. Old Tucson is a replica of Tucson in the 1860s with weathered adobe buildings, board sidewalks, and dusty streets. Stuntmen wear period clothing and stage blazing gunfights several times a day. Soundstage tours, the "Iron Door Mine," and stagecoach and train rides provide other excitement. Open daily 0900-1700; $7 adult, $4.50 children age 4-11; tel. 883-0100. Located 12 miles W of Tucson in Tucson Mountain Park. Drive west on Speedway Blvd. (not suited for large rigs) or take Ajo and Kinney roads.

**Old West Wax Museum:** About 40 wax ghosts of historical figures and movie greats inhabit this small museum next door to Old Tucson. Open daily 0900-1800; $2.10 adult, $1.05 children age 7-12; tel. 883-4203.

# NORTH OF DOWNTOWN

## SANTA CATALINA MOUNTAINS

The Santa Catalinas rise from the N edge of Tucson in ragged ridges of rock to the lush woodlands of 9,157-foot Mt. Lemmon. Hikers can choose among 150 miles of trail—ranging from easy strolls to extremely difficult climbs. Sabino Canyon and the Mt. Lemmon Highway (see below) are the easiest areas to visit in the mountains. The Santa Catalina topo map by the Southern Arizona Hiking Club shows all the main trails, distances, and trailheads. Pick one up ($2.65) at a U.S. Forest Service office or a hiking store. *Arizona Trails* by David Mazel has good writeups of trails in the Pusch Ridge Wilderness of the southwestern Catalinas, including Sabino Canyon.

**history:** In 1697, the tireless Jesuit priest Father Eusebio Francisco Kino visited a Papago village in what's now Tucson. He named it and the high ranges to the N and E "Santa Catarina." Spanish prospectors found gold in Cañada del Oro. They also reportedly mined gold in the Mine with the Iron Door, and silver in La Esmeralda, both "lost" mines lying somewhere in the range. Raiding Apache discouraged mining until the late 1870s, when Anglo gold-seekers began placer operations in Cañada del Oro and tunneled into the hillsides. Most of the mines were in the NE part of the mountains. Mt. Lemmon is named after botanist Sara Lemmon who, with her husband John, discovered many new species of plants on their 1881 expedition to the summit. As trails into the mountains improved, the citizens of Tucson more frequently headed to the hills for the cool air and scenery. The highway to the top was completed in 1949, built largely by federal prisoners.

## SABINO CANYON

A desert oasis in the southern foothills of the Santa Catalina Mountains. Sabino Creek begins its journey on the slopes of Mt. Lemmon and bounces down through the canyon, supporting lush greenery and trees in which deer, javelina, coyotes, birds, and other animals find food and shelter. In the Visitor Center, at the entrance to the canyon, you'll see exhibits about the canyon and Santa Catalina Mountains and you can buy books and maps about the area. Naturalist-led walks might be scheduled, or take the self-guiding nature trail behind the Center. The Visitor Center is open weekdays 0800-1630 and weekends 0830-1630, free; tel. 749-3223 for recorded announcements.

The road through Sabino Canyon winds in 3.8 miles, crossing the creek many times. Private motor vehicles are prohibited beyond the Visitor Center to protect the beauty and peacefulness of the area. You can explore the canyon by hiking, bicycling, or hopping on the shuttle bus. The shuttle leaves the Visitor Center daily every 30 min. from 0900-1630, except midsummer when departures are hourly from 0900-1600. Fares are $4 adult, $1.25 ages 3-12. You can get on and off as often as you choose at any of the 9 stops. Hiking, birding, picnicking, and swimming are the big attractions. The Forest Service provides picnic areas and restrooms, though drinking water is found only at the Visitor Center and the first 2 stops. Camping isn't allowed in the canyon; to camp, backpackers must hike at least ¼ mile past the end of the road or ¼ mile past Seven Falls.

Hikers have a choice of many destinations at the last stop: back to the Visitor Center via the Phone Line Trail high on the E slopes of Sabino Canyon (5½ miles OW), to Lower Bear Canyon via Seven Falls (12 miles OW), up the West Fork of Sabino Canyon to Hutch's Pool (8 miles RT), or to Mt. Lemmon's summit (13 hard miles OW). Enjoy the special magic of Sabino Canyon on a moonlight ride, offered several times a month, Mar. to December. Moonlight Shuttle fare is $3 adult, $1.50 children; reservations needed: tel. 749-2861.

**Bear Canyon:** Another shuttle bus leaves the Visitor Center for the 2½ mile ride E to Bear Canyon, a picnic area and trailhead for the Catalinas. Seven Falls, a series of cascades 2 miles up the Bear Canyon, is the most popular hiking destination. The good scenery doesn't begin until you leave the road, so there's no point in taking this shuttle unless you'll be hiking. Bear Canyon shuttle leaves hourly every day from 0900-1600; fare is $2 adult, $1 ages 3-12. Sabino Canyon is 13 miles NE of downtown Tucson. Take Tanque Verde Rd. to Sabino Canyon Rd. and turn N 4½ miles to the canyon entrance.

## MOUNT LEMMON HIGHWAY

In just an hour you can drive from the lower Sonoran Desert Zone to a Canadian Zone forest. Meadows bloom with wildflowers in spring and summer. Enjoy camping, picnicking, and hiking in the warmer months, skiing in

*Sabino Canyon*

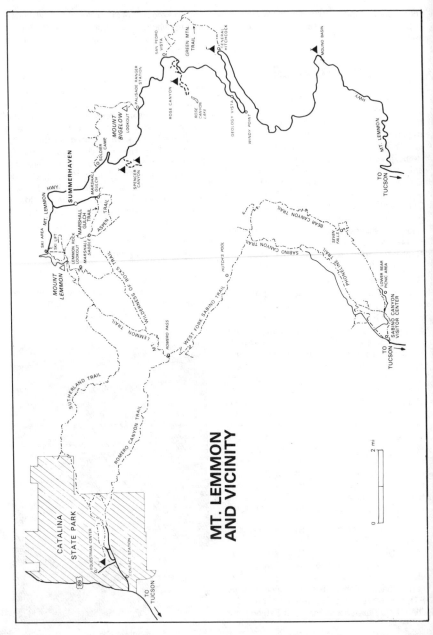

MT. LEMMON
AND VICINITY

winter. The 40-mile drive from Tucson leaves the saguaro, palo verde, and cholla behind, passes through juniper and pinyon, and enters pine forests at about 7,000 feet. Firs and aspen cling to the cool north-facing slopes above 8,000 feet.

**sights and campgrounds:** Molino Basin, 18 miles from Tucson, has the closest campground. It's open all year (elev. 4,500 feet) but doesn't always have drinking water; free. General Hitchcock Campground, 21 miles from Tucson, is higher (elev. 6,000 feet), and is usually open all year. Water is not always available; free. In another 2 miles you'll come to Windy Point, whose sweeping panorama of the southern foothills and Tucson is pretty day and night. Geology Vista, one more mile, has a good view to the SE and a sign describing the forces that created these mountains. Rose Canyon Lake, 33 miles from Tucson, has camping and trout fishing. It's open mid Apr. to mid Oct.; has drinking water; $5/night. You can see many mountain ranges rising in the E from San Pedro Vista, ½ mile beyond Rose Canyon turnoff. A sign identifies the ranges. Green Mountain Trail connects San Pedro Vista with General Hitchcock Campground. Allow 3 hours for the 4-mile (OW) hike.

At Palisade Ranger Station, 36 miles from Tucson, you can hike to the top of 8,550-foot Mt. Bigelow, a 1½ mile RT climb of 600 feet. The Butterfly Trail also begins at this trailhead and winds through ponderosa pine, Douglas fir, and juniper-oak woodlands to Soldier Camp, 5¾ miles to the NW; allow 4-5 hours between trailheads. Spencer Canyon Campground, 38 miles from Tucson, is open early May to the end of Oct.; has drinking water; $5/night. Soldier Camp is 39 miles from Tucson and ¼- mile N of the highway. Cavalry troops from Fort Lowell camped here in the 1870s while tracking rebellious Apache. Later the soldiers used the site as a summer resort.

You'll come to a fork in the highway about 41 miles from Tucson; keep L ½ mile for the tiny village of Summerhaven or R one mile to Ski Valley. Mt. Lemmon Alpine Lodge, in Summerhaven, has just 4 rooms ($45 d) and you'll need reservations at least 2 weeks in advance (Box 693, Mt. Lemmon, AZ 85619; tel. 576-1500). Its

restaurant serves "home-style" breakfast, lunch, and dinner. A pub has live entertainment on Sat. nights, Fri. too in the summer. Limited groceries are sold at the Lodge, but no gasoline (fill up before leaving Tucson). Horseback riding in the Catalinas can be arranged by Mt. Lemmon Alpine Lodge; costs range from $10 for a one-hour ride, to $45 all day, to $95 overnight with meals. You can often rent summer cabins tucked in the woods; contact Mt. Lemmon Realty, Box 1, Mt. Lemmon, AZ 85619; tel. 576-1333 or 576-1300.

**trail:** The 4-mile Aspen Loop Trail, beginning near Summerhaven, is a good introduction to the high country. Begin at Marshall Gulch Picnic Area, one mile S of Summerhaven. A gate blocks the road so you'll have to park and walk the last half mile. A sign, "Aspen Trail #93, Marshall Saddle 2.5," marks the start. The trail climbs through aspen, fir, and ponderosa pine forests with some good views. At Marshall Saddle turn R down Marshall Gulch 1 mile back to the picnic area.

**ski:** Mount Lemmon Ski Valley is the southernmost ski area in the United States. The double-chair lift takes summer visitors and winter skiers from 8,200 to 9,100 feet. Skiers have a choice of 16 runs, including a "bunny slope" for beginners. Rentals (skis, boots, and poles) cost $12, lessons are $16/hour (private) or $10/2 hours (group), and lift tickets cost $18/day ($12 for children 12 and under). You can get a recording of current ski and road conditions by calling tel. 576-1400 (call tel. 576-1321 for the business office). In summer you can take the lift up to enjoy the views and cool forests; $3.50 ($1.50 children 12 and under). A hiking trail also goes to the top through fir and aspen forests from the bottom of the ski lift. It's unsigned, so ask someone to point out the start. Season is about May to Oct.; allow 2-3 hours for the 2 miles RT. Several more hiking trails radiate from the summit, accessible by trail or the ski lift. The Iron Door Restaurant across the highway is open daily for lunch and dinner and on weekends for brunch. The highway continues past Ski Valley to an infra-red observatory near the top of Mt. Lemmon, but both the road and observatory are likely to be closed to visitors.

# EAST OF DOWNTOWN

**Reid Park Zoo:** Small but good collection of flamingos, lions, tigers, hippos, polar bears, and other exotic life. The zoo is active in breeding rare animals. Open daily 0930-1630; $1.50 adult, $.50 ages 5-14; tel. 791-4022. Reid Park is 3½ miles E of downtown. Enter from Randolph Way off either E. Broadway or 22nd Street. (Sun Tran Bus #7, 11, 14, or 17)

**Tucson Botanical Gardens:** Plant lovers wanting to see a variety of flora, both native and exotic, will enjoy a visit. Open Mon. to Fri. 0900-1600, Sat. 1000-1400, and Sun. 1200-1600; closed weekends June-Aug.; admission $1. Tours are given on weekends during the cooler months; tel. 326-9255. The gardens are about 6 miles NE of downtown at 2150 N. Alvernon Way, just S of Grant Road. (Sun Tran Bus #9).

**Fort Lowell Museum:** When the U.S. Army was chasing troublesome Apache in the 1860s, the troops needed a supply base. The Army established one near Tucson in 1862 and later named it Camp Lowell in honor of an officer killed in the Civil War. The camp moved to this site in 1873 and became a fort in 1879. It was a busy place during the Geronimo campaigns

until the famous Apache chief surrendered in Sept. 1886. With the Indian wars finally over in Arizona, the Army no longer needed this fort and abandoned it in 1891. The commanding officer's quarters have been rebuilt and are now furnished as they were in the 1880s. Exhibits of maps, documents, and photos show life of the frontier soldier. Ruins of the adobe hospital and other buildings are nearby. Open Wed. to Sat. 1000-1600; free. The museum is in Old Fort Lowell Park about 8 miles NE of downtown, off Craycroft Road. (Sun Tran Bus #34)

**Davis-Monthan Air Force Base:** Curious about what's going on at the local base? Tours are given twice weekly by an informative Air Force guide. Charles Lindburgh dedicated Davis-Monthan in 1927 as one of the country's first municipal airports. During WW II it became a training ground for crews of B-17 bombers and other aircraft. The base now has 2 distinct operations: one part trains pilots in combat aircraft, while the other, known as AMARC (Aerospace Maintenance And Regeneration Center), stores a staggering number of surplus planes. The dry climate of Tucson is ideal for both activities. The WW II birds have all left for museums but a great variety of

*scrapyard at Davis-Monthan A.F.B.*

*F-104 at Pima Air Museum*

postwar fighters, transports, and bombers stretches for blocks. The rows of giant B-52 bombers are quite a sight. Bus tours (free) are given on Mon. and Wed. at 0900, lasting 1 to 1½ hours. A special 4-hour tour of AMARC is given on the 2nd Sat. of every month. Some walking is involved on this one. Call the Public Affairs Division as far in advance as possible to make reservations and to check on tour times; tel. 748-4570. Tours start near the main gate at Craycroft Rd. and Golf Links Rd., 7 miles SE of downtown. Ask where to park. (Sun Tran Bus #30 or 34)

**Pima Air Museum:** More than 130 historic aircraft display the dramatic advances in aviation technology. Many famous planes from WW II through the Vietnam era can be seen. The Norden bombsight, cut-away engines, uniforms, and other memorabilia are also exhibited. A gift shop sells aircraft models, books, and posters. Open daily 0900-1700; $4 adult, $2 ages 10-17, under 10 free. This museum is about 12 miles SE from downtown. Take I-10 East, exit at Valencia Rd., turn L and go 2 miles.

**Saguaro National Monument/East:** This is the older and larger part of the Monument. The Visitor Center, just inside the boundary, has exhibits of desert geology, ecology, flora, and fauna. A 10-min. slide program is shown every half hour. Special programs and walks are given on weekends in the winter months. The cactus garden has a variety of labeled desert plants. Saguaro grow very slowly, taking about 25 years to grow just 2 feet, and need protective shade. Their arms don't appear until they are about 75 years old. The old-timers live over 200 years and reach 50 feet. Creamy white blossoms, the state flower, appear in early May. The fruit, which matures in midsummer, resembles a flower with shiny black seeds surrounded by a bright red shell. For many years, grazing cattle cut back the palo verde and other shade plants needed by the young saguaro. The cattle were removed in 1958, but it will be a long time before the saguaro forest recovers. Today it has only very old and very young specimens.

The 8-mile Cactus Forest Drive winds through foothills of the Rincon Mountains with many fine views. After 2½ miles, look for the Desert Ecology Trail on the left. On this 485-yard trail you can learn how plants and animals cope with the environment. Freeman Homestead Nature Trail begins on the R, 200 yards after you turn onto the spur road to Javelina Picnic Area. The Freeman Trail is a one-mile hiking loop through groves of huge saguaro and along a wash. Javelina Picnic Area has shaded picnic tables and toilets, but no water. The Tanque Verde Ridge Trail begins here and climbs into the rugged Rincon Mountains. Mica Mt., at 8,666 feet the highest peak, is

17½ miles away by trail. *Arizona Trails* by David Mazel has detailed hiking info and maps for for this and several other routes in the Rincons. Spring and fall are the best hiking times. A free permit from the Visitor Center is needed for overnight hikes. The Cactus Forest Drive is open daily 0800 to sunset and the Visitor Center daily 0800-1700; tel. 296-8576. The Saguaro National Monument/East is just off Old Spanish Trail, about 16 miles E of downtown. Bicyclists enjoy riding the scenic loop, which can be reached from Tucson on the bike path along Old Spanish Trail.

**Colossal Cave:** A dry limestone cave with authentic outlaw history. The tour guide will point out the large dusty formations and explain the geology, but won't tell where the $60,000 in gold is hidden! More than 6 miles of passageway have been mapped so far. The tour covers only ¾ mile, but many steps have to be climbed up and down. Tours leave every ½ hour and last about 45 minutes. A snack bar and gift shop are outside the entrance; a free campground is nearby. Open daily Oct. to Mar. 0900-1700 (until 1800 Sun. and holidays), daily Apr. to Sept. 0800-1800 (until 1900 Sun. & holidays). Admission: $4 adult, $3 ages 11-16, $1.50 ages 6-11; tel. 791-7677. The cave is 22 miles E of downtown Tucson. Take I-10 east to Vail-Wentworth Exit #279, then 7 miles north; or take the Old Spanish Trail to Saguaro National Monument/East, then 12 miles south.

**R.W. Webb Winery:** Arizona wine? Yes, and this commercial winery is the state's largest. You can learn about wine making on tours and tastings here lasting 30-45 min.; $1 charge. Open Mon. to Sat. 1000-1700 and Sun. 1200-1700; tel. 629-9911. Located 14 miles SE of Tucson; take the I-10 Vail-Wentworth Exit #279, and turn E 1½ mile on the north frontage road.

# TUCSON ACCOMMODATIONS

**youth hostel and Y's:** A new hostel is planned for Tucson; contact the Phoenix Valley of the Sun Hostel for details: 1026 N. 9th St., Phoenix, AZ 85006; tel. 1-262-9439. The L.A. Lohse Memorial Y.M.C.A., 516 N. 5th Ave. (corner of 6th St.), has single rooms for men only: $11/night or $65/week, bath down hall; tel. 623-7727. Rates are same whether member or not. Location between the university and downtown is convenient. Guests get a discount to use the swimming pool, raquetball courts, and gym.

**bed and breakfasts:** These are private homes open to travelers in the European tradition. The degree of luxury varies, but the hosts offer a personal touch not found in the usual motels. Advance reservations are requested. Barbara's Bed and Breakfast (Box 13603, Tucson, AZ 85732; tel. 886-5847) has a list of about 20 B&Bs in Tucson and the foothills from $20-$40 s, $25-$60 d. Bed and Breakfast in Arizona, Inc. (4533 N. Scottsdale Rd., Suite 108, Scottsdale, AZ 85251; tel. 1-995-2831) has a list of 240 Arizona B&Bs including many in Tucson; prices range $20-$90 s, $30-$110 d. Mi Casa Su Casa (Box 950, Tempe, AZ 85281; tel. 1-990-0682) is Spanish for "My house is your house"; the statewide listings include a variety in the Tucson area with rates ranging $30-$100 s, $35-$125 d.

**hotels and motels:** Congress Hotel is located at 311 E. Congress St., just around the corner from Greyhound and Trailways terminals and across the street from Amtrak. It's the last of the good but inexpensive downtown hotels. Singles are $15.12, doubles are $18.36; all with bath and a/c; tel. 622-8848. Handy location but travelers have been bothered by street people after dark. Note that most downtown restaurants close by 1800. Tucson has over 50 other hotels, motels, and resorts near the freeway, downtown, at the airport, near the University, and scattered around the valley. Look for listings in: *The Official Visitors Guide to Metropolitan Tucson* and *Arizona Accommodations Directory* all free at the Tucson Convention and Visitors Bureau. The Yellow Pages are another source.

*Tucson and the Santa Catalina Mountains*

**guest ranches:** Enjoy western hospitality and activities with high-quality accommodations and food. Horseback riding, hiking, birding, socializing, and relaxing are popular with guests. Many ranches have a heated pool and tennis courts; a golf course is usually nearby. Meals are included with your stay and often served family style. Advance reservations are usually required. Most guest ranches close during the hot summers though a few remain open for hardy visitors. Add about 20% service charge and tax to the following prices.

Hacienda del Sol Ranch Resort offers luxury in the desert just NE of Tucson, 5601 N. Hacienda del Sol Rd. (off River Rd.), Tucson, AZ 85718; tel. 299-150l. Guests have tennis, a pool, riding stables, and other facilities; a 27-hole championship golf course is nearby. Daily rates range $85-$275 s, $148-$335 d; an 11 percent discount is given from early May to the end of September.

Tanque Verde Guest Ranch lies in the foothills of the Rincon Mountains 24 miles E of Tucson (near the end of Speedway), Route 8, Box 66, Tucson, AZ 85748; tel. 296-6275. The old ranch (founded 1862) has 2 pools, a spa, tennis courts, horseback riding and many other activities. Daily rates are $130-$165 s, $160-$195 d from 16 Dec. to 30 Apr.; and $100-$135 s, $130-$165 d the rest of the year.

Lazy K Bar Guest Ranch is an informal family ranch 16 miles NW of Tucson at the foot of the Tucson Mountains, 8401 N. Scenic Dr., Tucson, AZ 85743; tel. 297-0702. Guests can choose among horseback riding, swimming pool, tennis courts, other games, and hiking. Rates run $85-$95/day s, $130-$150/day d; a 3-day minimum stay is requested; closed July and August.

White Stallion Ranch sprawls over 3,000 acres 17 miles NW of Tucson, 9251 W. Twin Peaks

Rd., Route 28, Box 567, Tucson, AZ 85743; tel. 297-0252. The ranch has a pool, tennis courts, horseback riding, and varied ranch activities from early Oct. to the end of April; rates: $91-$109/day s, $142-$164 d.

Middleton Ranch is a small guest ranch 37 miles S of Tucson, Box 504, Amado, AZ 85640; tel. 398-2883. Guests enjoy horseback riding and a pool from Sept. to Apr.; $40-100/day s, $60-150 d.

Rancho de la Osa Guest Ranch dates back 200 years to the time it was a Spanish hacienda; it's located 68 miles SW of Tucson near the Mexican border, Box 1, Sasabe, AZ 85633; tel. 823-4257. Guests have horseback riding, a pool, and lots of peace and quiet. Weekly rates (6 nights) are $450 s, $780 d; lower rates apply mid-May to mid-October. Weekend rates (2 nights) are $135 s, $195 d. Open all year (elev. 3,800 feet).

**spa resort:** Canyon Ranch Spa is a health and fitness vacation resort offering an active program of exercise classes, tennis, raquetball, swimming, hiking, biking, yoga, and meditation. Gourmet meals are of natural ingredients. The 28-acre grounds are NE of town (near Sabino Canyon) at 8600 E. Rockcliff Rd., Tucson, AZ 85715; tel. 749-9000, or (800) 742-9000. A 4-night package costs $1,045 s or $845/person d. Seven-night packages run $1,840 s or $1,510/person d. There's a 4-day minimum stay during the high season, but off season you can stay at a daily rate of $175 s and $140/person d.

**campgrounds and RV parks:** Catalina State Park is located 12 miles N of Tucson on Oracle Rd. (US 89). The 5,500-acre park in the foothills of the Catalinas is popular for picnicking, camping, birding, hiking, and horseback riding. Hikers can do a 1 or 1½-mile nature trail, a 2.3-mile Canyon Loop Trail, or climb all the way to the top of Mt. Lemmon (14 hard miles OW) via the Sutherland or Romero Canyon

Trails. Natural swimming holes along the lower parts of the Sutherland and Romero Canyon Trails make good day hikes; higher up both trails become very steep. Rates: $2 for day use, $5 camping (no hookups, but showers are planned); $1 extra per vehicle for out-of-state residents. Your horse is welcome to stay too, in the stables; tel. 628-5798.

Mt. Lemmon Area (Coronado National Forest) campgrounds are described under "Mt. Lemmon Highway." The first of several campgrounds is at Molino Basin, 18 miles from Tucson. Get camping info from the Forest Service office; tel. 629-6483. Gilbert Ray Campground is in Tucson Mountain Park, 8 miles W of town; $4.50 (or $6.00 w/hookups) for tents or RVs; no showers; tel. 883-4200. Justin's RV Park is 8 miles W of town near Tucson Mountain Park at 3551 San Joaquin Rd.; $8 w/hookups; tel. 883-8340. Prince of Tucson Trailer Park is at 3501 N. Freeway on the W side of I-10, 4 miles NW of Tucson; take I-10 Exit 254 (Prince Rd.); swimming pool and rec. room; RVs are $15 w/hookups (no tents); tel. 887-3501. Tratel Tucson RV Park Home Park is also 4 miles NW of Tucson; take I-10 Exit 254 (Prince Rd.) then S on the W side of I-10 to 2070 W. Fort Lowell Rd.; pool and rec. room; RVs $11.31 w/hookups (no tents); tel. 888-5401. Rincon Country West RV Park is 4 miles S of Tucson at 4555 S. Mission Rd.; take I-19 Exit 99 (Ajo Way), go ½ mile W on Ajo Way then ½ mile S on Mission; adults only; has a spa; $14 w/hookups (no tents); tel. 294-5608. Crazy Horse Campground is SE of downtown at 6660 S. Craycroft Rd. (I-10 Exit 268 then ¼-mile N on Craycroft); heated pool, spa, RV repairs, and horseback riding; $11 tent or RV w/hookups; tel. 574-0157. Cactus Country Trailer Haven is 19 miles SE of downtown off I-10, take Exit 275, then ¼-mile N to 10195 S. Houghton Rd.; heated pool and spa; $8 tents, $10.58 RV w/hookups; tel. 298-8428. Many other RV parks and trailer parks are listed in the Yellow Pages.

# TUCSON RESTAURANTS

The Mexican food in Tucson could hardly be beat in Mexico. Or a visitor can choose from Chinese, Middle Eastern, Greek, Italian, German, French, and more! Elegant service and food are presented by the 7 or so continental restaurants. The more expensive places may require coat and tie for the men; ask when making the reservation. And of course Tucson has cowboy food—the old standbys of steak, potatoes, beans, and biscuits. The following is only a small selection; see the Visitors Bureau for a longer listing.

Restaurants are marked: ★ = Bargain; ★ ★ = Moderate; ★ ★ ★ = Expensive.

## AMERICAN

★ ★ ★ Cork 'n' Cleaver: One of the best steak houses in Tucson; also a choice of seafoods and an excellent salad bar. Eight miles E of downtown at 6320 E. Tanque Verde Rd.; tel. 296-1631. Open daily for lunch and dinner.

★ Egg Garden: Eggs go in almost everything—omlettes, quiches, seafood, hamburgers, salads. Just E of downtown, 509½ N. 4th Ave. at 6th St.; tel. 622-0918. Open daily for breakfast, lunch, and dinner.

★ to ★ ★ Furr's Cafeterias: A super selection of courses at 3 locations: Six miles E of downtown at 5910 E. Broadway; tel. 747-7881. Four miles N of downtown at 4329 N. Oracle Rd.; tel. 293-8550. Just N of downtown at I-10 and St. Mary's Rd.; tel. 624-1688. Open daily for lunch and dinner.

★ Garland: Good place for American, Mexican, Italian, and vegetarian food. Located ¾ mile NE of downtown, 119 E. Speedway Blvd. at 6th Ave.; tel. 792-4221. Open daily for breakfast, lunch, and dinner.

★ ★ Cafe Sweetwater: A variety—steaks, seafood, chicken, veal, and more in an art deco setting. Located just E of downtown at 340 E. 6th St., at 4th Ave.; tel. 622-6464, reservations requested. Open Mon. to Fri. for lunch and Mon. to Sat. for dinner.

★ ★ Pinnacle Peak: Don't wear a tie to this informal family-style steakhouse—or else! Thousands of severed ties decorate the ceilings. Located in "Trail Dust Town" 8 miles E of downtown at 6541 E. Tanque Verde Rd.; tel. 296-0911. Open daily for dinner.

Besides the restaurants, Tucsonans also enjoy snacking, as at this stall in the Fourth Avenue Street Fair.

★ to ★ ★ **Sizzler Steak Houses:** Good value on steak dinners. Four miles E of downtown at 4330 E. Broadway; tel. 326-5133. Also just W of downtown at 470 W. Congress; tel. 623-2888. Open daily for lunch and dinner.

## CHINESE

★ **China Wall:** 2547 E. Broadway; tel. 323-2024. Open daily for lunch and dinner with Hunan, Szechuan, and Mandarin styles.

★ to ★ ★ **Old Peking:** 2522 E. Speedway Blvd. (½ block E of Tucson Blvd.); tel. 795-9811. Also open daily for lunch and dinner with Hunan, Szechuan, and Mandarin cuisine.

## CONTINENTAL
### (reservations requested)

★ ★ ★ **Arizona Inn:** The elegant dining room is open daily for breakfast, lunch, and dinner; 2200 E. Elm St. (between Campbell and Country Club), 2 miles NE of downtown; tel. 327-7646.

★ ★ ★ **Charles:** An old English manor sets the mood for elegant dining. Located 8 miles E of downtown at 6400 E. El Dorado Circle (near intersection of Speedway Blvd. and Wilmot Rd.); tel. 296-7173. Open for dinner, weekdays for lunch.

★ ★ ★ **Gold Room:** Noted for excellent food and service with a sweeping view of the city. Located at the Westward Look Resort, 9 miles N of downtown, 245 E. Ina Rd.; tel. 297-1151. Open daily for breakfast, lunch, and dinner.

★ ★ ★ **Iron Mask:** A suit of armor and Old English decor provide atmosphere. Four miles NE of downtown, 2564 E. Grant Rd. (E of Tucson Blvd.); tel. 327-6649. Open Tue. to Fri. for lunch and Tue. to Sat. for dinner.

★ ★ to ★ ★ ★ **Palomino:** Has one of the longest menus in town and some of the best continental, American, and Greek food as well. Eight miles NE of downtown at 2959 N. Swan Rd.; tel 795-5561. Open for dinner only; closed Sun. and holidays.

★ ★ ★ **Tack Room:** This highly rated restaurant is in an adobe hacienda. Ten miles NE of downtown at 2800 N. Sabino Canyon Rd.; tel. 298-2351. Open daily for dinner only.

## FRENCH

★ ★ ★ **Penelope's:** Personal service and excellent food. Three miles E of downtown on 3619 E. Speedway Blvd.; tel. 325-5080, res. requested. Open Tue. to Fri. for lunch and Tue. to Sun. for dinner. No smoking allowed.

## GREEK

★ ★ to ★ ★ ★ **Olive Tree:** Generous portions and a choice of indoor or patio tables. Located 7 miles E of downtown at 7000 E. Tanque Verde Rd.; tel. 298-1845. Open Mon. to Sat. for lunch and dinner.

## ITALIAN

★ ★ **Caruso's:** Southern Italian cooking in a Tucson institution dating back to the 1930s. Located just E of downtown at 434 N. 4th Ave.; tel. 624-5765. Open daily for dinner.

★ ★ to ★ ★ ★ **Scordato's:** Perhaps the best Italian restaurant in town, with a wide selection. Six miles W of downtown at 4405 W. Speedway Blvd.; tel. 624-8946, res. requested. Open daily for dinner only; extensive wine list.

## MEXICAN

★ ★ **Carlos Murphy's:** Downtown at 419 W. Congress; tel. 628-1956.

★ ★ **El Adobe:** Sonoran cuisine in one of Tucson's oldest buildings, 40 W. Broadway Blvd. (see downtown walking tour map); tel. 791-7458. Open daily for lunch and dinner; closed Sunday. Ask for a table on the patio if the weather is fine.

★ ★ **El Charro:** A longtime favorite (founded 1922), now in the historic Le Flein House downtown, 311 N. Court Ave., (see downtown walking tour map); tel. 622-5465. Open daily for lunch and dinner.

★★ to ★★★El Parador: A garden atmosphere and live music embellish the dining room. Located 2 miles E of downtown, 2744 E. Broadway; tel. 881-2808. Open Mon. to Sat. for lunch and dinner, Sun. for dinner only.

★El Torero: Popular place with generous servings. Located in South Tucson at 231 E. 26th St. (near S. 4th Ave.); tel. 622-9534. Open for lunch and dinner; closed Tuesdays. You'll find other Mexican restaurants in the neighborhood. South Tucson is a one-mile-square city-within-a-city just S of downtown Tucson.

★ to ★★La Fuente Restaurant & Lounge: Mariachi bands serenade diners in the evenings. At 1749 N. Miracle Mile Strip; tel. 623-8659. Open for lunch and dinner; closed Monday.

## MIDDLE EASTERN

★ to ★★Sheik Cafe: Lebanese and Syrian recipes are used to create fine meals. Shish kebab, stuffed cabbage rolls, and baked kippi are some of the specialties. Six miles E of downtown at 6350 E. Broadway (just past Wilmot); tel. 790-5481. Open for lunch and dinner; closed Sunday.

## ENTERTAINMENT

**movies:** Newspapers list what's new, but to see something different try the New Loft Theatre for old classics and foreign films; it's at 504 N. Fremont Ave. (near 6th St.), about ¾ mile E of downtown; tel. 624-4981. Gallagher Theatre has inexpensive movies every evening when the University is in session; on campus at the E end of the Student Union; tel. 621-3102.

**theatre and concerts:** The University of Arizona offers many productions (tel. 621-1162 for recorded announcement; tel. 621-7008 for further info). Performing groups include the University Theatre (Oct. to April), Studio Theatre (inexpensive student productions on Park Ave., next to the U of A campus; Oct. to Apr.), and University of Arizona Repertory Theatre (summer productions). Chamber music concerts are given on campus by Arizona Friends of Music from Oct. to Apr.; tel. 298-5806. The following companies perform in the Tucson Community Center Music Hall: Arizona Ballet (Nov. to Apr.; tel. 628-7446); Tucson Symphony (Thur. & Fri. evenings Oct. to May.; tel. 792-9155); Arizona Opera Company (Oct. to Jan.; tel. 293-4336); and Southern Arizona Light Opera Company (Oct. to June; tel. 323-7888). Arizona Theatre Company presents a series of plays from Oct. to May; tel. 622-2823. The experimental Invisible Theatre presents about 6 performances (Sept. to June, one mile NE of downtown at 1400 N. 1st Ave.; tel. 882-9721). For hilarious family entertainment, take in an old-fashioned melodrama at the Gaslight Theatre, Wed. to Sun., 7000 E. Tanque Verde Rd. (8 miles E of downtown); tel. 886-9428.

**social spots:** At the Cushing Street Bar, you'll find a relaxed atmosphere with 1880's decor; downtown at 343 S. Meyer St. and Cushing St.

(across from Tucson Community Center); tel. 622-7984. Funk and soul groups perform at the Stumble Inn nightclub, ½ mile E of downtown at 136 N. Park Ave.; tel. 792-1250. The Wildcat House has loud "Top 40" music, 1½ miles N of downtown at 1801 N. Stone Ave.; tel. 622-1302. The Bum Steer Bar plays loud rock; (check out the collection of oddities on the walls) 1½ miles N of downtown at 1910 N. Stone Ave.; tel. 884-7377. The Shanty is beer drinkers' heaven with nearly 300 brands of brew, downtown at 401 E. 9th St.; tel. 622-9210.

**sporting events:** The University of Arizona Wildcat teams compete in football, basketball, baseball, tennis, swimming, track and field, and other sports during the school terms. For ticket info call the McKale Center; tel. 621-2411; or the Sports Information number; tel. 621-4163. Hi Corbett Field in Reid Park (tel. 791-4096) hosts 2 baseball teams: the Tucson Toros from Apr. to Aug., and the early spring training of the Cleveland Indians. Greyhounds (dogs, not the Bus!) hit the track year-round, except for 5 July to 5 Aug. and 2 weeks at Christmas, at Tucson Greyhound Park; the park is in South Tucson (2 miles S of downtown Tucson) at 2601 S. 3rd Ave. (and E. 36th St.); tel. 884-7576.

## SHOPPING

**downtown mercado:** A Mexican-style market with fresh produce, food stalls, and local crafts comes to life on Fri. about 0900-1500. The market takes place downtown in La Placita Village.

**Fourth Avenue:** The section of 4th Ave. between 4th and 7th Sts. has many unusual craft & antique shops and restaurants. Big street fairs are held here in late April and early December. Also, the Salvation Army, Goodwill, and Tucson Thrift Shop stores on 4th Ave. (at 7th St.) offer used clothing and other items. For health foods, visit the Food Conspiracy Co-op; they have an herb room, whole-grain flours, etc.; open daily; nonmembers welcome; 412 N. 4th Ave. (between 6th and 7th Sts.)

**shopping centers:** Tucson has 4 malls open daily with department stores, specialty shops, and restaurants; all but Tucson Mall have movie theaters. All are enclosed and air-conditioned. El Con Mall has 130 stores, 3 miles E of downtown at 3601 E. Broadway; tel. 327-6053. Park Mall has 110 stores, 6 miles E of downtown at 5870 E. Broadway; tel. 748-1222.

*downtown mercado*

Tucson Mall has 200 stores, 4½ miles N of downtown at 4500 N. Oracle Rd.; tel. 293-7330. Foothills Center has 55 stores, 10 miles N of downtown at 7401 N. La Cholla Blvd. (W. Ina Rd.); tel. 742-7191.

**art galleries:**   Be sure to see De Grazia's Gallery in the Sun. Designed to blend into the desert, the building is made of adobe and surrounded by desert plants. You enter through a gate patterned after the one at Yuma Territorial Prison, then pass through a short mine shaft. DeGrazia, born in the Arizona mining district of Clifton, was fascinated from an early age by the desert colors and cultures of the Southwest. He became famous for his paintings, but created ceramics, sculpture, and jewelry and wrote books as well. He died in 1982 but the gallery continues as a museum. In a short movie, DeGrazia tells of his life and work. Local artists also have exhibits in the gallery. From downtown go 4 miles E on E. Broadway to Swan Rd., then N 6 miles to 6300 N. Swan Rd. (near Skyline Dr.); tel. 299-9191. Open daily 1000-1600; free; has a gift shop.

Old Town Artisans, in the middle of the downtown El Presidio District, is large and varied. Pottery, clothing, jewelry, wood carvings, and other crafts are available by local, Indian, Mexican, and international artists. Open Mon. to Sat. 1000-1700, Sun. 1200-1700. It's on the corner of N. Meyer Ave. and Telles St. (near Tucson Museum of Art); tel. 623-6024. Tucson has dozens of other art galleries and craft shops. See the Yellow Pages or the Visitors Bureau for a list.

## SERVICES

Main post office is 2½ miles SE of downtown at 1501 S. Cherrybell Stravanue. The downtown branch is at 141 S. 6th Avenue. Another is on E. University Blvd. (between Tyndall and Park Ave.), and there's one on the University of Arizona campus (in the basement of the Student Union). Exchange foreign currency at Valley National Bank, 2 E. Congress St. (downtown) or any branch; International Dept. tel. 792-7446. Or exchange it at First Interstate Bank, 150 N. Stone Ave. (downtown) or any branch; International Banking tel.

792-5444. Doctors' Central Directory, tel. 327-7471 (24 hours), will refer you to any doctor you might need. Down and out? Temporary Employment (Arizona Dept. of Economic Security), 22nd St., offers free services; tel. 628-5553.

**phone numbers:**

Emergency: tel. 911, 791-4452 (police info), or 622-3366 (sheriff info). Road Conditions: tel. 294-3113.

Crisis Counselling and Suicide Prevention: tel. 323-9373.

Information and Referral Service (community services): tel. 881-1794.

Tucson Parks & Recreation: tel. 791-4873.

Sun Tran (city bus): tel. 792-9222.

Tucson Community Center Box Office: tel. 791-4266.

University of Arizona Ticket Offices:
Sports Events: tel. 621-2411;
Concerts & Public Affairs: tel. 621-3341;
Theatre: tel. 621-1162.

Weather recording: tel. 623-4000.

## RECREATION

**Reid Park:**   This spacious green park in the middle of Tucson has a small zoo, Hi Corbett baseball field, soccer field, rose garden, lakes, and picnic areas. The park is 3 miles E of downtown; enter from Country Club Rd., Camino Campestre, or Randolph Way; tel. 791-4873.

**tennis:**   With over 150 courts spread around Tucson, it's not hard to find one. See "Recreation & Sports" in the Visitors Bureau's *Visitors Guide.* The Randolph Recreation Complex has 24 lighted public courts, instruction, and pro shop, as well as 10 racquetball courts; 3 miles E of downtown at 100 S. Alvernon Way (just S of E. Broadway); tel. 791-4896.

**golf:**   Another sport enjoyed by many Tucsonans. About 17 courses are open to the public; see "Recreation & Sports" in the

Visitors Bureau's *Visitors Guide.* Randolph Park, just E of Reid Park, has 2 18-hole courses at 602 S. Alvernon Way; tel. 791-4336.

**swimming:** Tucson Parks and Recreation has 19 swimming pools (open summer only). Addresses and phone numbers are in the telephone book under "Tucson City Government."

**horseback riding:** Tucson Mountain Stables offers a variety of trail rides and cookouts, they're about 15 miles NW of downtown in the foothills of the Tucson Mountains at 6501 W. Ina Rd.; tel. 744-4407 (reservations needed). El Conquistador Stables also have rides and cookouts, 11 miles N of downtown at 10,000 N. Oracle Rd., near the Santa Catalinas; tel. 742-4200.

**Southern Arizona Hiking Club:** Hikes organized by this active group vary from easy to challenging. The Club schedules dayhikes, backpacks, climbs, river trips, ski tours, and snowshoe trips. The group also promotes conservation and trail construction. Visitors are welcome on hikes. Contact the Club at Box 12122, Tucson, AZ 85732.

**skiing:** At Mt. Lemmon Ski Valley in the Santa Catalina Mountains you can enjoy downhill skiing during the late Dec. to late Mar. season. See "Mt. Lemmon Highway." One double chairlift and a beginner tow take skiers up the slopes. Longest run is ¾ mile, dropping from

9100 to 8200 feet through fir and aspen forests; tel. 576-1321. To check on snow and road conditions, call tel. 576-1400 (recorded message).

## EVENTS

Something's happening nearly every day, and the Visitors Bureau can tell you what it is. Ask for their *Tucson Events* brochure. The following are the best-known annual happenings: Tucson Gem & Mineral Show in Feb. is considered the world's best. Cowboys get together for a big 4-day rodeo and a colorful parade in La Fiesta de los Vaqueros in late Feb. or early March. Tucson Festival (Easter season), is an extravaganza of fiestas, concerts, theater, and music of the cultures and history of Tucson. Yaqui Indians of Pascua Village in Tucson stage the Yaqui Easter Ceremonials, a passion play, during the Easter season; the ceremony is a mixture of Catholic and tribal beliefs about the forces of good overcoming evil. At the Spring Fling in April, University students put on a carnival with rides, games, and food. Even though the sandy bed of the Rillito River is pretty dry, that doesn't stop the Rillito River Regatta in May; the "boats" are decorated 4WD vehicles in a benefit parade for charities. At the Tucson Junior Rodeo in Aug., youngsters

*Fourth Avenue Street Fair (held in April and December)*

(5-19) compete in riding and roping skills. The Papago All-Indian Rodeo and Fair takes place

*Fiesta de los Vaqueros*

in Oct., featuring a parade, singing, dancing, crafts, and food—all put on by the Indian tribe on their reservation near Sells, 58 miles SW of Tucson. Tucson Meet Yourself celebrates the diverse cultures of the city in Oct. with music, dance, food, and crafts. College students compete in Nov. at the University of Arizona Rodeo.

# INFORMATION

**tourist office:** Metropolitan Tucson Convention & Visitors Bureau is very helpful, 450 W. Paseo Redondo, Suite 110, Tucson, AZ 85701; tel. 624-1817. Open Mon. to Fri. 0830-1700; brochures can be picked up outside on weekends. Be sure to get the free *Visitors Guide.*

**Coronado National Forest:** Camping and hiking info for the Santa Catalinas is available from the downtown office in room 6A of the Federal Bldg. at 300 W. Congress St.; tel. 629-6483; or the Sabino Canyon Visitor Center; tel. 629-5113.

**libraries:** The main city library is downtown at 200 S. 6th Ave.; tel. 791-4010. Open Mon. to Thurs. 0900-2100, Fri. to Sat. 0900-1700, Sun. 1330-1700. The library also has 13 branches (see phone book). University libraries are open to the public and include some outstanding collections. Pick up free library-information pamphets in the Main Library lobby. Main Library (see University map) is open Mon. to Thur. 0700-0200, Fri. 0700-2100, Sat. 0900-2100, Sun. 1000-0200; shorter hours during summer and vacations; tel. 621-6441. Hikers and travelers may want to visit the map collection where topographic maps of the entire country can be photocopied; open Mon. to Fri. 0800-1700 and Sat. 1200-1600 during regular semesters; located on the 1st floor of the main library. Other collections include: Arizona, Southwest, Government Documents, Music, Oriental Studies, and the Center for Creative Photography. This last has manuscripts and photographs by Ansel Adams, Paul Strand, and other famous photographers, as well as an extensive library of books and periodicals on

photography. There's usually a small exhibit and the staff can tell you of others in town. Open Mon. to Fri. 0900-1700 and Sun. 1200-1700. Located just W of the University campus at 843 E. University Blvd.; tel. 621-7968.

**newspapers:** Tucson's major dailies are the *Arizona Daily Star* in the morning and the *Tucson Citizen* in the afternoon. The *Star's* Friday Entertainment section reports nightlife, concerts, theater, and dancing. Sights and events are listed in its Tucson Today column (Mon. to Sat.). The Art Calendar in Sunday's Entertainment writes up the art galleries and shows. The *Tucson Citizen* lists local happenings and movies in the Living section (Mon. to Fri.) and more in-depth reporting in the Thur. Calendar section. There's no Sun. edition.

**bookstores:** The shopping malls have the popular book chains. The Southwest Parks and Monuments Association Bookshop, downtown at Court and Council, offers excellent books on history, Indians, wildlife, and flora, as well as parks and monuments of the Southwest. The University of Arizona has a good bookstore at the W end of the Student Union with books on Arizona and the Southwest together with general reading and textbooks; closed on weekends. For used books try: Bookman's Used Books, 2501 E. Broadway Blvd. (at Tucson Blvd.), open daily; tel. 325-5767 and Goodbooks, 431 N. 4th Ave., open daily; tel. 792-9551.

**maps:** For hiking, Natl. Forest, state, and Mexican maps visit the Hiking Center in the Student Union basement on the U. of A. Campus; tel. 621-7045; or Tucson Maps, 2610 N. 1st Ave.; tel. 623-1104.

# TRANSPORT

**tours:** See Tucson from a double-decker bus with the Tucson Tour Co., leaving daily Nov. to mid-Apr. on a 2-hour loop of the city; $5 adult, $3 children under 12; tel. 327-3333. Gray Line Tours has day trips to the Desert Museum, Old Tucson, Nogales (Mexico), Phoenix, or Tombstone for about $20/person. Longer trips of 2-5 days take you to the Grand Canyon and other sights of northern Arizona; costs start at $80 for an overnight Grand Canyon trip; Box 1991, Tucson, AZ 85702; tel. 622-8811. Sandpainter Guided Tours gives you a choice of historic and scenic tours in and near Tucson; $28/person for the 5-hour tour; Box 50501, Tucson, AZ 85703-1501; tel. 323-9290. Float through the air high over Tucson with Fox Balloon Adventures; flights last 1 to 1½ hours and cost $125/person; Box 17733, Tucson, AZ 85731; tel. 886-9191.

**taxi and rentals:** Allstate Cab Company is low cost; tel. 881-2227 (24 hours). Taxi fares vary greatly between different companies—you may want to shop around. Tucson has over 2 dozen car-rental agencies with several at the airport. See the Yellow Pages. Rent Bicycles from "A" University Bike Store, 1015 E. 6th St.; tel. 884-8700; or Morrison Bicycles, 3025 E. Speedway Blvd.; tel. 795-1342.

**auto driveaways:** These are cars that need delivering to another city. If it's a place you're headed, you have a "free" car rental. But the driveaway companies do place some restrictions on time and mileage; also you need to make a deposit. Ask for an economy car if that's a consideration. Try: A-American Auto shippers (tel. 881-7307); AAACON Auto Transport (tel. 889-8805); or Auto Driveaway (tel. 323-7659).

**local bus:** Sun Tran takes you to the parks, sights, and shopping areas within the city and to the airport for only 50 cents. You must have exact change; transfers are free. Unfortunately, it does *not* go outside the city. Also, most buses go to bed about 1900, although a few routes run until 2200 or 2300, weekdays only. The Visitors Bureau has free route maps. The Weekend Pass (purchase from driver, $1) allows unlimited travel from Fri. night thru Sun. night. For Sun Tran info call tel. 792-9222.

**long-distance bus:** The Greyhound terminal is downtown at 2 S. 4th Ave. (at E. Broadway); tel. 792-0972. Some destinations and OW fares to: Los Angeles (4 x daily) $67; El Paso (5 x daily) $54; Phoenix (8 x daily) $15 local or $17 express; Flagstaff (3 x daily) $41.25; Douglas (1 daily via Benson, Fort Huachuca, Sierra Vista, and Bisbee) $14. Roundtrip fares may have a small discount. Lockers and a coffee shop (open daily 0600-2000) are at the station. The Trailways terminal is downtown (1 block from Greyhound) at 201 E. Broadway Blvd.; tel. 882-0005. Some destinations and OW fares to: Los Angeles (4 x daily) $56; El Paso (4 x daily) $35; Phoenix (3 x daily) $15; Flagstaff (2 x daily) $35; Nogales (9 x daily via Citizen Auto Stage) $5.85. Roundtrip fares may have a small discount. Lockers and a coffee shop (open daily 0600-1530) are at the station.

**train:** Amtrak has 3 eastbound and 3 westbound departures every week. Terminal is downtown at 400 E. Toole Ave. (2 blocks N of the bus stations); tel. 623-4442. For reservations and info call 1-800-872-7245. Westbound departs in the evening for Phoenix (2 hours, $22 OW), Yuma, and other points, arriving in Los Angeles the next morning (11 hours, $83 OW). Eastbound leaves in the morning: one train goes to New Orleans (1½ days, $212), the other to Chicago (2 days, $233). Amtrak gives large discounts on RT fares, making it more competitive with the bus and plane.

**air:** Tucson International Airport is 8½ miles S of downtown. Fourteen airlines and charters fly here. See the Yellow Pages for airline companies and ticket agencies. On the ground, there's a choice between taxis, airport limousine, and Sun Tran Bus #8. Arizona Stagecoach provides limousine service outside the terminal to your destination. For pickup to the airport, call tel. 889-9681 at least 4 hours before the flight.

# WEST TO ORGAN PIPE
# NATIONAL MONUMENT

## PAPAGO INDIAN RESERVATION

Heading W from Tucson on AZ 86, you reach the main Papago Reservation after 25 miles. The land appears inhospitable—dry sandy washes and plains, broken here and there by rocky hills or mountains. The first white men couldn't believe that people lived in such wild and parched desert, yet the Papago Indians have thrived on it for centuries. Close relatives to the Pima, the Papago once occupied a vast portion of the Sonoran Desert of southern Arizona and northern Mexico. Neighboring Indians called these desert dwellers "Papago," meaning "bean people," but the Papago have a more dignified term for themselves—"Tohono O'odham," meaning "desert people who have emerged from the earth." They believe that their tribe, like the plants and animals, belongs to the earth. Traditionally Papago had both winter and summer villages, staying near reliable springs in the winter, then moving to fields watered by summer thunderstorms. They gathered mesquite beans, agave, cactus fruit, acorns, and other plant foods, and hunted rodents, rabbits, deer, and pronghorn. Fields were planted with native tepary beans, corn, and squash.

After the 1854 Gadsden Treaty split their land between Mexico and the United States, the Mexican Papago population gradually withered away as it was absorbed by Mexican culture. Some families migrated into Arizona.

Today only about 200 Papago remain south of the border. In 1874, the U.S. government began setting aside land for the tribe in the 71,095-acre San Xavier Reservation. Papago land now totals about 2,800,000 acres (roughly the size of Connecticut). It's the 2nd largest reservation in the country, stretching across much of southcentral Arizona, and it's the home of more than 8,000 people. The old ways have largely disappeared upon contact with the white man's technology. Now most Papago, like anyone else in Arizona, live in modern houses; they farm, ranch, or work for wages. Skilled basketmakers, their attractive wares are in much demand. You'll see Papago crafts in trading posts and the Visitor Center at Kitt Peak. Early Spanish missionaries gained many converts—the Roman Catholic Church is the strongest on the reservation, though there are Protestant denominations as well. Almost all villages have a small chapel.

**visiting the reservation:** Most Papago are friendly, but the tribe has never shown much interest in tourism. Visitor facilities are sparse—gas stations are few and far between and campgrounds and motels nonexistent. Two attractions, in addition to the desert scenery, make a visit worthwhile: the Papago All-Indian Rodeo and Fair and the world-famous Kitt Peak Observatory.

**Papago All Indian Rodeo and Fair:** Papago cowboys show off their riding and roping skills

*greater roadrunner*
(Geococcyx californianus)

*McMath Solar Telescope*

in the tribe's big annual event, held in October. The Papago put on a parade, exhibit crafts, serve Indian fry bread, and perform songs and dances. You can get the dates from the tribal office in Sells or the Visitors Bureau in Tucson.

## KITT PEAK

Planning a national observatory, astronomers took 3 years to study 150 peaks in the Southwest before choosing this one in 1958. Large white domes, enclosing instruments that help to unravel the mysteries of the universe, cling to the 6,900-foot summit. The 19 telescopes come in many sizes and types, including one that uses radio waves. Some are owned by universities, foremost of which is the University of Arizona in Tucson. Nearly all the work is pure research, done by qualified astronomers who apply a year or more in advance to a panel that makes the selections. Before Kitt Peak was operating, students and women found it almost impossible to get time at a major telescope, but here they have an equal chance.

Astronomers use the equipment free of charge but no rain checks are issued! Workers learn to be philosophical after waiting many months and then getting clouded out. Instruments are controlled by computers; the scientist can even operate his telescope from Tucson. It's rare for an observer actually to look through telescopes these days; some instruments don't even have an eyepiece. Kitt Peak is funded by the National Science Foundation and managed by a group of 17 universities, the Association of Universities for Research in Astronomy.

**Visitor Center:** You're welcome to drive up and see the observatory and astronomy exhibits. A short self-guiding tour leads around the grounds and to 3 of the most impressive telescopes, which you can step inside. These are the McMath Solar (which doesn't look like a telescope at all), the 2.1-meter (84-inch), and the Mayall 4-meter (158-inch) telescopes. Most telescopes at Kitt Peak are not designed for magnification as much as for light-gathering power (a distant star looks the same pinpoint size through even the biggest 'scopes). An exception is the McMath Solar Telescope, which produces a 30-inch image of the sun by using mirrors in a slanted 500-foot corridor. Three hundred feet of this length runs below ground. You can step inside to see the interior; a TV screen shows the sun's image. This telescope won an architectural award in 1962, rare for observatories! The 2.1-meter telescope nearby was the first large instrument on Kitt Peak for nighttime viewing. It's used to observe distant stars and galaxies in both the visible and infrared spectra. The Mayall 4-meter, one of the world's largest telescopes, is housed in a building 19 stories high. An elevator takes you to the 10th-floor observation deck offering panoramic views of southern Arizona and northern Sonora. Inside is a gallery where you can see the telescope and a short video tape about its construction.

Kitt Peak Observatory is open daily 1000-1600, except Dec. 24th and 25th; no charge. A shop in the Visitor Center sells Papago basketry and astronomy-related posters, slides, and T-shirts. Films are shown daily at 1030 and 1330. On weekends and holidays (except Christmas) you can go on a free guided tour of the Observatory, lasting about 1½ hours, following the film. On the drive up, you'll pass a picnic area on the L, 1½ miles before the Visitor Center. Bring your own picnic supplies as no stores or restaurants are on Kitt Peak. The air is cool up here (15-20 degrees colder than Tucson), so a jacket or sweater will be useful most of the year. Kitt Peak is 50 miles SW of Tucson via AZ 86. The last 12 miles are on a paved and well-graded mountain road. Winter storms can close the road for short periods; check by calling tel. 623-5796.

## SELLS

Tribal headquarters and largest town on the Papago Reservation. The dependable water here has made the place a popular stop for travelers since prehistoric times. Sells was originally known as Indian Oasis, but the name was changed in 1918 to honor Indian Commissioner Cato Sells. The town is 58 miles SW of Tucson via AZ 86 (20 miles past the turnoff for Kitt Peak). Offices, schools, and shops are 1½

miles S of the main highway. Papago Trading Post in Sells has a room of Papago baskets whose prices range from ten to several hundred dollars. It also has a general store and gas pump. Pick up a copy of the *Papago Runner* (in English) to learn about the tribe's current concerns. The Papago Cafe is on the main highway just W of the turnoff for Sells. You'll find another trading post with Papago crafts 22 miles W at Quijotoa. Before camping or exploring the backcountry, check to see if you'll need a permit. Contact the Papago Tribe Administration, Sells, AZ 85634; tel. 383-2221. Ask about road conditions if you plan to venture off the main highway; dirt roads can become impassable after rains.

## ORGAN PIPE CACTUS NATIONAL MONUMENT

The Sonoran Desert is at its finest in this remote area of Arizona. Some desert plants, such as the senita cactus and elephant tree, occur only here and in Mexico. The name of Arizona's largest national monument honors

*senita cactus (Lophocereus schottii)*

*Quitobaquito Oasis*

the giant organ pipe cactus, which grows well in this area. In appearance it's similar to the saguaro, but the organ pipe's many branches all radiate from the base. Animals adapt to the heat by hiding out during the hottest part of the day. They're most active at night or in the mornings and evenings. Wildlife you might see include lizards, birds, kangaroo rats, kit foxes, ringtailed cats, bobcats, javelina, bighorn sheep, and pronghorn. The 5 species of rattlesnakes are nocturnal—a good reason to use a flashlight at night! About 30 species of birds stay year-round, and more than 260 others drop in on their migrations. Quitobaquito Oasis is a prime birding spot.

If you're lucky enough to be here in Mar. or Apr. after a wet winter, you'll see the desert ablaze with yellows, blues, reds, and violets. First to bloom are annual plants, which must quickly germinate and produce seeds before the summer heat, followed by the smaller cacti such as the chollas and prickly pears. Last to bloom are the big saguaros and organ pipes, whose blossoms peak in May or June. Scenic drives and hiking trails provide a chance to ex-

perience and learn about the Sonoran desert.

**Visitor Center:** For an introduction to the highly adaptable plants and wildlife that live here, start at the Visitor Center located 22 miles S of Why. A short slide program shows native animals and the effects of seasonal changes on the land. Another slide program shows desert wildflowers. Exhibits describe plants and animals of the region, while illustrating man's effect on the desert. Just outside, a short nature trail identifies common plants and gives more info on the desert environment. Rangers can answer your questions and issue camping permits. Books, prints, and a topo map are sold. Naturalist programs are presented during the cooler months at the Visitor Center, on trails, and at the campground. Summer is the quiet season at the Monument, as daytime highs commonly range from 95 to 105 degrees F, but it gives you a chance to experience that season in the desert. Thunderstorms appear in late summer, bringing about half of the annual 9½ inches or so of rain. Winters are cool to warm with occasional gentle rains. The Visitor

Center is open daily 0800-1700; $3/vehicle; tel. 387-6849.

**Puerto Blanco Scenic Drive:** Varied desert environments, Quitobaquito Oasis, and rare desert plants of the Senita Basin are highlights of this 53-mile loop. Numbered stops are explained in a pamphlet; pick it up at the Visitor Center or at the start of the drive, just W of the Visitor Center. Nearly all the route is graded dirt, designed for slow speeds—allow at least half a day. Note that a section of the drive is one way (counter-clockwise) and that you can't turn back! Quitobaquito, one mile off the loop, has a large man-made pond surrounded by large cottonwoods. The springs are 100 yards N up a trail. Ducks and other waterfowl, not what you'd expect in the desert, drop in during the spring and fall. Coots stay here year-round.

Father Kino and other early Spanish missionaries and explorers stopped here on their way to the Colorado River. The 49ers headed for the California gold fields took this southern route to avoid hostile Indians farther north. Many goldseekers perished from thirst on the fearsome Camino del Diablo or "Devil's Highway" between Sonoita and the Colorado River. Quitobaquito was one of few sources of water on the route. Senita Basin, 4 miles off the loop, is home of the senita cactus and elephant tree. Similar in appearance to organ pipe cactus, the senita is distinguished by its gray "whiskers"

and far fewer ribs on each arm. The elephant tree looks like the root system of an upside-down tree! See if you can find the resemblance to an elephant.

**Ajo Mountain Drive:** Heading into more rugged country in the eastern part of the Monument, this drive skirts the base of 4,808-foot Mt. Ajo. Part of the 21-mile gravel loop road is one way; pick up a pamphlet describing the drive at the Visitor Center or at the start, just across the highway from the Visitor Center; allow at least 2 hours. You'll have good views from Diablo Canyon picnic area and from the Bull Pasture Trail (beginning at Estes Canyon).

**hiking:** Several trails begin at the campground, located 1½ miles from the Visitor Center. Desert View Nature Trail travels up a wash, then climbs onto a ridge with a good panorama. Victoria Mine Trail, 4½ miles RT, takes you to an historic mine that produced lead, silver, and gold. Also beginning at the campground are a 1-mile trail encircling the camping area and a 1⅓-mile trail to the Visitor Center. Estes Canyon-Bull Pasture Trail, off Ajo Mt. Drive, is the most spectacular established trail. The Estes Canyon portion follows the canyon while the Bull Pasture portion climbs a ridge. The trails meet and then continue to Bull Pasture, where ranchers once grazed cattle. The entire loop, including the spur trail to Bull Pasture, is 4.1 miles RT; some sections are

Arch Canyon, Ajo
Mountain Drive

*cristate growth
on an organ pipe
cactus*

steep and have loose rock. Carry water. Count-less other cross-country hiking trips are possi-ble in the Monument's open terrain. Rangers can help you plan. You'll have to get a permit from them for any climbing or overnight hikes.

**accommodations, camping, and food:** The large 208-site campground near the Visitor Center is open all year (trailers to 35 feet). It has drinking water but no hookups or showers; sites cost $6/night. Tenters who want to leave the asphalt and flush toilets behind can also camp at Alamo Canyon Primitive Camp-ground, 14 miles away. This is a pretty spot and a good base for day hikes. It's free but the only facilities are pit toilets — get the required permit and directions beforehand from a ranger. No trailers or RVs permitted here. For motels, stores, gas stations, and restaurants, you have to leave the Monument; Lukeville (AZ), 5 miles S, and Sonoita (Mexico), 2 miles farther, are the nearest towns.

## VICINITY OF ORGAN PIPE CACTUS NATIONAL MONUMENT

**Lukeville:** Just a wide spot on the road next to the Mexican border, Lukeville was named for WW I flying ace Frank Luke. Besides the im-migration and customs offices, Lukeville has a

gas station, small store, and the Gringo Pass Motel ($25 s, $30 d) and Trailer Park ($10 w/hookups; no tents).

**Sonoita:** Several restaurants, motels, curio shops, and an attractive little plaza are 2 miles SW of the Mexican border in Sonoita. Beach-es, fishing, and seafood lure many visitors 63 more miles to Puerto Penasco on the Sea of Cortez. Here you'll find seaside motels, restaurants, and trailer parks. A permit is need-ed to travel beyond Sonoita. Auto insurance is sold at the border on both sides.

**Why:** Why Why? Why, because it used to be called "the Y" by motorists. Why is the junc-tion of AZ Hwys. 85 and 86 just N of Organ Pipe Cactus National Monument. Why has a motel ($18 s or d), a trailer park ($8 w/hookups; no tents), grocery store, gas station, and a couple of bars.

## AJO

This pleasant small town appears lost in a sea of desert. It's 10 miles NW of Why and 42 miles S of Gila Bend. The town's name (pronounced AH-ho) may have come from the Papago word for paint, because the Indians collected copper minerals here to paint their bodies. Prospectors settled as early as 1854 but Ajo didn't really get going until early in this century when suitable ore-refining techniques were available. The New Cornelia Copper Company started in 1917 and was later purchased by Phelps Dodge. Squeezed between current low copper prices and high costs, Phelps Dodge has shut down the mine and smelter. Now in hard times, Ajo waits for higher copper prices. The downtown plaza and many public buildings were built in a Spanish Colonial style and are surrounded by graceful palms and flowering trees. The miners' tiny houses are also decorated with greenery and trees.

**sights:** The New Cornelia open pit mine just S of town is one of the world's largest, 1 ½ miles across. To reach the mine lookout from downtown, turn SE on La Mina Ave., then R on Indian Village Rd., and follow signs to a ramada with exhibits overlooking the pit. The nearby Ajo Historical Museum houses pioneer and Indian exhibits in a former Catholic church. Hours are daily 1300-1630 but closed 15 July to 15 August. From the mine overlook continue to the end of Indian Village Rd. and turn L.

**accommodations and food:** Three motels are N of town on AZ 85: the Ajo, La Siesta, and Copper Sands. The Copper Coffee Shop, on the plaza, serves Mexican-American food. Other restaurants are N on the highway: Pizza Hut, Su Casa (Mexican), Dairy Queen, and Dago Joes Pizza (steaks and seafood).

**recreation and information:** A public swimming pool (open in summer) and tennis courts are next to the high school on Well Road. The Ajo Chamber of Commerce, library, and post office are in the plaza. The helpful chamber office is open Mon. to Fri. 1300-1700; tel. 387-7742.

## CABEZA PRIETA NATIONAL WILDLIFE REFUGE

The 860,000 acres of desert wilderness W of Organ Pipe National Monument remains much as it has always been. Nobody lives here. There're no facilities, no paved roads, and no running water. Only jeep tracks and remnants of the old El Camino Diablo cross the landscape. Twelve small mountain ranges rise above the desert floor. Wildlife and vegetation are similar to those in Organ Pipe Natl. Mon., but the climate is harsher here. The Cabeza's annual rainfall averages about 9 inches in the E but tapers to only 3 inches in the west. Some areas go more than a year without rain!

You can visit this land with a permit, a suitable vehicle, and supplies for desert travel. Summer can be dangerous. Cabeza doubles as a gunnery range for Luke Air Force Base, so you'll want to time your visit carefully! Its schedules are made up 2 or 3 weeks ahead and known by the Refuge headquarters in Ajo and Yuma. Permits are required for entry and you'll have to sign a liability release for the military. Four-wheel-drive vehicles are recommended, though a dune buggy should be OK. Anything else is likely to get bogged in the loose sand. Vehicles must stay on designated roads and be licensed for highway use. Ajo is the main administration office but you can also get information and permits in Yuma. Write or visit the U.S. Fish and Wildlife Service at 1611 N. 2nd Ave., Ajo, AZ 85321; tel. 387-6483 (in a funny-looking building on the highway just N of town) or at 356 W. 1st St., Yuma (Box 1032, Yuma, AZ 85364); tel. 783-7861.

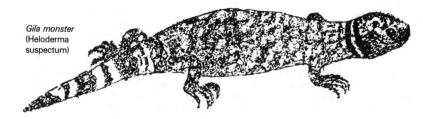

*Gila monster (Heloderma suspectum)*

San Xavier del Bac

# SOUTH FROM TUCSON TO MEXICO

Mexico is a short drive S from Tucson via I-19, just 63 miles or 100 km—all of I-19 is signposted in metric. Except for the speed limits, that is. The Highway Patrol doesn't want you getting confused by the sight of a 90 km/h sign! You'll be following the Santa Cruz River Valley, one of the first areas in Arizona to be colonized by the Spanish, and you may want to stop for the historic and scenic sights on the way. The Jesuit priest Eusebio Francisco Kino began mission work at Guevavi (near Nogales) and Tumacacori in 1691, and moved later to San Xavier and other sites. Livestock, new crops, and the new religion brought by Kino caused great changes in the lives of the Indians here.

## MISSION SAN XAVIER DEL BAC

This gleaming white church rises from the desert as a testimonial to the faith of early Spanish missionaries and the Papago Indians. Its beauty gave rise to the name "White Dove of the Desert." One of the finest pieces of

Spanish colonial architecture in the United States, the mission was founded in 1700 by Padre Kino, who named it after his patron saint, Xavier. Bac was the Indian village name, meaning "where the waters gathered." Raiding Apache destroyed the original buildings of Kino's mission after the Pima Indian revolt in 1751. Franciscan missionaries began construction of the present church in 1783, finished 14 years later. The architect used a mixture of Byzantine, Moorish, and late Mexican baroque styles. Adobe brick walls 3 to 6 feet thick keep the interior cool even on hot summer days. Some mystery surrounds the church: who designed it? Why was one tower left unfinished? Only legends supply the answers. Visitors are welcome inside the church, where a recording tells of the history and identifies the many saints and symbols. Above the altar, a statue of St. Francis Xavier is the central figure; above him is the Virgin of the Immaculate Conception; highest of all is the figure of God. Flash photos are permitted unless a service is in progress. Indians should not be photographed during worship. The church is still a spiritual

Grotto of Lourdes (replica) on Hill of the Cross          altar inside San Xavier del Bac

center for the Papago. Masses are held Sun. at 0800, 1030, 1200; weekdays at 0830; Sat. at 1900.

The small hill to the E has a replica of the Grotto of Lourdes. To the W is a former mortuary chapel where 2 early Franciscan friars lie buried. Major celebrations are the San Xavier Pageant and Fiesta (Apr.), the Feast of St. Francis of Assisi (Oct.), and the Feast of St. Francis Xavier (Dec.). The Mission has a small gift shop inside, and the Papago sometimes set up food stalls outside, especially on Sundays and religious holidays. San Xavier Plaza across from the Mission has shops selling Papago, Zuni, Hopi, and Navajo crafts. Mission San Xavier del Bac is 10 miles S of downtown Tucson. Take I-19 S to exit 95B (Valencia Rd.), go W 2 miles on Valencia Rd., turn L 2 miles on Mission Rd., then L onto San Xavier Road. The

Mission is open daily 0900-1800; donation; tel. 294-2624.

## SANTA RITA MOUNTAINS

Birdwatchers flock to Madera Canyon in the Santa Rita Mountains, 38 miles S of Tucson. The Santa Ritas, surrounded by a sea of desert, provide an attractive habitat for unusual wildlife, of which the coppery-tailed trogon bird *(Trogon elegans)* is the star attraction. During summer this colorful parrot-like bird flies in from Mexico to nest in tall trees in the canyon bottoms. More than 200 other birds have been spotted in Madera Canyon. April and May are best for bird-watching; hummingbirds are most numerous in June and September. Bear, deer, mountain lion, coatimundi, and javelina also share the spring-fed canyon.

**hiking and camping:** The Santa Ritas have over 70 miles of hiking trails, many suitable for horseback riding. Mount Wrightson, 9,543 feet, crowns the range and makes a challenging 13-mile RT hike. Two trails to its summit start at Madera Canyon's Roundup Picnic Area (elev. 5,400 feet): Old Baldy Trail (Forest Trail #94) and Super Trail (#134). Super Trail is easier, as its name implies. Allow a full day (10 hours) or backpack. A popular day hike is the 4½-mile loop from Bog Springs Campground to Bog Springs and Kent Springs. The trail elevations range from 5,100 feet at the campground to 6,600 feet at Kent Springs. For topo maps see the 7½-minute "Mount Wrightson" quadrangle or the Southern Arizona Hiking Club's 1:62,500 Santa Rita map. David Mazel's *Arizona Trails* has detailed trail descriptions. Bog Springs Campground is open all year, $4/site, trailers OK. The Santa Rita Lodge in Madera Canyon, Box 444, Amado, AZ 85640, tel. 625-8746, operates 12 rental units with kitchenettes, a gift shop, and information center. From Tucson take I-19 just past Green Valley to Madera Canyon Exit 63, then go 13 miles southeast.

**vicinity of the Santa Rita Mountains:** Green Valley is a retirement village on rolling hills overlooking the Santa Cruz Valley. Visitors can enjoy the 18-hole golf course, tennis courts, pool, and other amenities by staying in Fairfield's Desert Casitas Lodge, Box 587, Green Valley, AZ 85622-0587; tel. 625-2010. Rates start at $63 s, $74 d from Jan. to Mar.; and $45 s, $54 d from Apr. to December. Green Valley is 25 miles S of Tucson; Exit 65 or 63 from I-19.

## TITAN MISSILE MUSEUM

The U.S. Air Force maintained 18 Titan missile sites near Tucson, with other sites in Kansas and Arkansas. While all have been deactivated now, this one has been preserved as a memorial. Now you may step inside the missile complex, operational from 1963 until 1984, to see

the Titan 2 missile, silo, and controls. One-hour tours depart Wed. to Sun. hourly 0900-1600 (possibly on Mon. & Tue., too). Call first for reservations to be assured of a space; tel. 791-2929 (Tucson) or tel. 625-7736 (Green Valley). Admission: $4 adult, $3 seniors and military, $2 age 10-17. The museum is located about 20 miles SE of Tucson near Green Valley; take I-10 to Duval Mine Rd. Exit 69, then turn W 1/10 mile to entrance.

## TUBAC

Following the Pima Indian Revolt in 1751, the Spanish decided to provide protection for their missions and settlers in this remote region. Tubac Presidio was founded the following year, making it the oldest European settlement in what's now Arizona. Apache raids and political turmoil in following decades made life unbearable at times, and Tubac's citizens fled on 8 occasions. When the United States took over after the 1854 Gadsden Purchase, Tubac was only a pile of crumbling adobe ruins. Prospectors and adventure-seekers, fired by tales of old Spanish mines, poured in. Mines were found, and by 1860 Tubac was a boom town with Arizona's first newspaper, the *Weekly Arizonan*. The Civil War brought the good times to an end when the troops guarding the town headed east to fight. Apache once again raided the settlement, and the inhabitants once again had to flee. Tubac came back to life after the Civil War but the boom days were over.

Much later, when an art school opened in 1948, Tubac was on its way to becoming an artists' colony. Today, the village of Tubac has about 50 studios and galleries displaying modern jewelry, ceramics, wood carvings, prints, batiks, paintings, and other works. You'll see the Tubac motto: "Where art and history meet." During the week-long Tubac Festival of the Arts in Feb., residents and visiting artists celebrate with exhibitions, demonstrations, and food. Tubac is 45 miles S of Tucson; take I-19 Exit 34.

**Tubac Center for the Arts:** This gallery displays a variety of excellent work by local artists. It's open Tues. to Sat. 1000-1630 and Sun. 1200-1630; free. Located on Plaza Rd. in the middle of Tubac.

**Tubac Presidio State Historic Park:** A museum, just E of the artists' colony, shows the ups and downs of Tubac's history since its founding in 1752. The printing press used for Arizona's first newspaper is here and you can buy a reproduction of the first issue, dated 3 Mar. 1859. Other exhibits show how early residents made their own clothing, furniture, tools, and medicine. Models illustrate how the presidio appeared in the early years. Stairs lead underground to excavations of the original foundation and wall. Behind the museum is a schoolhouse built in 1885. (Tubac had Arizona's first school in 1789, but it no longer exists.) The Historic Park is open daily 0800-1700; admission $1 adult. A mesquite-shaded picnic area is across the street; no camping.

**accommodations and food:** Tubac Valley Country Club, one mile N, offers rooms ($50.40 s, $56.70 d and up from 1 Jan. to 30 Apr., lower prices in off seasons), The Stables Restaurant (breakfast, lunch and dinner; mod. to exp.), an 18-hole golf course, tennis court, and pool; tel. 398-2211. Take I-19 Exit 40.

# TUMACACORI NATIONAL MONUMENT

This massive adobe ruin evokes visions of Spanish missionaries and devout Indian followers. Father Kino first visited the Pima village of Tumacacori in 1691 and said mass under a brush shelter. Kino's successors continued the mission work of teaching religion and farming, but the present church was not

*Tumacacori Mission Ruin*

*Pena Blanca Lake*

begun until about 1800. Franciscan Father Narciso Gutierrez, determined to build a church as splendid as San Xavier del Bac, supervised the construction by Indian laborers. Work went slowly, and although never quite finished, the building was in use by 1822. Then the new Mexican government restricted funds for mission work and began to evict all foreign missionaries. Tumacacori's last resident priest, Father Ramon Liberos of Spain, was hauled off in 1828. Indians continued to care for the church and were occasionally visited by missionaries from Mexico, but raiding Apache made life hard. The last devout Indians finally gave up in 1848, packed the church furnishings, and moved to San Xavier del Bac.

Tumacacori fell into ruins before it was protected as a National Monument in 1908. A museum gives the history of the Indians and Spanish, shows architectural features, and displays some of the original wooden statues of the Mission. A self-guided tour tells about the circular mortuary chapel, graveyard, storeroom, and other ruined structures surrounding the church. Picnic tables are on the grounds but no camping. Across the street is Tumacacori Restaurant, serving Mexican food and steaks. Wisdom's Cafe, ⅓ mile N, also offers Mexican food. Tumacacori Fiesta, with Indian dances, crafts, and food, is held the 1st Sun. in December. Tumacacori Mission is 48 miles S of Tucson near I-19 Exit 29, or just 3 miles S of Tubac. The Monument is open daily 0800-1700; admission $1/car; tel. 398-2341.

## PENA BLANCA LAKE

A scenic 49-acre lake in the hills 16 miles NW of Nogales. Pena Blanca (Spanish for "white rock") is named for light-colored bluffs overlooking the water. Fishermen come to catch bass, bluegill, crappie, catfish and, from Nov. to Mar., rainbow trout. At an elevation of 4,000 feet, the lake area is a bit cooler than Tucson. A trail leads around the lakeshore. A lodge with motel, restaurant, bar, boat rentals, groceries, and fishing supplies sits beside the water. Reservations are recommended for lodging and boat rentals, especially on weekends; $26.25 s, $26.25-$31.50 d; tel. 287-5251. To reach the lodge, take the Ruby Rd. Exit 12 from I-19 and drive 11 miles W on AZ 289, a paved road.

**Atascosa Lookout Trail:** Forest Trail #100 climbs steeply from 4,700 feet through desert vegetation, oaks, juniper, and pinyon pine to the summit at 6,255 feet. Allow ½ a day for the 6-mile RT. Trailhead is 5 miles W of Pena Blanca Lake on Forest Route 39, a gravel road. Look for a parking area on the S side of the road; trailhead (unsigned) is on the N side. From the top, mountain ranges in Mexico can be seen to the S, Pena Blanca Lake and Nogales to the E, the Santa Ritas and Rincons to the NE, the Santa Catalinas to the N, and the Baboquivaris to the west. The trail is shown on the 7½-minute Ruby topo map. You can hike year-round except after snowstorms.

**Sycamore Canyon Trail:** This trail is rough in spots but can be followed downstream all the way to the Mexican border, a distance of 6 miles OW. The scenic canyon contains plants and wildlife rarely found elsewhere in the United States. The trail crosses Gooding Research Natural Area, named for a prominent Arizona botanist. The first 1¼ miles is easy walking, but then boulder-hopping and wading are necessary. Toward the end, the canyon opens up and saguaro appear on the slopes. A barbed-wire fence marks the Mexican border. The trailhead is about 10 miles W of Pena Blanca Lake on Forest Route 39; turn L ¼ mile on Forest Route 218 to Hank and Yank Historical Site. These adobe ruins were part of a ranch started in the 1880s by 2 former Army scouts. Hiking in Sycamore Canyon is good all year. Elevation ranges from 4,000 feet at the trailhead to 3,500 feet at border. Depending on how far you go, the hike can be an easy 2-hour stroll or a long (10-hour) 12-mile RT dayhike all the way to Mexico; see Ruby topo map. No camping allowed along the trail.

**camping:** White Rocks Campground is in Pena Blanca Canyon upstream from the lake. There's drinking water and room for trailers to 22 feet; $3. Turn L 1/10 mile onto Forest Route 39 at Milepost 10, one mile before the lodge.

**Arivaca Lake:** A beautiful 90-acre lake, 24 bumpy miles W on Forest Route 39 from Pena Blanca Lake. Fishermen catch largemouth bass, bluegill, and catfish while enjoying the solitude of this remote spot. Facilities are minimal: just parking areas, a boat ramp, and toilets. The best road is from Amado (I-19 Exit 48, 37 miles S of Tucson) to the village of Arivaca, 20 miles (paved). From Arivaca go S 5 miles on Forest Route 39 (gravel), then L 2½ miles to the lake. The other route is from Pena Blanca Lake on Forest Route 39; go 21 miles W from the lake then turn R 2½ miles. This route

winds through the Atascosa Mountains past the ghost towns of Ruby (fenced off), and Oro Blanco.

## NOGALES

Nogales, sitting astride the U.S. and Mexican border, is a truly international city. Most visitors to Mexico have shopping on their minds, and Nogales offers a huge selection of handicrafts. You'll also discover fine restaurants and serenading *mariachi* bands. Mexicans too like to cross the border for shopping and sampling foreign culture—you'll see them trooping into Safeway, McDonalds, and Pizza Hut.

**history:** Nogales Pass has been used by Indians for at least 2,000 years for migration and trade. The Hohokam came through to reach the Gulf of California for shells prized as bracelet and necklace material. Pimas, thought to be descended from the Hohokam, settled and traveled in the Santa Cruz River Valley and Nogales area after A.D. 1500. During the Spanish era, missionaries, soldiers, ranchers, and prospectors also passed through. Apache used

Gen. Fierro    Gen. Villa    Gen. Ortega

*Pancho Villa (center) and associates, 1915*

*Nogales (Sonora) and border, about 1920*

the pass on their raiding forays until well into the 19th century. Traders on the Guaymas-Tucson route knew the spot as Los Nogales (Spanish for "The Walnuts"). A survey team marked the international line here in 1855, one year after the Gadsden Purchase.

The town — or rather, the 2 towns (one in each country) — was started by 2 men in 1880. Juan Jose Vasquez established a roadhouse (refreshment and food for travelers) on the Mexican side, and some months later Jacob Isaacson set up a trading post on the American side. The first railroad line anywhere across the border came through Nogales in Oct. 1882. Trade, silver mining, and ranching kept Nogales growing. In 1898 its population of 1,500 on the U.S. side made it the 5th largest city in Arizona. When Pancho Villa threatened Nogales in 1916, the worried U.S. Army established Camp Little on the edge of town. Relations between the 2 halves of Nogales remained good despite the political turmoil in Mexico, and Camp Little was closed in 1933. Tourists "discovered" Nogales in the 1940s and tourism, along with trade, keeps the border busy today.

**sights:** Most visitors to Ambos Nogales ("Both Nogales") park on the American side near the border ($2/day) and set off on foot. This saves delays in crossing the border by car and finding parking spots in Mexico. The Pimeria Alta Historical Society Museum gives a good introduction to Nogales. Artifacts and old photos illustrate the long and colorful history of southern Arizona and northern Sonora (Mexico). The building, put up 1914 to house the Nogales (Arizona) city hall, police, and fire departments, is itself an attraction. You can see the old jail, horse-drawn water pumper, mining office, and other exhibits. The Society's research library has a wealth of books on regional history, and is open to the public. Museum and library are open Mon. to Fri. 0900-1700, Sat. 1000-1600, and Sun. 1300-1600; tel. 287-5402. The distinctive mission-style building is on the corner of Grand Ave. and Crawford St., ¼-mile N of the border. Local artists display their work in the Hilltop Art Gallery from Sept. to May, Hilltop Dr. (see map); tel. 287-5515. The square granite structure with a shiny aluminum dome, on the hillside to the NE, is the Santa Cruz County

Courthouse. Built in 1904, it is the oldest courthouse in Arizona still in use.

**accommodations:** La Hacienda Motor Hotel is a good value and has a Mexican-American restaurant, 1118 Grand Ave. (at AZ 82, 1 ¾ mile N of the border); $17.33 s, $19.43 d.; tel. 287-2781. Motel 6 is a mile farther N at 2210 Tucson Hwy. (just S of AZ 189); $18.85 s, $23.05 d; tel. 281-2951. Five other motels are on Grand Avenue. Sheraton Rio Rico Resort has golf, tennis, a pool, and horseback riding, 12 miles N of town (take I-19 Exit 17); $47.25 s, $57.75 d and up; tel. 281-1901. About a dozen hotels are on the Mexican side, but can be hard to find as streets aren't signposted. Three are

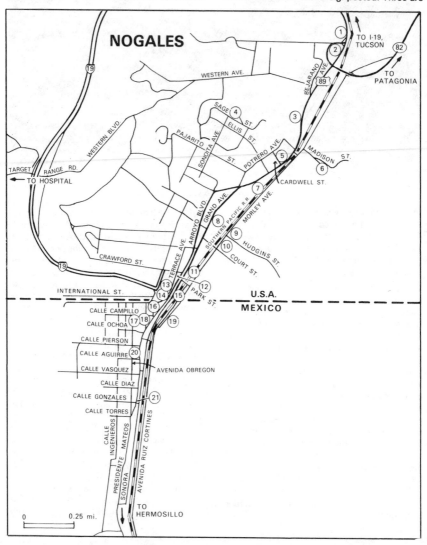

*Chief Tully with police officers behind City Hall, Nogales (Arizona) about 1936*

on Av. Juarez, 2 blocks to the R after crossing the border. Prices usually run US$10-20.

**camping:** Mi Casa RV Park is 4½ miles N of the border at 3420 Tucson-Nogales Hwy. (US 89); tel. 281-1150; tents or RVs $13.10 w/hookups. Bird Hill Trailer Park is 3 miles N of the border at 2428 Tucson-Nogales Hwy.; tel. 281-0078; (no tents), RVs $10.60 w/hookups. Campgrounds are also at Pena Blanca Lake and Patagonia Lake.

**food:** Grand Ave. is home for most of the restaurants on the Arizona side. You'll find Zula's (zulaburgers, steaks, Mexican; 1267 Grand Ave.), Denny's (920 Grand Ave.), Pizza Hut (624 Grand Ave.), and others. Molina's PK Outpost has many historical artifacts on display and a long Mexican menu in the historic Pete Kitchen Ranch N of Nogales on the I-19 frontage road. Pick up deli-style foods at the Arroyo Market, next to Garrett Wray Curios at 492 Grand Avenue. In Mexico, La Roca offers excellent Mexican food (entrees US$5-10) and nightly live music; 3 blocks to the L after the border crossing. Pancho Villa Restaurant in Hotel Olivia has mariachi music (corner of Av. Obregon and Aguirre). Cantonese cuisine is served at Mi Wah Restaurant (Av. Obregon, 3 blocks to R after the border crossing). Other restaurants are scattered around town; many have English menus and all accept US dollars.

**events:** The Mexican side celebrates Cinco de Mayo (May 5th) with a parade. Biggest annual event is the Santa Cruz County Fair in Sept. or Oct.; see a cow-chip chucking contest, fiddlers' competition, rooster crowing contest, animal exhibits, and entertainment. In Oct. the

---

**NOGALES**

1. La Hacienda Motor Hotel
2. Nogales-Santa Cruz
   Chamber of Commerce
3. Denny's Restaurant
4. Hilltop Art Gallery
5. Pizza Hut
6. War Memorial Park
7. public library
8. First China Restaurant
9. post office
10. County Courthouse
11. Pimeria Alta Museum
12. Consulado de Mexico
13. bus station (AZ)
14. Federal Building
    (U.S. Immigration and Customs)
15. border crossing
16. Mexican bus stations
17. Hotel Fray Marcos de Niza
18. Mexican post office
19. La Roca Restaurant
20. Hotel Olivia
21. Hotel Granada

---

*across the Border
in Nogales,
Sonora*

Arizonans throw an Oktoberfest with beer, German food, and entertainment. The Arizona side also has a Christmas Parade in late Nov./early December. Bullfighting takes place on the Mexico side in the Guadalupe Plaza de Toros; ask the Nogales-Santa Cruz Chamber of Commerce for dates.

**shopping:** When you cross into Mexico, all the shopkeepers know why you're there! Mexican craftsmen turn out an astonishing array of products, from Tiffany-style lampshades to saddles. Because a day's wages in Mexico comes close to an hour's wages in the U.S., most crafts are real bargains. Be sure to shop around and haggle before laying out any cash! Even in the large fixed-price stores, it's worth asking for a discount. English is spoken by all the eager salespeople. There's no need to change money into Mexican pesos either; dollars are happily accepted, major credit cards too. Crafts come from many corners of Mexico and merchants usually know their origin. Popular buys include: chess sets of carved onyx (a soft stone with a layered pattern), clay reproductions of Mayan art, painted vases, embroidered clothing, glassware, hand-tooled leather (bags, purses, and belts), wool blankets, and woodcarvings (including furniture). A few items are *very unpopular* with

U.S. Customs and will be confiscated: guns & ammo, fireworks, illegal drugs, switchblades, meat, poultry, and sea-turtle oil. Adults can bring back other goods totalling US$400, plus one quart of liquor—all duty-free—every 31 days. You can also shop for Mexican crafts on the AZ side of the border; Garrett Wray Curios (492 Grand Ave.) offers a large and varied selection.

**crossing the border:** No permit is needed to walk or drive across the border for visits in Nogales of 72 hours or less. To go beyond Nogales, U.S. citizens need proof of citizenship to get a tourist permit (good for 90 days) at the border. Visitors from other countries should check with a Mexican consulate for entry requirements; they should also see U.S. Immigration about re-entry before stepping across. In Nogales, AZ, the Consulado de Mexico is at 137 Terrace Ave.; tel. 287-2521. A separate permit is needed for driving a car in Mexico beyond Nogales. Pick it up at the border by showing proof of car ownership. When an accident occurs in Mexico, all parties involved are considered guilty until proven innocent; having insurance can prevent a stay in jail. Most U.S. policies are worthless, so you'll need to purchase Mexican insurance. Numerous agencies along Grand Ave. in Nogales, AZ, advertise Mexican insurance; they have daily and longer rates. You don't need to change money within Nogales; dollars or pesos are welcomed on both sides of the border. For longer trips into Mexico, the local currency is essential. You can save a little by purchasing pesos on the U.S. side. Safeway and other stores near the border almost always have a surplus of Mexican currency and will sell it at a better rate than banks.

**services:** The U.S. post office is just E of the border station (see map). Holy Cross Hospital is W of town on Target Range Rd.; tel. 287-2771. You'll find a public swimming pool and tennis courts near the War Memorial Park on Madison St. (see map). Golfers can tee off at: Meadow Hills, 3425 Country Club Rd. (NW of town); tel. 281-2165; Rio Rico Golf., 12 miles N (I-19 Exit 17); tel. 281-8567; and Kino Springs Country Club, 5 miles NE on AZ 82 (Patagonia Rd.); tel. 287-8701.

**information:** The Nogales-Santa Cruz Chamber of Commerce is helpful with local events, facilities, and sights. Open Mon. to Fri. 0900-1700 and Sat. 0900-1500; tel. 287-3685. When entering Nogales from the N on Grand Ave. (US 89), turn R on the street just *past* the Patagonia Rd. interchange (AZ 82). The Mexicans also have a tourist office (on the R just after crossing the border). The U.S. Forest Service office can tell you about hiking, camping, and road conditions in the Coronado National Forest to the W and E of Nogales; the office is 3 miles N of the border on US 89; tel. 281-2296. Nogales (AZ) has a library at 748 Grand Ave.; tel. 287-3343.

## TRANSPORT

**tours:** Headed for Mexico? The Coronado Inn can arrange train and air tickets and make hotel reservations; 900 Grand Ave., Nogales, AZ 85621; tel. 287-2785.

**bus:** Citizen Auto Stage sends 8 buses to Tucson ($5.85 OW), 3 of which go on to Phoenix ($24.35 OW). First departure is at 0700, last at 2000. The trip to Tucson takes 1¾ hours, and stops at Tumacacori, Tubac and other places along the way. Citizen Auto Stage is just 2 blocks from the border at 126 Terrace Ave. (next to Safeway). On the Mexican side 2 companies, Transportes Norte de Sonora (TNS) and Autotransportes Tres Estellas de Oro, provide extensive bus services at low cost. Each has about 15 daily departures from about 0730 to 2100. The stations are on opposite sides of Pesqueira St., one block to the R after crossing the border.

**train:** An express train leaves every afternoon for Mexico City (42 hours) via Hermosillo (4 hours) and Guadalajara (28 hours). Sleeping cars are available. A ticket office is located in the Mexican Tourism Building (open 0830-1100) near the border. The train station itself is about 4½ miles S; take a taxi or the Av. Obregon bus.

**by air:** The nearest major airports are at Tucson (64 miles N) and Hermosillo (174 miles S). Nogales has a small (but international!) airfield on Patagonia Road.

*Pimeria Alta Historical Museum*

# PATAGONIA AND VICINITY

The rolling hills of grass and woodlands surrounding Patagonia make up some of the state's choice cattle and horse lands. Patagonia, 19 miles NE of Nogales, is on the alternate route from Tucson to Nogales. Many people like to make a loop between the 2 cities by driving through Sonoita and Patagonia in one direction (I-10, AZ Hwys. 83 and 82), and the Santa Cruz Valley (I-19) in the other.

## SIGHTS

**Patagonia Lake State Park:**  A pleasant place for picnicking, fishing, and camping. The large, 275-acre reservoir is stocked with largemouth bass, crappie, bluegill, and channel catfish. Rainbow trout are released in winter. The marina (open daily 0800-1800) has a boat ramp, gas, boat and canoe rentals, and camping and fishing supplies. Swim at Boulder Beach (no lifeguard). Hiking trails go around the lake; ask a ranger to point them out. Petroglyphs on the far side are reached by boat or on foot. At an elevation of 4,000 feet, the park stays open all year with spring and fall the favorite times. Campground fee is $5/day ($7 w/hookups); day use is $2; nonresidents pay $1/vehicle extra.

**Museum of the Horse:**  Anne Stradling's lifelong love of horses is reflected in this amazing collection. Immaculate horse-drawn carriages, saddles, harnesses, Indian artifacts, Western art, even a 400-year-old Mexican ox cart fill 6 large rooms. Open daily 0900-1700; $2 adult, $.50 under 12. Located in Patagonia next to the Stage Stop Inn.

**Patagonia-Sonoita Creek Sanctuary:**  The Nature Conservancy maintains 312 acres along

*adobe ruin near Harshaw*

Sonoita Creek as a wildlife preserve. Year-round water and a variety of habitats attract a diverse birdlife with over 200 species identified. White-tailed deer, *chulo* (coati), javelina, bobcat, badger, and other animals also live in the thickets and woods. The public is welcome to visit, but no picnicking, camping, or pets. In Patagonia turn NW off AZ 82 onto 4th Ave., then L on Pennsylvania Avenue. The pavement ends and you'll have to ford the creek (don't cross if you can't see the bottom), and then you're in the sanctuary. Park near any of the 4 gates on the L along the next 1½ miles and start walking. An information board is just in from Gate 2.

**Cave of the Bells:** A "wild" cave in the Santa Rita Mountains to the north. The variety of minerals and an underground lake attract experienced spelunkers. Obtain gate key and directions from the Forest Service Office in Nogales or the supervisor's offices in Tucson or Phoenix. Onyx Cave, nearby, can be visited with permission of the Escabrosa Grotto Inc., Box 3634, Tucson, AZ 85722.

**ghost towns:** Decaying houses, piles of rubble, cemeteries, and old mine shafts mark deserted mining camps in the Patagonia Mountains to the south. Some of these are visited in daily tours from the Stage Stop Inn at Patagonia. On your own, you'll want the Forest Service map or topo maps to find the old sites. In a 45-mile loop drive, you can see the sites of Harshaw, Mowry, Washington Camp, and Duquesne. These ghost towns are described in *Arizona's Best Ghost Towns* by Philip Varney, and *Ghost Towns of Arizona* by Jim and Barbara Sherman. You can also drive E to the Huachuaca Mountains, Parker Lake, or

*coati* (Nasua narica)

Coronado National Memorial on the back roads. Most are dirt and should be avoided if it's been raining or snowing.

**accommodations and food:** The Stage Stop Inn (Box 777, Patagonia, AZ, 85624) is in the middle of sleepy Patagonia; $30.89 s, $36.29 d; tel. 394-2211. Hitching rings on the front are for tying up your horse. The restaurant next door has Mexican and American food including steaks, salad bar, and an all-you-can-eat Sun. buffet; open daily 0630-2100. Circle Z Ranch is a working cattle ranch with guest accommodations, 5 miles SW of Patagonia. The ranch features horseback riding and guests are welcome to come along on the roundups and other ranch work. A swimming pool and tennis court are other attractions. Write c/o Patagonia, AZ 85624; tel. 287-2091.

# COCHISE TRAIL

Chief of the Chiricahua Apache, Cochise was highly respected by white man and Indian alike for his integrity and leadership skills. He was never defeated in battle. The SE corner of Arizona was named Cochise County in his honor in 1881, despite the fact that he had waged war against troops and settlers for 11 years (1861-1872). Many historic sites of the Old West can be visited on a 206-mile loop through this varied country. Tourist offices call this drive the "Cochise Trail."

## TOMBSTONE

When prospector Ed Schieffelin headed out this way in March of 1877, friends told him that the only thing he would find among all the Apache and rattlesnakes would be his own tombstone. But he set out anyway, alone, and staked a silver claim, naming it Tombstone. When Ed struck it rich nearby, his brother Al said, "You're a lucky cuss." And the Lucky Cuss mine became one of Arizona's richest. Other claims were equally descriptive: Contention, Tough Nut, and Goodenough. The town was laid out in 1879 and blossomed to a population of 15,000 just 2 years later. It was said that saloons and gambling halls made up 2 of every 3 buildings in the business district. The famous OK Corral gunfight took place in 1881, and its details are still being debated by historians (see below). Shootings and hangings in the 1880s made Boot Hill Graveyard a busy place. Tombstone's rough and wild times have fueled the imagination of countless novelists and script-writers. Fires nearly wiped out the town on 2 occasions, but it was flooding in the mines in 1886 and 1887 that sent the town into a swift decline. Tombstone, "the town too tough to die," managed to survive and is now popular with visitors seeking out the Wild West.

## SIGHTS

**Boot Hill Graveyard:** Lying here are "Dutch Annie" (a widely admired prostitute), the losers of the OK Corral shootout, hanging (or lynching) victims, and assorted gunslingers. Many of the estimated 276 graves are unmarked; those that are have much to say about life in old Tombstone. Boot Hill is on the N edge of town; enter through the Boot Hill Gift Shop; open daily 0730-1800; free.

**St. Paul's Episcopal Church:** Built in 1881, this is the oldest standing Protestant church in Arizona.

**Allen Street:** Guns still blaze and bodies hit the dust on Allen Street, where gunfights and barroom brawls are staged. The action takes place on the 2nd, 4th, and 5th Sundays of the month at 1400. The show is free but you can make donations. On the 1st and 3rd Sundays of the month the OK Corral has a demonstration culminating in the famous shootout; $2 admission.

**Tombstone Courthouse State Historic Park:** Dating from 1882, this red-brick building was the scene of many emotional trials. Some of the convicted were hanged in the courtyard to the northwest. Not everyone was lucky enough to get a trial. A mob seized John Heath, accomplice to a robbery and murder in Bisbee, from jail and lynched him in 1884. The 6-man coroner's jury later declared that the unlucky fellow died "...from emphysema of the lungs —a disease common to high altitudes—which might have been caused by strangulation, self-inflicted or otherwise." Tombstone's courthouse was abandoned in 1929 when the county seat moved to Bisbee. The courthouse has been restored and now houses a museum of artifacts and photos of the old days. A gift shop has a good selection of books on Arizona history. Open daily 0800-1700; $1 adult 18 and over; 3rd and Toughnut Streets.

**The OK Corral:** The Earps and Doc Holliday shot it out with the Clanton cowboys on this site in Oct. 1881. Markers and life-size figures

*the lynching of John Heath*

show how it all happened, or at least one version of it. Other things to see are the studio and photos taken by Camilius S. Fly of early Tombstone, the old stables, a hearse that carried many a passenger to Boot Hill Graveyard, and even a red-light-district shack. You can "walk where they fell" daily 0830-1700 for $1 admission (children under 6 free). Located off Allen

*the OK Corral*

St. between 3rd and 4th Streets.

**Historama:** This 45-minute show recreates the old days with movies and animated figures. Presentations are given hourly from 0900-1600; $1 (under 6 free). Located next door to the OK Corral entrance.

**Schieffelin Hall:** Major theatrical companies

of the day performed in this large adobe building dating from 1881. John Sullivan and a company of boxers gave exhibitions here. On the corner of Fremont and 4th Streets. Not currently open to the public.

**Rose Tree Inn:** A rose slip sent as a wedding gift in the spring of 1885 from Scotland has

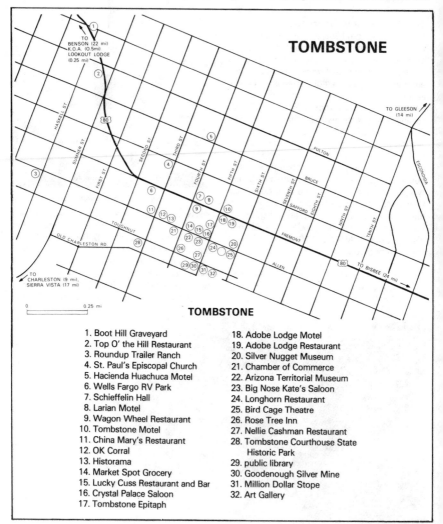

**TOMBSTONE**

1. Boot Hill Graveyard
2. Top O' the Hill Restaurant
3. Roundup Trailer Ranch
4. St. Paul's Episcopal Church
5. Hacienda Huachuca Motel
6. Wells Fargo RV Park
7. Schieffelin Hall
8. Larian Motel
9. Wagon Wheel Restaurant
10. Tombstone Motel
11. China Mary's Restaurant
12. OK Corral
13. Historama
14. Market Spot Grocery
15. Lucky Cuss Restaurant and Bar
16. Crystal Palace Saloon
17. Tombstone Epitaph
18. Adobe Lodge Motel
19. Adobe Lodge Restaurant
20. Silver Nugget Museum
21. Chamber of Commerce
22. Arizona Territorial Museum
23. Big Nose Kate's Saloon
24. Longhorn Restaurant
25. Bird Cage Theatre
26. Rose Tree Inn
27. Nellie Cashman Restaurant
28. Tombstone Courthouse State Historic Park
29. public library
30. Goodenough Silver Mine
31. Million Dollar Stope
32. Art Gallery

grown to cover an amazing 7,000 sq. feet. The "tree," claimed to be the world's largest, is a Lady Banksia. Its sweet-scented white blossoms usually appear in early April. Rooms exhibit a collection of antique furnishings belonging to a pioneer who arrived by wagon train in 1880; $1 adult (under 14 free); 4th and Toughnut Streets.

**Goodenough Silver Mine:** A guide will outfit you with a hardhat and lamp, then lead the way underground into this old silver mine for a one-hour tour. After descending 85 steps, the route leads past the Million Dollar Stope and then actually under the streets of Tombstone. Enter at the Rocksmiths, 5th and Toughnut; open daily except Wed. 1000-1600; $3.50 adult, $2.50 under 18; tel. 457-3691.

**Million Dollar Stope:** Miles of tunnels were dug out around Tombstone by hand to recover silver ore, and this particular chamber collapsed. A horse-drawn delivery wagon was passing overhead when the roof gave way; the driver managed to jump to safety but the horse, still alive, had to be led out a mine entrance 2 miles away. The stope is at the corner of 5th and Toughnut Streets.

**Crystal Palace Saloon:** Built in 1879, this watering hole and gambling house was the height of luxury in early Tombstone. As many as 5 bartenders stood on duty to serve the thirsty customers 'round the clock. The clientele has changed over the years but the Saloon still serves up drinks; corner 5th and Allen Streets.

**Tombstone *Epitaph*:** As one story goes, the town's newspaper was named when one of its founders, John P. Clum, was taking the stagecoach home from Tucson. Clum asked the passengers what they thought would be a good name. By coincidence, Ed Schieffelin was on board. He replied, "Well, I christened the district Tombstone; you should have no trou-

*John P. Clum*

ble furnishing the 'Epitaph.' " Clum founded the paper in 1880 and it's still being published. "Every Tombstone should have an Epitaph," residents say. You can visit the office to see the original press and other printing exhibits; free. Souvenir copies are sold—read your own *Epitaph*. Located on 5th St. (between Freemont and Allen Streets).

**Bird Cage Theatre:** This 1881 dance hall, gambling house, saloon, brothel, and theatre was the favored hangout of local characters and desperados. During its first 3 years, the doors never closed. Birdcage-like stalls suspended from the ceiling gave the place its name. See if you can count the reported 140 bullet holes in the walls and ceiling. The well-preserved building is open daily 0830-1730; $2 adult, $.50 children 8-12; Allen and 6th Streets.

*Bird Cage Theatre*

**Silver Nugget Museum:** See exhibits of outlaws, the law, Nellie Cashman—"Angel of Tombstone," photos, old documents, guns, and furnishings from pioneer homes. Admission $1, children under 12 free; Allen and 6th Streets.

## PRACTICALITIES

**accommodations and camping:** Tombstone Motel ($21.20 s, $25.20 d), 502 E. Fremont St. (US 80); tel. 457-3478. Adobe Lodge ($23.54 s, $25.68 d), corner 5th and Fremont Sts., has an Italian-American restaurant; tel. 457-3641. Larian Motel ($19.08 s, $25.44 d), 410 E. Fremont St.; tel. 457-2272. Hacienda Huachuca Motel ($15 s or d, $25 efficiencies), 320 E. Bruce (at 4th St.), has a pool; tel. 457-2201. Lookout Lodge ($33.92 s, $37.10 d), a Best Western, is ¾-mile N on US 80, has a pool; tel. 457-2223. Wells Fargo RV Park ($8 tent, $11.10 RV w/hookups) is right in town at 3rd and Fremont Sts.; has laundromat and showers; tel. 457-3966. Round Up Trailer Ranch ($10.50 tent or RV w/hookups) is at 201 W. Allen St.; has laundromat and showers; tel. 457-3738. Tombstone Hills KOA is 1½ miles N on US 80; $10 tent or RV; has a pool, laundromat, showers, and store; tel. 457-3829.

**food:** Not surprisingly, most restaurants feature Western decor and food. The Nellie Cashman Restaurant and Pie Salon is Tombstone's oldest, established in 1882. Breakfast, sandwiches, and dinners (shrimp, chicken, steaks, etc.) are served; 5th and Toughnut Streets. The Longhorn Restaurant offers Mexican, Italian, and American breakfasts, lunches, and dinners; 5th and Allen Streets. Adobe Lodge Restaurant dishes up breakfast and Italian-American meals; 5th and Fremont

Streets. The Lucky Cuss Restaurant and bar has sandwiches and dinners "1880's style;" on Allen St. between 4th and 5th Streets. The Wagon Wheel is open for lunch and dinner with steaks, chicken, and seafood; has live entertainment Thur. to Sun.; corner of 4th and Fremont Streets. Top O' The Hill Restaurant serves up Mexican and American meals; open for breakfast, lunch, and dinner; N on US 80 just before Boot Hill Graveyard.

**events:** Shootouts are held every Sun. afternoon (see "Allen Street," above). Tombstone's biggest celebration is the annual Helldorado Days, a 3-day event with shootouts, parades, square dancing, and other lively entertainment beginning on the 3rd Fri. of October. Smaller scale festivities are thrown for: Territorial Days (1st weekend in Mar.), Wyatt Earp Days (Memorial Day weekend), International Order of Old Bastards Parade (3rd Sun. in June), Nellie Cashman Day (Aug. 15th), and the Wild West Days on Labor Day Weekend.

**shopping, services, and information:** Allen Street is lined with shops selling Old West souvenirs, books, clothing, jewelry, and crafts. Some also have small museums, usually free, that often are worth a look. You can ride a stagecoach for a 15-min. spin around Tombstone; $3 adult, $2 age 6-12; trips start from Big Nose Kate's Saloon on Allen St. between 4th and 5th Streets. Tombstone Association of the Arts supports an art gallery in the original firehouse, next to the One-Million-Dollar Stope at 5th and Toughnut Streets. Pick up groceries at the Market Spot on Allen St. between 4th and 5th Streets. The Chamber of Commerce is on the corner of 4th and Allen Sts. but it's open on an irregular basis (Box 268, Tombstone, AZ 85638). The public library is at 5th and Toughnut Streets.

## VICINITY OF TOMBSTONE

Ghost-town enthusiasts will want to explore remnants of former mining towns. Gleeson, 15 miles E on a graded gravel road, flourished by mining copper from 1909 until the 1930s.

Operations ended in 1953. A saloon on the old main street is still open and you can see ruins of the jail, cemetery, school, adobe hospital, and other buildings. Mine tailings and machinery rest on the hillside. Courtland, one mile E and 3 miles N on good gravel roads, is occupied solely by ghosts. A jail, several buildings, and numerous foundations remain. Watch out for open mine shafts in this area.

At the site of Pearce, 9 miles N of Courtland, Jimmie Pearce found gold in 1894. The Commonwealth Mine was a success and the town's population reached 1,500 before dying back in the 1930s, when the mine closed. Pearce's Old Store is still open with a collection of antiques, many of which are for sale. Other things to see are the cemetery (W on the road just N of the store), old post office (across from store), Pearce Church (SW of the store), abandoned houses, and the Commonwealth Mine ruins. Pearce is also reached from I-10; take Exit 331 and head S 22 miles on US 666. In *Arizona's Best Ghost Towns,* Philip Varney devotes a whole chapter to these and other sites of the Tombstone area.

*a stall in the Bird Cage Theatre*

## FORT HUACHUCA

When raiding Apache were threatening settlers and travelers in the San Pedro Valley in 1877, the Army ordered a temporary camp set up near the Huachuca (wa-CHOO-ka) Mountains. In 1886 Fort Huachuca became the advance headquarters for the campaign against Geronimo, until the famous Apache chief surrendered in Aug. of that year. Although the Army later closed more than 50 forts and camps in the Territory, Huachuca was retained to deal with outlaws and renegade Indians near the Mexican border. World Wars I and II and the Korean War saw new duties for the Fort; finally in 1954 it was assigned its current task of testing electronic and communication gear. The town of Sierra Vista grew up outside the gates as a service center for the fort. Many army retirees have settled here; they like the climate and social and recreational opportunities, and they can continue to use base facilities. Sierra Vista now includes Fort Huachuca and is the largest and fastest growing community in Cochise County.

**Fort Huachuca Museum:** The museum's large collection of photos, Indian artifacts, dioramas, and memorabilia date from Apache-fighting days to the present. One room is dedicated to the Fort's Black troops, known as Buffalo soldiers. Barracks and administrative buildings dating back to the 1890s line the parade ground outside. Museum is open weekdays 0900-1600 and weekends 1300-1600 (closed holidays); free. The collection is housed in 2 buildings on either side of Hungerford at Grierson. From the Main Gate in Sierra Vista, it's about 2½ miles in; when you come to the Community Center Annex, turn L on Mizner and follow signs. Be sure to pick up a free visitor's pass at one of the gates (a driver's license and vehicle registration must be shown).

**accommodations and food:** When driving through Sierra Vista, you have a choice of taking the bypass route or going downtown on Fry Blvd. and Garden Avenue. Fry Blvd. has a Motel 6 and several other motels. Restaurants on Fry Blvd. include the Beef Baron (prime rib, seafood), Joy Garden (Chinese), Bar 'B' Que Pit, Golden Corral Family Steak House, Denny's, Imperial Garden (Chinese), and a platoon of fast-food places. Safeway, K-Mart, and Sears are in shopping centers on this busy road.

## HUACHUCA MOUNTAINS

The Huachucas, E of Sierra Vista, have many hiking possibilities and some scenic drives,

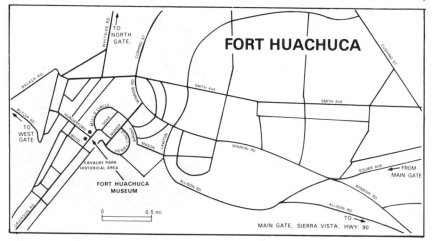

*aerial view of Fort Huachuca, 1929*

although part of the mountain range is controlled by the Army. The road through the Fort between Sierra Vista and the semi-ghost town of Canelo passes over the northern foothills and has some fine views. Secret electronic installations cap mountaintops. Upon entering the fort, pick up a pass and drop it off at the other end when leaving.

**Ramsey Canyon:** A year-round stream and an elevation range from 4,200 feet to 9,466-foot Miller Peak provide habitats for many kinds of wildlife. More than 14 species of hummingbirds congregate here from spring to early autumn. The Nature Conservancy has purchased 280 acres as a sanctuary for the hummers and other wildlife. The Mile Hi/ Ramsey Canyon Preserve's Bird Observation Station and a mile-long nature trail are open to the public 0800-1700; free. You're asked to visit on weekdays if possible, to reduce congestion and parking problems; no pets. Groups should obtain advance permission. No picnicking or camping, but visitors can stay in rental cabins at The Mile Hi, $42/night or $252/week (s or d). Write: R.R. 1, Box 84, Hereford, AZ 85615; tel. 378-2785. The nearby Apache Pointe Ranch offers trail rides; Box 1713, Sierra Vista, AZ 85635; tel. 378-6835 or 378-6800.

Ramsey Canyon is 4 miles off AZ 92, just 6 miles S of Sierra Vista.

**Coronado National Memorial:** Francisco Vasquez Coronado marched through this area in 1540 in search of the 7 Cities of Cibola. Although his quest was judged a failure by his backers, it was the first major European expedition into the American Southwest. Both this park in the Huachuca Mountains and the adjacent National Forest are named in his honor. Outstanding views of Arizona and Mexico can be seen from the top of 6,880-foot Coronado Peak, reached by a ½-mile nature trail from Montezuma Pass. The trail ascends 280 feet but has many shaded benches for resting. Signs describe Coronado's expedition and natural features of the Huachuca Mountains. Joe's Canyon Trail, 3 miles OW, connects Montezuma Pass with the Visitor Center in the valley below. You can reach Miller Peak (9,466 feet), the highest point in the Huachuca Mountains, on a 12-mile RT hike N from Montezuma Pass. A Visitor Center, staffed by National Park Service rangers, has historical, plant, and wildlife exhibits; open daily 0800-1700. A picnic area is nearby but there's no camping. In April the Memorial hosts the Coronado International Pageant—a day of Apache, Pima, Mexican, and Western dancing with music and crafts. The turnoff for Coronado Natl. Mem. is about midway between Sierra Vista and Bisbee on AZ 92. The Visitor Center is 4½ miles in, then another 4 miles and 1,300 feet higher on a gravel road to Montezuma Pass. You can also take the back roads (mostly dirt or gravel) from Patagonia or Nogales. Snowstorms occasionally close the pass in winter.

**Parker Canyon Lake:** This 133-acre fishing lake E of the Huachucas is a rarity in a land of little surface water. Trout are stocked in the cooler months to join the year-round population of bass, bluegill, sunfish, and catfish. Lakeview Campground is open all year; $3 day use, $5 camping; drinking water but no showers or hookups. Parker Canyon Lodge nearby has cabin rentals; tel. 455-5367. A marina has groceries, fishing supplies, licenses, boat ramp, and boat rentals. You can rent a canoe for $18/day (or $5/hr.), a rowboat for $15/day, and boat with electric motor for $22/day. A 4½-mile hiking trail goes around the lake. Boat motors are limited to 8 horsepower. Parker Canyon Lake is 28 miles S of Sonoita on AZ 83, 23 miles SW of Sierra Vista and 15 miles NW of Coronado National Memorial.

## BISBEE

Squeezed into Mule Pass Gulch, the old mining town of Bisbee is one of Arizona's most unusual towns. A tiny mining camp in 1877, Bisbee grew into a solid and wealthy town by 1910. The fine Victorian houses built in the boom years remain, so a visit to Bisbee is a step back in time. Brewery Gulch, a side canyon with more than 50 saloons in the early 1900s, earned a reputation for the best drinking and entertainment in the territory. Bisbee's riches, mostly copper ore, were dug from underground chambers and giant surface pits —tours take visitors to both types. Bisbee is in the Mule Mountains, 24 miles S of Tombstone and 95 miles SE of Tucson.

**history:** The story of Bisbee began over 100 million years ago, when a giant mass of molten rock deep in the earth's crust expelled great quantities of steam and hot water. These mineral-rich solutions slowly worked their way upward and replaced the overlying limestone rock, leaving rich copper ores. While looking for silver in 1875, Hugh Jones was the first to discover minerals here, but annoyed to find

*Bisbee and the Mule Mountains*

only copper, he soon left. Jack Dunn, an Army scout, found ore 2 years later. Dunn couldn't leave his Army duties to go prospecting, so he made a deal with George Warren to establish a claim and share the profits. Warren, a tough old prospector and heavy drinker, brought in friends and began mining, but "forgot" to share proceeds with Dunn. The new electrical industries needed copper, and investors became interested in Warren's camp. Judge

DeWitt Bisbee and a group of San Francisco businessmen bought the Copper Queen Mine in 1880, although the Judge never did visit the mining community named for him.

From the East, Dr. James Douglas of Phelps Dodge and Company came to Arizona and purchased property near the Copper Queen. After the 2 companies discovered that the richest ores lay on the property boundary, they merged rather than fight it out in court. A

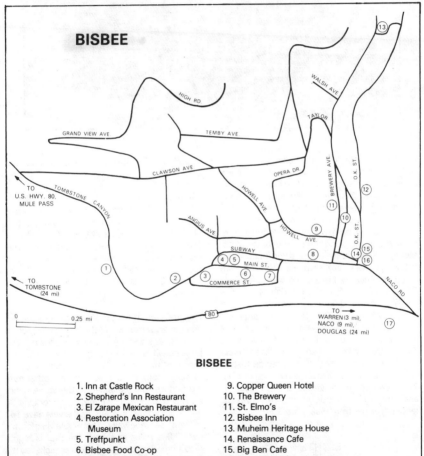

## BISBEE

1. Inn at Castle Rock
2. Shepherd's Inn Restaurant
3. El Zarape Mexican Restaurant
4. Restoration Association Museum
5. Treffpunkt
6. Bisbee Food Co-op
7. post office; public library
8. Mining and Historical Museum
9. Copper Queen Hotel
10. The Brewery
11. St. Elmo's
12. Bisbee Inn
13. Muheim Heritage House
14. Renaissance Cafe
15. Big Ben Cafe
16. Chamber of Commerce
17. Copper Queen Mine Tours

*early Bisbee smelter*

smelter was built, filling the valley with smoke and the clatter of machinery. Streets were paved and substantial buildings went up. Labor troubles between newly formed unions and mine management culminated in the infamous Bisbee Deportation. In July 1917, more than 1,000 striking miners were herded at gunpoint into boxcars and shipped out of the state. Mining conditions for workers improved in the following years, but Bisbee's economic life rolled with copper prices. The giant Lavender Pit closed in 1974, when the rich ore bodies finally ran out, and underground mining ended the following year. The district had provided more than 8 billion pounds of copper! The town wasn't about to dry up and blow away, though. People liked it here — the climate (elev. 5,300 feet), the scenery, the character. Bisbee is now popular with visitors and retired people. Although mining has ended, a small leaching and precipitation operation continues to recover copper from waste ore.

## SIGHTS

You can learn the history of the many early 1900's buildings downtown with the Chamber of Commerce's Bisbee Walking Tour pamphlet.

**Mining and Historical Museum:** Mining dioramas, old photos, and artifacts illustrate life in Bisbee's early years. Open Mon. to Sat. 1000-1600, Sun. 1300-1600, free. The Shattuck Memorial Archival Library inside has extensive material on local history. The Museum and Library are housed in the former Phelps Dodge General Office Building (1895) in Queen Plaza downtown.

**Copper Queen Mine:** Don a hard hat, lamp, and yellow slicker for a ride deep underground on a miner's tram. A guide, probably a miner himself, will issue the equipment and lead you through the mine. History, drilling tools, blasting methods, ore loading, and other mining features are explained in the stope (work area) and tunnels. The mine, in use for over 60 years, shut down in 1943. Its 4 levels have 147 miles of passageways. The whole district has over 2,000 miles of them! The tour is highly recommended; bring a sweater or jacket as it's cold inside (47 F). There are some steps to the stope area but the rest of the walking is level. The 1½-hour tour leaves daily at 1030, 1200,

1400, and 1530, $4 adult, $2.25 children 7-11, and $1.50 children 3-6, a discount is given if taken with one of the other tours (see below); tel. 432-2071. Buy tickets at the Queen Mine Building, just S of downtown off US 80.

**Lavender Open Pit:** A total of 380 million tons of ore and waste have been scooped out of this giant hole, which can be viewed from a parking area off US 80, one mile S of downtown. Press the button for a recorded description of the geology and mining of the Lavender Pit. A tour of the pit and still-operating leaching facilities is given daily at 1200 from the Queen Mine Building; 1 ½ hours; $3.

**Historic Bisbee Tour:** Guided tour of the historic districts of Bisbee and Warren. A guide tells the history and stories of the area; stops are made at viewpoints. Leaves Queen Mine Building daily at 1030, 1400, and 1530; lasting 1 ½ hours; $3.

**Restoration Association Museum:** You can see the old clothing, household items, and mining gear used by Bisbee's early settlers. Open Mon. to Sat. 1000-1500; closed Sun. & holidays; free. The museum is downtown at 37 Main Street.

**Muheim Heritage House:** Tours are given in this restored and furnished dwelling. Open Fri. to Mon. 1300-1600; tours are by appointment;

*stope area in Copper Queen Mine*

tel. 432-7071 or 432-4461; $1; at 207 Youngblood Hill.

## PRACTICALITIES

**accommodations and camping:** The Copper Queen Hotel has been *the* place to stay

*riding the "mule" into the Copper Queen Mine*

since its construction in 1902 by the Copper Queen Mining Company. Rooms vary in size and features, but all have been attractively restored and furnished in 1940's style. John Wayne once stayed in room 10, which has been the most popular since. Prices start at $27 s, $30.74 d.; reservations: Box Drawer CQ, Bisbee, AZ 85603; tel. 432-2216. The hotel has a saloon and swimming pool. A shop in the lobby sells jewelry made of turquoise and malachite, both copper minerals. The elegant 4-story hotel is downtown on Howell Ave., behind the Mining and Historical Museum. The Bisbee Inn offers bed & breakfast in a restored hotel, formerly the LaMore, opened in 1917. Baths are shared; $31.24 s, $41.84 d; (no smoking, no pets). Reservations: Box 1855, Bisbee, AZ 85608; tel. 432-5131; downtown on 45 OK Street, overlooking Brewery Gulch. The Inn at Castle Rock has bed & breakfast in a former miners' boarding house. Rooms, some with private bath, start at $18.35 s, $32 d; reservations: Box 1161, Bisbee, AZ 85603; tel. 432-7195; downtown at 112 Tombstone Canyon Road.

San Jose Lodge and RV Park has modern motel rooms ($30 s, $35 d) with a swimming pool and 26 RV spaces ($10.60 w/hookups) situated 6 miles SW of Bisbee at 1002 Naco Highway (Box 4577, Bisbee, AZ 85603); tel. 432-2226. Double Adobe Trailer Park offers tent spaces ($5) and RV hookups ($7); showers. Location is 8 miles E; take US 80 towards Douglas 4 miles, then L on Double Adobe Rd.; tel. 364-9976.

**food:** The Copper Queen Hotel's restaurant has continental and American cuisine, serving breakfast, lunch, and dinner. Renaissance Cafe, next to the Lyric Theatre, offers sandwiches, pizza, and subs. The nearby Big Ben Cafe has meat pies, quiches, soups, sandwiches, and coffees. Dine Chinese at Golden China, 15 Brewery Gulch. Treffpunkt, 25 Main St., serves standard American fare. El Zarape, 46 Main St., is a Mexican-American cafe (breakfast, lunch, and dinner). Shepherd's Inn, 67 Main St., has a variety of offerings — sandwiches, salads, and dinners. Lillie's Cafe, 4½ miles S of town on AZ 92 (near turnoff for

Naco), is a popular spot with locals. The Outback Supper Club and Antique Emporium is N of Bisbee over Mule Pass, serving seafood, beef, and other dishes with a European touch; open Wed. to Sat. for dinner, and Sun. for brunch and dinner; tel. 432-2333 (reservations suggested). Buy natural foods at Bisbee Food Coop downtown at 22 Main Street. Safeway supermarket is out of town at the turnoff for Naco.

**shopping:** Bisbee's mines have also yielded turquoise and other beautiful copper minerals. Several shops downtown sell stones set in silver as well as loose and rough stones. Another shop is at the Lavender Pit overlook. See paintings, ceramics, and other work of local artists in art shops downtown.

**entertainment:** See the Chamber of Commerce to find out what's playing in town. The Copper Queen Hotel's Saloon has live easy-

*Brewery Gulch*

*a faro game running full blast at the Orient Saloon, Bisbee in 1903*

listening music Thur. to Sat. evenings. For a variety of music, try the Brewery in Brewery Gulch Wed. to Saturday. St. Elmo's, also in Brewery Gulch, has country and rock music on some weekends.

**events:** The dust flies as cowboys perform in Bisbee's March rodeo. Vuelta de Bisbee is a tough multi-stage bicycle race held in April. Bisbee gets in a medieval mood in June during the Renaissance Festival with music, art, and crafts. Rock hounds come to town for the Bisbee Mineral Show the 1st weekend in October. In December the town decks out in lights and has a Christmas parade.

**services and information:** Copper Queen Community Hospital is at Bisbee Rd. and Cole Ave., 3 miles S in Warren; tel. 432-5383. The post office and city library are at 6 Main St. in downtown Bisbee. The Chamber of Commerce is on 10 OK St. (Box BA, Bisbee, AZ 85603); open Mon. to Fri. 0900-1700, Sat. 0900-1400; tel. 432-2141.

**transport:** Greyhound Bus stops at the old train station depot on AZ 92 near the traffic circle; tel. 432-7258. Butterfield State goes twice daily to Douglas and the Tucson airport from Warren, 3 miles S of Bisbee; tel. 432-2511. For a taxi, call Sun Arizona at tel. 432-5757.

**vicinity of Bisbee:** Naco is a sleepy Mexican border town just 9 miles S of Bisbee. There's little to see or do here; the Mexican side is much like rural communities of interior Mexico. TNS buses will take you to Hermosillo, Juarez, Nogales, Casas Grandes, and other Mexican destinations.

## DOUGLAS AND AGUA PRIETA

The prettiest sight in Douglas, some residents used to say, was the billowing steam and smoke from the giant copper smelter just W of town. The busy ore-processing plant meant jobs. In 1900, the Phelps Dodge Company, finding Bisbee's smelter too small and inconvenient to handle ores from recently purchased mines in Mexico, began looking for a new smelter site in the Sulphur Spring Valley. They chose this spot and named the hastily built new town for Dr. James Douglas, president of the company. Douglas and its sister town in Mexico, Agua Prieta, boomed when prices of copper were high and suffered when they were low. Mexican government troops battled it out in Agua Prieta with revolutionaries—Captain "Red" Lopez in 1911 and Pancho Villa in 1915.

Pancho Villa even made threats against the town of Douglas before retreating. An international airport—part of the runway was in the United States and part in Mexico—opened here in 1928.

Smokestacks of the Phelps Dodge smelter puffed their last in Jan. 1987, but the 2 cities have diversified into other industries. American companies operate manufacturing plants in Agua Prieta under the "twin plant" concept, using Mexico's inexpensive labor to assemble American products. With these new opportunities, Agua Prieta's population has tripled in the last 10 years to more than 60,000. Douglas and Agua Prieta have few "sights," but many visitors and retired people choose Douglas as a base to explore the historic and scenic places nearby in Arizona and Mexico. The Chamber of Commerce has a self-guided driving-tour leaflet of historic sites in Douglas. Pioneer and Indian artifacts can be seen in a tiny museum in Room 3 of The Bakery Bldg., 1116 "G" Ave.; open Mon. to Fri. 0900-1200 and 1400-1600, and Sat. 1400-1600.

**accommodations:** The massive 5-story Gadsden Hotel dominates downtown Douglas and is a sight in itself. Built in 1907 and rebuilt in 1928, the hotel calls itself "the last of the grand hotels." The lobby has massive marble columns decorated with 14K-gold leaf supporting a vaulted ceiling with stained-glass panels. A Tiffany stained-glass mural 42 feet long decorates one wall of the mezzanine, reached by a white Italian marble staircase. Over 200 authentic cattle brands embellish the walls of the Saddle and Spur Lounge, just off the lobby. Rooms start from $23.76 s, $28.08 d; 1046 "D" Ave., Douglas, AZ 85607; tel. 364-4481. Douglas also has a Motel 6, a Travelodge, and several other motels.

**camping:** Copper Horseshoe Trailer Park is ½ mile N on US 666 from US 80; tel. 364-2130. Double Adobe Trailer Park is 17½ miles NW (head W 8½ miles on Double Adobe Rd. from US 666); tel. 364-9976. Douglas Trailer Village is on the N side of town at 1206 21st St.; tel. 364-4326. Hidden Valley Mobile Rancho is to

*Gadsden Hotel lobby*

the NW of town at 1900 N. "G" Ave.; tel. 364-9651.

**food:** The Gadsden Hotel has a coffee shop and a Mexican-American restaurant. The Jaya Bakery & Deli prepares sandwiches and baked goodies, 843 "F" Ave.; closed Sunday. Next door is La Casa Mexicana Restaurant at the corner of "F" and 9th. Several other Mexican restaurants are scattered around town, and Agua Prieta has more. You'll pass Burger King, McDonalds, Sunshine Pizza House, and Pizza Hut on the west side of town on US 80.

**shopping:** Shops just across the border in Agua Prieta sell Mexican crafts, but on a much smaller scale than in Nogales. Arizona artists exhibit in the Little Gallery in Douglas, Pan American Ave. at 11th St., near the Chamber of Commerce; open Tue. to Sat. 1330-1600, closed July and August.

**services:** The post office is at the corner of 10th St. and "F" Avenue. Southeast Arizona Medical Center is W of town; tel. 364-7931. No permits are needed to visit Agua Prieta. For longer trips into Mexico, obtain papers at the border station or in Douglas at the Consulado de Mexico, 515 10th St. at "G" Ave.; tel. 364-2275. Mexican auto insurance is sold by Jones Associates, 561 10th St. at "F" Ave.; tel. 364-8496.

**information:** The Chamber of Commerce is helpful and has maps. Located at 1125 Pan American Ave. at 12th St.; open Mon. to Fri. 0900-1700; tel. 364-2477. Douglas Ranger District of the Coronado National Forest can tell you about camping, hiking, and backroads of the Chiricahua and Dragoon Mountains; Rt. 1, Box 228R, Leslie Canyon Rd., Douglas, AZ 85607; tel. 364-3468.

**transport:** Greyhound's daily bus to Tucson stops en route at Bisbee, Sierra Vista, and Benson. Bus station is at 538 14th St. at "G" Ave.; tel. 364-2233. In Agua Prieta, Transportes Norte de Sonora heads out to Cananea, Nogales, Hermosillo, Ciudad Obregon, Tijuana, Guadalajara, and Mexico City. A train line also goes to Nogales, but the bus is easier and faster. Rent cars from Southern Arizona Auto,

1200 "G" Ave.; tel. 364-2424; or Zane's Ford, 8 miles W on AZ 80; tel. 364-2485. For taxi service, call Gadsden Taxi; tel. 364-5555; or Taxi 21; tel. 364-5221. Sierra Vista Aviation flies to Fort Huachuca and Phoenix from Bisbee-Douglas Airport, 9 miles N on US 666; tel. 1-458-2855.

# THE CHIRICAHUA MOUNTAINS

Rising from dry grasslands, the Chiricahua (chee-ree-KAH-wah) Mountains are a wonderland of rock formations, spectacular views, diverse plant and animal life, and a variety of hiking trails. Volcanic rock, fractured by slow uplift of the region, has eroded into strangely shaped forms. Heavier weathering at the base of some columns leaves giant boulders balanced delicately on pedestals. The Chiricahua and other Apache tribes once hid among the pinnacles and canyons before attacking early European settlements on the plains below. Raids and skirmishes with the white man lasted until 1886, when Geronimo surrendered.

## CHIRICAHUA NATIONAL MONUMENT

In 1924, President Calvin Coolidge signed a bill turning the most scenic part of the wilderness into a national monument. The entrance is 70 miles N of Douglas, 36 miles SE of Willcox, and

*"duck on a rock,"* Heart of Rocks Trail

Sugarloaf
Mountain (on left)
from Sara
Deming Canyon
Trail

120 miles E of Tucson. Fort Bowie National Historic Site is nearby, on the gravel road S from Bowie. A narrow mountain road from Portal on the E side of the range crosses the Chiricahuas, but is not recommended for trailers; snows close the road in winter.

**Visitor Center:** A short slide show introduces the Monument and its sightseeing possibilities. Exhibits tell of the geology, ecology, wildlife, Chiricahua Apache, and early ranching in the area. Rangers can answer questions and advise on road and hiking conditions. Guided nature walks are led daily early Apr. to mid-June; campfire programs are held mid-Mar. to mid-Sept.; check for times. Books, prints, and maps are sold. Open daily 0800-1700: tel. 824-3560. A $3/car entrance fee is collected for the Massai Point Drive. This 6-mile paved mountain road climbs through Bonita Canyon to Massai Point (elev. 7,000 feet). Massai Point has a geology exhibit and offers sweeping views. A short nature trail and longer day hikes start here. Look N to see the profile of Cochise Head. Winter storms can close the road, but snowplows are out as soon as a storm is over.

**hiking:** The Chiricahuas are best appreciated on foot, whether on a short nature trail or on an extended hike. Pace yourself to allow for the altitude and rough terrain. Water should be car-

ried on the longer trips. Thunderstorms are a hazard in July and August; if caught, stay low and avoid exposed areas. Watch for rattlesnakes, too, this is their most active season, though they're also out in the spring and fall. You can hike any time of the year, but conditions are usually ideal from Mar. to May and Oct. to November. Snow sometimes blocks trails from Dec. to February. Monument trails are for day hikes only (no permit needed). Camping is restricted to the campground near the Visitor Center, but many backpack trips are possible in the nearby Coronado National Forest. Horseback riding is permitted in both the Monument and National Forest, but the Monument rangers like to be told if horses are brought in. Maps sold at the Visitor Center include a Chiricahua topo map showing hiking trails, a geologic map, and the National Forest map.

**trails:** The free Monument brochure has a map showing all the trails. Campground/Meadow Trail, an easy ½-mile walk between the campground and Visitor Center, winds through lush vegetation watered by a small seasonal stream. It's a good place for birdwatching. A short side trip leads to Silver Spur Meadow. The Rhyolite Canyon Nature Trail, from the Visitor Center, is an easy ¼-mile, self-guiding trail introducing local plant life; pick up a trail guide from the Visitor Center. Birdwatching is good too. Learn about some of the higher altitude plants on the ½-mile Massai Point Trail, at the end of the drive. The most impressive scenery awaits hikers on the Echo Canyon Loop and Heart of Rocks trails. Echo Canyon Trail winds through spectacular rock formations in a 3½-mile loop; begin from Echo Park or Massai Point trailheads, both near the end of Massai Point Drive. Heart of Rocks Trail passes famous rock formations—Punch & Judy, Duck on a Rock, Totem Pole, Big Balanced Rock, and others—on a 7-mile out-and-back trip from Massai Point. With half a day, you can make a 9-mile loop by returning on the Sarah Deming and Echo Canyon Trails. Inspiration Point is a one-mile RT side trip off Heart of Rocks Trail with views over the whole length of Rhyolite Canyon. You could also hike all the way down to the Visitor Center via Rhyolite Canyon Trail. The 7,307-foot Sugarloaf Mountain is the highest in the Monument, with great views over Arizona, New Mexico, and the Chiricahuas. It's a 2-mile RT hike to the summit from the Sugarloaf trailhead. The Natural Bridge Trail, off Massai Point Drive, offers pleasant but less spectacular hiking to a small rock bridge, 2½ miles from the road.

**Faraway Ranch:** Members of the Erickson Family lived on this ranch for 91 years before its purchase in 1979 by the National Park Service. The Park Service plans to open exhibits at the old homestead in 1988. Rangers sometimes give talks here. Faraway Ranch is 1½ miles W of the Visitor Center.

**camping:** Bonita Campground, ½ mile from the Visitor Center, costs $5/night (no hookups or showers); trailers to 26 feet OK. Another possibility is to drive up Pinery Canyon Rd. into Coronado National Forest. The turnoff for Pinery Canyon is on the R just before entering the Monument. Look for a likely spot after about 6 miles; no water or facilities; no charge. The nearest supplies are 26 miles SE in Sunizona, at the jct. of AZ 181 and US 666. You'll find Hatch's grocery store, gas, and motel ($21 s, $26.50 d), and an RV park ($7 w/hookups). Sunizona Cafe serves Mexican-American meals but is closed on Sun. afternoon and Monday. Willcox, 36 miles N of the Monument, also has motels, restaurants, stores, and trailer parks.

## CORONADO NATIONAL FOREST

The National Forest has numerous hiking and horseback opportunities. A road crosses the range through Pinery Canyon (on the W) to Onion Saddle (7,600 feet) and E to Cave Creek Canyon and Portal. The road is narrow and bumpy (mostly unpaved) but OK for cautiously driven cars. Snow and fallen trees close the road from Dec. to Mar. or April. A side road from Onion Saddle goes S along a ridge and climbs to Rustler Park (8,400 feet). From here, hikers can take the Crest Trail S to Chiricahua Peak (9,796 feet), a wilderness area and highest point in the range. Many other trails branch off in all directions. Forest trails in the Chiricahua Mountains total about 111 miles, but their conditions vary widely. Trails and trail lengths are shown on the Chiricahua Mountains Trail and Recreation topo map (scale 1:62,500), available from Tucson hiking stores, Forest Service Offices, and Chiricahua National Monument. The Coronado National Forest (Douglas Ranger

*'kissing rocks," Heart of Rocks Trail*

*Cochise, from Samuel Cozzen's 1873 The Marvellous Country*

District) map shows trails but lacks contour lines and fine detail. *Arizona Trails* by David Mazel is the best source for trail descriptions of the Chiricahua Wilderness.

**camping:** The Coronado National Forest has 15 campgrounds; see the Forest map for locations, seasons, and facilities. A $5/night fee is charged for sites with water; others are free. No permits are needed for backpacking or hiking.

## FORT BOWIE
## NATIONAL HISTORIC SITE

When the Butterfield Stagecoach line began to carry mail and passengers from Missouri to California in 1858, a station was built at a spring near Apache Pass. Although it was in the middle of Indian country, Cochise and his Chiricahua Apache allowed the station and stage to operate unhindered. All this changed 2½ years later when 2nd Lt. George Bascom falsely accused Cochise of kidnapping and theft. An attempt was made to capture Cochise by trickery, but the Indian chief escaped. Hostages were executed by both sides, and the war was on. Life became precarious for settlers and travelers in the region. Cochise was determined to kill or drive out from the region all white men. Unfortunately for the settlers, many Army troops left Arizona to fight the Civil War in the East.

On 15 July 1862, Brig. Gen. James Carleton and his California Column, fresh from their Arizona victory in the Union cause, were attacked by Indians at Apache Pass. Carleton saw the need for a fort and had Fort Bowie constructed within the month. Indian raids continued until 1872, when Cochise made peace with the Army in exchange for reservation land. However, bad management by the Indian Bureau, followed by the government's taking back the reservation, were too much for some of the Apache. Cochise had died while at peace on the reservation, but in 1881 Geronimo, the wily Apache chief, led bands of followers into Mexico and started new raids. Army cavalry and scouts from Fort Bowie sought out the elusive Indians until Geronimo surrendered 5 years later, in 1886. Arizona's Indian wars were over and the fort was abandoned on 17 Oct. 1894.

**visiting the fort:** Modern highways have bypassed the area and only crumbling ruins and memories remain. The National Park Service maintains the historic ruins and has a ranger station with a few exhibits; open daily 0830-1600. A brochure and signs identify the

*Geronimo, 1887*

*Fort Bowie, 1885*

fort buildings, the stage-station site, and battle and massacre locations. Old photos show how the fort appeared in its heyday. To preserve the historic setting, visitors must approach the site by foot. From the main road, follow a 1½-mile OW trail past the stage-station site, a cemetery, Battle of Apache Pass site, and Apache Spring to the extensive ruins of Fort Bowie. Pick up a brochure near the start of the trail. From the town of Bowie, on I-10, drive 12 miles S on a gravel road; parking is on the R, trailhead on the left. From Willcox (22 miles W) or Chiricahua Natl. Mon. (25 miles S), take AZ 186 to Apache Pass Rd., drive over the pass, then look for the signposted parking on the left. In bad weather Apache Pass Rd. becomes slippery and is not recommended. The fort site has water but no picnicking or camping facilities.

## WILLCOX AND VICINITY

Started in 1880 as a construction camp for the Southern Pacific Railroad, Willcox became a supply and shipping point for local ranchers.

*Fort Bowie, 1985*

For travelers, Willcox has a good selection of motels, restaurants, RV parks, and a large Visitor Center. The town, just off I-10, is a convenient base for visiting the scenic and historic sights of the area. The Chamber of Commerce and Museum of the Southwest, in Cochise Visitor Center, have historical exhibits, an information desk, and a gift shop. Open Mon. to Sat. 0900-1700, Sun. 1000-1400; free; take I-10 Exit 340 (AZ 186) then turn NE ½ mile on Circle I Rd; tel. 384-2272.

**Willcox Playa:** This giant lake bed is S of Willcox and visible from I-10. After heavy rains it becomes a shallow lake but usually is dry. You may see mirages on the surface in summer.

**Cochise Stronghold Canyon:** A beautiful wooded area of towering pinnacles in the heart of the Dragoon Mountains, 30 miles SW of Willcox. During the 15 years when the great Apache chief Cochise and about 250 warriors hid out here, no white person was safe in the valleys below. Cochise was never defeated in battle; he only agreed to peace in 1872 when land was promised for his tribe. The Dragoon Mountains took their name from the 3rd U.S. Cavalry Dragoons. Today the mountains offer picnicking, hiking trails, and a campground that has water except in midwinter. A self-guided nature trail, starting from the S end of the campground, explains the diverse plant life and other features of the area. Cochise Indian Trail continues up the valley past Cochise Spring and Halfmoon Tank to Stronghold Divide, 6 miles RT. It's also possible to continue down the other side of the range into West Stronghold Canyon. A rough but scenic drive crosses the range to the S at Middlemarch Pass, connecting the ghost town of Pearce with Tombstone to the west.

**Amerind Foundation:** Amateur archaeologist William Fulton started the Foundation in 1937 to increase the world's knowledge of American Indian cultures. The name comes from a contraction of "American" and "Indian." Especially active in research of Southwest and Mexican archaeology, the Foundation has amassed an outstanding artifact collection and a large library. Museum exhibits show clothing, masks, jewelry, weapons, and tools from many tribes. The Amerind Art Gallery displays paintings and sculptures by western and Indian artists of the 19th and 20th centuries. A museum store sells artworks, crafts, and books of native American cultures. Open daily 1000-1600 (closed major holidays) from Sept. to May; call for summer hours; $2 adult, $1 ages 12-18 and seniors; tel. 586-3666. The Amerind Foundation is 64 miles E of Tucson between Willcox and Benson; take I-10 Dragoon Exit 318, go S one mile, and turn L at the sign "FF Ranch — Amerind Foundation."

## BENSON

Benson is 36 miles W of Willcox and 45 miles E of Tucson. The Butterfield Stage crossed the San Pedro River nearby in the early 1860s, but the town didn't really get going until the railroad arrived in 1880. Benson became a busy town, whose saloons filled with cowboys, miners, Mexicans, and Chinese. The community is quiet now and has motels, restaurants, and campgrounds for travelers. A bit of the past is preserved in the San Pedro Valley Arts and Historical Museum. Photos and artifacts show life in the early railroad, mining, and ranching days. Local hand-made crafts are sold. Open Tue. to Fri. 1000-1600, and Sat. 1000-1400; in summer hours are 0900-1200, same days; free. From 4th St., the main street through downtown, turn one block S on San Pedro to the Museum.

# BOOKLIST

## DESCRIPTION AND TRAVEL

Abbey, Edward. *Down the River.* E.P. Dutton, 1982, 242 pages, $7.95. Abbey expresses his joys of and concerns about the American West in thoughtful, witty, and wide-ranging essays.

Babbitt, Bruce (editor). *Grand Canyon, An Anthology.* Northland Press, 1978, 258 pages, $15.95. Twenty-three authors from the Spanish days to the present relate their experiences with the Grand Canyon.

Belknap, Buzz. *Powell Centennial Grand Canyon River Guide.* Westwater Books, 1969, 1983, 52 pages (waterproof), $10.95. A map atlas with many historic photos and notes on the river from Lees Ferry to Lake Mead.

Bogert, John and Joan. *100 Best Restaurants in the Valley of the Sun.* Arizona Desert Minerals Co., 1985 (revised annually), 200+ pages, $4.40. Handy guide to many of the best-value restaurants in the Phoenix area.

Bower, Peter L. *Bicyclist's Guide to Arizona.* Phoenix Books, Box 32008, Phoenix, AZ 85064; 1980, 80 pages, $4.95. Short rides in the Phoenix and Tucson areas and longer rides throughout the state; gives advice on riding and equipment.

Butler, Ron. *The Best of the Old West, An Indispensable Guide to the Vanishing Legend of the American West.* Texas Monthly Press, 1983, 229 pages, $9.95. A lively guide to the places and institutions where the West lives on—towns and ghost towns, saloons, museums, dude ranchs etc.; covers the western states.

Cook, James E. *Arizona 101.* Cocinero Press, Box 11583, Phoenix, AZ 85061; 1981, 70 pages, $3.25. Enroll in this humorous but factual short study of Arizona.

Crumbo, Kim. *A River Runner's Guide to the History of the Grand Canyon.* Johnson Books, Boulder, CO; 1981, 55 pages & 26 maps, $4.95. Highly readable guide with a foreward by Edward Abbey.

Dutton, Allen A. and Bunting, Diane Tayor. *Arizona Then and Now, A comprehensive Rephotographic Project.* Ag2 Press, Phoenix, AZ; 162 pages. A photo album comparing old photographs with present-day scenes; enjoyable to flip through.

Hammons, Lee. *Mineral and Gem Localities in Arizona.* Arizona Maps and Books, Box 1133, Sedona, AZ; 1977, 112 pages. An introduction and 30 color maps cover the entire state, showing locations of rocks, minerals, gems, and fossils. It's written for both rock-hounds and prospectors.

Hoefer, Hans (and others). *American Southwest.* APA Insight Guides, 1984, 305 pages. Outstanding color photography illustrates this travel guide of Arizona, New Mexico, and adjacent areas. Numerous authors have contributed to the text.

Klinck, Richard E. *Land of Room Enough and Time Enough.* Peregrine Smith Books, 1958, 1984, 136 pages, $10.95. The land, legends, and peoples of Monument Valley.

The Story Behind the Scenery series: *Grand Canyon. Canyon de Chelly. Petrified Forest. Lake Mead-Hoover Dam.* KC Publications, Las Vegas, NV; 32 to 64 pages, $3.75. Introductions and beautiful color photos.

Lesure, Thomas B. *All About Arizona.* Harian Publications, 1981, 193 pages, $5.95. The title is presumptuous but this little guide is crammed with useful information. Emphasis is on living and retiring in the state but there's good travel and sightseeing coverage.

Leydet, Francois. *Time and the River Flowing: Grand Canyon.* Sierra Club-Ballantine Books,

1968, 160 pages. Essays and color photos of the Grand Canyon.

Lockard, Peggy Hamilton. *This is Tucson, Guidebook to the Old Pueblo.* Pepper Publishing, 2901 E. Mabel St., Tucson, AZ 85716; 1983, 271 pages, $8.95. Excellent guide to the culture, sights, and restaurants of Tucson and vicinity.

Loving, Nancy J. and Bean, Tom. *Along the Rim, A Road Guide to the South Rim of Grand Canyon.* Grand Canyon Natural History Assoc., 1981, 53 pages, $2.95. Beautifully done booklet about the viewpoints, history, and ecology along the Rim Drive.

Simmons, George C. and Gaskill, David L. *River Runner's Guide to the Canyons of the Green and Colorado Rivers—With Emphasis on Geologic Features, Vol. III.* Northland Press, 1969, 132 pages, $5. This volume covers Marble Canyon and Grand Canyon.

*Visitors Guide, Phoenix-Scottsdale & Valley of the Sun in Arizona.* Phoenix and Valley of the Sun Convention & Visitors Bureau, 502 N. 2nd St., Suite 300, Phoenix, AZ 85004; revised annually, 80 pages, free.

Sherman, James and Sherman, Barbara. *Ghost Towns of Arizona.* University of Oklahoma Press, 1969, 208 pages, $10.95. Brief histories of about 130 ghost communities. Well-illustrated with b/w photos, but maps are poor.

Stevens, Larry. *The Colorado River in Grand Canyon, A Guide.* Red Lake Books, Box 1315, Flagstaff, AZ; 1984, 107 pages (waterproof), $11.25. Maps and concise guide to geology, Indian history, exploration, flora, and fauna.

Thollander, Earl. *Back Roads of Arizona.* Northland Press, 1978. Attractive sketches illustrate this road guide to the scenic but seldom-traveled roads of the state. Edward Abbey wrote the introduction.

*The Official Visitors Guide to Metropolitan Tucson.* Tucson Convention and Visitors Bureau, Box 3028, Tucson, AZ 85702; updated annually, 44 pages, free.

Varney, Philip. *Arizona's Best Ghost Towns, A Practical Guide.* Northland Press, 1980, 142 pages. Explore the ruins of Arizona's boom and bust towns with this easy-to-use guide.

Wallace, Robert. *The Grand Canyon.* The American Wilderness/Time-Life Books, New York, 1972, 184 pages, $8.95. A well-illustrated book covering many aspects of the Canyon. Ernst Haas provides the excellent photography.

Writers' Program of the WPA. *Arizona, A State Guide.* Hastings House, 1940, 1956, 530 pages. This classic guidebook is still good reading.

# HIKING

Aitchison, Stewart W. *A Naturalist's Guide to Hiking the Grand Canyon.* Prentice-Hall, 1985, 172 pages, $8.95. The author introduces you to the Canyon's climates, geology, "critters," and plants, then takes you on 30 hikes. Good maps make the descriptions easy to follow.

Aitchison, Stewart W. *Oak Creek Canyon and the Red Rock Country of Arizona, A Natural History and Trail Guide.* Stillwater Canyon Press, Flagstaff, AZ; 1978, 142 pages. A well-illustrated guide to backroads and 24 hiking trails of the Sedona area. You also learn about Indians, early settlers, geology, plants, and wildlife of the region.

Bowman, Eldon. *A Guide to the General Crook Trail.* Museum of Northern Arizona Press and the Boy Scouts of America, 1978, 31 pages, $2.50. Trail guide to Crook's historic military road. The route begins in Camp Verde (north-central Arizona) and goes E along the Mogollon Rim for 113 miles. Trail was cleared and re-marked by the Boy Scouts and others as a bicentennial project.

Butchart, Harvey. *Grand Canyon Treks, A Guide to the Inner Canyon Routes.* La Siesta Press, 1976, 72 pages, $2.50. The classic hiking guide to the Canyon; this is the most useful of his 3 books.

Butchart, Harvey. *Grand Canyon Treks II, A Guide to the Extended Canyon Routes.* La Siesta Press, 1975, 48 pages, $1.95. Butchart describes rarely used trails and routes of Marble Canyon and western Grand Canyon.

Butchart, Harvey. *Grand Canyon Treks III, Inner Canyon Journals.* La Siesta Press, 1984, 72 pages, $3.95. Additional material adds to his earlier books.

Fletcher, Colin. *The Man Who Walked Through Time.* Random House, 1967, 239 pages, $3.95. Well-written adventure tale of Colin's 2-month solo hike through the Grand Canyon. He was the first to travel the entire length of the Park on foot.

Ganci, Dave. *Hiking the Southwest: Arizona, New Mexico, and West Texas.* Sierra Club Books, 1983, 408 pages, $9.95. A handy guide with a good introduction, practical hints, and a variety of trails.

Kals, W.S. *Land Navigation Handbook.* Sierra Club Books, 1983, 230 pages, $8.95. After reading this book you'll be able to confidently explore Arizona's vast backcountry. This handy pocket guide not only has details on using map and compass, but tells how to do altimeter navigation and use the sun and stars.

Mazel, David. *Arizona Trails, 100 Hikes in Canyon and Sierra.* Wilderness Press, 1981, 1984, 312 pages, $11.95. An excellent hiking guide to many of the designated wilderness areas of the state: the Grand Canyon, Superstitions, Chiricahuas, Mazatzals, and others. The maps are so good you won't need to buy any others.

McMoran, Charles W. *Hiking Trails of the Huachuca Mountains.* Livingston's Books, Sierra Vista, AZ 85635; 1981, 36 pages, $4.95. Useful guide to the peaks and canyons of the Huachucas in SE Arizona.

Morris, Larry A. *Hiking the Grand Canyon and Havasupai.* AZTEX Press, Tucson, 1981, 144 pages. Background on the Grand Canyon and Havasupai Indians, hiking tips, and trail descriptions.

Nelson, Dick and Sharon. *50 Hikes in Arizona.* Tecolote Press, 1981. A sampling of easy to difficult hikes with trail descriptions and maps.

Sheridan, Michael F. *Superstitions Wilderness Guidebook, An Introduction to the Geology and Trails including a Roadlog of the Apache Trail and Trails from First Water and Dons Camp.* Lebeau Printing Co., 1972, 52 pages.

Thybony, Scott. *A Guide to Hiking the Inner Canyon.* Grand Canyon Natural History Assoc., 1984, 43 pages, $1.75. Introduction and guide to best-known trails of the Grand Canyon; less detailed than Butchart's *Grand Canyon Treks,* but easier to use and has better maps.

# HISTORY

Cline, Platt. *They Came to the Mountain, The Story of Flagstaff's Beginnings.* Northern Arizona University with Northland Press, 1976, 364 pages, $18. Highly readable account of Flagstaff's founding and early years.

Coolidge, Dane. *Arizona Cowboys.* University of Arizona Press, 1938, 1984, 160 pages, $7.95. Tales of working the range in the early 1900s.

Dellenbaugh, Frederick S. *A Canyon Voyage, A Narrative of the Second Powell Expedition down the Green-Colorado River from Wyoming, and the Expeditions on Land, in the Years 1871 and 1872.* University of Arizona Press, reprinted 1984; 277 pages, $9.95. Dellenbaugh was an artist and assistant topographer of the expedition.

Faulk, Odie B. *Arizona, A Short History.* University of Oklahoma Press, 1979, 266 pages. Popular account of Arizona from the first days of European exploration through the territorial years and statehood.

Forrest, Earle R. *Arizona's Dark and Bloody Ground.* University of Arizona, 1936, 1984, 385 pages, $11.95. An account of the ruthless Pleasant Valley War between cattlemen and sheepmen.

Hinton, Richard J. *The Handbook to Arizona, Its Resources, History, Towns, Mines, Ruins, and Scenery.* First published by Payot, Upham & Co. in 1878; reprinted by Arizona Silhouettes in 1954, 431 pages. This is what you might have been carrying 100 years ago. The volume gives a good insight into Arizona's early years.

Hilzinger, George. *Treasure Land, 1897, A Handbook to Tucson and Southern Arizona.* 160 pages. Another grand old book to look for in the library.

*The Heart of Ambos Nogales.* The Journal of Arizona History, vol. 17, #2, summer 1976, page 161. The story of Nogales.

Hughes, J. Donald. *In the House of Stone and Light.* Grand Canyon Natural History Assoc., 1978, 137 pages, $7.50. A well-illustrated history of the Grand Canyon from the early Indians to the modern Park.

Johnson, G. Wesley, Jr. *Phoenix: Valley of the Sun.* Continental Heritage Press, 1982, 240 pages. Excellent text and photos trace the development of Phoenix from the ancient Hohokam civilization to the modern metropolis.

Mitchell, John D. *Lost Mines of the Great Southwest.* Rio Grande Press, 1933, 1984, 174 pages, $10. Who isn't enthralled by legends of lost treasure? You'll be reaching for a pick and shovel after reading these!

Parker, Lowell. *Arizona Towns and Tales.* Phoenix Newspapers, Inc., Phoenix, AZ; 1975, 292 pages. Entertaining tales of personalities and places in the yesteryears.

Pattie, James Ohio. *The Personal Narrative of James O. Pattie.* University of Nebraska Press,

1984 (reprint of 1831 edition), 269 pages, $6.95. An early fur trapper tells of his experiences in the wild lands of the West during the 1820s. He claimed to be the first white American to see the Grand Canyon.

Powell, J.W. *The Exploration of the Colorado River and its Canyons.* Dover Publications, reprinted 1961 (first pub. in 1895), 400 pages, great illustrations, $5.95. Powell's 1869 expedition—the first running of the Colorado River through the Grand Canyon; also a description of the 1870 Uinta Expedition.

Rusho, W.L. and Crampton, C. Gregory. *Desert River Crossing, Historic Lee's Ferry on the Colorado River.* Peregrine Smith Books, 1975, 1981; 126 pages, $5.95.

Sikorsky, Robert. *Fools Gold, The Facts, Myths and Legends of the Lost Dutchman Mine and the Superstition Mountains.* Golden West, 1983, 143 pages, $5. History of the most famous lost mine of all.

Summerhayes, Martha. *Vanished Arizona.* University of Nebraska Press, 1979 (reprint of 1911 Salem Press 2nd edition), 307 pages, $7.95. A young New England woman marries an Army officer in 1874, then sets out for some of the wildest corners of the West. Her accounts bring life of frontier Arizona into sharp focus.

Trimble, Marshall. *Arizona Adventure, Action-Packed True Tales of Early Arizona.* Golden West, 1982, 160 pages, $5. Nineteen stories from Arizona's Old West.

Wagoner, Jay J. *Arizona Territory, 1863-1912, a Political History.* University of Arizona Press, 1970, 587 pages. Excellent history of the territorial years.

Woody, Clara T. and Schwartz, Milton L. *Globe, Arizona.* The Arizona Historical Society, 1977, 262 pages. Stories of the early miners, pioneers, Indian battles, and the Graham-Tewksbury feud (Pleasant Valley War).

# ARIZONA INDIANS OF TODAY

Courlander, Harold. *Hopi Voices, Recollections, Traditions, and Narratives of the Hopi Indians.* University of New Mexico, 1982, 255 pages, $17.50. A selection of 74 Hopi narrations explaining their mythology, history, exploits, games, and animal stories. One of the best books on Hopi culture.

Dedera, Don. *Navajo Rugs: How to Find, Evaluate, Buy and Care for Them.* Northland Press, 114 pages, $8.95. Dedera gives the history of Navajo weaving, illustrates how it's done, shows regional styles, and gives practical advice on purchasing.

Dittert Jr., Alfred and Plog, Fred. *Generations in Clay: Pueblo Pottery of the American Southwest.* Northland Press, 1980, 156 pages, $14.95. An introduction to pottery of the pueblo Indians, both prehistoric and modern. Well-illustrated with B/W and color photos.

Dozier, Edward P. *Hano, A Tewa Indian Community in Arizona.* Holt, Rinehart and Wilson, 1966, 104 pages. A study of the Tewa's history, society, religion, and livelihood.

Dyk, Walter (recorded by). *Son of Old Man Hat, A Navajo Autobiography.* University of Nebraska Press, 1967 (original copyright 1938), 378 pages, $7.95. A Navajo relates the story of growing up in the late 1800s. He was born during his family's return from 4 years of internment at Fort Sumner.

Evers, Larry (editor). *The South Corner of Time.* University of Arizona Press, 1980, 240 pages, $17.50. Stories and poetry by contemporary Indians of the Hopi, Navajo, Papago, and Yaqui tribes.

Fontana, Bernard. *Of Earth and Little Rain, The Papago Indians.* Northland Press, 1981, 140 pages, $27.50. Essays and photos on Papago life and their land.

Forrest, Earle. *The Snake Dance of the Hopi Indians.* Westernlore Press, 1961, 172 pages.

Detailed look at Hopi mythology and ceremonies, illustrated with many old photos.

Gillmore, Frances and Wetherill, Louisa. *Traders to the Navajo.* University of New Mexico Press, 1983, 265 pages, $8.95. The Wetherills lived in and explored the Monument Valley region and traded with the Navajo. These are some of their stories about lost mines, early travelers, and the Navajo people.

Gilpin, Laura. *The Enduring Navajo.* University of Texas Press, 1968, 505 pages, $37.50. Excellent photo book about the Navajo, their homes, land, ceremonies, crafts, tribal government, and the trading posts.

James, Harry C. *Pages from Hopi History.* University of Arizona Press, 1974, 258 pages, $8.50. Beginning with the Hopi's mythological entrance into this world, their history is traced through early migrations, encounters with the Spanish, difficulties with Mexicans and Navajo, resistance to U.S. authority, and living today.

Kammer, Jack. *The Second Long Walk: The Navajo-Hopi Land Dispute.* University of New Mexico Press, 1980, 265 pages, $9.95. Background on both sides of the long-running land dispute between the Navajo and Hopi.

Kavena, Juanita Tiger. *Hopi Cookery.* University of Arizona Press, 1980, 115 pages, $8.50. Learn how to make *piki* bread, bake a prairie dog, fix a squash & fresh corn casserole, make a yucca pie, and more!

Locke, Raymond F. *The Book of the Navajo.* Mankind Publishing, 1976, 464 pages. Navajo legends, art, culture, and history from early to modern times.

Mooney, Ralph. *The Navajos.* National Geographic Magazine, Dec. 1972, page 740. The Navajo people and how they have balanced their traditions with life in 20th C. America.

Mullet, G.M. *Spider Women Stories.* University of Arizona, 1979, 142 pages. Selected stories from Hopi mythology.

Page, Jake. *Inside the Sacred Hopi Homeland.* National Geographic Magazine, Nov. 1982, page 607. A rare look at the spiritual life of the Hopi.

Page, Susanne and Page, Jake. *Hopi.* Harry N. Abrams, Inc., 1982, 240 pages, $30. An unprecedented project recording the Hopi and their spiritual life. Everyday life, ceremonies, and sacred places rarely seen by outsiders are described and illustrated with large color photos.

Powell, Major J.W. *The Hopi Villages, The Ancient Province of Tusayan.* Filter Press, Palmer Lake, Colorado, 1972 (first pub. about 1891), 36 pages, $1.50.

Shaw, Anna Moore. *Pima Indian Legends.* University of Arizona Press, 1968, 1983, 111 pages, $6.95. Folktales of the Pima Indians.

Simmons, Leo (editor). *Sun Chief, The Autobiography of a Hopi Indian.* Yale University Press, 1942, 460 pages, $8.95. A Hopi tells of his experiences growing up in both the Hopi and white man's worlds, then returning to traditional ways.

Suntracks, Larry Evers. *Hopi Photographers/Hopi Images.* University of Arizona Press, 1983, 111 pages. Photography of the Hopi, 1880-1980, with historic photos by Anglos and modern work by Hopi photographers; b/w and color.

Titiev, Mischa. *Old Oraibi, A Study of the Hopi Indians of Third Mesa.* Peabody Museum, vol. XXII—No. 1, 1944 (reprinted by Kraus Reprint Corp. 1968), 277 pages. Detailed account of Hopi society and ceremonies.

Webb, George. *A Pima Remembers.* University of Arizona Pess, 1959 (reprinted 1982), 126 pages, $7.50. Traditional stories of the Pima Indians.

Wright, Barton. *Hopi Kachinas, The Complete Guide to Collecting Kachina Dolls.* Northland Press, 1977, 139 pages. From clowns to ogres, a great many dolls are illustrated and their functions explained.

Wright, Margaret. *Hopi Silver.* Northland Press, 1982, 113 pages, $8.95. History and examples of Hopi silversmithing.

Yava, Albert. *Big Falling Snow.* University of New Mexico Press, 1978, 178 pages, $9.95. A Tewa-Hopi reports the history and traditions of the Tewa and Hopi peoples, including the conflicts with missionaries and government officials who tried to Americanize the tribes.

# ARCHEOLOGY

Ambler, J. Richard. *The Anasazi: Prehistoric Peoples of the Four Corners Region.* Museum of Northern Arizona, 1977, 50 pages, $5.95. One of the best overviews.

Grant, Campbell. *Canyon de Chelly, Its People and Rock Art.* University of Arizona Press, 1978, 290 pages, $12.50. The geology, archeology, and history of the canyons are well-illustrated. Nearly half the text is devoted to the wealth of petroglyphs and pictographs left by the Anazazi, Hopi, and Navajo.

Gregonis, Linda and Reinhard, Karl. *Hohokam Indians of the Tucson Basin.* University of Arizona Press, 1979, 48 pages, $4.95. Introduction to the prehistoric Hohokam Indian archaeology and their life.

Lister, Robert and Lister, Florence. *Those Who Came Before.* University of Arizona Press, 1983, 184 pages, $10.95. A well-illustrated guide to the history, artifacts, and ruins of Southwest prehistoric Indians. Describes parks and monuments containing their sites.

McGregor, John C. *Southwestern Archaeology.* University of Illinois Press, 2nd ed., 1982, 511 pages, $16.95. Are you curious why archeologists like their work and how it's done? This book presents motivations and techniques of the scientists. It describes cultures and artifacts from the earliest known peoples to the present in a readable and useful form.

Noble, David Grant. *Ancient Ruins of the Southwest.* Northland Press, 1981, 156 pages, $8.95. Well-illustrated guide to prehistoric ruins of Arizona, New Mexico, Colorado, and Utah, with practical info on getting to sites, nearby campgrounds, and services.

Oppelt, Norman T. *Guide to Prehistoric Ruins of the Southwest.* Pruett Publishing Co., Boulder, CO; 1981, 208 pages, $6.95. Introduction to ancient cultures with descriptions of more than 200 sites in Arizona, New Mexico, Colorado, and Utah.

Viele, Catherine. *Voices in the Canyon.* Southwest Parks and Monuments Assoc., 1980, 76 pages. Highly readable and well-illustrated book about the ancient Anasazi and their villages of Betatakin, Keet Seel, and Inscription House (now all in Navajo Natl. Mon.).

## NATURAL SCIENCES

Arnberger, Leslie P. and Janish, Jeanne R. *Flowers of the Southwest Mountains.* Southwest Parks and Monuments Assoc., 1982, 139 pages, $7.95. You'll find descriptions and illustrations of flowers and common trees found at 7,000 feet and above.

Barnes, F.A. *Canyon Country Geology for the Layman and Rockhound.* Wasatch Publishers, Inc., 1978, 160 pages. Geologic history and guide to rockhounding; emphasis is on SE Utah and adjacent Arizona.

Chronic, Halka. *Roadside Geology of Arizona.* Mountain Press Publishing Co., 1983, 314 pages. Well illustrated with photos, maps, and diagrams. Organized along major highway routes; also covers the National Parks and some Monuments.

Dodge, Natt N. *100 Desert Wildflowers in Natural Color.* Southwest Parks and Monument Assoc., 1963, $3.50. Introduction and brief descriptions with a color photo for each flower.

Dodge, Natt N. *100 Roadside Wildflowers of Southwest Uplands in Natural Color.* Southwest Parks and Monuments Assoc., 1980, 64 pages, $3.50. Introduction and brief descriptions with a color photo for each flower, usually found above an elevation of 4,500 feet.

Dodge, Natt N. *Poisonous Dwellers of the Desert.* Southwest Parks and Monuments Assoc., 1981, 40 pages, $2.50. Creatures to watch out for: poisonous insects, snakes, and the gila monster. Advice is given on insecticides and bite treatment. Some nonvenomous animals often mistakenly thought poisonous are listed too.

Dodge, Natt N. and Janish, Jeanne R. *Flowers of the Southwest Deserts.* Southwest Parks and Monuments Assoc., 1980, 112 pages, $2.50. Desert plant and flower guide for elevations under 4,500 feet.

Doolittle, Jerome. *Canyons and Mesas.* Time-Life Books (American Wilderness Series), 1974, 184 pages, $12.95. Text and photos give a feel for the ruggedly beautiful country of northern Arizona and adjacent Utah and Colorado.

Earle, W. Hubert. *Cacti of the Southwest.* Desert Botanical Garden (Phoenix), 1980, 208 pages, $11. The 152 known species of cactus in the SW are listed with B/W and color photos, classification, and cultivation.

Elmore, Francis H. and Janish, Jeanne R. *Shrubs and Trees of the Southwest Uplands.* Southwest Parks and Monuments Assoc., 1976, 214 pages, $7.95. Color-coded pages help locate plants and trees above 4,500 feet elevation (from the pinyon-juniper belt to treeline).

McKee, Edwin D. *Ancient Landscapes of the Grand Canyon Region.* Northland Press, 1982, 52 pages, $2. Brief account of how the Grand Canyon area came to be.

Manning, Reg. *What Kinda Cactus Izzat?* Reganson Cartoon Books, Box 5242, Phoenix, AZ; 1969, 108 pages, $3. A fun-to-read book on "who's who in the desert" — the cacti and other desert plants in the Southwest.

Nelson, Dick and Sharon. *Easy Field Guide Series of Arizona: Snakes, Insects, Birds, Mammals, Cactus, or Trees.* Primer Publishers, (various dates), about 32 pages, $1/each. Easy to carry mini-guides.

Olin, George. *House in the Sun.* Southwest Parks and Monuments Assoc., 1977, 236 pages, $3.95. A guide to the Sonoran Desert, why it exists, and how life has adapted to it. Also tells how *you* can adapt to the sometimes harsh conditions and enjoy the desert in safety. Many color photos.

Olin, George and Thompson, Dale. *Mammals of the Southwest Deserts.* Southwest Parks & Monuments Assoc., 1982, 97 pages, $6. Well-illustrated with b/w and color drawings.

Patraw, Pauline M. and Janish, Jeanne R. *Flowers of the Southwest Mesas.* Southwest Parks and Monuments Assoc., 1977, 112 pages, $2.50. Flowers and trees of the Upper Sonoran Zone (pinyon-juniper belt) are illustrated and described.

Powell, Lawrence Clark and Collier, Michael. *Where Water Flows: The Rivers of Arizonas.* Northland Press, 1980, 64 pages, $25. Essays and beautiful color photos about 7 of Arizona's rivers.

Smith, Robert L. *Venomous Animals of Arizona.* University of Arizona, 1982, 134 pages, $5. Ever wonder about a scorpion's love life? Good descriptions of the fascinating poisonous insects and animals, with medical notes.

Stokes, William L. *Scenes of the Plateau Lands and How They Came to Be.*. Starstone Publishing Co., 1969, 66 pages. How mesas, canyons, volcanoes, and other geologic features were formed.

Sweet, Muriel. *Common Edible and Useful Plants of the West.* Naturegraph Publishers, Happy Camp, CA; 1976, 64 pages, $2.50. Nontechnical descriptions of plants and trees that have food, medicinal, and other uses. Most of these were first discovered by Indians and used by pioneer settlers.

Whitney, Steve. *A Field Guide to the Grand Canyon.* William Morrow, 1982, 320 pages, $12.95. Excellent, well-illustrated guide to the Canyon's geology, early Indians, flowers, trees, birds, and animals. Most of the information also applies to other canyons on the Colorado plateau. Practical advice for visiting and hiking in the Grand Canyon is included too.

# ONWARD TRAVEL

Franz, Carl. *The People's Guide to Mexico.* John Muir Publications, 1986, 555 pages, $11.95. This hefty guide is about experiencing Mexico. It's crammed with useful advice on driving, public transport, accommodation, cantinas, markets, and staying healthy.

Richmond, Doug. *Mexico, A Travel Survival Kit.* Lonely Planet Publications, 1985, 255 pages, $7.95. Handy guide with an introduction, the sights and cities, where to stay, and how to get around.

# REFERENCE

Comeaux, Malcolm L. *Arizona, A Geography.* Westview Press, 1981. Geographies of the United States series. A 336-page volume full of info on Arizona's physical geography, settlement, population, resources, and agriculture.

*Arizona Statistical Review.* Valley National Bank, Box 71, Phoenix, AZ 85001; revised annually, 80 pages, free at any bank office. Maps and tables summarize population, finances, education, climate, and mining in Arizona.

Walker, Henry P. and Bufkin, Don. *Historical Atlas of Arizona.* University of Oklahoma Press, 1979, 130 pages, $12.95. Clear maps and concise text illustrate the geography, Indian tribes, exploration, and development of Arizona.

# MISCELLANEOUS

Fischer, Al and Fischer, Mildred. *Arizona Cook Book.* Golden West, 1974, 142 pages, $3.50. A culinary guide to the state—Indian, Western, barbeque, and backpacking. Learn how to make cactus jelly and other delicacies.

# INDEX

*Italicized* page numbers indicate information in captions, call-outs, charts, illustrations, or maps. (Inclusive page numbers, i.e., "147-169," may also include these types of references.) **Bold-face** page numbers offer the primary reference to a given topic.

# ABOUT
# THE AUTHOR

Back in school, Bill Weir always figured that he'd settle down to a career job and live happily ever after. Then he "discovered" traveling. After graduating with a B.A. degree in physics from Berea College in 1972, Bill wound up as an electronic technician in Columbus, Ohio. But the very limited vacation times just weren't enough for trips he dreamed of. So, in 1976 he took off with his trusty bicycle and rode across the United States from Virginia to Oregon with Bikecentennial '76. The following year he did an even longer bicycle trip — from Alaska to Baja California. Then the ultimate journey — a bicycle cruise around the world! That lasted from 1980 to 1984, with most of the time spent in the South Pacific and Asia. Naturally Bill used Moon Publications' excellent *South Pacific Handbook* and *Indonesia Handbook*. Correspondence with the authors led to some text contributions for their books and the idea of doing a guidebook for Arizona. From New Delhi, Bill returned to his home base of Flagstaff, Arizona, and set to work researching and writing this guidebook. The project took 1 ½ years. In it, he hit the road again with ol' Bessie the bicycle to visit the Indian lands of NE Arizona, then covered the rest of the state by car and by hiking. Still free and single, Bill's major interests continue to be the diverse worlds of the American Southwest and Asia.

## MOONBOOKS TRAVEL CATALOG
*Free Total Trip Planner*

Smart travelers plan ahead. Whether you're heading to Kathmandu, Rio de Janeiero, or Disneyland, *Moonbooks Travel Catalog* has the right guide for you. Our catalog includes travel guides, maps, travel literature, language aids, and accessories for all sorts of adventurous, exotic destinations as well as traditional vacation places. *Moonbooks Travel Catalog* specializes in the unusual, hard-to-find item such as an Indonesian language course or map to Vanuatu. This catalog is just plain entertaining reading in itself! And, of course, care has been taken in the format too. It's easy to use, with a table of contents, complete index, hundreds of photos, and detailed descriptions of each item. Ordering is simple by phone or mail, with check, money order, or credit card. So be adventurous and get yours now! 178 pages. **Code MN27**

# DID YOU ENJOY THIS BOOK?
## Then you may want to order
## other MOON PUBLICATIONS' titles.

**SOUTH PACIFIC HANDBOOK, 3rd edition** by David Stanley. Here is paradise explored, photographed and mapped — the original comprehensive guide to the history, geography, climate, cultures, and customs of the 19 territories in the South Pacific. No other travel book covers such a phenomenal expanse of the Earth's surface. 12 color pages, 121 illustrations, 195 b/w photos, 35 charts, 138 maps, booklist, glossary, index. 588 pages.
**Code MN03**                                                                                      **$13.95**

**BLUEPRINT FOR PARADISE: How to Live on a Tropic Island** by Ross Norgrove. Do you dream of living on a tropical island paradise? *Blueprint for Paradise* clearly and concisely explains how to make that dream a reality. Derived from his own and others' experiences, Norgrove covers: choosing an island, owning your own island, designing a house for tropical island living, transportation, getting settled, and successfully facing the natural elements. Breathtaking illustrations complete this remarkable guide. 202 pages. Available November 1987.
**Code MN36**                                                                                      **$14.95**

**MICRONESIA HANDBOOK** by David Stanley. Apart from atomic blasts at Bikini and Enewetak in the late '40s and early '50s, the vast Pacific area between Hawaii and the Philippines has received little attention. *Micronesia Handbook's* 238 packed pages cover the seven North Pacific territories in detail. All this, plus 58 maps, 12 charts, 8 color pages, 77 photos, 68 drawings, index. 238 pages.
**Code MN19**                                                                                      **$8.95**

**FINDING FIJI** by David Stanley. Fiji, everyone's favorite South Pacific country, is now easily accessible either as a stopover or a whole Pacific experience in itself. This guide covers it all — the amazing variety of land and seascapes, customs and climates, sightseeing attractions, hikes, beaches, even how to board a copra boat to the outer islands. *Finding Fiji* is packed with practical tips, everything you need to know in one portable volume. 20 color photos, 78 illustrations, 26 maps, 3 charts, vocabulary, index. 127 pages.
**Code MN17**                                                                                      **$6.95**

**JAPAN HANDBOOK** by J.D. Bisignani. Packed with practical money-saving tips on travel, food and accommodation. *Japan Handbook* is essentially a cultural and anthropological manual on every facet of Japanese life. 35 color photos, 200 b/w photos, 92 illustrations, 29 charts, 112 maps and town plans, an appendix on the Japanese language, booklist, glossary, index. 504 pages.
**Code MN05**                                                                                      **$12.95**

**INDONESIA HANDBOOK, 4th edition** by Bill Dalton. The most comprehensive and contemporary guide to Indonesia. Discover the cheapest places to eat and sleep, ancient ruins and historical sites, wildlife and nature reserves, spiritual centers, arts and crafts, folk theater and dance venues. 12 color pages, hundreds of photos, illustrations, maps, charts, booklist, vocabulary, index. 900 pages. Available in December 1987.
**Code MN01**                                                                                      **$12.95**

**NEW ZEALAND HANDBOOK** by Jane King. New Zealand is nature's improbable masterpiece, a world of beauty and wonder jammed into three unforgettable islands. Explore white-water rapids, ski the slopes of a smoldering volcano, cast a flyrod in an icy stream, or have a bet on "the trots." 8 color pages, 99 b/w photos, 146 illustrations, 82 maps, index. 512 pages.
**Code MN35**                                                                                      **$13.95**

**HAWAII HANDBOOK** by J.D. Bisignani. Offers a comprehensive introduction to Hawaii's geography, vibrant social history, arts, and events. The travel sections inform you of the best sights, lodging and food, entertainment, and services. J.D. Bisignani has discovered bargains on excursions, cruises, car rentals, and airfares. Maps, charts, illustrations, color and b/w photos, index. 650 pages. Available November 1987.
**Code MN34** $14.95

**MAUI HANDBOOK** by J.D. Bisignani. Boasting historic Lahina, sensitively planned Kaanapali resort, power center Haleakala, and precipitous Hana Road, Hawaii's Maui is one of the most enchanting and popular islands in all of Oceania. 6 color and 50 b/w photos, 62 illustrations, 27 maps, 13 charts, booklist, glossary, index. 235 pages.
**Code MN29** $8.95

**GUIDE TO JAMAICA: Including Haiti** by Harry S. Pariser. No other guide treats Jamaica with more depth, historical detail, or practical travel information than *Guide to Jamaica*. 4 color pages, 51 b/w photos, 39 illustrations, 10 charts, 18 maps, booklist, glossary, index. 165 pages.
**Code MN25** $7.95

**GUIDE TO PUERTO RICO AND THE VIRGIN ISLANDS: Including the the Dominican Republic** by Harry S. Pariser. Discover for yourself the delights of America's "51st states," from the wild beauty of St. John, an island almost wholly reserved as a national park, to cosmopolitan San Juan. 4 color pages, 55 b/w photos, 53 illustrations, 29 charts, 35 maps, booklist, glossary, index. 225 pages.
**Code MN21** $8.95

**GUIDE TO THE YUCATAN PENINSULA** by Chicki Mallan. Explore the mysterious monolithic cities of the Maya, plunge into the color and bustle of the village market place, relax on unspoiled beaches, or jostle with the jet set in modern Cancun. 4 color pages, 154 b/w photos, 55 illustrations, 53 maps, 68 charts, appendix, booklist, vocabulary, index. 300 pages.
**Code MN32** $10.95

**ALASKA YUKON HANDBOOK: A Gypsy Guide to the Inside Passage and Beyond** by David Stanley. The first true budget guide to Alaska and Western Canada. 37 color photos, 76 b/w photos, 86 illustrations, 70 maps, booklist, glossary, index. 230 pages.
**Code MN07** $7.95

**CALIFORNIA DOWNHILL** by Stephen Metzger. Gives complete, detailed listings of all of California's 40 downhill ski areas, from the bunny slopes of Big Bear to the near-vertical faces of Squaw Valley — and everything in between. 15 color and 37 b/w photos, 21 illustrations, 30 maps, 41 charts, index. 144 pages.
**Code MN31** $7.95

**BACKPACKING: A HEDONIST'S GUIDE** by Rick Greenspan and Hal Kahn. This humorous, handsomely illustrated how-to guide will convince even the most confirmed naturophobe that it's safe, easy, and enjoyable to leave the smoggy security of city life behind. 90 illustrations, annotated booklist, index. 199 pages.
**Code MN23** $7.95

# BOOKS OF RELATED INTEREST

**Arizona Trails**
by David Mazel
The 100 hikes described in this book range from short dayhikes to 50-mile treks. Most are on well-maintained, easy-to-follow trails, but a few trace routes that were blazed a century or more ago by Indians or prospectors, and have rarely been used since. There are plenty of challenges here for the experienced back-country traveler, yet this is also a guide the beginner can use right away. This book includes accurate, updated maps (most of them inaccurately mapped on U.S Geological Survey topo maps). Purchased separately, the maps needed for just a small selection of hikes would cost more than the book itself, which contains all the maps you will need. Index. 320 pages.
Size: 5 x 8.
**Code WI40** $12.95

**Insight Guide American Southwest**
by Apa Productions
The American Southwest attracts a special kind of traveler. The vast expanses and terrible natural beauty intimidate some, but inspire others who love the region. The hardy cultures that have settled here share this fascinating mix of self-reliance and humility that the landscape instills. Not all of the Southwest is somber, of course; there is plenty of fun to be had. To the lover of the outdoors, the entire region is a playground. To the gambler, Las Vegas is a mecca. To the tourist, the Grand Canyon may well be the ultimate sight. To the student of Native American Culture, the area offers art, ceremony and reservations the size of New England. The fine maps, lush photography and lively writing make for a book as bold and beautiful as the Southwest itself. Index. 305 pages. Size: 6 x 9.
**Code IS02** $15.95

## MOONBELTS

A new concept in moneybelts. Made of heavy-duty Cordura nylon construction and strong water-resistant fabric, the *Moonbelt* offers maximum protection for your important papers. This pouch, designed for all-weather comfort, slips under your shirt or waistband, rendering it virtually undetectable and inaccessible to pickpockets. Many thoughtful features: 1-inch-wide nylon webbing, heavy-duty zipper, and a 1-inch high-test quick-release buckle. No more fumbling around for the strap or repeated adjustments, this handy plastic buckle opens and closes with a touch, but won't come undone until you want it to. Accommodates travelers cheques, passport, cash, photos. Size: 3½ x 8. Available in black or white.          **$6.95**

# IMPORTANT ORDERING INFORMATION

**1. Codes:** Please enter book and/or map codes on your order form. This will assure accurate and speedy delivery of your order.

**2. Prices:** Due to foreign exchange fluctuations and the changing terms of our distributors, all prices are subject to change without notice.

**3. Domestic orders:** We ship UPS or US Postal Service 1st class. Send $3.00 for first item and $.50 for each additional item. Please specify street or P.O. Box address, and shipping method. Deliveries are subject to availability of merchandise. We will inform you of any delay.

**4. Foreign orders:** All orders which originate outside the U.S.A. **must** be paid for with either an International Money Order or a check in U.S. currency drawn on a major U.S. bank based in the U.S.A. For International Surface Bookrate (8-12 weeks delivery), send U.S. $2.00 for the first book and U.S. $1.00 for each additional book.

**5. Telephone orders:** We accept Visa or Mastercharge payments. **MINIMUM ORDER U.S. $15.00.** Call in your order: (916) 345-5413. 9:00 a.m. - 5:00 p.m. Pacific Standard Time.

**6. Noncompliance:** Any orders received which do not comply with any of the above conditions will result in the return of your order and/or payment intact.

---

# MOON BOOKS MAKE GREAT GIFTS!